AMERICAN CIVILIZATION

A PORTRAIT FROM

AMERICAN

TEXTS BY

EDITED BY DANIEL J. BOORSTIN

McGRAW-HILL BOOK COMPANY
NEW YORK

THE TWENTIETH CENTURY
CIVILIZATION

WILLIAM H. GOETZMANN

NATHAN GLAZER

MARTIN E. MARTY

FRANK FREIDEL

W. W. ROSTOW

PHILIP B. KURLAND

WALTER MUIR WHITEHILL

MARCUS CUNLIFFE

EDMUND N. BACON

RICHARD SCHICKEL

R. W. B. LEWIS

HAROLD ROSENBERG

ERNEST R. MAY

565 illustrations

139 in color

426 photographs, engravings and maps

Designed and produced by THAMES AND HUDSON, London
MANAGING EDITOR: Ian Sutton BA
DESIGN: Ian Mackenzie-Kerr ARCA, MSIA
EDITORIAL: Christine Cope BA, Jennifer Rusden BA
RESEARCH: Millicent Greenberg BA, Emily Lane BA, Sheila Lee BA
MAP: Shalom Schotten
BLOCKS: Gilchrist Brothers Ltd, Leeds
TEXT FILMSET in Great Britain by Keyspools Ltd, Golborne, Lancs
PRINTED in West Germany by H. Stürtz, Würzburg
PAPER supplied by Papierfabrik Schleipen GmBH, Bad Duerkheim, West Germany,
and Gerald Judd, Ltd, London
BOUND by Van Rijmenam NV, The Hague, Holland

Library of Congress Catalog Card Number: 72–1129
SBN: 07–006497–0

CONTENTS

INTRODUCTION

DANIEL J. BOORSTIN

WHEN William Bradford landed on American shores in 1620, he observed that he and his fellow Pilgrims were now separated 'from all the civil parts of the world'. They were risking a New World wilderness to redeem an Old World civilization. Three and a half centuries later, these shores had themselves become a very proto-type of civilization. Whether or not the United States had in other respects become a modern Rome, in the 20th century this nation had become a pole-star by which peoples around the world guided themselves and took their bearings. American civilization stirred them to visions of what they might be, of what they wanted to be, or of what they feared they might become.

In the 20th century the United States had become a celebrity-nation, about which literate men everywhere were supposed to have an opinion. From their judgments of American civilization people became accustomed to speculate on the meaning, the promise, and the threat of civilization itself. There was good reason to see the United States as an extrapolation, a preview, or even perhaps a caricature, of what the future held for mankind. For this continent had offered Western man an opportunity to broaden his very notion of civilization, to give new emphasis to man's restless quest for novelty.

American civilization was in many ways a world-civilization. The nation was the product of an unprecedented ingathering of peoples across oceans and from remote continents. Here was a testing-place for what Old-World ways could do in a vast and rich New-World setting. The United States thus became a laboratory for the reasoned hopes, the casual collisions, the untried enterprises of men from everywhere. It was a place of second chances, oppor-tunities, revivals, revisions, and rebirths. A place for trying out what elsewhere was only imagined, or could not even be imagined elsewhere because it could not be tried. The United States was both a product and a producer of a New World. And much of the specula-tion about America was a wondering about how new this New World really was, about how much renewal was possible for man.

In this late 20th century, while the American appetite for novelty remains unsated, and while hopes become more extravagant than ever, we may ask a more old-fashioned, more Old-Worldly ques-tion. What does it all add up to? Has the New World lived up to Old World expectations? By now, what has man in the United States, adding together the old and the new, actually succeeded in accomplishing? What has he fashioned in the way of new attitudes to his land, new forms of government and law, new shapes of enterprise and art and architecture, new modes of thinking about God and community?

This volume aims to help answer this question. Since so much of the American achievement has been outward and visible, we need the copious illustrations in this book. We have tried to offer a kind of vivid critical inventory of the civilization of the United States, viewed from the late 20th century. We have been less con-cerned with the varied historical experience of being an American than with the American achievement. And we have chosen topics that might help the reader reflect on how this achievement compares with the achievement of men elsewhere.

The present volume offers the assessments of thirteen experts, selected for their informed scholarship, their vigor of judgment, their feeling of nuance, and their ability to interpret their subject for the layman. They have been chosen, too, for their shared assumption that there has been something distinctive about the civilization of the United States which is worth describing to the world. Each author has written from his own point of view, which does not necessarily accord with that of the editor or of the other authors. Since all the authors, except one, are Americans, their work also shows how these different aspects of American civiliza-tion look from within.

We call this book a *portrait* because we hope to offer—in words and pictures—a vivid, recognizable, and subtle likeness of American civilization. We would hope that we have helped the reader find something unfamiliar in the familiar. A portrait selects and re-creates visible features to reveal character. Each of our authors has been chosen because he does have his own special style of portraiture.

We have aimed not at being complete, nor at laying out the whole anatomy or physiology or history of this vast subject. Instead we have aimed at emphasis—to underline some features of this civilization which are remarkable, interesting, and character-istic. Earlier history is recounted, for the most part, only as a portrait painter would fill in background. Our authors have been asked not to tell the whole story but rather to describe and assess the 20th-century product—in institutions, in ways of producing and distributing, in the shape of city and countryside, in works of art and literature and architecture.

The subjects of the chapters have been chosen to provide foci of exploration, promising points of departure for feeling out the character of this civilization. We have tried to avoid a coverage of subject-matter simply because it is there. We hope too that we have avoided the repetition which might have come from assigning a chapter to every conceivable subject. Some subjects—for example science and technology, labor, and the role of women—are so pervasive that they are explored throughout many of the chapters.

American civilization has been characterized by a peculiar, dynamic miscellany, by its own special contradictions, by a unique brand of unpredictable creative chaos. We would have been untrue to our subject if we had made our topics too neat or our divisions too sharp. American civilization has specialized in the dissolving of Old World specialties, in the breaking down of categories sacred to learned men and textbook writers of other places.

Among the many themes that emerge from this thirteen-part inventory, at least two might command the special interest of the student of civilizations. They are *Transformation* and *Popularization*.

In one chapter after another we see the consequences of the American Transformation. Old World institutions and ways of thinking and organizing, of making and doing, take on unpredicted new significance here, with unpredictable consequences. The universal human need to explore the land, the sea—and the air—which shaped earlier American history, becomes (as William H. Goetzmann observes) a major American institution, with conse-quences which, by the later 20th century, shape American educa-tion, the American economy, and the American imagination. The problems of loyalty and hatred, of the confederation of peoples, of differences of language and religion, of war and peace, here become transformed into problems of cultural pluralism, of federalism, of law and constitutionalism (as Nathan Glazer,

Martin E. Marty, Frank Freidel, and Philip B. Kurland all remind us).

And we see, too, what happens in a society that popularizes its politics, its religion, and all its culture. Martin E. Marty shows us the new cast given to the doctrines and institutions of Christianity. Politics acquires new forms, gives the people new powers of command, and the governors new incentives to obey, as Frank Freidel notes. An American 'Aristocracy' comes to be created by money, which, in theory at least, any American can acquire and the distinctions of success and money (Walter Whitehill observes) tend to displace more hereditary distinctions. Education, elsewhere a mark of tradition-bound ruling classes, becomes (as Marcus Cunliffe explains) the great equalizer, and, in the process, the very subject matter of education is revised almost out of recognition. A great new democratized drama—motion pictures—comes into being and music and other forms of entertainment art (Richard Schickel observes) are reshaped while audiences are enlarged to become coterminous with the population. Literature takes on a new cast, becoming the vehicle for questing minorities (as R. W. B. Lewis notes). Art (according to Harold Rosenberg) becomes almost everything to almost everybody, while artists reach for the mass market.

Americans then worship the gods of growth and change. Flux becomes an established American institution. Novelty, no longer merely the spice of life, becomes the very meat and potatoes of daily American experience. Enterprise (Walt Rostow tells us) dominates the continent. Cities expand and multiply (described by Edmund Bacon) in a nation which (Ernest May notes) is increasingly tempted to see itself as a world missionary, destined to save the world by the latest American prescriptions.

These are only a few of the themes. The *meaning* of American civilization—what all these remarkable efforts of men in the present boundaries of the United States signify for mankind—each reader will have to assess for himself.

Just before the beginning of this century Mark Twain observed, 'It was wonderful to find America, but it would have been more wonderful to miss it.' Of course he was not the first to suggest that American civilization was nothing more remarkable than the result of an error in navigation. Whatever else might be said about American civilization, it surely has been one of the great surprises of man's history. And only a misanthrope could suppose that we have seen the last of these surprises. The authors and the editor of this volume do not pretend that today they or anybody else can convey—in a phrase or in a book—what the American achievement really adds up to. But they do hope that this volume will help the reader rediscover for himself the grand technicolor spectacular that might have been missed if those early navigators had not made their lucky mistake.

My close collaborator in editing the volume has been my wife, Ruth F. Boorstin. I wish also to express my thanks to Mr Ian Sutton and the extraordinarily competent and imaginative staff at Thames and Hudson.

Mr Edmund Bacon wishes to thank his friend and associate Peter Mahony for working with him in the development of many of the concepts contained in Chapter IX.   D. J. B.

Acknowledgments
The illustrations sections have been the responsibility of the publishers, who would like to thank all the authors for their unfailing help and advice in the choice of pictures and wording of the captions, and also the following individuals and institutions for their generous co-operation in the collection of photographs: Arno Jakobson of The Brooklyn Museum; Leo Castelli Gallery, New York; the staff of the Chicago Historical Society; The American Museum in Britain, Claverton Manor, Bath; Professor Carl W. Condit; Mr and Mrs James D'Angelo, New York; Col. Edgar William and Mrs Bernice Chrysler Garbisch; Robert Hallock of *Lithopinion*, New York; Mrs Angela Smith, Librarian of the Institute of United States Studies in London; Miss Elizabeth Zyman, of the United States Library, University of London; Marlborough Gallery, New York, and Marlborough Fine Art Ltd, London; Andrew Poggenpohl of the *National Geographic Magazine*; the staff of Photograph Services, The Metropolitan Museum of Art, New York; Mrs Charlotte La Rue of the Museum of the City of New York; Wilson G. Duprey and Martin Leifer of The New-York Historical Society; Harold W. Raumbusch of the Raumbusch Decorating Company, New York; the United States Information Agency in Washington and the United States Information Service in London; Jerry Kearns of the Prints and Photographs Division, Library of Congress, Washington, D.C.; and Mrs Eleanor Snyder of the National Collection of Fine Arts, Smithsonian Institution, Washington, D.C.

The excerpt on p. 264 is from William Carlos Williams' COLLECTED EARLIER POEMS. Copyright 1938 by William Carlos Williams. Reprinted by permission of New Direction Publishing Corporation and MacGibbon & Kee Ltd. The excerpt from 'To Brooklyn Bridge' by Hart Crane, on the same page, is reprinted with the permission of Liveright Publishing Corporation, from *Complete Poems*. Copyright 1933, 1958, 1966 by Hart Crane.

I

EXPLORATION'S NATION

The role of discovery in American history

WILLIAM
H. GOETZMANN

*'In the United States there is more room where nobody is
than where anybody is. That is what makes America
what it is.'*

GERTRUDE STEIN

The discovery of America

has been going on for four hundred years, and the experience has molded the character of a nation. In a sense, it has never ended. The lunar expeditions of today are the natural successors of the early explorers' sea voyages and the great land journeys of the pioneers. The frontier has been pushed to its terrestrial limit, and man sets out, in President Kennedy's phrase, across the 'new ocean' of space.

The history of 18th- and 19th-century America can never be understood without keeping this frontier constantly in mind. It provided an exploratory dimension within and on the very borders of the nation that was lacking in older countries. It postulated growth, expansion, progress. For those in search of independence, for those determined to make their fortunes through hard work and enterprise, for those (like the Mormons) set on starting a whole

new society, the natural and only advice was 'Go West'. In the West anything was possible.

Exploration and settlement went hand in hand, and the pattern remained in many respects constant. In 1780 the pioneer farmer was gathering his crops and building his log cabin in Kentucky, in 1880 in Idaho. Bingham's painting (opposite) of Daniel Boone escorting settlers across the Cumberland Gap is a tribute from one generation to another. Boone was an 18th-century pathfinder, who had penetrated the Cumberland Gap in the Appalachian Mountains (from Virginia to what was to become Kentucky) in 1769. Thereafter he acted as guide to bands of settlers; by the end of the century over a million people had passed through. Bingham was himself a frontiersman. He lived in Missouri, which in 1851, when the painting was made, had been for thirty years a frontier state. (1)

The first map known to show America dates from about 1440: it is the so-called Vinland Map (left), based, at five hundred years' remove, on the tradition of Viking visits to Newfoundland in the 10th century. (2)

Columbus's ships, the *Santa Maria,* the *Pinta* and the *Niña,* left no pictorial record, but they were of the same type as this contemporary Catalan *ex-voto* (right). The largest was less than 120 feet long. Land (an island of the Bahamas) was first sighted on 12 October 1492. (3)

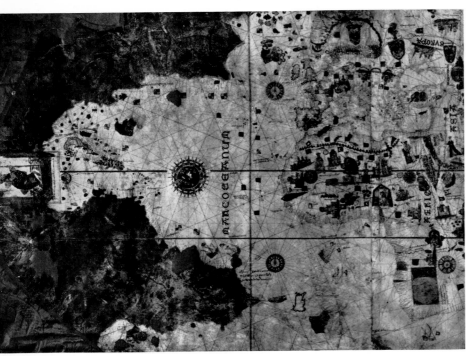

Juan de la Cosa, 1500. In eight years the outline of the eastern seaboard had been filled out by Spanish, Portuguese and English discoveries, and the land had been recognized as a new continent. La Cosa had been Columbus's pilot in the first voyage. (4)

Sebastian Münster, 1540. The woodcut map added to Münster's very popular edition of Ptolemy's *Geography* is more ornamental than informative, though Münster was interested in the new discoveries. Note the position of Japan ('Zipang'). (5)

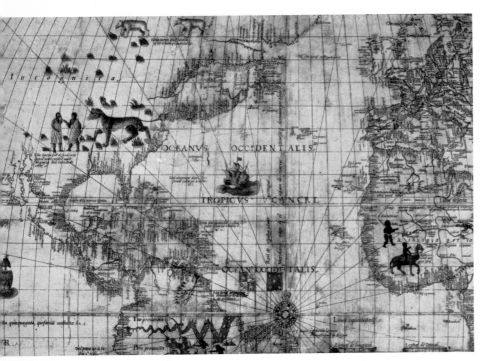

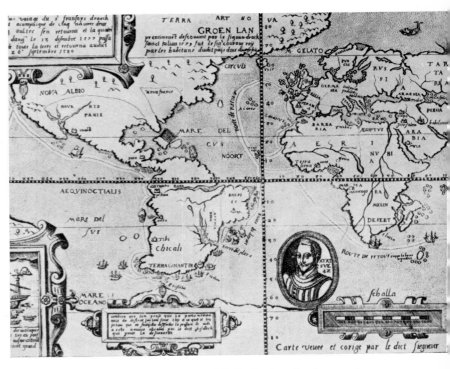

Sebastian Cabot, 1544. John Cabot explored three hundred miles of coastline in North America in 1497. His son Sebastian, who had accompanied him on this voyage, later spent three years in South America. In this map Sebastian summarized the knowledge available from all sources, adding fanciful animals. (6)

Francis Drake, 1577–80. The world had already been circumnavigated by Magellan's expedition (1519–22), but Drake's was the first such voyage by an Englishman. This engraving shows him and the course of his voyage around South America and as far north as California. (7)

The Northwest Passage, or sea route to the Indies north of Canada, haunted the imagination of European explorers for a hundred years. Martin Frobisher claimed to have found it in 1576. He certainly reached Frobisher's Bay and brought back an Eskimo. Left: a watercolor made by John White in the 1580s. (8)

The interior was still mysterious in 1748 (below). The area to the west of the Mississippi and Great Lakes is here wildly underestimated, and southern California is shown as an island. (9)

Greater accuracy is attained in Humboldt's 1811 map of New Spain (below), based on the explorations of Lt Zebulon Pike. Lower California is now again shown as a peninsula. (10)

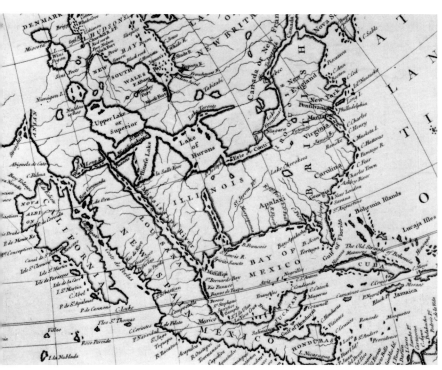

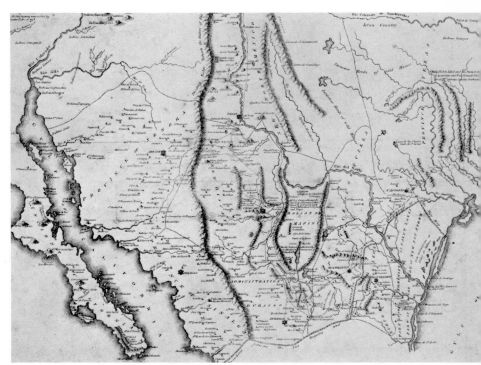

From a satellite (below) the continent lies open and visible at last, confirming the picture that cartographers on the earth have so painstakingly built up. On this composite photograph of 1966 some of the main cities have been marked. (11)

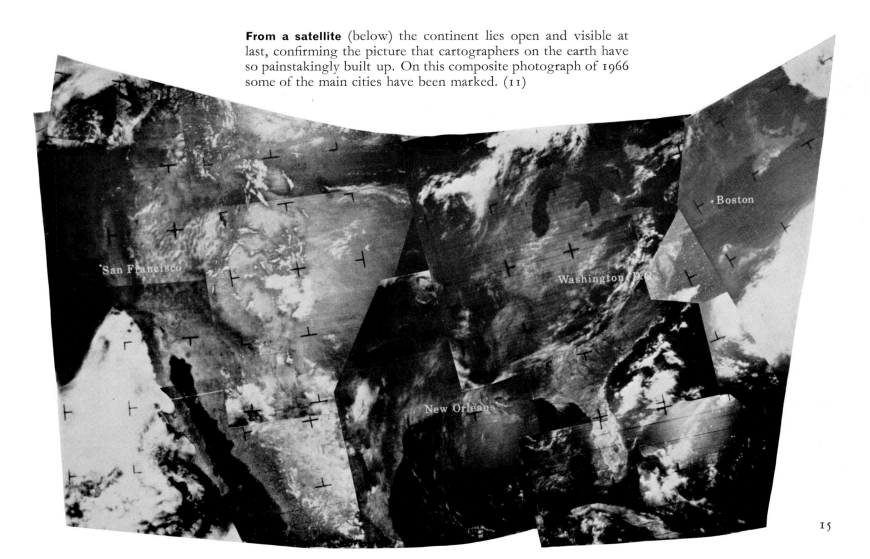

15

'American Progress' (1872): columns of settlers and prospectors start the long trek westward. Behind them, the lights of New York; before them, the wilderness and fleeing Indians; above them – allegorically – 'Columbia' conjuring up railways and telegraph wires as if by the touch of magic. (12)

'The Promised Land' (right) celebrates the moment in 1846 when a settler family, the Graysons, emerged from their crossing of the Rockies to see the rich landscape of California spread out before them. (14)

The new land was not an Eden, as some of the accounts written in the east suggested. Above: a typical early settlement, 1822. The house has been built of logs cut from the forest; other trees have been girdled and burnt to clear fields. Right: a ranch on the gold rush route in Idaho, 1882. Far right: a characteristic 'new town' of the West, Parsons, Kansas, in 1873. (13, 15, 16)

the most vivid evocation of that moment of awe and wonder – *The Grand Canyon of the Yellowstone*. In the far distance he showed the white line of the Tetons, and on the plateau to the left the steam rising from geysers. This was the psychological reality of the West, as it entered the minds of Americans everywhere. Moran's paintings and Jackson's photographs helped to strengthen the government's resolve to preserve the whole region as an unspoiled national park. (22)

Before the frontier had reached the west coast, the lure of exploration drew Americans north and south to the limits of the world. Captain Charles Wilkes led an expedition which was away four years (1838–42), traced fifteen hundred miles of frozen Antarctic coastline in the south and established the US as a future Pacific power. Left: Wilkes's ships anchored off Antarctica. (23)

Arctic exploration claimed many lives. Elisha Kent Kane (above) reached 80° 10′ in 1853–55 but suffered grueling hardships. (24)

Alaskan gold drew thousands north in search of wealth. Below: prospectors, crossing the Chilkoot Pass, 1898. (26)

A few miles more were conquered by Charles Hall in the *Polaris* (above), but his expedition ended in disaster in 1871. (25)

Only six men survived the failure of A. W. Greely's attempt on the Pole in 1884 (below). (27)

The Pole conquered: Robert Peary and his Negro partner Matt Henson (above) reached the North Pole by boat and on foot in April 1909. (28)

The new technology of the 20th century soon made traditional methods of exploration obsolete. In 1926 Richard Byrd and Floyd Bennett (above) flew from Spitzbergen to the Pole in a Ford trimotor plane. Two days later Nobile, Ellsworth and Amundsen (seen above on the left, greeting Byrd) successfully took the dirigible *Norge* (left) over the Pole. (29, 30)

Exploration is still a science. Below left: US scientists on the Ross Ice Shelf in Antarctica positioning trail-mark flags, using a vehicle equipped to detect crevasses. Below: the nuclear-powered submarine *Skate* surfaces at the North Pole, 17 March 1959. (31, 32)

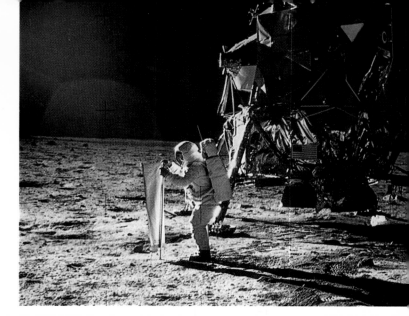

The moon landings are only one more stage in the long saga of American exploration. One of the pioneers of space travel was Robert H. Goddard, who had already by 1909 worked out the whole theoretical basis for a multi-stage-rocket carrying men to the moon. His first liquid-fuel rocket (left) was launched in 1926. Forty-three years later, on 20 July 1969, Neil Armstrong stepped on to the surface of the moon. Right: his companion, Buzz Aldrin, setting up a solar wind collector — in the same tradition as the surveyors of a century ago. (33–35)

The role of discovery in American history

WILLIAM H. GOETZMANN

IN 1927, the year of Lindbergh's transatlantic solo flight to Paris, in a book entitled *Time Lock*, the American designer Buckminster Fuller published the first of his revolutionary views of the globe. The 'Dymaxion Traffic Chart', as he called it, addressed the whole question of efficient world air traffic in the coming 'aviation age'. In facing this question of the future, Fuller, like some modern Mercator, drastically altered the conventional globe to suit his own purposes. The French Riviera he placed at the center. The North Pole was a fifth of the way down from the top of the map at the center. The Aleutian Islands rested at the very top, where the North Pole normally would have been, while the rest of the map was filled in by parts of the Americas, Africa, Europe and Asia. Most of the southern latitudes were missing. Fuller's main purpose was to indicate the prevailing air currents and the most direct lines of flight relative to the most heavily populated and advanced technological areas of the globe. But, in a characteristically American way, Fuller could not help relating his abstract concept to aspects of practical technology that suggested the settlement of a global frontier. Almost gleefully he related:

> Numbers of little airplanes are shown, flying the logical world air routes—circling the Arctic as a major traffic turntable, as well as crossing through Europe to Dakar, over the Atlantic to Natal and up the chain of the Americas. Spotted all through the then-unpenetrated Arctic and tropics are shown a number of dwelling machines, modern environmental control devices which would make possible maintenance of service-conditions for the airports in these then-unlivable areas.

In 1934 he invented still another map which he published in 1938 in a second non-fiction scientific shocker, *Nine Chains to the Moon*. As he described it, the map was 'a one-continent map in which all visible error was massaged into the ocean areas. . . . Its main purpose was to clarify the one-continent concept which joins the chain of continents together over the Aleutian route.' On other occasions, he devised a world map with the North Pole at the center and one for 'sailor-men' that focussed on the idea of one great world ocean and virtually ignored the land masses.

The visionary as pragmatist

Unlike Jules Verne, Fuller was not a visionary for romantic purposes. Rather, he was addressing himself to a series of practical world problems that required him to see the earth in a flexible, instrumental way. He was the visionary as pragmatist on a global scale, and whether he knew it or not, the perfect symbol of over four hundred years of American experience. Relying largely on a prodigious futuristic imagination, Fuller had invented the most accurate, least distorted of all global projections—a new precision tool, so to speak. But, most important symbolically, he represented the paradoxical working of the American mind, which had roots in the twin forces of Renaissance imagination and practical ingenuity. Fuller, like some intellectual adventurer of the Age of Discovery, looked to the unbounded future and a new Age of Discovery. He was thinking on a global scale, as Americans and their European forbears had always done, and like them he was not afraid to alter what had been considered fundamental realities to suit his purposes. At the same time, he demonstrated a practical

interest in rapidly changing technologies, a manipulative attitude toward nature, focussing on problem-solving, and a concern for the needs of societies in migration over the planet.

As Fuller's work illustrates, the processes of exploration and discovery are perhaps as much a matter of mind—of abstract vision and even somewhat mystical imagination—as they are of heroic adventure and practical achievement. This was never more true than in the long series of episodes that led to the discovery and gradual emergence of the United States onto the horizon of human knowledge.

For America is the product of an Age of Discovery that never really ended. From the Viking voyages in the 10th century to the lunar voyages of the 20th, much that is held to be American derives from a sense of the ongoing and complex process of exploration that has made up so much of its history. First Western Europeans, then Americans themselves came to participate in what can only be described as a gigantic learning process that was centrifugal, even boundless in scope and so basic to the processes of thought as to resemble the Scientific Revolution. Indeed, it is perhaps no accident that the European Age of Discovery and the first loomings of the Scientific Revolution virtually coincide in time. Their intellectual thrusts, though not overtly related, were much alike in their bold rejection of old authorities, their empirical and experimental tempers, their rooting in the humbler arts of the practitioner rather than the schoolman, their cumulative results, and the fundamental intellectual and cultural alterations which they invariably generated.

These two great world revolutions form the heritage of America —a nation of visionary traders and explorers and movers—of adventuresome, but practical and effective men, whose tradition it has been to build new systems adapted to remote and seemingly improbable places, which in turn may be only stepping stones to some further adventure beyond the horizon, perhaps even the new *oikumene* of outer space. The explorer therefore stands as a kind of archetypal American, bred out of the momentous experiences that came to ripeness in the Renaissance when men first learned through travel and communication of remote Cathay beyond the Mongol hordes from Karakoram to Samarkand, of the immensity and depth of learning in the Arab world, of Muscovy, Malacca, the Golden Ceronese, Cipangu, and Africa south of Ceuta.

Groping towards America

It is customary to date the beginning of the Age of Discovery in 1419 with the establishment by the Portuguese prince, Henry the Navigator, of his maritime observatory at Sagres on the southern tip of the Iberian peninsula. In retrospect however, Prince Henry's venture should undoubtedly be seen simply as the beginning of the accelerated or 'take-off' phase of a culture that had become increasingly fascinated with the possibilities of oceanic exploration.

The ancient world, with its limited vessels, had of course been concerned with exploration. The Carthaginian Hanno's circumnavigation of Africa, the celebrated Egyptian voyages to the Land of Punt in East Africa, the gradually accumulated knowledge of the coastlines of lands bordering the Indian Ocean, the precise knowledge of the Mediterranean from the Black Sea to the Phoenician port of Gades (Cadiz)—beyond the Pillars of Hercules—all attest to the exploring energies of the ancient world. By the second

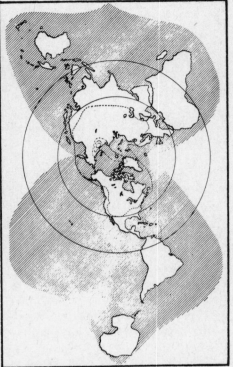

Buckminster Fuller's maps have treated the world as something flexible, to be represented in any way that suits man's purpose. His 'Dymaxion Traffic Chart' (left) demonstrated as early as 1927 his concept of the 'one-town' Air Ocean World, in which aircraft circle the Pole and huge prefabricated buildings can be transported to remote places by previously unoperated air routes. Another map of 1934 (above) showed all the dry land of the earth as one continent, 'similar to a three-bladed propeller with the hub at the North Pole. The winding dotted line is that of our population isotherm.' (1, 2)

century AD, Mediterranean men had edged around Iberia and were regularly sailing their galleys northward to ports in northern and western Europe, to England, and Ireland, the Shetlands, the Orkneys and even Iceland, situated, according to authorities, in the Sea of Cronos and known as Ultima Thule—the Land's End of the world. A few bold sea adventurers moved out west onto the broad Atlantic in search of its namesake, Atlantis, the lost kingdom beneath the sea, said by some to be marked by sludge and dangerous shallows that could wreck an unwary vessel. These men, mostly Phoenicians, did not find Atlantis but they found the Madeiras and the Canaries. And they generated myths and legends of further islands and kingdoms west over the ocean—such places as the Islands of the Blessed mentioned by Pindar, the Fortunate Isles described by Horace, the Hesperides where grew the golden apples of the sun, and somewhere out there, past the fearful guardians of the deep—the Elysian Fields.

As ancient times grew into medieval times, these mythical places did not change much except in name. Thule remained as such for a long time, as did the Islands of the Blessed and the Fortunate Isles, but new areas of major importance were added: Antillia, the Seven Golden Cities (the seven Canary Islands?) of the Moorish bishops of Spain, El Dorado, and Brazil Rock, which was

not removed from British Admiralty charts until 1873. Such hypothetical places, of course, gradually migrated to America and stimulated further exploration. One remembers Coronado's futile quest for the Seven Cities of Cibola, and who could forget Raleigh's tragic search for El Dorado—the river of gold and its fabled cities— somewhere in the exotic jungles of South America? There were other such quests for imaginary places in America, just as futile, perhaps not so tragic, but in the long run powerful stimulants to continental exploration.

Spurred on by myth and the development of crude navigational instruments such as the compass, the portolano chart and the sun staff, the succession of voyagers to the West never ceased, nor did knowledge of their voyages really die out. Papal Bulls and other medieval documents of the 9th century, such as the Irish cleric Dicuil's *De Mensura Orbis Terra*, mentioning Greenland, and a proclamation of Louis the Pious in 834 appointing missionaries to Dicuil's new lands, indicate that Celtic people fleeing from Viking and other northern sea raiders reached Iceland and then, crossing the Sea of Cronos, reached 'Gröenland'. There is some indication that they went on from there to a place called 'Hvitramannaland' which could only be North America. This was over one hundred years before the Norse discovery of America, and these people were sufficiently well-known to merit the attention not only of the ruler of the Frankish kingdom but of the Pope himself. Further, at least one Viking saga records the discovery by Viking explorers of evidence of settlements of the Celts or 'Westmen' in Greenland and North America.

The achievements of the Vikings themselves in the 10th century can hardly be dismissed, as they seem to have been, as being of no consequence in the meaningful discovery of America. Due to a mass of literature and recent archaeological excavation, the voyage of Eric the Red to Greenland in 981 is now well established. Even the plans of the remote eastern and western Greenland outposts have been traced to the point where we know the actual site of the Bishop of Greenland's See. Likewise, the wind-blown voyage of Bjarni Herjolfsson to America and Greenland, the joint venture of Leif Ericsson and Bjarni to Vinland, the tragic voyage of Leif's brother Thorwald in search of Vinland, and the New World colonizing ventures of Thorfinn Karlselfni have emerged from the Sagas into sharper historical focus. We know too that direct knowledge of the Greenland settlements, as well as the existence of the coasts of Helluland, Markland, and Vinland, persisted as late as Bishop Erik's visit to Greenland in 1121. Beyond that, the sagas and the Icelandic histories carry the tale, and, as it appears from the p 14 (2) recent discovery of the Vinland Map, a cartographic tradition persisted in some form until at least 1440, or well after Prince Henry launched his ambitious Portuguese ventures to the Indies and the New World.

The most important of the latter was the voyage of Don João Vaz Corte Real, as super-cargo aboard a ship bound from Denmark for Greenland and North America under the command of Captains Pining, Pothorst, and Scolvus. According to Corte Real, they reached Greenland and lands beyond. All this suggests that the Portuguese and the Norse at least, and possibly any knowledgeable seaman engaged in the sailing trade between Portugal, England and Scandinavia, knew of the existence of not only Greenland, but a sizable, mysterious and doubtless forbiddingly cold land mass beyond. This traditional knowledge passed down through the Corte Real family, so that in 1501 Gaspar Corte Real, Don João's son, began a regular series of family voyages to the Newfoundland fishing banks.

Columbus, sailor and scholar

No one, of course, epitomizes all the many aspects of the Age of Discovery quite so well as Christopher Columbus. It is perhaps only natural that he should do so, for of all the great explorers he combined wider experience and more of the traditions of learning than any of the others. He grew up in the mid-15th century seaport of Genoa with sailors, shipbuilders, traders, chartmakers and master mariners at every hand. At an early age he sailed in Genoese and Venetian ships to ports around the Mediterranean. Then on his first voyage out into the Atlantic, he was shipwrecked off the coast of Portugal, and he went to Lisbon to settle down for a time as a maker of portolano charts (coast charts showing bearings and distances between ports). He was soon joined by his brother Bartholomew and together they gathered all available information from the Portuguese and Italian navigators of the Mediterranean and Atlantic for incorporation into their charts. During this time, too, Columbus made voyages to the African coast, to the Madeiras and Azores, and important voyages to the British Isles, Iceland, and north in the frozen seas toward the Arctic Circle. As a chartmaker and sailor, Columbus was in a position to know virtually all there was to know, from the North Atlantic lore of the Bristol fishermen to the details of winds and currents out on the wide Atlantic beyond the Azores. He knew charts and philosophical *mappae mundi*. He knew navigation and the use of all the latest instruments. He knew about the construction of ships and their p 14 (3) handling in all situations. And he knew the many-faceted natural lore of the sea.

In addition to all this practical knowledge, Columbus avidly read nearly everything pertaining to exploration and the Indies. As a chartmaker it was his profession to do so. As an explorer it was his great enthusiasm. Among the most important books that he read were *The Travels of Marco Polo*, Ptolemy's *Geography*, the great compendium of Marinus of Tyre, the works of Aristotle, Strabo,

Roger Bacon, and particularly Cardinal Pierre d'Ailly's popular *Imago Mundi*, which Columbus covered with marginal annotations. He also corresponded with many people, including the learned physician Paolo Toscanelli of Florence, who, believing that Marco Polo's estimate of the size of Asia was correct, reasoned that by sailing west some three thousand miles one could reach Japan.

Basing his broadest calculations on these authorities, Columbus made several critical errors. He underestimated a degree of longitude, calculating it to be 45 nautical miles. He overestimated the width of Asia, making it some 283 degrees. And he was strongly influenced by Toscanelli's calculations; consequently he believed that Japan and the Indies lay some 2400 nautical miles west of the Canaries, whereas they are actually some 10,600 miles. Upon such optimistic calculations derived from what he considered to be the very best authorities, and upon his vast knowledge and experience, Columbus predicated his plan. He may have been wrong in detail, but he was by no means the unlearned visionary sailor that history has sometimes made him out to be. Instead he represented in one man all the best knowledge, both practical and theoretical, that was available in the Age of Discovery.

The story of Columbus's rejection and disappointment at the Portuguese court in 1484, and of his subsequent success in securing aid from Spain, is well-known, as are most of the details of his epic voyages. Sailing out from the Canaries on 6 September 1492, he followed the easterlies across the Atlantic some thirty-seven days until he sighted an outpost of 'Japan'—Watlings Island in the Bahamas, now better known as San Salvador. On that first voyage, too, he made passage through the Bahamas to Cuba, coasted its northern shores and then crossed over to Santo Domingo where he founded the first settlement in the New World since the Norse experiment of the 11th century. Losing the *Santa Maria* to a reef on Christmas Day, 1492, he sailed back to Spain via the Azores and Lisbon in the *Nina* which was freighted with gold and Indian passengers. When he returned in triumph to Barcelona, Columbus stunned the imagination of the world as no explorer ever did before.

In all, Columbus made four voyages to the New World, discovering many of the islands of the Caribbean and coasting the shores of Central and northern South America. However, he never knew that he had discovered a new continent and a new world of far greater significance than the goal he sought, which had already been attained by Da Gama and the Portuguese in 1498. Instead, the full discovery and outlining of North America (as well as South America) had to be left to other men in the decades to come.

A continent takes shape

While Columbus was suffering the disappointments of his last two voyages, a number of other Spanish explorers had already begun the fifty-year process of limning the outlines of what they came to recognize was a new world in two continents. In 1499–1500 Alonso de Ojeda, Juan de la Cosa (Columbus's pilot on the first voyage), and Amerigo Vespucci (a Venetian in the service of Spain) explored the whole northern coast of South America, and Vespucci recognized it for what it was—a continent. The fruit of their labor and that of Columbus was Juan de la Cosa's monumental map of the World drawn in 1500, on which were represented all the p 14 (4) Spanish, Portuguese and English discoveries after Columbus. It was the most important map drawn in the Age of Discovery.

In 1513 Juan Ponce de Leon from his base in Puerto Rico sailed north and discovered Florida—the first Spanish landing in North America. While he was doing this, Vasco Nuñez de Balboa led a small band of tough adventurers across the Isthmus of Darien where, from a mountain peak, they looked out upon the waters of the Pacific. For the first time the realities of New World geography as they related to Asia began to be apparent to the Spaniards.

Between 1517 and 1519 other men discovered Yucatan and Mexico. Francisco de Cordova reached the Mayan province in 1517; Juan Grijalva cruised northward along the Mexican coast, and Alvarez Piñeda sailed even further northward around the Gulf to Florida passing the mouth of the Mississippi. Gradually the contours of the North American continent became apparent—the more so when in 1524 Esteban Gomez completed a voyage along the east coast of North America from Nova Scotia to Florida. By this time another Spaniard, Ferdinand Magellan, succeeded after

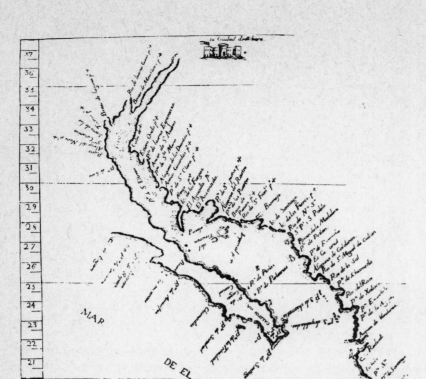

One of the earliest maps to show conclusively that lower California was a peninsula, not an island, was drawn in 1541 by Castillo, pilot of the mission sent to co-operate at sea with Coronado's expedition of 1540. (3)

his tragic death by his lieutenant Sebastian del Cano, had crossed through the Strait of Magellan and voyaged across the Pacific to the Indies, completing the mission that Columbus had started. When del Cano reached Seville, the global dimensions of the world were apparent.

With respect to that part of North America which was eventually to become the United States, only the voyage of Francisco Ulloa in 1539 to the head of the Gulf of California, which proved lower California was not an island, and the west coast voyages of Ferrelo and Cabrillo north to the 42nd degree of latitude were needed to complete the picture. Indeed, as early as 1520, with Cortez's ferocious conquest of the Aztec capital Tenochtitlan, the major shift in Spanish focus was toward the interior where, for over a century, another set of adventurers would pursue many of the same myths and legendary Golcondas that had lured the Spaniards across the ocean to the New World in the first place.

f 3

Cabot, Frobisher and Drake

While the Spanish were intent on locating a passage to India in the southern latitudes, a Venetian named John Cabot arrived in Bristol with a map and a globe, and a scheme for succeeding where Columbus had apparently failed. He knew of the discovery of land to the west by the Bristol fishermen, and he proposed sailing the same route until he struck land, then coursing southwest until he rounded what he took to be a peninsular extension of northern Asia. Once he had rounded this peninsula, the way to Japan and the Orient would be clear. He convinced the merchants of Bristol, who supported him, and with their help he secured a commission from King Henry VII of England to sail west on a voyage of discovery.

He got under way from Bristol in 1496, but was forced to turn back. The following year, in May of 1497, he set out again and after a rapid voyage of about five weeks he sighted North America which he coasted for about three hundred miles in the region of Nova Scotia and Newfoundland. Then he returned home to England, announced his discovery of the land of the Great Khan, and prepared for another voyage more ambitious in scope. In 1498 he sailed west with five ships. One turned back because of a storm. The rest were never heard of again.

On his first voyage Cabot had made one landing in the New World, no one knows where, and claimed it for England. He was the first European after the Norsemen to land in North America and the British claims to right of discovery in that region rest on his voyage. For a long time, historians were forced to depend on accounts of the voyage given by Cabot's son, Sebastian, who

cast himself in the role of discoverer, though he was only a boy at the time. This caused the voyage to be viewed with a great deal of scepticism until the discovery in 1956 of a letter written in the winter of 1497–98 by John Day, an English merchant in Seville, which described and confirmed the first voyage of the much-maligned John Cabot.

p 14 (5)

After Cabot, England's interest in a Northwest Passage lapsed for nearly seventy years. It was not until 1575 that Martin Frobisher, a pirate and slave trader, secured the backing of Michael Lok, formerly of the Levant and Muscovy Companies, for a voyage to the northwest. In all, Frobisher made three voyages. On the first, in 1576, he made for Greenland, crossed over to Baffin Island and coasted south, discovering Frobisher's Bay which, upon his return, he declared to be the Northwest Passage, or the Strait of Anian as it came to be called. His account was especially convincing because he returned with a Mongol-looking Eskimo whom he had hoisted kicking and screaming from his kayak by the sweep of one mighty arm. Frobisher also found what he took to be gold ore, and on his second voyage devoted his efforts almost exclusively to loading his ships with the ore and returning to England, ignoring the search for Anian. On his third voyage, a harrowing experience among the ice floes where he skirmished with Indians and lost both men and boats, Frobisher discovered and sailed into Hudson's Bay for two hundred miles. This was his most important geographical discovery. It changed English maps so that they showed no land (formerly a tip of Asia) north of the Strait of Anian, only a clear passage via Hudson's Bay to China.

p 15 (8)

f 4

While Frobisher was questing for gold and a Northwest Passage, Sir Francis Drake was having better success to the south. Leaving England in 1577, he rounded the tip of South America and cruised up the west coast of that continent, plundering the Spanish settlements in spectacular fashion. On this voyage Drake sailed as far north as San Francisco Bay and a little beyond before he crossed the Pacific to the Orient and a triumphant round the world return to England. His was the first English view of the 'backside' of America.

p 14 (7)

In the late 16th and early 17th centuries, however, prodded by the skilful propaganda of Richard Hakluyt, a number of English captains continued to test the cold northwest for the elusive passage to India. Between 1585 and 1587, John Davis, a skilled seaman from Dartmouth, sailed the coasts of Labrador and reached Cumberland Sound of Baffin Island. Eventually he got as far north as 72° 12′, tracing the true relationship of Greenland to the mainland and coming as close as anybody to finding the only northwest passage available through the Arctic Sea.

In 1610 Henry Hudson perished when he, along with his small son, was cast adrift by mutineers in the midst of the immense bay which bears his name. His expedition had already reached the deep southern arm of James Bay, which pointed directly into the heart of the rich Canadian fur country, before he met his sad fate. Thomas Button led an expedition into the Bay which searched in vain for the marooned navigator, but at least contributed further knowledge of the region. In 1616 Robert Bylot and William Baffin explored Baffin Bay, and in 1631 Luke Fox discovered and explored Fox Basin to the north of Hudson's Bay, while Thomas James probed the southern and eastern limits of the great inland sea.

Despite the fact that Foxe explicitly recognized that they were 'out of the way to Japon', the primary result of English exploration to the northwest was to establish more firmly the existence of the Strait of Anian—a myth which affected British, French, Spanish and American exploration for the next 150 years, and brought to sharp focus an imperial struggle for the continent of America. Even as late as 1607, the first successful Jamestown colonists in Virginia were strictly enjoined to search for a strait leading to Cathay as their first order of business. The intrepid Captain John Smith consumed much valuable time in doing so.

A passage to India

Though by the beginning of the 17th century the main outlines of the North American continent were apparent, reality did not seriously conflict with mythical and global objectives for the next 250 years. The Strait of Anian or some feasible passage to the Indies remained a primary objective of European and American rivalries. While the English searched Hudson's Bay and confronted the problem of the Appalachian barrier, the French under Jacques Cartier and later Samuel de Champlain opened up the St Lawrence gateway to the west. In 1634 Jean Nicollet reached Green Bay on the western shore of Lake Michigan and reported the 'Western Sea' to be three days distant. In the 1650s Pierre Radisson and Sieur de Groseilliers not only explored Lake Michigan and discovered the Illinois River, but they also followed Lake Superior to its western extremity and crossed overland to the upper Mississippi. None of these French explorers found the passage through the heart of the continent that they sought, though in 1680 Father Louis Hennepin as he sailed down the Mississippi noted the Missouri flowing in from the west and believed he had at last found it, and Baron Louis de la Hontan in 1688, though he had never been west of the Mississippi, spread detailed reports about the 'Long River' leading upstream to the Western Sea. His fictitious reports about Lake Timpanogos and its westward-flowing river, together with the strange inhabitants he claimed to have seen, managed to confuse explorers and geographers for a century.

f 5

Meanwhile, between 1669 and 1687 Robert Cavelier de La Salle had descended the Mississippi from the Great Lakes to the Gulf and established an ill-fated settlement at Matagorda Bay in Texas. La Salle's reports of his findings changed French geopolitical strategy. Control of English expansion through control of the Mississippi became much more important for a long time than the search for the Western Sea, though as late as the 1740s the Vérendryes were casting about in the Black Hills of South Dakota for a way west.

To the south, the Spaniard De Soto trekked all over the southeast and crossed over and sailed up and down the Mississippi, but he too failed to find the fabled strait, nor did he find El Dorado or even another Tenochtitlan in the manner of Cortez. The closest any Spaniard came to a transcontinental passage was the tortured, stumbling journey of the cunning Cabeza de Vaca, who, shipwrecked on the Texas coast in 1535, made his way across the entire Southwest to the Mexican province of Sinaloa. His account of his trials and tribulations among the plains and pueblo Indians focussed not on the passage to India but on the cities of Cibola. This momentarily distracted the Spanish, who, with the experience of Cortez always before them, and the myth of the Seven Cities of Cibola still very much alive, sent out two expeditions northward to search out the fabled empires. The first under Fray Marcos de Niza reported success and heightened the myth. The second under Coronado in 1540 could report only failure. Though he and his men explored most of the Southwest, discovering the Grand Canyon and coursing out onto the plains, Coronado's Seven Cities turned out to be the disappointing seven pueblos of Zuñi along the Rio Puerco, a branch of the Rio Grande. And in Kansas he found

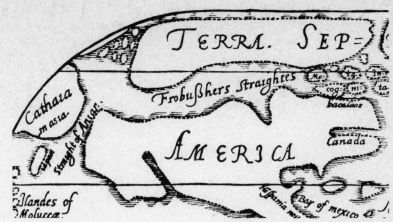

This detail of a 1578 map of the world illustrates the Northwest Passage which Frobisher thought he had found. In 1576, reaching Frobisher's Bay, which he took to be a strait, he decided to sail westward to see 'whether he mighte carrie himself through the same into some open sea on the backe syde.' The Strait of Anian is seen to the north-west, between America and Cathay. (4)

not Gran Quivira as his guide told him he would, but a wretched plains Indian town instead. Coronado and those who followed him, such as Sosa and Oñate and Kino, did, however, open up the Southwest to settlement well in advance of rivals to the north on the east coast of America.

The myth of the garden

Though for a time Spanish, French and British alike were all stymied in their search for Anian and turned their attention to more immediate problems of exploitation, colonization and imperial confrontation, the Northwest Passage dream never really faded. In 1776 Escalante marched northward from Santa Fe into the rugged country of southern Colorado, crossed over the Colorado River and penetrated the Wasatch Mountains to Utah Lake in the Great Basin. His map drawn by Miera y Pacheca included a Timpanogos River (later changed to the Rio Buenaventura) flowing westward from Utah (Timpanogos) Lake to the Pacific. Miera y Pacheca's map became the basis for all subsequent maps of the early American West, especially that of Alexander von Humboldt, published in 1811, which was the most influential of its day. As a result of this cartographical information, even after the collapse of the French empire in North America, Spaniard, Briton and American alike continued to search for the Rio Buenaventura, the Timpanogos or some other river passage across the continent to the sea until 1845 when Lt John C. Frémont, after circling the entire Great Basin, reluctantly reported that no such river passage existed.

f 11

p 15
(10)

Even then hope did not die. Lewis and Clark's earlier monu-

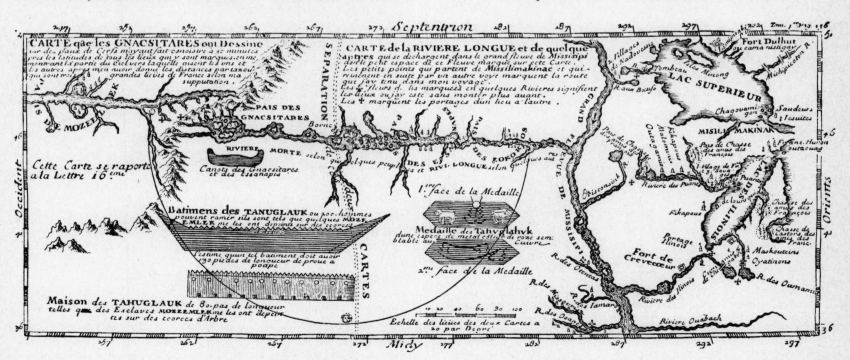

The French explorer La Hontan claimed that the left-hand half of this map had been drawn for him on deerskins by Indians. He shows a 'Rivière Longue', probably the Missouri, and on the other side of the mountains a completely fictitious river flowing west. (5)

f 6 mental voyage up the Missouri, their crossing over the mountains, and their voyage down the Columbia River suggested that somewhere, just north of the Great Basin, such a river might exist, and the Columbia became a precious geopolitical pawn of international politics until the mid-19th century.

The importance of all this activity was twofold. It accelerated the march across the continent, which without the passage to India concept might have been more leisurely. And it inevitably focussed attention on the heart of the continent. French exploration had demonstrated the obvious strategic quality of the Mississippi and its tributaries, not to mention the economic potential of its valley. Likewise, French fur traders from the Vérendryes onward dramatized the economic potential of the Missouri and its tributaries. Christopher Gist, Simon Kenton, Daniel Boone and others like *p 13 (1)* them, crossing over the Cumberland Gap into Kentucky and the Ohio River country on their way west, opened up that territory for economic exploitation and Indian warfare. Long hunters—buckskin-clad explorers who stayed out in the wilderness for a year or two at a time—moved south beyond the Appalachians into Alabama and as far west as Memphis. The most traveled of these hunters was a poor retarded boy who wandered south to the Gulf and possibly west to the Mississippi in the company of friendly Indians. Unfortunately he was quite unable to make himself understood in the white community when he attempted to tell of the marvels he had seen.

By the late 18th century, news of the new-found Adamic world in the interior of the continent was filtering back to Europe where imaginative writers like François René de Chateaubriand took their cue from works like William Bartram's *Travels* and John Filson's *The Discovery, Settlement and Present State of Kentucke* in which Daniel Boone emerged as a full-fledged American hero, and the romantic writings of Gilbert Imlay, the Kentuckian who retired to Paris where he inflamed the imagination of French romantics. The European writers, in turn, with Rousseau's notion of the state of nature before them, conceptualized wild America into myth, created an Eden out of the Dark and Bloody Ground, a noble savage out of the relentless red foe, and a Bois de Boulogne out of the entire vast trans-Appalachian country.

This series of literary images fitted in well with American nationalistic pretensions and an emerging self-image of national innocence in a state of nature. It also reinforced the practical claims of American land speculators and promoters. And so, as Henry Smith has pointed out in *Virgin Land: the American West as Symbol and Myth*, the explorers' accounts became transfused into mythical descriptions of the continental interior as an Edenic garden of the world with Daniel Boone its primitive pathfinder and the sturdy yeoman as its central hero. It was a powerful myth that enabled promoters to transform reality to suit their purposes and in so doing to draw thousands of settlers west out onto the treeless Great *f 11* Plains and over the forbidding Rockies to California's advertised

Lewis and Clark, who made the first crossing of the continent in 1804–06, were commissioned not only to explore possible routes, but also to collect information about natural features and native inhabitants. In this rather fanciful engraving they negotiate with Indians. (6)

pastoral valleys. Even the Mormons were persuaded by John *p 17* Charles Frémont's description of the desolate Great Salt Valley as *(14)* 'a bucolic place', and they migrated there, appropriately naming *p 64* their kingdom 'Deseret'—a kingdom which through hard work *(11)* came eventually to match Frémont's version of reality.

So powerful a force was the myth of the garden that settlers moving west largely ignored the reports of army explorers like Zebulon Pike and Stephen H. Long who termed the High Plains a 'Great American Desert', or Captain Randolph Barnes Marcy, who in 1849 called parts of Oklahoma and Texas the 'Great Zahara of North America'. Rather they preferred to believe the reports of fertile soil, soft zephyrs, and incredible abundance advertised in

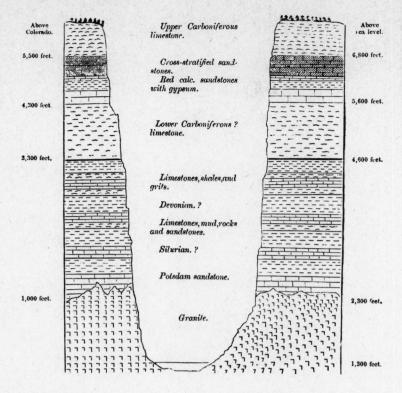

An expedition led by Lt J. C. Ives in 1857 was the first to make a scientific survey of the geology of the Grand Canyon. This cross-section (above) was drawn by John Strong Newberry, who with Hayden and others began the compilation of a stratigraphic column for the American West. The same party also included the Prussian artist F. W. von Egloffstein, whose impossibly romantic drawings (left), the first ever made of the Canyon, owed as much to Doré as to natural observation. (7, 8)

Kennedy's *Texas* and the promotional materials of Stephen F. Austin and other Texas empresarios. Only the Federal government took men like Pike and Long seriously, and under President Jackson moved the Cherokee and Choctaw Indians into the regions scientifically designated as desert.

The last mountains

Still other aspects of exploration in the interior of North America drew settlers west at an incredibly rapid pace. The dramatic events of the Rocky Mountain fur trade captivated the American imagination in the 1820s and 1830s. Mountain men such as Robert Stuart, Jedediah Smith, Zenas Leonard, Etienne Provost, Robert Ferris and Jim Bridger penetrated the Rockies during this period and located passes through the mountains to Oregon and California. They served as guides to emigrant wagon trains and occasionally drew maps of that vast complex region through which the settlers would have to pass to reach the Pacific. In addition, the fur trade itself created bustling settlements in St Louis and a number of Missouri River towns and led eventually to the opening of the Santa Fe trade which in turn brought Americans into and across the Southwest. The Rocky Mountains and the arid escarpments of the far Southwest were hardly gardens or Edens, but they did represent hypothetical abundance. This potential was duly reported by mountain men, Santa Fe traders, land speculators, European sportsmen and romantic painters, not to mention army explorers of the 1840s and 1850s sent out by the Federal government to make maps and determine scientifically what the Louisiana Purchase and Mexican cessions (following the war with Mexico in 1846) were good for.

p 17
(14)

In the latter respect, after Frémont's determination of the true nature of the Great Basin, the most important army exploring ventures of the mid-19th century were the survey of the new boundary with Mexico (1848–57) and the search for a railroad route across the mountains to the Pacific. The Mexican Boundary Survey was largely the work of Major William H. Emory and Lt Amiel Weeks Whipple of the United States Topographical Engineers, whose government report with its map was the most accurate and complete ever made of the Southwest. The railroad

f 10

explorations were also conducted by the Corps of Topographical Engineers under the direction of Colonel John James Abert and Secretary of War Jefferson Davis.

In 1853 five separate expeditions moved through the West. Four of them ran laterally from east to west, while the fifth moved up and down the Pacific coast. It was the largest such exploring expedition ever attempted up to that time by the United States. Predictably, each of the expedition leaders reported that his was the most feasible route for a transcontinental railroad, so the country, torn by sectionalism on the eve of civil war, was faced with a choice it could not make. But the result was not complete failure. In the reports of Lt Isaac I. Stevens, Captain John W. Gunnison, Lt James Beckwith, Lt Amiel W. Whipple, Lt John Pope and Lt John G. Parke was a vast compendium of scientific information about the West, including comprehensive maps, geological drawings, plant inventories, meteorological data, classifications of animal life, mineralogical surveys, and ethnological descriptions that for the first time provided a complete and relatively accurate picture of the American West. From their work a whole new view of the continent emerged.

f 9

As a counterpoint to these sober scientific assessments of the West, Frémont, now in disgrace and driven from the Army, during the same period led two spectacularly disastrous railroad expeditions into the West on his own. The first floundered in the deep snows and mountain passes of the San Luis Valley and the southern Rockies, and the survivors were reduced to cannibalism. The second came to grief in the mountains further west where the men were frozen and the survivors barely escaped with their lives. The day of the spectacular individual explorer in North America had almost passed.

The last important individual feat of exploration within the continental United States was, however, perhaps the most spectacular of all. In May of 1869 one-armed Major John Wesley Powell and nine amateur companions set off from Green River, Wyoming, down the unknown Colorado River in four specially made longboats, braving 1,500 miles of broiling rapids, mile-deep canyons and tumbling waterfalls. For a hundred days they traveled down the river, alternately propelled at lightning speed through the rapids and narrows, or slowly and laboriously lining their boats downstream on ropes. When they emerged at the Mormon settlement of Callville on 30 August, Powell and his men, less one English visitor who had given up early and three who had been massacred by Shivwit Indians when they tried to climb out of the river canyons and walk back to civilization, had explored the last unknown territory within the continental United States. They had discovered the last unknown mountain range and the last uncharted river.

p 18
(18)

Reports compiled by the Pacific Railroad Survey teams in 1853 contained a vast mass of information on a wide range of subjects. This page illustrates varieties of reptile. (9)

The Mexican Boundary Survey, conducted by Major Emory and Lt Whipple, was a mission fraught with danger. In this 1852 sketch, Apache Indians attack the expedition's convoy. (10)

p 18
(17, 19)

But they did more than fill in blank spaces on the national map. In the course of his river trip and subsequent expeditions to the Colorado plateau country in 1870 and 1871–72, Powell conceptualized virtually the entire structural geology of the inter-montane region, defining many of the terms relating to faulting, uplifting and river erosion that are still in use throughout the world today. More important, Powell applied his empirically derived concepts to the whole question of human ecology in regions of aridity and economic scarcity. His *Report on the Lands of the Arid Regions of the United States* published in 1878 was one of the most important books ever written by an explorer. In it the Major spoke out against the myth of the garden and forcefully pointed out that much of the American West was an arid region without enough water to sustain settlement in the traditional yeoman fashion. Instead, like Buckminster Fuller in 1927, he argued that American institutions must be specially adapted to the arid lands before settlement would be possible. He proposed a new land classification system adapted to grazing more than farming, a whole system of water conservation and river basin control, and the careful conservation of timber and mineral resources. In short, he called for a planned economy in the late 19th-century halcyon days of unrestrained free enterprise and devil-take-the-hindmost *laissez faire*.

Moreover, Powell's efforts did not stop short with white settlement. He was also scientifically fascinated by the Indians, by their

way of life, their myths, their language, and by the question of their survival. His grand scheme for the West included the conservation of people as well as the land. Out of his efforts arose not only the US Geological Survey in 1879 and the whole blueprint for conservation in America during the Progressive era after 1900, but also the Bureau of American Ethnology, the first government agency for the scientific study of mankind. Powell was one of those rare explorers whose dramatically changed view of the realities of nature helped significantly to revise the views of a whole culture.

While Powell was exploring the plateau province and expounding his doctrines, other late 19th-century explorers were also in the field bent on other missions. The flamboyant Clarence King of Yale led a survey across the West along the 40th parallel and opened up the interior of the Great Basin to a fantastic mining boom. Ferdinand Vandiver Hayden, a physician and geologist, led another survey of the Rocky Mountains that emphasized their geological variety and resulted in the creation of Yellowstone National Park. The expedition's photographs of mountain and park scenery, made by the incomparable William H. Jackson, plus Moran's equally dramatic paintings, helped to confirm in the public's mind the national park idea—a uniquely American contribution to world culture. In addition, the photographer, Jackson, and Hayden's artist, W. H. Holmes, explored and publicized to the outside world the lost prehistoric Pueblo civilizations of the Southwest. A short while later in 1881, a rancher, Robert Wetherill, discovered the fantastic cliff palaces of Mesa Verde and hundreds of other important sites in the Southwest. Abandoning his ranch, Wetherill, sometimes alone and in winter, rode through canyons and over mesas locating and dramatizing the lost Indian ruins to people back east. He was eventually murdered by Navahos a short distance from his homestead, which stood in the shadow of the largest prehistoric Indian complex north of Mexico—Chaco Canyon, New Mexico. 'Anazazi', or the Ancient One, he was called by the Indians, and more than any other man he took American exploration into another realm—the time-out-of-mind realm of ancient America. Much of the continuing exploration of the American West today takes place in this realm and that of another discoverer of ancient America who cannot be forgotten— Othniel Charles Marsh, the master paleontologist.

Marsh, who eventually became curator of the Peabody Museum at Yale, began his career as a western explorer one day in 1868 when he stepped off the Union Pacific in Nebraska and discovered the remains of the extinct fossil horse of North America. He went on to many other discoveries, however, from pterodactyls to dinosaurs, until he was shipping whole train-loads of extinct beasts back to Yale in a furious competition with Edward D. Cope of Pennsylvania. Together and somewhat scandalously, these two men,

p 18
(18)

p 19–
(20–2

p 19–
(21, 22
p 164
(34)

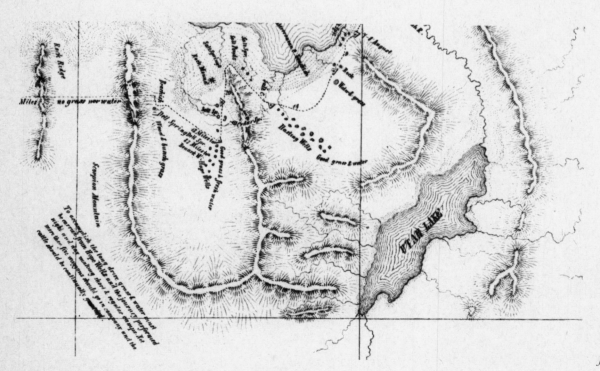

The journey west was not as easy as promoters and artists suggested. In this detail of the Utah desert from a 'Map of the Emigrant Road to San Francisco' careful instructions suggest the hardships to be expected. Utah Lake, seen here, is the 'Lake Timpanogos' of earlier accounts, from which a mythical river flowed west. (11)

'Professor Marsh's Primeval Troupe. He shows his Perfect Mastery over the Ceratopsidae.' Othniel Charles Marsh, seen as a paleontological showman in a 'Punch' cartoon of 1890. (12)

charging one another with quackery, hijacking train-loads of specimens, wheeling and dealing frantically and entrepreneurially in the sober commerce of science, made paleontology seem the most exciting science in 19th-century America. And somewhere along the way, Marsh's primitive horse cycle proved to be the most substantial piece of evidence for the validity of Charles Darwin's theory of evolution through natural selection.

To the south

It is obvious then that exploration and the discovery of America have not been simply a matter of geography. They involved the constant imaginative redefinition of America that is in itself a characteristic expression of the American mind. In a sense, America has been almost anything its explorers or their 'programmers' wanted it to be at the time. And yet constant discoveries and re-discoveries have continually changed the meaning of the country for its citizens.

Changing definitions of America by explorers, however, have by no means been confined to the continental United States. A fundamental aspect of its existence is the fact that the present United States was first discovered and emerged into human consciousness during an age of global discovery. For most of its history the United States has also taken part, along with the principal nations of Europe, in extra-territorial global exploration, in part as a means of defining itself and its position in the world.

Early in the 19th century American explorers solved the ancient problem (dating from Magellan's voyage in 1519–22) of *Terra Australis Incognita* or the location of a southern continent below Cape Horn. As early as 1819 sea lion hunters from Stonington, Connecticut, sighted the Antarctic coast. In that year James P. Sheffield in the *Hersillia* was the first to see the southern continent. He was followed in early 1820 by Edward Bransfield in the *Williams* and in November of that year by Nathaniel Palmer in the *Hero*. The first landing on Antarctica was made by John Davis of New Haven when he rowed ashore from the *Cecelia* in February of 1831. Though they are relatively obscure now, these men made a dramatic impact on 19th-century American thought, which saw America looking toward a boundless horizon. In 1849 the country's foremost novelist, James Fenimore Cooper, dramatized the exploits of the Antarctic explorers in his book *The Sea Lions*. Somewhat earlier, fired by the lectures of John Cleves Symmes on polar whirlpools at the frozen ends of the earth, and the attempts of his friend Jeremiah N. Reynolds to promote a United States exploring expedition to the South Pole, Edgar Allan Poe wrote his most ambitious work, *The Narrative of A. Gordon Pym*—the story of a man rushing irresistibly to his doom in the whiteness of Antarctica. To the end of his life images of exploration and disaster in the ice-bound Antarctic remained with Poe, and the connection of whiteness and death was his continuing obsession.

Between 1819 and 1831 there appears to have been a continuous and general American interest in the southern continent, capped by the American Antarctic Exploring Expedition of 1829–31 led by Capts Benjamin Pendleton and the experienced Nathaniel Palmer. However, the most important of all American expeditions to the southern seas was the great Federally-sponsored United States Exploring Expedition of 1838–42 commanded by Captain Charles Wilkes. This consisted of six ships and included a whole coterie of scientists, mapmakers and artists. It had a three-fold purpose: scientifically to verify the existence of an Antarctic land mass, to range out over the South Pacific charting whale migrations and mapping the exotic islands of the South Seas, and to explore the coasts of Oregon locating ports on the Pacific and the possible outlet of a Northwest Passage.

Capt. Wilkes's expedition was gone for four years on one of the great voyages in modern history. During the course of the expedition Wilkes and his men definitely proved the existence of Antarctica and mapped its frozen shoreline for 1500 miles. They also mapped the South Pacific so accurately that many of Wilkes's charts are still in use today. And due to the wreck of the *Peacock* off the mouth of the Columbia River, United States negotiators pushed their demands for a territorial boundary with Canada north of Puget Sound so as to secure its safe harbors. More than any other, the Wilkes Expedition dramatized the role of the United States as a future Pacific power. Further exploration of the Antarctic by the United States was neglected, however, for nearly one hundred years or until the Wilkins-Hearst Expedition of 1928 long after Amundsen and Scott discovered the South Pole.

p 22 (23)

Instead the United States turned westward across the wide Pacific and southward to South America for much of the 19th century. The most significant American ventures across the Pacific were, of course, Commodore Matthew Calbraith Perry's expedition to the China Sea and Japan in 1852–54, and the Rodgers and Ringgold North Pacific Exploring Expedition of 1853–56. Perry's expedition, an unambiguous product of Manifest Destiny, not only opened up Japan to American trade, but also established coaling stations in the China Sea to service the new steam warships of the United States Navy. The demand for trade, international competition for the China market, and the exigencies of a new technology thrust the United States into the Pacific and the Far East in a permanent way. And Perry as explorer was not only the advance scout, he was the chief theoretician.

f 13

The Rodgers-Ringgold Expedition followed on the heels of Perry's expedition and mapped the entire North Pacific with an eye to the most efficient sailing routes to China, further emphasizing America's Far Eastern and global orientation. Voyages like these laid the groundwork for Dewey's presence in Manila Bay in 1898 and the acquisition of a series of Far Eastern outposts which eventually became hostages to Japan and now China.

A Japanese view of the arrival of Commodore Perry's expedition of 1852–54. Above, eight American ships (three of them paddle steamers) in Yokohama harbor; below, the landing of Perry's party. (13)

During the same period, in the mid-19th century, American explorers also looked to South America. From 1849–52 Lt Melville Gilliss conducted a US Naval astronomical expedition to the Southern Hemisphere in an attempt to measure from a post in Chile the transits of Venus across the sun and, in so doing, accurately to measure the circumference of the earth. And while Gilliss was in Chile, Lts Lardner Gibbon and William Herndon led an expedition to the Valley of the Amazon in search of suitable land to colonize American Negro slaves. A bit later, in 1859–61, Dr Martin Delaney, who was to become the first Negro officer in the US Army, explored the coast of West Africa and concluded a treaty with the Yoruba chiefs of the Niger for the same purpose.

Also in the mid-19th century, official and unofficial American explorers surveyed the Rio de La Plata in South America, the Dead Sea, the Amur River in Siberia, the Bering Straits, and the coasts of Central America from Tehuantepec to Atrato, the last in search of a canal route to insure two-ocean status.

Back in Washington, Lt Matthew Fontaine Maury at the Naval Observatory issued his all-important charts and books on the winds and currents of both the Atlantic and the Pacific Oceans, based on reports from ocean-going vessels, which enabled American clipper ships to outdistance ships of all nations in the race for distant ports. His *The Physical Geography of the Sea*, published in 1855, was, according to one writer, 'the first textbook of modern oceanography'. Like Fuller in the 20th century, Maury and Perry in the 19th already saw America as a global nation basing its pretensions on a scientific knowledge of the principles of oceanography and a command of clipper ship and steam warship technology.

The lure of the Pole

American attention has also centered on the Arctic where, for most of the 19th century, explorers searched for an open polar sea which would again provide a long-sought Northwest Passage. Though intrepid British explorers such as Hearne, McKenzie, Franklin, Ross, Simpson, Perry and Back had led expeditions through the Arctic regions north of Canada since the beginning of the 19th century, the event that most vividly focussed attention on the Arctic was the disappearance in 1846 of Sir John Franklin and all his men aboard the discovery ships *Erebus* and *Terror* as they were searching for a Northwest Passage somewhere west of Baffin Island. When the likelihood of an Arctic disaster's having befallen Franklin and his men dawned on Britons and Americans alike in 1848, a whole series of rescue and search expeditions were mounted that continued as late as 1880, when US Army Lt Frederick Schwatka's expedition marched overland from Hudson Bay to King William Island hunting the remains of Franklin's lost party. During this period British naval expeditions under R. J. N. McClure, Sir Edward Belcher, Richard Collinson, John Ross, Horatio Austin, H. R. N. Kellet and Henry McClintock crossed and re-crossed the frozen seas north of Canada between Baffin Island and Point Barrow, Alaska. During the course of their dramatic search, McClure, in September of 1850, almost succeeded in forcing a Northwest Passage by sea between Bank and Victoria Islands, while McClintock, as a result of his investigation of Peel Sound and the vicinity of King William Island, where Franklin's party actually perished, pointed the way to the practicable Northwest Passage traversed by Roald Amundsen in 1906.

The search for Sir John Franklin also inspired the most famous of 19th-century American expeditions to the Arctic. The first, sponsored by the American philanthropist Henry Grinnell, departed in 1850, commanded by Lt Edwin de Haven of the US Navy, and returned within a year without having found any trace of Franklin, though Lt Elisha Kent Kane's narrative of the expedition so captured the popular imagination that Grinnell outfitted a second expedition in 1853. Commanded by Kane, the expedition stayed out two years in search of the lost explorer, suffered unbelievable hardships, and reached the highest known point of north latitude, 80° 10′, at Cape Constitution on the Kennedy Channel between Greenland and Ellesmere Island. Kane died in 1857 shortly after his grueling experience, but he had laid out the route which his successors, A. W. Greely, Charles F. Hall and Robert E. Peary, were to follow as they painfully inched their way across Arctic wastes to the discovery of the North Pole.

p 22 (24)

Kane's primary achievement was his demonstration that the Kennedy Channel was practicable for navigation and pointed straight to the Arctic Sea. This changed the emphasis in Arctic exploration from a search for the Northwest Passage to a race for the North Pole. In 1861 Dr Isaac Hayes explored Smith Sound and Kane Basin. Ten years later, after participating for five years in a fruitless search for Franklin's remains, Dr Charles Francis Hall sailed the *Polaris* up the passage between Greenland and Ellesmere Island as far north as 81° 37′ N, from which point he ascended a peak at Cape Brevoort and saw the Robeson Channel opening out into the long-sought polar sea. Hall perished on the expedition, and a party of survivors marooned on an ice-cake drifted, almost unbelievably, for two thousand miles before they were saved.

p 22 (25)

By 1879 N. A. E. Nordenskiold of Sweden had completed a Northeast Passage across the top of Siberia to Alaska, and the nations of Europe, along with America, began collectively to turn northward. After a series of international conferences in Hamburg and Berne, a co-operative effort at the scientific examination of the Arctic developed, and the year 1881 was designated the International Polar Year. Unfortunately in that year A. W. Greely of the United States started out from Greenland northward up the Kennedy Channel to one of the most spectacular Arctic disasters of the day. Marooned for over a year on Sabine Island, after having reached Cape Washington at 83° 24′ N on the northern coast of Greenland, the farthest point north reached to that time, all but six men of the Greely expedition perished under horrible circumstances. Greely himself survived and attempted to dominate American activities in the Arctic for the next thirty years.

p 22 (27)

However, from 1886 onward, Robert E. Peary of the US Navy began a ceaseless effort to reach the North Pole. In 1892, Peary returned to Greenland which he had explored in 1886 and systematically searched it for a jumping-off point for the Pole. By 1900 he had traversed that frozen island to its northern tip and sailed around it, demonstrating once and for all its true character. After that he poised for a dash for the Pole. He failed in an expedition from Cape Hecla in 1902, and he failed a second time in 1906, though he reached 87° 6′ N latitude. Finally, in a masterfully organized expedition across frozen ice floes and treacherous open stretches of water, Peary reached the North Pole on 6 April 1909, accompanied only by Matt Henson, his intrepid Negro partner, and two Eskimos. It was one of the great feats of exploration, and among other things, Peary demonstrated that the polar sea was by no means open water at any point along the route.

p 23 (28)

Alaska and the northern frontier

Two further northern developments were meanwhile taking place. After 1860, and following earlier efforts by the Russians, Americans had begun to explore Alaska. As a result of the fifty-year process of Arctic exploration, all northern explorers also began to look more closely into Arctic nature and the possibilities it afforded for sustaining human life. Science and scientific adaptation became increasingly important. Among the most significant American explorations in Alaska was the Western Union Telegraph Expedition of 1866 designed to run a line of communications around the world from the United States across Alaska, the Bering Straits and Siberia. This resulted in the excellent work of William Healy Dall and Frederick Wymper. Dall became perhaps the most expert and experienced of all American explorers of Alaska.

After the purchase of Alaska in 1867, American exploring activity in that vast territory underwent several phases which paralleled, in many ways, previous experience in the American West. For a time the United States Army and the Coast and Geodetic Survey spearheaded exploration. Typical of such work were Captain Charles Raymond's reconnaissance on the Yukon and the marches of Lts Frederick Schwatka and George M. Stoney into the Alaskan interior in the 1880s. Gradually, however, the United States Geological Survey took over the work in a more systematic fashion, concentrating on careful mapping and the search for mineral resources. Sober professional efforts like these were occasionally punctuated by more sensational ventures such as Edward S. Harriman's seaborne reconnaissance in 1899, in which he took a yachtful of leading Alaskanists on a scientific pleasure cruise that returned little more than trivial information and perhaps a few observations concerning the possibility of a globe-encircling railroad. By implication the mighty Gilded Age transportation magnate meant to resurrect singlehandedly the once important land bridge to Asia, lost in the mists of time and the Bering Sea. Gold strikes in the Klondike, rich salmon fisheries in the interior and the limitless resource potential of Alaska and other parts of the Arctic country made this an appealing possibility to the American imagination.

p 22 (26)

No one did more to fix in the popular mind the idea of a new Arctic frontier, which could be, in effect, a new kind of 'garden', than the American-educated Canadian, Vilhjalmur Stefánsson. In a series of dramatic single-minded expeditions east from Point Barrow and north from the MacKenzie River estuary, Stefánsson, between 1906 and 1918, explored the icebound Beaufort Sea and mapped the frozen archipelagoes of the far north, west of Ellesmere Island. Most important, however, Stefánsson viewed the Arctic not as a hostile place, but as 'the Friendly Arctic'. He proved that careful study of the Eskimo culture enabled a man to live with ease off the land and even the incredibly cold winter became friend instead of foe. Stefánsson's ideas, purveyed through his extensive writing and his influence on a whole generation of Arctic explorers, made the Arctic analogous to the 19th-century Rocky Mountain frontier where the survival techniques of the mountain men were of prime value. He provided one last frontier of the traditional sort understood by Americans and Canadians alike, and he along with others helped to re-orient what had once been an Atlantic- and Pacific-focussed continent toward a northern frontier on the shores of the Arctic Sea.

Men and machines

But at virtually the same time technology was racing ahead, and men were developing new machines to conquer rather than adapt to the Arctic, much along the lines that Fuller was to suggest on his 'Dymaxion Air Traffic Chart'. In 1896 a Swede, S. A. Andree, attempted a balloon flight from Spitzbergen across the North Pole. He crashed, and the remains of his party were not found until 1930. Nothing daunted, an American newspaperman, Walter Wellman, between 1907 and 1909 tried three times to reach the Pole by means of specially designed French airships. Though he failed, the age of air travel and specialized machines was making it possible for modern man to skip in giant steps over the whole traditional frontier settlement process. An Italian, General Umberto Nobile, accompanied by Lincoln Ellsworth of the US Air Service and Roald Amundsen successfully took a dirigible over the North Pole in 1926. And in the same year, just two days prior to Nobile's trip, Richard E. Byrd and Floyd Bennett in a trusty Ford trimotor plane made a successful flight from Spitzbergen over the Pole. Charles Lindbergh's flights to Alaska and the Far East via the northern route in 1931 and 1933 further dramatized the utility of the airplane in bringing about settlement on the northern frontier. Bombers of the US Army Air Force Ferry Command in World War II repeatedly demonstrated that the Arctic 'Great Circle Route' was the shortest route to Europe and parts of Asia. And all through the 1920s and 1930s, partially due to work in the Antarctic as well as the north, men developed a host of machines to cope with the elements, ranging from motorized sleds and tank-tracked snowmobiles to sophisticated solar radiation gauges, and radio and electronic communications equipment. In short, and on a larger scale with big and relatively complex machines, the technologists were once again transforming global geographic thinking. Americans were very much a part of this process.

p 23 (30)

p 23 (29)

Due to a newer and more sophisticated northern frontier concept, a heightened scientific curiosity on the part of physicists about the behavior of men and machines in extremely low temperatures, and the strategic exigencies of the Cold War, the United States government has launched no fewer than thirty-seven major postwar expeditions to the Arctic. The most dramatic of these were the voyages of the atomic submarine *Nautilus* underwater to the North Pole in 1958 and the underwater negotiation of the Northwest Passage by the atomic submarine *Skate* in 1959. In 1969, due to the discovery of immense oil deposits on Alaska's north slope, the specially designed supertanker *Manhattan*, equipped with lasers, cut its way through the ice on still another Northwest Passage.

p 23 (31)

p 23 (32)

Space, 'the new ocean'

But even as the Arctic frontier became technologically practicable, forcing a conceptual redefinition of North American geography, the infinitely more complex science of rocketry and space technology arose to force a redefinition of all global geography. As early as the 1890s, the Russian Konstantin Tsiolkovsky began to consider the problem of space travel. By 1898, dreaming large dreams of interplanetary travel, Tsiolkovsky had worked out most of the basic concepts of rocket propulsion. In 1903, while men were still struggling with sledges and balloons in the Arctic, and the Wright brothers were successfully testing the world's first heavier-than-air flying machine at Kitty Hawk, North Carolina, Tsiolkovsky unobtrusively published his papers on rocketry in little-read Russian scientific journals.

Meanwhile, an American, Robert H. Goddard, in 1899 at the age of seventeen had also begun work on extra-terrestrial travel. By 1909, after taking a PhD at Clark University, he had worked out independently the entire theoretical basis for a multi-stage rocket that would carry man into space. Like Tsiolkovsky he concealed most of his visionary imagination behind the dry-sounding title of a scientific paper published in 1920, 'A Method of Reaching Extreme Altitudes'. The Patent Office records reveal, however, that from 1914 onward Goddard had designed the hardware for virtually every aspect of rocket propulsion and guidance. In all, between 1914 and 1920 he had secured some two hundred patents before he revealed his ideas to the outside world.

The scientific paper, nevertheless, secured him a grant of $5000 from the Smithsonian Institution, and from that point on, he was able to put his ideas to a practical test. In a field near Auburn, Massachusetts, on 16 March 1926, Goddard launched the world's first successful liquid-propelled rocket to an altitude of 40 feet, by which point it had already accelerated to a speed of 60 miles per hour. In 1929 Goddard's spectacular rocket experiments attracted the attention of Charles Lindbergh who secured him support from the Guggenheim Fund for the Promotion of Aeronautics, and Goddard moved his whole experiment station to Roswell, New Mexico. There, throughout the 1930s, working with his wife and a small team of mechanics, Goddard quietly perfected a rocket that reached an altitude of 9000 feet.

p 24 (34)

The third pioneer of rocketry was Hermann Oberth, a German. Oberth, inspired by Jules Verne's novels, also independently worked out the principles of rocket propulsion. His first paper, published in 1923, had a dramatic title, *The Rocket into Planetary Space*. Later Oberth corresponded with Tsiolkovsky, and, more important, he gathered around him a group of young space enthusiasts who formed 'The Society for Spaceship Travel' in 1925. In 1929 Oberth further dramatized his work in a book, *The Road to Space Travel*. Thus the Germans, in contrast to the Russians and Americans, instantly captured the popular imagination in terms of space exploration.

It took a war, however, and the dreadful results of the Peenemünde V-2 laboratory that produced the unstoppable rocket vehicles of the second London blitz to alert the world to the new technology that would one day change the entire orientation of the globe. After World War II, Russia, conscious of its long tradition of expertise in rocketry, lost no time in exploring the potential of German technological breakthroughs. Russian scientists immediately concentrated on the development of very large rockets or intercontinental ballistic military missiles as a counterpoise to the American discovery of the atomic bomb.

Likewise, the United States hardly 'returned to normalcy', as it did after World War I. Virtually the entire German Peenemünde team, under the direction of Wernher von Braun, who had visited Goddard in the 1930s, moved to the United States and continued work on the development of the space rocket and such related fields as space medicine. American scientists attached to the Air Force and the Navy also worked along parallel lines, fully intent upon exploring the potential of outer space.

Ironically, in view of the intense competition between nations, it was an international co-operative venture—the International Geophysical Year—that provided the occasion for man's first real penetration of space. As part of its program for that year, the United States announced plans for the launching of an artificial earth satellite that would aid in more accurately mapping the globe. Russia, however, actually performed the feat on 4 October 1957, when it launched *Sputnik I. The New York Times* headline for the next day captured something of the excitement felt by men around the world for the first time made forcibly aware of a new frontier for exploration:

SOVIET FIRES EARTH SATELLITE INTO SPACE
IT IS CIRCLING THE GLOBE AT 18,000 M.P.H. . . .

In November, the Russians launched a second *Sputnik* carrying a dog, demonstrating that life could be sustained in outer space.

On 6 December 1957, the American launch vehicle, *Vanguard*, blew up spectacularly on its launch pad in Florida. Von Braun and his army team from the Redstone Arsenal in Huntsville, Alabama, however, finally managed to launch a United States satellite on 31 January 1958, using a *Jupiter* rocket missile made up of elements of the *Redstone* military ballistics missile. Just as in the Renaissance, a new Age of Discovery began—born of competition between men and nations, dependent alike on abstract theory, applied science, now called 'engineering', visionary imagination and the faith of whole cultures who invested billions of dollars or rubles in the great adventure out into the frontier that President John F. Kennedy called 'this new ocean'.

On 12 April 1961, Russia again startled the world when it launched the first space explorer around the earth. The cosmonaut Yuri Gagarin orbited the globe in eighty-nine minutes aboard the spherical spaceship *Vostok I*. The first American orbital flight took place on 20 February 1962, when John Glenn rode three times around the earth in the Project Mercury Capsule *Friendship 7*. From this point on, both nations took ever bolder steps out into space in a race for the moon. They were motivated only in part by national pride and considerations of international security, for once the new knowledge of space and space technology appeared on the horizon of human knowledge, there was no ignoring it—no putting it back into the Pandora's box whence it came. Knowledge was neutral, but implacably pervasive in the minds of men. They could do with it what they wished, but they had no choice but to do something, hopefully in the best interests of all mankind.

Exploration in the 1960s, then, became the product of gigantic machines, enormous conglomerates of scientists, bureaucrats, technicians and test pilots as well as an astoundingly complex technology which ramified everywhere and paradoxically depended as much on miniaturization (in circuits, computers, cameras, etc.) as upon giantism in rocketry. The public heroes were the astronaut and cosmonaut explorers who should not be forgotten—pioneers such as Gagarin, Titov, Shepard, Glenn, Carpenter, Tereshkova, Komarov, Leonov, Grissom, White, Lovell, Armstrong, Conrad, Aldrin, Chafee, Schirra, Beregovoi, Bykovsky and Borman. But hundreds of artificial satellites, unmanned space flights, space cameras, spectroscopes, and tiny irrepressible beeping radios also expanded human knowledge to an incredible degree. The Van Allen radiation belt, composed of particles of solar energy circling around the earth, was discovered. The biological effects of weightlessness and other space phenomena became known. The earth was photographed *in toto* and in detail for the first time, as was the moon with all its craters and pockmarks. The mysteries of Mars began to be revealed, and likewise those of Venus, while, as the 1970s began, space probes moved out toward Jupiter and its lonely satellites first seen by Galileo. The practical utilities of celestial mechanics and Einstein's theories became more fully understood, along with the nature of space itself, light, and solar radiation. Spacemen learned to live and navigate in a new medium and with a whole new celestial orientation. Beyond this, science seemed on the verge of understanding the origins of the galaxy. A new age of cosmology had been thrust upon earthmen by the accelerated force of rocket propulsion.

p 24
(35)

Along with this new knowledge came, in the United States and presumably in Russia, a whole series of massive new space indus-

tries and innumerable spin-off or tangential industries reaching out into medicine, communications, weather forecasting, computers, teaching machines and even the 'new math' and other devices for restructuring all available educational systems and tools. Artificial satellites provided nearly instant world telecommunications. Gradually with *Telstar* and *Comsat* they became commercially practical vehicles, owned by millions of stockholders, that flashed everything—from the Tokyo Olympic Games to the horrors of battlefield combat—to a worldwide audience.

In terms of earthbound economics, the return on governmental expenditures was multiplied so extensively as to be virtually incalculable. By the simple yardstick of Keynesian economics, every public dollar invested had a 'multiplier effect' of approximately seven times, which meant that it did the work of seven dollars in the economy. This in the United States alone provided a tax base so greatly increased as to make the space program in reality profitable to the public economy. $1,000,000,000 invested and multiplied by the Keynesian formula yielded $7,000,000,000 of taxable income, which at an average tax rate of 20% yielded nearly $1,500,000,000, not to mention hundreds of thousands of jobs for workers of all kinds in a greatly stimulated and dynamic economy.

Moreover, the space venture was a 'service' venture whose products were in most cases not the endless flow of useless, unimaginative durable goods and luxury items that glutted the market in times past, but instead were related to knowledge potentially consumable by all. In America the 'brain industry' began to emerge as predominant, just as 'big steel' had towered over the late 19th and early 20th centuries, and the automotive industry, after Ford, had assumed command by mid-century. Out of the space adventure and the burgeoning space industries came new knowledge, new techniques, a new global awareness and potentially a whole new style of life which, given proper direction, could bring about the solution of many of the planet's most pressing problems. Clearly, given the inexorable pull of the space frontier, and the rapidly accelerating world scientific cast of mind, society on earth could never remain static.

p 116
(28)

At the end of the 1960s, that miraculous decade, the climax of space exploration was reached in full view of the entire world. On 20 July 1969, communications satellites relayed around the globe the unforgettable ghostly video pictures of man's first landing on the moon as American astronauts Neil Armstrong and Edwin (Buzz) Aldrin, clad in bulky space suits, climbed awkwardly down from their lunar spacecraft and set first foot on the moon's luminous and eerie surface. They found it a wasteland, as did their successors Charles Conrad and Alan Bean who landed in a second expedition on 19 November 1969. The legendary 'Mountains of the Moon', once located in *mappae mundi* in remote Africa, had now become reality in the form of gigantic craters and towering peaks that stood empty and silent, unfrequented by any living creature perhaps since their creation.

p 24
(33)

To some, the moon and the planets are new worlds like 'the friendly Arctic' of Stefansson, which man's technology, in the spirit of Buckminster Fuller and Buck Rogers, will some day make inhabitable. Thus astronauts Armstrong and Aldrin are the new Columbuses, and the moon, the new America. To many, however, the analogy with Columbus seems false. What Armstrong and Aldrin and all their heroic space predecessors have revealed is not a series of new worlds for escape and habitation, but a profounder knowledge of the earth's true place in the universe. They have changed once again the entire perspective of the globe and man's place on it. As a nation of explorers, both visionary and pragmatic, even sometimes mystical, 20th-century Americans have discovered what was perhaps always there—a vastly shrunken earth that in the future will force men to look inward with intensity and concern, even as they face the infinite horizons of outer space. Once again, as it was in the original Age of Discovery, American history is world history and America's destiny is inextricably bound up with that of the entire planet.

II

A NATION
OF NATIONS

Who are the Americans?

NATHAN
GLAZER

'Give me your tired, your poor,

Your huddled masses yearning to breathe free,

The wretched refuse of your teeming shore

Send these, the homeless, tempest-tost, to me.'

LINES ENGRAVED ON THE BASE OF THE STATUE OF LIBERTY

The mixture of peoples,

which gives so characteristic a quality to American life and causes so many uniquely American problems, is comparatively recent in origin. The Age of Immigration follows the Age of Discovery with hardly any overlap. In this chapter we will be concerned almost entirely with events since 1870.

During the 18th and early 19th centuries settlement was predominantly from Britain. Germany and the Scandinavian countries were also represented, but their peoples were also Protestant and found it easy to share the values of their neighbours. Irish immigrants were the only numerous Catholic group. There were also two large groups aside from the free immigrants—the Negroes and the Indians who remained second-class citizens.

The great wave of 'new immigrants' came in the second half of the 19th century: first the Irish, then Italians, Poles, Russians, Central and Southern Europeans, Japanese, Chinese. The first immigration act, directed against the Chinese, was passed in 1882. In 1924 the ethnic composition of the nation was fixed by the imposition of quotas, a system which remained in force until 1965.

After 1945 immigration rose and became quite heavy, but thousands were refused because their quotas were filled. Ben Shahn's mural (opposite) painted in 1937–38 for the Community Center of Jersey Homesteads, Roosevelt, New Jersey (a Federal housing development for workers in the garment industry) expresses succinctly both what America could do for the immigrant and also what the immigrant could do for America. Among the anonymous crowd taking refuge from persecution and poverty strides the dynamic figure of Einstein, clutching his violin case.

There are two ideals for a multi-national state. One is for all citizens to forget their differences, to discard their old identities and take on another, that of 'Americans'—the philosophy of the 'melting pot'. The other is for each to preserve his own culture, style and outlook, but for all to live peaceably together—the philosophy of the 'nation of nations'. The first has been tried and failed. Now, as not only national minorities but the previously underprivileged blacks and Indians begin to assert their cultural independence, the second faces its greatest test. (1)

Arriving: having satisfied the officials, immigrants wait to be transferred to New York itself (below, 1912). There, every national group had its own particular district, to which the new arrival naturally gravitated. (4)

Crossing: a ship-load of immigrants nearing the end of their journey in 1906. (2)

Waiting: in New York immigrants landed not on Manhattan itself but on Ellis Island, a few hundred yards off-shore, where they were scrutinized to ensure that the national quotas and other regulations were being adhered to. The island became an immigration station in 1892, and its 'pens' (right, 1906) were the first welcome that most new American citizens experienced. Before it closed in 1954 over twenty million people had passed through it. (3)

Living: parts of New York were hardly distinguishable from Europe. Orchard Street (right, *c.* 1900) was a Jewish area, signs in Hebrew proclaiming the ethnic identity of the inhabitants. (6)

Working: the immigrant was on the bottom rung of the ladder, and had to accept whatever work was offered. Above: an Italian woman carries home cloth for the family to make up at starvation wages. New York, 1909. (5)

Moving on: after a short spell in New York, many immigrants moved west, to states which were still developing and which offered more to the pioneer. Right: an immigrant train on the Baltimore and Ohio line, *c.* 1910. (7)

The Irish were the first immigrants to pose problems as a specific national group. Arriving in large numbers in the years after the potato famines of 1848–49, they were hard to assimilate: they were very poor and they were Catholic. Non-acceptance made them less ready to compromise and their 'Irishness' became a quality to cherish, not to forget. Below: a St Patrick's Day Parade in Union Square, New York, 1874. (8)

End of the voyage: passengers from Ireland disembarking in New York about 1855. In the background is Castle Garden, used for the processing of immigrants until Ellis Island was opened in 1892. Note, on the trunk on the right, 'Pat Murfy for Ameriky'. (9)

Irish power had grown to such an extent by the 1880s that it was arousing resentment among the rest of the population. A cartoon in *Puck* (above) of 3 April 1889 – 'They all do it' – shows politicians and other public figures bowing low before the personification of Ireland. (10)

43

'The melting pot' meant that cultural differences were boiled down to produce uniform American products. It was an ideal that applied equally to everyone though of course the transformation would be more radical in some cases than in others. A Navajo Indian, for instance, could be turned – it was hoped – from a 'barbarian' warrior to a sober industrious citizen, by three years' training at an Indian School. Above: the same boy, before and after this process, in the 1880s. (11, 12)

'The Thing won't melt!' (above). In 1915 it was held against the Germans that they had failed to renounce their national loyalties and undergo the expected transmutation. (13)

Round the same table sit the family of nations that make up America. Uncle Sam carves the turkey; the centerpiece is Universal Suffrage; American presidents look down benevolently from the walls. In this cartoon by Nast national differences are stressed for the sake of the visual point, but ideally the Chinaman will soon give up his pigtail and the Spanish lady her mantilla. (14)

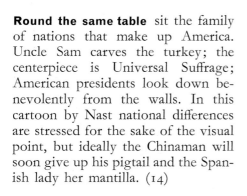

UNCLE SAM'S THANKSGIVING

In the schools (right) 'Americanization' was an important part of the curriculum. It aimed at giving children of various ethnic groups a new positive tradition to replace what they were losing. (15)

The failure of the 'melting pot' was tacitly confessed in 1942, when Americans of Japanese origin were assumed to be untrustworthy and 'relocated' (above). These fears, springing from hostility towards Japanese immigrants on the West Coast, proved to be without foundation. (16)

'**Welcome to All**' (above) – a lithograph by Keppler of 1880 which tells its own story. Below the picture was printed a quotation from the *New York Statistical Review*: 'we may safely say that the present influx of immigration to the United States is something unprecedented in our generation.' At that time this was still seen by most Americans as a good thing, but the day of immigration quotas was about to dawn. (17)

The frontier was tolerant: in a gambling saloon in Sonora, California, *c.* 1850, Europeans, Mexicans and Chinese mingle. (18)

The men who prospered were among those who advocated the control of fresh immigration. In another Keppler cartoon (above right), of 1893, the shadows behind the rich Americans reveal the poor Europeans they once were. In the words of the sub-title, 'they would close to the newcomer the bridge that carried them and their fathers over'. (19)

The new loyalty felt by the immigrant for the land that gave him shelter and opportunity was called upon in the First World War. This 1917 poster for US Government Bonds perhaps contains an extra appeal to help carry the blessings of American freedom back to Europe. (20)

Remember Your First Thrill of AMERICAN LIBERTY

'**A Nation of Nations**' was the title of a book by Louis Adamic published in 1945. The four pictures on the right form a double-spread from it. The message was in many ways the opposite of the 'melting pot'. Cultural differences were valuable and ought to be preserved. 'Americanization' did not mean suppressing such differences, but allowing them to co-exist. It is this ideal which now seems to be the more promising for the future. Far right: a sample of the innumerable foreign-language newspapers published in the States. (21, 24)

HISPANO AMERICANS: The Lopez home at Trampas, New Mexico, is many generations old.
(Photo by John Collier. Library of Congress)

GERMAN AMERICANS: Farm family in Lincoln County, Nebraska.
(Photo by John Vachon. Farm Security Administration—Library of Congress)

Black Americans constitute a special case, in that they came involuntarily and for three hundred years suffered oppression and exploitation. Slavery and its heritage cannot be easily overcome. Above: four generations of slaves, photographed on a Southern plantation in 1862. World War II contributed to overcoming discrimination against blacks. In a national emergency white and black fought and worked side by side (right). (22, 23)

AMERICAN FAMILIES: From Holland (*above*); from Russia (*below*).
(*Photos by Alexander Alland*)

Chinese Americans never subscribed to the 'melting pot' and have always maintained a culturally distinct existence while peacefully co-operating with their neighbours. Above: a grocery store in San Francisco's Chinatown, *c.* 1906. Left: celebrating the Chinese New Year in New York today. (25, 26)

49

The Indians form the other large group of 'involuntary Americans', and for long received treatment different from but little better than that of the Negroes. The 'melting pot' solution to their problem has already been illustrated (pls. 11, 12). Modern attitudes are gradually changing to respect for Indian tradition and way of life. Left: Navajo children in Arizona being collected by a school bus of the US Bureau of Indian Affairs. The Navajo language, formerly neglected, is beginning to be encouraged and taught. (27)

Films reflect the changing popular image of the Indian. Stories in which Indians are villainous sadists have practically died out, but until recently when Indians were to be portrayed sympathetically they were often played by white actors (above, *White Feather*, 1955). By the seventies (above right, *Little Big Man*, 1971) something like historical objectivity was being attempted with real Indians in the cast. (28, 29)

POWER TO THE PEOPLE

FREE THE NEW YORK PANTHER 21

How far can separatism go? Extremist groups like the Black Panthers (left) attack 'cultural pluralism', indict America for failing to build a genuine 'nation of nations', and demand power for themselves. (30)

Who are the Americans?

NATHAN GLAZER

PERHAPS no social structure in the world is as complex as that shaped by American society and government in the 360 years following the first settlement on the eastern shores of the present United States. Certainly no contemporary society has received as much and as sustained attention, from its own citizens and scholars and from those in other nations, and none is as problematic—in every sense of the term. There is no agreement as to whether this nation was founded on freedom or on slavery; on whether the defining character of its social development was to fasten exploitation, in one or another form, on one people after another, or to expand opportunity and freedom, in one form or another, for one people after another; nor is there agreement as to whether its future form will be one in which its various groups live apart from one another, in suspicion and hostility; or in a rigidly ordered and forcefully imposed hierarchy; or in harmony and equality. The very term 'a nation of nations' indicates our dilemma in understanding the American achievement—or, as some would put it, disaster—in creating one nation of many peoples and races.

The term 'a nation of nations' was perhaps most widely used in the years just before and during the Second World War, and its chief publicist was the American immigrant writer Louis Adamic. 45 (21) The term then had an optimistic air. It emphasized that, while Hitler expanded his power in Europe and imposed German rule over 'inferior' races, here in the United States all peoples were—or potentially were—equal. The coming of the Second World War, which saw Hitler menacing all the peoples of Eastern Europe, had led to a tremendous reawakening of dormant feelings of ethnic identity among immigrants from Eastern Europe and their children in this country. The public recognition of ethnic backgrounds, it was generally believed, served to strengthen American commitment to the Second World War. Thus, during World War II immigrant groups were *encouraged* to feel and express their connection to their homelands, instead of being criticized or punished for doing so, as had frequently been the case in the past.

Admittedly some groups in the population were in an ambiguous situation. Those of German, Italian and Japanese origin, and other 45 (16) groups, too (Hungarian, Rumanian), were torn between the support of fascist regimes at home and the support of the war of the United States and its allies against Hitler. Nevertheless, during World War II the meaning of the phrase 'a nation of nations' could be spelled out as follows: While Germany and Japan insisted on the primacy of one race, with lesser races marked for various roles from extermination or servitude to minor leadership in a system strictly guided by the leader race, in this country full equality prevailed. This equality was not only an equality between individuals, who were given opportunities whatever their ethnic and racial background to advance as far as their talents permitted. It was also in good measure an equality between peoples, who were allowed to preserve, to the extent they wished, their languages, their cultures, P 49 their religions, their schools, their customs, their associations. 25–26) This was the meaning of the term 'a nation of nations' during the period of the Second World War. Of course Louis Adamic and others who used the phrase would have been the first to admit— indeed to insist—that there was much discrimination on the basis of ethnic background, religion, accent, and in particular race. Yet it was clear that they saw the direction in which America was

moving as a positive one: one in which these differences would not disappear, would not be merely tolerated, but would be in some active sense celebrated, as contributing to the strength, the democratic character, the healthy diversity, of the nation.

In order to indicate something of the history of America's own understanding of its ethnic and racial diversity, let me contrast this optimistic usage of the term 'a nation of nations' around 1940–45 with the period twenty-five years earlier, when another war, the First World War, was raging, and the period twenty-five years later, our own day.

Immigrant quotas

During the First World War, the concept of 'a nation of nations' was also raised, even if different terms were used. But then the concept was attacked by the leading statesmen of the time— Theodore Roosevelt and Woodrow Wilson—and it was defended, ably and brilliantly, really for the first time, by only a few intellectuals on the left, Horace M. Kallen and Randolph Bourne. World War I, like World War II, created powerful reverberations among the immigrant peoples of the United States. The war had brought to a sudden end the greatest migration in history: the p 46 (17) steady movement, year after year, of a million or more immigrants from all the countries of Europe, but principally Italy, Russia and Austria-Hungary. Inevitably, when Europe tore itself apart in the greatest war in its history, the immigrant peoples were also involved. It was nothing so simple as the Germans and Austrians and p 47 (20) Hungarians against the English, French and Russians. For these were also imperial powers, and the immigrants drawn from the subject peoples were often passionate enemies of the governments of their home countries. Thus, Czechs and South Slavs supported the allies, the Irish were drawn to Germany, the enemy of England, the Jews were against Russia but also hoped England might grant them a small piece of the collapsing Ottoman Empire for Palestine, and so the tangle went. Those national leaders who wanted the United States to play a clear and powerful role in world affairs determined only by the 'national interest' saw this tangle of loyalties as only complicating their task. They also felt that the United States quite properly was a nation identified with its original and largest group of settlers, those from England, and thus while they accepted the legitimacy of agitation to support England—'the mother country'—they could not see the legitimacy of agitation in support of other nations.

In this confusion, Kallen and Bourne argued that America had *not* become—and indeed, from the point of view of the welfare of its people and humanity *should not* become—simply 'America', one nation, owing loyalty to a single origin. The 'melting pot' (the p 44–5 dream of Israel Zangwill, in a popular play of the beginning of the (13) century) had not worked. By all reason, it should not. Origins were not insignificant, to be discarded. They made up culture, style, outlook. In some measure they were being preserved in America, and indeed they ought to be preserved, and the resulting diversity should be welcomed, not deplored. If it was, the United States might offer a new model to the world, not the model of a uniform homogeneous nation, but the model of 'a nation of nations', of, in Kallen's term, 'cultural pluralism', in Bourne's 'a transcultural America'.

xenophobic periods in its history. The chief concrete result of the xenophobia was the erection of barriers to mass, unrestricted immigration.

Immigration had been totally unrestricted until 1882: in that year Chinese were excluded, and individual undesirables—lunatics, idiots, convicts and persons likely to become public charges. In 1907, under a 'Gentlemen's Agreement' with Japan, the Japanese government agreed to limit Japanese immigration, in order to prevent the insult of a legal restriction. In 1917, during World War I, a 'barred zone' was set up by which immigrants from the Asiatic and Pacific regions were excluded, and a 'literacy' test was finally, after many years' agitation, imposed.

But all these would have been merely modest dampers on the great flow of immigrants which had poured into the country until 1914. In 1921 a temporary immigration act, and in 1924 a permanent immigration act finally adopted a ceiling limit on the number of immigrants that should be accepted, and in effect determined, as a matter of national policy, that the racial or ethnic composition of the nation should not be allowed to change as a result of immigration. Congress established an annual maximum quota of 150,000 immigrants from eligible countries. Asia and the Pacific were not included within the quota; no immigration from those areas was allowed at all. Countries in the Western Hemisphere were also left outside the quota system—but there no limit on the number of immigrants was set. Each country's yearly quota was to bear the same relationship to the total quota (150,000) as the number of persons derived from that country by birth or descent bore to the total white population in the United States in 1920. The determination of the 'contribution' each nation had made to the population of the United States by 1920 was no mean task, and one can argue whether it was in any meaningful sense possible to determine such a figure. In any case, the attempt was made, it became law, and as a result, more than half the available quota positions went to Great Britain and Ireland, a very large share to Germany, and only small proportions to Italy, Poland, Czechoslovakia, Russia and other East European nations. This system, though modified many times, in particular to bring in Asians under less discriminatory features, prevailed roughly in this form until 1965.

What had happened to bring about such a radical change in a key national policy? Many things. Among the most important was the change in the major countries of origin of European immigrants around 1880. Until then, the majority of immigrants came from the British Isles, Ireland, Germany and the countries of Scandinavia. Most of these were of Protestant religion, which conformed to the religion of the great majority of the earlier, settled white population, itself largely of English, Scottish, and Irish origin, with a substantial German component. Many spoke English. Many were seen as linked culturally, through religion or language or customs, to the earlier settled population. The strongest antipathy was felt by the earlier settlers to the Irish, who were Catholic, impoverished and considered inferior. But by the end of the 19th century this prejudice, while still strong among the older elite of English origin, had lost all political force. Indeed, by the 1880s, the Irish power in the cities of the northeast was such that there was more danger in antagonizing the politically well organized and effective Irish than benefit to be gained from attacking them. Thus, in the election of 1884, it was widely believed that the Republican Blaine had lost because one of his supporters had denounced his enemies as supporters of 'rum, romanism and rebellion'. In the language of the times, this meant clearly the Irish—hard drinkers, Catholics, and supporters of rebellion against England. The angry Irish reaction to this characterization may have cost Blaine the election. Ten years later, President Cleveland took a high-handed attitude toward the British in their dispute with Venezuela. Again, historians believe that one factor was his desire to appeal to the anti-English Irish.

While then immigration was a matter of English, Scottish, Irish, German, Swedish and Norwegian immigrants, it was not much of a national issue. The matter was quite different when it came to Chinese, and later Japanese, immigrants. These settled largely in California, where there was violent antipathy to the Chinese, particularly among workingmen who believed they undercut their

The Chinese were the first to suffer from anti-immigration feeling. By 1882 both parties—the Democrat (Tammany) tiger and the Republican elephant—were courting popularity by urging restriction. To liberals like Thomas Nast it was at the cost of uprooting the tree of Liberty. (1)

The defenders of the immigrant cultures were fighting against not only the charge of 'hyphenated Americanism' that was made by Theodore Roosevelt; they were also fighting against the 'Americanization' movement which insisted on stripping from the immigrant children the languages, cultures, habits, they had brought with them, and on turning them, in the schools, into 'Americans', whatever that was. They were fighting, too, against a rising tide of opposition to the policy of free immigration—or near to free immigration—that had characterized this nation's immigration policy from the beginning.

The supporters of the idea of 'a nation of nations' during World War I lost. After the war, America entered into one of the most

52

wages, but in truth among all parts of the population. In 1882, as we pointed out earlier, Chinese immigrants were excluded, except for officials, businessmen, and students. During the first decade of the 20th century there was substantial Japanese immigration to California, and in 1908, by Gentlemen's Agreement, their immigration was limited, too.

p 47 (19)

But when, after 1880, Southern and Eastern European immigrants began to outnumber those from Western and Northern Europe, agitation against further European immigration also became strong. The new immigrants were denounced as uneducated, impoverished, accustomed to despotic and authoritarian government, inclined to criminality. Race theories rose to prominence to explain their inferiority, and indeed dominated American scholarship in sociology and anthropology through the 1920s. The labor movement had always opposed unrestricted immigration because it meant increased competition for jobs, and lower wages.

When, to this complex of forces, were added the fears raised by the victory of Bolshevism in Russia in 1917, and its threats of worldwide revolution, free immigration was doomed. Immigrants from Europe after the war, everyone knew, would be predominantly from Eastern and Southern Europe. Many would be Jews. Eastern Europeans and Jews were prominent in the membership of the Communist Party and other radical groups. Together with the earlier arguments—the opposition of the labor movement, and the opposition of American patricians who believed the new immigrants to be of inferior races—the fear of revolution finally led to the victory of immigration restriction in 1921.

Anti-Catholicism played a role, as did anti-Semitism. Al Smith met a powerful anti-Catholic trend in his race for the Presidency in 1928. Henry Ford published the 'Protocols of the Elders of Zion' in his *Dearborn Independent* in the 1920s. During the earlier part of the decade, the xenophobic, anti-Catholic, anti-Jewish and anti-Negro Ku Klux Klan swept through the country and came near to dominating both presidential conventions in 1924. And during the same period, a national policy of prohibition of alcoholic beverages was adopted. Once again, it was the white Protestant Anglo-Saxon heartland that demanded such a policy, to the confusion and non-comprehension of Catholic and Jewish immigrants.

p 65 (14)
p 155
(12)

'A nation of nations' was not a popular slogan in the twenties. Leading sociologists discoursed on the inferiority—inherited or acquired—of the recent immigrant peoples. Americanization was an unchallenged trend in the public schools. But with the 1930s,

'The only way to handle it': the Act of 1921 reduced the flood of immigrants to a mere trickle. Its supporters had two main justifications—the overcrowding of the labor market and the entry of 'undesirables inoculated with the virus of Bolshevism'. (3)

as we pointed out, a change began. The reputation of the new immigrant groups rose; matter-of-fact denigration became more and more difficult. A new orientation to the new immigrant groups developed.

Many things contributed to the change. First, the immigrants' children were already moving through the public schools, into the working class and the lower middle class; they were becoming voters. Just as by the 1880s it became dangerous to attack the Irish, by the 1930s criticism of the newer groups, directly or by implication, was in many areas becoming politically hazardous. Franklin D. Roosevelt became President in 1932 largely because of the disastrous depression that took place under the administration of Herbert Hoover. No special appeal to the immigrant groups was necessary, in a time of national disaster, and none was made. But by 1936 Roosevelt had already demonstrated a special appeal to the new immigrant groups. He had shown his opposition to Hitler, he had appointed individuals from the newer groups to important positions, he had shown his sympathy for the workingmen in the mass-production industries—who were overwhelmingly of the newer immigrant groups—and Samuel Lubell has demonstrated that by 1936, Roosevelt already had gained an ethnic base in fashioning his new electoral victory. In 1940, as the war approached, the ethnic base was even stronger—Jews, Poles, Czechs supported him, Irish and Italians drew away.

The new immigrant groups came of age in the 1930s. In the 1940s, with the coming of a war that took on some of the character of the crusade of 'a nation of nations' against the nations that wished to establish 'master races', their position became firmer. A movement for 'intercultural education' spread in the schools. The schools, many educators declared, at least in the larger cities where immigrant groups predominated, were no longer purely Anglo-Saxon and Protestant. They must recognize all groups, and must teach the children that America was made up of more than the descendants of those who fought the Revolution. Indeed, the movement to incorporate the immigrant groups into the popular image of American society went to the point where each group had to find, in the Revolution, an early representative who fought with the colonists against the British—a Haym Solomon, a Kosciuszko or Pulaski—and in this way to legitimate its presence and role in American society.

'Tain't their color I mind s'much—it's their habits, I 'bject to.' A cartoon of 1879 ridicules Irish contempt for the Chinese, by inviting contempt for the Irish. (2)

During and after World War II, a characteristic type of movie emerged in which a single platoon of soldiers or the crew of a single airplane is shown as being composed of all the peoples of the United States (for example, in the 1942 movie *Air Force*). It is true that an Anglo-Saxon—or possibly an Irishman—generally captains the plane or leads the platoon, that the Italian is often a comic character, the Jew a neurotic one, and yet it was clear what was happening: an effort was being made to portray the country as 'a nation of nations'.

Pressures for reform

The Immigration Act of 1924 had set for itself an unachievable goal: to fix the ethnic composition of the American population at a single point in time, 1920. Many things were to happen to make that goal quite unrealistic. It is true that in the latter part of the 1920s immigration dropped by half. In 1924 707,000 immigrants entered, in 1925 294,000. Immigration dried up almost entirely in the 1930s, as the United States suffered through a great depression and became unattractive to immigrants. In the entire decade of the 1930s, only 528,000 immigrants entered the country (compared with more than 4,000,000 in the 1920s, almost 6,000,000 between 1911 and 1920, almost 9,000,000 between 1901 and 1910). Immigration would have been even less had it not been for the rise of Hitler. The Jews of Germany could enter under the ample German quota. Those of Eastern Europe were not so fortunate.

p 39 (1)

It appeared as if the hope of the framers of the Immigration Act of 1924 might be realized, for the number of immigrants in the 1930s was the smallest that had entered this country for more than one hundred years—one had to go back to the decade of the 1820s to find a smaller figure! With the coming of World War II, immigration was reduced to only a trickle. The great age of immigration seemed undoubtedly past.

But this was, it turned out, only a temporary phenomenon. With the end of the war, new pressures developed to increase the number of immigrants into the country. First, there were hundreds of thousands of war refugees who wished to leave Europe—Jews, Ukrainians, Poles, and others. They had relatives in this country and supporters in this country. A series of special acts permitted many of them to enter outside the quota limits. More than one million immigrants entered the country during the 1940s, almost all in the second half of the decade, after the war.

Second, world developments made it very embarrassing to maintain the 'barred zone', which included our wartime ally China, the newly independent nations of India and Pakistan with whom we wished to ally ourselves, and Japan, a nation that rapidly rose from the destruction of war, and with which it was important to maintain good relations. A revision of the immigration laws was clearly in order, and it was carried out in 1952. All previously ineligible countries were given token quotas of 100, but the national-origins

quota system affecting Europe was unchanged. Thus Congress started reversing the racist elements of previous legislation, though the ethnic preferences of the Act of 1924 remained firm. The act was important as marking the beginning of a policy that was to lead, by 1965, to the removal of any race or ethnic distinction at all in American immigration legislation.

Third, we must record increasing pressure against the whole system of national-origins quotas. In the early 1920s, when the system was fashioned, the recent immigrant groups consisted in large measure of poor and illiterate workingmen and their children. They contributed relatively few voters. At the end of the war, the situation was quite different: they now formed powerful voting blocs. We have pointed out that from 1936, and even more, 1940, Roosevelt was increasingly dependent for election on an ethnic coalition. After the war, as these groups became more and more important, agitation for a basic change in the laws became ever stronger. Special arrangements were made for special groups. Thus, Hungarian refugees from the failed revolution of 1956 were allowed in outside the quotas. Senator John F. Kennedy, later President, became one of the strongest advocates of immigration reform. After his assassination the reforms he had proposed received the vigorous support of President Johnson, and became law in 1965. A completely different approach to immigration now came into effect, one in which the national origins or race of a prospective immigrant played no role at all: instead, such factors as the immigrant's skills and occupation, and the presence of family relations in this country determined his priority among prospective immigrants. Thus, the attempt to stabilize the proportions of various national elements in the American population by limiting immigration was abandoned.

Fourth, the Immigration Act of 1924 did not control immigration from the Western Hemisphere, nor of course did it control movement from American possessions overseas. These two sources were able to provide important components of the American populations. During the 1920s, almost a half-million immigrants were recorded from Mexico. Immigration continued, after the Depression, at a heavy rate into California, Texas, and other states. A Mexican–American community developed in the southwest that in 1970 numbered more than five million. On the Eastern Coast there was an equivalent movement from Puerto Rico, and by 1970 one and a half million Puerto Ricans and their children lived in New York and other cities. After Castro came to power, hundreds of thousands of Cubans entered the country. Thus the pattern whereby new substantial elements have been added to the American population has not come to an end. The United States is still the leading country of immigration in the world. The attempt to stop mass immigration, which seemed to have succeeded in the 1920s and 1930s, has been abandoned. In the ten years from 1959 to 1968, 3,116,000 immigrants were admitted to this country. The

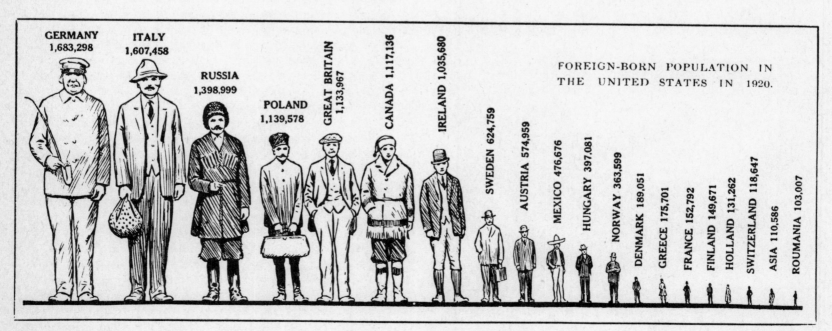

FOREIGN-BORN POPULATION IN THE UNITED STATES IN 1920.

GERMANY 1,683,298 · ITALY 1,607,458 · RUSSIA 1,398,999 · POLAND 1,139,578 · GREAT BRITAIN 1,133,967 · CANADA 1,117,136 · IRELAND 1,035,680 · SWEDEN 624,759 · AUSTRIA 574,959 · MEXICO 476,676 · HUNGARY 397,081 · NORWAY 363,599 · DENMARK 189,051 · GREECE 175,701 · FRANCE 152,792 · FINLAND 149,671 · HOLLAND 131,262 · SWITZERLAND 118,647 · ASIA 110,586 · ROUMANIA 103,007

Immigrant quotas for each country were fixed in such a way as to keep the proportion of foreign-born Americans the same as it was in 1920. In practice it proved superfluous, since in the thirties immigration dropped to an average of just over 50,000 a year. (4)

The mutual bitterness between races and religions is blamed in a cartoon of 1870 on the sectarian schools, all supported on state funds. The remedy is for all children to attend the same common schools. (5)

annual rate of immigration in recent years, since the 1965 act has taken full effect, has run above 350,000 a year.

But does this mean America is 'a nation of nations', or, to use another descriptive phrase that has been used to characterize the relationship of the different immigrant strands to each other in the United States, is it a 'melting pot'? We have pointed out that in the 1940s, the term 'a nation of nations' was used optimistically, to describe America's success in integrating many peoples, in contrast to Germany's regressive effort to establish a hierarchy of peoples. The optimistic mood did not last long.

Actually, the full implications of the term had never been thought through. It was one thing for the immigrants and their descendants to find toleration for a fragmentary culture and religion maintained in the new world. It was quite another to demand equality for each of the cultures, and in particular, equality with what was the central people in the making of America, the colonists from England and their descendants. Nor was it clear what equality might mean.

The problem did not come up, however, because the ethnic groups derived from the later immigrants actually did not make strong claims for a full equality. Thus, they did not demand that their languages (which in any case they had abandoned) be granted equal status with English. They did not insist on autonomy or political recognition, as did many of the minority groups of Europe, and other parts of the world.

The demands of the ethnic groups descended from the later European immigrant peoples were fairly modest, and thus could—even if it took a long time and there was some dragging of feet—be met. They demanded the right to independent associations and independent schools, often under religious auspices. They demanded, in the areas in which they were numerous, some recognition in the public schools, in the form of acknowledgment of special holidays, and some identifiable role in public celebrations, and they demanded particularly the suspension of derogatory remarks, so common in the schools, in the mass media, in the speeches of politicians, in the 1920s and later. On occasion, their demands were more serious: political support for the homeland, for example, which might conflict with the demands of other groups. Even these demands were acknowledged and responded to in various ways by the pluralistic patterns of American politics. Each of these groups, where it was numerous, could elect its own representatives, or influence the political representatives even of other groups. Derogatory remarks in the schools and elsewhere declined as the groups became more numerous, as they themselves supplied teachers and principals and newspaper reporters and filmmakers and politicians. The issue of discrimination in employment and housing, which varied in significance from group to group, declined with increasing prosperity and education, and eventually the ethnic groups—in particular, the Jewish group, which suffered most of all the European immigrant groups from such discrimination—became strong enough so that anti-discriminatory legislation was passed in the cities and states where they were numerous.

The acculturation of the immigrants, and their educational and occupational rise, in a society which seemed, with little conscious effort, to change immigrants into new men, turned the immigrants and their children into patriots, supporters of American institutions and American foreign interests. This prevented any great difficulty in accepting the concept of 'a nation of nations', in the relatively mild form in which it was put forward. In effect, the nation of nations concept could be accepted because so little was asked. If, for example, the Americans of German descent had been active supporters of German interests in the two world wars, there would have been a really radical challenge to the American system of incorporation and accommodation of ethnic groups. Strangely, there was not. Germans and those of German descent were drafted and expected to fight like everyone else, and did. Only in the case of the Japanese in World War II was there suspicion of disloyalty on ethnic and racial grounds. There was actually hardly anything to support such suspicions, no more than in the case of the Germans and Italians. Yet owing to the fierce antipathy to the Japanese on the West Coast, the entire population, citizen and non-citizen, men, women, and children, were rounded up and confined in concentration camps for most of the war. They were allowed to fight only in Europe, and then only on the basis of volunteering.

In only one area did the immigrant groups as groups really make

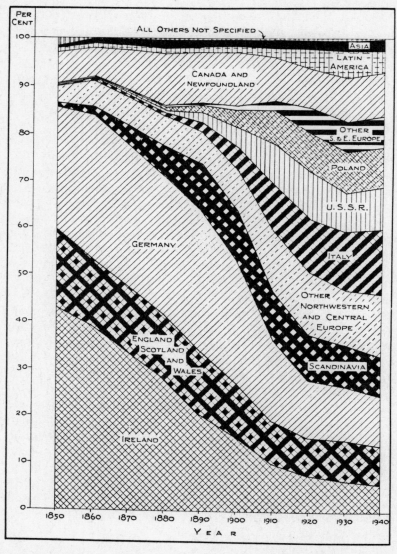

Composition of the foreign-born population of the United States by country of birth, 1850–1940. Immigration from Ireland declines steeply; from Britain, Canada and Germany remains fairly constant; from other European countries significantly rises. (6)

p 45 (16)

55

a strong claim for full equality—that was in the case of their religions. They insisted that the Catholic religion should be placed publicly on the same level as the Protestant faiths of the early settlers, and the Jews made the same claim for Judaism. To this claim, the American system eventually deferred. The holidays of all three religions were accepted as public holidays in the areas where their adherents were numerous; their observances were acknowledged in various ways; they were given public recognition in the religious ceremonies that opened the deliberations of Congress and the meetings of national political conventions.

Where the blacks fit in

Despite the accommodation and incorporation of the groups of European origin in American society, by 1970 the American system was widely considered a failure, and the term 'a nation of nations' was heard no more. The tone of self-congratulation over the ability to accommodate different peoples had quite disappeared. Now one heard of 'two nations, one white, one black, drifting apart'. And one heard of other nations, too: a brown nation of Mexican-Americans and Puerto Ricans, a red nation of American Indians, and others. The American system, which seemed so successful in the decade after World War II, now was widely accounted a failure, one in which nations, instead of coming together as an integrated society, were moving farther apart from each other, into separatism and whatever dangers might flow from it.

One very large component of the American population had from the beginning been excluded from the history of free immigration and of relatively free internal development in this country: that is the American Negro. Negroes came to this country almost as early as the first English settlers did. But they were brought, they did not come willingly. They came as slaves, not as free men. Historians have unraveled a good deal of their early history in this country, and much evidence suggests that initially there was no general expectation that Negroes and their children would be slaves forever. But in a relatively short time they were defined as slaves, they and their children, without rights, and this status was written into a complex web of law and custom, that, after three hundred years, despite one frightfully destructive civil war, and decades of the most intense political conflict, still exists in some measure to limit the status and freedom of Negroes in America. By 1790, the time of the first census, almost 20% of the population was black, almost all slaves. This proportion dropped as white, free immigrants entered the country in increasing numbers during the 19th century. In 1860, on the eve of the Civil War, 14% of the population was black, by 1900 only 10%. Today 11 or 12% of the population is black.

How could America reconcile its openness to the white immigrants from Europe with its enslavement of a huge black population, brought involuntarily from Africa? It tried: the Constitution was one effort, the development of theological and sociological justifications of slavery was another, the institutionalization of a strong streak of racism throughout American society was a third. In the end, the two could not be reconciled. The presence of a free black population—10% of the entire black population on the eve of the Civil War—was a constant embarrassment. This was a free black population, in the sense that they were not slaves. Yet they were not fully free, because even in the free states of the United States, free blacks were hemmed in by a patchwork of discriminatory legislation and practice, which often prevented them from p 48 (22) voting and limited their rights in schooling and marriage.

Through the Civil War, the status of slavery was abolished, and the Constitution was amended to root all color discrimination out of American society. In 1865, the thirteenth amendment to the Constitution declared, 'Neither slavery nor involuntary servitude . . . shall exist within the United States.' In 1868, the fourteenth amendment declared that 'All persons born or naturalized in the United States . . . are citizens of the United States and of the State wherein they reside. No State shall make or enforce any law which shall abridge the privileges and immunities of citizens of the United States; nor shall any State deprive any person of life, liberty or property, without due process of law; nor deny to any p 136 (19) person within its jurisdiction the equal protection of the laws.' In 1870, the fifteenth amendment added, 'The right of citizens to vote

shall not be denied or abridged by the United States or by any State on account of race, color, or previous condition of servitude.' This seemed as clear a grant of full citizenship as possible to the former slaves, and indeed to any other person born or naturalized in the United States. Despite this, by 1876, the United States had withdrawn Federal troops from the South, and the process of stripping away the rights of Negroes in the South proceeded with little interruption. By the end of the century, their right to vote and participate in politics was radically restricted, through various subterfuges, to the point indeed where Negroes had no political force at all; their right to equal education was nonexistent; their right to equal treatment in public facilities had been taken away through a specious doctrine of 'separate but equal' facilities accepted by the Supreme Court; their right to life itself was not secure as thousands were lynched for real or imaginary infractions of the rigid code of racial etiquette, more powerful than any law, which restricted their movements, their language, their attitudes, the very way they looked at a white man or woman.

Racism, particularly in the South, was strong enough to make the amended Constitution ineffective. The Southern Negro, released from the abysmal status of slavery, still suffered, through the effects of rigid custom and thousands of local and state laws, from an inferior status. He was not allowed to enter or was driven out of occupations that paid well and offered high status. He could enter professional status only when, as a professional, he dealt with other Negroes—as a teacher in the segregated Southern school systems, as a preacher in segregated churches, as an occasional doctor or lawyer with a Negro practice. He could not vote, for the most part, nor participate in the critical primary elections of the dominant Democratic Party. Since he was without political power, he was in effect without legal redress. The courts existed for him only to enforce the white-made law and white-made codes of racial etiquette.

While freed from slavery, many blacks still lived on white-owned plantations. Under the new system of 'sharecropping', adapted to their legally free status, they were in effect bound by debt through life. But there was one big difference from slavery—they were free to move, to the towns and to the north and west, and many did.

In the North, the situation was quite different. At the turn of the century, only 10% of American blacks lived in the North. But when World War II cut off white European immigration, a steady migration to the North began, one which ebbed and flowed with economic conditions but which has not yet ceased. By 1970, almost half of American blacks lived in the North and West. There they lived in the cities, in enormous urban areas that had recently housed—and for some time still did—white European immigrants. And they began to move through political, social and economic developments that in many ways paralleled those of earlier immigrants. Thus, from the 1920s on they began to elect their own representatives and to control their own local political organizations. Black men, who had not been seen in Congress and in state legislatures since the abandonment of the post-Civil War effort to guarantee rights to the blacks, now were seen again—but this time representing the Northern, not the Southern Negro. Negroes moved into heavy industry—steel, autos, rubber—and with the establishment of powerful industrial unions in these industries in the late 1930s, they began to earn the high wages of mass production industry. They began to buy their own homes, to enter Northern and Western colleges and universities.

But while in some respects their rise paralleled that of the white immigrant groups, the parallel was far from complete. At certain times an optimistic mood pervaded the black communities: in the 1920s, as they moved into Harlem and launched a Negro renaissance in the arts; in World War II, as they demanded and gained a measure of equality in employment; in the postwar period, as antidiscrimination legislation was passed in Northern states and as their national organization, the National Association for the Advancement of Colored Peoples, began to win judicial victories in the courts, which started the long, slow, painful rollback of the legal structure establishing and supporting racial separation, culminating in the Supreme Court decision banning separate facilities in schools in 1954. Lynching declined, and in the 1950s just about disappeared.

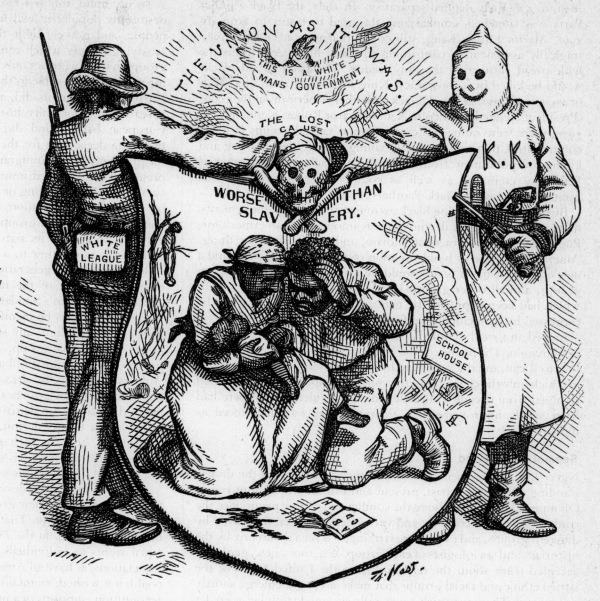

The Negro's coat-of-arms, by Thomas Nast, 1874. The Civil War had ended slavery as a legal institution, but in fact Negroes seemed only to have exchanged one form of oppression for another—their school burned down, their people lynched. (7)

In the North, for fifteen or twenty years after the end of World War II, it appeared as if the course of the American Negro would parallel that of white immigrants, that Negroes would be integrated into the larger society. One did not hear so much then of the strength of American racism as a national phenomenon. It is true it was strong in the South, but there had been a phenomenally rapid decline in racial prejudice against the Japanese Americans, who returned to their homes in California and were able to re-establish their communities, to enter higher education and the professions, to restore their businesses. There was an equally rapid drop in 49 (26) discrimination against Chinese. Jews found, perhaps as a result of the war against Hitler, that anti-Semitism had suffered a strong decline, and occupations and residential areas that had been previously closed to them were now open. Similarly, anti-Negro feeling seemed to be on the decline. President Truman offered strong leadership against discrimination, despite his Southern origins, and desegregated the armed forces.

Perhaps one can date the beginning of the evaporation of this general feeling that the problem of forced Negro inferiority and segregation would be overcome to 1954. The South raised massive and furious resistance to the desegregation of the schools. In the p 186 North, the economic rise of the Negroes which had accompanied (34) World War II and the Korean war came to a halt—indeed, relatively to whites, there was a decline in the Negro economic position. Simultaneously, with the rapid freeing of the nations of Africa, expectations were created for a new status for Negroes—expectations that were not fulfilled. In addition, the Negro communities themselves developed serious problems, which could undoubtedly be ascribed, in various degrees, to the racism of the past and the racism of the present, and the consequent institutionalization of self-defeating modes of behavior. Thus, criminal acts occurred at a very high rate in black neighborhoods, bringing fear to black families. Desertion and illegitimacy were common, leading to many

families without men, and a typical pattern in poor black areas in which working women had to raise large families without help. Economic and educational opportunities were taken up at only a slow and faltering rate. Negroes did not establish businesses in the ghettos, as white immigrants had done, did not attend the free and state colleges in substantial numbers. Nor did they exploit the political opportunities open to them. The proportions registering   p 138 and voting were low, lower than that of white ethnic groups, and   (23) it was difficult to raise money in black communities for political campaigning. Thus the number of black representatives grew slowly, increasing frustration over what was felt as powerlessness.

The effects of these developments took perhaps ten years to reach fruition. Martin Luther King suddenly rose to national prominence   p 139 by leading the Montgomery bus boycott of 1956, and became the   (26) most prominent leader of a new, activist Civil Rights movement. He led campaign after campaign for Negro rights, and in 1959, for the first time since Reconstruction, a Civil Rights act was passed to implement constitutional guarantees in the face of bitter Southern resistance. Further Civil Rights acts were passed in 1964 and 1965. Through the 1960s, and particularly in the second half of the 1960s, there were rapid Negro gains in employment, income, higher   p 131 (7) education enrollment, and voting and political representation. Presidents Kennedy, Johnson and Nixon all supported policies designed to improve the position of Negroes. But black expectations, in part because of the Civil Rights movement, in part because of the promises of new legislation and presidential leadership, in part because of the massive response of the mass media to the black condition, exceeded gains, and anger and despair spread. In 1964 there came the first of four successive years of massive rioting in the northern and western black urban areas. In 1965, Stokely Carmichael launched the ambiguous slogan 'Black Power', in effect   p 50 (30) denying the validity of the gains of the recent past and moving away from integration, the objective of the Civil Rights movement until then, to a vaguely defined separatism. In 1967, the Black Panther Party was launched, emphasizing the need to resort to arms. In 1968, Martin Luther King, still committed to non-violence, was tragically assassinated, confirming to many black Americans the widespread conviction that any leaders who tried to aid blacks would be killed by a conspiracy. King's was the fourth of a series of assassinations that shook black and other Americans in the 1960s (President Kennedy, Malcolm X and Senator Robert Kennedy). By 1970, there were numerous extremist and radical groups in black communities, particularly among young people; the shooting and killing of policemen from ambush in black urban areas was becoming common, as well as counter-violence against black militants such as the Black Panthers.

p 50 (28, 29) By this time, paralleling black extremist and militant movements, there were growing similar movements among Mexican-Americans, Puerto Ricans, and American Indians, and all said the same thing: America's promise to build 'a nation of nations' was a sham and a delusion, the United States could integrate only white European groups, and all other groups were subject to a pervasive racism which had been expressed by genocide in the past and would be expressed by genocide in the future.

Indeed, in 1970 the entire American past was subject to intense re-examination. The history of the Negro, the Mexican-American, the Puerto Rican, and the American Indian was increasingly seen as one in which only the character of the suffering imposed upon them had changed from decade to decade, and any evidence that there had been steady improvement in their position was denounced as illusory.

Separatism renewed

Never has any ten-year period seen such a reversal in the understanding of a nation's past, present and future. One cannot rise in Olympian detachment above the conflict and simply pronounce the truth. The truth is complex and variegated, and seen differently by different groups, and even more striking, it is seen differently by the historians and sociologists of each group. Whether a new, generally accepted truth about the relationship to the United States of the varied ethnic and racial groups that make it up will emerge shortly is doubtful. There was such a generally accepted truth between, let us say, 1890 and 1930. It was that the Anglo-Saxon colonists had created what was good and distinctive in this country, and that while West European immigrants of Protestant background could be assimilated to the Anglo-Saxon center, it was doubtful that East European immigrants, let alone those of other races, would ever become the equal, in intelligence, contribution to American society, understanding and support of American democracy and institutions, of the Anglo-Saxons, the Germans, and the Scandinavians. This view crumbled as the new immigrants rose to a greater measure of political and economic power and social acceptance. A new view came into being that dominated American thinking, scholarly and popular, in the 1940s and 1950s. It was that all groups were equal before the eyes of the law, and American civilization could accommodate all groups and make them part of itself. Neither religion, nor language, nor color, nor distant origin, was any bar to becoming a full citizen and participant, in law and in custom, in American civilization.

p 50 (27) Now we see another view emerging. The incorporation of groups of other colors, and in particular of groups who have had something like a colonial relationship to the United States (American Indians, confined to reservations; Negroes, brought here as slaves; Mexican-Americans, conquered or immigrants from a country under American domination; Puerto Ricans, subjects of the United States) had been hampered by race prejudice and by prevalent disdain. These groups were 'colonized'. To speak of 'integrating' them was illusory. Only 'freedom' could satisfy them.

To my mind, this is a radical exaggeration of the truth, which despite its popularity will fasten new illusions on the American people, and gravely limit their capacity to continue to build a satisfying society which can find a place for every group. These groups in truth were not only 'colonized'. They are also immigrants, for many of them came to this country willingly and freely, just as European immigrants did, and most of them moved to our cities in search of opportunity, just as farmers and small town dwellers of European background did. The problems they have faced in making a decent life for themselves have much in common with the problems white immigrants faced. White immigrants also knew prejudice, and colored immigrants also faced problems of acculturation and overcoming of class habits and practices independent of color. The integration of earlier immigrants was always a complex thing. Each group had a different history, based on its culture, the time of its arrival, the degree of prejudice it met, its own tastes in relating to a complex modern civilization. Thus, Poles of the second generation were predominantly of the working classes, and Jews of the middle classes, but this could not be ascribed to 'racism'. Similarly, one had to expect that differences would continue to be manifest among groups of other races.

Nor was 'freedom' any sufficient definition of the desires and hopes of an ethnic group. The comparison with truly colonized groups that demanded full autonomy or independence is illusory. American society is already too subtly integrated and interdependent for any group to demand meaningfully this kind of freedom. What it can demand is freedom for each individual to go as far as his talents permit, in an open society with democratic institutions, and for each group to have the right to maintain whatever institutions it wishes to, as long as these do not undermine the minimal loyalty to the state that any society requires.

American society has developed a subtle and complex process for the incorporation of new groups. They have been given no public, corporate recognition. That had been decided at the beginning of mass immigration, in the 1820s and 1830s. They have been given equal rights as individuals, and the freedom to form voluntary associations, as have all Americans. This has meant that each group could, if it wished, maintain a corporate identity, but without state recognition, support, or sanction. These corporate identities have sometimes been unsatisfying and then the institutions that supported them would fall into decay; in other cases they have been maintained vigorously through a number of generations.

This is a unique way of accommodating the facts of ethnic and racial diversity. It is difficult to say that it is worse than others, as one sees other multi-ethnic societies—Canada, Belgium, Russia, and all the rest—struggling in their own ways with the problem of ethnic diversity. The anger of the poorer groups owes less to the concrete, current facts of discrimination and prejudice—though certainly this does exist—than to the great expectations aroused in them by America's open society, its relatively free system of education, its open government service, its ease of mobility, geographical and social, its remarkably multifarious mass media, with their amazingly easy access to and full coverage of government policies and varied social realities.

Thus the crisis in group relations that the United States is enduring in the present day can be seen not as a crisis resulting from failure, but one which is itself the result of success—success in opening America to as many groups as it has done, in attempting to make each an equal part of the social fabric, and partial success in doing so, and in thus creating in each group organization, leadership, demands, anger and frustration. New demands have been raised, demands which press against the established patterns of group accommodation. Only the future can tell whether these demands will be moderated, or whether, on the other hand, the established patterns themselves can be modified to accommodate them.

III

FREEDOM AND FAITH

Spiritual attitudes in a New World

MARTIN E. MARTY

'Get religion like a Methodist.

Experience it like a Baptist. Be sure of it

like a Disciple. Stick to it like a Lutheran.

Conciliate it like a Congregationalist. Be proud of it

like an Episcopalian. Simplify it like a Quaker.

Glorify it like a Jew. Pay for it like a Presbyterian.

Practice it like a Christian Scientist.

Work at it like the Salvation Army. Propagate it like

a Roman Catholic. Enjoy it like a Negro.'

EDGAR DEWITT JONES

A church planted in the wilderness

symbolizes the original role of religion in the United States. Whatever the motives of later immigrants, those of the first settlers were largely religious. 'There was never a generation that did so perfectly shake the dust of Babylon', said Increase Mather, 'as the first generation of Christians that came to this land for the Gospel's sake.'

This pioneering spirit—the sense of making a new beginning in a new land—ran through all the early religious movements that entered America from Europe, and can later be recognized in the numerous evangelistic and utopian denominations from Mor-

monism to Christian Science that have arisen, and still arise, on American soil. Today there are probably more competing religious groups in America than in any other comparable population, though in this century the division between the progressives and conservatives of each group has become in many ways more significant than the divisions between groups.

The church shown here is the Catholic Chapel of the Holy Cross, in the Arizona desert at Sedona. Built in 1956 by Ashen and Allen, it rises from a spur of red sandstone at the base of a 1500 foot cliff. (1)

The Pilgrim Fathers, the first permanent settlers in North America, were Puritan separatists seeking a freer religious life in the New World. A party from Lincolnshire is seen here disembarking from the *Speedwell* in Holland in 1620. They later transferred to the *Mayflower* for the Atlantic crossing. (2)

Anabaptists, believers in adult baptism by total immersion, came chiefly from Germany. This ceremony (left) was sketched about 1812 in Philadelphia. (3)

Quakers (below) were among the most politically distinctive of the early sects. Pennsylvania, founded in 1682, was a Quaker colony, dedicated to their ideals of liberty and peace. Later they pioneered the antislavery movement. (5)

Catholic missions were established by Spain. Above: visitors to California in 1786 welcomed by Christian Indians. Below: the church of San Xavier del Bac, Tucson, Arizona. (4, 6)

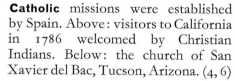

The diversity of faiths existing side by side in early America is reflected in this vivid photograph by Dorothea Lange. On the Great Plains of South Dakota stand three once neat wooden churches: Catholic, Lutheran, Baptist. (7)

Baptists, mostly derived from New England Congregationalists, established themselves with the very earliest settlers. Below: the Seventh Day Baptist Church of Newport, Rhode Island, built in 1729. Already divided in Europe, the Baptists split into more parties in America. Today the black National Baptists and the Southern Baptists are among the main groups. (8)

Lutherans in America in many respects kept more closely to their original traditions than their brethren in Europe. Below center: a scene in the Lutheran church of York, Pennsylvania, in 1800. (9)

Jewish settlers were at first refugees from Spanish and Portuguese persecution. The Touro Synagogue (Touro was the first cantor) at Newport, R.I., (below right) was designed by Peter Harrison in 1759–63, a century after their arrival in the colony. (10)

The Mormons, driven by persecution, set out in 1846 to found a new kingdom in the West. At their first camp (above) they were fed by a miraculous descent of quail. (11)

Camp meetings lasting several days became a feature of frontier religion. Below: as Methodist preachers address the crowd, a man in the foreground falls in an ecstatic trance. (12)

64

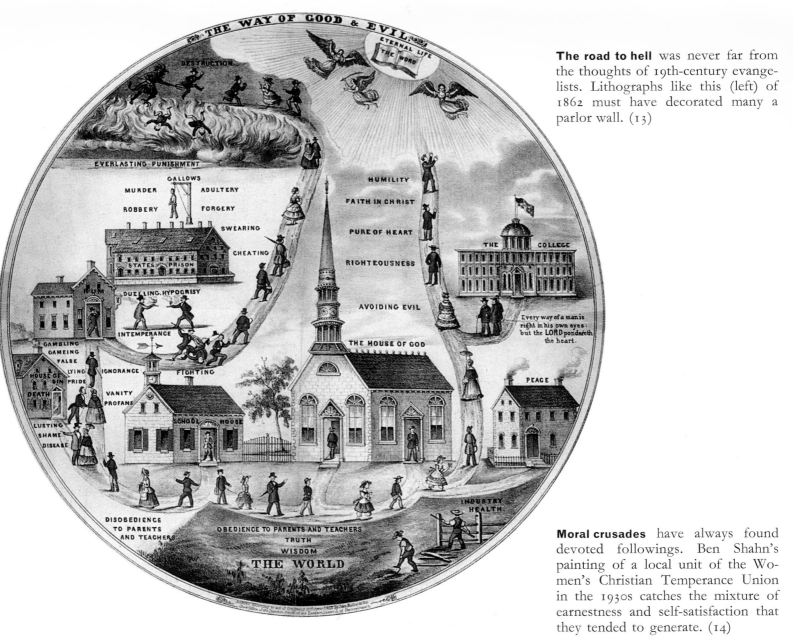

The road to hell was never far from the thoughts of 19th-century evangelists. Lithographs like this (left) of 1862 must have decorated many a parlor wall. (13)

Moral crusades have always found devoted followings. Ben Shahn's painting of a local unit of the Women's Christian Temperance Union in the 1930s catches the mixture of earnestness and self-satisfaction that they tended to generate. (14)

On American soil the transplanted denominations often assumed an evangelistic tone, turning readily to mass emotionalism. George Whitefield (above left), visited America seven times, rousing his congregations to violent enthusiasm. A century later, Moody and Sankey carried their back-to-the-Bible message all over the world. Above, a meeting in London in 1875. (15, 16)

Christian Science, founded by Mary Baker Eddy in 1879, revived primitive Christian healing. Below left: the Biennial College Conference in the Mother Church of Boston, Mass. (17)

Black Muslims, a sect based loosely on the Mohammedan faith and advocating strict separation of the races, combines black nationalism with a strict ethical code. (13)

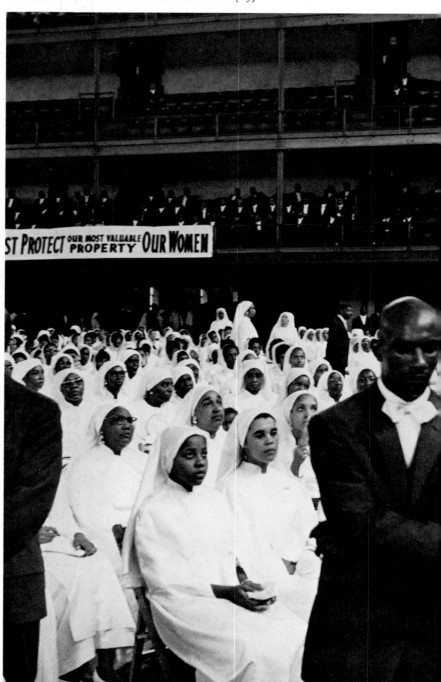

Modern revivalists see themselves as rescuing their disciples from a doomed world. In the 1920s and 1930s Aimee Semple McPherson (right) and Billy Sunday (far right) drew enthusiastic audiences by their message of moral renewal without material renunciation. 'It pays to serve God', said Sunday. (19, 20)

Billy Graham's campaigns are organized with elaborate precision. Through his use of the mass media and of mass publicity techniques, the revival meeting has been enlarged to international dimensions. Below: converts in Anaheim Stadium in California walk up to the rostrum to make their 'decisions for Christ'. (21)

The latest 'Jesus Revolution' is more fundamentalist than ever. Followed mainly by young people, it represents a protest against material values and a return to poverty, simplicity and faith. Here a California girl points upward with the 'Jesus sign' (photo Julian Wasser). (22)

Pass the Lord and PRAISE THE AMMUNITIO

Even the Catholic church, the largest single denomination in America, has its progressive and conservative wings. The late Cardinal Spellman, Archbishop of New York, was alleged (top) to have carried his support of the Vietnam War, to unchristian lengths, but Catholic priests have also been active in anti-War movements. In 1965, for the first time in history, the Pope visited the United States, celebrating mass in St Patrick's Cathedral, New York. (23, 24)

Spiritual attitudes of a New World

MARTIN E. MARTY

In 1742, New England's most highly regarded evangelist and
theologian, Jonathan Edwards, provided the classic religious expression of the promise of America. Setting down *Some Thoughts
Concerning the Present Revival of Religion*, he suggested that 'probably
that will come to pass in spirituals, which has taken place in
temporals, with respect to America'. Whereas until recently the
world had been supplied with its silver and gold and earthly
treasures 'from the old continent, now it is supplied chiefly from the
new; so the course of things in spiritual respects will be in like
manner turned'.

Visitors from the Old World have never ceased to be fascinated
by the spiritual turns of North Americans. Settled in centuries
when many Europeans were turning their backs on historic
religion, America refused to become a simply secular society.
Even today, in the last third of the 20th century, citizens of the
United States belong to, attend, support, and defend religious
institutions with a devotion rarely matched elsewhere. Divided
into more competing religious groups than any other population,
the American people at the same time seem to be able to draw
upon generalized and common sentiments which have served and
still serve to unite their nation. The characteristic form of church
life is the denomination, and church-going people cling to their
own denomination with considerable tenacity. Yet inquirers find
that on most issues these more than 250 denominations do not serve
to explain the substance of their members' beliefs and hopes.

To explain this situation in American religion it is not enough to
trace denominational histories, nor to postulate the growth of a
single 'civic religion'. One has to look at the way in which a sort of
two-party system is emerging, a system in which two elements
contend for place and power within most religious groups and
unite across their boundaries. No new denominations have emerged
as a result of the contention. No schisms within old denominations
have occurred as a result of the conflict. Neither side is formally
organized, but both claim that they are legitimate heirs of their
spiritual traditions. In a nation where a high premium is often
placed on novelty, both groups like to claim a longer history.

Josiah Strong, a Protestant promoter at the beginning of the
20th century, clearly defined the two groups in his book *The Next
Great Awakening* (1902). He wrote: 'There are two types of
Christianity, the old and the older. The one is traditional, familiar,
and dominant. The other, though as old as the Gospel of Christ,
is so rare that it is suspected of being new, or is overlooked altogether. They are not to be distinguished by any of the old lines of
doctrinal or denominational cleavage. Their difference is one of
spirit, aim, point of view, comprehensiveness. The one is individualistic; the other is social.' Needless to say, the individualists, by
whatever name they would have called themselves, would also have
claimed to be the older and purer.

The ability of American believers to cluster across and not
within the lines of their communions and to blur 'the old lines of
doctrinal or denominational cleavage' is turning out to be as
distinctive a contribution to religious forms as were the invention
of the denomination or the formation of a unifying consensus
religion in a pluralist society. Both contemporary and historical
analysis will confirm the presence of this contribution and suggest
something of its depth.

Denominations and divisions

A tour of American religion on institutional lines would reveal how
confusing the New World's spiritual attitudes have become. When
asked about their religion, most interviewees begin by identifying
themselves as Methodist, Jewish, Lutheran, Catholic, or something
else, whether or not they attend or support the life of the institutions
implied by these terms. Adherents channel most of their religious
energies through them. Denominations remain the most efficient
means of gathering and disbursing funds, training ministers, sending missionaries, effecting charities, and publishing. It is common
knowledge that funds for interdenominational or ecumenical work
are the last to be added to budgets of local congregations and are the
first to be dropped when people fail to meet the budgets.

Yet sociologists Charles Y. Glock and Rodney Stark, after
having assessed the attachments nominal Baptists have for Baptist
doctrines or Pentecostalists have for Pentecostalist teachings, have
spoken of a 'new denominationalism'. They might more appropriately have spoken of a 'residual denominationalism', of a people's
reminiscence of distinctive teachings which once played a part in
shaping life, but which no longer do so.

When one speaks of what really shapes life, denominationalism
becomes much less significant. An inquirer about the spiritual
attitudes of the United States' largest denomination, the nearly
fifty-million-strong Roman Catholic Church, would find vast
differences within that body. During the early years of the Vietnam War he would have heard New York's Cardinal Francis
Spellman speaking of the military action there in the terms of a
holy war, a crusade on the part of Christ's soldiers. But just as much
public attention was being given at the same time to the Jesuit
Father Daniel Berrigan, a college chaplain and poet utterly opposed
to the war, in the name of the same God. The Catholic War Veterans
invoked God, Christ, and Mary in defense of the American military
and moral positions and found the poet's brother, Philip Berrigan,
to be virtually treasonous when, as a priest and in the name of the
Church, he helped storm a draft board office and violate its records.

Father James Groppi of Milwaukee, as a priest in good standing,
identified completely with the cause of Black Power in race relations
but would not have been acceptable, or even physically safe, had
he been assigned to say Mass in his boyhood parish a few miles
away. Were the curious visitor to consult the Catholic press, he
would find the *National Catholic Reporter* finding warrant for
political and theological radicalism in papal encyclicals. But *Twin
Circle*, a reactionary and well-financed paper chartered to oppose
tendencies like those expressed in the *Reporter*, disagreed utterly on
all political, social and theological positions—and similarly invoked
papal encyclicals in support.

When Pope Paul VI issued *Humanae Vitae* in the summer of 1968,
almost all American bishops expressed enthusiasm in varying
degrees for the papal anti-birth-control statement. Just as readily,
the majority of the men and women who teach theology in American colleges and seminaries vigorously opposed these teachings
and claimed the Catholic tradition of doctrinal development for
their positions. Progressives often embrace the evolutionary
theology deriving from the French Jesuit paleontologist Pierre
Teilhard de Chardin, while conservatives see his teaching as a

Richard Mather, born 1596, emigrated in 1634 and soon became one of the most renowned preachers in New England. Increase and Cotton Mather were his son and grandson. (1)

denial of the faith, a repudiation of the supernatural, and a contribution to anti-Christian collectivism. To say 'Catholic' in the closing decades of the 20th century is to say little about a position or a person.

f ʃ Every fifth American can be identified as a Baptist, a member of the second largest cluster. The Baptist denomination existed originally to support adult immersion as the form of baptism, congregationalism in church polity, and religious freedom in relation to the government. Most Baptists may still hold to these tenets, but their public attitudes and stances are what have become visible to the world, and on these they are hopelessly divided.

The two largest Baptist groups are the National Baptist Convention and the Southern Baptist Convention. Most of the 5,500,000 members of the National Baptist Convention are black. They tend to revere a traditional otherworldly theology, to eschew unsettling social positions, and to favor only very cautious policies toward racial integration. Few of them were at home with the progressive theology of the century's best-known Baptist cleric, Martin Luther King. King combined old Baptist church modes with the non-violent approach of Mohandas Gandhi and modern theology picked up at the Boston University School of Theology. He was too much interested in reform of the social order to attract many of the more quietistic and cautious National Baptists. If King was suspect in their eyes, the following generation of Baptists who caucused in movements of Black Power are anathema to them.

Neither the National Baptist conservatives nor Martin Luther King and his kind would be welcomed in thousands of congregations of their fellow-believers in the largest Protestant group, the eleven-million-strong Southern Baptist Convention. Many of these remain utterly devoted to racial segregation and in many southern communities their churches serve as organizing centers for white racist organizations. Many of these Southern Baptists, whether in rural or suburban settings, will tolerate no preacher who 'meddles in politics' by expounding unpopular views on race, war, housing, or legislative actions. Yet members of the Convention's Christian Life Commission are widely respected by other church leaders for their astute analysis of modern social problems and their endeavors to have Southern Baptists face up to social complexities. Not less otherworldly in their fundamental theology than the intransigents, they are convinced that Christianity is also to transform this world.

A visitor to the pulpit of the denomination's President W. A. Criswell in 1969 or 1970 would hear the preacher condemn all

those who did not accept his particular theory of the literal inerrancy of the Bible. Yet if further visits took him to any of a number of Southern Baptist seminaries, he would find respected teachers differing significantly from Criswell on this doctrine which he regards as most basic of all.

Methodism, the third largest cluster, has since 1908 found its *f ʃ* officials, seminary teachers, and many ministers involving the church with social issues. The Methodist Social Creed of 1908 reproduced many of the Protestant Social Gospel's teachings about the conversion of American society into conformity with the Kingdom of God as proclaimed by Jesus. Some Methodist leaders, such as Harry F. Ward, are admittedly as influenced by Karl Marx as by John Wesley. But while some Methodists adhere to views like Ward's, a visitor to many a suburban Methodist congregation will find that the leading laymen are more likely to be organizing a Billy Graham crusade than following Methodist positions on open housing or revolution in the Third World.

Two of Presbyterianism's best known representatives in the late 1960s were William Sloane Coffin, Jr, the Chaplain at Yale University, and Robert McAfee Brown, professor at Stanford University. Whoever consults the historic textbooks would expect that their careers should be devoted, at least some of the time, to defense of divine predestination, presbyterial church polity, and a distinctively Calvinist view of the Lord's Supper. But they were in fact better known for criticism of American military policies, support for selective conscientious objection to the draft, and contending for change in race relations. At the other extreme, J. Howard Pew, President of the Sun Oil Company, was during the same years a spokesman for many influential Presbyterian laymen. On his reading of Calvin, the churches are to avoid involvement with the social order. They are to convert people out of the world, to prepare them for heaven, to equip them for personal holiness, and to permit them as individuals to take citizens' roles—which Pew hoped would be on the side of the economic *status quo.* On almost no significant issue would he be recognizable as a member of the same denomination as Coffin and Brown, nor would the followings of these two kinds of leaders have much in common.

The New World's spiritual attitudes would be most confusing were a visitor to try to use historic denominationalism to make sense of the century's best-known Protestant evangelist, Billy p 67 (2 Graham. He, too, holds some ties with the Presbyterian clergy, though he would have agreed with little in Coffin's or Brown's views. But he is at the same time a Baptist, and thus—following the traditional textbook approach—should be committed to contradictory views of Baptism, the Lord's Supper, and other teachings over which his Baptist and Presbyterian forefathers in faith fought holy wars. Graham is closer to Pew in his general view that Christians should not expect to transform a sinful world—they should extricate people from it and prepare them for the life to come. Changing the world is thus a fortunate possibility as a bonus or afterthought from changed individual lives.

Most members of the churches of Continental provenance, the Lutheran and the Reformed, organize their church lives around the *f ʃ* themes of man's sin and God's grace, the problems of earth and the p 63 (9 promise of heaven. They have often been described as traditionalist or quietistic in the political realm. Indeed, they have chosen to repudiate most of the noted theologians of 19th- and 20th-century European Lutheranism and the Reformed Churches, where the most radical innovations in religious thought have occurred. Yet in the United States the most formidable theological experimenters of the 20th century, men like Paul Tillich and Reinhold and H. Richard Niebuhr, have drawn on the same Continental rootage and source.

Episcopalians, deriving impulses from British Christian Social- *f ʃ* ism and a century of American social theology, are often in the front rank of churchly endeavorers trying to transform the existing world in the name of the Kingdom of Christ. In continuity with historic Anglicanism, they allow for great breadth and comprehension of Christian doctrine. For years, the maverick Bishop James Pike was at home in this communion. But the Episcopal congregations and dioceses are filled with economic individualists and doctrinal precisionists. Episcopalianism is one of the few groups in which 20th-century heresy trials occurred. The United

Jonathan Edwards (1703–58), theologian and evangelist, saw America as the divinely chosen setting of God's new revelation. His vision, however, included salvation in the world, and not merely rescue from it. (2)

Church of Christ includes and tries to live with the whole range of Congregationalism's theological and social positions.

Non-Christian organized religion in America is represented chiefly by Judaism. Because of a heritage of ghetto life and suspicion on the part of the Christian majority, the Jewish believers would be expected to possess a solidarity that Christian groups do not know. There is, of course, denominationalism within the Orthodox-Conservative-Reform-Reconstructionist spectrum. But while most Jews see religion as the transformer of society, they recognize significant differences of opinion on most aspects of Jewish life and thought—and these do not often follow the denominational lines. Very often the issues of assimilation and integration *versus* segregation and isolation in a Gentile environment serve to define them, though almost all historic Jewish expression has shared the Christians' affirmation of the American environment for ritual and mission.

Some attempts have been made to characterize the American religious who do not feel at home in any of the denominations. Some choose to be called secular humanists or merely humanists. Like the Unitarians and Universalists, they are, of course, not bound or defined by any precise doctrines. But like these denominations, even their community is torn. On one hand there are many who share the philosopher John Dewey's sense of *A Common Faith*. In Dewey's spirit men like the Reverend A. Powell Davies believe in the democratic faith and its limitless potential for raising the level of life and 'making the world increasingly more happy, more just, and more good'. In the writings of Professor J. Paul Williams, this social common faith calls for Americans to look on their democratic ideal 'as the Will of God, or, if they please, the Law of Nature' and democracy will 'become an object of religious dedication'.

On the other hand, this advocacy of a common faith can also follow politically reactionary lines, as in the evolutionary vision of Robert Welch, the founder of the John Birch Society, or in the practices of any number of nationalistic organizations where American symbols are regarded with a sense of ultimacy and celebrated with quasi-religious ritual. For them, the generalized American religious tradition exists not to transform the world into a common social faith but to equip autonomous individuals to withstand the corrosive and enervating effects of such social approaches.

Denominational categories, then, are more confining than helpful to people who want to determine what Americans believe and hope for. Yet few new institutional schisms based on competing and even opposing points of view have resulted from the religious

two-party system we have been discussing. There is, instead, sometimes creative and sometimes frustrating coexistence between groups that hold alternative visions of the role of religion in American mission and destiny. A more useful distinction is between those who believe that religion exists primarily to *transform* the American environment into some ideal like the Kingdom of God, and those who believe that religion should first of all *rescue* people from that environment for the sake of heaven later or cultic life now.

In American history the specific appeals of the would-be transformers and rescuers have inevitably taken on the color of their particular religious communities. Protestants, Catholics, Jews and humanists have invoked different myths, symbols, revelations, or traditions to substantiate their cases. For an understanding of recent American religious history, a concentration on Protestantism is most useful.

Protestantism deserves attention because of its priority and predominance in most areas of the United States through most of its history. Today, two-thirds of all Americans identify themselves as broadly Protestant. French Catholicism in eastern Canada formed one arm of a kind of pincers from the north, and Iberian Catholicism formed another, based in the southeast (Florida) and southwest. In the thirteen colonies almost no Catholics were represented for much of their history—fewer than 25,000 being present in a population of several millions by 1776. Only in Maryland had they played a decisive role in shaping public institutions. Not until the great Irish and German immigrations near the middle of the 19th century did Catholicism rise to prominence as the largest single church body and not until the great immigrations were finished around the First World War did Catholicism come to have a strong and positive impact on the national ethos.

Judaism, in the late decades of the 20th century, still numbers fewer than six million people, and many of these are not observant at synagogues. Only three per cent of Americans list themselves as Jewish. Not until the forty-four years of mass immigration after 1881 did significant numbers of Jews come upon the scene.

Statistical prominence and chronological priority thus give Protestantism a privileged position in the making of national myths. Novelists from Herman Melville and Nathaniel Hawthorne in the 19th century down through William Faulkner in the 20th have reworked and wrestled with Puritan-Protestant symbols. Much of the poetic imagery and significant elements of religion in the nation's folklore related to that tradition. Catholic or Jewish themes came into predominance only in the second half of the 20th century.

The Congregationalist historian Leonard Bacon in 1898 was still speaking for many when he wrote that 'by a prodigy of divine providence, the secret of the ages had been kept from premature disclosure' until the Protestant Reformation had occurred to purify the religion that would be transported to America. The grade school textbooks of the 19th century, when they presented maps identifying world population blocs, unanimously listed the United States as a Protestant nation, without specifying the criteria for the designation.

Conscious as they were of their Englishness, the founding fathers stressed that they were peculiar kinds of Englishmen—Protestants, purified by persecution in many cases—but also that some measure of repudiation of England had gone into the making of the American religious element. Governor William Bradford could teach his generation to say, 'Our fathers were Englishmen . . .' but later Cotton Mather, in the same New England tradition, began his major book on history, 'I write the *Wonders* of the CHRISTIAN RELIGION, flying from the Depravations of *Europe*, to the *American Strand*'.

The positive view of the American environment, the virgin 'wildernesse' that was also a Zion or a 'cittie set upon a hille', was born of a blending of reaffirmation and repudiation. New World religion was not to be wholly new; God had not left himself wholly without witness in Europe. Much has been made of the words purportedly spoken by Francis Higginson, a non-Separatist Puritan, in 1629: 'We do not go to New England as Separatists from the Church of England; though we cannot but separate from the corruption in it, but we go to practise the positive part of church reformation and propagate the gospel in America.' But equal weight must also be given to words such as Increase Mather's:

f s

f s

p 62 (4, 6)

p 40–41

developing a New World theology which saw America as the milieu for God's fulfilment. 'The latter-day glory, is probably to begin in America.' The 'Sun of righteousness' would 'rise in the west, contrary to the course of things in the old heavens and earth'.

Like Increase Mather, Edwards seemed to be saying that the Old World had had its chances. The New World was now prepared 'in order to make way for the introduction of the church's latter-day glory—which is to have its first seat in, and is to take its rise from, that new world'. No longer would America be a postscript to the Christian story that had moved from the Middle East through Europe. Instead, here was to be the climax; wherever revival was, there was the theater or arena for God's introduction of a new era of justice and peace. 'When God is about to turn the world into a paradise', he locates it 'in the wilderness'. The man who was known for talking about sinners in the hand of an angry God could speak as eloquently about the time when 'this whole great society shall appear in glorious beauty'. It was 'God's manner to keep things always progressive'. Far from being a dour pessimist, Edwards was actually writing a breathtakingly optimistic scenario for the world that would be saved through America.

Students of American religious history have to familiarize themselves with the language of the millennium, a thousand-year period of wonders. When Edwards thought of missionary work among the Indians, he considered that 'the discovery of so great a part of the world' was 'one thing by which divine providence is preparing the way for the future glorious times of the church, when Satan's kingdom shall be overthrown throughout the whole habitable globe, on every side, and on all its continents'. Edwards did not use the threat of hell or the promise of the millennium to contrive revivals of religion, but he did see revivals as a kind of anticipation of life and community in such a good age.

Millennial imagery came more and more to the fore early in the national period, when American Protestants took over the custodianship of religion in what looked to them like an evangelical empire. They did not want merely to save men *from* the world but to save men *in* it, to remake their lives and through these lives to remake society, to carry on a mission to the whole world. Samuel Hopkins, who inspired much of the benevolent and charitable movement, argued that Jesus Christ who was condemned in the world 'should have this reproach wiped off in the sight of all men, and that the cause in which he suffered and died, should prevail and be victorious in this same world, where he suffered and died'.

The foremost revivalist of the first half of the 19th century, Charles Grandison Finney, brought the Protestant millennial doctrine or myth to the center. The propagation of Christianity would lead the world toward perfection. Then would come the thousand years of peace, after which Christ would return and God's reign would be permanent on earth. 'If the church will do her duty, the millennium may come in this country in three years', he said in his *Lectures on Revivals*. Christian reform was spreading—how could men be gloomy and pessimistic? 'Are these evidences of the world's growing worse and worse? The world is not growing worse, but better', was the word of the *Oberlin Evangelist* in 1843. This point of view came to be known as postmillennialism, and was the mythic backdrop for the approach of those who would see religion chiefly as a power to transform the world.

Rescue from the world

While Finney was speaking of progress, one of his contemporaries, William Miller, described and foresaw cataclysm. In fact Miller, *f4* from whom the modern Seventh Day Adventist denomination traces its rise, predicted that Christ's Second Coming would occur in 1843. This view, called premillennialism, tended toward a more pessimistic view of the world. Christians were to be rescued, saved, from the world. Holiness was called for, but it did not pay for men to be stained by compromise in the public and political realms. Christ's second coming alone would bring in peace and order.

Outside his own denomination, Miller remained a minor figure in American Protestantism, but the idea to which he witnessed came to parity with the postmillennial view. To moderns, the controversy between the two must seem arcane and theologically obscure. An American could go about his business for years and,

MAMUSSE
WUNNEETUPANATAMWE
UP-BIBLUM GOD
NANEESWE
NUKKONE TESTAMENT
KAH WONK
WUSKU TESTAMENT.

Ne quoſhkinnumuk naſhpe Wuttinneumoh *CHRIST*
ᴸᴼh aſoowelit

JOHN ELIOT·

CAMBRIDGE:
Printeuoop naſhpe *Samuel Green* kah *Marmaduke Johnſon.*
1 6 6 3.

Title-page of the Massachusetts Indian Bible, translated by John Eliot, the first Bible printed in the US, and the earliest example of the translation of the whole Bible as a means of evangelization. (3)

'There never was a generation that did so perfectly shake the dust of Babylon . . . as the first generation of Christians that came to this land for the Gospel's sake.'

The New World transformed

The purified Protestant colonizers of New England did not always live up to their sense of 'errandry', and by the 1730s a Great Awakening was needed to vivify religion there and to help people clarify their sense of mission. It was in this time that Jonathan *f2* Edwards emerged to comment on the New World's spiritual turn. He stood at the head of a tradition in Protestantism as he looked out with favor at the possibilities in the environment around him. Two centuries later, when discussing 'Christ the Transformer of Culture', H. Richard Niebuhr was to say that Edwards 'with his sensitive and profound views of creation, sin, and justification, with his understanding of the way of conversion and his millennial hopes, became in America the founder of a movement of thought about Christ as the regenerator of man *in* his culture'. [Italics mine.] Neibuhr saw that Edwards' approach was later perverted in a banal 'theurgism' in which men were deluded into thinking they could 'channel the grace and power of God into the canals they engineered'. On the other hand, it was also bastardized to 'justify the psychological mechanics of a shabby revivalism' and in the shallow sociological science of one part of the Social Gospel.

What was at the heart of the Edwardsean picture of the environment? Those who have a superficial acquaintance with this Protestant giant usually know his words of warning about God's judgment and impending hell. It is true that Edwards was capable of talking in terms of Biblical apocalypse about the end of the world and the natural phenomena which would suddenly end the human story. But throughout his career he worked just as hard at

William Miller calculated that the end of the world would take place between 21 March 1843 and 21 March 1844. After the latter date passed without incident, he revised it to 22 October. This satirical print, published in the same climacteric year, shows the Boston Tabernacle ascending to *heaven, a few followers clinging on and himself sitting on the chart (based on Daniel and Revelation) from which his dates were derived. Joshua V. Himes, Miller's chief publicist, is left behind in the Devil's clutches, surrounded by moneybags. (4)*

unless he was in range of a pulpit in a fundamentalist Protestant church, almost never even hear the words premillennial or post-millennial. But their use was fateful in the 19th century. For reasons not yet wholly explained, the evangelists in the urban and industrial period gravitated toward the premillennial option. While Protestantism was helping a population move into a whole new stage of history, its most popular spokesmen were coming to see Christianity chiefly as a rescue agency from a complex world.

66 (16)   In the late 19th century the major spokesman for premillennialism was the evangelist, Dwight L. Moody. Moody may have picked up premillennialism under the subtle influence of some conservative Bible scholars in the Plymouth Brethren. Perhaps he gravitated to the idea in the reaction to progressivism that came with the period immediately after the Civil War. Whence postmillennialism? Moody: 'Where do you get it? I can't find it. The word of God nowhere tells me to watch and wait for the coming of the millennium, but for the coming of the Lord. I don't find any place where God says the world is to grow better and better, and that Christ is to have a spiritual reign on earth of a thousand years. I find that the earth is to grow worse and worse and that at length there is going to be a separation' between the saved and the damned.

Moody's formal theology amounted to a call for Christians to separate from the evil world. The classic expression of Moody's alternative to Edwardseanism was: 'I look on this world as a wrecked vessel. God has given me a life-boat, and said to me, "Moody, save all you can."' He was sure that nothing would 'take the men of this world out of their bonds and stocks quicker than' the idea that our 'Lord is coming again'.

67 (20)   The professional revivalist ever after normally tended to view his work not as transforming but as rescuing men. Billy Sunday was the prime example early in the 20th century. While open to some kinds of social reform, his first task was to extricate people from the world. And after mid-century Billy Graham was announcing in the public press that 'the Bible teaches that justice and peace will ultimately triumph. Utopia is going to come. Man himself cannot bring this about. He cannot build a perfect world on the cracked foundation of human nature, but God is going to bring it about.' 'Jesus will return, and His coming will mark the end of Satan's supremacy, abolishing all human misery such as disease, poverty, and war.'

Concentration on the historic controversies over post- and premillennialism would be beside the point were it not that they reveal a subtle and surprising shift in attitudes about the American milieu and religion in American history. The transformers, purportedly optimists as Edwards had been, came to take an increasingly negative view of the *status quo*, while the reputedly pessimistic premillennialists, men on Moody's kind of mission, sounded carping, but came to be typed as positive thinkers about America as it was.

The postmillennial tradition after the Civil War was enlarged upon by Social Gospel thinkers, many of whom minimized the mythic references, but all of whom worked for progress and reform of the world. In order to 'Christianize the social order', as Walter Rauschenbusch was to put it, they had to show how short of Christianization America was. Affirmative about some orders of life, such as the family, school, and church, they engaged in radical criticism of *laissez-faire* economics, labor policies, and an individualism which they felt kept the world from improvement.

Meanwhile, the men who spoke of rescue from the world were increasingly supported by aspiring businessmen, entrepreneurs, and affluent new urbanites. The Marxist interpreter comes upon this scene and decides that the premillennialist, the rescue-man, by offering 'pie in the sky' and rejecting plans for social reform, rendered religion into opium. Naturally, in this reading, well-off people who exploited others would be drawn to this kind of evangelistic preaching. It soothes people with bad consciences, justifies people who like the world as it is, serves to remind them of the ordered life of their childhood, and in no way inconveniences them. Meanwhile, the evangelist replies: people who are 'saved' and ready for Christ's coming will be most motivated to be holy and to want to serve him in the world. And even though that world is under Satan's power, if it is the New World of America, it provides a wonderful theater for God's rescue work.

The later premillennial mythology, then, has produced people with views at least as positive as Jonathan Edwards ever held. Dwight Moody was a patriot, a nationalist, a businessman identi-

p 67 (20)

fied with business interest. Billy Sunday, who, like Moody, attacked the Social Gospel and some other reformist movements, echoed Moody's 'I don't see how a man can follow Christ and not be successful'. He said, 'Christianity is your character and character is your capital.' 'It pays to serve God.' 'We are citizens of the greatest country in the world and we will admit it.' Billy Graham, decrying individual evils and announcing that reform will come only with Christ's return, golfs with Presidents, is regarded as part of the affluent society, and represents a threat to few upholders of 'the American Way of Life'.

The historian William McLoughlin mused over the paradox or confusion in Moody, who was overly optimistic about 'evangelization of the world through human agency and . . . overly pessimistic . . . that the world was getting worse and worse'. Pessimism about social reform was coupled with optimism about another world and both appeared curiously against a background of affirmation of this world when this world happened to be America.

Those who sought to rescue people from the world began with a pessimism about what man could do. But closer examination of America as a place where good men had left a deposit of holiness and good works and as a free nation where men were allowed to make religious choice led to an ever less critical understanding of America. The world was still described as a distracting allure for would-be saints, but the American reality in the world came to be a positive good. America looked more and more like the Kingdom and few who preached for conversion found reason to plead for a far-reaching transformation of American society but only for change of individuals in it.

Catholic Americanization

The second-largest religious cluster, Roman Catholicism, is divided on similar lines, though its spokesmen use other terms, doctrines, and myths than those associated with the millennium. The Catholics' two parties divide over the issues of 'nature' and 'supernature'. Both saw the slow rise of social reformism in terms of a theology which was chiefly concerned with getting to heaven and avoiding hell. The 'Americanizers' were originally like Protestant postmillennialists, who wanted to be transformers of their world, without, of course, denying Catholic teaching about a life to come. The 'anti-Americanists' were like the premillennialists who wanted to rescue people from the world, with its hostile Protestant environment; to keep them faithful to the Pope; to stress the supernatural. America was thus often a symbol for both parties.

The Americanizers were progressives, were optimistic—though doctrinally thoroughly orthodox. They made a great point of their love for the environment. John Ireland, a bishop of St Paul after 1884, was effusive: 'Republic of America, receive from me the tribute of my love and of my loyalty. With my whole soul I do thee homage. . . . Thou bearest in thy hands the hopes of the human race, thy mission from God is to show to nations that men are capable of highest civil and political liberty.' John Spalding and James Gibbons, two of his colleagues, spoke in similar terms. They were accused by European parties and by American conservatives like Michael Corrigan of New York of being too adaptive, guilty of an 'Americanist heresy'. Father Andrew Greeley characterized the transformation-minded party as optimists, democrats, socially conscious, eager for amity with non-Catholics, proud of the American church, cultural assimilationists, educators, activists—

and loyal to Rome. When the French priest Charles Maignen helped bring about the condemnation of their general views, John Ireland wrote, 'Read the letter carefully and you will see that the Americanism condemned is Maignen's nightmare. Whoever preferred natural to supernatural virtues? Whoever taught that the practice of natural virtues was not to be vitalized and supernaturalized by divine grace?'

For the next half-century a band of social reformers worked in the context of Catholicism, only to be attacked by those who wanted the Church to devote itself chiefly to 'supernatural virtues'. But just as Jonathan Edwards embraced America and still appealed for a transcendent reference, the Catholic radicals could immerse themselves in the complexities of modern life and still, as John E. Reardon put it in 1939 while defending radicals like Dorothy Day and Peter Maurin, argue that Catholics should 'promote the uncompromising advance of supernatural Catholicism along every sector of the Catholic front and around every side of Catholic individual and social life'. Just as for the heirs of Edwards, among whom the idea of the postmillennium was to breed discontent with the world as it was, their Catholicism eventually led them to express discontent over America as it was and served as their lever for moving or changing it.

Catholic partisans of the cause of rescue from the world, also in the name of supernatural virtues, countered these Americanizers and radicals. They began by expressing suspicion toward the New World environment. Having arrived late on the scene, they were surrounded by people of other faiths who had set the terms of life for them. Robert D. Cross, in *The Emergence of Liberal Catholicism in America*, noted that, 'hostile to the Protestant majority, suspicious of governmental enterprise, and averse to the active melioristic spirit of the times, these Catholics met secular culture so far as possible only on their own terms'. Catholicism was a symbol and seal of separation from that culture, and this party opposed all innovations except those that would strengthen the defensive armor of the Church.

Except for their minority status, these 'Anti-Americanists'' point of view was originally similar to that of Moody-Sunday-Graham and the premillennialists. Men could be tainted if they had to compromise with people who held other religious views. There were hostile and satanic forces present, along with seductive attractions. Father John Tracy Ellis later pondered how this negativism, which he saw to be directed against scholarship, came about. Could it be because of the 'too literal interpretation which many . . . have given to St Paul's oft-quoted statement that "Here we have no permanent city, but we seek for the city that is to come" . . .'?

Yet just as the Protestant rescuers paradoxically came to affirm the American environment as an excellent theater for their activity, Catholics who stressed otherworldliness and supernature and who rejected environmental optimism finally came to be more contented with the American Way of Life than were the Americanizers. The hyper-patriotism of the Knights of Columbus and the Catholic War Veterans is as well-known as their distaste for Catholic theological and social progressivists. 'Half suspect—they bow too low', according to John Tracy Ellis (in an allusion to Huguet, an officer of Richelieu's guard), such Catholics felt constantly pressed to prove their love for their new-found home and did so with ardor.

Nationalism has been the mark of the orthodox Catholic, as has been eventual contentment with the approved social contract. When the Jesuit professor Walter J. Ong called for Catholics to pick up the best from the Protestant-progressive-evolutionary vision in America, he had to warn at the same time against their grafting this on to a chauvinism or an 'Americanology', based on the belief that this country is called by God to lead the rest of a benighted world to salvation. One of the difficulties facing the Catholic sensibility in the United States 'is precisely the tendency of many Catholics to let their understanding of the United States be defined by something like such jingoism'. Jingoism can only be an expression of people who find their environment congenial in almost all respects and who do not want it tampered with or transformed. Those who had once wanted through 'supernature' to protect the faithful from America later found themselves fanatically affirming America.

The Jew and the promise of America

The smaller but significant Jewish community has not been divided on lines quite like these, but the struggle to come to terms with the environment is similar to those of Catholics. The 'otherworldly' motif has been less strong in Jewish conservatism, because Jews are less precise about definitions of after-life and less decisive in anything like heaven-and-hell choices. In every case, however, articulate Jews have had to make up their mind about what to be and do in the New World.

Jews could not share the Christian vision of millennium or Messiah. While most Jews might not associate themselves with the 'death of God' theology of Rabbi Richard Rubenstein, they might tend to agree with his attempt to disassociate himself from the Christian views of historical purpose. Rubenstein, in criticizing a 'Christian atheist', Thomas J. J. Altizer, found even in him too much of the traditional views. Altizer had identified himself with Jesus, who 'represented the promise of a new beginning, a fulfilment, a radical change in man's tragic and broken condition. The sad answer of the rabbis was that nothing new has happened. The world in its sadness goes on.' So Rubenstein criticized Altizer's view of the future. Altizer 'has also spoken hopefully of America's vocation as being cut off from the past and oriented toward the future'. But countering this vision, as old as Increase Mather and Jonathan Edwards, Rubenstein envisaged America's destiny 'to become Europeanized. What we are experiencing in Vietnam is a sense of limit, defeat, and the ironies of history'—something for which Christianity had not prepared American religionists.

The American Jew has been more preoccupied with space than with time. After Peter Stuyvesant advised New Amsterdam's Jews to build houses 'as close together as possible', they were to be cramped in ghettos imposed or chosen, while surrounded by great spaces lightly filled with non-Jews, many of them hostile. But Jews have been divided about how to regard that environment. The ghetto mentality advocated something comparable to what Christian rescuers and otherworldly types sought: to keep the faithful apart, defended, unspotted. Jewish ritual and modes of life, it was agreed, would help build walls against intermarriage, assimilation, and the acquisition of values from the Christian American environment.

The New World was overpowering in the Jewish case, too. Even the most sequestered Jews preferred their America to the Europe they had fled. And before long spokesmen were celebrating the positive features of the new nation. Ludwig Kempert, a German Jewish poet, wrote, 'It is to America that our longing goes forth.... No help has come for us, we are not saved. Seek help in faraway America.' But involvement with America meant the subtle seductions that came with exposure to a Christian ethos. The Jews were ready to take that risk.

p 63 (10)

By the time significant anti-Semitism developed, after 1881, Jews were free to be of two minds about religious or social policies because they were so clearly attached to so much of American life and its values. With a sense of the transforming power of religion, the Jewish Justice Louis Brandeis was able to say that 'The twentieth-century ideals of America have been the ideals of the Jew for more than twenty centuries.'

When Zionism came to attract American Jewish sympathies, the new kinds of loyalties to 'Jerusalem' or Israel did not compromise the attachments Jews felt for America. Few migrated. Few joined the American Council for Judaism, which wanted to make Judaism into a vague spiritual system but not a people's defense of Israel.

Through the years the Jewish thinkers and activists who had originally been more involved with the dynamics of the larger American society came to apply ever more rigorous tests to it. In the process, they were to become more critical of the way Americans practiced justice. Meanwhile, Judaism also produced out of the

Distribution of religious adherents in 1965. The letters represent the main religions in each state; those in brackets the secondary ones. (5)

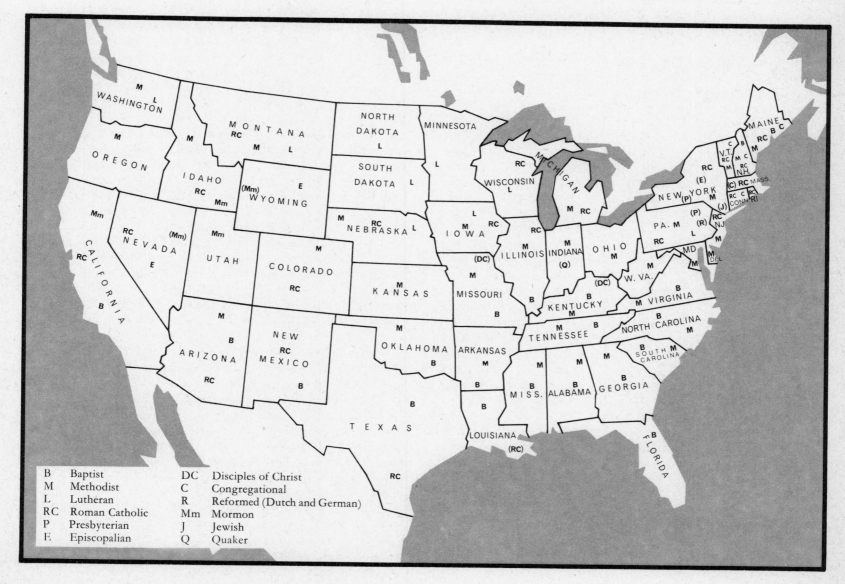

B	Baptist	DC	Disciples of Christ
M	Methodist	C	Congregational
L	Lutheran	R	Reformed (Dutch and German)
RC	Roman Catholic	Mm	Mormon
P	Presbyterian	J	Jewish
E	Episcopalian	Q	Quaker

memory of the ghetto more conservative organizations which were given to a rather uncritical endorsement of American society, despite residual complaints about anti-Semitism in it.

Anti-Semitism remained a potent force, and the Jew remained surrounded by alien ideas; the post-World War II movement to the suburb meant the end of the ghetto and an increase of intermarriage, with the accompanying threat of assimilation. But the old ghetto sense of withdrawal, designed to protect or rescue Jews from the hazards of the environment, was supplanted by an exposed Judaism, one which largely sided with Christians and other Americans who worked for the transformation of an environment which they could affirm.

Public and private religion

The denominations were the distinctive invention in New World religion, but they told us little about how religious forces moved in America. We have seen that they have followed basically two lines. Protestants who worked with the postmillennial myth, Catholic 'Americanizers' and Jews who favored exposed religious life began with an essentially positive view of America and rated it increasingly negatively as they set out to transform society. Premillennialist Protestants, Catholic 'otherworldly supernaturalists', and Jews who clung to ghetto existence began with essentially negative views of the world, but when they looked around and saw that the world was an America rich with promise for them they rated it more positively, even as they set out to rescue individuals from what evil remained in the world. The two 'schools' or approaches propagated themselves in different ways in the 20th century.

Those who seek the transformation of society might be called the political (' = of, belonging, or pertaining to the . . . body of citizens') or 'public religionists'. They may attend church or synagogue, but they transmit their religious teachings through more public media. Most of religion's better-known literary and intellectual figures, members of activists' elites, and theologians at seminaries and universities disseminate their views through denominational pronouncements, the press, public acts, and involvement with 'page one' issues. The Central Conference of American Rabbis, the National Catholic Welfare Council, or the National Council of Churches are often staffed by people who hold to the 'public' point of view.

Only occasionally does one glimpse the intersection of the public and private spheres. Martin Luther King was at home on magazine covers, at demonstrations, in meetings with politicians. Not until his funeral in a Baptist Church in Atlanta were citizens made aware of his deep roots in traditional personal religion. While Father James Groppi regularly says Mass, Chaplain Coffin preaches to collegians, and Abraham Joshua Heschel faithfully follows Jewish observances, their ministry is essentially one that has to do with religious and moral exertions of power, or expressions of viewpoint on matters which visibly exercise the whole community, issues like peace or race.

The logical question for the outsider to ask would be, 'Why, if the differences within denominations are so deep and if they cut across the lines of religious organizations, do not some people leave each group and re-cluster with more congenial company?' The answers given are many, from cynical versions having to do with jurisdiction, ownership of church property, and even mundane matters like ministerial pension plans, to more probing ones. Among these is the already mentioned fact that each side has some legitimate claim on the traditions. Each has reason to claim that it is faithful to the intentions of its founders and fathers. Most Western religion was fashioned before the era of modern individualism, when religion had to do directly with all of life; the party that favors 'political' religion trades on this history. But the group accenting personal faith also can point to aspects of traditions which were designed to keep believers unspotted by the taint of political compromise.

The two groups need each other. The 'public' party is not self-perpetuating. It draws on personnel formed by private and pietistic religion. On the other hand, while the debt is seldom acknowledged, those who favor personal and otherworldly religion justify their presence in a free society on ethical bases, and their competitors within their own communions have often done much to present these ethical credentials. Most of all, the two parties trade on a common pool of spiritual symbols; both give evidence of truly believing that their own are the authentic interpretations of their religious heritage and that the other element has either denied it or aborted its development.

To these reasons must be added a final one: the two parties do overlap. There are shared beliefs and emphases. Within Christianity, for example, those who work for the transformation of man's world do so in the context of eternal and spiritual values as well as in the setting of ministry to individual persons. They do not see themselves as downgrading such values and ministries but as upgrading the task of participating with God in creative and sustaining work. On the other side, those who want to deliver men from the world are not necessarily heartless or unthinking about world problems. Many of them have distinguished themselves by participation in that world and others have tried to find theological bridges to it. They simply believe that such tasks are secondary to their mission. Those who would seek resolution of conflict between the parties in the future would have to lead them to see the common pool of symbols and the overlap of beliefs and mission. Until that occurs, a pattern of drift and separation is likely to continue.

Joseph Pulitzer, the journalist, once advised newspapermen to 'afflict the comfortable; comfort the afflicted'. Public religionists generally came to accent the former mission. While they would say that they had a vision of a peaceable Kingdom and the reign of justice in mind, they find religion to be a prophetic element to disrupt life as it is established. Only thus will the exploited and the overlooked be noticed and served by religious forces. In this prophetic attitude, much of their criticism is directed not to 'secular man' but to people who appear to them to be complacent men and women in church pews and synagogue seats.

On the other hand, those who want to rescue people from the world but to leave the social fabric of America pretty much alone propagate their views through what might be called personal or private religion. While the doings of public religionists are reported on the front pages, these have a reserved section on a religion page in metropolitan newspapers. To most such people, worship is the center of their religion. Ceremony, ritual, sacrament, and preaching provide them with a universe of meaning and discourse to which to relate and through which to order their lives. These services are not ordinarily reviewed by critics or noticed in the papers. In one sense, 'nothing ever happens' at such rites, nor is it intended to. Instead of comment on public issues, people find there a center for interpreting the major stages, crises, and joys of daily life.

Personal and private religion is more concerned to support religious institutions—off which, it must be said, public religion in part lived. Religious institutions might find difficulties in a secular world. They compete; they devote many energies to fund raising; they find their supporters distracted by a world of increasing leisure; young people focus their dislike on religious institutions. Yet in America, at the beginning of the last third of the century, these institutions flourish. Over 60% of the people claim to belong to them, and over 40% claim to attend one each week, and spend almost one billion dollars a year erecting buildings to house them.

They enjoy tax exemptions for these institutions and, in return, they serve society by supporting its existing order. Comment on the controversial issues of the day is not expected and might be proscribed. And for all their otherworldliness or language of withdrawal from the secular, their moral or reformist concerns concentrated only on individual faults and vices: personal lovelessness, 'the seven deadly sins', and violations of mores. David Martin, the British sociologist of religion, has suggested that the phrase 'Texas Baptist millionaire' conjures up a very 'thisworldly' kind of man who wants a very otherworldly kind of Gospel. American society here and now is endorsed as the nearest perfection—if only the people in it would live up to national and religious visions.

In Pulitzer's phrase, while many would say that they want to 'afflict comfortable' persons, their basic mission is to 'comfort the afflicted'. Instead of a prophetic role, theirs is priestly. In place of a disruptive vision, theirs is integrative. In this attitude, much of their criticism is directed not only at 'secular man', who violates the nation's religious character, but also at the advocates of a trans-

Separation of church and state was an essential part of religious freedom. The First Amendment (1791) stated: 'Congress shall make no law respecting an establishment of religion, or prohibiting the free exercise thereof.' A cartoon by Thomas Nast in 1871 shows the various churches arriving with buildings in their own chosen architectural styles, and the state firmly refusing to favor any. (6)

formed American society, the theological innovators and social radicals in church and synagogue. Yet there is occasional interaction with public religion. Evangelist Billy Graham, throughout the 1960s, found himself more and more drawn to comment on social structures. Not a few religious conservatives take active roles in the movements for racial change. Some people tending chiefly to 'rescue from the world' belong to what are called 'historic peace churches' (Mennonite, Brethren) and are thus involved in criticism of war and advocacy of the end of the military draft.

Two approaches to consensus

While there is overlapping, intersection, interpenetration and interpermeation between the two styles of religious community—indeed, some individuals give half a heart to both—they are essentially in conflict. One celebrates the America that could be, if only a certain theological vision and social passion were to transform its whole way of life. The other celebrates the America that is, purged only of the individual faults which prevent the national religious covenant from becoming evident, and the American mission and destiny from becoming manifest in the world.

At the same time, American religious forces of both kinds contribute to elements of national consensus. The transformers have been the chief agents of ecumenical and interfaith activities. Not lightly regarding their theological and denominational differences, they have submerged these for purposes of practical alliance on public issues and for theoretical ideals, such as the expression of religious concord. The Protestant world in particular has been filled with such movements: the Federal Council of Churches (1908), the National Council of Churches (1950), American participation in the World Council of Churches (1948), an interdenominational Consultation on Church Unity, and endless denominational mergers along religious family lines—all these have ordinarily been inspired chiefly by people with the transforming vision.

The Second Vatican Council made possible Roman Catholic participation in theological dialogue, local councils of churches, and elements of joint worship. In general, the 'Americanizers'' heirs, the socially involved and theologically adventurous, have pioneered in these enterprises. Through them, Catholics work with non-Catholics in their attempts to express religious unity and to help change the world. Through the National Conference of Christians and Jews and similar organizations, interfaith activities receive support. Many of these activities are rejected by 'fundamentalists' in the various communities and by intransigents who issue warnings about the indifference to denominational doctrines on the part of people who man and inspire ecumenical and interfaith organizations.

On the other hand, personal and private religion more readily contributes to a national consensus through its support of the symbols of the political body. The flag, the pledge of allegiance to that flag with the words 'under God' latterly inserted, the words 'In God We Trust' as a motto on coins and currency, the presence of chaplains at legislatures and civic gatherings, the invocations and benedictions at gatherings of supporters of the American Way of Life—all these are more often in the hands of people who are officially described as seeking to rescue, reform, and inspire individuals in a society which they have come basically to endorse.

This is not to say that advocates of social transformation through religion are unpatriotic, non-nationalist, and generally negative types. Some of them have played distinguished roles in public life or have informed schools of political thought. Thus a generation of statesmen like George Kennan and Dean Acheson acknowledged their debt to Reinhold Niebuhr. But men like Niebuhr were more ready than were their religious antagonists (e.g., Billy Graham around 1957) to see an irony in American history. Niebuhr chose to comment readily on the pride and pretensions of nations, on their tendency to arrogate to themselves divine prerogatives, or to in-

77

voke religious symbols to justify their least attractive acts. In the Niebuhrian tradition, men chose to speak, as Abraham Lincoln did, of Americans as 'an almost chosen people'. In Graham's school, Americans are more readily identified as 'the chosen people'.

Both of these very informal clusters of religionists find allies not only outside their own communions but also outside the whole field of organized religion. In so doing, they express differing visions of the meaning of the secular order.

The social transformers in American religion have been more ready to give a positive valuation to the possibilities in the whole secular order. In referring to non-believers who were passionate for justice, Reinhold Niebuhr liked to quote St Paul, 'These have a zeal for God, but not according to knowledge.' Thus he gave theological expression to the idea that, as he saw it, God worked through men who did not explicitly express faith in him. John Courtney Murray, a Jesuit Father, in *We Hold These Truths*, worked out sophisticated bases in natural law for Catholic identification with the good man in civil society, whether or not Catholic, or even religious. Rabbi Abraham Joshua Heschel frequently reached into Hebrew resources for the idea that 'chosenness' is not an exclusive property of people who worship God in a particular way.

While Judaism had long before worked out a system of thought which affirmed 'the world' in such terms, Protestantism and Catholicism in America gave new expression to what was called a secular theology in the mid-1960s. Professor Harvey Cox, in the bestselling interpretation on these lines, has described *The Secular City*. In it, the Church is God's advance guard. People are motivated by certain Biblical symbols, like the Exodus and Servanthood. But they can find profound alliances available among agnostics, the godless, and others through whom God might assert His Lordship more readily than through 'the noise of solemn assemblies' and complacent pew-sitters.

Such theological visions have been largely rejected by those who support personal or private religion. Not that they continue in complete withdrawal from the taint of public involvement. They vote, run for office, serve in the military, pay taxes, and take positions on public issues. But they do this as individuals, and they unite with other individuals of other religious persuasions or with no visible religious means of support.

The secular order in general, in their eyes, could continue to be interpreted negatively but American order was a positive good because of a religious deposit there. Secular meant not 'potential', or even 'neutral', but rather that which distracted men from God or tried to thwart God's purposes. When in 1962 (*Engel v. Vitale*) and 1963 (*Abington School District v. Schempp*) the United States Supreme Court ruled out organized devotions and Bible reading in public schools and public institutions, there was a considerable hostile reaction. In opposition to the Court's interpretation, some congressmen advocated a constitutional amendment. During hearings on the subject, with a few surprising exceptions, spokesmen for what we are calling public religion were critical of public provisions of religion in secular institutions. In the Court's phrase, they wanted the State to remain 'wholesomely *neutral*', with the accent on the adjective. Private religionists, who were critical of 'secularism' in American institutions, wanted it '*wholesomely* neutral', with the accent on the adverb, and desired that a public provision be made. Once again, the denominational background of the spokesmen made less difference than did their commitment to the ways America was to be transformed.

Today, proponents of both viewpoints find much to make them uneasy in the American future. Both envisage new troubles for religious institutions in a secular age. After the religious revival of the 1950s had added persons, buildings, and vocations to America's religious assets there was a stabilization in the 1960s. The controversies in national life rent the churches and synagogues, often along the two-party lines that have been described here. A new generation found the concerns of both to be irrelevant. Many gifted and restless people, young and otherwise, were turning to Eastern and primitive religions to tap resources that had been lacking in Western Euro-American religion, which had long been dominant in the United States. For every analyst who prophesied a secular future there was another who, looking at phenomena from Astrology to Zen, envisioned a religious future on which Americans could draw.

What seems not to be at issue among the religiously observant of most denominations and schools and parties is a view in which the American environment and history is itself revelatory and redemptive. America provides the raw material for world-transformation or is the theater for God's greatest rescue work. Given such understandings, little that occurs in the public realm is exempt from the application of religious symbols.

In such a view, the denomination appears as a rather ingenious invention for channeling conflict into harmless paths. (I use 'invention' here in the dual sense: it was found and it was fashioned.) When Americans brought about a new thing in the New World by *f6* separating the religious from the civil realms (during the half century before 1833, when Massachusetts finally disestablished religion), they devised a voluntary system for support of religion. But they also found it necessary to see to it that men could hold to their particular visions of religious ultimates without being constantly involved in holy wars. The denomination performed this function precisely.

Americans were weary of holy wars, crusades, and religiously-based conflicts of the kind 17th-century Europe had known. The denomination led to the reduction of physical conflict by controlling it in verbal channels. The rhetoric of American denominational strife has been vitriolic: Protestants against Protestants, Protestants against Catholics, Christians against Jews, religious against 'infidels'. But there are almost no dead bodies as a result of the warfare. The denomination was the organizing center for private conflicting visions, while religious people ordinarily worked at the same time to promote civil concord.

If conflict between religious institutions has been largely verbal, Americans have certainly employed religious symbols to heighten conflict on matters which divided them. Theological interpretations of the origin of the American Indian were used to justify policies of removal. Religious visions have been regularly associated with the ways men looked at the facts of race, particularly in black-white enmities. Religions provided the chief sources of morale and rationales when North and South divided and were at war. The missionary language of the churches has regularly been associated with the declarations of America's manifest destiny in foreign affairs. Christian anti-Communism and Christian-Marxist dialogues have been expressions of alternative approaches to life in the Cold War. When calls for law and order confronted calls for revolutionary upheaval in the latter decades of the 20th century, they were frequently accompanied by claims that God willed one or the other.

So long as conflict remains part of the American story, religious symbols will probably be involved on both sides. Yet whenever consensus prevails, religious interpretations serve as a bond and provide depth. The language of America's public documents, its Declaration of Independence and Gettysburg Address and Presidential Inauguration speeches are cadenced with religious language, and it is difficult to picture the complete disappearance of these uniting symbols from national life.

While conflict remains between parties in American religion itself, the words of Abraham Lincoln in reference to civil strife have been invoked as a judgment on both. 'In great contests each party claims to act in accordance with the will of God. Both *may* be, and one *must* be wrong. God cannot be *for*, and *against* the same thing at the same time.' 'The Almighty has his own purposes.' His words were intended to help people place themselves in perspective so that they could take part in fulfilling the vision of America, in the time of risk when they might 'nobly save or meanly lose the last, best hope of earth'.

Over a century later, Americans of many religious persuasions and parties choose to identify with this language as being part of what Edwards had foreseen as 'the latter-day glory' now begun in America.

IV

POPULAR POLITICS

The government of the people in action

FRANK FREIDEL

'All the ills of democracy can be cured by more democracy.'

ALFRED E. SMITH

'Government of the people,

by the people, for the people' was Lincoln's definition of democracy. The various ways in which that ideal has been interpreted and codified are described in Chapter VI. It involved the delegation of legislative power to the two assemblies, of executive power to the President and of legal power to the Supreme Court. But beneath all these the ultimate arbiter was still the will of the people, and this was largely true from the very beginning of American history, even before the Revolution. This chapter will concentrate on the expression of the people's will, how it was organized into factions and how factions became parties whose leaders—in a way unforeseen by the framers of the Constitution—were automatically candidates for the Presidency. By the mid 19th century, presidential elections, which had originally been conceived as above 'faction', constituted the main arena of party rivalry.

A presidential campaign today is a matter of complex organization, vast expense and an amount of technical expertise that would have puzzled Washington or Lincoln. Whether these developments are beneficial to democracy is an open question, but it is probably true to say that politics is now more truly 'popular' than at any time in the past. The illustration opposite shows the culmination of a recent election, the inauguration of President Johnson on 20 January 1965. Behind the platform, erected for the occasion, rises the dome of the Washington Capitol, seat of the Senate and the House of Representatives. (1)

Hotly disputed Town Meetings (left) managed the affairs of the larger New England towns, before the Revolution. They formed the centers of opposition to 'court' rule, and sought to win influence in the elected lower houses of state legislatures. 'Whigs' at that time meant those who stood for the colonists (in such disputes as that over the Stamp Act of 1765, by which a tax had to be paid on all newspapers and legal documents), 'Tories' those who supported the English government. (2)

The tea controversy aroused sympathy abroad. In this French engraving of about 1775 Father Time shows lantern slides to the Continents. In the blaze of a bonfire the tea-pot explodes, driving the British lion and his cubs off to the right while young America advances, seizing the cap of Liberty. (3)

A Tory exciseman who collected the unpopular tea duty in Boston in 1774 was tarred and feathered and made to drink the health of all the royal family in scalding tea. This is a British view of American 'patriotism'. (4)

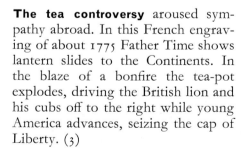

The fall of George III: a band of patriots pulled down the equestrian statue of the King in New York in July 1776, on the same day as the Declaration of Independence was proclaimed. (5)

The Boston Tea Party (left), one of the incidents leading to full-scale rebellion, was a protest against the fact that the East India Company enjoyed a monopoly of tea imports. A group of the 'Sons of Liberty' disguised themselves as Indians and threw 18,000 lbs of British tea into Boston harbor. (6)

The first President took the oath – in the open air, before the assembled people, as it is still taken – on 30 April 1789. New York was the original capital, and the ceremony (right) was held on the balcony of Federal Hall, the first meeting place of the Senate. (7)

Winning votes was the first concern of every politician. There were fewer short cuts to power than in Europe, and the art of popular appeal blossomed early. In this festive scene in Philadelphia, 1816, voters hand ballots through the windows of Independence Hall in the center (each ward had its own window). In the foreground an infirm elector is lifted out of a carriage. The building on the left is the Republican Party headquarters. (8)

A victory fan (left) was carried by the wife of James K. Polk, eleventh President of the United States, in 1844 at his inauguration. It shows the first ten Presidents plus her husband, who is labeled 'President Elect'. (9)

Banners, ribbons, pins, buttons, slogans, catch-phrases and every sort of gimmick to catch popular attention are especially characteristic of American politics and are by no means recent phenomena. Above right: campaign ribbons of 1876, when Samuel J. Tilden ran against Rutherford B. Hayes. The result was a disputed election in four states, settled by an 'Electoral Commission' which found in favour of Hayes. Right: Republican badges of 1888, proclaiming the names of Benjamin Harrison and his running-mate Levi P. Morton. Symbols include the 'presidential chair', the log-cabin and a sheep standing for protection. (10, 11)

Jacksonian democracy was another step towards the popular politics of today. During the first three decades of the 19th century voting qualifications were lowered until in some states almost all adult males were enfranchised. Andrew Jackson, elected 1828, broke the tradition of 'gentlemen' Presidents, though his enemies accused him of tyranny and portrayed him (left) as 'King Veto' because of his disrespect for the decisions of the Supreme Court. (12)

The log-cabin image (above and below) was taken up boldly by William Henry Harrison, grandfather of Benjamin, in 1836, on the slender justification that he lived in a mansion called *The Log Cabin*. (13, 14)

Violence often marked the course of politics at the grassroots. In 1849 the militantly Protestant Native American Party, or 'Know-Nothings', began burning Catholic churches and battling (above) with militiamen sent to restore order. (16)

The Ship of State (below) forms part of the inaugural procession in Washington of President Buchanan in 1857. (17)

The dirtiest election of American history is reputed to have been the contest between James G. Blaine and Grover Cleveland. Blaine's shady deals with railroad bonds are satirized in this cartoon, parodying Phryne before the Athenian judges. (15)

'Another Voice for Cleveland': the stick used to beat Cleveland was the discovery that he had an illegitimate child. Cleveland won the election in part because Blaine offended the Irish by referring to 'Rum, Romanism and Rebellion'. (18)

Popular politics in action: in 1890 a new party, the Populists, came into power in the Midwest, calling for economic reforms and the introduction of a currency based on silver rather than gold. After a disputed election in Kansas in 1893 the Populists barricaded themselves in the state house, to be driven out by armed Republicans (above) who eventually won the day. (19)

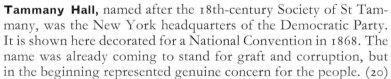

Tammany Hall, named after the 18th-century Society of St Tammany, was the New York headquarters of the Democratic Party. It is shown here decorated for a National Convention in 1868. The name was already coming to stand for graft and corruption, but in the beginning represented genuine concern for the people. (20)

Bryan's 'Cross of Gold' speech was regarded as blasphemous by his opponents because of its use of Biblical imagery. (22)

'The Lost Bet'. Cleveland ran for a second term in 1892, when he defeated Harrison. This painting (Courtesy Chicago Historical Society) shows a scene in Chicago just after the result was announced. A Chicago Republican had offered to pull his Democrat friend through the city in a cart if Cleveland won. Note, in the banner above them, that Cleveland's running-mate was Adlai Stevenson, grandfather of Eisenhower's opponent. (21)

Two views of T. R. Roosevelt. Left: as seen by his own party, the Apostle of Progress, the distributor of prosperity, justice and all the virtues. Right: as seen by the Democrats, a Roman tyrant, dragging his enemies, including Bryan, in triumph behind his chariot. (23, 24)

Modern campaigning begins with F.D. Roosevelt. Besides taking over the 'whistle-stop' speech (above left) from earlier politicians, he was the first to use an airplane to accept nomination (left: arriving at Chicago, 1932) and the radio (above) as a tool of government. He quickly realized that oratory was out of place on the air, and his 'fireside chats' were heard sympathetically by the whole nation. (25, 26, 28)

Opinion polls occupy growing attention, though they make occasional spectacular errors. Above: victorious Truman holds a paper prematurely announcing his defeat in 1948. (27)

The results go up on the night of 7 November 1956, to show that Eisenhower has beaten Stevenson. With him on the stand is Vice-President elect, Richard Nixon. (29)

A Goldwater supporter proclaims his loyalty (below). Barry Goldwater's campaign against Johnson in 1964 revealed the split between liberals and extreme conservatives even within the ranks of the Republican Party. (30)

The increasing complexity of modern elections has made them largely the province of publicity men and 'image' makers, the leaders ensuring party unity and endorsing local parties throughout the country. Above: Hubert Humphrey speaking as Vice-Presidential candidate at Santa Fe in 1964. Around the stand are portraits of Democrats seeking state and local offices. (31)

Television brought a new challenge. The debates between Kennedy and Nixon in 1960 (left) are thought to have been decisive in swinging the vote towards Kennedy. Television time now accounts for a large proportion of the money spent on elections, but Nixon has prudently avoided further direct confrontations. (32)

91

The government of the people in action

FRANK FREIDEL

POPULAR POLITICS have given life to the American system of government. The ultimate power which rests with the people finds expression through politics. The political history of the United States must, unlike that of ancient Rome or some European dynasties, focus upon a large electorate as well as upon a handful of leaders. True, leaders loom large, and one of the most common-place ways to organize American history has been through a presidential synthesis. But the vital base is popular politics.

The origins of American politics lie in British traditions which began to undergo modifications as soon as the settlers sought participation in their own governments. The first legislative body in the New World, the Virginia House of Burgesses, initially met in 1619, and the shaping of Colonial politics was soon well under way. Settlers repeatedly challenged the governing elite, seeking to break away from British models. In 1635 when the royal governor of Virginia threatened their economic interests, they forced his return to England. It was only after several eruptions of disorder, culminating in Bacon's Rebellion in 1676, as successive waves of newcomers sought to gain control, that an emergent planter aristocracy came firmly to dominate Virginia politics. These leaders, who served as Justices of the Peace, controlled local politics, and in the House of Burgesses defended planter interests against British incursions. Similar developments took place elsewhere.

'The meanest inhabitants'

In most colonies, the political leaders were allied in what might be called a party. They usually called themselves Whigs, and like the Whigs of England tried to counter what they thought to be undue royal authority. They sought control of the elected lower house of the legislature, where through exercising the power of the purse they tried to prevent the royal governor from acting against colonial interests. Sometimes there was a smaller party of those who, enjoying the favor of the governor, supported his policies. From among its leaders, the governor would appoint his council, which served as the upper house of the legislature. These sup-porters of royal authority came usually to be known as the Tories. So it was that John Adams once wrote that from the beginning in every colony a 'country' and a 'court' party vied with each other. These were by no means clear-cut political parties; it is an indica-tion of their shifting, rather nebulous nature, that the words 'party' and 'faction' ordinarily had the same meaning. Both were suspect. The so-called Whigs and Tories of the Colonial period and the revolutionary crisis were by no means analogous to later national parties in the United States.

As in Virginia, colony-wide politics focussing in the lower house of the legislature was primarily a defense of the dominant economic interests of the colony against interference from London. The Whigs resembled their British counterpart in being a loyal opposi-

tion—at least until the crisis of the 1770s. At this level, politics seemed predominantly a gentleman's avocation, with the alliances and clashes among great families as much as among special economic interests. To be sure, there were notable clashes, and even shots fired between the planter aristocrats of the Carolinas and the up-country small-farmer Regulators. But the history of Colonial politics was not, as an earlier generation of scholars liked to envisage it, a struggle between colonial dominant and debtor classes as much as a widening breach between all the colonists and the mother country.

Among humbler people also—small farmers and artisans in towns—political habits were developing in the 18th century that continued long thereafter. Some small farmers along the frontier, like the Regulators, even resorted to arms against the planter aristocrats they regarded as oppressors. But many more small farmers throughout the colonies, together with northern towns-people, voted for the members of great families whose names were familiar to them. In part it was deference toward, for example, the Randolphs of Virginia and Livingstons of New York; in part, especially in the South where regard for dominant families con-tinued as a political factor through much of the 19th century, a mixture of motives may well have led poor people habitually to vote for their powerful neighbors. At the polls they made common cause (whether against the British in the late 18th century, or in favor of white supremacy in the late 19th century) and through the sharing felt a rise in their own standing. Deference or fear may have influenced some. Undoubtedly many more were voting for a patron who could be expected to provide small favors when needed, beyond the immediate one of recognition and apparent familiarity on election day. The Southern gentry long continued as patrons much in the tradition of some European nations, ruling the county courthouses and the state capitols.

In towns, especially Boston, the basic patterns of urban politics were becoming established long before the American Revolution. Resentment against royal repression manifested itself both in town meetings and in mob action. During King George's War, in 1747, a mob of several thousand Bostonians protested against a press gang seizing men to serve in the Royal Navy, forcing Governor William Shirley to flee to a fort in Boston Harbor. To the authorities in London, Governor Shirley explained the political base for the rioting:

> The principal cause of the Mobbish turn in this Town is it's Constitution; by which the Management of it is devolv'd upon the populace assembled in their Town Meetings; where . . . the meanest Inhabitants who by their Constant attendance there are generally in the Majority and outvote the Gentlemen, Merchants, Substantial Traders and all the better part of the Inhabitants to whom it is Irksome to attend.

p 82 (2)

Governor Shirley was correct in his description of Boston politics, but failed to explain why it boiled over into mob action—resentment against the encroachment upon their freedom.

Popular leaders could not only incite a mob, but through gathering votes and dispensing favors also determine in advance the actions of the Boston municipal government. John Adams expressed shock over the operations of a political club in the 1760s:

Party conventions arouse almost as much passion and publicity as the elections themselves. Here, under a flood of lights, sur-rounded by cameramen and microphones, Adlai Stevenson addresses the Democratic convention at Los Angeles, 1960. (33)

This day learned that the Caucus club meets at certain times in the garret of Tom Dawes, the Adjutant of the Boston regiment. He has a large house, and he has a moveable partition in his garret which he takes down, and the whole club meets in one room. There they smoke tobacco till you cannot see from one end of the garret to the other. There they drink flip, I suppose, and they choose a moderator who puts questions to the vote regularly; and selectmen, assessors, collectors, firewards, and representatives are regularly chosen before they are chosen in the town.

Popular politics intensified, and developed extensive apparatus during the revolutionary crisis. It also came to appear sinister to the gentry. In 1765, political clubs, the Sons of Liberty, organized the protest against the Stamp Act. Many of their techniques foreshadowed later party procedure in the United States: political insignia, petitions, manifestos, rallies, picnics and dinners with songs and toasts, and a turning out of every eligible voter at the polls. Other of their methods spilled over into the extralegal and violent. They would summon recalcitrant Tories or royal officials to appear under the local Tree of Liberty to give an accounting of their actions. Sometimes they hanged and burned effigies of the officials, or tarred and feathered them in person and sacked their homes. Thus the Sons of Liberty might appear on some occasions as a local political faction or party, and on others as a coercive, destructive mob. The gentry, including many who favored the patriot cause, took alarm at the mob actions. In the aftermath of the Boston Massacre, John Adams was one of the attorneys who defended the squad of British soldiers who had fired into the patriot mob.

p 82 (4)

Throughout the colonies it was the combined efforts of the Sons of Liberty with their frequently rough tactics and of the Enlightenment gentlemen in the colonial assemblies, expounding political theory, that withstood British threats to American rights. Combined, they challenged the Tories at home and the royal authority from overseas.

Among the first links in intercolonial co-operation against the British were the Committees of Correspondence which the Sons of Liberty began to form among themselves in the 1770s. These came to include the colonial assemblies. Out of these links came the first Continental Congress. The second Continental Congress after the beginning of hostilities in 1775 became the *de facto* revolutionary government.

In retrospect, men like Jefferson were ready to characterize the struggle as having been a struggle between the Patriots representing the people, and the Tories standing for aristocracy. Jefferson considered the split between a popular party and a party of privilege as having continued in the Continental Congress. Years later he wrote to Adams:

There you and I were together, and the Jays, and the Dickinsons, and other anti-independants [sic] were arrayed against us. They cherished the monarchy of England; and we the rights of our countrymen. When our present government was in the new, passing from Confederation to Union, how bitter was the schism between the Feds and the Antis. Here you and I were together again.

Parties and factions

Such was Jefferson's backward glance from 1813. Reality was a good bit different during the Revolution and Confederation years. There were indeed factions or parties within each state—in some only two; in others, three or four. Some of these groups seemed to have only one primary aim, sometimes to prevent creditors from obtaining full payment of debts due to them. Sometimes these factions seemed ready, like the Sons of Liberty, to break the bonds of electoral process and resort to violence. There was the shock in the winter of 1786–87 when debt-ridden farmers in western Massachusetts, failing to gain cheap paper money or tax relief through the petitions they sent from town meetings and county conventions, took up arms against the state courts. It was precisely to prevent factions or parties like these from escalating into violence that the Constitutional Convention was called.

Further, at the national level, there had never been clear-cut parties in the Continental Congress nor the Confederation Congress. The delegates to these, as in the United Nations Assembly, depended upon their home states for instruction. They represented a considerable diversity of state interests.

That brilliant assembly of successful men of affairs who framed the Constitution were fearful of popular politics as it was flourishing on the state level. Nor were they ready to accept the legitimacy of a national two-party system. To them the Tories had been the corrupt defenders of unlawful encroachment upon their liberties; only the Patriots had been legitimate. So, too, on the state level the only lawful political groups were those dedicated to maintenance of property rights against debtor onslaughts. The delegates were especially fearful of the tendency of popular politics to break the bounds of the law. The frame of government they drafted, as Richard Hofstadter has pointed out, was to be 'a constitution against parties'.

James Madison emphatically argued, on behalf of the new Constitution, that it would curb parties and factions—terms that he used interchangeably. In the classic tenth essay in *The Federalist*, his opening words were: 'Among the numerous advantages promised by a well-constructed Union, none deserves to be more accurately developed than its tendency to break and control the violence of faction.' There were complaints everywhere, he declared, 'that the public good is disregarded in the conflicts of rival parties'. The very size of the new Federal Union, and the diversity of interests it would encompass, Madison argued, would neutralize these factions and prevent the formation of a majority party that might threaten the rights of a minority.

The paradox of the founding of the Federal government was that the framers carefully devised a constitution to curb popular politics, but that it took popular politics to make the new Constitution work. Madison and Hamilton, who had inveighed against faction and party, were to be the prime founders of two competing national political parties.

When the new government began operation, the long-standing fears that popular factions or parties might carry the taint of potential mob violence, and that a national party of opposition threatened treason, continued to be entertained. In part, the large-scale military action against the Whiskey Insurrection, and the punitive legislation against the Jeffersonians, the Alien and Sedition Acts, are indicative of the old traditions. So too are some of Jefferson's subsequent partisan acts.

Other, and more important, old tendencies helped bring rapid party development in the Federalist era. It was, after all, through a combination of parties or factions in colonial assemblies, backed by popular machinery to elect those legislators, that Americans had always gained their political ends. Even in *The Federalist* No. 10, Madison had not advocated a suppression of these means; that would entail a worse evil, the destruction of liberty. Further, Madison conceded that most legislation would involve the regulation of various competing economic interests, 'and involves the spirit of party and faction in the necessary and ordinary operations of government.' Hamilton even granted in *The Federalist* No. 70 that 'the differences of opinion, and the jarrings of parties' in the legislature, 'though they may sometimes obstruct salutary plans, yet often promote deliberation and circumspection, and serve to check excesses in the majority.' Nor were these views entirely novel. Even earlier than in England, Bernard Bailyn has pointed out, some Americans had come to appreciate the advantages of political parties. In 1733, a writer in the *New York Gazette* declared: 'Parties are a check upon one another, and by keeping the ambition of one another within bounds, serve to maintain the public liberty.'

The Federal Union did indeed seem to be born without parties, or with only one big party, the Federalists. During the struggle over ratification, the Federalists were well-organized, cogent, and effective. The anti-Federalists were often confused and conflicting in their ideas and techniques, a weak negative coalition. Even leaders as popular and powerful as Patrick Henry in Virginia and George Clinton in New York could not stem the Federalist tide. Upon ratification, the anti-Federalist opposition disappeared. Within the new government, everyone at first was a supporter of President Washington's administration. The President, firmly opposed to parties, was in some respects a transitional figure

Election day in Philadelphia 1764. Benjamin Franklin lost his seat in this election. Pennsylvania was then a proprietary colony owned by the *Penn family. Party divisions were based not only on economic differences but on religious conflict between Quakers and Presbyterians. (1)*

between constitutional monarchy and later Presidents exercising power as heads of their parties. He was an American George.

Even the prestigious Washington could not prevent the rise of national parties. It was logical if not inevitable. Gradually, after the initial sessions, the members of both houses of Congress came to align themselves in voting patterns. Some most often voted for the measures President Washington and Secretary of the Treasury Hamilton favored; others more often than not voted against them. Party machinery could help elect to Congress men who would support (or block) these measures. Slowly, only very slowly after decades, party discipline served ordinarily to control the votes of these men once elected. There never came a time when all men in Congress voted according to party policy.

The beginnings of party apparatus

By 1792, Madison was reluctantly looking to a party as the means of achieving the political principles in which he and Jefferson believed: an administration meeting the agrarian interests through a strict construction of the powers of the Constitution. For some time Madison and Jefferson continued to regard party building as a necessity forced upon them by the opposition. Even as President, Jefferson hoped for a fading away of parties, that is, of the Federalist opposition.

Hamilton, for his part, organized the Federalists toward the great end of serving the mercantile and financial interests, and through them the entire nation, by means of a broad construction of the Constitution.

Both the Federalists and Jeffersonian Republicans organized in quest of the noblest ends of government, yet, in keeping with their prejudice against parties, ascribed to the opposition base factionalism. They set forth their own aims in high-flown language and described those of their opponents as encompassing depravity.

The unloveliest aspects of political parties were all too apparent during their emergence in the 1790s. They began to take shape against the backdrop of the French Revolution, with its Declaration of the Rights of Man, its Reign of Terror and the bitter war between England and France. The Republicans, espousing the ideals of the French Revolution, favored France, and attacked the Federalists as a pro-British, monarchist aristocracy. To the Federalists, the

Republicans were veritable French Jacobins, certain if they came to power to make a mockery of law and order. A Delaware pamphleteer warned voters in 1800:

> Can serious and reflecting men look about them and doubt that if Jefferson is elected, and the Jacobins get into authority, that those morals which protect our lives from the knife of the assassin—which guard the chastity of our wives and daughters from seduction and violence—defend our property from plunder and devastation, and shield our religion from contempt and profanation, will not be trampled upon and exploded.

On the other hand, parties had the beneficent effect of ameliorating more extremist tendencies. As the Republicans sought to win the votes of those who had been Federalist, they veered away from the Democratic Clubs, too reminiscent of the Sons of Liberty (and the Jacobins). Adams Republicans likewise wooed the voters in the center—those to whom Jefferson was attractive. Centripetal forces were at work.

The opposing party did become a check, forcing responsibility upon the party in power. Less noticed than Hamilton's brilliant establishment of a financial program for the new nation, but also important, was the contribution of the Republican Albert Gallatin. In the House of Representatives, through the Washington and Adams administrations, he kept a close watch upon the Treasury Department, insisting it be accountable for the funds at its disposal.

Rudimentary party apparatus rapidly developed. From Jefferson himself, who behind the scenes wrote letters of suggestions and distributed pamphlets, it extended through party editors disseminating propaganda, to state and county organizations. There were manifestos, rallies, insignia such as red-white-and-blue cockades to wear in hats—and political ruses of considerable intricacy. Republicans of Charleston, South Carolina, were angered in 1800 because the Federalists distributed ballots on green, blue, red and yellow paper, then stationed men to watch the casting of these ballots. But in New York, Republicans under Colonel Aaron Burr were equally resourceful in creating new voters, and with the strength of Tammany Hall behind them, won the state election. Jefferson himself was willing to stand by some of the promises of office his lieutenants proffered during the campaign.

By the time Jefferson took his oath of office as President in 1801, the first national party system was proving its worth. His inauguration was in itself a proof that Americans were accepting the legitimacy of a political opposition. The party of the 'outs' was for the first time coming into power. The nation was changing, and the party system was a vital factor in making change possible. The Constitution had been so carefully fabricated to counter popular turbulence through its many checks and balances that it is difficult to see how, except through political parties, the Federal government could have grown and developed. National political parties could reconcile some differences between states and regions; they could provide some amalgam among the President, Congress, and judiciary. A strong President as party leader, with popular backing and a firm majority in Congress, could put into effect a program. President Jefferson demonstrated this positive worth of political parties in the early 1800s, enhancing his effectiveness as chief executive through his additional power as leader of his party. He was a hero of the people. Federalists complained over the political feasting that marked his inauguration in words that sound like the shock, a generation later, over the advent of President Jackson. A New Yorker wrote in March 1801:

Our people in this country are running perfectly mad with enthusiasm about the man of the people, the savior of his country (as they term him). Drunken frolics is the order of the day, and more bullocks and rams are sacrificed to this newfangled deity than were formerly by the Israelitish priests.

In the relatively new, uncertain system of parties and politics, quite possibly Jefferson's personal popularity was his greatest asset. He responded quickly to requests to cut taxes and government expenses drastically. Resentment against the heavy Federalist taxes to fight the naval war against France had been the issue tipping the election of 1800 in his direction. Later, Jefferson reaped the political benefits of the war between Britain and Napoleon, which created prosperity for the United States. But the war also brought trouble for Jefferson when the warring nations violated American neutral rights. Jefferson's solution in 1808 was the Embargo. The cutting off of trade with Europe ended both the prosperity and Jefferson's popularity. It diminished his control over his cabinet and Congress. Nor did his successors through President John Quincy Adams exercise much control.

Jefferson's setback in 1808 and his successors' ineffectiveness seem attributable to the weakness of the Republican party. Republican machinery in Congress was ill-formed or non-existent. Jefferson could make no real use of party discipline and had little patronage at his disposal. Republican congressmen seldom if ever caucused upon issues or agreed in advance upon strategy. Indeed, their voting patterns often indicated that their greatest loyalty was to other congressmen with whom they shared rooming-houses in the half-built, miserable city of Washington. The few caucuses were those they held every four years to nominate a President. The nominating caucuses were barely effective and made a President feel more dependent upon Congress than upon the people.

In the first three decades of the 1800s the first party machinery gave way to a second set of parties. The Federalists never again won the Presidency; the Republicans soon made inroads in New England, and by the 1820s only the one big Republican party remained. Factionalism within it, usually along sectional lines, made it ineffective.

Interesting questions arise concerning the collapse of the first system of popular parties in the United States. Their rudimentary nature and lack of firm discipline doubtless contributed. Was it not also due to the reluctance of the electorate and of many politicians themselves to look upon parties as scarcely legitimate, as at the best a necessary evil? It was Federalists during the Jeffersonian era who were forever charging the Republicans with operating a highly efficient organization, averring that Republican congressmen were binding themselves in caucuses. In part to avoid stigma, some congressmen refused to admit to a party label. On the other hand, the most cohesive factor in the Republican party was its popular national leader Jefferson and his attractive program. President Madison, whom Washington Irving dismissed as a withered little applejohn, and President Monroe, occasionally appearing in his

faded Revolutionary uniform, were scarcely men with whom to rally the rank and file to the polls. Nor could the Federalists find a successor to President Washington, who had been the *aegis*, the means to ends, to Hamilton (who admitted it) and to every other Federalist political leader. The Federalists withered away nationally, and the Republicans, winning by default, showed signs of disintegrating into sectional factions.

While national politics were languishing in the decade after the War of 1812, new political parties began to burgeon in the states. In several states, two-party political systems evolved fairly early; others, especially in the South, were one-party states until the 1850s; and in Tennessee for many years there were only factions rather than parties at the state level. These state parties came to form loose coalitions in favor of one or another national presidential candidate, leading to the formation of the second system of national parties.

Wooing the new voter

Democratization was the theme in the development of the new state parties. Older states lowered voting restrictions, and one state after another to the west entered the union with all qualifications for voting stripped away save that a voter must be a free white male citizen at least twenty-one years of age. The citizenship requirement was not always firm; the South Carolina constitution of 1810 limited suffrage to white males of two years' residence but was silent on citizenship. There was a sizable increase in the electorate, but not as spectacular a rise as vehement political debates in state constitutional conventions seemed to indicate. The increase has been estimated as ranging in various states from 10% to 50%. In New York, a relatively conservative state, a reform measure in 1821 increased the number of adult males qualified to vote for the assembly from 78% to 90% of the total; in 1826 the remaining 10% acquired the ballot. Only a third had been able to vote for the state senators and the governor; after 1826 all could vote for them. Conservatives complained bitterly that voters lacking in education, culture, or property would not respect the property rights of the well-to-do. One newspaper editor commented, 'In plain English . . . the electoral character of the country goes now upon all fours.'

The tide of democratization swept from state to state during the 1820s and 1830s despite the conservative efforts to contain it. Except in three states few restrictions remained upon white male suffrage. Democratization spread from the franchise to touch almost every aspect of government. Since the 1630s written ballots had been used in Massachusetts, and voice balloting survived in only parts of the South after 1800—in Kentucky to 1890. At the polling places, the three-day election with voting by voice or by handwritten ballot slowly gave way to single-day elections in smaller precincts where voters cast printed ballots. It was easier to get to the poll, and to cast one's vote free of intimidation. p 84–5

Voters gained the right to vote directly for more government officials. In 1800 voters chose presidential electors in only two states; by 1832 only South Carolina entrusted selection of electors to the legislature. In every state except South Carolina and Virginia, voters after 1824 directly chose the governor; earlier, in six states legislatures elected the governor. Numerous other offices came to be filled by popular vote.

Democratization spread to political party techniques. At both the national and state levels, caucuses of the members of a party in a legislature often selected the party slate. The congressional caucus, by 1824 when it last operated, had come into disrepute as the means of nominating a President. 'King Caucus' was undemocratic and unpopular. State legislatures not only nominated their state slates but made nominations for the Presidency. They too were open to charges of being undemocratic levied against them by those out of power. For the 'outs' there was the alternative technique of state conventions. As early as 1788 Pennsylvania politicians had met in convention. County politicians similarly nominated slates at mass meetings. By the mid-1820s, whenever an 'out' party in a state held a convention, the other party in order not to appear undemocratic usually responded by holding its own convention. By this time conventions were regular procedure in the mid-Atlantic states, and by the mid-1830s they were being held in almost all states. The extension of the convention to the national nominating process was logical. In 1808 and 1812, Federalists held what were rudimentary national conventions, bringing together delegates from about half the states. It was a third party, the Anti-Masonic party, that in 1831 held the first significant national nominating convention. The two major parties followed, and the tradition of national nominating conventions was established. In national elections, the traditional 'Address to the People', primarily praising the qualifications of the candidates, gave way to the party platform. The Democratic convention of 1840 drafted the first national platform, consisting of only nine brief resolutions. By the 1850s, the parties also had established national executive committees which were custodians of the party machinery between elections, selected convention sites, and ran campaigns.

p 88 (20)
p 92 (33)

The democratization of politics also led to more formal and abundant machinery at the state and local levels—committees of all sorts responsible for the numerous elections and still more numerous candidates.

Patronage in the form of both honors and emoluments became the incentive to spur these legions of party workers toward victory. In New York State, where DeWitt Clinton and his supporters battled against Martin Van Buren and the Albany Regency, there were at stake, Richard P. McCormick calculates, 'over eight thousand military appointments and nearly seven thousand civil offices. In the latter category were judges, justices of the peace, court clerks, public notaries, commissioners of deeds, public auctioneers, district attorneys, sheriffs, coroners, county treasurers, and mayors and clerks of cities.'

Political campaigns focussed upon bringing out a winning margin of voters. Through the 1820s, in one-party areas, or where there was no real contest, the percentage of voters remained light. In Virginia, in the uncontested presidential election of 1820 when Monroe ran for a second time, only 4% of the white adult males bothered to vote. Throughout the nation, the four-cornered presidential race of 1824 brought hot contests in only a few states; in most, one or another candidate was the overwhelming favorite. Hardly more than a quarter of those eligible bothered to vote. The excitement of 1828, as adherents of Adams and Jackson exchanged epithets, more than doubled the number of voters. The circus atmosphere of 1840 increased the turnout to 78% of those eligible.

p 85
(10, 11)

The more highly organized campaigns became the first great national sport, the forerunner of organized baseball and football. There was an intensification of slogans, songs, posters, buttons and tokens, rallies, and torchlight processions. In many states there were yearly elections for the governor as well as local and municipal offices; there were the biennial congressional elections, and capping the excitement, the presidential elections every four years.

Party machinery tended to solidify. Workers, even when they lost, were eager to recoup their defeat in the next election. The rank-and-file of voters too remained loyal to the parties and leaders to which they had given their affection. From this core of support, the leaders sought to build enlarged followings, to sweep into office and retain power.

A basic faith in this democratic participation in popular politics underlay the shifting slogans and issues and the annual hullabaloo. In these years that brought the election of President Jackson and the triumph of Jacksonian democracy, Americans, whatever their party loyalties, hailed their system as the means of attaining a near-utopia at home and as a model for the rest of the world.

'The decisive opinions of the people'

The American ebullience came from a belief that individual enterprise and energy, encouraged by state and local governments, could bring an unprecedented level of well-being for all the people. As for the governments, they derived their ultimate power from the people, and were run on behalf of the people by a citizenry boasting generations of experience. The toppling of revolutionary movements in Europe in 1820, 1830, and 1848 saddened sympathetic Americans but confirmed their belief that it was the peculiar genius of the American people to be adept in self-government. Levi Woodbury, one of President Jackson's cabinet officers, expressed this view succinctly in his private correspondence, writing in 1831:

I must confess, that my confidence in European revolutions is not very strong. There is intelligence enough in the higher ranks; but the middling and lower classes seem to . . . [need] a participation in the whole machinery of the government with knowledge of their practical duties while so participating: and then will Liberty indeed be not *la mère de la license, mais la fille des lois.*

Our people have been thus participating and learning almost two hundred years and in that rested our great security at the Revolution and in that will it continue to rest.

The corollary, for Woodbury and his generation, was to place one's faith in the American voter. During the campaign of 1832 Woodbury privately wrote:

We have very satisfactory political information from the whole West—and await calmly the decisive opinions of the People as expressed at the ballot-boxes next month.

Ours is an agitating life under institutions so thoroughly popular. But the great mass of society is very sagacious about its interests and rights and, though liable to be misled for a time, soon acquire further light—bring judgment to the correction of feeling—and place the Ship of State in the true track to ensure the *greatest good for the greatest number.*

Although these views (including the utilitarian end) are usually referred to as those of Jacksonian democracy, they permeated the thinking of most Americans of the era, regardless of their political persuasion. It was an age of ambitious native-born white Americans firm in their entrepreneurial aspirations. It was a nation 'on the rise'—of farmers, artisans and shopkeepers in the countryside and small towns, expanding their enterprises and speculating on the rising value of land. Even the workingmen in the cities along the Atlantic coast, hoping to become entrepreneurs, shared their views. It was a politics shaped to a 'boom and bust' economy in which the national dream was to make a fortune—or if a depression and calamity came, to wipe out one's losses through easy bankruptcy laws so that with an economic upturn one could start over again.

The role of government was to aid these entrepreneurs, whatever their local or regional interests, and to place no impediment in their way. It was a politics, therefore, that revolved around the pros and cons of protective tariffs, the opening of new lands to farmers, planters, and speculators, acquisition of still more territory, improvement of transportation, improvement of the money supply and banking. Subsidiary were reform questions like free public education. Since frequently politicians could not meet these issues head-on without antagonizing blocs of potential voters, many elections from the municipal to the national level skirted issues and concentrated on personalities. Beneath the superficial nationalism following the War of 1812, serious sectional differences had intensified. Party managers within states sought to strengthen their parties and to gain national honors through attaching themselves to national presidential candidates. It was in this way that two major national parties again came into existence. But these national parties could bridge sectional issues, like the protective tariff favored in the North and abominated in the South, only by drawing attention away from them.

General Jackson was the ideal presidential candidate of the 1820s because he was a symbol of national unity—of supposed victory in the War of 1812—and because little was known about his views on specific issues. As the people's hero he was elected. Once in the White House, Jackson's views became exceedingly well known indeed. From among the Republicans those supporting him came to form the Democratic Republican or Democratic Party.

Jackson's opponents, agreeing on little but their opposition to Jackson, made him their main issue, and coalesced into the National Republican Party. By 1834, with some slight changes it had become the Whig Party. The Whigs emphasized that like their English counterparts who had sought to curb the power of the King, they were the defenders of the people against presidential tyranny. They liked to portray Jackson as 'King Veto', garbed in royal robes, and to glorify themselves as the surrogates of the voting public to whom the Constitution had entrusted all policy-making power. It was in this guise as the party of the people,

p 86 (12)

avoiding the economic issues upon which there were sectional differences, that the Whigs put forward General William Henry Harrison as the 'log cabin' candidate in 1840, and won.

p 86
(13, 14)

The role of the first significant third party, the Anti-Masons, deserves note. It grew out of the democratic furore over the alleged murder of a New York State printer who had threatened to reveal the secrets of the Masonic order. Its adherents attacked Masonry for its secrecy and purported privileges. Anti-Masonry attracted a number of ambitious young anti-Jackson politicians who had not found a niche in the National Republicans, men like Thaddeus Stevens of Pennsylvania and William H. Seward of New York, who were to become leaders in the 1850s when a new Republican party emerged.

Whether through the Democratic, Whig, or Anti-Masonic Parties, astute politicians emphasized or muted issues as might be most expedient to gain votes. Parties moved toward the center rather than the extremes, since the center was where the voters were. Whigs might assail Jacksonians as the party of the mob, and Democrats the Whigs as the party of privilege, but their appeals to voters often overlapped. About 1840, Horace Binney, one-time Federalist, complained:

The Whigs are at this day more democratic in their devices and principles than the Democrats were in the days of Jefferson. There are few or no sacrifices of constitutional principle that the Whigs will not make to gain power, as readily as the Democrats. Their very name is Democratic Whigs; that is to say, they have entered into full partnership with those who trade upon the principle that . . . the masses are always right, and that nothing else is fundamental in government but this. What the Whig affix means, I think it is difficult to say. It is certainly nothing more than a badge of preference for some matter of administration wholly independent of constitutional principle, and varying consequently from day to day. Today it is tariff; the next day, internal improvements; the day after, something else. . . . The only question is how to obtain most of the sweet voices and emoluments of government, and this is as much a Whig object as a Democrat object, and there is no obvious nor characteristic difference in the nature of their respective bids.

Both the Whigs and the Democrats were gingerly in their approach to troublesome national questions, not only out of an eagerness to win but out of a fear of disintegration. Over the issue of the extension of slavery into territories, the Whigs did disintegrate in the 1850s. Most Southern Whigs had been moving into the Democratic Party, and most of the South became what it remained well into the 20th century, a one-party area. The Democratic Party continued to hold a national constituency, of slaveholders and their supporters in the South, and of various Northerners who did not insist upon curbing the extension of slavery. Some of these Northerners were states'-righters who objected to Federal intervention over slavery in the territories; some were from the South or Southern sympathizers; some were merchants with Southern business interests; many were urban working people, often of immigrant origin and Catholic, whose party ties had always been with the Democrats, and who had no desire to liberate black labor to compete with themselves.

Many middle-class people, especially reformers, looked upon the Democratic Party as a combination against them on the part of the plutocracy allied with the working man. Ralph Waldo Emerson commented in 1854, 'We know that wealth will vote for the same thing which the worst and meanest of the people vote for: rum, tyranny, slavery, against the ballot, schools, colleges, etc.'

The new Republicans

A new Republican Party emerged in the 1850s as a challenge to the Democratic Party. It was the most successful of several third parties forming against the slaveholders of the South and the Catholic immigrants of the North. The Free Soil Party which preceded it was active in 1848 and 1852, attracting opponents to the extension of slavery from both the Whig and Democratic parties. The more successful third party, the American Party, popularly known as the

p 86 (16)

Know-Nothings, flourished in the 1850s, in response to the widespread middle-class fear of the large numbers of Catholic Irish and

Germans arriving in American cities. But it was fear of the extension of slavery that most upset Northerners, leading to the establishment in 1854 of the Republican Party. The Republicans soon came to encompass many former Free Soilers, Know-Nothings, Whigs, and anti-slavery Democrats. It was solely a Northern party, but the North had grown so much more rapidly than the South that, in 1856, in the first presidential election in which it participated, the Republican Party came close to winning.

The Republican Party stood foremost against the extension of slavery. Its leadership went even further in its dislike or even opposition to slavery. Like the original Republicans and Federalists, it stood forthrightly for a clear-cut group of ideological principles, since it did not try to straddle the Mason-Dixon Line. Everywhere in the North its principal appeal was that of 'free soil'. In the East it was the advocate of protective tariffs for manufacturers, and in the West the proponent of free homesteads for farmers and subsidies to hasten the construction of railroads. All these the Southerners, acting through the Democratic Party, had blocked. Large numbers of those voting for the Republican ticket in the 1850s and 1860 were voting primarily for one or another of these economic measures, or out of dislike for Catholics and immigrants, and not necessarily against slavery. In total their votes in 1860 brought the election of Abraham Lincoln.

Southern militants, interpreting the election of the Republican Lincoln as a threat to their agrarian, slaveholding system, put into operation the machinery of secession. In the crisis winter of 1860–61, one state after another in the deep South left the Union, forming the Confederate States of America. Border-state and Northern politicians tried to negotiate a compromise. Lincoln, as spokesman for the Republican Party, was willing even to accept an irrevocable constitutional amendment that Congress passed, forbidding the Federal government to interfere with the domestic institutions of a state, including slavery. Further than this, Lincoln would not go. He would not back down on opposition to extension of slavery. 'The instant you do they have us under again,' he warned; 'all our labor is lost, and sooner or later must be done over.' Even had the Republicans made this concession, the organization of the Confederacy would have continued. There was no compromise the Republicans could have offered that would have been acceptable to the secessionists. Nor would Northerners allow peaceable secession. By the time the Confederates fired on Fort Sumter in the spring of 1861, all parties in the North, Democrats and a few remaining ex-Whigs (Constitutional Unionists) as well as Republicans, preferred to resort to arms.

p 130 (3

p 134
(13)

The Civil War brought a political revolution within the United States. The Confederacy operated much like the United States political system. The two differences were that there was only one political party and the states asserted their rights in an exaggerated way against President Jefferson Davis and central authority. It has been suggested that the Confederacy died of an excess of states' rights.

In the North, President Lincoln successfully out-maneuvered the powerful war governors within the Republican Party, and established national party supremacy. He also succeeded in maintaining some semblance of control over the radical Republicans in Congress, who tried to push him toward emancipation faster than he felt the Northern and border-states electorate was ready to go. He was cautious but shrewd in his political sense. Through patronage he built firm personal support, and as party leader he held together factions ranging from conservative ex-Whigs from border-states to fiery abolitionist radical Republicans. Through keeping the Republican Party relatively united, and even more through General Sherman's capture of Atlanta, Lincoln won re-election in 1864 against strong Democratic opposition.

The Republican Party entered Reconstruction as the party of victory, but holding only a thin majority of supporters in the North. During the war it had put through its program—not only containment but abolition of slavery, a protective tariff and national banking act on behalf of manufacturers and financiers, and a homestead act and railroad land grants to maintain the support of farmers in the Middle West and West. When President Lincoln was assassinated in April 1865, it lost its greatest spokesman and most astute leader.

'Another such victory and I am undone.' The words of King Pyrrhus are attributed to Thomas Nast's Republican elephant, seen here resting after the closely won election of 1876. (2)

After the Civil War

Immediately after the Civil War it seemed as though the Democratic Party might again become the majority party. President Andrew Johnson began the rapid reconstruction of the ex-Confederate states under Democratic leadership. The Southern white electorate, stripped of its most prominent planters and Confederate leaders, voted Democratic. Throughout the Middle West, farmers in southern Ohio, Indiana, and Illinois were still Democratic, and opposed the Republican financial policies. Workingmen of immigrant background in the growing cities were loyal voters in Democratic organizations. Their wages had gone up far less rapidly than prices; they had not favored emancipation; and in New York City they had participated in bloody rioting against the draft.

The radical leadership among the Republicans in Congress took drastic action to retain power and thus the Republican program. It barred from their seats in Congress the new representatives and senators from the formerly Confederate states, several of whom had been serving in the Confederate Army or Congress in Richmond. Large numbers of Northern voters, distressed by Southern state enactment of 'black codes' for the repression of ex-slaves, and by riots against Negroes in Memphis and New Orleans, in 1866 elected an overwhelmingly Republican Congress. By gradual stages the Republican Congress enacted measures over the objections and vetoes of President Johnson to take over Reconstruction.

Radical Republican reconstruction left its mark on popular politics even far into the 20th century. Its aim was first to guarantee the civil rights of the freed slaves, and second to extend to them the right to vote. Senator Charles Sumner pointed out that there could be 'no substantial protection for the freedman except in the franchise'. Further, through its reorganization and readmission of the Southern states, the Republican Congress obtained a reconstructed South which voted Republican. p 136–7 (19)

Reaction against radical Republican reconstruction of the South set in by the early 1870s. Although most of the new state governments in the South were the handiwork more of white than black voters, and although few of the office-holders were black, the corruption of these governments—grossly exaggerated—was blamed upon black voters. White supremacy became the rallying cry of 'redeemers', some of them hooded members of the Ku Klux Klan, who swayed white voters and intimidated Negroes.

Northern opinion at first backed enforcement of civil rights measures against the Ku Klux Klan. But soon the stories of corruption together with the unwillingness of Northern whites to view blacks as equals caused the North to look with sympathy upon the 'redeemers'. They were ready to accept the ending of Reconstruction and the re-establishment of the Democratic Party in the South with its emphasis upon white supremacy. Some Negroes continued until the end of the century to vote in the South; it was only then that states by various tactics barred them entirely from the polls. The usual reason, that blacks were ignorant and their votes frequently purchasable, was acceptable in the North.

Although the post-Reconstruction 'solid South' was Democratic, there were serious struggles for power within the party in state after state. The agrarian political leaders of the poor white farmers, the 'rednecks', contended for power against the spokesmen for the 'New South', the politicians representing the new commercial and manufacturing interests of Atlanta, Louisville, and Birmingham, often allied with the old-fashioned 'Bourbon Democrats'. Several times the farmers won, but in the end the business and Bourbon interests were predominant, rallying voters with nostalgic oratory about the 'lost cause' of the War between the States and the evils of Reconstruction. As late as the 1920s this oratory still sounded like distant thunder throughout Dixie. A disgusted woman political leader in Texas wrote a friend, after attending the state Democratic convention in 1928, about the old-fashioned politicians who declaimed on and on about the '"gallant soldiers who wore the gray" and "the wicked and iniquitous carpet baggers" who oppressed them—and the "dirty black niggers" who were elevated to rule over the "noble womanhood"—no I mean "*pure* and noble womanhood of the South" by those same naughty carpet baggers'.

Nationally, the Democratic Party continued to be basically an alliance between the Southern politicians and Northern urban machines and gentlemen. In the farming areas of the Middle West, pre-Civil War voting patterns persisted. Counties near the Ohio River were heavily Democratic, and prairie counties solidly Republican. The Democratic program in Congress, despite much oratory about states' rights and free trade, was not frightening to businessmen and did not differ widely from that of the Republicans.

The Republican Party was strong enough, although just barely, after the loss of the reconstructed South, to dominate the White House for a generation. The Democrats won the Presidency only twice (with Cleveland). As Southern states disenfranchised blacks, they created a thin Democratic majority which held into the 1890s. Thanks to this majority the Democrats frequently controlled one or both Houses of Congress. f 2 p 89 (21)

The most important difference between the Republican and Democratic Parties seemed to be that the Democrats were primarily Southern, and the Republicans almost totally Northern. The Republican leadership, like that of the Democrats, heavily represented the business community, and was threatened by farmer interests. Republican policies did not in reality differ sharply from those of the Democrats, although Republicans did emphasize the blessings of a protective tariff. It was useful, therefore, for them to rally the faltering Northerners and turn out the veterans' vote with emotional appeals which were the Northern counterpart of white supremacy. The Republican appeal was referred to as the 'bloody shirt'. Robert G. Ingersoll gave it its classic expression in the 1870s, declaiming to Union veterans: f 4

> Every man that tried to destroy this nation was a Democrat. . . .
> The man that assassinated Abraham Lincoln was a Democrat. . . .
> Soldiers, every scar you have on your heroic bodies was given you by a Democrat.

Ideals compromised

There was, in the view of many critics, little real difference between the Democratic and Republican Parties, with each of them depending upon emotional appeals, party loyalty, personality, and the traditional techniques of campaigning to pull the voters to the polls. Even in 1884 when the Democrats ran a 'good government' candidate, Governor Grover Cleveland of New York, against the Republican Senator James G. Blaine, the 'plumed knight from Maine', the reform editor, George William Curtis, complained:

A popular Democratic cartoon of 1896 shows the great American cow, fed by Western and Southern farmers, giving all her milk to Wall Street and big business in the East. (4)

'The platforms of the two parties are practically the same.' Both promised civil service reform and improvements in the tariff. But the campaign focussed upon Blaine's allegedly incriminating letters concerning some railroad bonds, and Cleveland's paternity of an illegitimate child. To Democratic torchlighters shouting against Blaine, 'continental liar from the state of Maine', Republicans retorted: 'Ma, ma! Where's Pa? Gone to the White House, ha, ha, ha!' Because of Cleveland's reform record, clean government Republicans, calling themselves 'Mugwumps', defected to him in considerable numbers. There was the likelihood, on the other hand, that numerous Irish Catholics would defect from the Democratic Party to Blaine, who had long delighted them with his attacks upon the British. But the Republicans slipped. Late in the campaign, a spokesman for some Protestant ministers, Samuel D. Burchard, referred to the Democrats as the party of 'Rum, Romanism, and Rebellion'. Democrats immediately spread the damning words on broadsides and in headlines. Cleveland carried New York by 1,149 votes, and with New York and other states with small majorities, carried the election. But it is possible that Cleveland won in New York not because of the anti-Catholic slogan, but because his supporters managed to buy more floaters than the Republicans. A floater was a man of no fixed party affiliation whose vote was for sale.

Henry Adams had long since looked upon American politics as a hopeless business. He had given up writing reviews of congressional activity at the end of the session of 1869–70, and he explained years later:

He could have said no more, had he gone on reviewing every session in the rest of the century. The political dilemma was as clear in 1870 as it was likely to be in 1970. The system of 1789 had broken down, and with it the eighteenth century fabric of *a priori*, or moral, principles.

To Adams, the outcome had been dismal:

One might search the whole list of Congress, Judiciary, and Executive during the twenty-five years 1870 to 1895, and find little but damaged reputation. The period was poor in purpose and barren in results.

'Let us Prey'. 'Boss' Tweed, the head of Tammany Hall in the 1860s, and his cronies are shown as vultures, waiting out the storm raised against them by Thomas Nast in his cartoons. (3)

Reformers seeking to purify government and political processes might share Adams's conclusions, but worked incessantly through the period to eliminate opportunities for evil from politics. In the 1870s they smashed the Tweed Ring in New York City; thereafter they fought corrupt bosses elsewhere. They also tried to stop machine domination at the polls. After the Cleveland–Blaine election of 1884, most states began to use the secret or Australian ballot, which made it harder to purchase votes or intimidate voters. Above all, reformers tried to eliminate the spoils system, the main means of rewarding party workers. In the aftershock following the assassination of President James A. Garfield by a mentally unbalanced office-seeker, Congress enacted legislation creating a Civil Service Commission and excepting officeholders from political assessments. Slowly a number of Federal positions came under civil service protection. These reforms in total made some difference, but city and state political machines and national leaders became adept at circumventing them when public attention lagged.

The anomaly of the late 19th century was the high level of public excitement over national politics, and the relatively low esteem in which politicians were held. Lord Bryce, writing brilliantly about the American system, disagreed with Henry Adams and gave the politicians considerably higher marks:

There are all sorts among them, creatures clean and unclean . . . but that one may say of politicians in all countries. What characterizes them as compared with the corresponding class in Europe is that their whole time is more frequently given to political work, that most of them draw an income from politics and the rest hope to do so, that they come more largely from the poorer and less cultivated than from the higher ranks of society . . . many are proficients in the arts of popular oratory, of electioneering, and of party management.

They show a high average level of practical cleverness and versatility, and a good deal of legal knowledge. They are usually correct in life, for intoxication as well as sexual immorality is condemned by American more severely than by European opinion, but are often charged with a low tone, with laxity in pecuniary matters . . . Even if the last thirty years have furnished some grounds for accusing the class as a whole, there are many brilliant exceptions, many leading politicians whose honour is as stainless and patriotism as pure as that of the best European statesmen.

The achievements of Congress and the Presidents during the last quarter of the 19th century corroborate Bryce's view. True, there was often little clear-cut distinction between the major parties, and legislation like that reforming the civil service seldom made more than a beginning, in setting basic precedents. Yet the era was as legislatively rich as almost any in American history. There were beginnings in civil service reform, railroad rate regulation, dissolving (or regulation) of trusts, improvement of agriculture, and conservation of public lands as National Parks and Forests. While rivers and harbors bills were labelled as the 'pork barrel' for congressmen, much of the money went into needed improvements of inland waterways, especially those linking the Great Lakes.

p 86–7 (15)
p 87 (18)

f 3

p 20–2 (21)

Much of the political struggle during the late 19th and early 20th centuries was within each of the major parties. At first it was between urban and agrarian wings of the parties. Farmers in the 1870s, suffering from low crop prices, deflationary governmental politics, and high railroad rates, reacted in two ways. Through farmers' clubs associated with the Grange they succeeded in winning control of several state legislatures in the Middle West and obtaining railroad rate regulation. Nationally, they fought for cheap paper money, the Greenbacks. After the price of silver dropped drastically at the end of the 1870s they changed their agitation to one for unlimited coinage of silver as a means of obtaining a plentiful cheap money supply. When they failed to win control of either major party, in the 1890s they organized themselves into the People's or Populist Party, which fought for silver and an array of other reforms. Farmers' parties won numerous local victories in the Middle West but could raise only small amounts for campaigns. They were hard pressed in their struggles against the major parties which had elaborate machinery and substantial financing. In 1896, William Jennings Bryan, espousing the issue of free and unlimited coinage of silver, captured the Democratic nomination, but lost the election to the well-financed Republicans.

p 88 (22)

Only a few years later, reform-minded young civic and business leaders who had looked askance at Bryan and the silver campaign were ardently espousing the progressivism of the early 1900s, fighting for some of the same reforms the Populists had favored. The Emporia (Kansas) editor, William Allen White, granted years later that the progressive boy had caught the Populist boy in swimming and had stolen all his garments except for the ragged underwear of 'free silver'. Why a man like White, an ardent progressive, earlier rejected Populism was clear in his famous editorial, 'What's the Matter with Kansas?', in which he berated the Populists as a bunch of uncouth failures, turning their backs on progress.

Progress and progressivism

Progressivism brought into both parties an energetic young middle-class leadership dedicated to democratizing government and making it run more scientifically, regulating large-scale corporations and finance, and bringing social justice to the underprivileged. They wished to wipe out the urban slums and conserve the nation's resources. They led an exciting crusade within the p 88 (23) Republican Party under the leadership of President Theodore Roosevelt. Under Roosevelt's successor, President Taft, the schism between the 'old guard' and progressives widened. When progressives failed to win in the 1912 Republican convention, they bolted and formed a third party, the Progressives, with a Bull Moose emblem, and with Roosevelt as their candidate. Democrats

New Hampshire is traditionally the first state to hold presidential primaries. Here the Democratic donkey and Republican elephant peep at the results. (6)

in 1912 nominated another progressive, Governor Woodrow Wilson of New Jersey, whose progressivism differed from Roosevelt's in being more concerned with states' rights and small business. Wilson was elected, and within four years had enacted not only his own New Freedom program but also much of Roosevelt's New Nationalism. It was a great burst of reform, coming to an end not long before the United States entered the First World War.

Progressives brought vital changes to urban politics. To break machine control over cities, they developed city-manager and commission plans of city government, with notable reform administrations in cities like Cleveland and Toledo, Ohio. Men like Newton D. Baker and Brand Whitlock proved that, with continued vigilance on the part of reformers and voters, clean city governments could improve living conditions for poor people. City bosses also learned that their poor constituents favored social justice legislation. Boss Charles F. Murphy of New York allowed his Tammany delegation in the New York state legislature to vote for these measures—and two Tammany leaders in the legislature, Robert Wagner and Alfred E. Smith, thus embarked on notable reform careers.

At the national level, progressivism also brought political changes. The Seventeenth Amendment to the Constitution, ratified following several scandals, took away from state legislatures the election of senators and gave it to the voters of each state. p 140 (31)

The Nineteenth Amendment, adopted in 1920, extended suffrage to women. It was the victorious conclusion of a battle p 138 (22) begun in 1869 when two women's suffrage organizations came into existence, and women won the right to vote in Wyoming Territory. By the First World War, women could vote in eleven states west of the Mississippi. Resistance in the East from liquor interests who feared that women would vote for Prohibition, and in the South from those who thought woman suffrage would bring renewed Negro suffrage, made the battle for the amendment difficult. The women gained political allies during the war, and were victorious soon thereafter.

Slowly women gained standing in politics. Many of them had

A new role for the President—that of television personality. TV was first used to film a presidential press conference in 1955. (5)

been active in the social justice movement during the progressive era. Jeannette Rankin of Montana in 1916 became the first woman elected to Congress, and Frances Perkins in 1932 the first woman cabinet member. Both the Democratic and Republican Parties created women's divisions, and appointed a national committeewoman from each state. As women engaged increasingly in party work, they were able to make their voices heard at committee meetings and conventions. In local and state politics, the League of Women Voters, a non-partisan organization, became a significant force. Nevertheless, over fifty years after the passage of the suffrage amendment, women still hold relatively few offices in the United States.

Organized labor moved into the forefront of American politics during the New Deal in the 1930s. During the depression year 1932, when Governor Franklin D. Roosevelt of New York ran for President against Herbert Hoover, Roosevelt campaigned as a former progressive, the champion of the middle-class 'forgotten man'. Roosevelt did indeed bring much of Theodore Roosevelt's and Wilson's progressivism to the New Deal. By 1935, the base of his political coalition was shifting, and he came to depend considerably upon poorer people and organized labor. The National Labor Relations Act was giving protection to the new C.I.O. as it undertook the organization of the steel, automobile and rubber industries. In return, the C.I.O. in 1936 and thereafter contributed heavily to Roosevelt's campaign. In subsequent elections, organized labor continued to be an important factor in the Democratic coalition.

Negro voters in the North, through 1932 preponderantly loyal to the party of Lincoln, by 1934 were switching their allegiance to Franklin D. Roosevelt and the Democratic Party. Heavy black migration to Northern cities during the Second World War gave this vote added importance to the Democrats. President Truman in 1948 tried, without alienating Southerners, to court the Northern Negro vote. He delivered a campaign speech in Harlem. Black votes were part of the combination which brought him victory; in several key states they provided the vital margin.

During the civil rights revolution of the 1960s, Northern black voters helped keep the pressure upon Washington which brought legislation and administrative action to enable Southern Negroes to p 138 (23) register and vote. By the 1970s, large numbers of Southern Negroes were voting, and had elected some local officials. Several large Northern cities had elected Negro mayors, and for the first time since Reconstruction, a Negro had been elected to the United States Senate. Negroes were becoming a key factor in American politics.

Techniques of electioneering

Through the 20th century, technological changes brought modifications in political techniques. Campaign trains took candidates criss-crossing through their states or the nation. William Jennings Bryan in 1896 traveled eighteen thousand miles, speaking to as many as five million people, the first presidential candidate really p 90 (25) to canvass the country. Whistle-stopping was Franklin D. Roosevelt's favorite mode of campaigning, taking him to countless cities and towns, to greet crowds and inspire increased efforts from local politicians. As late as 1956, the train was an important piece of presidential campaign apparatus.

p 90 (26) In 1932, Roosevelt made the airplane an instrument of politics, when he startled the nation by flying from Albany, New York, to Chicago to deliver his acceptance address in person before the nominating convention. Previous candidates had waited decorously for some weeks for a ceremony of official notification, so the effect was doubly dramatic. It was a single episode. Roosevelt hated planes and did not again use one for political purposes. By the time his successor, President Truman, began campaigning, planes were commonplace, an ordinary means of making political appearances

far from Washington. By the 1960s, jets had given a dizzying speed to presidential campaigns, enabling candidates to appear in all fifty states, and sometimes in several states from coast to coast in a single day.

Communications also wrought a political revolution. Part of the attraction of Bryan was the remarkable carrying quality of his mellifluous voice in an age before the invention of public address systems. Delegates sitting high in the gallery at Chicago in 1896 had to put rolled-up newspapers to their ears to hear the speakers on the platform. Then Bryan's voice came ringing out with the 'Cross of Gold' speech; they put down their papers and cheered. At later conventions, amplifiers piping in music and speeches could have the opposite effect, of overwhelming the delegates. At the Chicago Democratic convention of 1940, an unknown voice took over the public address system and began an incessant chant, 'We want Roosevelt', in an effort to stampede the delegates into an immediate nomination of the President.

Radio in the 1920s brought an additional dimension to politics. Some of the most skilful politicians, accustomed to the winning of live audiences, were suspicious of the microphone in front of them. At the 1924 convention, Al Smith referred to it derisively as a 'pie plate'. Roosevelt, recognizing its potential as early as 1928 when he delivered the address at Houston nominating Smith for the Presidency, shaped his remarks and style of delivery for the national radio audience rather than for the delegates in front of him. As President, through the medium of the 'fireside chat', a p 90 (28 relatively intimate form of address, he effectively rallied his following.

Television after World War II superseded radio, becoming a f 5 significant factor by the campaign of 1952. Gestures and facial expressions as well as intonations became important; it was not an easy medium to master. In 1960 it was perhaps the decisive factor, p 91 (32 when Senator John F. Kennedy of Massachusetts, the Democratic presidential candidate, apparently lagging behind Vice President Richard M. Nixon, engaged Nixon in several televised debates, and closed the gap.

The possibility of applying social science and through scientific techniques manipulating politics became apparent in the 1930s with the development of the first public opinion polls. These not only gave a rough prediction of the elections, beginning in 1940, but also gave approximations of voters' views on key issues. The prestige of the polls dropped temporarily in 1948 when they incorrectly predicted the victory of the Republican presidential candidate, Governor Thomas E. Dewey of New York, over p 90 (2 President Truman, but they became ever more important in political planning and campaigning. Through polling devices and the use of computers, experts could tell candidates for either local or national office what issues they might best emphasize, what views were most likely to win votes, and where they might best expend their campaign efforts. In 1970, several congressional campaigns were thus computerized.

Use of the computer, television and other media, and of airplanes has inflated the expense of campaigns. The cost of running for mayor or sheriff is usually many thousands of dollars, and for President, many millions. Observers have been fearful that the new politics would mean the application to all elected officials of the humorist Will Rogers's wisecrack concerning United States senators, that they were the best money could buy.

As yet, election returns do not reflect entirely the expenditure of money or the predictions of polls. Even the smoothest-running, most heavily financed political organizations do not always succeed. A majority of voters in several states habitually split their party tickets. The American voters might not, as the Jacksonians thought, be always right, but they are continuing to demonstrate their independence. The future of popular politics rests upon that independence.

V

STAGES
OF ENTERPRISE

The business of America

W. W.
ROSTOW

'The will to grow is everywhere written large
and to grow at no matter what
or whose expense.'

HENRY JAMES

'Not a change for the better in our human housekeeping
has ever taken place that wise and good men
have not opposed it—have not
prophesied that the world would wake up to find
its throat cut in consequence.'

JAMES RUSSELL LOWELL

America welcomed the machine.

Individual initiative, social mobility, willingness to submit every-thing to the test of experience, and a relative shortage of labour, made the Americans uniquely fitted to take advantage of techno-logical progress. Inventions from Europe were eagerly copied and improved; new ideas were tested; and by the second half of the 19th century purely American industry was overtaking that of the Old World.

Already in 1851 visitors to the Great Exhibition in London had been impressed by American precision work on a small scale. By the time of the great Philadelphia exhibition held to celebrate the centenary of independence in 1876, America could show her capacity for major engineering. George H. Corliss's steam engine (opposite) was the most powerful ever built. Weighing 1700 tons, with cylinders more than a yard across and gear-wheels of thirty feet, it was capable of 2500 horsepower, and drove all the other mach-inery in the exhibition. It was the symbol of America's future. (1)

America's Crystal Palace followed London's in the space of two years. The exhibition of 1853 (above) brought the rest of the world to New York to see the fruits of American progress on its home ground. Some of the inventors who made it possible are seen in the group portrait (right) of *c.* 1860. Bogardus, Colt and McCormick are second, third and fourth from the left. Below left: one of the annual fairs held by the American Institute in New York to publicize and market American products. (2, 3, 5)

McCormick and Whitney are two examples of inventors who combined business ability with technical brilliance. McCormick's reaper (above) revolutionized farming. Eli Whitney, having gained painful experience through his cotton-gin, used the system of mass-produced interchangeable parts in his arms factory (left, Yale University Art Gallery) at Springfield, Mass. (4, 6)

Canal traffic developed on a grand scale during the early 19th century before being killed, as it was all over the world, by the railways. The most ambitious venture of all was the Erie Canal, connecting the Great Lakes with New York. This naive painting of 1832 (left) shows some of its eighty-two locks. (7)

'By industry we thrive': America as a German immigrant saw it in 1873. The industrious workers – blacksmiths, miners, engineers, masons, carpenters, farmers, surveyors – build a new society by their own labor; in the corners are their tools of trade, including those of the artist. (8)

'The World's Railroad Scene' (above) is an advertisement showing the coverage of the Illinois Central Railroad in 1882. The modern steam train is contrasted in the vignettes on the right with older ways of transport. (9)

'Ten Minutes for Refreshment' (right) of 1886 offers a more sardonic view of the railway age (Courtesy Chicago Historical Society). It was through such pressures as this that the 'quick lunch' became an American institution. (10)

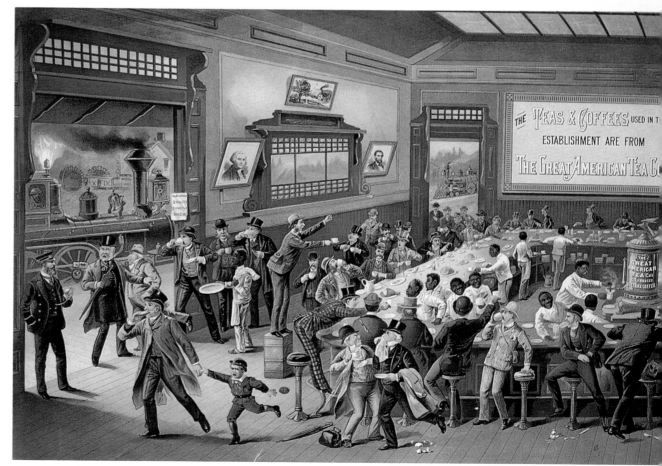

Fortunes were made by men of ideas and energy who could foresee the ways in which industries would develop. The Studebaker brothers (right) built up a large automobile business from a wagon-tire shop. John D. Rockefeller (seen, below right, with his wife in old age) assisted at the birth of the new industry of 'oil-refining'. By 1911 he was worth a thousand million dollars. (12, 13)

'Bell Time' (above) by Winslow Homer, 1868. Men, women and children, clutching their lunch-boxes, stream out of a New England factory after the long day's work. (11)

Steel rapidly outgrew the stage where it could be controlled by a single owner. Above: the Bessemer process at Bethlehem Steel, Pittsburgh, in 1895. Right: the dinner held in 1901 to celebrate the formation of US Steel by the merging of the Carnegie and Morgan Companies. Eighty-nine executives sit round a table shaped like a huge rail. (14, 15)

Mechanized man confronts nature (above) – a photograph of 1902 that seems to symbolize much of America's aspiration and confidence. (16)

The Astor empire had been built up by John Jacob Astor on the fur trade. With the proceeds he and his son bought real estate in New York, both slum property and fashionable shops. Above: Park Row, New York, all owned by Astor, nearly all selling ready-made goods. (17)

111

Aviation was pioneered in America by the brothers Wibur and Orville Wright. Their early experiments with gliders (right) in 1902 led in the following year to the first powered flight. As an industry, however, it was curiously slow to develop. Its earlier phase was characterized more by enthusiastic amateurs than by businessmen. Far right: the program of the first Aviation 'Meet', held in 1910 at Los Angeles. (18, 19)

The assembly line was to revolutionize industry when Henry Ford introduced it into his automobile works at Detroit in 1913. But he did not invent it. It was foreshadowed (in what has been called the 'disassembly line') by the meat-processing yards of Chicago (below: chromolithograph Courtesy Chicago Historical Society, 1880). Here every process from slaughtering the pig to labeling the can is a separate specialized operation. (20)

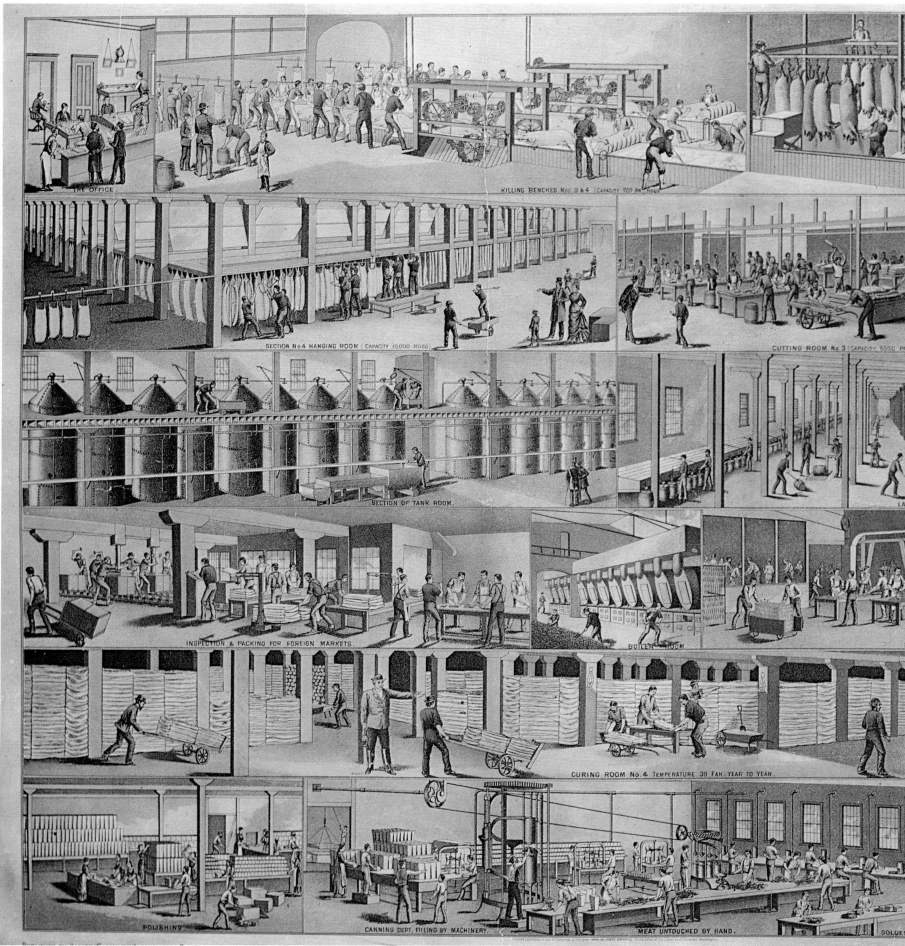

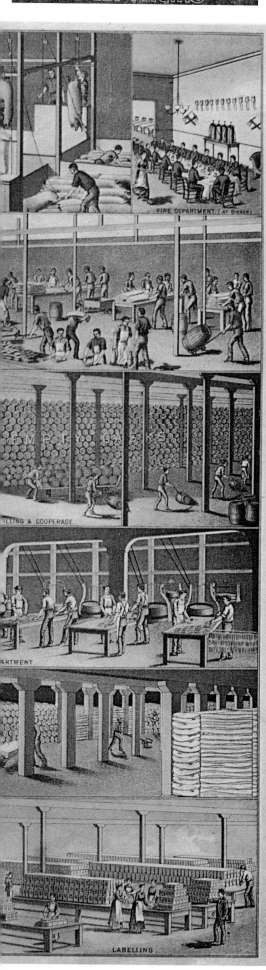

Broadway, 1880 (above). Apart from the plethora of advertisements, the most noticeable feature is the jungle of wires that criss-cross the street – signs of the rapidly expanding telephone and telegraph industries. This lithograph was itself a commercial enterprise: the various businesses paid handsomely for the privilege of having their names included. (21)

New markets were tapped by mail-order firms like Sears, Roebuck. Right: a catalogue cover of 1897. (22)

The national style of enterprise took new forms after 1918. As the individual business gave way to the big corporation, so the latter gave way to the public authority and to enterprises requiring public-private co-operation. Below: building the Norris Dam in the Tennessee Valley, one of the sponsored projects of the 1930s to combat the Depression. (23)

A strange new world is being evolved by modern technology, creating shapes unforeseen by the past. Above: the Los Angeles Freeway, with its pattern of interlocking roads. Right: automated mining. The wheeled components, stored in a mobile container, are for transporting the coal while it is still underground. (24, 26)

Three men and a computer control the vast oil refinery of Tyler, Texas. Americans still 'expect an improvement to be found in everything', but industry now must incorporate research programs involving disciplines from every field. (25)

The jumbo-jet, Boeing 747, the largest passenger plane in the world, capable of holding 450 people, emerges from a hangar as big as a cathedral. (27)

The business of America

W. W. ROSTOW

SPEAKING OF the American space effort, in San Antonio on 21 November 1963, President Kennedy said:

We have a long way to go. Many weeks and months and years of long, tedious work lie ahead. . . . But this space effort must go on. . . .

Frank O'Connor, the Irish writer, tells in one of his books how, as a boy, he and his friends would make their way across the countryside; and when they came to an orchard wall that seemed too high to climb, too doubtful to try, too difficult to permit their journey to continue, they took off their caps and tossed them over the wall—and then they had no choice but to follow them.

My friends, this nation has tossed its cap over the wall of space—and we have no choice but to follow it. Whatever the difficulties, they must be overcome. Whatever the hazards, they must be guarded against. . . . We will climb this wall with both safety and speed—and we shall then explore all the wonders and treasures that lie on the other side.

For almost two hundred years now American enterprise has been marked by the counterpoint between men, drawn by 'wonders and treasures' beyond, tossing their caps over the wall, in adventurous strategic decisions, and then climbing over the wall to try to make good their gambles, through 'long, tedious work'.

The pattern is discernible, in different forms, from the 1790s to the present: from Eli Whitney to Edwin Land; from a pre-industrial nation of less than four million, scattered along the Atlantic periphery, to an urbanized America of more than two hundred million, struggling to shape a life of quality in the wake of the automobile revolution—and in all the stages of growth between.

The national style

Three deeply rooted, interwoven strands yielded in the 19th century a distinctive style, as Americans went about their national business—a style modified, but still recognizable in the 20th.

First, American unity was achieved not through the continuity of geography or race or shared memories reaching long back in the past, but through a shared commitment to ideals which transcended the nation's borders. The coming to America itself was associated with a sense of religious mission; down to the present, American nationalism has been imbued with a sense of higher sanction for the particular forms of social individualism, political democracy, and private enterprise which evolved. The Calvinist and deist traditions converged in this matter, permitting Americans to derive this higher sanction from either divine or natural law.

As Tocqueville perceived, this special sense of mission was

The conquest of space can be seen as the logical culmination of the American style in enterprise. In President Kennedy's words, 'This nation has tossed its cap over the wall'. But in contrast to the self-made, self-sufficient image of earlier years, progress now is linked to co-operation (between, for instance, industry, universities and government), long-term planning, and agreed national objectives. (28)

reinforced by the initial task of taming and organizing an empty continent: '. . . the American people views its own march across these wilds, draining swamps, turning the course of rivers, peopling solitudes, and subduing nature. This magnificent image of themselves does not meet the gaze of the Americans at intervals only; it may be said to haunt every one of them in his least as well as in his most important actions and to be always flitting before his mind.' The transition from America as a religious sanctuary to a setting of unique material opportunity can be observed as early as the end of the 17th century, in the works of Cotton Mather and others.

The 'magnificent image' was thus linked to the second strand in the national style: a philosophic pragmatism appropriate to a life of hard, absorbing, material pursuits, executed on the basis of individual initiative, conducted to individual advantage.

The nation presented for more than two and a half centuries the challenge and possibility of an open frontier; and, for a full three centuries, the American environment made economically attractive to many—at home and abroad—a virtually unobstructed flow of immigration. In this setting individual effort and competence yielded high returns in economic welfare, the attainment and expansion of which drew off the bulk of the society's talent and energies.

p 16 (12)

f 1

The attraction of economic life was, moreover, negative as well as positive. Down to 1914—notably after the Civil War—the society's internal structure and relations to the outside world were such that positions in neither church nor state represented roles of great national prestige and authority, let alone affluence. Men came to seek in the adventure of the American economy—in the test of the market—status elsewhere granted by a less monolithic, more heterogeneous scale of values.

The mobility of American life heightened the attraction and psychological importance of individual achievement. The divorce of the individual from a sense of direct connection with a stable, structured community was further increased by the flow of immigrants. The problems and pace of adjustment varied, of course, with each wave and source and social class of immigration, as well as the region and community within which the immigrant settled. Despite great variation, however, between the Hungry Forties and World War I, each wave of immigration faced a pattern of adjustment to the prevalent values and culture of the nation which was, by and large, accomplished by generational stages. And, except for the slaves, a natural process of selection operated to some degree among the immigrants, tending to draw the more ambitious and adventurous, as well as those hard pressed in their old settings.

In his adjustment to American society, the individual's demonstration of effective performance in economic and political markets played a substantial role. The man who could solve palpably urgent material problems, organize and operate profitably a productive enterprise, deal effectively with the day-to-day compromises and accommodations of local and political life, thus rose in status; his operational cast of mind came to dominate the American scene, a cast of mind empirical in method, pragmatic in solutions.

But men have a need and instinct to generalize their experience, to organize, somehow, the chaos around them; and when Americans, busy with limited practical chores, building a new continental

'*The Lure of American Wages.*' *In the 1850s more than two and a half million immigrants left their homes in search of a better life in America. Before the Civil War labor was scarce and wages were high by comparison with Europe, so that laborers could easily save enough in a short time to buy their own land and become financially independent. With the expansion of the textile industry, women too were needed for work in the mills. (1)*

society, reached out for larger abstractions, they tended to base them on concepts derived from personal, practical experience. They generalized what they intimately knew. In Tocqueville's phrase, Americans have continued, in a substantial part of the nation's intellectual life, 'to explain a mass of facts by a single cause'.

In both its dimensions—a devotion to the ordering of fact in terms of low-order abstraction and a certain vague disorder at high levels of abstraction—the classic American intellectual style has reflected the operator's biases and fitted his needs. Committed to do the best he can in terms of goals defined by the concrete task he has undertaken or the institutions of which he is a part, the operator desires to know in detail his field of action but wishes to be as eclectic as he need be and as unhampered as possible by considerations outside those implicit in his operations.

The third strand in the American style arose from the need to bridge two gaps: first, the gap between a heightened reliance on idealism to define and maintain a sense of nation and community and a heightened reliance on the vigorous interplay of individual, regional, and group interests to do the day's work; second, the gap between a concentration of effort on particular chores, perceived in terms of low-order abstractions and the rich but somewhat disorderly kitbag of higher abstractions into which Americans reached for their general organizing principles.

Americans have bridged these gaps by building their operational style around problem-solving. In politics, for example, Americans have been content to leave implicit the moral and philosophic ambiguities which flowed from the method of compromise and experiment. Relatively little attention in formal thought or articulation was given to the common law formulae which emerged from these living processes because of two massive facts: first, the extraordinary continuity of the American experience down to 1914,

a continuity which persists in many domains down to the present; second, the distinct success of the United States as a national society. Men are more inclined to re-examine a system which is confronted with radically new problems or which is failing than a going concern. And when, toward the close of the 19th century and the early years of the 20th, some Americans became more reflective and articulate about their society, they tended (in Morton White's words) to elevate 'life, experience, process, growth, context, function' over 'logic, abstraction, deduction, mathematics, and mechanics'. Justice Holmes described the national style, as well as the law, when he said: 'The life of the law has not been logic: it has been experience.'

But the intellectual content of a process is immensely complex. Many factors interact over time. The number of unknowns is likely to be greater than the number of equations that can be formulated. Conventional logic can grip only limited elements within a process; and it is likely to give them a rigid and static cast. Men successfully operate process by accumulating experience, feel, judgment, by sensing recurrent patterns rather than by isolating clean-cut, logical connections of cause and effect. This is how good captains of sailing vessels have worked—good politicians, good businessmen. This has been the typical American style in operating and developing the nation's society—including its economy.

So far as the American style in enterprise is concerned, then, we would expect to find a 'magnificent image' of the possibilities, leading to bold strategic decisions in which men threw their hats over the wall; a concentration within those strategic decisions on specific practical problems to be solved, rather than on the refinement of theoretical approaches to them; and, then, a vigorous, dogged reduction of the operational problems resulting from the strategic decisions to an ongoing process that worked.

The economic context

The character of the American economy helped both to shape the national style and to determine the problems and possibilities with which it had to come to grips.

The essential features were these:

—a high rate of population growth and, generally, in growth of real income per head;

—a relative abundance of good land in relation to the supply of labor, especially of skilled labor;

—consequently higher real wages for industrial labor than in Europe;

—an agriculture which lent itself to maximizing output per man rather than output per acre outside the cotton South—and, to some degree, even within the pre-1860 South, given the rising price of slaves;

—a social structure and income distribution which encouraged production for a mass market;

—great distances and obstacles to transport to be overcome before an efficient national market could be created;

—the need for elaborate production, financing, and marketing organizations, once a national market had been created, notably after the Civil War.

Taken together, these factors made attractive a precocious introduction into the American economy of labor-saving machinery; mass production of standard items, such as coarse textiles and ready-made clothing; relatively advanced methods of specialization and attention to labor efficiency; and farm machinery.

p 107 (6)

These factors decreed also that Americans would exhibit early, with respect to machinery in general, a tendency now notorious with respect to automobiles—a tendency to scrap rather than to maintain for long periods.

In part, this tendency arose from expectations that new, improved machinery would soon be available, as many ingenious hands tinkered and refined existing models; and they were encouraged by the patent system which took shape in the 1790s. An American friend told Tocqueville in 1832; 'there is a feeling among us about everything which prevents us aiming at permanence; there reigns in America a popular and universal belief in the progress of the human spirit. We are always expecting an improvement to be found in everything.'

In part, this bias made sense because skilled labor was scarce and the maintenance and periodic rebuilding of machines was expensive.

Finally, Americans tended to run their machines intensively, getting as much as possible out of them by way of labor-saving, at the cost of accelerated obsolescence.

In the organization of markets, a watershed occurred at about the time of the Civil War.

Until the railway net was thrown into the Middle West during the 1850s, the markets for labor, capital, and manufactures tended to be fragmented by distance, transport costs, and, indeed, information about market conditions. After the Civil War a more sensitively interacting national market emerged in all three dimensions. After 1865, immigration accelerated and industrial labor became somewhat less scarce; but by that time the American addiction to labor-saving machinery was deeply ingrained and the imperatives and enticements of a mass national market were even stronger than before.

The transition was, like most, more gradual than the word watershed would suggest; for example, the Erie Canal (1825) had already had extensive consequences in tying New York to Buffalo and beyond; and the Eastern railway boom of the 1840s had altered market interconnections profoundly in the most populous region of the country. But there is underlying truth in the conventional view that an era ended in 1860 (I would call it the Take-off); another began in 1865 (I would call it the Drive to Technological Maturity). p 108 (7)

So far as American enterprise is concerned, the first period was marked generally by firms run by single men, families, or intimate partnerships; the second, by the emergence of big corporations. p 110 (12, 15)

We turn now to illustrate the unfolding of the American style in enterprise in these two periods and, then, in the stages beyond.

Before 1860: preconditions and take-off

It was in 1851 at the Crystal Palace Exhibition in London that the British—and others—became generally conscious of American virtuosity in machine-building and in sophisticated manufacture with interchangeable parts.

A lock, a revolver, and a reaping machine became symbols of the new America that emerged before visitors to the glass monster. The London *Daily News* reported the trend of interest:

'The Grain Movement from the West', a wood engraving from Frank Leslie's 'Illustrated Newspaper' 1877, shows huge quantities of grain arriving by rail at the New York Central and Hudson River Elevator.

The growth of the railroad, more than any other factor, opened up the national market and abolished the limitations enforced by distance and the cost of transport. (2)

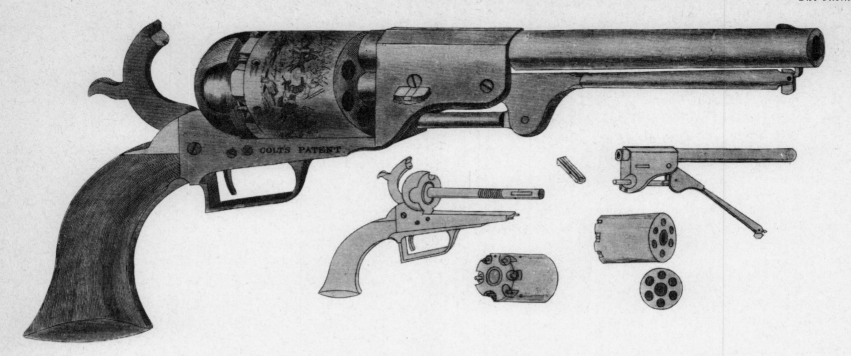

The 'revolving, cylinder-firing pistol' which became famous as the Colt revolver was one of the most impressive exhibits at the Crystal Palace in 1851. Samuel Colt had studied the technique of interchangeable parts at Whitney's factory, later opening his own at Hartford, Connecticut. (3)

f 3

A great change has taken place in the comparative attractiveness of the various departments. Formerly the crowds used to cluster most in the French and Austrian section, while the region of the stars and stripes was almost deserted—now the domain of Brother Jonathan is daily filled with crowds of visitors. In the front, trim mercantile men crowd around Hobbs' lock; right opposite the click of Mr. Colt's revolvers is unceasing, as the exhibitor demonstrates the facility with which they can be made to perform their murderous task; and in the rear jolly broad-shouldered farmers gather about McCormick's reaping machine, and listen in mild stupidity to the details of its wondrous prowess at Tiptree Hall and at Leicester, over rough and smooth land, ridge and furrow.

p 107 (6)

But there were also American ice-making machines, corn-husk mattresses, fireproofed safes, meat biscuits, india-rubber shoes and life-boats, railroad switches, nautical and telegraph instruments, a special grease-removing soap usable with either salt or fresh water, and artificial eyes and legs.

This technical success was capped psychologically by the easy victory of the schooner *America* over British rivals.

The pattern discernible at the Crystal Palace had been developing, in fact, for sixty years. The initiating figure—in symbol and, to a degree, in substance—was Eli Whitney. He is worth attention, even though revisionist historians emphasize properly that he belongs, in effect, with a whole school of less famous inventors and practitioners of the early American system of manufacturers, including Simeon North, John Hall, and others who contributed to the development of the milling machine and turret lathe on which so much of modern manufacturing techniques depended.

Whitney was a pre-take-off figure; that is, it was not until the 1820s that a sustained industrial surge began in New England and not until the period 1843–60 that the railroads laid the foundations for industrialization on a more nearly national basis. Caught up in an authentic vision of how modern industry should be conducted, Whitney suffered in trying to bring that vision to life before the nation's economic institutions, attitudes, and habits could sustain it.

Whitney began, of course, by glimpsing with truly incredible speed a solution to a major problem: how to cut the costs of cleaning cotton. Inspired by the possibilities, he tossed his hat over the wall —cutting himself loose from his teaching career, and plunging ahead with the cotton gin.

f 4

He belonged to a generation which had read with morbid fascination Lord Sheffield's *Observations on the Commerce of the American States With Europe and the West Indies*. It comforted the British in 1783, as American independence was accepted at Paris, by asserting that the prospects for the new nation were economically dim outside the British Navigation System; and it concluded that America could never establish extensive manufactures. As a penurious student at Yale (1789–92), Whitney had debated both sides of the question: 'Does the National Security depend on fostering Domestic Industries?' He certainly read Lord Sheffield and, almost certainly, what was, in effect, Hamilton's response: his *Report on Manufactures* of 1791—with its abiding doctrine of aspiring underdeveloped nations that 'not only the wealth but the independence and security of a country appear to be materially connected with the prosperity of manufactures'. Whitney's bent, in any case, was technical. And Yale, under Ezra Stiles, provided some stimulus.

From Yale he headed south as a tutor to a planter's family. He had been hired by the manager of General Greene's estate, Phineas Miller, who was a friend—later the husband—of the General's widow.

What happened immediately upon Whitney's arrival in South Carolina he only revealed to his family almost a year later, on 11 September 1793:

There were a number of very respectable Gentlemen at Mrs. Greene's who all agreed that if a machine could be invented which would clean the cotton with expedition, it would be a great thing both to the Country and to the inventor. I involuntarily happened to be thinking on the subject and struck out a plan of a Machine in my mind, which I communicated to Miller . . . he was pleased with the Plan and said if I would pursue it and try an experiment to see if it would answer, he would be at the whole expense, I should loose nothing but my time, and if I succeeded we would share the profits. . . . In about ten Days I made a little model, for which I was offered, if I would give up all right and title to it, a Hundred Guineas. I concluded to relinquish my school and turn my attention to perfecting the Machine. . . .

I returned to the Northward for the purpose of having a machine made on a large scale and obtaining a Patent for the invention. . . .

In half-interest partnership with Miller, Whitney left to seek his patent in May 1793. In June he made his application to the Secretary of State, Thomas Jefferson, forwarding in October a description of a full-scale model; and, then, in March 1794 the model was delivered and the patent received.

Thus, the British industrial revolution was mightily accelerated, the South converted to the Cotton Kingdom, and slavery consolidated—dashing the hopes of many of the Founding Fathers that it would naturally fade away.

For Whitney and Miller, however, there followed not triumph but a protracted and heart-breaking struggle to translate their patented machine into a working enterprise that could make money. The means did not exist on the American scene to finance, manufacture, and market a piece of equipment for which the demand was urgent and intense but for which the monopolist's price was high in terms of the planter's normal cash holdings.

In the face of these problems, they tried to create a business in which they could hold to their monopoly and exploit it by setting up gins around the country which would process the cotton, payment to be made in kind. But the enterprise was hit from all directions. Despite Mrs Greene's help, they lacked financial resources; Miller was caught up in a fraudulent land speculation in an effort to gain a quick cash profit to expand their slim working capital; their factory burned to the ground; the monopoly was broken by the manufacture of gins by others; the British manufacturers resisted the ginned cotton; a suit in the Georgia courts for patent infringement was lost.

Whitney entered in 1795 a period of deep despair and of withdrawal, out of which he emerged in 1798 to launch his second phase of invention and innovation—a phase marked by Miller's death in 1803, and by the purchase of the gin patent by the State of South Carolina for fifty thousand dollars, after a protracted struggle which ended only in 1805.

Having thought through the nature of his vicissitudes with the cotton gin, Whitney's second key strategic decision was economic, not technical:

Instead of taking a partner, he would enter into an agreement with the Federal Government; instead of the limited cash and credit at the command of any individual, the Treasury would finance his project. He realized also that, instead of being overwhelmed by more customers than he could supply, he would be producing for a single buyer. That he made this basic decision first and then looked about for a likely vehicle is clear.

In May 1798, after one false start, he proposed to Secretary Oliver Wolcott of the Treasury (an old Yale man, with whom he had dealt before) that he 'undertake to Manufacture ten or Fifteen Thousand Stand of Arms' for the government. The idea of converting a group of workers who had made a handful of cotton gins to the mass manufacture of arms was, on the face of it, outlandish. In its first four years the Springfield armory had produced just over one thousand muskets. But President Adams's administration faced a crisis as acute as the private crisis of Whitney: it looked like war with France, and America had no adequate domestic source of arms. Thus, both parties stepped off into the dark with a contract of 14 June 1798, which committed Whitney to deliver four thousand weapons before the end of September 1799, six thousand weapons by a year later.

He proceeded to set up his plant on the basis of interchangeable parts of great precision—a notion circulating on both sides of the Atlantic, but never put to the test of substantial factory production. He ran into every kind of difficulty that might be predicted, as well as

p 106–7 (4)

Whitney's cotton gin (seen here in an engraving from 'Harper's Weekly', 1873) could easily be operated by two men, and increased from one pound to fifty per day the amount of fiber that could be separated from the seed.

Demand for the machine was enormous. Whitney and Miller started a factory to manufacture it, but its marketing presented problems they could not solve. (4)

plague and bad weather. He sought and was granted delay and further advances by Wolcott. In January 1801 he was able to display impressive samples to both the outgoing and incoming Presidents, Adams and Jefferson. He was advanced more money and more time. And by the end of September 1801 the first batch of five hundred muskets was delivered. The War Department complained of flaws in 1808; but, essentially, in the first decade of the new century Whitney translated his concept and his contract into a working and revolutionary manufacturing system. And, equally, he solved his private problem of innovation: how to become a successful manufacturer, without private capital, in a society still predominantly made up of farmers and handicraftsmen.

What these government contracts brought to life was a system in which, in Whitney's words, 'the tools themselves shall fashion the work and give every part its just proportion—which, when once accomplished, will give expedition, uniformity, and exactness to the whole'. There were others, in parallel, working in this direction; and there were many quick to seize on the method and to apply it in other directions, when its efficacy was proved. That process of application and diffusion was reflected at the Crystal Palace in 1851 and accelerated during the 1850s as the national market widened.

Whitney, before he was finished, was to feel the vindictiveness of bureaucracy at its worst, notably through Callender Irvine. But at critical moments the American style in enterprise was shared also in the Federal government: from Wolcott and his reprieves of time and money to the congenial understanding of Jefferson, whose enthrallment by the world of science and gadgeteering belied his vision of an American nation of yeomen untainted with Hamilton's vision of industry. And, in the end, Whitney, the War Department, and the talented new men at the national armories got on well. The imaginative leap of the inventor and the terrible anxieties of innovation gave way, at last, to an ongoing process.

Not until its patronage relation to aircraft design and the aircraft industry did the Federal government play again so direct and critical a role in American industrial development—if one excludes the more oblique effects of the Morrill Act of 1862 and the land grant colleges.

Whitney died in 1825, in precisely the period when New England was caught up in the first solidly based major surge of American industrialization. Its focus was cotton textiles. The period of Embargo and War (1806–15) had seen a good deal of manufacture of consumer goods in substitution for British imports. But the war babies mainly perished with the coming of peace and normal trade in the Atlantic.

Francis Cabot Lowell, however, had found as early as 1813 the formula for viable textile manufacture on the American scene: the recruitment for the labor force of farmers' unmarried daughters, living in a setting of gentility that included lectures by Mr Emerson; the exploitation of cheap accessible water power; the use of advanced machinery; the concentration on production of relatively coarse grades of textiles where the American demand was strong; and the concentration of marketing in the hands of a single agent. Lowell's profits were immediate and high. Unlike gun production, here was an industrial base capable of rapid expansion: the market was growing and managerial skill plus tariffs could cut into British imports. One hundred and sixty-four cotton mills were erected in New England in the 1820s. Moreover, the machinery requirements for the factories could spread far beyond the armories the approach which Whitney symbolized and helped pioneer.

Then, as men tinkered on both sides of the Atlantic, the railroads began to come in during the 1830s, one of the first linking the new, vital textile center at Lowell to Boston. In the 1840s New England and the Middle Atlantic states developed fairly dense railway nets. In the great boom of the 1850s, American railway mileage more than tripled (to something of the order of thirty thousand miles), as the network was thrown out over longer distances, notably to link the East and the Middle West.

By 1860 the United States had moved beyond its industrial status reflected at Crystal Palace: it was producing the iron and engineering products required to build and maintain its railroads. The earlier inventors and pioneers of interchangeable parts now had a mass private market, efficiently tied together. In this environment the United States began to face, on a substantial scale, the task that was

to dominate enterprise in the years after 1865: the management of organizations beyond the reach of a single man.

As A. D. Chandler notes, there were always forerunners; for example, John Jacob Astor's far-flung American Fur Company and Nicholas Biddle's Second Bank of the United States. And, one can add, there was the quietly influential precedent of the management of the Army. Nevertheless, Chandler's dictum is just: '. . . with the completion of the great east-west trunk lines early in the 1850's administration became a full-time task in American business.'

Some clearly perceived the problem at the time; for example, the General Superintendent of the Erie railroad, Daniel C. McCallum:

A Superintendent of a road fifty miles in length can give its business his personal attention and may be constantly on the line engaged in the direction of its details; each person is personally known to him, and all questions in relation to its business are at once presented and acted upon; and any system however imperfect may under such circumstances prove comparatively successful.

In the government of a road five hundred miles in length a very different state exists. . . . I am fully convinced that in the want of a system perfect in its details, properly adapted and vigilantly enforced, lies the true secret of their [the large roads'] failure. . . .

On this perception a group of imaginative railroad engineers designed the organizational structure for the first large-scale American industrial enterprise, based on the centralized management of specific functions, broken down by departments, its unity maintained by the prompt and uniform reporting and standardized operating instructions permitted by the telegraph.

1865–1920: towards technological maturity

The half-century after the Civil War saw the United States move from the modest but sturdy industrial base created in a predominantly agricultural society before 1860 to an urban society dominated by industry. Its private enterprises rapidly absorbed the new technologies and materials generated on the world scene: steel and chemicals, electricity, refrigeration, and the internal combustion engine, rubber and oil. And they organized themselves to make the most of the unique, rapidly expanding continental market which emerged.

Drake's oilwell, the first ever drilled, in 1859, near Titusville, Pennsylvania. By 1870, five million barrels of oil a year were being pumped, and in that year John D. Rockefeller and his partners formed the Standard Oil Company, which was to dominate the industry from then on. (5)

p 112 (18)

There were men still in the inventive tradition of Whitney and the cotton gin: Edison and Berliner and the Wright brothers, for example. But the era was dominated by those who threw their hats over the wall in a different sense, more like Whitney's approach to the government for the gun contract; that is, men who perceived possibilities of large profit by some marriage of existing technology and the immense national market, through new forms of industrial organization.

Writing of John D. Rockefeller in *The Robber Barons*, Matthew Josephson notes:

f 5

In the life of every conquering soul there is a 'turning point', a moment when a deep understanding of the self coincides with an equally deep sense of one's immediate mission in the tangible world. For Rockefeller, brooding, secretive, uneasily scenting his fortune, this moment came but a few years after his entrance into the oil trade, and at the age of thirty. He had looked upon the disorganized conditions of the Pennsylvania oil fields, the only source then known, and found them not good: the guerrilla fighting of drillers, of refining firms, of rival railroad lines, the mercurial changes in supply and market value—very alarming in 1870—offended his orderly and methodical spirit. But one could see that petroleum was to be the light of the world. From the source, from the chaotic oil fields where thousands of drillers toiled, the grimy stream of the precious commodity, petroleum, flowed along many diverse channels to narrow into the hands of several hundred refineries. . . . Now what if the Standard Oil Company should by further steps of organization possess itself wholly of the narrows?

The upshot in 1882 was the first great trust, in which forty-one participating owners turned over the bulk of their shares to a self-perpetuating board of nine trustees. This yielded not only a famous protracted national political debate but also an enterprise reaching throughout the national market with strong centralized and institutionalized management, no longer dependent on one man, backed by a substantial central staff, and uniform accounting procedures.

The critical 'immediate missions'—the strategic decisions—of the new innovating leaders varied.

There was Gustavus Swift who saw that the new technology of refrigeration could unite the growing urban demand for fresh meat and the sprawling herds of cattle on the western plains. The heart of the new integrated operation was a distributing and marketing organization that reached into every major city.

James Duke seized on a new cigarette manufacturing machine to move into mass production and mass distribution of the newly popular product.

General Electric and Westinghouse moved briskly, in the wake of Thomas Edison's incandescent lamp, to build up wide-ranging electric equipment industries, including engineering departments responsible for rapidly evolving designs.

Steel moved both towards integration (back to its raw material sources) and to diversification (beyond rails into structural steel and other products). And then, under Elbert Gary, a sprawling billion-dollar empire was loosely formed into a holding company—the United States Steel Company.

p 110 (14)

As these and other massive new units emerged, they experimented with various forms of consolidation, horizontal as well as vertical. The central problem was to combine the imperatives of unified management with the advantages of scale—notably in respect to the cost of raw materials; efficiency of plant operations; mobilization of labor supply; marketing; and working capital. The railroads—especially the Pennsylvania—provided the model adopted most often. And sometimes railroad executives moved over directly to apply their management and accounting experience to other fields. Central operational units related to each function were created, with general managers for each such department. Co-ordination and broad policy-making decisions governing finance, mergers, efforts to extend markets, etc., fell to a small group of commanding figures supported by small staffs.

The vitality of the enterprise as a whole hinged on the quality of a few men at the top. Part of the relative strength of Standard Oil, for example, stemmed from the fact that Rockefeller assembled at

'*The modern ship of the plains*' (1886). *As immigrants streamed into America, the railroad networks which stretched across the nation transported them to their new homes, with their families goods and chattels.* (6)

the top a larger group of men of business talent than most of these early imperial efforts. Generally, however, these corporations depended on the qualities of a single, major, dominating leader.

These were organizations exploiting the rapidly increasing scale of the American market—notably, the urban market; although Sears, Roebuck and others found new methods for tapping the rural markets, as well, with the revolutionary mail-order catalogue.

p 113 (22)

The great new firms (except in electricity) did not generate much technical innovation at the center of their organizations. 'Scientific management' was focussed by Frederick W. Taylor and others around efficiency in the small, not the large; that is, how, by specialization of function in a machine shop or other narrow operation, maximum efficiency could be achieved in routine, regularly repeated operations. Taylor's classic work is focussed around shop management. Taylor's image of innovation was the small, incremental improvement, arising from imaginative men working in or directing the shop. His symbol was not the laboratory but the stop-watch.

Just as the railroads of the 1850s foreshadowed the problems and solutions of the next phase of American enterprise, a crisis at du Pont in 1902 and its resolution foreshadowed patterns of strengthened central staffs and decentralized production units that were to be widely diffused in the 1920s and beyond.

When Eugene du Pont, the firm's president, died, three younger men of the family resisted the impulse to sell out the firm, already a century old. Alfred, Coleman and Pierre du Pont bought it for twelve million dollars. Their reorganization of 1903 involved, within the production department, separate, relatively decentralized units for producing high explosives, black powder, and smokeless powder. Special development laboratories were set up. And by 1919 the technologically vital and inherently diversified nature of the chemical business had yielded departments for manufacturing cellulose, dyestuffs, and paints, as well as explosives. Decentralization by product, rather than merely by function, plus the acceptance of research and development as part of the firm, required greatly strengthened executive management at the top, supplied by an enlarged Executive Committee and staffs to mobilize data for it.

The interest of du Pont in the automobile industry, via the investment of a substantial volume of its profits in General Motors in the period 1910–20, set the stage for the application of these principles to the most important industry of the next stage of American development.

1920–55: the age of mass-consumption

The railroad was the most powerful innovation of the 19th century. It simultaneously created an efficient national market; set up large demands for heavy industry and engineering products, providing, for example, the principal initial demand for steel; brought new agricultural areas and sources of raw materials into an economical relation to domestic and foreign markets; accelerated the pace of urbanization; induced large capital imports; and stimulated the development of the American capital market.

Thus far the mass production, sale, and use of the automobile has been the most powerful innovation of the 20th century, also because of its multiple effects. It became a significant, if not dominating, market for steel and engineering products, rubber, glass, oil, and light electronics; it restructured American life along suburban lines; it linked rural to urban markets in new, more flexible ways; it created a requirement for large-scale sales and servicing industries; it set up extensive requirements for roads and parking facilities; it played a critical role in a social revolution touching patterns of American life from courting habits to the getaway methods of bank robbers. It was accompanied by—and, in various indirect ways, related to—a surge in the production of various durable consumer goods and processed foods which came to fill American homes, as rising incomes and suburban life made personal service expensive and inaccessible: washing and drying machines; vacuum cleaners; the electric ice box; the oil furnace and then air conditioning; canned and, then, frozen foods.

The revolution—which I have called the stage of High Mass-Consumption—came logically first to the United States because of the persistence of higher income per capita in America than in Europe and other more advanced industrial nations. But it was triggered, against this background, by one of the great insights—or strategic decisions—in the history of American enterprise; that is, Henry Ford's 1908 definition (announced in 1909) of his immediate mission as the production and sale of a cheap, reliable, single model 'for the great multitude' so that every man 'making a good salary' could 'enjoy with his family the blessing of hours of pleasure in God's great open spaces'. And, then, after considerable experiment, in 1913 the moving assembly line for the Model T was set in motion. Ford's strategic concept of 1908 was now matched by a working process.

Its success—and the parallel success of others—posed major questions of industrial organization, as the number of private automobiles in use moved from 306,000 in 1909 to 8,000,000 in 1920; 23,000,000 in 1929; 26,000,000 in 1945; 54,000,000 in 1955; 78,000,000 in 1966. The critical transition in scale was that which occurred in the decade before 1920, when a twenty-five-fold increase occurred in private automobile ownership; something like a ten-fold increase in annual sales.

The motor car which had begun as the plaything of the elite, became the liberator (and enslaver) of the common man.

While Ford met this expansion by enlarging his factories and sales operations, under essentially one-man control, the other great innovator, William C. Durant, pulled together a holding company for making and selling automobiles, parts, and accessories. Ford's was an engineer's solution to the challenge and opportunity, Durant's that of an organizer of finance and men.

Built into the General Motors structure under Durant was a considerable degree of autonomy for the various manufacturing units; but a brief recession in 1910 suggested the financial vulnerability of this sprawling, loosely managed empire; and it was caught hard, in the midst of ambitious postwar expansion plans, by the sharp recession of 1920.

Durant withdrew and the du Ponts moved in to make sense of the operation, after putting up, with others, the funds necessary to avoid catastrophe. Chandler describes as follows the historic reorganization, designed by Alfred P. Sloan, Jr, and put into effect by Pierre du Pont:

Under his [Sloan's] proposal the operating units—the car, truck, parts, and accessories divisions—retained their full autonomy.... What was new ... was the creation of a general office, consisting of general executives and advisory staff specialists, to assure overall coordination, control, and planning.

... they labored at developing a mass of statistical information to flow through these channels to provide the general staff and operating officers with a clear and continuous picture of the performance of the many divisions and of the corporation as a whole....

By 1925 General Motors' innovations in management had produced a new decentralized type of organization for the large industrial enterprise.

The relative decline of Ford's sales from 40–50% of the market in 1920–25 to 20–30% in the 1930s and the rise in this period of General Motors' from 10–20% to 40% or better clinched the point; and after the Second World War Henry Ford's grandson clapped 'the G.M. organization garment onto the Ford Manufacturing frame' (*Fortune*, May 1947).

American enterprise found its way, then, to a new pattern. It balanced the financial and other advantages of centralization with quasi-autonomous production divisions. It provided the advantages of both manageable scale and clear accountability. The pattern was not universally accepted; and, where accepted, it was modified to fit the special requirements of particular markets and firms. But it commended itself, in general, to an industrial complex which was moving to diversified lines of capital and consumer goods.

These are the large but flexible structures, commanding vast resources of working capital, managerial skill in depth, a sense of competitiveness among their various divisions as well as in relation to other firms, which constitute *Le Défi Américain* that Europe and the world have had to face.

After 1955: the search for quality

By the mid-1950s a new stage in American growth began to take shape. The diffusion of the automobile and durable consumer goods continued, of course, and surged with the boom of the 1960s; but it was clear that the gadgetry of the stage of High Mass-Consumption had been absorbed by such a high proportion of American families that further extension of the pattern could no longer constitute the long-term basis for American growth.

In both private and public outlays Americans began to spend relatively less on manufactures, more on certain services. Between 1956–58 and 1959–66 the average proportion of disposable income spent on services rose from 34% to 37%. Employment in services, as a whole, came to absorb more than half of the working force.

Private expenditures, for example, have increased disproportionately for medical services, education, recreation, and foreign travel. In 1970 national parks and other Federal recreation areas will have served an estimated 793 million visitors, a figure increasing at the rate of 7% a year. On the public side, in the course of the 1960s Americans turned to deal with some of the social havoc wrought during the stage of High Mass-Consumption. They suddenly became aware of the concentration of Negroes in rotting urban ghettos, living in a subculture which conventional institutions of education, welfare, and private industry did not effectively penetrate. Public allocations for urban redevelopment, education, and medical services were expanded. Public measures were taken to move the Negro to full citizenship, which yielded both accelerated progress and increased tension in American society. And first inadequate steps were taken to come to deal with the air and water pollution that had been permitted to build up in the previous generation.

The shift to certain services fitted well the existing industrial structure. Automated data processing, for example, is revolutionizing banking, insurance, and other services; and the International Business Machines Corporation and other firms producing the new equipment are structured along the now classic balance between centralized executive leadership and decentralized, diversified divisions. But in areas such as education and medicine, there is a need for innovation and pioneering. And new patterns of business organization may be required, given the peculiar institutional nature of the markets.

One may devise and manufacture—as is now happening—all manner of imaginative teaching devices, based on modern technology, designed to improve the quality of instruction in an age of mass higher education. It is a quite different matter to induce teachers to adopt them and to use them well. The Lockheed Aircraft Corporation, for example, has designed an efficient experimental hospital; but it is likely to be accepted only slowly by the medical profession.

Moreover, the actions and policies of government interweave these new dynamic sectors, quite aside from the government's enlarged role in medicine. The international race in new aircraft—including supersonic transport—may help determine where the balance of payments gains and burdens fall in the coming era of mass international travel. In turn, that race in the United States, as elsewhere, hinges on a partnership between government and private enterprise. New, rapidly growing firms, full of bright young men, seek to apply modern analytic and data processing methods to education and urban problems, among others; but they must find their markets in an intricate public-private maze of institutions, not by direct appeal to a mass market, in the tradition of the classic industrial giants. Similar public-private links may have to emerge if the clearing of air and water pollution is to be accomplished and rational transport schemes devised for the great cities.

In short, patterns of industrial organization devised for supplying military and space programs may come to characterize widened areas of more conventional civil activity as well.

The new phase of American growth raises a second problem of enterprise; that is, the distortion of creative, innovating talent within the American economy. Three major American industries grew with substantial research and development components built into their initial structures: chemicals; electricity and electronics; and the aircraft industry. Others followed in various degrees. But it was for long true in many industries that directors and managers who were comfortable and skilful with problems of finance and marketing, labor and plant efficiency, were awkward and uncertain in dealing with the organization of creativity involved in research and development departments. It was harder there to reduce policy issues to a palpable problem to be solved. Great industries, absorbing vast resources, have gone their way with relatively minor attention to institutionalized invention and refinement of techniques; for example, steel, construction, textiles, automobiles, railroads and mass transit in general.

The accompanying table reflects the distortion in research and development outlays. In 1960, 83% of all research and development expenditures in the industrial sector of the American economy was undertaken in five industries: aircraft and missiles; electrical equipment and communication; machinery; chemicals and allied products; motor vehicles and other transport equipment. Something like this pattern had persisted over the previous thirty years.

The technologies of High Mass-Consumption are being efficiently absorbed in Western Europe and Japan. Management has emerged (or is emerging) which combines strong executive leadership with ample working capital, modern research and development, and efficient diversified production units. If the old American primacy in productivity is to persist, innovations will be required in certain service sub-sectors and modern science and technology will have to be applied over a much wider front than in the past.

Public enterprise

In the new era now beginning to take shape, where men gradually turn to seek lives of higher quality rather than merely increases in conventional material income, the outcome for the American growth rate and the balance of payments may well hinge somewhat less than in the past on the performance of the private sector and rather more on enterprise in the public sector of society; that is, on Federal, state, and local governments, the public servants who man them, and the officials the people elect.

It is worth looking back briefly, then, at the American style as it has been reflected in public enterprise.

As one would expect, the American styles in private and public action have much in common: the same tendency for bold strategic decisions, and then the laborious reduction of policy to working process by trial and error. There is also the tendency to innovate by facing and solving practical problems, rather than by the elaboration and debate of theory.

American political life, in fact, has typically waited until problems took the form of major crises before innovation was undertaken. The political market, based on an approximation of one-man one-vote, was generally a less sensitive index of danger and opportunity than the private marketplace. Indeed, the founding of the nation itself followed the pattern of the national style: the Declaration of Independence—the ideological hat thrown over the wall; the Constitution—the organizational structure that worked, found after the wall had been painfully climbed, and the Articles of Confederation found wanting as a form of government; and then, two centuries of operating, adjusting, refining the process within it, in the face of a succession of new problems thrown up by the dynamics of history.

In economic policy the Federal government operated before 1861 against the background of the 'magnificent image' of America and its possibilities, although Federal action was held back by regional opposition to excessive expenditures on 'public improvements'. In the pre-Civil War period this spirit, nevertheless, led not only to the Cumberland Road (1817) but to the pathfinding expedition of Lewis and Clark (1804–06), and to other germinal explorations.

The States were less inhibited in pursuing their grand designs—the Erie Canal among them. In throwing their hats over the wall, on occasion some of the state governments could not, in fact, make the climb: for example, a number of the state-financed railway lines of the 1830s failed.

But there was a clear image of where the nation was heading in the Congress of the early 1860s when it met without the Southern-

PERCENTAGES OF EACH INDUSTRY'S EXPENDITURE SPENT IN PARTICULAR PRODUCT FIELDS

Industry	Expenditure in all product fields (in millions of dollars)	Guided missiles	Communication equipment and electronic components	Aircraft and parts	Chemicals except drugs and medicines	Machinery	Motor vehicles and other transportation equipment	Atomic energy devices	All other product fields
		%	%	%	%	%	%	%	%
Aircraft and missiles	3,577	48.9	15.1	19.1	0.4	a	0.6	3.1	12.8
Electrical equipment and communication	2,355	5.8	51.6	10.5	0.4	a	a	14.1	17.6
Machinery	927	13.7	17.4	2.5	0.6	51.5	2.7	1.7	9.9
Chemicals and allied products	882	a	a	a	61.7	a	a	2.9	35.4
Motor vehicles and other transportation equipment	844	6.6	10.3	9.1	0.6	4.6	58.2	0.7	9.8
All others	1,576	n.a.	n.a.	n.a.	12.9	n.a.	n.a.	4.1	n.a.
All Industries	**10,161**	**22.0**	**21.2**	**11.1**	**7.7**	**7.3**	**5.5**	**5.5**	**19.7**

a ... not available separately but included in 'All other product fields'.
n.a. ... not available.

This table shows the areas in which research expenditure was applied in 1960 in American industry. The first column gives the totals in millions of dollars for each industry, the other columns the percentages of those sums allotted to each product field within each industry. (7)

ers: tariffs to protect industry; colleges to encourage agriculture, mining and industrial technology; and the transcontinental railroads. And in the Civil War itself the North, exploiting its industrial machine and its new railway net, translated into dogged military process Lincoln's commitment to maintain the unity of the nation—a commitment rooted in hard regional interests and political realities, but also in a determination that the special experiment of America must not fail.

Aside from the Spanish-American War, the direct enterprises of the Federal government were limited down to 1917. But Washington—and the state governments—acquired progressively a widened range of administrative functions as the nation gradually insisted on policies of industrial control and human welfare which would mitigate the harshnesses of the age. Through the Federal Reserve System and other institutions, the government moved to set the climate and the terms on which private enterprise would operate; although government enterprise, in the narrow sense, remained limited.

As the modern Federal civil service evolved, after the Act of 1883, its style and structure came to reflect the criteria of specialization and efficiency in the small which marked Taylorism. The object was to set standards of technical competence to defeat the spoils system, not to build creative staff work into the government. The pioneering innovations in welfare policy came in the States, notably Massachusetts, New York, and Wisconsin.

In the First World War the skills and management generated in industry and finance over the previous half-century were brought for the first time into the Federal government through the War Industries Board. The nation's imperial industrial style was reflected in the plans for the great American offensive of 1919—which never took place.

p 114 (23) The New Deal was, obviously, the greatest period of civil enterprise since 1787 and the years which immediately followed. In its experimental vigor and theoretical eclecticism, the New Deal remains a classic American exercise in innovation by crisis.

In the Second World War, bold—almost extravagant—gambles of policy were made good by the capacity to mobilize American energies and resources in long, tedious work; for example, the commitment to build a massive daylight precision bomber force; the decision to invade the European continent directly on a single front; the decision to build the atomic bomb. And so, also, after the war, with the Marshall Plan and NATO.

In the 1960s the McNamara reorganization of the Pentagon—the largest American public enterprise—brought, at last, the format of the large modern corporation to military organization. The functional departments (the three services) were grouped, via the program budget, in terms of the products their components were supposed to supply: strategic forces; air defense forces; general purpose forces. And top management was strengthened by enlarged staffs and accounting devices. But McNamara was the fourth to try: Elihu Root's reforms were ultimately blunted by the Bureau Chiefs; the reforms of Peyton March in the First World War and George Marshall in the Second were substantially diluted with the coming of peace and the assertion of primacy by the services. The fate of the McNamara reforms is still to be determined.

The wars in Korea and Vietnam were conducted in ways less typical of the national style than others since 1861. The limitation of objectives and tactics required in a nuclear age and the inherent and appropriate political and military role of the Koreans and South Vietnamese imposed disciplines and constraints which prevented the American hat from being thrown over the wall in the old sense. But in Korea the minimal object was achieved after much trial, error, and travail; and, I would guess, it will, in the end, be achieved in the even more difficult circumstances of Vietnam.

p 112 (18) The space program, after the psychological and political crisis created by the initial Soviet advantage of the late 1950s, represented a more classical American problem. And there—once the critical decision was taken in 1961 to send men to the moon—its Director sought and succeeded substantially in reducing the revolutionary enterprise to an ongoing enterprise with many decentralized points of initiative and decision, combined with a strong directing hand:

I think [said James Webb] the forces of democracy are dynamic forces. They ought to be constructed organizationally so that they are like an airplane—they're stable, they return to a predetermined course, and they don't have to depend on a hierarchical structure of decision. I wanted to construct a dynamically stable administrative machine for this agency.

In its weaving together of industry, universities, and government, the space program may provide a prototype for future enterprises—Federal, regional, and state—designed to deal with unsolved problems of urban life, mass transit, air and water pollution.

American political leadership has, then, reflected the national style. It has remained loyal to Grover Cleveland's dictum: 'It is a condition that confronts us—not a theory.' The banners of reform were not sharp, lucid, ideological slogans. They were phrases evoking a general sense of direction: the Square Deal and the New Freedom; the New Deal and the Fair Deal; the New Frontier and the Great Society. Their spaciousness permitted government to grapple experimentally with specific contemporary problems on a pragmatic basis.

In plunging, late in the day, into the new array of challenges in the 1960s—posed by issues of race and the cities; the pollution of the environment; the emergence of mass higher education; and the delicate balances between justice and order raised by white and black protest and the rising crime rate—the national style in public enterprise was consistent with the long sweep of the American past. A revolutionary series of strategic decisions was taken in the form of new legislation followed by trial and error operations over a wide front. Clearly, the scale of the effort has not yet matched the scale of the problems; and experiment has not yet yielded the organizations and strategies that would permit these problems to be dealt with confidently, through ongoing processes. In dealing with this agenda, the United States has only just begun.

It is an agenda that confronts deeply rooted attitudes and institutions that may not yield as easily as some of the problems of the past; for example, archaic urban and suburban jurisdictions; university faculties deeply conservative with respect to educational method, whatever their political stripe; state governments and legislatures geared neither in personnel nor in political balance nor in tax structures to carry the large part of the load Washington ought not to assume; the psychological resistance to accepting Negroes in the suburbs.

But the success or failure of America in dealing with that part of the agenda of the Search for Quality that falls on the public sector is not likely to depend on the quality of enterprise, in the narrow sense, of which the public sector is capable. The American public sector is, evidently, able to play its role in the curious partnership society the nation has created and operates, but which it has never formulated with theoretical rigor.

The outcome will be determined by the political process that lies behind the public sector in a democracy. That means it depends on the will of a majority of American citizens to face these potentially degenerative problems, discipline inflation without an excessive damping of the growth rate, and forego the private income necessary to deal with them. And this must be done at a time when the blandishments of High Mass-Consumption retain their appeal for many, but when a potentially creative minority has rejected the values and institutions which have brought the United States to a point where a society of quality might be possible.

It is the American style as a whole—and 'the magnificent image' itself—that is now undergoing perhaps its severest test since the 1850s, in the early phase of the Search for Quality.

VI

A CHANGING
FEDERALISM

*American systems
of laws and constitutions*

PHILIP B. KURLAND

'No matter whether th' constitution follows
th' flag or not, th' supreme coort
follows th' iliction returns.'

MR DOOLEY (FINLAY PETER DUNNE)

'Out of many, one'

is the motto held in the eagle's mouth on the Great Seal (upper left, opposite). One of the greatest merits of the Constitution of 1789, in the eyes of those who framed it, was the fact that each former colony preserved most of its sovereignty, while partaking in a voluntary union. It was England's claim to intervene in the internal affairs of the colonies that had provoked rebellion; and the new states had no wish now to substitute for the English monarchy a new form of tyranny in the shape of a powerful central government. Each state ruled itself, making collective decisions on those issues that affected the Union, but living under its own laws.

Such was the Federal ideal, which is still vigorously alive—in the loyalties of the people as well as in the apparatus of state legislatures and governors. This shield was designed for the centennial year of independence. The thirteen original states occupy the top rows. Lower down come those which joined between 1790 and 1876. At the bottom are 'territories' to be admitted to statehood only later (the Cherokee Nation Indian Territory became Oklahoma). The two most recent states, not shown here, are Alaska and Hawaii, both admitted to the Union in 1959.

The Constitution upon which the Union was founded remains valid in virtually all its clauses, plus 26 Amendments. But values as well as circumstances change, and with them America's view of what the Constitution should mean. Through successive decisions of the Supreme Court it has been so drastically re-interpreted that it is necessary to speak not of one Constitution but of at least three. (1)

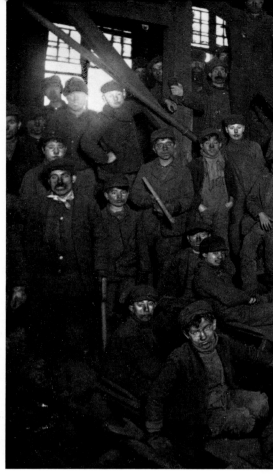

The second Constitution spanned the period between the Civil War and the Depression. Secession was prevented, slavery and the denial of the franchise to Negroes were pronounced unconstitutional. The central government extended its power but still did not consider it its duty to interfere in commerce or to protect the laborer

The first Constitution, lasting from the establishment of the Union in 1789 to the outbreak of the Civil War, embodied the ideals of local self-government for which the States had fought. Top: Congress voting independence in 1776. But one vital question was never settled: Did a state have the right to leave the Union if it chose? That issue came to a head in 1861 over slavery. The first state to secede was South Carolina. A mass meeting at Institute Hall, Charleston (above), calling for a State Convention led eventually to the attempt to establish the whole of the South as a separate republic, and to war as the only answer. (2, 3)

from exploitation. This view of the Constitution has been called 'Social Darwinism' – the economic survival of the fittest or *laissez-faire*. Above: breaker boys in a coal mine, 1909. Below: striking textile workers at Lawrence, Mass., who stopped work in protest against wage reductions in 1912, are met by the state militia. (4, 5)

The third Constitution began when F. D. Roosevelt came to power in 1933. Faced with the unprecedented economic crisis, the central government began to take control in a way which completely contradicted the dogmas of the second Constitution. Federally sponsored schemes, like that of the Tennessee Valley Authority (top), provided employment not only for its builders and its users but for artists like William Gropper who recorded them. Today, few areas of life are immune from government supervision. Above: the Bureau of Census, Washington, where computers can sort people by age, education, and many other criteria. (6, 7)

The separation of powers is also a concept that has meant different things at different times. The Constitution provided that 'the judicial power of the United States shall be vested in one Supreme Court' (and other courts to be erected by Congress) and 'the Executive power ... in a president'. The president's house (below) in the center of Washington was burnt by the British in 1814, rebuilt and painted white to conceal the marks of fire – hence its present name. This sketch is by the architect Benjamin Latrobe, 1817. (8)

'**All legislative powers** herein granted shall be vested in the Congress of the United States which shall consist of a Senate and House of Representatives.' The Capitol (below), where both houses meet, was begun in 1793; the central portion with the dome was added by Charles Bulfinch from 1818 to 1824. Later enlargements after 1850 gave it the grandiose appearance that it has today (see p. 81). (9)

The House of Representatives consists of members elected every two years, the number from each state based on the population rather than size. The original chamber, by Latrobe (above), has now been replaced by a larger one similar to the new Senate (pl. 31). This painting of 1821 shows a moment when the candles of the chandelier are being lit. Justices of the Supreme Court are present at the back of the dais. (10)

Each state has its own constitution, operating through a governor and – with one exception – two legislative houses. Right: a Virginia Constitutional Convention held in 1829. James Madison is speaking. Constitutional Conventions were called to consider such questions as the extension of the franchise. (11)

The Civil War meant the end of the old Federalism and the beginning of the new. It answered two vital questions: Could the central government impose its will on the States by prohibiting slavery? and Was the Union voluntary or binding?

Chief Justice Taney handed down the decision in the Dred Scott case (1857), which included the ruling that Congress could not prohibit slavery even in the territories, i.e., areas not incorporated as states. It was conflict over slavery that led to war. (12)

The Confederacy, a rival independent Federation, was proclaimed by the Southern states in 1861. Left: its president, Jefferson Davis, was inaugurated at Montgomery, Alabama, on 18 February. (13)

The Union under Lincoln was eventually able to impose its Federalist view on the South after a long and bloody war. Left: Lincoln with General George McClellan at the latter's headquarters near Antietam. Above: Ulysses S. Grant, who was finally given command of all the Union armies and led them to victory. (14, 15)

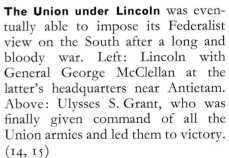

Grant's supply base at City Point, Virginia (above), enabled him to isolate the Confederate capital of Richmond and bring the South to surrender. (17)

'Prisoners from the Front' (left) by Winslow Homer, a sober and sympathetic painting of Confederate prisoners with their Union guards, typified the desire of the North for a firm peace, nonretributive terms and the welding of all the states into a single nation. (16)

The war left many Southern towns in ruins. Right: Charleston, South Carolina, where it had all begun with the bombardment of Fort Sumter. (18)

'The right of the citizens of the United States to vote shall not be denied or abridged ... on account of race, color or previous condition of servitude' – the Fifteenth Amendment (1870). The Thirteenth, five years earlier, had abolished slavery. This ideal-ized vision of the Negroes' future was not fulfilled. By a variety of means – poll taxes, literacy tests, fraud and violence – they were gradually deprived of the vote in the Southern states and had difficulty in exercising in the North. (19)

'The Bosses of the Senate', a cartoon by Joseph Keppler published in 1889, indicates popular discontent with a government that seemed unable or unwilling to interfere with the monopolists. In the year following, however, Congress did pass the Sherman Antitrust Act. (20)

The Depression caused sweeping increase in government initiatives and in the extent to which the Supreme Court allowed such initiatives. This poster by Ben Shahn publicized the efforts of the Resettlement Administration to aid families impoverished by the dust storms. Public money began to be spent in vast amounts on 'general welfare'. (21)

Modern democracy – the 'third Constitution' – is characterized by an emphasis on rights of the individual – economic, social and political.

Votes for women came with the Nineteenth Amendment (1920) but only after years of campaigning by suffragettes. Above: a woman posts bills in Cincinnati, 1912. It took another forty years, and far more determined protest, before Negroes in the South began reclaiming their rights. Below: registering at Haynesville, Alabama, in the 1960s. In many districts the campaign still continues. (22, 23)

Organized labor existed in America from the end of the 19th century. The 1930s saw its steepest rise in membership, from three to nearly nine million, but the Ford plant of Detroit held out against it until 1942, when the first election of union officials (top) took place. In 1955 the two biggest unions, the American Federation of Labor and the Congress of Industrial Organizations (above) merged. (24, 25)

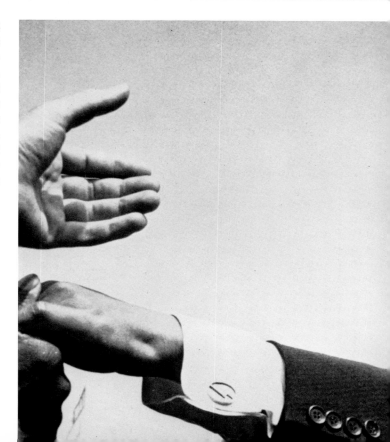

The Poor People's Campaign in Washington, May 1968 (right), underscored the now almost universal demand that government play a paternal role, regulating society to ensure security as well as freedom. (28)

Freedom of speech has been endangered more by fear of foreign enemies than by pressures from within. Senator McCarthy's harassment of suspected Communist sympathizers was opposed by the courts only timidly, when at all, and it was his confrontation with the army (above) that brought his downfall. (27)

'**The Negroes and the Whites** must either wholly part or wholly mingle', wrote Tocqueville in the 1830s. The first phase of the Negro civil rights movement aimed at 'mingling'. Left: Martin Luther King greets a fellow marcher in Washington, August 1964. But after his assassination in 1968 there was a growth of Black militancy, exemplified by the Black Panthers under Eldridge Cleaver (right) who won increased support for a policy of 'wholly parting'. (26, 29)

When the Supreme Court ruled that
state or local laws requiring separate
schools for Negro and white children
were unconstitutional, a crucial stage
was passed in the move toward total
integration and equality. It was one
more example of the way in which the
Court, by simply interpreting the law,
could operate as a force for change.
Ben Shahn's *Integration* (above) shows
Earl Warren (center) and his colleagues who handed down the historic decision in 1954. (30)

The Senate today (right) preserves
one of the few features of the old
Federalism, since there are still two
Senators for each state, irrespective of
size or population. Their method of
selection, however, was modified in
1913. Instead of being chosen by the
state legislatures, they are elected by
the people. (31)

American systems of laws and constitutions

PHILIP B. KURLAND

'THE LIFE OF THE LAW has not been logic; it has been experience.' Mr Justice Holmes's famed dictum about the common law is equally applicable to America's highest law, the Constitution. Experience explains its original content; experience justified its changing construction in the past; experience is the guide to its present-day evolution. Because experience and not textual analysis has given meaning to the Constitution, it has been possible for a single document to provide what has been, in effect, three different constitutions, without the political chaos that usually accompanies the making of a new constitution.

The first American Constitution can be measured temporally from the establishment of the Union to the War between the States; the second followed the Civil War and lasted until the accession to the Presidency of the second Roosevelt; the third originated in the New Deal and is still in the process of operative change.

The remarkable adaptability of this single body of words has been due in some measure to the originally unique device of judicial review and the use of the Supreme Court as a 'continuing Constitutional convention', interpreting the document and rationalizing its words and phrases to fit the times. Judicial review is in itself a remarkable aspect of American constitutional law, since not a single word in the Constitution authorizes the assumption of that power. Here, too, experience—or 'necessity' to use Learned Hand's word—afforded the justification. Thus, Charles Evans Hughes was almost right when he described the Constitution as meaning whatever the Justices of the Supreme Court want it to mean. It is experience—history if you will—that demonstrates what Hughes forgot to add, that the Justices' interpretations are only the penultimate ones, for they are in fact subject to the acquiescence of the American people.

The American Constitution is the embodiment of two fundamental concepts. The first is based on experience that goes back at least as far as Coke and possibly to Magna Carta, the concept of the rule of law, as a right of the people and an obligation of government. The second derives from the colonial experience that taught the need for limited government and more particularly for limited central authority. Thus, the Constitution when it came into being was framed, in anticipation of Lord Acton's dictum that power corrupts and absolute power corrupts absolutely, to divide such power as it authorized. First, the Constitution provided for a limited delegation of powers to the central government, thus dividing such government as was to be tolerated between the States on the one hand and the nation on the other. A new kind of federalism was thus created. Second, it provided for dividing the relatively few powers that the central government was given among three branches and then added to this separation of powers a series of checks and balances of one branch on the others. Third, by amendment of the original document, almost as soon as it became operative, provisions were made to prohibit certain governmental actions, particularly those where the colonial history demonstrated abuses by the Crown and Parliament, further to assure the new Americans the 'liberties of free-born Englishmen'.

Federalism: law and experience

Federalism, like other forms of government, has a multiplicity of shapes. What K. C. Wheare has described as the classic form of

Federalism was acknowledged a century earlier, by Tocqueville, to be an American origination. Thus, Wheare tells us;

> What is necessary for the federal principle is not merely that the general government, like the regional governments, should operate directly upon the people, but further, that each government should be limited to its own sphere, and within its sphere, should be independent of the other.

Tocqueville, in his never-equalled study of the American people, recognized the genius of the proposed American system in this regard:

> This Constitution, which may at first sight be confused with the federal constitutions that have preceded it, rests in truth upon a wholly novel theory, which may be considered as a great discovery in modern political science. In all the confederations that preceded the American Constitution of 1789, the states allied for a common object agreed to obey the injunctions of a federal government but they reserved to themselves the right of ordaining and enforcing the execution of the laws of the union. The American states which combined in 1789 agreed that the Federal government should not only dictate the laws, but execute its own enactments. In both cases the right is the same, but the exercise of the right is different; and this difference produced the most momentous consequences.

This novel arrangement must again be attributed to experience, experience of two kinds: that which derives from the time when the colonies were peopled by acknowledged subjects of the Crown and that which followed the formation of a confederation of the colonies, first to wage the War of the Revolution and then to effectuate the common interests of the newly independent states.

The American colonies, unlike most colonial empires, were not cultivated for the wealth that could be taken from them by a trading company or a military government that conscripted native labor and local resources. The American colonies were colonies of settlement, not colonies of exploitation. Because of this, they were peopled by partners of and equals to the inhabitants of the motherland. While they acknowledged fealty to the Crown, they also asserted their rights of self-government. And distance and its attribute of time served the colonists well in this regard. While the Crown and Parliament could send viceroys, direct government from Westminster was impossible, for neither the people nor the problems of the new land lent themselves to controls that could be simply effected by royal emissaries. Possibly Great Britain could have ruled the American colonies by military force, but eschewing that choice it could do no more than treat with local authorities rather than control them.

As Daniel J. Boorstin has pointed out, the colonial experience was in fact an experiment in Federalism within the British Empire. It was only when Westminster attempted to reject this American Federalism that the war of secession became a necessity:

> American experience had far outrun English (or European) theory. Colonial legislatures, in control of local and internal matters over which faraway London was powerless, were content to leave to London the broad questions of imperial policy, trade,

p 82 (2)

The progress of ratification of the Constitution is shown in this cartoon from the 'Massachusetts Centinel' (1788). The eleven upright pillars are states which had ratified before Washington's inauguration in 1789. North Carolina followed seven months later, and Rhode Island in 1790. (2)

and navigation which required the power of the British navy. Americans had worked out a *modus vivendi* [a federalism] which, with occasional adaptations to the shifting needs of empire, might have continued to function indefinitely. When, in the 1760's, the British government tried to tighten its rein on the American colonies, London was defying the facts of life.

As the conflict sharpened, British writers, hoping to exorcise the mysterious spirit of American rebellion, simply chanted more insistently their beautiful absolutes. The British chorus became a liturgy. The colonies, wrote one Briton in 1769, "must either acknowledge the legislative power of Great Britain in its full extent, or set themselves up as independent states; I say in its full extent, because if there be any reserve in their obedience, which they can legally claim, they must have a power within themselves superior to that of the mother country; for her obedience to the legislature is without limitation." "It is impossible," insisted Governor Hutchinson of Massachusetts in 1773, "there should be two independent Legislatures in one and the same state." In these loyal phrases, Britons asserted the impossibility of what had long since come into being.

The English were not wrong in theory but only in the application of theory to the contemporary facts. Two hundred and fifty years later, the assertion that two independent legislatures could not exist in the same state would prove to be true. But by then time had worked its changes.

If the colonists were short on theory to explain the Federalism that they sought to maintain, they were well-versed in the writings of Sidney and Harrington, of Locke and Coke. Jefferson's immortal phrases in the Declaration of Independence have been read, therefore, against the background of the theories that were familiar to America's learned men, as an expression of the Crown's infringement of the rights of Englishmen among whom the colonists numbered themselves. The Declaration could, however, be read in terms of the rights of local government rather than the rights of individuals. The charges equally support the proposition that the incursion by the central government on the authority of the colonial governments was a violation of that custom that was of the essence of the British constitution. Certainly the parade of 'horribles' in the indictment of King George III could be so read, as can one of the less-famed paragraphs toward the end of the Declaration:

Nor have we been wanting in attentions to our British brethren. We have warned them from time to time of attempts by their legislature *to extend an unwarrantable jurisdiction over us.* We have reminded them of the circumstances of our emigration and settlement here. We have appealed to their native justice and magnanimity and we have conjured them by the ties of our

common kindred to disavow these *usurpations*, which would inevitably interrupt our connection & correspondence. They too have been deaf to the voice of justice & consanguinity. We must therefore acquiesce in the necessity, which denounces our separation, and hold them as we hold the rest of mankind, enemies in war, in peace friends. [Emphasis added.]

If the experience of the colonists led to rejection of central governmental authority, experience with the Articles of Confederation led to recognition of the need to move beyond the traditions of Federalism toward the innovation acknowledged by Tocqueville. As Merrill Jensen has put it: 'The "weakness" of the central government under the Confederation was the weakness of any government that must achieve its ends by persuasion rather than by coercion. There was a large group of citizens of the new nation who believed in persuasion; a smaller but equally powerful group believed in a central government with coercive authority.' It was the latter group that ultimately prevailed to bring about what Madison described as a government both national and Federal.

Strangely enough, the high point of state power under this newly created Federalism came with the presentation of the Constitution for ratification by the people at State conventions. From the time *f 2* that nine States ratified the proposed Constitution, State power was on the wane. *E pluribus unum* was the motto, the goal, and ultimately the achievement.

The first Constitution

During the period of the first Constitution, from 1789 to the Civil War, there was much debate as to whether the document that was called the Constitution was a compact among the States, from which a contracting party could withdraw at will, or at least *p 130* whenever another party was in default, or a deed of power directly from the people to the central government, a grant that could be withdrawn only by the grantors, the people of the United States. Both North and South—the interests of the States tended to be separated in this manner almost from the beginning—argued at different times for the right of secession that was implicit in the compact theory. But, as with the Revolution, this issue was not to be resolved by contending theorists but only through the clash of arms. The North prevented the secession by the successful prosecution of the Civil War and established the nationalists as the pre- *p 134* dominant force in the country once and for all.

At the new nation's infancy, the same forces that protected the colonies from interference by the Crown and the Parliament also sheltered the state and local governments from interference from Washington. The country was spread too far and too wide, the interests of its citizens were too disparate, to permit government from a central capital. All the more so when government had so limited a role to play in the lives of the American citizens.

With the improvement of communications and transportation, with the development of industry and commerce, the national interests grew and so did the national power. And the elastic clauses of the Constitution were found to provide more authority to Washington and more inhibitions on the States. The Supreme Court—through the clause that guaranteed the supremacy of national laws and treaties, through provisions for adding to the specified powers of the central government those that were 'necessary and proper' to execute the ones that were specified, through the discovery of a broad if not total negative implication as to state power from the grant to the nation of power over commerce, through a ban on impairment of contracts that was expanded to protect all sorts of corporate endeavors from state government control, and through the insistence on the power of judicial review over state actions—afforded a powerful means for transmogrifying the 'sovereignty' of the several states into the sovereignty of the nation. As the country grew stronger, international affairs and war powers, which only the national government could indulge, became more important elements in American life and helped strengthen the nation vis-à-vis the States. After the Civil War put an end to the claims of state sovereignty, Federalism was to become an empty slogan for rhetorical rather than practical use.

It is not clear who or what killed American Federalism, or even when it died. Like the victim in Agatha Christie's *Murder on the Calais Coach*, Federalism was struck down by so many causes that none alone can be credited with or blamed for the ultimate demise, although each had a part to play in bringing it about.

In this regard, as in so many others, Jefferson proved prescient about the role of the judiciary when he said:

> The judiciary of the United States is the subtle corps of sappers and miners constantly working underground to undermine the foundations of our Confederated fabric. They are construing a Constitution from a coordination of a general and special government to a general and supreme one alone. This will lay all things at their feet, and they are too well versed in English law to forget the maxim "*boni judicis est ampliare jurisdictionem.*"

A contemporary Justice of the Supreme Court, William O. Douglas, has found in retrospect more causes for the decline of Federalism than did Jefferson in prospect:

> In America the trend has been toward the development of a strong and powerful national government. The impetus of that growth has in part been decisions of the Supreme Court from the time of Chief Justice Marshall to date. It has in part been the increased use by Congress of the great arsenal of power contained in the Constitution. Powers long neglected, *e.g.*, powers over interstate commerce, have been increasingly used by Congress since the turn of the twentieth century. The increased complexities of American life, the growth of industrialism, the disappearance of the frontier, the increase in the population, the growing dependence of one part of the nation on the others—these were all powerful pressures creating the need and demand for federal regulation in fields where previously only the States had legislated. The depression of the 1930's emphasized the need for planning by central government. The advent of two World Wars made necessary the close integration of the national economy under the National Government. And the war powers of Congress and the President . . . were ample for that purpose.
>
> The Federal income tax which came to use as a result of the Sixteenth Amendment has also given centralization a powerful push.

The movement toward centralized government was slow during the period from the Civil War to the New Deal—the period of the second Constitution—largely because the role of government was belittled and the powers of both state and national governments were restrained by the courts whenever they were exercised in such a way as to interfere with the control of the market. Mr Justice Holmes to the contrary notwithstanding, Herbert Spencer's *Social Statics* was, during this period, at least as effective a portion of the

Constitution as any of the language placed in it by the founding fathers. The guarantee of due process of law set out in the Fourteenth Amendment as well as in the Fifth was found to include Social Darwinism as the highest law of the land.

The acceleration of centralization that began with the New Deal resulted from a crisis that local government was both unable and unwilling to confront. The Great Depression and the advent of the Second World War made it necessary for a more powerful and more universal government to take the reins of power which have never p 131 (6) since been surrendered. Technology combined with Keynesian economic theory has doomed Federalism, at least as its essence was described by K. C. Wheare in the quotation already cited.

Nevertheless, the essence of Federalism is still abroad in the land. Demands are growing for a return of authority and power to local units of government where they are subject to more direct control by the people affected and less control from Washington. The demand is, however, not for a return of sovereignty to the States, or even to the governments of the cities, but to even more local units. The problem is not confined to the United States, as the recent report of the Redcliffe-Maud Commission in Great Britain makes clear. That commission has recommended sweeping reforms of local government in that country. And even so, the dissent of Mr Derek Senior is based on the failure of the report to make local government local enough.

Lip service continues to be paid to the merits of Federalism in the United States, but the only constitutional vestiges of any importance are: (1) the continued utilization of the Electoral College system in the choice of a President, where the ballots are cast by state and under which an election thrown into the House of Representatives for lack of a majority in the Electoral College will be decided by a vote by states; and (2) the fact that the United States Senate is still composed of two senators from each state, p 140 (31) without regard to population. The Electoral College is about to disappear through constitutional amendment; presumably the Senate is not in immediate danger of similar extirpation.

Tocqueville's prescience will be tested once again now that Federalism has become moribund in the United States. He had suggested: 'It is generally believed in America that the existence and permanence of the republican form of government in the New World depend upon the existence and duration of the federal system.' And it was Lord Acton who credited Federalism with being the only viable defense against the excesses of democracy:

> Of all the checks on democracy, federalism has been the most efficacious and congenial. . . . The Federal system limits and restrains sovereign power by dividing it, and by assigning to Government only certain defined rights. It is the only method of curbing not only the majority but the power of the whole people, and it affords the strongest basis for a second chamber, which has been found essential security for freedom in every genuine democracy.

The danger of the end of the republican form of government suggested by de Tocqueville and the danger of the loss of individual freedom to rampant democracy predicted by Acton are not imminent but they are immanent in contemporary American society.

Separation of powers

As with the term Federalism, so, too, with the phrase separation of powers. It is subject to many more meanings than one, and to different meanings at different times. Clearly the first three Articles of the Constitution provide for three separate branches of government and assign the functions that each is to have. But the tripartite division was no mere adaptation of Lockean theory. Certainly, as already suggested, the authors of the document knew the arguments of Aristotle, Locke, Montesquieu, and Harrington on the subject of separation of powers. Equally important was their knowledge of the British model, parts of which they liked but most of which they rejected. Perhaps most important was the experience of the colonial and state governments which had enough variations of tripartite governments among them to afford good comparative data. Here again the Constitution represented a composition based on experience and compromise, compromise between those who would choose a government dominated by the legislature and those who preferred a government under the tight command of a strong executive.

Constitutional lawyers and historians will probably never stop arguing the question of the intent of the framers. All that can be clearly discerned, however, is that the division was made; that in addition to a separation of powers, there were provisions for checks and balances, thus introducing the legislature into the executive domain, as with the need for approval of the Senate in executive appointments, treaty-making, and of the President into the legislative area, by calling for his recommendations and providing for his veto; and that there was enough play left in the joints to allow for some shift of power among the three branches, dependent in large measure upon who could and would use it.

In looking back to the origins of the Constitution, the reader is denied clear meaning because, among other things, the strongest of constitutional features originated after the drafting and promulgation of the instrument. The party system, which showed some of its attributes in Jefferson's day, but came to fruition in the Jacksonian era, has had an extraordinarily important role in the assignment of constitutional function. When the President became the party leader, his powers were enhanced by his public constituency and his party following in the legislature and outside it. When the presidential nomination was dependent on congressional caucus, the relationship between the executive and legislative branches was not unaffected by the exercise of that congressional power. The party system is extraconstitutional in terms of the written document, but not in the sense of custom that also makes for American constitutional rules, albeit unwritten ones.

It should be recognized that the constitutional division of powers was clearly not intended as a device to make government efficient. It was not an anticipation of specialized functions so much as a system of restraints on government. As Professor Andrew McLaughlin once told us:

If it be asked why people were so unwise—and the question is often asked—as to hamper government by division of authority and by checks and balances, the answer is simple: such was the kind of government the leaders and probably men in general wanted. Who are a free people? Those who live under a government so constitutionally checked as to make life, liberty and property secure. That would have been the most explicit answer of the Revolutionary days. In some ways the most marked development of the idea of popular government from that time to this has been the development of the belief that governments, strongly directed by popular opinion, should be competent and active—a change from the belief that governments should not do things to the belief that they should do things.

Of the three branches of government, the national judiciary, however much greater its ken than the judiciaries of other nations of that time and this, has been the most confined and the most consistent in the powers that it exercises. Essentially its function is a negative one: to naysay other parts of government, state or national, that threatened to stray or strayed beyond the bounds set for them. Certainly the bounds are amorphous and were often the creation of the courts rather than constitutional exegesis by the courts. But, as Hamilton pointed out in selling the Constitution to the conventions through the Federalist Papers, the judiciary had neither the purse nor the sword at its disposal. Its power was the power of reason and persuasion, certainly weak reeds by comparison with the control of the fisc or of the military establishment.

To acknowledge this deficiency of power is not to denigrate the role of the judiciary in the government of the United States. Having taken unto itself the power of judicial review of the national government as well as of the States, the judiciary and particularly the Supreme Court was able, over a period of time, despite the opposition of some strong Presidents, like Jefferson, Jackson, Lincoln, and F. D. Roosevelt, to establish itself as the living voice of a living Constitution: the Delphic oracles who had but to be understood in order to be obeyed. As already indicated, the judicial power to limit state authority contributed mightily to the decline of Federalism. And the Court has had no small role in

most of the constitutional crises of American history. Its disastrous judgment in the Dred Scott case, for example, was not a small factor in bringing on the Civil War. p 134

It should also be noted that the power of the judiciary derives not only from its function as arbiter of constitutional issues. To the courts is also attributed the authority to interpret national statutes. Over and over again, the courts have proved the validity of Bishop Hoadley's dictum: 'Whoever hath an *absolute authority* to *interpret* any written or spoken laws, it is he who is truly the lawgiver to all intents and purposes, and not the person who first wrote or spoke them.'

As Robert Jackson told us, when he was Attorney General of the United States, the Supreme Court has had its share of conflicts, particularly with the executive branch of the national government:

[The Court] has been in angry collision with most dynamic and popular Presidents in our history. Jefferson retaliated with impeachment; Jackson denied its authority; Lincoln disobeyed a writ of the Chief Justice; Theodore Roosevelt, after his Presidency, proposed a recall of judicial decisions; Wilson tried to liberalize its membership; and Franklin D. Roosevelt proposed to 'reorganize' it. It is surprising that it should not only survive, but with no might except the moral force of its judgments should attain actual supremacy as a source of constitutional dogma. f 3

Nor did the Court contest the field only with the executive branch. American history is filled with similar contests for power with Congress. The Court's survival, indeed, has depended on the fact that it did not challenge and was not challenged by both at the same time. It could protect itself against one or the other, but hardly against both. Its existence and its constitutional power may therefore be attributed to the fact that the two other branches have been in conflict with each other more often than with the Court.

The Supreme Court as arbiter

Indeed, on rare occasions the Court has been called upon to arbitrate the contests for power between Congress and the President. This has not often been the case; political questions of this magnitude seldom lend themselves to judicial resolution. But we do have expressions from the Court on the division of function between the other two branches, and on the whole, in recent times, the Court has spoken for legislative dominance rather than executive hegemony. This is seen, for example, in the outcome of the Steel Seizure Case. There, President Truman had 'seized' the steel mills to prevent their shutdown during the Korean War because of a labor dispute. The mills sought and secured the intervention of the judiciary on the ground that the President had exceeded the constitutional powers at his disposition. Congress had clearly refused to authorize such power of seizure when it was asked to do so prior to the crisis in question.

The Court was thus presented with the choice between two primary theories of the meaning of Article II's grant of the executive power. The William Howard Taft theory was stated thus:

The true view of the Executive function is, as I conceive it, that the President can exercise no power which cannot be fairly and reasonably traced to some specific grant of power or justly implied and included within such express grant as proper and necessary to its exercise. Such specific grant must be either in the Federal Constitution or in an Act of Congress passed in pursuance thereof. There is no undefined residuum of power which he can exercise because it seems to him to be in the public interest. . . . The grants of Executive power are necessarily in general terms in order not to embarrass the Executive within the field of action plainly marked for him, but his jurisdiction must be justified and vindicated by affirmative constitutional or statutory provision, or it does not exist.

In opposition to this approach was that of Theodore Roosevelt who asserted that it was not only the President's 'right but his duty to do anything that the needs of the Nation demanded unless such action was forbidden by the Constitution or by the laws.' The President acts 'for the common well-being of all our people, whenever and in whatever manner . . . necessary, unless prevented by direct constitutional or legislative prohibition.'

In the Steel Seizure Case, the Court clearly opted for the Taft view of the executive power, although most contemporary political scientists espouse that of Roosevelt. Excerpts from Mr Justice Jackson's opinion in that case are instructive:

> That comprehensive and undefined presidential powers hold both practical advantages and grave dangers for the country will impress anyone who has served as legal adviser to a President in time of transition and public anxiety. While an interval of detached reflection may temper teaching of that experience, they probably have a more realistic influence on my views than the conventional materials of judicial decisions which seem unduly to accentuate doctrine and legal fiction.

For Mr Justice Jackson, as for Justices Black, Frankfurter, and Douglas, the answer was not a simple one. 'Presidential powers are not fixed but fluctuate, depending upon their disjunction or conjunction with those of Congress.' With the action of Congress or the chosen inaction of Congress in mind, however, the seizure was invalid. 'When the President takes measures incompatible with the expressed or implied will of Congress, his power is at its lowest ebb, for then he can rely only upon his own constitutional powers minus any constitutional powers of Congress over the matter.' Certainly, the Roosevelt-like claim of an unlimited executive power had to be rejected, both for historical reasons and for the dangers implicit in such a notion:

> The example of such unlimited executive power that must have impressed the forefathers was the prerogative exercised by George III, and the description of its evils in the Declaration of Independence leads me to doubt that they were creating their new Executive in his image.... I cannot accept the view that this clause is a grant in bulk of all conceivable executive power but regard it as an allocation to the presidential office of the generic powers thereafter stated.
>
> ... emergency powers are consistent with free government only when their control is lodged elsewhere than in the Executive who exercises them. That is the safeguard that would be nullified by our adoption of the 'inherent power' formula. Nothing in my experience convinces me that such risks are warranted by any real necessity, although such powers would, of course, be an executive convenience.
>
> In the practical working of our Government we already have evolved a technique within the framework of the Constitution by which normal executive powers may be considerably expanded to meet an emergency. Congress has granted extraordinary authorities which lie dormant in normal times but may be called into play by the Executive in war or upon proclamation of a national emergency....
>
> In view of the ease, expedition and safety with which Congress can grant and has granted large emergency powers, certainly ample to embrace this crisis, I am quite unimpressed with the argument that we should affirm possession of them without the statute. Such power either has no beginning or it has no end. If it exists, it need submit to no legal restraint. I am not alarmed that it would plunge us straightaway into dictatorship, but it is at least a step in the wrong direction.

Nevertheless, history reveals that, just as the power of the States has atrophied and that of the nation has blossomed, so too the national legislative power has become subordinated to the power of the Presidency. For the relative power of these two branches has depended not so much on the terms of the Constitution or the elusive intentions of the founding fathers, but on the personalities of the office-holders and the exigencies of the times. The division of power between Congress and the President is essentially dependent upon the public will and, in recent times, at least, it is the President rather than the Congress who has secured the support of the people. In periods of crisis, the American public has tended to turn to the executive for leadership. And, since the ascendancy of the second Roosevelt to office, the country has been in an almost perpetual state of crisis.

Moreover, here as in the instance of the decline of the States, power has flowed not only to the governmental agency that seeks it, but away from that which chooses rather to avoid its responsi-

Franklin D. Roosevelt was elected for a second term in 1936, by a sweeping majority, but much of his New Deal legislation was vetoed as unconstitutional by the justices of the Supreme Court. This 'Punch' cartoon (1937) optimistically shows FDR on the merry-go-round of success, taking the Supreme Court for a ride. He had proposed to add up to six justices to the Court, in order to reduce the odds against his policies. In the event, he failed, but the Supreme Court itself soon became more sympathetic to the New Deal. (3)

bilities. Governmental power has not so much been usurped by the nation and its chief executive as it has been largely abdicated by the States and the Congress.

Thus, in 1967, an astute English journalist, Louis Heren, could accurately describe the American Presidency in these terms:

> I do believe that the modern American Presidency makes sense as a political system only when it is seen to be a latter-day version of a British medieval monarchy, and I commend this approach to its loyal American subjects. Thus armed, they will be less bothered by the frustrations that usually attend the conventional method of measuring the incumbent against the constitutional yardstick. I am not denigrating the United States Constitution; as a foreign correspondent who has worked in too many countries, I am immensely respectful of it. Nevertheless, it is not always helpful when discussing the modern Presidency, and therefore the modern American system, and for a fuller understanding one must return to the medieval past of the British monarchy.
>
> ... the main difference between the modern American President and a medieval monarch is that there has been a steady increase rather than diminution of his power. In comparative historical terms the United States has been moving steadily backward.

Certainly the system is no longer with us that Woodrow Wilson described long before his Presidency as 'Congressional Government'. Certainly 'Presidential Government' would be a more accurate label today. The comparison between the Presidency and the English monarchy that preceded Magna Carta may well be valid. There are a few indications, however, that the pendulum may yet swing once more. The era of the one-term Presidents may be approaching. The barons are restless and especially ambitious senators, who have done in Caesars before, are beginning to assert the prerogatives of the representatives of the people that once-proud Congresses asserted in the past. Whether the power of the Presidency is to return to the cyclical pattern that existed before the

New Deal or to continue on its steady course of expansion is a question that will be answered anew for each generation unless and until the presidential office swallows the Constitution. If, however, Congress is to reassert itself, it must first reform itself. It needs a far greater efficiency than it now has to confront the President in a struggle for power. It must raise its prestige in the eyes of the electorate. And it must organize itself so that the control is shifted to those who are most likely rather than least likely, as is the case today, to confront the authority of the President with the will of the people.

In the early 1970s, however, the President continued to enjoy, in fact, exclusive control in the domain of foreign relations to the point, as Heren noted, that he could wage war without congressional declaration. The legislative program of the Congress is, in fact, the legislative program of the President, even with a Congress made up of a majority of members of the opposition party. By a principle known as impoundment, the President even feels free to pick and choose from among the programs Congress enacts those that he will administer and those that will remain unexecuted. And, as leader of his party, as well as President of his country, he controls the political destinies of all those who need the party's support to remain in office. His access to the news media affords an enormous power. And his patronage, not merely in terms of governmental offices, but in terms of governmental grants and contracts, is an immensely potent weapon.

We have come a long way, indeed, since Thomas Jefferson assumed the Presidency with the commitment to execute the will of his congressional master. The path has not been a straight one. But there has been no turning during the last four decades.

The second Constitution

Federalism and separation of powers, even in their new clothes of 1787, were but the means by which the aspirations of the people of this new nation were to be attained. What Professor George Sabine once wrote about the Levellers is equally appropriate to the spirit of the American Constitution:

> From the Leveller's point of view there was no more merit in parliament's claim to sovereign power than in the king's. Like the king, parliament has merely a delegated power, and it is as important to protect individual rights against a legislature as against an executive. . . . The plan . . . was substantially that of a written constitution with its bill of fundamental right. . . . Parliament must not repudiate debts, make arbitrary exceptions to the operation of the law, or destroy the rights of property and of personal liberty.

'The rights of property and personal liberty' were not regarded as disparate but as conjunctive. From the Levellers, from Harrington, from Locke, from many other masters, and from experience, the American creators of the Constitution learned and accepted that the most important ingredients of liberty, at least for that time, were the rights to secure, to create, to use, to control, and to alienate property. There was no liberty without property nor, of course, any property without liberty. And, however benighted that proposition may seem today, it holds promise of return as a fundamental concept of American society. What is changing is not the recognition of property as an inherent aspect of personality, but the concept of property itself. The new kinds of rights to be asserted by an individual against other individuals and, more important, against the state will be recognized as property rights whose infringement will also be considered as violations of the 'Blessings of Liberty', which the Constitution was framed to protect.

Implicit and explicit in the Constitution, then, were protections for the interests of property as they were then defined—the definition has forever been changing. The rules against impairment of contracts, against taking of property without compensation, against state bankruptcy laws, etc.—the list is extensive—were all for the purpose of protecting what modern contemners of the Constitution call the creditor and landed classes. What these erstwhile historians forget is that the society of which they speak was one in which equality as a fact rather than an imposed rule of law was great: the economic society was an open one, even when one recognizes the advantages that accrued from provident

forefathers who had acquired strategic realty or entered on flourishing commercial enterprises.

It is, therefore, not surprising that in terms of giving meaning to the new Constitution, the problems that arose during the Federalist period were not problems of civil liberties, except insofar as civil liberties may be deemed to include rights of property. A catalogue of the Supreme Court's constitutional opinions between the new nation's founding and the Civil War is one of constitutional protection afforded property rights or of decisions between two claimants to those rights. Even the appalling Dred Scott decision was concerned with the issue of property, the issue of one man's property in another man. The right to do business free of government restraint was the primary claim brought to the Court, and the Court, by one device or another—the Commerce Clause in the New York steamship case, the Contract Clause in the Dartmouth College case, the Necessary and Proper Clause in the Bank of United States cases, and so on—framed the Constitution to protect that claim.

When the Fourteenth Amendment, after the Civil War, added a proscription against state action as well, in terms of protection against deprivation of life, liberty, and property without due process of law, an even more effective weapon was handed to the Supreme Court for the protection of business interests. At a time when the industrial state was burgeoning, the Court lent great *f 4* support to protect that growth against interference by the nation and the States.

After the Civil War, *laissez-faire* dominated constitutional doctrine. Freedom of contract became the new standard. Laws that furthered such freedom, like those that forbade organization of labor to interfere with the contractual relations between the laborer and the employer, were valid under the terms of the evolving Constitution. But laws that inhibited freedom of contract, like *p 130–1* those specifying minimum wages or maximum hours, were found *(4, 5)* to violate the terms of the basic document. Zoning laws were improper interferences with a man's right to use his property. So were building codes, except after catastrophes like the Chicago fire, the San Francisco earthquake, and the Triangle Shirt Factory fire. The courts were always pragmatic and the Supreme Court had forgotten, if it ever knew, that Mill contended that the concept of liberty did not include the power to contract away that liberty.

As was always the case with the American Constitution, the interpretation was not fixed and unwavering. Decisions did permit price-fixing for businesses affected with a public interest, primarily utilities and their equivalents. But the rate-making was made subordinate to Supreme Court review to assure that the stockholders, however watered their shares, received a 'fair return' on their investments. Essentially, however, the Court thought that government regulation of business activities was unnatural and, therefore, unconstitutional. If such regulation was indulged by the States, it violated the Fourteenth Amendment's protections against infringement of life, liberty, or property without due process of law. If attempted by the nation, it was found to be beyond the powers specifically granted by the Constitution and an invasion of those that the Tenth Amendment reserved to the States and the people. (It must have been the people because they were not allowed to the States.)

Certainly there were exceptions: the police power, the power to protect the citizens' health and safety and welfare was occasionally invoked to justify legislation to those ends. But, except where political organizations with these goals became dominant, which was not a frequent occurrence, the legislatures were little more amenable to state control of business—monopolies excluded—than were the courts who struck down the little legislation that was passed.

The third Constitution

All this was changed by the crisis of the Great Depression and what has followed. A Constitution that had provided a barrier to government interference with business activities suddenly became, without a single word in the document being changed, a license for such laws—a license not only to the States but to the national government as well. The Tenth Amendment became a dead letter and the Fourteenth Amendment was read as if the word property had been all but deleted from the due process clause.

Professor Edward S. Corwin put the proposition of change in this way:

> Whereas the [earlier] period was marked by the concept of the priority of the rights of property, the decades immediately following [1935] have been distinguished by a restoration of emphasis on the rights of persons and an increasing disposition on the part of the Court to invalidate legislation, not on substantive grounds, but rather in terms of governmental infringement with the basic liberties protected by the Constitution.

It is doubtful that there was a 'restoration of emphasis', as Corwin suggests. The development of non-property rights of persons was essentially a new enterprise.

The decline of Federalism and the end of judicial restraint of national government power over economic affairs marked the beginning of the new constitutional period, the era of the service state. All of a sudden, the 'general welfare' became a concern of the central authority and the Court was not prepared to interfere. Social security, labor legislation, bank laws, farm production, the securities market, you name it, the government in Washington would regulate it. And what they could not achieve directly, they could effect by so-called 'grants-in-aid'. The power of the purse, based on the power to tax, was as effective as direct legislation.

One consequence was the vast increase in government. An extraordinary proportion of the American populace became dependent for its livelihood either directly or indirectly on the governments, national, state, and local. Even more important, almost no area of life was left unaffected by government regulation. From birth control to death certificates, an American's life had become the constant subject of government power. If we had not yet reached Orwell's 1984, we were well on the road.

The Constitution, however, specifically recognized that tyranny consisted of inhibitions on freedom of speech and press; of established churches and restraints on the non-established; of unreasonable searches and seizures; of cruel and unusual punishments; of deprivation of the privilege against self-crimination; of suspension of the writ of *habeas corpus*; of denial of bail and speedy trials and jury trials; of a myriad things, at least some of which could be summed up as deprivation of life, liberty, or property without due process of law. And as the government began to mushroom, so did some of the safeguards that the framers wrote into the Constitution start to come into play.

In the days of John Marshall, the Court decided that the Bill of Rights inhibited only national action and not state action and the decision, as a reading of legislative intention, was a sound one. In the 1880s, the Court decided that the due process clause of the Fourteenth Amendment was essentially a ban on substantive economic legislation, and the reading was an unsound one. By the 1920s, the Court began to find that some of the Bill of Rights was indeed applicable to the states through the Fourteenth Amendment. And by the 1970s, it was difficult to find the protections of the Bill of Rights that were not held to be so applicable.

There were problems with this development. Essentially, it placed on the weakest branch the obligation to inhibit the strongest branches of the government, not merely in matters that affect the purse but in matters that are frequently regarded as basic to the survival of the nation. One man's free speech is another's seditious treason. One man's privilege against self-crimination is a threat to another's safety. The press can be protected by the courts, at least for a while; but the courts cannot make the press responsible, which is the only reason for its freedom. Safeguards of criminal procedure are to some only trivial technicalities that permit criminals to escape the punishment of the law.

The most basic of our freedoms, freedom of speech and press, have been critical problems in this country's past only when it believed itself threatened by foreign enemies. The Alien and Sedition Laws were limitations imposed on those who were thought to be in league with an enemy country. The Palmer raids and anti-syndicalist and anti-Communist laws between the two World Wars saw foreign power as the danger. So, too, with the McCarthy era after World War II. To the extent that protection from harassment was necessary, the courts provided it, if somewhat timidly. They recognized their own limitations. Today's American

'*The Rising of the Usurpers and the sinking of the liberties of the people*' —a protest by Thomas Nast in 1889 against the control exercised over the '*necessaries of life*' by the trusts. Monopolies flourished and the Court upheld '*laissez-faire*', refusing to apply regulation to big business. The cartoon shows a blindfolded Statue of Liberty, with the foundered vessel of the '*People*' at her feet. (4)

problem is that we now believe, with some cause, that we are always the object of foreign attack. Restraints to preserve the nation from a foreign enemy will always be more acceptable than those that are limitations on domestic wrongdoers.

The last part of the 20th century, however, has also brought a new self-styled enemy of government: those who demand more government services with less government control. They are the enemy because they see that a system that connects government authority with government beneficence cannot tolerate the freedom without responsibility that is every man's dream and no man's reality but some men's foolishness. The threat that these nihilists bring to contemporary United States is not that their views will prevail, but that in preventing their foolishness, the government may repress and destroy freedoms that we all now enjoy. The courts alone cannot preserve our constitutional liberties against an assault not only by those who detest them but invoke them, but also by those who purport to revere them but would dispense with them in dealing with the dissidents.

When this country was in the depths of a war, when men were dying not only that others might live, but that others might live in liberty, Judge Learned Hand delivered a speech on 'I Am an American Day', 21 May 1944, to a large gathering who were to take their oaths of American citizenship. His speech was entitled 'The Spirit of Liberty', and it epitomized the provision in the constitutional preamble that asserted that one purpose for which

147

WHAT DID YOU SAY YOUR NAME IS?

723-411-606

After the Great Depression, Government legislation was introduced to control almost every sphere of individual life. This cartoon referring to the Social Security Act of 1935 suggests that the US citizen had become depersonalized and reduced to a number. (5)

the Constitution was framed was 'to secure the Blessings of Liberty to ourselves and our posterity'. Judge Hand said this:

We have gathered here to affirm a faith, a faith in a common purpose, a common conviction, a common devotion. Some of us have chosen America as the land of our adoption; the rest have come from those who did the same. . . . We sought liberty; freedom from oppression, freedom from want, freedom to be ourselves. . . . What do we mean when we say that first of all we seek liberty? I often wonder whether we do not rest our hopes too much upon constitutions, upon laws and upon courts. These are false hopes; believe me, these are false hopes. Liberty lies in the hearts of men and women; when it dies there, no constitution, no law, no court can save it; no constitution, no law, no court can even do much to help it. While it lies there it needs no constitution, no law, no court to save it. And what is this liberty which must lie in the hearts of men and women? It is not the ruthless, unbridled will; it is not freedom to do as one likes. This is the denial of liberty, and leads straight to its overthrow. A society in which men recognize no check upon their freedom soon becomes a society where freedom is the possession of only a savage few; as we have learned to our sorrow.

What then is the spirit of liberty? I cannot define it; I can only tell you my own faith. The spirit of liberty is the spirit which is not too sure that it is right; the spirit of liberty is the spirit which seeks to understand the minds of other men and women; the spirit of liberty is the spirit which weighs their interests against its own without bias; the spirit of liberty remembers that not even a sparrow falls to earth unheeded; the spirit of liberty is the spirit of Him who, near two thousand years ago, taught mankind that lesson it has never learned, but has never quite forgotten; that there may be a kingdom where the least shall be heard and considered side by side with the greatest.

This essay—and it is only an essay—should end at this point. After Judge Hand's words, anything must be anticlimax. But if the lesson of this essay is that law, even constitutional law, is not the master of a society but its servant, then the clearest of the examples is yet to be stated. The relationship between the black and white races in this country is the essential flaw in the history of American liberty; for it gives the lie not only to the Declaration of Independence but to the ambitions of the Constitution itself. It is the flaw that once almost caused the foundering of the nation and the flaw that may yet rend asunder what remains, I believe, the world's greatest hope for a free society, an open society in a world that tolerates very few such societies.

It is perhaps noteworthy that, of all Americans, it is the blacks whose forefathers did not choose to come here but were brought against their will. And so, contrary to Judge Hand, of all Americans, the blacks cannot be seen as immigrants or the children of immigrants. For neither they nor their ancestors came to this country for a freedom that they could not secure elsewhere. The problem of the two races has been the cross that this country has been required to bear from the beginning.

Those who noted the realities of the problem from an early perspective in our history were gloomy about their predictions. In 1835, Tocqueville anticipated the problem with which the country is now faced: 'If ever America undergoes great revolutions, they will be brought about by the presence of the black race on the soil of the United States, that is to say, they will owe their origins, not to the equality but to the inequality of condition.' His analysis was cogent:

As long as the Negro remains a slave, he may be kept in a condition not far removed from that of the brutes; but with his liberty he cannot but acquire a degree of instruction that will enable him to appreciate his misfortunes and to discern a remedy for them. Moreover, there exists a singular principle of relative justice which is firmly implanted in the human heart. Men are much more forcibly struck by those inequalities which exist within the same class than by those which may be noted between different classes. One can understand slavery, but how allow several millions of citizens to exist under a load of eternal infamy and hereditary wretchedness? . . .

As soon as it is admitted that the whites and the emancipated blacks are placed upon the same territory in the situation of two foreign communities, it will be readily understood that there are but two chances for the future: the Negroes and the whites must either wholly part or wholly mingle. . . . I do not believe that the white and black races will ever live in any country upon an equal footing. But I believe the difficulty to be still greater in the United States than elsewhere.

Tocqueville's doleful prediction was shared, as he told us, by Thomas Jefferson, who wrote:

Nothing is more clearly written in the book of destiny than the emancipation of the blacks; and it is equally certain, that the two races will never live in a state of equal freedom under the same government, so insurmountable are the barriers which nature, habit, and opinion have established between them.

And yet it is clear that the very life of the American nation is dependent upon disproving the predictions of these early thinkers. Or, at least, dependent on achieving one of the two alternatives proffered by Tocqueville: 'the Negroes and the whites must . . . wholly mingle.' The second half of the 20th century in the United States has witnessed the mighty effort of the law, through the Constitution itself, to provide the grounds for that achievement. For the first time in American history, it is recognized that all legal barriers to the intermingling of the white and black races are invalid. The Supreme Court can change the law; but it can change the law only to the extent that its decrees will be followed. For the Court's is the power of persuasion and not the power of coercion. In this regard, it can act as the conscience of a nation, but of a nation whose conscientious scruples, in this area, have too long been buried from sight. p 140 (30)

There are those who reject the Court's actions toward settlement of the racial problem as too little. They should recognize that three centuries of disabilities cannot be compensated for by fiat or eliminated by pretending that there are no disabilities consequent upon this history. There are those who condemn the Court's actions as too much. They, in turn, ignore not only the letter but the spirit of the Constitution and they reject the Holmesian formula that the solution for most of the problems of a society is for that society to become more civilized.

Law is of the essence of American society. It is being tested to its limits, and perhaps beyond, by two problems that are difficult if not insoluble. For the first time, American liberty is threatened because of a danger to American society from within rather than from without the country. For the first time, the country is being forced to face up to what Gunnar Myrdal so aptly termed 'The American Dilemma'. These are not issues that will be resolved either by the substance or machinery of the laws; the laws will, however, respond to the wishes of the American people. When the people choose, we shall likely enter upon our fourth constitutional period. It will be a period of liberty and equality, if we choose well; it will be one of repression and chaos if we choose badly.

VII
SOCIETY, INEQUALITY AND MANNERS

The new aristocracies of success

WALTER MUIR WHITEHILL

*'While in Europe the mutual entertainments of
an inherently stable upper class create society,
in New York the constant contortions
of Society are indispensable to create and maintain
a precarious upper class.'*

RALPH PULITZER

The new society

envisaged by the early colonists and proclaimed in the Declaration of Independence soon bred a new 'society'. The word in this sense implies a structure, and structure implies inequality. American society was a copy of European but with a fundamental difference. In the early days, inherited wealth and family meant less than they had in the Old World. The 'aristocracy' tended to be one of accomplishment and the distance between the extremes was neither so great nor so impassable. European visitors, during the late 18th and early 19th centuries, commonly praise the culture and manners of their American hosts, but within certain limits. Sir Augustus Foster, shortly before 1812, wrote of the 'very

pleasant evening parties' to which he was invited in Washington. 'Compared with the society of many an English provincial town, I confess I thought they were seen to much advantage.'

Henry Sargent's painting *The Dinner Party* (opposite) belongs to the following decade, but the English atmosphere is still there. It is the Boston milieu to which the artist himself belonged, comfortable, respectable but without pretensions to high gentility. The decoration is fashionably Neo-classical, and the details of costume, furniture tableware—down to the wine bottles in their case under the table—provide an inventory of contemporary taste and manners. (1)

Europe transplanted: the social history of America consists of an evolution, during the 18th and 19th centuries, from a purely European way of life to one unique to America. Below: the Sargent family, 1800, with English-style clothes and furniture. Right: the Haven family of Massachusetts, about seventy years later. The scene now, set on a characteristic veranda, is unmistakably American. (2, 3)

England and Holland mingle in the architectural styles of 18th-century New York (above). This view of 1797 looks down Broad Street towards Wall Street; the building at the end is Federal Hall. (4)

Spain was recreated in the early villages of New Mexico, and they remain astonishingly Spanish to this day. Right: the adobe village of Chimayó. (6)

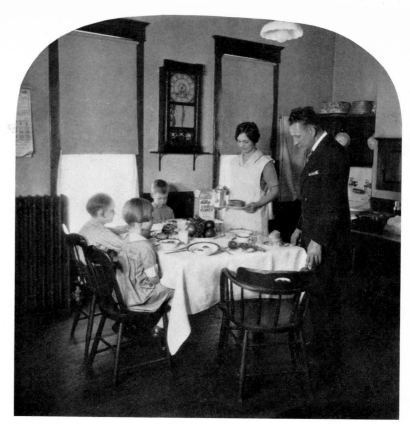

The American way of life defined: in the 1920s a series of 'Citizenship Lessons' was produced for the benefit of immigrants by the Keystone View Company – stereo cards showing how a model American (lower middle class, married, three children) spent his day. This is breakfast, a meal consisting partly of packaged cereals, eaten in the kitchen. (7)

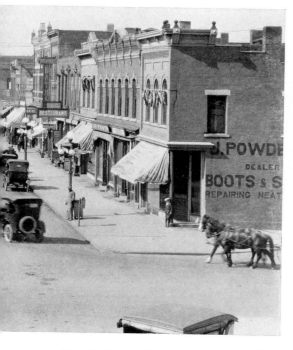

Small town America soon had its own style and atmosphere, conditioned by rapid commercial expansion, grid-planning and *ad hoc* building. The main street was typically straight and wide and lined with shops, hotels and restaurants. Rochester, Minnesota, is seen here (above) in the 1920s; the automobile is already posing a parking problem. (5)

As commuter living becomes the pattern for most Americans, suburbs multiply round the cities — neither town nor country, often neither picturesque nor efficient. Right: residential Los Angeles, 1971. (8)

Social gatherings, are endlessly varied, and yet each epoch produces its own highly characteristic forms. Above: New England picnic to mark the Fourth of July, about 1845. (9)

Roller-skating (left), late 19th century – a typically American combination of exercise, ingenuity and fun. (10)

The speakeasy (right) represented a low social ebb, when prohibition tended to make gourmet conviviality into something illicit and sordid. (12)

The State Fair (above right: Des Moines, Iowa) was the social event of the year in farming areas – both meeting-place and agricultural show. (11)

Money became the key, the symbol and the challenge of social success, and America provided a full exegesis of how fortunes could be made, displayed and spent. **John Adams** (below left), who entered Harvard in 1751, represents the first generation of 'the aristocracy of accomplishment' that replaced in the colonies the English aristocracy of birth. **Amos Lawrence** (below center) made his money in Boston from 1807 onwards in drygoods and textile production, founding a mill-town. **Mrs Potter Palmer** (below right) belonged to the later part of the century, when business had moved west, to Chicago. The wife of a department store tycoon, she threw herself into improving the position of women and collecting works of art. A 20th-century phenomenon was the newspaper millionaire, **William Randolph Hearst** (right). Hearst sat with his mistress, Marion Davies, on his right, at a luncheon party given for Hollywood celebrities in 1930. Note, amidst the splendour, the sauce bottle on the table. (13–15, 18)

Wealth moved west throughout the 19th century. In the 1880s in San Francisco the upper slopes became fashionable, particularly the district known, because of its concentration of mansions, as Nob Hill. Above: the Stanford and Hopkins houses, two creators of the Central and Southern Pacific Railroads. (16)

Imitation Renaissance palaces expressed the cultural ambitions of their owners. Above: the Astor House, Fifth Avenue, New York, by Richard Morris Hunt. Like other present-day galleries and museums J. P. Morgan's Library (left, with Morgan's portrait over the fireplace), containing priceless European treasures, began as the private collection of a rich man. (17, 19)

The American home has been, and continues to be, open to technical innovations of all kinds. Coal-gas, used early in the century for street lighting, was becoming common for interiors (right) in the 1870s and 80s. The advertisement for a washing machine (below) dates from 1869. (20, 21)

The heroism of ordinary life (below). Andrew Carnegie sponsored prizes for heroism. *Puck,* in 1904, suggested that surmounting the hazards of everyday living in the American city deserved such an award. (22)

THE MIDNIGHT HERO.

THE KITCHEN HERO.

THE EIGHT-HOUR OPERA HERO.

THE SUBURBAN VARIETY.

PERSONALLY CONDUCTED HEROES.

THE PREDIGESTED HERO.

HEROES OF THE STRAP.

HEROES À LA BROOKLYN.

THE HEROIC SUMMER HERO.

RECOGNITION AT LAST.

The ultimate in mechanized living is the experiment at Coral Gables, Florida, being developed under the aegis of Westinghouse Electric Corporation. The old kitchen has gone, to be replaced by a 'food preparation center' operated by a control panel. (24)

Leisure in the 20th century is in danger of becoming as standardized as work. Since the mass of people can now afford amusements from which they were previously barred, mass-production has stepped in to provide them. Above: eating at one of the roadside restaurants that have sprung up in response to American mobility. Right: to enable more people to enjoy high society by the sea, Miami beach is now packed with nearly indistinguishable luxury hotels. (23, 25)

The constituents of 'Americanness' are infinite and are constantly shifting and changing. On these two pages we show four tiny facets from those that together make up the great mosaic of America: the snack-meal, 'spectator sport', popular culture, and the automobile.

The drugstore with soda fountain was a purely American creation, a combination of pharmacy and quick, informal eatery. Above: the interior of Collins Pharmacy at Islip, Long Island, in 1900. This period also saw the invention of the Automat (right, 1903), a self-service restaurant with coin-in-the-slot machines. The drugstore itself diversified yet further to make a whole range of goods available under one roof, until the modern drugstore (below, at Lafayette, Louisiana) is hardly distinguishable from a supermarket. (26–28)

Football has become a powerful ritual, a focus of emotions and loyalties. Below: the band of Ohio State University spells out 'Ohio' while playing a college song during half-time. (29)

The rise of the automobile has probably altered the face of America more than any other single recent factor. In seventy years it developed from an amusing plaything to an uncontrollable giant. Right: the days of motoring chivalry, 1914. 'Why! Good afternoon! Yes, it is a shame. He should have fixed that before we came.' Horse and buggy win the girl. By the thirties (center: billboard on Highway 99), the automobile was a symbol of the good of life. By the mid century, it had produced the superhighway and the suburban 'shopping-center' (below), was drawing away population, and was changing the character of urban life. (31–33)

WORLD'S HIGHEST STANDARD OF LIVING

There's no way like the American Way

Art in the backwoods: this mobile museum (above) was sponsored by the Virginia Museum of Fine Arts in Richmond to circulate in remote areas of Virginia. (30)

ART MUSEUM

Landscape cherished, landscape desecrated. America was the first nation to conceive the idea of national parks. The valley of the Yellowstone River in Wyoming has been kept in its natural state since the Hayden Survey (pp. 19–20) a century ago. Here tourists watch the ever-predictable performance of the geyser 'Old Faithful'. But where nature is unprotected waste-products spread pollution at an alarming rate. Below: automobile wrecks abandoned in the desert near Shoshone, California. (34, 35)

The new aristocracies of success

WALTER MUIR WHITEHILL

A GOOD CENTURY before the first English settlers founded James-town, Virginia, in 1607, Spaniards were busily conquering the New World. Methodically they reproduced the physical and archi-tectural setting, as well as the bureaucracy of Spanish life in the more remote and improbable reaches of the Americas. Whether in Santa Fé, New Mexico, or Bogotá, Colombia, the principal church, the *plaza mayor*, the municipal buildings stand in a relation to each other and to the mountains rising behind them that makes their derivations from the homeland instantly and abundantly clear. And when one sees high in the Andes just such a colonial bridge crossing a stream as might be found in Castile—complete with grandiloquent inscription setting forth the builder and the reign of some distant Most Christian Majesty—one realizes how far the Spanish Empire perpetuated the systematic habits of its Roman predecessor. Thus in Texas, New Mexico, Arizona, and California there are buildings that continue the tradition of this Spanish imperial conquest, often in a landscape strongly reminiscent of the Castilian plateau. If one visits the church at Chimayó, New Mexico, as I did on a January day in 1966, and finds the *señor cura parroco* and his sacristan, enjoying the afternoon winter's sun on a bench outside the church, smoking cigarettes, and watching a big dog and a big goose solemnly and alternately chase each other across the *plaza*, one seems to be in Spain rather than in the United States.

Reflections of Europe in the wilderness

Much of the Atlantic seaboard from New England to Georgia was once as English as Chimayó still is Spanish. Although greater density of population in eastern states has obliterated all but a few colonial survivals, there are still striking resemblances between the old and the New Englands. In 1934 I crossed the Thames at Gravesend one day, after visiting the burial place in St George's Church of Pocahontas, daughter of the Indian king Powhatan, who had married the English settler John Rolfe, was brought by him to England in 1616, created a London sensation as *la belle sauvage*, only to die of tuberculosis late in March of the following year, as she was on the point of embarking for her native Virginia. On my way to the spare and grim little 7th-century church of St Peter at Bradwell-on-Sea, I soon found myself in an unfamiliar part of Essex. What struck me incidentally but all the more forcibly was the number of wooden clapboarded buildings with gabled or gambrel roofs that resembled the earliest surviving dwellings in Essex County, Massachusetts. I subsequently found that Martin S. Briggs had devoted his *The Homes of the Pilgrim Fathers in England and America (1620–1685)* to demonstrating the close kinship between the 17th-century timber houses of New England and those of certain parts of south-east England. Briggs's drawing of a street of wooden houses might almost be mistaken for a part of a New England coastal town, were it not plainly labeled as Great Wakering, Essex, while his drawing of a cottage at Kingsbury Green, Middlesex, takes one into the world of the Parson Capen House in Topsfield, Massachusetts, or the Paul Revere house in Boston. From early 19th-century engravings of buildings now destroyed, like Benjamin Franklin's birthplace, one can readily see how much the 17th-century Boston that has disappeared resembled some English counterparts that have survived. That is what one would expect, for Englishmen have generally shown strong resis-

tance to 'going native'. Just as the first British soldiers in India continued to wear busbies in defiance of climate and vulgar con-venience, and their civilian brethren, both in Africa and the Far East, kept up many of the formalities of the Victorian boarding house, so the Puritan Englishmen who came to the Massachusetts Bay from 1630 onward, reproduced, to the best of their resources, and abilities, the houses and surroundings with which they were most familiar.

Carl Bridenbaugh in *Cities in the Wilderness* and *Cities in Revolt* has recorded the manner in which Boston, Newport, New York, Philadelphia, and Charleston rapidly evolved from wilderness settlements to be the metropolises of the British North American colonies. For want of any other means of supporting themselves, Bostonians early turned to the sea, and by the second half of the 17th century had achieved respectable maritime commerce, intimately bound to the city of London. By the end of the century the tonnage of Boston shipping was exceeded only by that of London and Bristol. Boston was the largest place in British North America until the middle of the 18th century, when it fell behind the faster growing ports of Philadelphia and New York. As Boston is the oldest British settlement in North America that has continuously retained the character of an urban seaport through which newcomers have entered, it will provide numerous specific examples that are pertinent to this chapter.

The sea is a hard master, but it can bring fortunes, which in their turn diminish equality. Thus within a few decades of the first settlement, some recent English immigrants in New England were a great deal richer than others. Goods 'lately come from London', as colonial advertisers phrased it, found a ready sale in Boston. Daniel Neal, in his *History of New England*, published in London in 1720, wrote: 'Conversation in Boston is as polite as in most of the Cities and Towns in England, many of their Merchants having travell'd into Europe, and those that stay at home having the Advantage of free Conversation with the Travellers; so that a Gentleman from London would almost think himself at home at Boston, when he observes the numbers of people, their Houses, their Furniture, their Tables, their Dress and Conversation, which, perhaps is as splendid and showy, as that of the most considerable Tradesmen in London.' Note the comparison to 'that of the most considerable *Tradesmen* in London'. This is not aristocracy in the traditional European sense, but neither is it communal egalitarian-ism. Some English immigrants had clearly moved faster and further than others.

The sea provided a ladder that the ambitious and daring colonial New Englander might climb. A boy in his teens might ship before the mast, for want of an easier future, with the possibility of rising to command and eventually establishing himself ashore as a merchant. Many did in the first two centuries of Massachusetts, and at a speed that in these days seems incredible.

A certain number of people went back and forth between New England and England for reasons of trade, politics, or family ties. Some had surprising histories, like Governor John Winthrop's nephew, George Downing. Born in the British Isles in 1625, he went to school at Maidstone in Kent before coming to New England with his parents in 1638. He entered the newly founded Harvard College, took his bachelor's degree with the first class in 1642 and

p 152 (3)
p 202–3

152 (4)

f 1

f 2

A 17th-century American timber house could easily be mistaken for its English counterpart. The cottage at Kingsbury Green Middlesex (above), and a Colonial house such as Paul Revere's in Boston (below), are both constructed with overhanging upper storeys and clapboard sidings. (1,2)

George Downing's name to the street which has long contained the residence of the Prime Minister. Thus the address 10 Downing Street owes its origin to a member of the first class to be graduated from Harvard College.

John Davie, of the Harvard class of 1681, returned to England through the good fortune of inheritance. One day in 1707, while hoeing corn barefoot on his farm in Groton, Connecticut, Davie received word that he had inherited a baronetcy, 'which Honor', as Judge Samuel Sewall reported in his diary, 'is supported with an Estate of Four or Five Thousand pound per annum.' The new baronet promptly returned to England where he settled on his inherited property, becoming eventually high sheriff of Devon. Although he stayed in England until his death in 1727, Sir John Davie sent books to the Yale Library in 1713 and only sold his Connecticut farm in 1722.

But for every colonist who returned to England permanently, there were many who made brief journeys for medical study, religious improvement, political preferment, or the simple desire to see the great world. A few of the sons of the more influential Virginia tobacco planters, rather than attending their own College of William and Mary, matriculated at Oxford or Cambridge. But for every one of these travelers, there were hundreds who, for lack of funds or inclination, never budged from the colonies. Henry Adams (c. 1583–1646), the American progenitor of a remarkable family with a passion for keeping documents, was a first settler of Braintree, Massachusetts, but as L. H. Butterfield, Editor-in-Chief of *The Adams Papers*, has observed, 'for more than a century after 1639 there remain only a few wills, deeds, receipts, printed fast-day proclamations, and scraps of correspondence to document the history of a family of farmers, maltsters, and holders of town offices who lived their lives below the level of historical scrutiny.' The first of the family to return to England, or indeed, to stray far from Braintree, was the settler's great-great-grandson, John Adams, the second President of the United States. It was only in October 1783, a few weeks after he had signed the definitive treaty of peace with Great Britain in Paris, that John Adams set foot in England. Although he 'was never before so Sea sick' as in crossing the straits of Dover on 23 October, and found London expensive, he noted in his diary concerning his lodging at Osborne's Adelphi Hotel that 'the Rooms and furniture are more to my taste than in Paris, because they are more like what I have been used to in America'. What John Adams had 'been used to in America', that is the architecture and furniture of New England of the decades immediately preceding the Revolution, had been English in origin or inspiration. Some of the household effects that to him seemed right and proper had doubtless 'lately come from London', as the newspaper advertisers represented. More had been made on the spot, for over one hundred and fifty cabinetmakers, chair-makers, and carvers had been active in Boston prior to the Revolution, but their object was to duplicate, as best they could with what they had, the amenities of the more elegant world overseas.

Although some colonial Anglican parish churches, like Christ Church (1723) and King's Chapel (1750) in Boston would have passed muster creditably enough in the British Isles, most colonial houses were on a smaller scale and built of simpler materials than their English Georgian contemporaries. Suitable details like pilasters and Palladian windows there were in abundance, but brick, clapboards, or wood sanded and painted in imitation of stone, were the normal building material for façades, while indoors wall-papers made do in place of tapestries. Down to 1775 most colonists reproduced English life as best they could. With the American Revolution all this changed. 'Home' was now in North America rather than in the British Isles. A number of colonists, loyal to the Crown, including some of the most stylish, decamped for good to Halifax and England, leaving places to be filled by new men, who had risen from the obscurity of the farm by way of revolutionary military or political service, or through successful ventures at sea. But the British tradition died hard. Sir Augustus John Foster, British Minister to Washington just before the War of 1812, noted the gentlemen—'all good English names'—who 'feasted us in their turn, or had occasionally very pleasant evening parties. Compared with the society of many an English provincial town, I confess I thought they were seen to much advantage.'

p 156 (13)

p 151 (

settled down for a few years as a tutor 'to read to the Junior pupills as the President shall see fit'. Offering instruction in Harvard College did not hold him for long, as Downing soon made his way back to England, where he found employment on Oliver Cromwell's staff. In 1657 Cromwell made him Minister to Holland. Although his credentials, written by no less a civil servant than John Milton, described him as 'a person of eminent quality', Samuel Pepys called him 'a perfidious rogue'. Downing certainly had the flexibility of the Vicar of Bray, for although Cromwell sent him to Holland, he later represented Charles II (who in 1663 made him a baronet) in the same post. New England saw him no more, although a useful London real estate transaction in the early 1680s gave Sir

Banker and philanthropist George Peabody, who founded the many museums and institutions that bear his name in Great Britain and the United States, distributing prizes for the Working Classes Industrial Exhibition, at the Guildhall, London, in 1866. (3)

American kinds of aristocracy

There are tracts of land in the eastern United States still owned by descendants of those who first settled on them in the 17th and 18th centuries. Sometimes they are being farmed by people who, like the early generations of Adamses, still live their lives 'below the level of historical scrutiny'. In other cases families have remained where their ancestors settled, but have changed their occupations with the times. In the town of North Andover, Massachusetts, where I live, the Stevens family were among the 17th-century founders. Early in the 19th century Captain Nathaniel Stevens (1786–1865), great-great-grandson of the John Stevens who in 1642 became the fifth man to make his home in the town, embarked on the manufacture of woolen goods. Although the present-day firms of M. T. Stevens and Sons Company and J. P. Stevens and Company, Incorporated, have offices in New York City and mills in southern states, the Stevens Mill in North Andover still operates. In 1960 great-grandchildren of Captain Nathaniel Stevens established and endowed the Merrimack Valley Textile Museum in North Andover, an institution preserving objects, books, and manuscripts that record the history of woolen manufacturing in the United States.

But for every family that stayed put, as Stevenses have in North Andover and du Ponts have in Delaware since Eleuthère Irenée du Pont started his powder mill on the Brandywine in 1802, there were many more who moved about looking for something better. If they found what suited them, they put down roots, as did Peter Jefferson at Shadwell. If people had less luck, they kept on going. But when they settled down and prospered, they soon developed manners and social habits that reflected the tastes of Europe. Even the author of the Declaration of Independence, who considered it self-evident 'that all men are created equal', sheltered himself from the weather in the forms of a hierarchical society. Before John Adams went to Harvard College in 1751, no Adams had shown his face conspicuously outside of Braintree; from his time to the present the family has maintained an extraordinary level of national distinction, generation after generation. This is the American

version of aristocracy, an aristocracy of accomplishment, achieved rapidly by conspicuous and intelligent effort, but imposing upon succeeding generations a responsibility quite as binding, and sometimes as hindering, as the traditional aristocracies of Europe.

John Adams in a single generation leaped from agricultural obscurity to national leadership because he went to Harvard College and got some education. This was an outstanding performance by a singularly able man. But in general in the United States not more than three generations separate a man with mud on his boots from a descendant who can move in cultivated company anywhere, provided sufficient education or fortune— preferably a combination of both—has been achieved. Most of the names that one particularly associates with Boston today—Cabot, Lowell, Jackson, Higginson, Peabody, Gardner and the like—are those of Essex County farmers or seamen who moved to Boston after the Revolution to fill the places left vacant by the Loyalist migration.

Just as the first Henry Adams had settled in Braintree and begotten a race of farmers, Francis Peabody, on arrival from England in 1635, had done the same in Essex County. Through the 17th and 18th centuries, Peabodys, like Adamses, were farmers, deacons, militia officers, hog-reeves, and fence-viewers, unknown beyond their town boundaries. Then during the Revolution, Joseph Peabody, born in 1757, went privateering, and with his prize money took a winter off to improve his scanty reading and writing. He went back to sea, rose to command, came ashore to a counting house, and by his death in 1844 was the principal East India merchant of Salem. His distant cousin, George Peabody, born in 1795, by an even more remarkable metamorphosis, wound up in London as an international banker and the great philanthropist of the third quarter of the 19th century. Joseph had started as a simple farm drudge; George's career began by his sweeping out the general store in South Danvers and peddling from a pack on his back. As George never married, his name survives through the numerous museums and philanthropic endeavors that he endowed in England and the United States in the 1850s and 1860s. These

p 156
(13)

f 3

were of such repute that Victor Hugo remarked of George Peabody that 'having had a place near Rothschild, he found means to change it for one near St Vincent de Paul'. Among the numerous descendants of Joseph Peabody one finds not only bankers, businessmen and trustees, as one might expect, but Harvard professors, the founder of Groton School, an Episcopal bishop, and a Governor of Massachusetts.

In succeeding generations, manufacturing supplemented maritime commerce as a means of rapid social mobility. Amos Lawrence, a farmer's boy who came from Groton to Boston in 1807, went into the drygoods business with his younger brother, Abbott Lawrence, and soon reached as a commission merchant the state of comfortable success that is indicated by Chester Harding's huge portrait of him (in Paisley dressing gown) now in the National Gallery in Washington. The Lawrence brothers moved from importing to manufacturing textiles; the mill city of Lawrence, Massachusetts—created in the 1840s along the Merrimack River—bears their family name. Abbott Lawrence later in life became Minister to the Court of St James's and, incidentally, the grandfather of Abbott Lawrence Lowell, President of Harvard University. The energy and ability that these brothers and their sons put into mercantile and manufacturing pursuits was turned in the third generation to the service of the church, for Amos Lawrence's grandson, William, began to study for the ministry immediately after his graduation from Harvard College in 1871. His first parish was in Lawrence, which unlovely city he tried to improve. From 1893 until 1925 William Lawrence was Bishop of Massachusetts. Indeed election to the episcopate has become an occupational hazard in the family, for both of Bishop Lawrence's sons, as well as one of his sons-in-law, have been bishops in Massachusetts.

p 156 (14)

The instances cited of social mobility among New Englanders of English ancestry have been drawn from families whose progenitors emigrated in the 17th century. With national groups that came here two hundred and more years later one can almost see the process in action. President Kennedy's grandfather, Patrick Joseph Kennedy, born in East Boston of parents who had fled the Irish potato famine a decade earlier, began as a longshoreman, became by his own efforts the owner of saloons and a coal business, the founder of a bank, a state representative and senator, as well as the ward boss of East Boston. He enjoyed a reputation for honesty, fairness, and general decency. P. J. Kennedy's son, Joseph P. Kennedy, born in 1888, went to the Boston Latin School and Harvard College. After a meteoric business career, in which he had made a great fortune in the same rough-and-tumble familiar to men of English origins a few generations earlier, he followed in the steps of John Adams, John Quincy Adams, Charles Francis Adams, and Abbott Lawrence by becoming Ambassador to the Court of St James's in 1937. Among Joseph P. Kennedy's eight children one became the Marchioness of Hartington, and three were United States senators, one of whom also served as the first Catholic President of the United States.

p 91 (32)

The past three generations of the Kennedy family simply indicate that the descendants of Irish immigrants fleeing the potato famine, given the right combination of ambition, ability, education, and opportunity, can and do follow the same pattern as the descendants of English Puritan immigrants who put the ocean between themselves and the Church of England. It is simply a matter of time rather than of inherent difference. It should be remembered that the candidates opposing each other in the 1968 election for the vice-presidency of the United States were the American-born sons of men who had emigrated from Greece and Poland in the present century.

American kinds of inequality

Samuel Eliot Morison once observed: 'In 1860 the average American was a land-owning yeoman farmer; since 1900 he has been an employee.' In the Colonial period, farming and seafaring were the principal occupations of nearly all Americans. We have noted earlier how Lawrences, Stevenses, and the like, turned successfully from farming to textile manufacturing in the first quarter of the 19th century. While large industrial cities grew up around some major factories, many small New England towns surrounded by fields had a little factory tucked away by a river,

where some specialized product was produced. The manufacture of phaetons, gigs, tinware, joiner's planes, clocks, palm-leaf hats, stoves, scythe-snaths, chairs, and a multitude of other products, gave modest but steady returns in many small communities, without generating the filth and squalor that characterize large industrial cities.

Now and then special circumstances would provide opportunity for a man to prosper beyond such small expectations. Ezra Cornell (1807–1874), the son of a Massachusetts Quaker journeyman potter who had moved west into New York State, left school at seventeen and turned itinerant carpenter. In 1828, when he was twenty-one, he arrived in Ithaca, New York, where he was soon managing a plaster mill. Having lost his job, as a consequence of the panic of 1837, he bought the patent rights of a recently invented double mold-board plow, and walked as far as Maine and Georgia peddling the contraption. In the course of this uncertain activity, he stumbled into the development of the electric telegraph, recently invented by Samuel F. B. Morse, by devising a machine that would dig for, lay, and cover a cable in a single operation. Although telegraph wires eventually went overhead rather than underground, Cornell was in the game sufficiently early to become the largest shareholder in the Western Union Telegraph Company soon after its incorporation in 1856. Thus between 1860 and 1864 his annual income jumped from $15,000 to $140,000, and in 1865 he became, by gift of half a million dollars, the founder and chief benefactor of Cornell University in the Ithaca he had walked into as an itinerant carpenter thirty-seven years earlier.

p 179 (8–10)

The fluid developing economy of American life after the Revolution offered a scene in which even a first-generation immigrant could attain great wealth provided he were alert to opportunities. John Jacob Astor (1763–1848), born in Waldorf, Germany, met on his way to America in 1784 a fellow-immigrant who had traded furs with Indians. Exploiting this opportunity, Astor by the time he was twenty-three had his own shop in New York, and made frequent expeditions to Canada on fur-trading ventures. Within a few years he became the leading factor in the fur trade, accumulating a fortune of $250,000, with which he purchased New York real estate. The Louisiana purchase inspired him to open in 1811 a central depot at the mouth of the Columbia River in Oregon, named Astoria, from which furs collected on the northwest coast would be efficiently shipped to Canton, thereby getting him into the China trade with Europe and America. Although the War of 1812 spoiled this enterprise, and he never succeeded in monopolizing the fur trade, he had by 1834 achieved a fortune of twenty millions, which established him as a financial power in New York City. His son, William Backhouse Astor (1792–1875) expanded the family's Manhattan real estate (including slum tenements) to a point that gained him the title 'the landlord of New York'. John Jacob Astor's holdings, thus enlarged, were long administered by his grandson and namesake (1822–1890), and his great-grandson of the same name (1864–1912). Another great-grandson, William Waldorf Astor (1848–1919), moved to England in 1890 and, having become a British subject, was created Viscount Astor in 1917.

Throughout the 19th century great fortunes were achieved through transportation, the opening of natural resources, and the greatly expanded industrialization that resulted from this combination after the Civil War. The Vanderbilt fortune was based on several forms of transportation. Cornelius Vanderbilt (1794–1877) —descended from a Dutch Van der Bilt who settled on Long Island in the latter half of the 17th century—moved upward and outward from running a ferry between Staten Island and New York into the new coastwise steamboat business in 1829, with vessels plying the Hudson River and Long Island Sound. To meet the demands of the 1849 Gold Rush, he established a line of steamships to California, by way of Nicaragua. In the 1860s he moved into New York railroads; by combining three inefficient lines into the New York Central, he had by 1872 created a single excellent system. Through acquisition of the Lake Shore & Michigan Southern, the Michigan Central, and the Canada Southern roads, he achieved one of the great American networks of transportation. Having started from scratch, Cornelius Vanderbilt left an estate in excess of $100,000,000. His railroad network was carried on and

$28,000 IS PAID FOR A SALT CELLAR

Gem of Ashburnham Collection Brings a Record Price at Christie's.

$30,500 FOR A TOILET SET

MORGAN PAYS $42,800 FOR BOOK AT HOE SALE

Competitive Bidding to the Last for "Le Morte D'Arthur," Translated from the French.

ENORMOUS PRICES FOR OLD FURNITURE

$80,000 FOR A HELMET.
Specimen of Art Bought by Widener, of Philadelphia.

New York, February 26.—P. A. B. Widener, of Philadelphia, it was announced to-day, has acquired the famous Morosini helmet, said to be the finest specimen of its kind, for $80,000, from a firm of art dealers here.

This piece of armor is a product of a time when the making of armory was considered an art of equal importance to painting and sculpture. It belonged to Vincenzo Morosini, one of the most celebrated Venetian patr— the sixteenth century, and

WOMEN SHOW PET DOGS IN WALDORF-ASTORIA

Sawdust Ring Laid Out for Judging in the East Room.

ELEVEN FIRSTS FOR LAWSON.

servant.

HER $15,000 MUFF MISSING.
Mrs. Shainwald of New York Gives Notice to Scotland Yard.

Special Cable to THE NEW YORK TIMES.

$500,000 IN GEMS ON MRS. LEEDS AT PANTOMIME BALL

Maxine Elliott a Statuesque Bluebeard Wife — Craig Wadsworth Appears in Persian Attire.

LADY DIANA MANNERS AS A DANCING COLUMBINE.

Brilliant Processions in Great

GILDED ROOM FOR TOY SPANIEL SHOW

In spite of the philanthropy of men like Carnegie and Rockefeller, who had worked their way up from humble beginnings, the rise of the great tycoons steadily deepened the gulf between rich and poor. These details from 'A Tale of Today', a montage of newspaper clippings in a 'Harper's Weekly' of 1915, provide a telling contrast. Top: the diversions of the rich. Below: a grim story of unemployment, inadequate home and working conditions, and death from exposure and starvation. (4, 5)

DIE OF STARVATION, TOO PROUD TO BEG

Steven Farley and Wife Found When Their Passaic Home Is Broken Into.

HER DEAD BODY IN HIS ARMS

Couple, Once Church Workers, Had Refused Friends' Offers of Aid —Man Long Unemployed.

SAYS LACK OF WORK IS GROWING PROBLEM

Chamberlain Bruere Asks Help of Jewish Women at Emanu-El Mass Meeting.

AGED MEN DIE OF EXPOSURE.
Found Starving in a Farm House in Exeter, R. I.

Providence, R. I., Dec. 20.—After having been found critically ill in a lonely farm house in Exeter, without warmth, food or medicine, Thomas Peckham and Thomas Hazard, both over 80 years of age, died at the home of friends in that village today. The men were found at the Hazard homestead, which is in an isolated part of the village. Both were lying upon the floor, barely conscious. All efforts to revive the sufferers failed and they succumbed to the long ex-

DISTRESS OF POOR REVEALED BY COLD

Thousands Out of Employment Appeal for Food and Shelter.

MANY FAMILIES ASK AID

Charity Workers Report. Unprecedented Conditions Due to Warborn Idleness.

DEPICTS GIRLS' LIFE ON $5 TO $7 A WEEK

Miss Packard Tells Factory Commission How Clerks Feel the Pinch of Poverty.

LUNCH MONEY FOR SUITS

1,500 Men in Bowery Bread Line.

There were 1,500 men in the bread line at the Bowery Mission last night. Of these, 500 were sheltered overnight in the mission with the assurance that they would be fed in the morning. The mission sent 150 men to lodging-houses, 250 men to the University Settlement, 40 men to 155 Clinton Street, the Free Synagogue mission, and others to various other shelters. The mission also got jobs for 100 men to shovel snow.

ENDS LIFE BECAUSE HE COULDN'T FIND WORK

New Haven Man, Only 6 Cents Left, Was Supporting Mother and Sister.

New Haven, Nov. 16.—One of the most pitiful happenings that have come to the attention of the local charity organizations was that which became known this morning, when

expanded by his son William Henry Vanderbilt (1821–85) and grandsons Cornelius Vanderbilt (1843–99) and William Kissam Vanderbilt (1849–1920).

The California gold rush of 1849, which made some men rich almost overnight, underlined the need for a transcontinental railroad. In July 1862 the Pacific Railroad bill was passed by Congress, providing for the construction of the Union Pacific, to start on the one hundredth meridian and run west to connect with the Central Pacific Railroad of California—organized by the 'Big Four'—Collis P. Huntington (1821–1900) and Mark Hopkins, dealers in hardware and mining supplies, and Leland Stanford (1824–93) and Charles Crocker (1822–88), drygoods merchants of Sacramento. The two lines met at Promontory Point, Utah, on 10 May 1869. Once the two coasts were linked, a fever of competitive railway construction began to open up hitherto inaccessible areas of the great West. Congress chartered three other lines, the Northern Pacific, the Southern Pacific, and the Santa Fé, aiding each of them by grants of twenty square miles of public lands for each mile of track constructed. By 1884 all three had reached the Pacific coast. James J. Hill (1838–1916), the greatest of the railroad builders, opened much of the northwest with his Great Northern Railroad by developing the country as his tracks pushed west across the Dakota plains.

Transportation brought the iron orefields of Michigan and Minnesota and the distant coal deposits of Pennsylvania within manageable reach, thus making possible an American iron and steel industry. Andrew Carnegie (1835–1919) at the age of thirty jumped into the iron business in Pittsburgh. By 1873 he was concentrating on steel, to such purpose that in 1889 the steel production of America had passed that of Great Britain. So the glare and smoke of blast furnaces befouled a once clean countryside. In 1900 the profits of the Carnegie Company were $40,000,000, of which $25,000,000 was Carnegie's personal share. A year later he sold his company for $250,000,000 to the United States Steel Corporation, newly formed by the banker John Pierpont Morgan (1837–1913).

Transportation also brought the oil fields of northwestern Pennsylvania within reach of Cleveland, Ohio, where John D. Rockefeller (1839–1937) joined with partners in building a refinery in 1863. By the age of thirty-eight he dominated the fast growing business of piping, refining and marketing American petroleum, and Standard Oil of Ohio, which he had incorporated

p 110–11
(15)

in 1870, held a position close to monopoly. In 1892, as a result of the Sherman Anti-Trust Act, Rockefeller transferred Standard Oil's properties to companies in Ohio, New York, New Jersey, and Indiana, with control of the combination handed over to a holding company. At their highest point, Rockefeller's holdings fell only slightly short of \$900,000,000. Unlike the children of many self-made men, Rockefeller's son, John D. Rockefeller, Jr (1874–1960), and five grandsons have followed distinguished careers in business, philanthropy, and public service.

p 110
(13)

The last third of the 19th century was a period of rapid development and cut-throat competition, leading to great industrial monopolies, as well as to severe business panics. After the panic of 1873, J. P. Morgan, dominant in government financing and corporate reorganizations, including that of railroads, succeeded in restoring faith abroad in American securities. His personal activity was decisive in national recovery from the panics of 1893 and 1907, as well as in forming in 1895 the syndicate that successfully halted the drain of gold reserves from the United States Treasury. The creation of the United States Steel Corporation has been described as one of his 'most daring and imperial undertakings'. This was a period in which powerful individuals carried on their competitive efforts with the nonchalance of Norse gods

p 157
(17)

clouting one another with hammers. It was also the period that turned the average American from farmer to employee.

With vast fortunes, the chasm between rich and poor deepened, even though some of the fortunes were turned to corrective philanthropy. George Peabody, before his death in England in 1869, had founded numerous learned institutions that bear his name in this country and had given \$2,500,000 to build model workingmen's tenements in London. Andrew Carnegie in 1889 published 'The Gospel of Wealth', in which he set forth the theory that the rich man was in reality a 'trustee', holding surplus wealth for the benefit of his fellows. After Carnegie's retirement from business, he put this into practice by giving away not only his income but most of his capital; his benefactions amounted to \$350,000,000, of which \$62,000,000 were allotted to the British Empire and \$288,000,000 to the United States. John D. Rockefeller founded the University of Chicago in 1889 with a gift of \$600,000; ultimately it was to be endowed by himself and his son with over \$80,000,000. It has been estimated that the total of Rockefeller's benefactions in his lifetime reached \$550,000,000, and the whole value of his and his sons' gifts, down to 1955, came to more than two and a half billions.

From the fortunes of this period came also great collections of

f 4, 5

f 3

f 7

p 158
(22)

p 178 (5

A party given by Peter Manigault speaker of the South Carolina Commons House of Assembly, c. 1754. Manigault (left, holding a decanter): 'Your toast, Howarth.' To his left, an officer sings a song; to his right, the artist himself says, 'Pray less noise, Gentlemen.' (6)

works of art that brought objects of the highest quality to the United States from Europe. Although J. P. Morgan was a New Englander, devoted to the Episcopal Church, his combination of forceful action in great matters, combined with the assembly of great works of art, made him resemble a figure of the Italian Renaissance. His Medician qualities may still be seen in the collections of the Metropolitan Museum of Art, and in his magnificent library at 33 East 36th Street, which possesses the greatest holdings of medieval manuscripts outside Europe. Although the Pierpont Morgan Library is now a public scholarly institution, one may still see the superb Renaissance room in which its founder marshaled his forces to quiet the panic of 1907. The Pittsburgh coke and steel manufacturer Henry Clay Frick (1849–1919) assembled a great collection of paintings that are on public display in his New York house. The Pittsburgh banker, Andrew W. Mellon (1855–1937), whose father lent Frick the money that started him in business, became the greatest single national benefactor in this direction. Secretary of the Treasury under Harding, Coolidge, and Hoover, and Ambassador to England, Mellon gave his remarkable collection of paintings, including twenty-one masterpieces from the Hermitage which he acquired after the Russian Revolution, to the Federal government in 1937 as the nucleus of the National Gallery of Art, for which he further provided the building and endowment. His two children, Paul Mellon and the late Mrs Mellon Bruce, continued and enlarged his tradition of imaginative generosity to the arts and the humanities.

p 157
(17)

The national origins and family backgrounds of these 19th-century titans are so varied as to defy any pattern. For example, Andrew Carnegie and John D. Rockefeller both started from scratch. Carnegie, however, was a Scot, brought to the United States at thirteen, while Rockefeller's Germanic ancestors had been settled as farmers in Somerville, New Jersey, since 1722. More than a century later, Rockefeller's father left the New Jersey farm to become an itinerant vendor of patent medicines, moving about from place to place, finally settling in Cleveland. Henry Clay Frick was the son of farmers who had migrated to Pennsylvania in the 18th century; his father's family originally came from Switzerland, his mother's were Mennonites from the Palatinate. Charles M. Schwab (1862–1939), a younger associate of Carnegie, was the grandson of turn-of-the-century German immigrants; while Joseph Pulitzer (1847–1911), who through journalism (*St Louis Post-Dispatch* and *New York World*) exercised considerable influence on the political life and character of the press of this period, was a Jew born in Hungary, who obtained passage to the United States by enlisting in the Union Army in Hamburg, Germany. By contrast, J. P. Morgan was a New Englander of British origins, who did not start from scratch. His father, Junius Spencer Morgan (1813–90), after being in business in Boston and Hartford, went to London in 1854 as a partner in George Peabody's international banking firm, where his son began his career in 1856. After Peabody's retirement, the firm became J. S. Morgan & Co., and in due time, J. P. Morgan & Co. Andrew W. Mellon was also a second-generation banker; his father, Thomas Mellon, brought by his parents from County Tyrone, Ireland, to Pittsburgh in 1818 at the age of five, became a lawyer and a judge, but established a private banking house in 1869.

Transportation, in a new form, achieved one of the great 20th-century fortunes, that of Henry Ford (1863–1947), whose father, William, had left County Cork in 1847 during the Irish potato famine. Henry Ford's mass production of a low-priced automobile changed the face of the United States radically, for the worse, in the course of the 20th century. The Ford Foundation, administering the products of his success, is making imaginative attempts to improve the state of the world in many directions. Established in 1936 by Henry and Edsel Ford as a Michigan philanthropy, it became a national organization in 1950. From resources greatly exceeding those of earlier foundations, it has already committed sums in the neighborhood of three billion dollars to institutions and individuals in all fifty states, the District of Columbia, and seventy-eight foreign countries.

A little over a century ago Ezra Cornell felt himself rich when his annual income had mounted to $140,000. The magazine *Fortune* in November 1957 estimated that 155 individuals in the United States

Andrew Carnegie (1835–1919), born in Scotland, emigrated to the US with his father in 1846. He held strong views on rich men's responsibilities. Here, he holds four of the 2,505 libraries he had endowed by 1918. (7)

were worth $50,000,000 and that 45 of this number had property in excess of $100,000,000. A *Fortune* study of May 1968 suggested that there were 153 individuals then worth $100,000,000 or more, 66 of whom had property in excess of $150,000,000. In this latter list one finds, as one would expect, Mellon, du Pont, Rockefeller, Ford and Frick heirs, but also names like Joseph P. Kennedy, Dr Edwin H. Land (the inventor of the Polaroid camera), and DeWitt Wallace (the originator of the *Reader's Digest*). The list is topped by J. Paul Getty of the Getty Oil Company, and Howard Hughes, whose fortune is based on aircraft, tools, and real estate.

The equality of opportunity in the American scene cannot disguise the inequality of achievement that characterizes it, for the height of isolated peaks only emphasizes the depth of the wide valleys between them. Although these great fortunes have been amassed by only a fraction of one per cent of the population, the possession or lack of property has always in the United States influenced the holding of power over daily life. Now that the average American has become an employee, he is less free than ever before to determine the course of his life and thoughts or even where he lives. His pay is higher, his working hours shorter than his grandfather's; his wife possesses conveniences that her grandmother would have considered unattainable luxuries, and considers them as her right. But these conveniences are what other people manufacture on a large scale and persuade the average American family that they want and need, while their thoughts are often formed by the capsulizations of newspapers, radio, and television. And if a man works for a large organization, he may be frequently uprooted and transferred to a new scene in the course of his career. Aside from property, numbers control American life, for the churches, the political parties, the labor unions, have by this means exercised great power over the destiny of the average American.

p 162
(32)

p 158–9
f 8

At the top of the American scale today are perhaps fifteen per cent of the population: the possessors of great wealth, whether inherited or self-made, and the professional and executive classes. At the bottom are perhaps twenty per cent: the unskilled laborers, the unemployed, the poor, the ignorant, and the unemployable. Between these extremes lie almost two-thirds of the population: the white-collar workers, skilled craftsmen, and partially skilled workers. In the top group the influence of newspaper columnists, serious writers, some clergymen, some college presidents, some college professors, especially those who have moved into the service of the Federal government, bears little relation to the individual property that they may, or may not possess. In the bottom group abject poverty prevails, whether hidden away in remote clearings of Appalachia, or more visible in the decaying central cores of great cities. The steadily increasing, almost unthinking, prosperity of the middle sixty-five per cent in postwar decades has underlined the grave inequalities of American life. In the professional classes schoolteachers, actors, clergymen, rural doctors, and small-town professional people generally are poorly rewarded in relation to their skills and training, in comparison with hand workers like plumbers, carpenters, masons, construction and factory workers. The building trades are so generally unionized that members of them, if they choose, may become capitalists in their own right through the purchase of securities, while many highly trained professional men and women have nothing left when they have finished stretching their salaries to cover carefully planned expenses of life. The general prosperity of the middle sixty-five per cent, when flaunted in the faces of the urban poor, causes the lowest group to demand as an inherent 'right' things that were until recently conveniences or luxuries only attained by special effort and superior ability. Political rhetoric announcing a 'war on poverty' only excited unattainable and unrealistic expectations.

In spite of great national wealth, good intentions, and social legislation, we are further away from the millennium than we were a century ago, and it does no good to blink at the fact. But how we reach the millennium is another matter. It will certainly *not* be reached by cutting off the peaks to fill in the valleys, or by em-

bracing similar panaceas and nostrums. Professor Edward C. Banfield of Harvard, writing in *Daedalus* on why government cannot solve the urban problem, observed: 'If all Negroes turned white overnight, the serious problems of the city would still exist and in about the same form and degree; it is the presence of a large lower class, not of Negroes as such, that is the real source of the trouble.' An editorial in the *Boston Globe* of 9 August 1968, commenting on a recent 'Poor people's march', observed: 'There isn't any such thing as a just share of wealth. Some people have more wealth than others . . . a just share of dignity for all Americans is another matter.' Alas, even that is still to be attained.

p 139
(28)

'Society'

The earliest use of the word 'society', in the meaning of 'the aggregate of leisured, cultured, or fashionable persons regarded as forming a distinct class or body in a community, *esp.* those persons collectively who are recognized as taking part in fashionable life, social functions, entertainments, etc.' cited in the *Oxford English Dictionary* is Lord Byron's couplet of 1823 from canto XIII, xciv, of *Don Juan*:

> *Society is now one polished horde,*
> *Formed of two mighty tribes, the* Bores *and* Bored.

Matthews's *A Dictionary of Americanisms* defined the word only in special combinations. 'Society editor' is traced back to an 1880 mention in Joel Chandler Harris's *Uncle Remus*; 'society reporter' to the following phrase from the *St Louis Globe-Democrat* of 29 April 1888: 'the brainy paragraphs thrown off by one society reporter'. The earliest cited instance of 'society column' is from the *Kansas City Star* of 15 August 1931. This is as one might expect, for in the United States 'society' in this sense is a post-Civil War phenomenon.

In a world based on the ownership of land or of rural pursuits, people of given position or substantial holdings share numerous interests, and are likely to be at least acquainted with anyone similarly situated in the neighborhood. In the South, before the introduction of railroads, a well-mannered and literate traveler might break his journey at any plantation or country house he reached at nightfall, with the expectation of being made welcome. Some of Thomas Jefferson's financial problems sprang from the fantastic number of people who appeared at Monticello, sometimes with only the slenderest thread of introduction, and stayed more than overnight. Thus in the countryside most people of similar tastes and position were at least potentially acquainted, for the arrival of a traveler brought a welcome tie with the world beyond the horizon.

f 6

p 203
(7)

Even in cities and towns before industrialization and massive immigration, people who lived in the handsomest houses expected to know each other as a matter of course, save in cases of extreme misanthropy. Mrs Charles Pelham Curtis, writing of Boston of the second quarter of the 19th century, recalled that it 'was very limited in its residential region, and different streets were given over, as it were, to different clans. Summer Street was the home of the Sam Gardner family; Lees, Jacksons and Putnams, all related to each other, congregated about Chauncey Place and Bedford Street; Perkinses in Temple Place, Lawrences and Masons in Colonnade Row', and so on. New York and other cities had similar enclaves, where cousins married each other and lived in bonds of family proximity.

p 152–
(5)

Before the Civil War the pursuit of education or an agreeable climate created close friendships between northern and southern states. Numerous Virginians came to Harvard College and were warmly welcomed in Boston. South Carolinians would seek the sea breezes of Newport, Rhode Island, in summer while New Englanders might escape from winter's snow in Charleston. All this quite simply amounted to like-minded people enjoying the company of their relatives and friends. In this simpler world when a girl reached the age to put up her hair and put down her skirts, her parents might have a dinner, followed by dancing, at home for close relatives and friends. The balls of Charleston's St Cecilia Society or Philadelphia's Assembly, which have continued since the 18th century, were larger but still intimate gatherings of relatives, friends and neighbors.

Chic Young's 'Blondie', the archetypal featherbrained housewife, dazzled by the prospect of unlimited credit facilities. Her husband Dagwood is less enthusiastic. (8)

Charles Dana Gibson, the creator of the 'Gibson Girl', began his career as a humorist for 'Life' Magazine. In 1907 he published 'The Social Ladder', a collection of satirical, yet half-affectionate, drawings of the ostentation and materialism of the upper classes. Here, members of 'Society', showered with gold, through which they trudge ankle-deep, parade in an endless and joyless circle. (9)

The following extract from a letter written by a Bostonian in 1873 to explain the measures adopted by the Somerset Club in dealing with a troublesome member provides a limpid definition of social relations at the time.

I suppose what Society wants is agreeable sensations—peace plenty and politeness—and when anybody makes a noise and makes it unpleasant he is disliked, no matter how many real virtues he may possess. Social clubs are not established to protect men in their abstract rights, or to carry on disputes and controversies, but to promote cheerfulness, good feeling, harmony and pleasant intercourse, and when they don't do this they soon fade away. If a man makes himself agreeable, society goes no deeper and the same is true if he makes himself disagreeable—hence agreeable bad men and women are more highly prized than disagreeable good ones.

In the last third of the 19th century, as the number and size of great American fortunes multiplied, the possession of a handsome house no longer necessarily carried with it a corresponding position, for the occupant of such a house might, or might not, prove an agreeable companion to his neighbors. In a conscious effort to achieve congenial company at New York balls, Ward McAllister (1827–95) organized in 1872 the Patriarch Association, consisting of himself and twenty-four others of 'the leading representative men of the city, who had', in his self-appointed view, 'the right to create and lead society'. Each Patriarch, for his subscription, was entitled to invite four ladies and five gentlemen, including himself and family, to each ball. 'We then resolved that the responsibility of inviting each batch of nine guests should rest upon the shoulders of the Patriarch who invited them, and that if any objectionable element was introduced, it was the Management's duty to at once let it be known by whom such objectionable

party was invited, and to notify the Patriarch so offending, that he had done us an injury, and pray him to be more circumspect.' When Mrs William Astor, the wife of a grandson of the first John Jacob Astor, in 1892 asked Ward McAllister to help her make out the guest list for a ball, she reminded him that her ballroom at 350 Fifth Avenue would only comfortably accommodate four hundred people. McAllister, with a flair for the dramatic, alleged to newspaper reporters that there were 'only about 400 people in New York Society that one really knows'. Such statements soon gave rise to the notion that there was such a thing as 'society', and that people were or were not 'in' it. Moreover the appearance in the late 1880s of the *Social Register* (whose sombre black cover with orange lettering has not changed in eighty years), which has long proved a convenient address book and telephone directory for those listed in it, suggested once again the existence of a mysterious thing called 'society', to which many are called but few are chosen.

From the 1880s until World War I, Loire Valley châteaux and Renaissance and Baroque palaces sprang up along upper Fifth Avenue in New York City. William H. Vanderbilt and two of his sons built huge houses in the 51st–52nd and 57th–58th Street blocks, while in the mid-1890s Mrs William Astor abandoned her house on the corner of 34th Street (with its ballroom capacity of four hundred) for a château designed by Richard Morris Hunt at the corner of 65th Street. Hunt designed 'The Breakers' at Newport for Cornelius Vanderbilt, and for his brother, George W. Vanderbilt, who eschewed finance and devoted himself to scientific agriculture and forestry in North Carolina, the great French Renaissance house 'Biltmore', near Asheville.

Some of the great American houses of the late 19th and early 20th century were often more tasteful than their owners, thanks to architects like Hunt, Charles F. McKim, Stanford White, Ogden Codman, and Herbert Browne, who had a flair for elegance that

p 157
(19)

would have endeared them to the Italian grand dukes or German princes of a century or two earlier. Andrew Carnegie, soon after selling his business to the United States Steel Corporation in 1901, built a great house that occupied an entire block on upper Fifth Avenue, although it bore the address of 2 East 91st Street. Thus a Pittsburgh steel fortune came to require a vast house in New York. In 1905 Charles M. Schwab completed a French château, set in an entire block on Riverside Drive, with a façade derived from Chenonceaux. Although without a gallery on arches spanning the river, Schwab's house had numerous amenities—pipe organ, gymnasium, and bowling alley—lacking in the original. Henry Clay Frick moved in 1914 to 1 East 70th Street, a handsome low stone house whose windows opened on a terrace extending along Fifth Avenue from 70th to 71st Street. Other corners of Fifth Avenue were adorned with the great houses of German-Jewish bankers. Felix M. Warburg built a château at 1109 Fifth Avenue, at 92nd Street, completed in 1908, while Otto H. Kahn created an Italian Renaissance palace at 1100, between the Warburg and Carnegie houses. Lower down the avenue the Montana miner and senator, William Andrews Clark, achieved a corner house that carried the decorative exuberance of the Ecole des Beaux-Arts to limits undreamed of in France.

Against such an architectural background, New York life from the turn of the century until the outbreak of war had a stylish showiness reminiscent of Edwardian England. Handsome carriages or pioneer automobiles filled the streets; elegant private railway cars and steam yachts were available for more distant journeys. Ladies dressed to be seen and admired; their servants were outfitted in elegant liveries. Press photographs and the drawings of *f 9* Charles Dana Gibson and Howard Chandler Christy recall a decade of conspicuous ostentation that had little in common with what had preceded and was to follow it. This brief era of New York life, with its complementary migrations to Newport, Saratoga, and Europe, represented to the readers of the daily press, and especially of the scurrilous gossip sheets, 'Society' with a capital S. The extravagant and tasteless gyrations of some of the recent plutocrats, who were drawn as if by a magnet to the scene, have furnished congenial inspiration to journalists like Cleveland Amory and the late Lucius Beebe.

Even at the time, the scene was not as monolithic and homogeneous as it appeared from without. In 1910 Ralph Pulitzer, publisher of the *New York World*, amusingly satirized the New York dinner table, opera box, and ball in a little book, *New York Society on Parade*, with illustrations by Christy. His theme was that 'while European Society consists of a deep mill-pond of assured position with a froth of probationary parvenus, New York Society consists of a whirlpool of tentative novices with a sediment of permanent members.' He was better able to look at both sides of the coin than most, for he was not only a newspaperman and son of Joseph Pulitzer, but he had in 1906 married Frederica Vanderbilt Webb, a granddaughter of William H. Vanderbilt. Ralph Pulitzer continued his analysis thus:

> Instead, indeed, of having an aristocracy whose caste is beyond question and beyond change and whose mutual hospitalities constitute Society, New York has an 'Aristocracy' whose elevation is largely artificial, whose membership is largely arbitrary, and whose existence vitally depends upon those activities which are known as social functions. In other words, while in Europe the mutual entertainments of an inherently stable upper class create Society, in New York the constant contortions of Society are indispensable to create and maintain a precarious upper class; while in Europe the pleasures of Society are among the prerogatives of rank, in New York the pleasure of 'rank' is the inducement to Society. The contrast between the two species of Society is precisely the contrast between the amateur athlete who exercises for his amusement and the professional athlete who exercises for a living.

Although New York's Fifth Avenue was the most visible urban manifestation of the multiplication of American late 19th-century fortunes, a few other cities had regions of comparable ostentation. In San Francisco, Nob Hill in the late 1880s became the site of a remarkable concentration of great houses built by railroad and silver magnates. Its very name—a contraction of nabob—indicates the character of its residents; Robert Louis Stevenson, who saw it in its heyday, called it the Hill of Palaces. Although the approaches to the hill were steep and its top windy, the introduction of cable cars in 1873 made it tolerably accessible, whereupon Collis P. Huntington, Charles Crocker, James Fair, Leland Stanford, and Mark Hopkins built themselves gaudy houses, from which they could literally look down upon their fellow citizens. Whatever might be said about the taste of these buildings, no one could deny that they had cost a great deal of money, which in 19th-century San Francisco clearly lent distinction. The fire of 1906 levelled all but one of the Nob Hill houses. The single exception was that built in 1886 by the silver king James C. Flood, at a cost of a million and a half dollars, which was thought to be the first brownstone west of the Mississippi. It survives today, somewhat altered, as the house of the Pacific Union Club.

p 156–7 (16)

The hitherto neglected lake front on the North Side of Chicago became in the 1880s an area of conspicuous ostentation. Here in 1885 Mr and Mrs Potter Palmer built a brownstone mansion that had many of the bad points common to the imitation Rhenish castles built by homesick German brewers in other parts of the United States. Anders Zorn's portrait of Mrs Potter Palmer, painted in 1893 when as President of the Board of Lady Managers of the Chicago World's Fair she had consolidated her dominant position in the city, is considerably more attractive than the huge house in which she lived. The mansard-roofed, forty-five room house of Cyrus Hall McCormick, with ballroom, and Perry H. Smith's white marble mansion, with theater, symbolized a conspicuous way of life. Gossip had it that the Smiths delighted in showing their guests the butler's pantry, in which faucets furnished not only hot and cold water but well-iced champagne.

p 156 (15)

Few American cities after the First World War resumed life in its previous form. The quixotic idiocy of Prohibition, for one thing, killed off most of the good former restaurants and substituted clandestine night-clubs and speakeasies—a name given in the 19th century to unlicensed saloons. Now when everything was unlicensed and illicit, people drank more rather than less, for to many Americans it seemed a wise precaution, if not a moral duty, to drink what was at hand, lest one be involuntarily dry later. Such occurrences, to the detriment of good order, were all too common until the administration of Franklin D. Roosevelt disposed, one trusts definitively, of Prohibition.

p 155 (12)

Increasing taxes and diminishing supplies of servants numbered the days of the great houses of the turn of the century. A few lingered on, but most gave way to apartment houses or office buildings. Those that have survived with least alteration are the houses of great collectors who endowed them as continuing institutions, like Henry Clay Frick's, opened as an art gallery in 1935, the Pierpont Morgan Library in New York, Mrs Isabella Stewart Gardner's Fenway Court in Boston, or the Henry E. Huntington Library and Art Gallery in San Marino, California. This last contains the remarkable collections assembled by the nephew and business associate of Collis P. Huntington of the 'Big Four' railroad builders.

p 157 (17)

In Philadelphia the excellent train service on the Main Line of the Pennsylvania Railroad between the city and Paoli had, from the 1870s, led to an early development of suburban life. Eventually many families gave up living in Philadelphia at all, to the increasing detriment of parts of the city that had once been handsome. What occurred earliest in Philadelphia became general in many parts of the United States between the two world wars, as the automobile furnished a new means of living in the country and still working in the city. Many of the new suburban houses, even if large, tried their best not to look so. Their builders sought models in modest English Georgian houses, or American colonial derivations thereof, rather than in Renaissance palaces or Baroque villas. At the beginning of the 20th century the residences of most substantial citizens could be readily seen in orderly rows along city streets, with New York's Fifth Avenue as the most outstanding instance. By the middle of the century the homes of such people were scattered far and wide, often well-hidden in the country, for conspicuous ostentation had given way to an almost equally costly search for privacy.

THE BIBLE   FASHION MAGAZINE

'Progress'; the transformation of womanhood in 300 years, as seen by A. B. Walker. The English Puritan lady of 1615, dressed modestly, studies her Bible; her counterpart in 1915 smokes, drinks, and reads a fashion magazine. (10)

Women and learning

In front of the west wing of the Massachusetts State House stands a bronze statue of Anne Hutchinson (1591–1643), banished in 1638 for too vigorous teaching of unwelcome theological doctrine; in a comparable place before the east wing there sits a likeness of the Quaker Mary Dyer, hanged in 1660 when she persisted in returning to Boston after two banishments. 'And some there be which have no memorial, who are perished as though they had never been, and are become as though they had never been born.'

Among these is poor Ann Hopkins, wife of Edward Hopkins (1600–57), Governor of Connecticut, 'a godly young woman and of special parts' as Governor John Winthrop described her, who became insane and outlived her husband by forty-one years 'by occasion of her giving herself wholly to reading and writing'. Winthrop was perfectly specific about the cause of Ann's troubles;

'for if she had attended to her household affairs, and such things as belong to women, and not gone out of her way and calling to meddle in such things as are proper for men, whose minds are stronger, she had kept her wits, and might have improved them usefully and honorably in the place God had set her.'

John Winthrop to the contrary notwithstanding, reading and writing were not always a fatal handicap to 17th-century Puritan women, for Anne Bradstreet (1612–72) who came to New England in 1630 with her husband Simon Bradstreet (a future Governor of Massachusetts Bay) became the pioneer bluestocking of British North America by publishing in London in 1650 a volume of poems entitled *The Tenth Muse Lately sprung up in America*. Not only was she the first woman poet; she was a rather able one, whose verses have gone through seven editions (1650, 1678, 1758, 1867, 1897, 1932, 1967) and can still be read with pleasure. Moreover she was a happy and useful wife and mother of eight children.

Even in a Puritan colony, all was not piety, literature, and high-mindedness. The General Court of Massachusetts in 1660 was legislating against 'excess in apparel, both of men and women', especially declaring its 'utter detestation and dislike, that men or women of mean condition, should take upon them the garb of Gentlemen by wearing gold or silver lace, or buttons . . . or women of the same ranke, to wear silk or tyffany hoods, or scarfes, which though allowable to persons of greater estate, or more liberal education, yet we cannot but judg it intollerable in persons of such like condition'. Nevertheless John Josselyn, who visited Boston in 1663, described the Common, 'where the Gallants a little before Sun-set walk with their Marmalet-Madams, as we do in Morefields'. Here in the 17th century is a pattern that continued throughout American life wherever money was being made, even to frontier mining towns: wives of 'persons of greater estate' would import, from London or Paris, the current equivalents of gold or silver lace, 'tyffany hoods or scarfes'; 'women of mean condition' would imitate them as best they could, and there would be strumpets somewhere, whether walking in public with their gallants a little

'For the Benefit of the Girl who is about to Graduate', a cartoon by Charles Howard Johnson. A girl student, asleep at her studies, dreams of an advancing army of pots, pans, brooms and washtubs, who warn her that she will have need of them too. (11)

before sunset, or remaining in the more reticent obscurity of houses. Down to the First World War the products of Paris, the local dressmaker, and the home sewing-machine were markedly different, and could be distinguished at a glance. The growth and success of the wholesale garment industry eventually almost eliminated class distinction in dress. Although some women still go to Paris, close approximations of their purchases appear so rapidly in great numbers in every state that only the most discerning eye can tell the difference. Advertising and television almost instantly diffuse and dilute the novelty of even the most outlandish whim, while mail order catalogues bring an approximation of the latest mode even to the remotest farms. While many women still agree with Miss Cornelia Frances Forbes (1817–1911) of Milton, Massachusetts (as reported by Ralph Waldo Emerson) 'that the sense of being well-dressed gives a feeling of inward tranquillity which religion is powerless to bestow', the outward and visible signs of superiority in dress are no longer so immediately evident as they were before 1914. Today the only ultimate elegance left is an understated simplicity, so subtle that it cannot readily be imitated.

John Winthrop's notion that women should not go out of their 'way and calling to meddle in such things as are proper for men, whose minds are stronger' has been definitively disproved by a succession of literate (and sometimes *very* strong-minded) women over the past three centuries. An 18th-century Boston parallel to Anne Bradstreet appeared in the Negro slave Phillis Wheatley (1753–84), born in Africa and bought by a Boston tailor as a maid for his wife, whose *Poems on Various Subjects, Religious and Moral*, were published in London in 1773. Although collegiate education in Massachusetts did not extend to women for two centuries after the foundation of Harvard College, the lack of formal learning did not handicap the literary skills of Abigail Adams (1744–1818), wife of the second President of the United States and mother of the sixth, or of Mercy Otis Warren (1728–1814), poet, dramatist, and historical apologist of the American Revolution. Girls working in the textile mills of Lowell, Massachusetts, in the 1840s published their poems in *The Lowell Offering, written exclusively by females employed in the mills*, a periodical so unexpected that it was reviewed in *The Times* and provoked a debate in the French Chambre des Députés on the virtues of industrialization. Few writers anywhere have had more readers or stirred up the world more surprisingly than Harriet Beecher Stowe (1811–96). Her *Uncle Tom's Cabin, or Life Among the Lowly*, written while the author was tending her newly-born seventh child, appeared in book form in 1852, with sales of 300,000 copies within the year. English circulation eventually reached a million and a half.

Perhaps the most far-reaching, single-handed accomplishment of any 19th-century American woman was the creation of the Christian Science Church. Mary Baker Eddy (1821–1910) was born on a New Hampshire hillside farm, had only desultory schooling, but became the founder and evangelist of a religious body that has p 66 (17) spread far beyond the borders of the United States.

The alliance of Susan B. Anthony (1820–1906), Amelia Bloomer (1818–94), Lucretia Coffin Mott (1793–1880), Elizabeth Cady p 138 (22) Stanton (1815–1902), and Lucy Stone (1818–93), which brought about general recognition of women's rights, including that of suffrage, would have terrified Governor Winthrop. The activities of Frances E. Willard (1839–98) and the Woman's Christian p 65 (14) Temperance Union, aided by such unlovely allies as the ignorant, hatchet-wielding saloon-smasher Carry Nation (1846–1911), led eventually to the unfortunate Eighteenth Amendment which, when it officially came into effect in 1920, officially deprived all Americans of the right to drink. As even women can go too far, this misbegotten monstrosity was repealed in 1933. The Nineteenth Amendment, giving nation-wide suffrage to women, ratified in 1920, is the permanent accomplishment of this movement.

After the First World War the profusion of pictures, statuettes, vases, and knick-knacks vanished from the parlor along with the maid who had dusted them. The twenty-inch feminine waist cinched in by corsets having been allowed to expand more naturally, its enemy the twelve-course dinner was reduced. Floor- f 10 length skirts and feathered hats as big as trays got blown out of fashion as soon as a woman drove a motor car. One cannot help wondering what the dress-reformer, Mrs Bloomer, who gave her name to an article of costume now obsolete, would have thought of the miniskirt, which is the culmination of her efforts. Once there was a discernible difference between the costumes of 'nice' and 'naughty' ladies, for the latter, by no more than an extra inch of exposure, could exercise a powerful attraction. This distinction has been lost by the way, for now every schoolgirl normally exposes more than the naughtiest lady of the past would have attempted. The appropriateness of the miniskirt, like that of the picture-window, depends upon the view. As only a small percentage of thighs and knees are sufficiently young and well-shaped to benefit from it, it is perhaps as well that some young women take to blue jeans and baggy sweaters, dear to 'hippies'.

The creation of such institutions as Mount Holyoke (1837), p 179 (7) Vassar (1865), Wellesley (1870), Smith (1875), Radcliffe (1879), Bryn Mawr (1885), and Barnard (1889) gave American women their own independent colleges, comparable in academic standards to anything available to men. In addition women soon found their way into great numbers of state and private universities and colleges. Even Harvard, the oldest institution of learning in the United States, is today co-educational in practice if not yet completely so in theory.

In the 19th century visits to the poor, church meetings, lectures, and women's clubs had begun to supply a titillating change from feminine household routine. After the First World War came a multiplication of female groups concerned with cards, crafts, or music, art or literature, with schools and hospitals as well as churches, with politics and what today we call social welfare. These activities continue to be mostly local in scope and of varying success as the voluntary occupation and interest of women past child-bearing and not professionally employed. But of approximately seventy-three million employed persons in the United States today, close to a third are women. They work in every kind of job, and take things in their stride. Many college graduates marry young, and work to support their husbands through graduate school. As domestic service is almost unobtainable, young women cook and keep house with a competence that startles their less accomplished elders. Some exceptional women continue a career even with children. Others, alas, become so entrapped in ferrying children to school, attending PTA meetings, scrubbing, and tending house that excellent minds lie fallow for too many years. But the trend for a return of women to full or part-time work once all their children are in school is markedly increasing. Those who are able to continue without interruption in a profession do so simply as competent people, rather than specifically as women. The old time evangelism of the suffragette no longer has wide appeal. A dialogue reported by Vera Brittain in *Lady into Woman*, although of British origin, applies with equal pertinence to the United States. An old suffragette remarks, 'I like my committees to go on all day. You really feel then that you've got something done.' A young professional inquires: 'But when do you do your work?' 'But, you see, I think committees *are* work' is the surprised answer. There is, of course, an underworld of both men and women of limited intelligence who, agreeing with the old suffragette, waste endless time in committees, designing horses and producing camels. But most intelligent American professional women who accomplish anything haven't any more time for such nonsense than their husbands or brothers. This is what the higher education of women has brought about.

VIII

TEACHING THE NATION

The development of American education

MARCUS CUNLIFFE

'Education was free. That subject my father had

written about repeatedly, as comprising his chief hope

for us children, the essence of American opportunity,

the treasure that no thief could touch,

not even misfortune or poverty. It was the one thing

he was able to promise us when he sent for us;

surer, safer than bread or shelter.'

MARY ANTIN

Education's role

in American life has always been central, and markedly distinct from that in any other country. To the early colonists it was vital that the clergy of the future should be educated, and this was seen as a public responsibility. Yet this connection between church and school, which at one time seemed destined to be far closer than in England, began to dissolve with the Revolution. Hardly any colleges restricted entry to members of particular denominations, though the values upon which they were based did remain strongly religious. Also unlike their English counterparts, American universities and schools tended not to be national in scope. Each state undertook its own education; all but two of the original thirteen colonies had its own college. This has had certain drawbacks, in that no overall policy has been applied, but it has also meant that American education has been open to experiment.

This teaching chart (opposite) was one of a series produced in brilliant color by the Diamond Litho-Publishing Company of Minneapolis, Minnesota, in 1894. Described as 'simple, practical and scientific', these 'teaching machines' instilled into grade-school pupils 'all the primary and practical principles of arithmetic and bookkeeping'. This was done by means of ingenious techniques and the colorful presentation of fruits and vegetables, livestock, store interiors—familiar objects to children in small farming communities. Numbers were written in the 'blackboard' in the center to be multiplied by, added to, subtracted from or divided by the numbers in the 'spokes'. The spaces in between show various ways of making up standard coin values. However delightful these charts appear to us now, they must have caused much suffering to the children who were exhorted to 'Drill, Drill, Drill', and assimilate facts and figures through the drudgery of endless repetition. An accompanying 'educational axiom' informed them that 'It is better to do One Thing One Hundred Times, than One Hundred Things One Time'. (1)

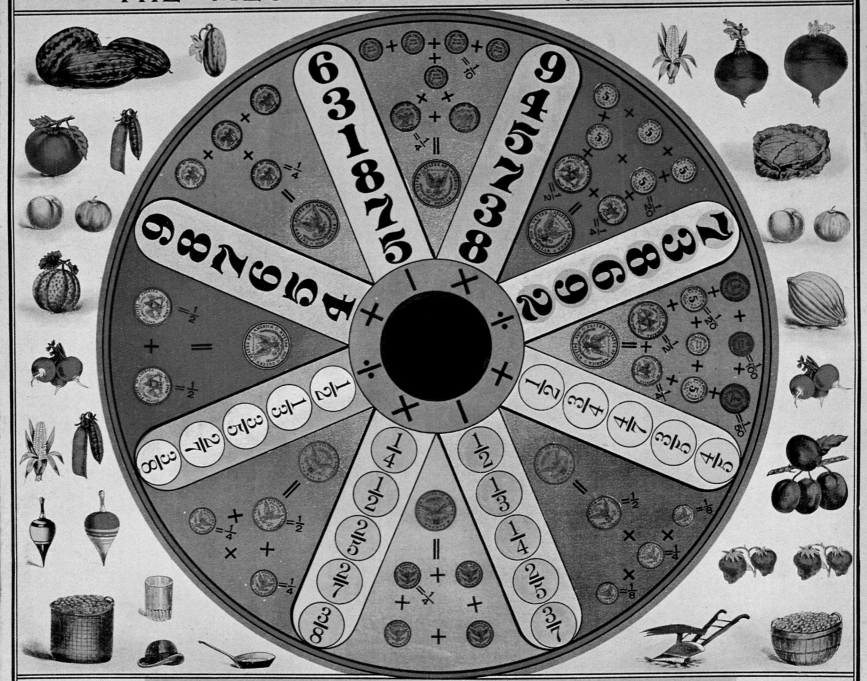

SUGGESTIONS TO THE TEACHER.

This Chart is a valuable device for teaching the pupil the application of the principles already learned. It is one thing to learn, it is another thing to apply. To obtain knowledge without knowing how to use it, is the play of Hamlet with the part of Hamlet left out. To *give* knowledge is less than half the work of the teacher. The varied uses of the Chart will suggest themselves to every teacher. The wheel with the blackboard in the center, has many uses. Three are prominent: I. A drill in the Addition, Subtraction, Multiplication and Division of Whole Numbers; II. A drill in the Addition, Subtraction, Multiplication and Division of Fractions; III. A drill in changing money. For the drill on whole numbers: Place say figure on the blackboard, point to the sign, and to the figure in the spoke of the wheel, above, that it may be desired to use. Change the figure on the blackboard, and the drill is changed. Follow the same course with the drill on fractions. The pupil should be taught to add, subtract, multiply, and divide fractions mentally. To make the mental drill successful only the small fractions should be used. The objects given in the picture below, and all the detached objects, are given to illustrate buying and selling. Buy and sell all these objects with the money given. This makes the work practical. The teacher will be surprised at the rapid progress made.

MEAT MARKET.   GROCERY STORE.

'A University for men instead of a college for boys.' This was the destiny its friends proposed for Harvard (founded in 1636), in the words of one of its eminent alumni, Emerson. Of the three buildings in the 1726 engraving (above left) only Massachusetts Hall, on the right, still stands. Kansas State University, Lawrence (above right, in 1867), at first had only one student and one professor, who then married each other. (2, 3)

Leadership and generosity helped the universities in their struggles for survival. Ezra Stiles (left), a clergyman, like almost every other college president until the early 19th century, guided Yale's recovery after the War of Independence. John D. Rockefeller, multimillionaire benefactor of the University of Chicago, is seen here (right) with its first president William Rainey Harper. (4, 5)

The first medical school in America was established in 1765 at the College and Academy of Philadelphia. Left: a lecture in 1888. (6)

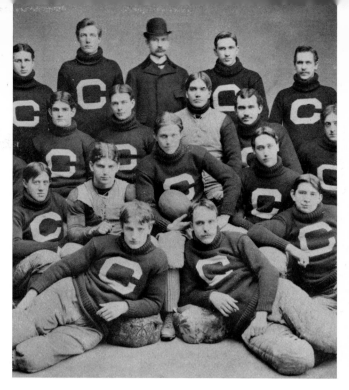

Cornell University (below) was established in 1868 by telegraph tycoon and senator Ezra Cornell, who found himself with 'about half a million dollars more than my family will need'. Its syllabus included everything from classical and modern languages to veterinary science, at first taught by Professor James Law in fields and barns. In 1894, the state financed a veterinary college at a cost of $50,000; the same amount bought an up-to-date dairy laboratory (far right). Athletic prowess had assumed unwarranted importance by the 1890s. Cornell President Andrew D. White condemned football as 'barbaric', and indeed Cornell's free-for-all style was notorious. Right: the heroes of Cornell in 1895. (8, 9, 10)

Graduates at Vassar (above) at first received only certificates of 'the first degree of liberal arts', since a woman 'bachelor' was considered unseemly. (7)

Co-education came in 1837 at Oberlin College, Ohio, also the first to accept students regardless of race (occasional Negroes had graduated elsewhere). Above: the class of 1891. (11)

Tuskegee, founded by Booker T. Washington, was an early attempt to bring the arts and sciences – including upholstery and mattress making – to Negroes. (12)

Young ladies' seminaries were the predecessors of the female colleges which began to emerge in the 1860s. In this detail from a painting by an unknown artist of about 1810 (left), a graduation ceremony is taking place. Some of the better seminaries later developed into colleges, such as Mount Holyoke (attended by Emily Dickinson) and Milwaukee-Downer College. (13)

'Self Culture' is good reading: an advertisement for a magazine launched in Chicago in 1901, which aimed at broadening the female mind by imparting knowledge painlessly. Nowhere was the value of education in attaining a higher standard of living given more emphasis than in America. (14)

In the country school painted by Edward Henry in 1890 (right), a class of unruly urchins is supervised by a young woman teacher. The professions, including teaching, were slow to open their ranks to women; it was thought that they would not be able to keep order effectively. However, the shortage of teachers in the public schools made their presence necessary, and by 1900 there were 42,290 college- or seminary-educated women at teacher-preparatory schools. (15)

'Il Libro dell' Emigrante', an English-language manual for Italians, illustrates the 'before' and 'after' stages of a success story of which education was the key. On the front cover the immigrant, shabbily dressed, is seen arriving with all his possessions in a carpet bag; on the back, bowler-hatted and prosperous, he departs for his native country, while a porter struggles under the weight of his trunk. (16, 17)

In schools for young children the Froebel Kindergarten method was adopted from Europe in 1857 and was well established by the 1890s. Left: educational play with geometrical blocks in an American kindergarten. (18)

National pride and a sense of American history were inculcated in the schools and gave unity to the educational system. From 1890 onwards, state after state passed laws obliging schoolhouses to fly the Stars and Stripes each day, and pledging allegiance to the flag (above, in 1908) became a national practice. (20)

The first Sunday school class (left) in North Market Hall, Chicago, was gathered from the streets by the evangelist Dwight L. Moody (see p. 73). (19)

Evening classes for adult immigrants helped first-generation Americans, who often could not speak English on arrival, to adapt themselves to the unfamiliar conditions of their new life. (21)

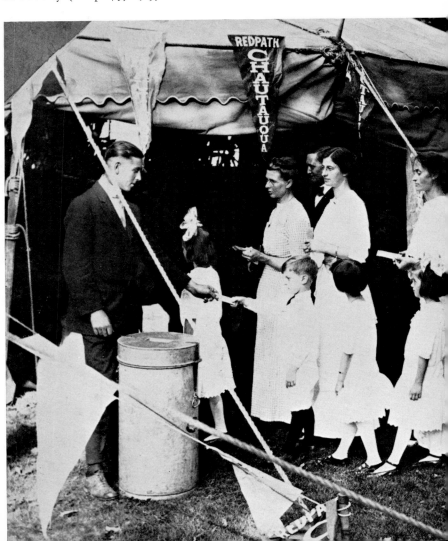

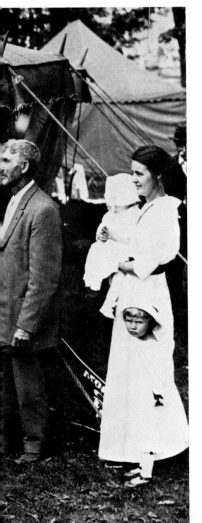

The focal point of learning in a small community was the schoolhouse. An example like this, at Alma, Wisconsin, in 1897, would have replaced a simple one-room shack managed by a single teacher, and before that, probably, tutoring – perhaps by a clergyman – in a private house. (23)

'The most American thing in America', Theodore Roosevelt said of the Chautauquas (left), the immensely popular tent shows that toured the country combining entertainment with culture. A typical program might include brass bands, Red Indian dances, a lecture on science or history, magicians and Hawaiian ukuleles. (22)

German methods involving division into classes or 'grades' by age-group, were introduced by the great educational reformer Horace Mann (1796–1859), after a five-month European tour. Right: a grade school in Valley Falls, Kansas. (24)

183

Schools of today offer a wide variety. In backward rural areas the one-room school house survives much as it did a hundred years ago. This one (right) is in Georgia. (25)

Television and other technological advances have supplied radical new methods of teaching. Film slides and synchronized records (above) are used to help children develop creative abilities. *Sesame Street*, an experimental TV series for children aged 3–5, teaches its young viewers to acquire the basic skills of literacy and numeracy, and to develop 'awareness of self and the world around us'. Its organizers claim particular success with racial and ethnic minorities. Left: Big Bird, one of the program's puppet characters, welcomes visitors to 123 Sesame Street. (26, 27)

The public high schools began to flourish after the middle of the 19th century, when the demand arose for a type of school that would rival the academies in providing a broader, more complete education, with highly qualified teachers and first-rate equipment. Starting in Massachusetts, the high school system eventually became established everywhere. Today, one of the most modern high school buildings in the United States is to be found in Carlsbad (right), New Mexico. (28)

State and university co-operation on scientific and military projects is now an established feature of academic life, though one increasingly open to criticism. This 'high-resolution radio interferometer' (left), consisting of five 60 foot dish antennae, was designed and built by Stanford University staff, headed by Professor Ronald N. Bracewell, with support from the Air Force Office of Scientific Research and the National Science Foundation. (29)

185

The **equalizing role** of education was embodied in the foundation of state institutions where, as for instance the Indiana constitution of 1816 puts it, 'tuition shall be gratis, and equally open to all'. The University of California, which commenced instruction in 1869 in Oakland, moved to Berkeley in 1873, when the settlement of the town began; it now has campuses all over the state. Right: the first graduating class of Berkeley in 1873. Below: an aerial view of the vast Berkeley campus today. (30, 31)

A new stage in Federal involvement in education was marked when the GI Bill provided college tuition grants to World War II veterans (left). The years that followed saw substantial Federal contributions to education, and loans and scholarships for students. (32)

Catholic schools long appeared to be excluded from Federal generosity, and Catholics tended to rely on their own educational system. But by the 1960s, they were beginning to receive their share of public funds. Right: a Catholic schoolroom with the ever-present Stars and Stripes. (33)

Racial equality became the burning issue in education in the 1950s, when the Supreme Court ruled that segregation was unconstitutional. At Little Rock, Arkansas, troops were called in to enforce the decision (top). Ten years later (above), the same setting shows blacks and whites peacefully studying and socializing together. Below: black children taken to school by bus in an attempt to overcome local segregation. (34, 35, 36)

Student unrest in action at a peace rally in Washington (above). Some of the older generation were alienated by the bitter attacks on Establishment values by militant student leaders who supported draft evasion, demanded a 'democratic' share in university government, and expressed disenchantment with what appeared to them as 'battery-farming' methods. Yet when viewed in the historical context, their demands for 'relevance', and for a part in governing the institutions are the continuation of characteristic American traditions in education. (37)

Young scientists attend a class in physics at the American University in Washington D.C. The founding fathers' dream of a national university situated in the nation's new capital was never precisely realized. But the Washington area has its full quota of colleges, universities and research establishments, for some of whose scholars the Library of Congress, the National Archives and the burgeoning Smithsonian Institution are important attractions. (38)

The shape of universities in present day America is made up of some of the most exciting works of modern architecture anywhere in the world. Philip Johnson's Kline Biology Tower (left) at Yale, of 1965–66, is the center of a whole complex of new science buildings. The cylindrical columns contain the ventilation shafts of the laboratories. Older universities like Yale reflect, through their buildings, the whole course of American education – from the original foundation of colonial days, through the varied contributions of 19th- and 20th-century private benefactors, to the great Federally financed projects of today. (39)

The architectural school of the Illinois Institute of Technology in Chicago traces its artistic pedigree back to the Bauhaus through its director Mies van der Rohe. His own design for Crown Hall (below) embodies the Bauhaus ideals of clarity, economy and logic. The interior is one unified space, the exterior merely the framework of steel supports for the roof and wall panels of glass. It was built between 1952 and 1956. (41)

A new library for the University of California at San Diego takes the eccentric shape described as 'a five-level spheroid, supported on 16 cantilevered concrete columns rising from a 200 ft square podium'. (40)

The development of American Education

MARCUS CUNLIFFE

A SOCIETY is exemplified in and also shaped by its educational system. Its view of human nature, its ideas on leadership and the masses, its present state and its conception of a desired (or dreaded) future: these can all be discerned from the actual structure of the system and from the literature that grows up inside and outside it. The graduation ceremonies of educational institutions in complex societies may be taken as symbolic counterparts to the *rites de passage*, the initiation ceremonies, in so-called primitive societies. In each case the culture dramatizes the culmination of the process by which the codes and texts, the inner lore, have been transmitted to the young. Secular schooling has literally assumed some of the instructional tasks that were once the responsibility of the church. Writings on education often have a sermonizing quality, for inquiries into the nature and purpose of education juxtapose the real with the ideal, *is* with *ought*. Sacred and secular texts may be almost interchangeable.

So education has been conceded a central and rather solemn importance among the institutions of mankind. Of no nation is this more true than of the United States. Indeed the recognition long antedated the achievement of independence, especially in New England. With the Revolution, and the beginning of a search not yet ended for a responsible and enlightened new social order, a heavier trust than ever before was placed upon education as the instrument of enlightenment. Thomas Jefferson again and again stressed its prime role: 'If the condition of man is to be progressively ameliorated, education is to be the chief instrument in effecting it.' The realization of this Jeffersonian dream was to be a protracted business. In the process the United States evolved educational devices—the public, tax-supported school and the college—that were seen to differ markedly from those of Europe. As with so many themes in American history, therefore, the story in broad outline is one of an initial implantation of European institutions; their gradual adaptation to American circumstances; and their transformation into distinctively native styles. Yet the development is in truth more complicated: European ideas continued to influence American practice, and American ones to exert a counter-influence in Europe and in other continents.

Some problems

However, before we turn to the unfolding of the story some other complications ought to be noted. The first problem is an apparent paradox. Though education is a subject of immense resonance, much of what is said about it—above all by professional educators—seems trite or tedious. 'It is ominous,' said Ralph Waldo Emerson (*Lectures and Biographical Sketches*, 1876) '. . . that this word Education has so cold, so hopeless a sound. A treatise on education, a convention for education, a lecture, a system, affects us with a slight paralysis and a yawning of the jaws.' Jacques Barzun echoed the sentiment in his *Teacher in America* (1944), whose opening sentence is: 'Education is indeed the dullest of subjects and I intend to say as little about it as I can'; and Barzun prefaces the chapter with a quotation from a novel by an English wit, Thomas Love Peacock: 'The bore of all bores was the third. His subject had no beginning, middle, nor end. It was education. Never was such a journey through the desert of the mind, the Great Sahara of intellect. The very recollection makes me thirsty.'

Why this dullness and opacity? In part because of the very immensity of the subject. Even if we restrict discussion to the realm of professional teaching the range of institutions where this is provided—from kindergarten to graduate school—is dauntingly wide. But there are other forms of education—Sunday schools, apprenticeship training, adult classes, lectures, concerts, libraries, museums, radio and TV programs, pieces of advice and information tendered by parents or friends—widening out still further, and all able to claim a place in a properly comprehensive estimate. Tom Paine, like many of his contemporaries at the end of the 18th century, believed education to be an essential right, and the next step in the liberation of mankind. 'One schoolmaster,' he declared with anticlerical gusto, 'is of more use than a hundred priests.' But Paine also remarked on another occasion: 'As to the learning that any person gains from school education, it serves only like a small capital, to put him in a way of beginning himself afterward. Every person of learning is finally his own teacher.' Emerson would surely have concurred.

p 182
(19)

p 184
(26, 27)

A second, related problem is that there has been continuous and sometimes ferocious disagreement over education in the United States. The balance sheet of gains and losses is always being redrawn; what one man regards as an achievement may appear to another as a disaster. A generation ago, American educationalists such as George S. Counts perceived the historical span of their subject as a grand, an unequaled success. As late as 1956, in the preface he contributed to someone else's text, Counts reiterated that the unique American contribution was the 'educational ladder' of elementary, secondary and higher schooling, supported by public taxation. It had been created earlier than comparable schemes in other countries, and was still embracing a higher proportion of the 15–21 age group than anywhere else in the world. Statistically, Counts was correct, and the process has continued since he wrote. By 1970 the majority of Americans remained in high school until the age of 17; and two out of every five of college age were enrolled in institutions of higher learning. Without the great American educational ladder, Counts concluded, 'a régime of liberty would not have been established over such a vast territory. Without it the fabulously productive industrial economy, with its insatiable demands for skills, . . . resourcefulness, and creative talent, would have been impossible. Without it the formation of a single people out of the many nations, races, and religious sects coming to our shores from the Old World would have faltered.'

As we shall see later, some scholars would dispute the *historical* accuracy of the Countsian kind of saga, which tended to interpret educational history narrowly and perhaps anachronistically, and to claim too much for the profession. But the 1950s saw the upsurge of another kind of attack on American educational orthodoxy. Instead of *achievements*, commentators began to speak of *crises*. Starting with a challenge to grade-school education, expressed in books with titles like *Educational Wastelands* and *Why Johnny Can't Read*, the new unrest spread to an often savage critique of higher education—mounted initially by the students themselves and then supported by various sympathetic professionals. The important point to the critics was not how many pupils were being processed, but how good the process was—usually with an underlying implication that standardization was the enemy of standards.

A In Adam's Fall We sinned all.

B Thy Life to mend; This Book attend.

C The Cat doth play, And after slay.

D A Dog will bite A Thief at night.

E An Eagle's flight Is out of sight.

F The idle Fool Is whipt at school.

A page from the New England Primer, published by Benjamin Harris in the late 17th century. It was known as 'The Little Bible of New England'. (1)

Three truisms

So accounts of the historical development of American education, and assessments of the degree of success attained, are now bewilderingly various. The truisms that dominated the pedagogical texts of thirty to forty years ago have been subject to sceptical questioning. Let us briefly consider three of these familiar propositions: the basic early American commitment to public education; the separation between church and state; and the principle of decentralized as against nationally controlled education.

p 178 (2) 1. *The basic commitment.* Here the conventional surveys lay heavy stress upon the founding of Harvard College in 1636, within a few years of the first settlements in the Bay Colony:

> After God had carried us safe to *New England*, and wee had builded our houses, provided necessaries for our livelihood, rear'd convenient places for Gods worship, and setled the Civill Government: One of the next things we longed for, and looked after was to advance *Learning* and perpetuate it to Posterity; dreading to leave an illiterate Ministry to the Churches, when our present Ministers shall lie in the Dust.

By 1650 Harvard had established the four-year course that still characterizes American colleges, and was conferring its own degrees: a remarkable achievement in a struggling new colony. Surveys point too to the provision made for schooling in some New England communities even before the celebrated Massachusetts law of 1647, whose preamble began:

p 180–1 (15)
p 183 (23)
> It being one chief project of that old deluder, Satan, to keep men from the knowledge of the Scriptures...; and that Learning may not be buried in the graves of our fore-fathers in Church and Commonwealth, the Lord assisting our indeavours....

p 184 (25) The law enacted that every Massachusetts town of fifty families should open a common school, whose master would teach the children to read and write; and that a grammar school, 'to instruct

youth so far as they may be fitted for the Universitie', should be instituted in every town of a hundred families or more. From these beginnings has been traced the subsequent spread of American popular education. From them has been deduced a passion for scholarship, especially in New England, whose motivation was by f 1 no means entirely religious.

2. *The separation between church and state.* Here the apparent contrast between England and the United States is certainly striking. Until early Victorian days England had only two universities, Oxford and Cambridge, and the colleges in them restricted admission to members of the Church of England. In the American colonies, Harvard, Yale and the other colleges that existed at the time of the p 178 Revolution were each tied to a particular denomination. The Revolution brought in the doctrine of separation between church and state, in educational as in other sides of public life. As new states came into the Union—sometimes, as in the case of Michigan, explicitly providing for higher education in the very initiation of statehood—the pristine state universities were avowedly nondenominational. Federal educational institutions, notably the United States Military Academy at West Point (1802), rotated their f 7 chaplaincies among the major Protestant denominations. Although a great many colleges came into being in the 19th century under denominational auspices, few attempted to confine student entry to members of the founder-church. And in the public schools— p 185 public in the usual meaning of the term, not in the peculiar inverted (28) British usage, in which 'public' connotes 'private'—the principle became established that, while generalized religious instruction might be provided, no one sect or denomination should be allowed to proselytize.

So much for the received view of church-state separation. But the record is far from simple. A diffused religiosity pervaded American education. Until the early 19th century college presidents p 178 were almost invariably ordained clergymen, and except in major centers the practice persisted until the last third of the century. Hundreds of colleges *were* founded under religious auspices, with the aim of promoting the growth in some new area of the Methodist or Presbyterian or Episcopal (Anglican) faith. Separation did not entail secularism, and certainly not the anti-clericalism that became a feature of the school systems of certain countries in continental Europe. Even the great Horace Mann of Massachusetts, a tireless p 183 advocate of universal public schooling, never contemplated god- (24) lessness in the nation's classrooms. The United States was, he once perhaps artlessly declared, a 'Protestant' country—by which he meant a religious one. Roman Catholicism, vastly extended through p 186 immigration in the second half of the 19th century, seemed to its (33) defenders to be subtly discriminated against, in public schools f 4 orientated—even if unwittingly—toward Protestantism. For this and other reasons American Catholics established a comprehensive educational network, ranging upward from parochial schools to universities. By 1970, with the American Catholic population as large as that of England, their educational domain was comparably vast, and constituted a system-within-a-system. Even the seemingly absolute rule of no public funds for Catholic (or other 'private') education was beginning to be modified. The Elementary and Secondary Educational Act of 1965, for example, authorized the spending of over one billion dollars in grants of Federal money to the States to raise the levels of instruction in backward areas; and the grants were available to church-supported as well as public schools.

3. *Decentralization.* Here too we must beware of oversimplified assertions. The principle of national control is undoubtedly far weaker in the United States than in most other countries. Proposals made by George Washington, James Madison and other Founding Fathers to create a national university met with less and less enthusiasm as the years went by, and were never implemented—at least, not in ways that the original proposers would have recognized. Outside America systematic education tended to grow up under the auspices of the national government. The school curriculum was so rigidly and so minutely administered in France, for instance, that until very recently administrators in Paris knew exactly what lessons were being imparted, age-group by age-group,

all over the country, at any given moment. In France and elsewhere, school and university teachers are regarded as civil servants. In the United States, on the other hand, the basic unit of school-administration is the local board of each school-district, whose members are laymen. Educational boards of individual states have long been accustomed to wield much greater power over educational policy than that of remote officials in the nation's capital. The officials who matter are district superintendents: they have no direct connection at all with Washington, D.C. About half of the 2,200 colleges and universities now existing in the United States were founded by private or religious groups, and they have maintained their governing autonomy. The remaining 1,100 institutions may be classified as state or city enterprises. Many of these latter foundations received scant support in their early days, in part because the funds available went to other 'educational' purposes. The University of Michigan was created in 1837. In 1860 the Michigan regents were still complaining that while the legislature readily provided appropriations for reform schools and lunatic asylums, the University had yet to receive any money from the very assembly that might have been expected to nurture it.

On the other hand it may be suggested that American education has historically been subject to a good deal of external control and influence, and that this has included legislative control. Federal policy promoted the spread of educational institutions through subsidy in the form of land-grants. The pattern—of turning over sections of public land to the States to supply an income earmarked for education—dates back to the Northwest Ordinance of 1785. It was reaffirmed in the Morrill Act (1862), which used Federal land-grants as a means of endowing new state 'A. and M.' (agricultural and mechanical) colleges. Subsequent Federal legislation—the Hatch Act (1887), the Smith-Lever Act (1914) and the Smith-Hughes Act (1928)—furnished grants to the States, sometimes on a matching basis, to stimulate vocational teaching and research, with p 179 (9) particular emphasis on agriculture and domestic science (or 'home economics'). The principle of Federal involvement thus remained alive. And however modest the beginnings or uneven the application, responsibility for education at *state* level was never in doubt. The relative remoteness of *Federal* control should not blind us to the authority entrusted to state governments. Every state except one or two of the original thirteen colonies created a state university at an early stage—Georgia in 1785, North Carolina in 1789, Tennessee in 1794, and so on. They did not become notable centers of learning for several decades; but then, not even Harvard or Yale or the other famous private foundations emerged as universities in the modern sense of the term until quite late in the 19th century.

p 185 (29) p 186 (32) As for the Federal involvement, the end of World War II marked a decisive augmentation. Veterans (ex-servicemen) received college tuition grants under the 'G.I. Bill'. Federal funds for research projects in natural and social science became major contributions to university revenue. The shock to national pride of the Russian Sputnik launchings of 1957 led to the National Defense Education Act (NDEA) of 1958. This appropriated 887 million dollars for improved instruction and study in science, mathematics and foreign languages, and included scholarships and loans for college students. President Lyndon B. Johnson gave a prominent place to education in his schemes for the 'Great Society'. The Higher Education Facilities Act (1963) provided funds for college building. An extended NDEA (1964) created grants for scholarships in the humanities. By 1964 the Federal government was spending over two billion dollars a year on education. This figure was substantially increased by legislation in 1965 to support elementary, secondary and college education, both through grants to the states and direct to students in the form of loans and scholarships. The trend toward increasing Federal involvement is almost certainly irreversible.

It is often said that the United States is a nation whose geographical vastness embraces startling differences of outlook between one region and another. This is undeniable. But in the circumstances it seems still more remarkable that the various regions have been so pervasively 'Americanized'; and this is as noticeable in education as in other respects. Some districts have comprehensive secondary schooling while others have split the secondary stage into junior and senior high schools. That is a

minor variation in face of the recognizable, national pattern. Imitation and competitive emulation, the drive to inculcate national pride through the public schools, the dissemination of doctrine through institutions like Teachers College of Columbia University, and the sheer utility of standardizing practices in grading, admissions, etc., to meet the needs of an extremely mobile population: all these have combined to create a pattern as homogeneous in its way as the deliberately centralized systems of some other countries. Localities have responded to a national mood to which they have been acutely attuned. In 1890, for example, North p 182 (20) Dakota and New Jersey, two states 1500 miles apart and with apparently almost nothing in common, passed laws to oblige schoolhouses to fly the national flag each day. Other states swiftly p 186 (33) followed. With equal rapidity in the same era state after state introduced legislation to compel the teaching of American history and civics in their public schools.

Taking these three proverbially unique aspects of American education, then, we can see that if the total pattern is unmistakably American, merely to emphasize uniqueness is misleading. The basic commitment to education preceded that of Europe and was more wholehearted. But it has not been quite so continuous and clearcut as some patriotic American chroniclers have urged. The diminution and in certain realms the disappearance of church control has not entailed an entire absence of religious influences in American education. And the localized, decentralized evolution of American education has nevertheless resulted in a nationwide system whose features are essentially the same in every state.

The historical perspective

The best way to put these difficulties into perspective, and to understand the controversies of the present day, is to retrace the historical development of education in the United States. One possible method would be to divide the past three and a half centuries into periods and to look for dominant impulses within each. Thus it could be argued that, whatever other elements were present, the *religious* impulse was the most powerful within Colonial America. The period from the Revolution to the Civil War could be seen as dominated by the *democratic* impulse. That from the Civil War to about 1900 might be taken as the era when *socializing and vocational* aspects were foremost—this era overlapping with the concern for specialization, especially in higher education, which has been so marked from about 1870 to 1970. But it is obvious that each impulse, having been generated, remained in being. It is salutary too to remember that before the present century, not only the theoretical treatises but the innovations in actual teaching practice or ancillary education have usually originated in Europe. Though quickly adapted to American circumstances, Sunday p 182 (19) schools and devices for adult education such as lyceums and mechanics' institutes were first launched in England; so was the Lancasterian system, by which bright older pupils were trained as f 2 monitors and then passed on their knowledge to the younger children. French formulations interested American educators from

The monitor system introduced by Joseph Lancaster, an English educationalist. Pupils form into a semi-circle at the command of their monitor (from 'The Lancasterian System of Education, with Improvements', 1821). (2)

p 183
(24)

Jefferson onward. All levels of German education enjoyed high prestige in 19th-century America. The systematic division of children by age-group, into classes or 'grades', was pioneered by Prussia and transmitted to Massachusetts in the 1840s by Horace Mann, secretary of the State Board of Education, after a tour of European schools. Even Tsarist Russia seemed to hold lessons for American education. The Philadelphia Centennial Exposition of 1876 provided an impressive display of national prowess in science and technology. But to the president of the Massachusetts Institute of Technology (MIT), the most instructive exhibit was one of objects produced by students of the Moscow Imperial Technical School. The combination of theoretical teaching and practical craftsmanship struck him as 'the philosophical key to all industrial education'; MIT immediately introduced engineering workshops on the Moscow model. In the 19th century American education-alists revealed a close awareness of the precepts of such European

p 182
(18)

mentors as Pestalozzi, Froebel (from whom the *kindergarten* derived: the first American example dates from 1857), and Herbart.

So the orchestration of American educational themes was never purely indigenous. This is no reflection upon American resource-fulness. In part it is merely to recall that colonial and early national America was a new society; from John Adams to Walt Whitman come frequent assertions that the present generation must concern itself with everyday necessities in order that future generations may have the leisure for learning and the arts. The historic role of the United States was, it appeared, to make actual what Europeans for the most part were only able to dream about. Ideas were abundantly generated in Europe: the plasticity of American life offered the opportunity to put them to the test.

Religious aspects. Well into the 19th century recurrent waves of alarm swept the nation: alarm that the nation seemed to be slipping into godless and mindless apathy. The peril appeared most serious in the new western settlements. Vigorous ministers such as the Yale-educated Lyman Beecher preached the need for urgent, large-scale remedies, in the shape of a great missionary campaign by the churches to plant the word of God in the backwoods. This missionary zeal, together with the West's own boosterish spirit of self-improving self-advertisement led (as Daniel J. Boorstin has shown in *The Americans: The National Experience*) to an extra-ordinary burst of college-founding through most of the 19th century. 'In every state a Baptist college' was a slogan much heard in the 1820s. The other denominations were equally thrusting. Boorstin cites the case of Wooster in Ohio. At the end of the Civil War, in 1865, the Presbyterian synod of that state, anxious to have a Presbyterian college in the area, sought pledges of support from suitable townships. Wooster defeated its rivals by producing a free site and $100,000 in promised cash donations. So arose from nothing the University of Wooster. 'What we desire', the board of trustees declared, 'is to make Wooster the great educational center of Ohio as Oxford and Cambridge are in England and the Universi-ties are in Germany and France.'

Ex nihilo nihil? This staggering development had ambiguous consequences. Far too many colleges were created in thinly settled districts where neither funds nor students were available in sufficient quantity. By 1860 more than 700 colleges had given up the ghost. Philip Lindsley, president of the new non-denominational University of Nashville, said in 1834:

> A principal cause of the excessive multiplication and dwarfish dimensions of Western colleges is . . . the diversity of religious denominations among us. . . . Of the score of colleges in Ohio, Kentucky and Tennessee, all are sectarian except two or three; . . . and the greater part are mere impositions on the public. . . . Must every State be divided and subdivided into as many college associations as there are religious sects within its limits? And thus, by their mutual jealousy . . ., effectually prevent the useful-ness and prosperity of any one institution?

p 186
(33)
f 4

But if religious aspects colored American education, the ultimate outcome was a secularization of these church establishments. Disagreement over religious instruction in schools, as we have seen, brought about the elimination of Bible classes from public education. One Catholic scholar speaks of 'the contradiction inherent in the very idea of one common school attempting to serve a religiously pluralistic society'. Certainly the implications were contradictory. In New York in the 1840s, controversy between Protestants and Catholics over the religious content of instruction in schools ended in the state taking over their adminis-tration from a private body known anomalously as the Public School Society. On the other hand Catholic dissatisfactions, and the creation of a separate Catholic school system, tended to reinforce the lingering protests of *laissez-faire* liberals who resisted state control. As late as the 1890s the Catholic Bishop of Trenton, New Jersey, was maintaining that 'the idea that the state has a right to teach . . . is not a Christian idea. It is a pagan one.'

At college level, as Boorstin points out, interdenominational rivalry paradoxically produced 'Nothingarianism'—a non-specific religiosity offering a welcome to all comers. Religious enterprise merged with other motives, to furnish a vigorous if chaotic multi-plicity of astonishingly similar institutions, neither public nor private but somewhere in between: *community* colleges in several senses of the word. Whether religious or secular in origin, each frequently had to struggle for survival in the first years. Under-enrollment was farcically apparent in western areas even where the infant foundation was officially conceived. There was a moment shortly after the Civil War when the brand-new state university of Kansas had only one professor teaching one girl student—and he reduced the student body to nil by marrying her. Local, community philanthropy therefore became essential, to found colleges and then to keep them going. With no inconsistency in their own eyes, colleges also sought and sometimes obtained grants from public funds. Casting about for money, American colleges soon perceived the importance of alumni (graduates). Princeton's alumni associ-ation dates back to 1826, that of Harvard to 1842. Since then, love for one's Alma Mater has been ingeniously nurtured, and become commercially indispensable to many institutions. The award of honorary degrees to potential benefactors, whether or not they were alumni, was another device put to early and wide use.

p 178

Religion did not vanish from the scene. If state universities lacked divinity schools, their presence on other campuses more than made up the gap. In the 20th century, fierce disagreements over religious rituals in schools or the use of public funds for church-supported schools continued to erupt from time to time, even reaching as high as the Supreme Court.

The democratic impulse

In achieving independence from the mother country the American colonies, which had never at first hand known an aristocracy of the European kind, opened themselves to the implications of the Jeffersonian proposition that all men are created equal. True, by this they understood *white* men, and men more than women. Even so the air of the late 18th century was full of promise, and promises. Jefferson's Bill for the More General Diffusion of Knowledge, introduced into the Virginia legislature in 1779, anticipated by more than a decade the French schemes of Condorcet and others.

The Ladies' Hall at Oberlin College, Ohio, from the 1854–55 Catalogue, which also listed the 'Ladies' Board of Managers' of the Female De-partment. (3)

'*The American River Ganges: the Priests and the Children*', *a cartoon by Thomas Nast (1871), illustrating the current controversy over the teaching* *of Catholic doctrine in schools. Nast saw it as a threat to the nation's youth.* (4)

Like them he envisaged a system of free public elementary schools; for the best way to guard against political tyranny was 'to illuminate, as far as practicable, the minds of the people at large'. By the time of the Civil War the idea of public schools, locally controlled and tax-supported, commanded fairly general assent, and in some states was firmly established. By 1900, of the one million American children undergoing secondary education, nearly 90% were enrolled in public high schools: the strictly private sector had dwindled into statistical insignificance. The same principle was enshrined in an increasing number of state institutions for higher education. The Berkeley campus of the University of California, for instance, had opened in 1873. Its catalogue proudly announced: 'Tuition in all departments of the University except the Medical College, is ABSOLUTELY FREE.' The names of professional educators such as Henry Barnard of Connecticut and Horace Mann of Massachusetts, who had helped to bring about this educational revolution, are commemorated appropriately in a number of educational establishments. Parts of Horace Mann's annual reports to the Massachusetts Board of Education are unsurpassed as examples of the democratic faith in pedagogy:

p 186
(30, 31)

> I believe in the existence of a great, immutable principle of natural law . . .,—a principle antecedent to all human institutions . . .,—a principle of divine origin, clearly legible in the ways of Providence . . .,—which proves the *absolute right* of every human being that comes into the world to an education; and which, of course, proves the correlative duty of every government to see that the means of that education are provided for all. . . .
> Education, . . . beyond all other devices of human origin, is the great equalizer of the conditions of men—the balance-wheel of the social machinery.

But the previous paragraph pays too little attention to the time-dimension. In fact progress was uneven: rapid in some areas, sluggish in others. Jefferson's bill never passed; by the Civil War Virginia still had no public school system. New England was by comparison far ahead, as was New York. Yet Mann's reports, on closer inspection, are a summons to action rather than a vote of thanks for what has been accomplished. He attributes the gains made by Massachusetts to things done two whole centuries ago by the Pilgrim Fathers, and indicates that the advance has been painfully slow. He is a propagandist for a cause yet to be put to a nationwide test. At his death in 1859 the majority of American students at the secondary stage were still in private schools, and the total figure was probably not more than about 70,000. Elementary schooling was much more widespread, but that was where the educational ladder stopped for the bulk of American children. Higher education for women was severely limited; Emily Dickinson's Mount Holyoke was as yet a seminary, not a college, and Vassar, the first academically distinguished college for women, did not open until 1865. The principle of co-education had started at Oberlin College, Ohio, in 1837, and been adopted at Antioch, also in Ohio, in 1853, and by the new state university of Iowa in 1855. For Negroes college education before the Civil War was almost impossible. Antioch—where Horace Mann had incidentally gone to be its first president—was still something of a pioneer in being ready to admit black as well as women students. True, a great many colleges for white youths *were* founded, and some of these— including Jefferson's University of Virginia, his brainchild—were admirable. He had conceived it as the summit of his plan for a comprehensive state system. But it took forty years to realize from the mention in his bill of 1779, and was the only part of the plan to be implemented. A summit without a base? It begins to appear that too many colleges were founded and not enough schools, or

p 178–9
(7, 11)
p 180
(13)
f 3

public schools, in the first half of the 19th century. Richard Hofstadter indeed regards this as the period of the 'Great Retrogression' in American higher education. In *The Development of Academic Freedom in the United States* (1955) he argues that too high a price was paid for the premature popularization of education. Standards actually deteriorated. Teaching and library resources were poor, discipline penally harsh, academic freedom flouted by boorish trustees.

This is probably too gloomy a view. Because of its special concern with academic freedom it omits a number of factors, and exaggerates the victory of egalitarianism, or of low-browism. The Texas legislator who in opposing an 1856 bill for a state university portrayed such institutions as 'the ovens to heat up and hatch all manner of vice, immorality and crime' was hardly a typical spokesman for his time—though it must be conceded that he is not the only American, then or since, to have harbored suspicions of that sort. More to the point is the hesitation of Jefferson and his contemporaries over the feasibility of a thoroughly egalitarian educational system. His scheme for Virginia was not a ladder but a pyramid. The 1779 bill spoke of illuminating people's minds 'as far as practicable'; and here Jefferson took for granted that only a proportion of those who emerged from elementary schooling would go on to the secondary level, from which again only the intellectual cream would rise to the final, university stage.

In one vital respect the ideals of Jeffersonian Americans did however anticipate the attitudes of their successors. The democratic imperative as such did not dominate their arguments. They put forward all sorts of reasons why the United States should educate as many of its citizens as possible. Egalitarianism was only one of the reasons. The same formulas were produced half a century later by Horace Mann, in his eloquent last annual report (1848). Education, he says, enables all men to be prosperous: 'It does better than to disarm the poor of their hostility towards the rich; it prevents being poor.' Education supplies an indispensable training in republican methods and principles—to be imparted solemnly and non-controversially. Wickedness and violence threaten societies: 'Now, how best shall this deluge be repelled? What mighty power, or combination of powers, can prevent its inrushing, or narrow the sweep of its ravages?' Moral education, is Horace Mann's answer. To be sure, there is nothing 'reactionary' in such observations. They embody a sort of diffusedly democratic emotion. But they claim so much that they lose definition. One begins to feel the 'yawning of the jaws' of which Emerson spoke. Democracy has become equated with America, and with the *status quo*. The cry is for more education, but there is a vagueness about what education *means*.

One of the problems faced by Mann's generation of educators—those, that is, who favored public education—was that theirs was the era of the private academies: state-chartered, fee-paying institutions, often with good teaching and flexible curricula. They could be defended as ideal American institutions. The Reverend Edward Hitchcock, president of Amherst College, sang their praises in 1845. Free from governmental influence, catering to all levels, they were the perfect instrument of education for the sturdy American who 'will not consent to have others tell him what course of study he shall adopt, and how far he shall pursue it'. Mann did not argue that they should have their charters withdrawn. He saw that the only way to combat them was to elevate public schooling to the same height. But in his first report (1837) he explained why academies were harmful. They sapped the energies and the financial and intellectual resources of their district:

p 180–1
(15)
p 183
(23)
p 184
(25)

All this inevitably depressed and degraded the common school. In this depressed and degraded state, another portion of the parents find it, in fitness and adequacy, inferior to their wants; and, as there is now a private school in the neighborhood, the strength of the inducement, and the facility of the transfer, overbalance the objection of increased expense.... Thus another blow is dealt; then others escape; action and reaction alternate, until the common school is left to the management of those, who have not the desire or the power either to improve it or to command a better.

Everyone who is familiar with an intermingling of public and

private schools can recognize the force of Mann's picture. Yet there are ironies in the story which suggest that force of circumstance rather than ideology determined the fate of the academies. Some, like Exeter and Andover, have remained in being. Others modulated into colleges. The majority disappeared. According to Theodore R. Sizer (*The Age of the Academies*, 1964) the reason was not that Americans became convinced they were undemocratic; indeed, those in western states had little social cachet. The reason was the growing density of population. The academy was above all a rural institution. So long as it was competing with the rural public school it could win, especially in states whose school systems were feeble. But it could not compete with the big urban high school with well-equipped plant and specialist teachers. Here too Mann was correct in understanding the terms of the contest. The 1880s, the decade that saw the 'closing' of the old continuous frontier of unsettled land, also marked the point at which for the first time in American history the number of children in public schools exceeded those being privately educated.

Socializing and vocationalism

With the tipping of the balance came a redefinition of the role of the school. Hitherto the public high school had tended to function as a tax-supported academy, aimed at preparing a fairly high proportion of its pupils for college entrance. Now, as the nation's high-school system began to approximate the conditions Mann had dreamed of, great effort was put into school-building, the proper training of teachers and so forth. Correspondingly, great things were expected of the nation's schoolrooms. Education in the widest sense had long been America's panacea. American writing on social questions, which grew greatly in volume after the Civil War in response to the newly urgent problems created by urbanization and industrialization and mass immigration, tended to be loftier, more genial and less specific than that of Europe. Elementary, secondary and higher education were expected to generate the enlightenment typified in their founding, like a perpetual-motion machine. The duty of education was to educate, in every conceivable way. For the schools of the eastern cities there was the task of turning hundreds of thousands of immigrant children, most of whose parents could not speak English on arrival, into acceptable young Americans. In 1909 over half the children at school in the nation's major cities were of foreign-born parentage. In New York the percentage was 71.5, in Chicago 67.3, in Boston 63.5. The schools were expected to make the children of native-born Americans into still better Americans. In recent years there has been a swing in the other direction: a feeling that the pluralism in American life—the ethnic and religious diversity—ought to have been left to flourish instead of being subjected to homogenizing or 'Americanizing' pressures with their melting-pot utopianism. But of course the alternative vision, of a happily heterogeneous society, is itself utopian. Out of a blend of motives—some crass, some exalted, but in the main well-meaning—the nation's educational system acknowledged and even proclaimed its role as servant of the community.

p 181
(16, 17
p 182
(21)

It followed, in the closing decades of the 19th century, that the public schools would be as public as possible. They would prepare young Americans to be adult Americans. It followed too that the acquisition of knowledge could be treated as a socializing activity, and carried forward on all fronts. The Chautauqua movement, which began as a summer training scheme for the religiously inclined in the 1870s, widened into a large-scale program of open-air learning. The combination of a hot climate and increased leisure and prosperity turned the summer months into an immense, multifarious season of recreation-cum-instruction for middle-class Americans of all ages. The fashion spread also in western Europe. Some of its manifestations—the Boy Scout movement (1908) and university extramural courses are instances—could be claimed to originate in Britain. But the spread of summer camps for children, summer drama and dance groups, summer university sessions, has gone further in the United States than anywhere else in the world during the past hundred years. The founding of libraries and museums, often in a burst of civic pride, and the attempt to make them attractively accessible to the public, is also a conspicuous feature of the post-Civil War decades.

p 182–
(22)

f 5

The interior of the Cincinnati Public Library, sketched by Feorge W. Rapp in 1869, the year after its opening. Originally designed as an opera house, it was sold while building was in progress and converted to its present purpose. (5)

In the schools and colleges, one of the most complicated issues was the degree to which formal instruction should directly serve the community. In its crudest form this meant the insistence that children and undergraduates should learn practical skills instead of 'useless' knowledge: household management, say, or at a subsequent stage shorthand-typing and car-driving. For some educators the establishment of separate technical high schools or of the land-grant colleges were dangerous concessions to popular sentiment. A few critics were appalled by the way American colleges, in the act of expanding, apparently enslaved themselves to the American business ethic. One of the most direct signs was business schools, of which the first in a long line, the University of Pennsylvania's Wharton School, was established in 1881. But the threat, according to the critics, was more subtly pervasive. John Jay Chapman, a Harvard graduate and a patrician of powerfully idiosyncratic temperament, refused to be rhapsodic about the expansionist reforms of the new breed of college presidents such as Charles W. Eliot of Harvard:

> Eliot's prominence is connected with the rise of the new education, that . . . blind battling for light, which began in America during the seventies, when the opinion prevailed that the commercial growth of the United States . . . compelled the pulling down of the old buildings and old curricula, and the making of all things anew. I have heard William James say, 'Yes, yes, we must have large things first, size first; the rest will come.' This was the unspoken philosophy, the inner compelling, dumb thought of the epoch. . . . In the case of Doctor Eliot the subjection of the administrator to his age was especially apparent; for Eliot's first great need was a need of money; and money could only come from State Street and Wall Street, and could only be expended in ways which the business men of America approved. The money question is the key to Doctor Eliot's career, merely because it is the key to his epoch. His very extraordinary nature could, I believe, have ruled a seventeenth-century theocracy. He cared nothing for money; he cared merely for power. But power in the United States between 1870–1910 meant money power: therefore Eliot's nature took on a financial hue.

Thorstein Veblen made a similar point in his caustic analysis of *The Higher Learning in America* (1918). Veblen did not deny that rich businessmen were munificent in their gifts. He had taught at two new universities, Chicago and Stanford, which at the outset were dependent respectively upon the oil wealth of John D. Rockefeller and the railroad fortune of Leland Stanford. His complaint, like that of Chapman, was that the socializing and vocational aspects of the public school system, the training for citizenship which he conceded was desirable for children, had swamped higher education. In his view, 'anything like an effectual university —a seminary of the higher learning, as distinct from an assemblage of vocational schools—is not a practicable proposition in America under current conditions.' Nor did he think things were any better in the state universities; state legislatures and boards of regents

p 178 (5)

p 179 (8)

were at least as narrowly materialistic as millionaire philanthropists, in fact often more so—Rockefeller for instance genuinely admired scholarship and made no attempt to interfere with the detailed running of Chicago.

f 6   The results could certainly be bizarre. The 1931 curriculum of the University of Nebraska listed courses in early Irish, creative thinking, American English, first aid, advanced clothing, ice cream and ices, third-year Czechoslovakian, football, sewerage, and a man's problems in the modern home. Offerings no less surrealistically miscellaneous can still be culled from American catalogues, especially those of some of the large state universities. But the situation was more complex than Chapman or Veblen were ready to admit. At all times and in all countries schools have sought to mold good citizens and colleges to train men in the professions—
p 178 (6)   teaching, preaching, law, medicine. To the extent that education in the United States was a community activity, it was inevitable that the nation's educational institutions should reflect national values and also strive to be useful to their society. Criteria of utility and relevance were in themselves perfectly sensible. The recurrent attacks from the 18th century onward on the teaching of Greek and Latin were often launched not by ignoramuses but by men who honestly regarded them as archaic vestiges, retained through conservatism at the expense of more intellectually satisfying and more vital subjects—including English. The argument that it was impossible to teach children things whose relevance they could not perceive, and that they should therefore link the activities of the classroom with those of their communities, was at the end of the 19th century not a businessman's slogan but the crusading contention of radically innovative educators like John Dewey. In fact, taking the century as a whole, the astonishing feature of American education was the conventionality not the novelty of the curriculum. Chapman and Veblen were protesting at the overthrow of a college system which many of their contemporaries had found narrow and rigid in the extreme. The idea of a state university applying its skills to the advancement of society seemed electrifyingly impressive in the Wisconsin of Robert M. LaFollette. The university and the state capital were both in the same town, Madison. In the early years of this century the University of Wisconsin was spoken of as the 'fourth branch' of the government; its faculty appeared to be indoctrinating the legislators rather than the other way round. The difficulty was to know where to draw the line between service to society and subservience to its material goals.

Specialization. On the whole, at least at the beginning, the recasting of higher education was enthusiastically welcomed. There had been too many parochial little colleges—places 'as stagnant as a Spanish convent, and as self-satisfied as a Bourbon duchy', in the words of
p 178 (2)   President Andrew D. White of Cornell. Ralph Waldo Emerson had been no slavish admirer of the old Harvard from which he had graduated. He noted with approval, in 1869, that 'the friends of

Harvard are possessed by the idea of making it a University for men, instead of a College for boys.' Looking back on what happened under Eliot another Harvard alumnus, Charles Francis Adams, was almost as disdainful as Chapman. His emphasis is however interestingly different. In the passage quoted above Chapman complains of the triumph of the business ethic. Adams's complaint was that the old Harvard of rote-learning and parrotlike recitation had been bad, but that Eliot's new structure of numerous 'elective' courses, to be chosen by students according to taste, introduced 'the yet more pernicious system of premature specialization. This is a confusion of the college and university functions and constitutes a direct menace to all true high education. The function of the college is an all-around development, as a basis for university specializations. Eliot never grasped that fundamental fact, and so he undertook to turn Harvard college into a German university—specializing the student at eighteen.'

America certainly did follow the German example. Johns Hopkins (1876), the first all-graduate American university, announced through the inaugural address of President Daniel Coit Gilman the intent to aim at the exploration of 'all useful knowledge; . . . the encouragement of research; . . . and the advancement of individual scholars.' The PhD was the new badge of professionalism. By 1900 any person of serious academic pretensions was expected to immerse himself in a lengthy period of research in pursuit of his doctorate. Half a century passed after that before American academic circles began to suspect that the PhD thesis requirement might have done as much to impede as to stimulate true scholarship. In the first decades there was something exhilarating in the expansive rigor of the new learning. Some foundations like Johns Hopkins and Chicago made their name almost overnight. Several of the state universities began to build first-rate departments. Smith, Bryn Mawr and other new women's colleges, while less grandiose in conception, quickly demonstrated their quality. The older colleges for men, notably Harvard, Yale, Columbia and Princeton, showed their determination to stay among the front-runners. As scholarship became more specialized college-teachers ceased to profess a multiplicity of fields. They now talked of 'disciplines'; and each discipline began to group itself into a national professional body, usually with its own learned periodical. Hence the Modern Language Association (1883), the American Historical Association (1884), and the American Economic Association (1885). Pedagogy itself became a professional subject, though it was regarded by other academics with a skepticism that has still not entirely vanished.

Not every college became a powerhouse of learning. And in those that did make big efforts there was a considerable gap between the researchers and the main collegiate mass. For this was also the era of the rise of college athletics. By the 1890s college football   *p 179*
generated intense excitement—in part because it had been dis-   *(10)*
covered that potential benefactors liked to identify themselves   *f 7*

A cartoon in a 1927 issue of 'Life' magazine ridiculed the subjects listed in many university curricula. 'Advanced sandwich-making' was hardly more far-fetched than some of the courses actually offered to students. (6)

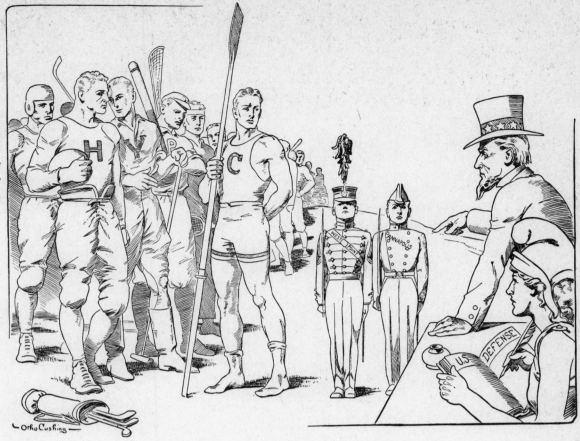

178 (5) with winning teams. President William Rainey Harper of Chicago, whose team was losing in a game with Wisconsin, delivered himself as follows: 'Boys, Mr Rockefeller has just announced a gift of three million dollars to the University. He believes the University to be great. The way you played in the first half leads me to wonder whether we really have the spirit of greatness in ambition. I wish you would make up your minds to win this game and show that we do have it.' For some professors sport and scholarship were not incompatible. In his pre-political days Woodrow Wilson helped to coach the Princeton team. Even football could be seen as a field for specialized work. The athletic side of college life was to grow to monstrous proportions. The president of a Middle Western state university made a revealing slip in a speech some years ago: his dream, he said, was 'to create a university that the football team can be proud of'. Once again, the line has proved difficult to draw between the right and the wrong kind of zeal.

Taking the whole picture of American educational development up to the 1950s however, the salient impression is of expansion, improvement and optimism. As in all branches of human endeavor, yesterday's reforms are apt to become today's stumbling blocks. The Harvard elective system brought in by Eliot was severely modified in the interests of coherence by President Lowell, Eliot's successor. Robert M. Hutchins, who later followed Harper as president of Chicago, abolished football there as one step in a sweeping critique of academic practices. His book *The Higher Learning in America* (1936) was as much a diatribe as Veblen's previous volume of the same title. But up to the 1950s, growth and achievement appeared to move in tandem. The statistics were formidable. By 1960 well over 3 million Americans were enrolled in higher education, as against 160,000 in 1890. In 1890 graduate schools were still in their infancy, enrolling only 2,400 students throughout the United States. The number soared to well over 300,000 by 1960, of whom incidentally about a third were women. In 1890, 150 students earned PhDs. In 1960 the figure was over 10,000. Other indices, such as Nobel awards in science and medicine, suggested how high the United States stood in relation to the rest of the world. A good deal of the world's best work scholarship in social science and the humanities emanated from American universities; and that mattered far more than the reflection that some of the world's annual output of trivial, tedious scholarship was also American in provenance. A similar unevenness was evident in the nation's high schools. Some were dismally sub-collegiate in spirit, or beset by terrible problems in the city slums. Many however were admirable; and though perhaps none was better academically than the best private schools, such as Exeter Academy, their cumulative quality was such that the private sector remained relatively tiny.

Current problems and proposals

Why then the spate of books since the 1950s with titles like *Educational Wastelands*, *The Berkeley Revolt* and *The Dissenting Academy*? Why has the word 'multiversity', of proud coinage only a dozen years ago, dropped into disuse or disrepute?

One reason is purely economic. Education is expensive, and the costs increase with every extra year of schooling. A high-school place costs more than a grade-school place. More money is needed for an undergraduate than for a high-school student, and more for a postgraduate than an undergraduate. However education is financed, someone has to pay. The more ambitious and the more genuinely democratic the system, the heavier the burden upon local, state and national taxes. Lyndon B. Johnson's Great Society announced not for the first time that all Americans had a right to as much education, including college education, as they felt they needed. Various similar statements had been made for well over a century. The difference came with the sheer spread of belief that college education was desirable: attainable: necessary. And of those who already took for granted the acquisition of a BA, an additional period of graduate school began to seem essential. Even if the nation's prosperity had continued to grow as much as in the 1940s and 1950s, the point would still have been reached at which even the richest nation on earth would find itself unable to foot the bill for an infinitely expanding educational universe. But economic recession and the costs of the Vietnam war forced the issue.

Hesitations over education have been apparent throughout American history because of the difficulty of defining its scope, or deciding between the claims of different parts of the system. There has always been dissatisfaction too on the part of some people over elements that others might take pride in. But recent circumstances have thrust together several kinds of dissatisfaction. One widespread criticism, lucidly outlined in Lawrence A. Cremin's *The Transformation of the School* (1961), is of so-called Progressive teaching, for which John Dewey has been held largely responsible. Each school, Dewey had said, should become 'an embryonic community life', reflecting in miniature 'the life of the larger society' and yet helping to change it into a 'worthy, lovely, and harmonious' society. He assumed, as did the exponents of the 'Wisconsin Idea', that there was something inherently ameliorative within the educational system—again a parallel with religious institutions. But this parallel could have served to show that the teacher like the preacher usually seeks to persuade men that whatever is, is best: his calls to reform, if any, are usually confined to unobjectionably broad moral precepts. The charge, in Arthur E. Bestor's *The Restoration of Learning* (1955), and Admiral Hyman Rickover's *Education and Freedom* (1959), was that Deweyite educationalists had ruined the nation's schools. Teachers were stuffed with pretentious nonsense about 'life-adjustment'. In the eyes of the angry Admiral Rickover, shocked by what Sputnik seemed to reveal of American inferiority to Soviet Russia, the nation's children had ceased to learn anything except how to fit in to a slack adult society. Mediocrity had fed reciprocally upon mediocrity. But now, said Rickover, the people were at last aroused to 'the need for reform. . . . Parental objectives no longer coincide with those professed by the progressive educationists.'

Energetic attempts were made to reinstate formal learning in the schools, and with considerable success. But the public's confidence in the experts had been shaken. Within a few years confidence in p 187
(37) university educators was also being shaken, though for very different reasons. It was students who led the way; and ironically their complaints could have been drawn from some of the writings of Dewey. Not all: they would have condemned the moral acquiescence in society's demands that had in fact stirred one of Dewey's former admirers, Randolph Bourne, to castigate him for supporting American involvement in World War I. Otherwise they echoed Deweyite assertions that education must be made 'relevant' to the current scene. Where Professor Bestor wanted education to provide systematic intellectual training, student militants maintained that universities had become impersonal, pedantic, authoritarian. They scoffed at the notion of their elders that to increase student numbers was *per se* a social gain. For those on the crowded campuses of the 1960s, who were bitterly at odds with everything traditional in American life, higher education was battery-farming, mechanical indoctrination, 'brainwashing'. Some of their fiercest attacks were aimed at government-sponsored programmes, including ROTC (military training), and at the activities of foundations and large corporations which they regarded as warmongering, 'Establishment' agencies. They threw many campuses into turmoil. In this bitterly warring atmosphere, few observers could summon up the necessary detachment to note how irony piled upon irony. As the dust died down scholars such as Robert Nisbet (*The Degradation of the Academic Dogma*, 1971) pointed out that universities in the United States had perhaps concerned themselves since 1945 all too much with 'relevance' to society—even if it was a different kind of relevance from that urged by student leaders. For twenty-five years the universities had been showered with government and foundation grants. Could it be, as campus radicals alleged, that the nation's professorate, at least in some of the natural and social sciences, had become subtly corrupted by this beneficence? Had the ancient ideal of research become entangled with entrepreneurial greed?

Only a small minority of students were active militants. Often their attacks on specific aspects of teaching and administration seemed to be pretexts, or the only available means of demonstrating their estrangement from the larger society. They displayed little or no historical awareness (perhaps with a sound instinct: radicals cannot afford to admit that they are re-enacting old dramas, where conservatives take comfort in the thought). Few of them probably would have been interested to know that academic freedom had at times been a heated faculty issue. Yet their arguments, in historical context, seem peculiarly American. They were exactly in line with generations of their forebears in contending that education has a dual task: to be relevant to its society and to improve it. Where they differed of course was on the definition of improvement. And they showed a characteristically utopian American faith that life could be transformed, although by means not quite defined or definable,

through the medium of education. Possibly too they were carrying out the logic of the democratic impulse, which implies not merely education of and for the people but education *by* the people. (Black p 179
(12) militants felt they had been denied all three, and were now telescoping the process so as simultaneously to demand black education p 187 for black people by black people. Some women felt the same way.) (34–6) Hence the claim to a share in university government. In democratic logic they had a case for arguing that it should be a dominant voice, since students formed the majority in each university community.

However altruistic their motives, though, student protest provided one more reason for America's temporary disenchantment with higher education. Some of the student complaints—for instance, that eminent professors were inaccessible and often absent—gained a sympathetic hearing from the taxpaying generation. Other signs of student unrest alienated the taxpayers and convinced them that institutions of higher education might indeed be 'ovens to heat up and hatch all manner of vice, immorality and crime'. Draft-evasion angered Middle America—though it should be said that a great many campuses remained Middle-American in composition and in sentiment. Faced with ever-increasing costs, college presidents found their alumni disapproving of campus unrest and disinclined to part with their money on the previous generous scale.

The 1970s then promised to be full of trouble for American education. In the larger society and within the educational system there was deep division and deep uncertainty over the aims of education, especially at the higher levels. Anyone who reviews the history of education in the United States may conclude that the uncertainty will not be resolved. It is conceivable that higher education has tried to do too many incompatible things, and that its whole pattern will have to be profoundly modified. No solutions are to be found in other countries, which are experiencing kindred difficulties. One proposal, commended by Martin Meyerson, focusses upon the financial problem but sees it as a possible key to other problems. This is to award money to students instead of institutions. In Meyerson's words:

> I can imagine few things that will give the students a greater influence over colleges and universities than their control over the dollar. If a student has through a grant or a loan . . . the funds to pay for his tuition, his living arrangements, and probably some kind of cost-of-education allowance to the institution, the vote of the student would determine the financial viability of many of our institutions. This would not be true of those . . . where the donors are dead, but it would hold for most other institutions.

In short, something like the British method, but applied to 2,200 institutions, many of them in dire financial trouble and some (Meyerson implies) not deserving to survive.

The dilemmas confronting American education are however more fundamental. Here the historical perspective brings a kind of negative consolation. Looking back over the whole span we can discern a series of dualisms or alternative answers. They are the result of the constant social change that typifies Western society. Modern man oscillates between fear and hope, the anchor and the sail, desiring innovation and then repudiating it. In American education as in American thought generally we find regular alternations: becoming and being, freedom and order, individuality and citizenship, feeling and knowing, contemporaneity and heritage. Though there has been an irreversible and enormous enlargement of the sphere of educational opportunity, every new step represents a reaction to its opposite dualism. Horace Mann, on the whole, opted for the 'becoming' set, his successor William Torrey Harris for the 'being' alternative. Dewey stood for 'becoming', Bestor once more for 'being'. And so *ad infinitum*? . . .

IX

NEW-WORLD CITIES

Architecture and townscape

EDMUND N.
BACON

'Only a few are able to live in delightful surroundings;
the rest have to take things as they come. But will
not the people of a continuing democracy awaken some time
to the fact that they can possess as a community
what they cannot as individuals?'

DANIEL H. BURNHAM

How and why

did the New-World city come into being? The first cities in America, as we have seen in Chapter VII, were a projection of European ideas on the terrain of the new continent. Three elements in particular soon began to modify those ideas. The first was the enormous size of the continent, a fact which only gradually seeped into American consciousness, but which eventually produced a dimension in American thinking which had not existed before. The second, which probably grew out of the experience of predominantly working-class settlers taming the wilderness, was a kind of resourcefulness and enterprise, a boldness in technical innovation on a large scale, which both stunted and reinforced urban development. The third has been the continuous insistence on viewing American society as a combination of individuals rather than as a mass pheomenon.

While it is difficult to observe directly the impact of these forces on the shape and character of an American city at any specific moment, their cumulative effect can be seen as cities grow. Indeed, the evolving city is a reflection of the interaction of these three often contradicting forces on the American environment and American institutions. The outcome of the struggle, and the form that will result, is still unclear.

This photograph (opposite) shows the 18th-century 'Shambles', or open air market of Philadelphia; behind it the 19th-century Headhouse, with its octagonal cupola and gold weather-vane, and behind that again the three 20th-century Society Hill Towers designed by I. M. Pei. (The fountain at the base of the towers is just visible through the Shambles.) Together they express one special characteristic of the American mind, an impatience with the purely historical, but at the same time, a deep respect for inherited tradition. The result here, and in some other American cities, is an amalgam of the old and the new giving a freshness to the urban scene. This is possible, however, only because the new respects the essential characteristics of the old. If the Pei Towers had been capricious and expressionistic in form they would have created a horrible dissonance. Because they are a pure expression of structure, reminiscent of the form of the many-paned muntined, 18th-century double hung window, they set up a kind of resonance with the older architecture despite the difference in scale.

These three works together not only constitute a harmonious juxtaposition of architectural forms, but also express in themselves and their mutual positioning the continuity of the flow of time through the city. (1)

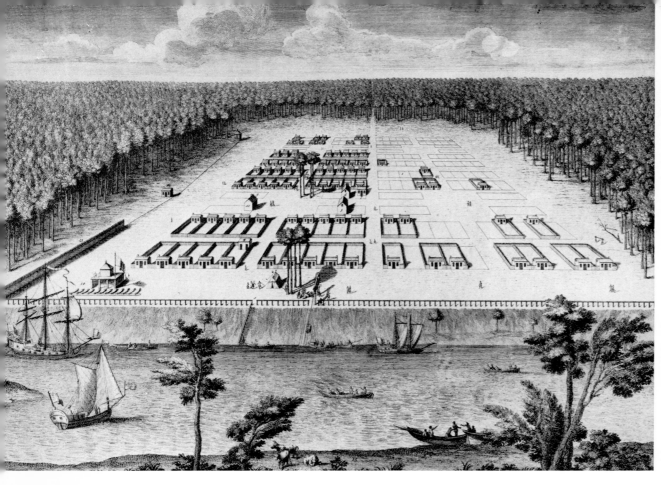

The first planners were men like William Penn and James Oglethorpe, who consciously aimed at creating ideal societies in a new environment. Oglethorpe founded Savannah (above) for ex-prisoners in 1733. It was divided into six cellular units, or 'wards', each of which combined residential and public buildings round a central open square. As the city was built up, the pattern emerged (above right: Savannah from the same viewpoint in 1837) creating a varied vista of architecture and park. (2,3)

A graceful neo-classicism, used with freedom and ingenuity, gave unity to American public architecture. Thomas Jefferson, an amateur but very knowledgeable architect, designed Monticello (right) in 1769, basing it primarily on Palladio. By the 19th century Greek influences were modifying Roman. Left: a house at Milan, Ohio. (4, 7)

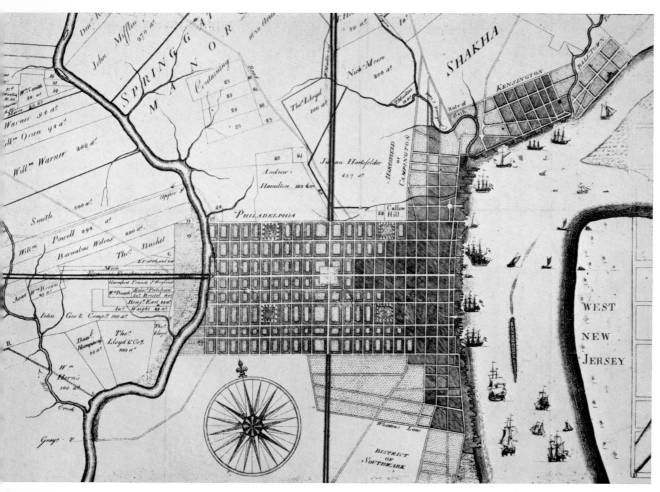

Penn's Philadelphia (1683) was to be 'a green country town', integrating the city and the farmland around it. High Street and Broad Street, meeting in the center, divided the whole area into four quarters. Each quarter had its own public park. The two main axes were capable of indefinite extension: these later developments are shown by heavy black lines. Above: the long straight vista of High (now Market) Street, from Ninth Street. (5, 6)

The cathedral-like vaults of Pennsylvania Station, New York, (right) of 1906–10 by McKim, Mead and White were a monument to the railway age, now destroyed. (17)

Architecture obliterated: the sudden boom in the telephone and telegraph in the 1880s resulted in streets being festooned in wires until the urban environment lost distinction. This photograph (below) of New Street, New York, looking towards Wall Street, was taken after a blizzard in 1888. Today overhead signs, traffic signals, street lights and trash baskets are having the same deadening effect (p. 221). (18)

To humanize the city, which unimaginative planning and the dominance of technology were fast making monotonous and harsh, Frederick Law Olmsted evolved a concept of landscaping which was first applied to parks but later influenced the whole process of urban growth. It was he who in 1857 created Central Park in New York – now an indispensable green 'lung', in the midst of the dense mass of buildings (left, looking north). Within its boundaries (below, looking south) Olmsted allowed for motor traffic but isolated it in special sunken roads. This view shows the lake with Bethesda Fountain. (19, 20)

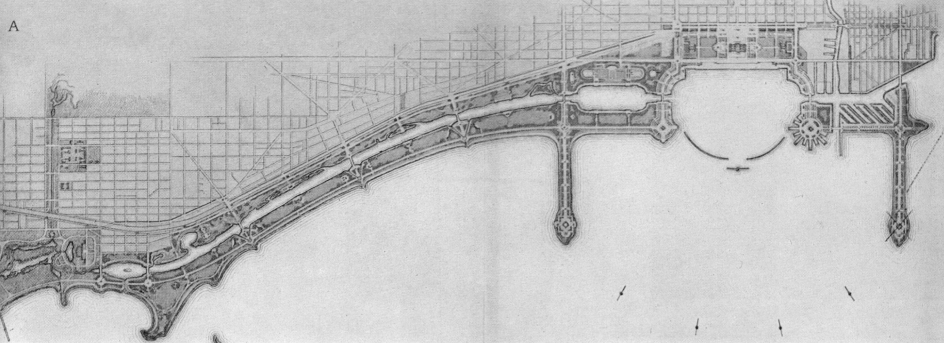

Olmsted's success in New York led to his being invited to lay out the World's Columbian Exposition at Chicago in 1893. Architecturally, this exhibition was retrogressive; in a city that led the world in the invention of new forms to meet modern needs (see overleaf) it was decided that the buildings facing the Court of Honor should be stucco-faced and classical (top). But in its planning it proved fertile for the future. The 'White City' in its verdant setting became an ideal. In 1909 Burnham and Bennett produced a plan (above) for uniting Jackson Park, where the exhibition was held, with Grant Park by a continuous belt of lakeside landscape – a scheme which has been mostly carried out. (21, 22)

Modern architecture began in Chicago. It was made possible by a booming economy, with vast commercial enterprises needing new offices and warehouses; an absence of inhibiting traditions, which enabled it to break with historicism; and the fortunate concurrence of half a dozen architects of genius. Every year saw the blocks reaching higher and higher, until new technical solutions were essential. In the old system of loadbearing walls the limit was reached with Burnham and Root's Monadnock Building of 1891 (right) – sixteen storeys, with walls six feet thick at the base. The way in which it renounces ornament (at the client's insistence) and yet achieves a satisfying form is typical of the new style being evolved in response to new requirements. (24)

Chicago's opportunity came in 1871 when fire swept through the city destroying the whole business district and an area of five square miles to the north in a few hours. Within ten years it was rebuilt on an even larger scale, and in fireproof materials. (23)

The iron skeleton frame was pioneered by William Le Baron Jenney, whose aims were purely functional. Above: his Fair Store in course of construction, 1890. Upon his basic grid elevation, other designers were able to construct a new aesthetic of architecture. A characteristic feature was the 'Chicago window' – two movable sections flanking a fixed center. Right: a group by Holabird and Roche (1898), the right-hand façade designed by Sullivan. (25, 26)

210

The mature Chicago style was attained in the partnership of Sullivan with Adler. Technical boldness goes hand in hand with confident, large-scale articulation and carefully calculated ornament. In the Guaranty Building, Buffalo (below), of 1894, the emphatic verticals are contained by a strong base and cornice. Sullivan's brand of Art Nouveau (right, from the Carson Pirie Scott Store, 1903–04) was the equal of anything being created in Europe. (27, 28)

The 'Prairie' style of Frank Lloyd Wright was in some ways a product of the Chicago School – Wright grew up in Sullivan's office. But he was not by temperament an urban architect. Houses like the Martin House, Buffalo, of 1904 (below) unite with the landscape rather than imposing themselves on it. (29)

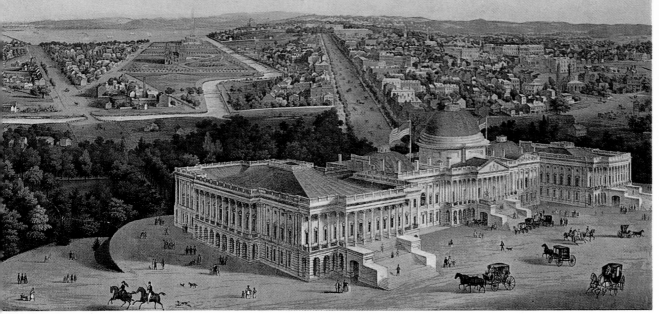

The New-World City *par excellence* is Washington, planned during the first years of the Republic, realized and extended ever since. L'Enfant's original plan had envisaged two vistas, one south from the President's House, the other (the Mall) west from the Capitol. Both would focus on the Washington Monument (marked A in the plan above), but beyond that the view would be open, across the waters of the Potomac River. A lithograph of 1852 (top) shows the vista from the Capitol. In the early 20th century these two vistas were 'stopped' by filling in parts of the swampy Potomac and building the Jefferson and Lincoln Memorials as shown by added black lines on the plan. (30, 31)

To bring the landscape into the heart of the city by means of open-ended vistas had been L'Enfant's ideal, expressed in this bird's-eye view (above). A quite different ideal – one of finite resolution, of monumentality, derived from the World's Columbian Exposition in Chicago on which they had all worked – animated the men of the MacMillan Commission in 1901 (left). It is this plan that has been basically followed in practice. (32, 33)

Other malls, other capitols throughout America bear witness to the continuing influence of the Chicago Exposition and its Washington offspring. Right: the civic center of Denver, Colorado. (34)

New York's growth was neither so rapid as Chicago's, nor so deliberate as Washington's. Starting at the southern end of Manhattan Island, it developed northward on a regular grid-pattern of streets but with surprisingly haphazard architecture. The three photographs below are all taken from the same point. Top: railroad tracks leading to the terminal of the New York Central (1906). Center: the tracks now covered over by Park Avenue, which is interrupted by Grand Central Station (after 1910). Bottom: the same vista now completely closed by the new Pan Am building by Gropius. (35–37)

The unique skyline of New York is due to the accumulation of individually conceived buildings, each competing against the next and subject to few effective planning regulations. The large photograph (left) looks south down Fifth Avenue, with the Empire State Building the dominant accent in the center. (Right: work in progress in 1931.) Since the photograph was taken, this has been outstripped by the two towers of the World Trade Center, at the southern end of the island in the financial district, seen here silhouetted against the water. The view above shows Castle Garden, and behind it skyscrapers built on the old irregular street pattern. (38–40)

At Rockefeller Center (below), planned in the 1930s, part of a valuable commercial site was given over to public 'plazas' and gardens. (41)

To restore the city to the pedestrian became an urgent task when the automobile threatened to destroy traditional urban values. New forms of environment had to be created. Rockefeller Center was one. Another was the Prado, Boston, laid out in 1933 between the Old North Church (left) and Bulfinch's St Stephen's. (42)

A riverside park (below) winds through the business center of San Antonio, Texas, happily oblivious of the bustling streets above it. (43)

Space for sculpture was created in Chicago when the new Civic Center was built in 1964–65. Here (above) we look through the open lower floor to a sixty-foot sculpture by Picasso. (44)

Sunken courtyards, linked below street level to form a single system of gardens and spaces for amusement, make Penn Center in Philadelphia a landmark in urban planning. It is Rockefeller Center carried a stage further: light and air are brought into the midst of the city, and people can enjoy them unmolested by the flow of traffic. (46)

The cascade in Portland, Oregon (left), created a new environment so involving that passers-by are inspired to plunge into the water. (45)

217

To the poor 'the city' meant dirt, darkness, overcrowding, disease and ugliness. Slum conditions in America at the turn of the century were as appalling as anywhere in the world. The writings and photographs of such men as Jacob Riis and Lewis Hine gave publicity to the problem but produced little in the way of solution. Above: lodgers in a tenement in Bayard Street, New York, *c.* 1889. Right: workers' homes and steel mills in Pittsburgh, 1909. The 19th-century legacy lingered on: every great city has its slums. The photograph of children playing under the 'El' (above right) was taken in Chicago in 1941. (47–49)

Public housing became a reality with Franklin D. Roosevelt's New Deal, and in the forty years since his election has probably changed the face of American cities more than any other single factor. Living standards have risen spectacularly. But at the same time something has been lost. Community sense has been replaced by statistics. The human scale has been dwarfed. Along with the over-crowding and the misery, the very values that make cities worth living in are in danger of being discarded. Below: Penn Station South Housing Project in New York, 1963. The photograph illustrates the contrast between the old small streets where the individual retains a sense of identity, and the anonymous block where he becomes part of a vast machine.

Another such scheme, which failed because it took insufficient account of social factors involved, was the Pruitt Igoe project, St Louis. After only eighteen years, wrecked and abandoned by its inhabitants, it became a hotbed of crime. To reduce the density, one whole block (right) was demolished in 1972. (50, 51)

Today's New-World city tries to avoid the faults of both old and new. Reston, Virginia (above), integrates city and garden, rich and not so rich, commerce and homes. (52, 53)

To be avoided: rigid zoning laws that separate residential from commercial areas and create 'neon-lit wastelands' (left) between the two. (54)

The assertion of individuality and of 'place' has led to the formation of community groups, notably in ethnic ghettos, which have recreated the environment in their own image. Below: paintings on a wall in the Lower East Side, New York, by a group of black teenagers. (55)

Architecture and townscape

EDMUND N. BACON

'WHO CAN DESIRE more content that hath small means, or but only his merit to advance his fortunes, than to tread and plant the ground he hath purchased by the hazard of his life?'

So wrote Captain John Smith in 1614, stating as clearly as anyone the question that would motivate Europeans, first a trickle, then a flood, to emigrate to the New World to seek its answer on American shores. The question persisted, and, in almost the same terms, inspired the thousands of adventurous people who moved westward from these settlements across the prairies seeking a new life for themselves during the 19th century. It persists today, and something of its spirit is being rekindled in the present wasteland centers of large cities, where the form of the community to come is being forged by a new kind of pioneer.

Smith went beyond the treading and planting of ground and asked the further question, 'What so truly suits with honor and honesty, as the discovering things unknown, erecting towns, peopling countries . . . ?' and indeed the settlements grew into towns and the towns into cities. Because the land on which they were built was untrammeled by any pre-existing roads or streets, structures, monuments or legal subdivisions, and because the people who built them had liberated themselves from the bonds of inherited European institutions, the forms which these cities assumed and the institutions they generated proved to be particularly responsive to the changing social, spiritual and political ideas of the American people. This was true of the 17th- and 18th-century seaboard settlements. It was true of the 19th-century settlements of the westward-moving pioneers. It is true of American cities today, as the acceleration of managerial and technological advance, and the ever-increasing tempo of American life give them their peculiarly American characteristics.

f2
p 154–5

The people

The people who built the first American cities had one quality in common: they had identified their environment as the principal impediment to self-fulfilment and had taken decisive and unconventional action to change it. While they constituted only a fraction of the malcontents of Europe, they were the ones who saw the answer to their frustrations not in self-destruction or violence against existing institutions, but rather in seeking a new environment in which they could fulfil their own vision of life for themselves and their families. Out of this grew a strong, individual sense of place which was influential in the form of early settlements and which remains a characteristic of American aspiration today.

It is generally acknowledged that the self-selection process which divided the Europeans who emigrated from those who stayed behind produced in America a group of people with special qualities and characteristics. What is not equally appreciated is the influence of the conditioning they went through in the process of getting to the new country. Modern techniques of 'sensitivity training', in which individuals are subjected to extremely intimate situations including physical contact and emotional confrontations which violate conventional notions of privacy, have become an accepted element in inter-personal relationships and even in the training of business executives. The personal intimacy and physical and emotional contact that were inevitably a part of the months spent on the Mayflower, and all of the other ships crossing the

Atlantic well into the second half of the 19th century, provided a kind of sensitivity conditioning to the people who arrived on these shores that would make any modern attempt pale in comparison.

It was in these circumstances aboard the crowded ship *Arrabella* in the Atlantic Ocean in 1630 that John Winthrop wrote of his Puritan band, '. . . wee must delight in each other . . . mourne together, labour, and suffer together, allwayes haveing before our eyes our Commission and Community in the worke, our community as members of the same body . . .' and then went on to visualize that community as a 'cittie set upon a hille', stating that 'the eies of all people are upon us'. It was here, aboard the *Arrabella*, and the other ships like it which crossed the Atlantic, and later in the wagon trains which crossed the western prairies, that was implanted in the minds and sensibilities of the people that special American sense of community, immediate, intimate, spontaneous, close yet fluid and changeable, which has been a hallmark of American society from the beginning, and which has had continually changing expression in the form of the 'cittie set upon a hille'.

The town

The character of the settlements which these people built has been an expression of the relationship between a sense of place and a sense of community. The sheer requirements for protection in the earliest settlements led to the houses being huddled together within a stockade. As the colonies became more secure the people moved out into villages, but these remained as residential clusters, usually around a village green which could be used for animals in case of attack. Beyond the village lay the land for intensive agriculture, divided into strips assigned to the villagers, and beyond that was land in common ownership, pasture and woodland open to any villager. It is evident that this system of land tenure would discourage extensive growth of the village because this would entail subdivision of the agricultural strips into building lots. It was the practice on occasion, when the pressures of population growth seemed a threat to the town, for a group of villagers to detach themselves and form a new settlement elsewhere.

The permanent legacy of the New England town lay not so much in its plan, which varied widely, as in its three-dimensional expression. As the original primitive methods of building construction gave way to the more refined frame buildings of the 18th century a remarkable harmony of environment was achieved. Wood clapboard siding of virtually identical dimension was used on practically all the buildings from the simplest to the most monumental. The windows with their wooden muntins were all multiples of practically uniform panes of glass. The number, not the size, of panes, varied with the importance of the building. As a result of these common modules and unified materials, each structure related to its neighbor, all of the buildings combining into one unified community fabric. The gradual introduction of more ambitious architectural elements—the enrichment of a house doorway with some Georgian detail based on memory of England or copied from a pattern book, a columned portico or Wren-inspired steeple for the church—made richer and more articulate the distinction between the functions of the various buildings, but never to the extent that the basic design connection between the simplest and the most elaborate building was broken.

p 203 (8)

f1

The cities of 18th-century New England possessed a remarkable consistency of scale, their differences lying in enrichment and multiplication of standard elements. Above: four buildings in Newport, the first two by Richard Munday (1724 and 1739), the second two—a library and a market—by Peter Harrison (1748 and 1761–72). Below: panorama of Boston in 1736, its skyline punctuated by steeples inspired by Wren and Gibbs. (1, 2)

p 82 (2)   Integral with the architecture was the New England town meeting, an assembly to deal with the communal problems of the town to which each person, regardless of age or status, was welcome, indeed, in some circumstances, was required to go. Sometimes inefficient, sometimes the vehicle for oppression or cruelty, nevertheless the New England town meeting provided a vehicle for individual participation in democratic decision-making with a degree of sensitivity and completeness that has not since been matched. It has given to all subsequent American experience the image of an individual sense of place in the decision-making. The institution and the town have blended together in the American consciousness to produce a kind of ideal model of community in which participatory democracy and sympathetic environment are integral. The significance of this vision in its impact on American cities today depends not so much on the degree of accuracy with which it represents the facts as they existed in 18th-century New England, but rather as a future ideal toward which to strive. In this sense it is a powerful force today.

Another way in which the New England town provides a model for current thought is that of response to growth. It is remarkable, as one visits many of these towns today, to observe their power of survival. In town after town the basic central green is still there, the trees grown to full stature, the essential public buildings which gave it its character remain intact. Within the matrix of the town streets, individual lots have been built and rebuilt over generations, and so the streets become a sort of museum of American notions of world styles. The junior castle, miniature Italian villa, 1920 version f 4   of colonial, sometimes even in brick, harmonize with the earlier, purer wood clapboard structure in ways that would be impossible in many of the more formal European towns and villages.

Thus, in addition to a sense of place and sense of community, there was added to the American consciousness the capacity of the community to absorb change over time without losing its integrity, and to replicate itself, even in the seemingly hostile environment of the big city.

The Vitruvians in America

Parallel with the unselfconscious, incremental growth of the great majority of settlements in early America there grew a few cities based on a clear, purposeful, geometrically defined plan, the most significant of which were Philadelphia in Pennsylvania, founded in 1682, and Savannah in Georgia, founded in 1733. Each had behind it a man imbued with a social purpose: William Penn who sought to foster religious and political tolerance, which was actually achieved at a high level in Philadelphia, and James Oglethorpe who had been concerned with prison reform in England, especially related to debtors, and who provided ex-prisoners with a place for a new life in Savannah. Each of these settlements was based on a comprehensive regional land policy, integrating town and farm, and each followed the kind of formal geometry that was developed by Renaissance architects attempting to translate the writing of the classical Roman architect Vitruvius into the ideal city for their own day.

Penn's purpose was to create a 'green country town, which will never be burnt, and always be wholesome', doubtless having London in mind on both considerations (the Great Fire had happened sixteen years before). At the beginning he laid out the regional hinterland in farm lots with five hundred acres as the basic unit, providing that 'each purchaser and adventurer shall, by lot, have so much land as will answer to the proportion which he hath bought or taken up with rent'. Between the two-square-mile central city and the farms an extensive tract of unsubdivided land was set aside as 'the Liberty Lands of Philadelphia'. The conditions of settlement further provided that each purchaser would receive land in the central city '. . . after the proportion of ten acres for every five hundred purchased, if the place will allow it'. While in practice the number of town lots proved insufficient for the purpose, and portions of the Liberty Lands were subdivided to augment the supply, this basic method of land tenure and land division was intended to encourage association between the rural and urban communities, and give the farmer a stake in the city's well-being.

p 203
(516)

The plan of the city itself, at the narrowest point between the Delaware and Schuylkill Rivers, had two principal streets a hundred feet wide—one, High (now Market) Street, connected the two rivers, and the other, Broad Street, at right angles to it extended along the watershed to the city boundaries. At the point of inter-

p 271
(46)

section Penn placed a ten-acre square for the 'publick buildings' where the 1870 City Hall with its 536-foot tower stands today, still dominating the skyline at Penn's original crossing. The boundary streets on the north and south established the limits of the city as he saw it, and with Broad and Market Streets defined four quadrants in the center of each of which Penn placed a square as a public park. These were eight acres in size, slightly larger than the city block defined by his orthogonal street grid, thus interrupting but not severing the regular street pattern.

Simple as it is, this plan has proved able to provide not only a remarkably articulate and orienting framework for building (it took nearly two hundred years for it to become completely built up), but also a powerful springboard for the extension of the city into the hinterland. Market Street was elongated westward and serves as the central spine for urban renewal today, and Broad Street was extended north and south to become, reputedly, the longest straight street in the world. These two co-ordinates, each dominated by its own particular vista of City Hall, give a continuous sense of orientation, and the center is still powerfully present in a city of two million people.

Within the residential areas a similar sense of orientation is produced by the street interruptions caused by the four squares, providing at key points terminating vistas of trees. These, along with the vistas of City Hall on the principal streets, provide a con-

nection between the smaller and larger elements of the city, and an awareness of position in the larger system. In the extension of the residential areas of Philadelphia only the gridiron plan of streets was repeated from Penn's layout, not the orienting elements, with the result that the long, straight streets frequently produce an overpowering monotony and in some parts the sense of place is almost totally destroyed.

f3

It is also unfortunate that the extension of Philadelphia did not continue Penn's idea of providing each new community with a park in its center. Yet this very thing did occur in the development which took place around the original 1733 settlement of Savannah, proving that Oglethorpe's original vision, in addition to its inherent merits, had the peculiar and valuable quality of expansibility.

The town which Oglethorpe laid out had as its basic unit a 'ward' which consisted of a central public square, four blocks of 'tythings' with ten house lots each, and four 'trust lots' facing the sides of the square, providing sites for the more important buildings such as meeting halls, churches and stores. The original layout had four of these cellular units to which two were added, the six 'ward' units serving the town needs until the American Revolution.

p 202 (2)

The regional plan consists of farm lots of forty-four acres, garden lots of five acres, and, adjacent to the garden lots, 'a common round the town for the convenience of air'. Unlike Philadelphia, this common was not allowed to be subdivided in a haphazard manner. As Savannah grew after the Revolution, wards were added one after the other to the city, identical in design with the original cellular plan of Oglethorpe, until by 1856, the entire common had been turned into a city with twenty-four connecting units centering on twenty-four public parks, providing a richness

p 202 (3)

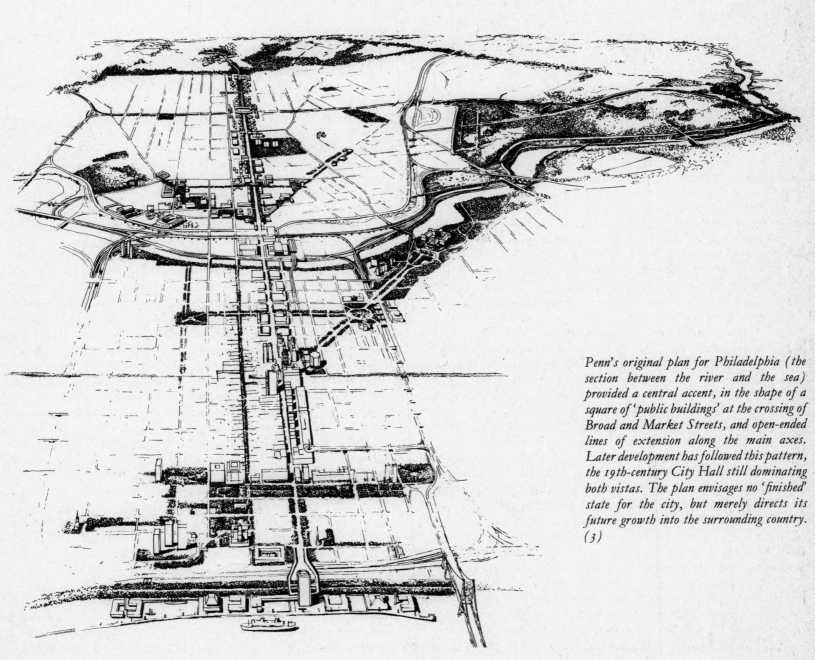

Penn's original plan for Philadelphia (the section between the river and the sea) provided a central accent, in the shape of a square of 'public buildings' at the crossing of Broad and Market Streets, and open-ended lines of extension along the main axes. Later development has followed this pattern, the 19th-century City Hall still dominating both vistas. The plan envisages no 'finished' state for the city, but merely directs its future growth into the surrounding country. (3)

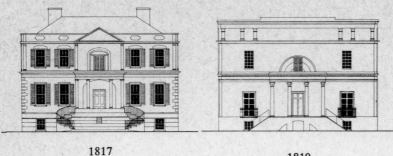

1817

1819

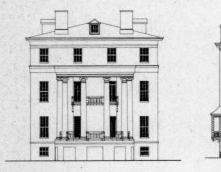
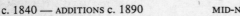
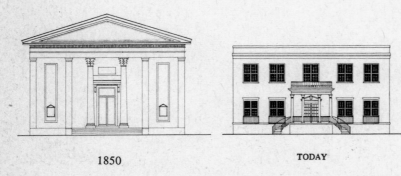

c. 1840 — ADDITIONS c. 1890

MID-NINETEENTH CENTURY

1850

TODAY

Architecture in Savannah: the South remained faithful to the classical style, though proportions became increasingly unorthodox. (4)

of living, of individual connection with the sub-unit and with the system as a whole, of varying vistas of parks and open spaces that is unmatched. Amazingly, the idea behind this plan, seemingly so fragile, proved to be so powerful in the public mind that only one square has been taken over for a public parking garage, and most of the squares have withstood the onslaught of modern traffic, the streets going around them rather than through their center. To the foresight of Oglethorpe we owe the repetition of a beautiful pattern for over a hundred years. Because all of the common was publicly owned, the public squares necessary for the plan could be acquired at no expense. When the common land was exhausted the Oglethorpe pattern of community ceased. The widespread restoration of old houses in the former commons area proves the relevance of the plan to the present day.

The New Athens

'The agricultural capacities of our country constitute its distinguishing feature, and the adapting of our policy and pursuits to that is more likely to make us a numerous and happy people, than the memory of an Amsterdam, a Hamburgh or a City of London', so wrote Thomas Jefferson in 1816, and during a brief period following the Revolution the new country did achieve a sort of equilibrium which made it seem possible that Jefferson's vision of an agrarian democracy actually would be achieved.

The nation's new sense of identity led to a reappraisal of the accepted style of architectural expression, including the primarily p 203 (7) Roman-based work of Jefferson himself. Robert Mills, architect

of the Washington Monument (designed 1836), said that only a few examples of the Greek style were necessary to convince the citizens '. . . of its superiority over the Roman . . .' and that it '. . . exactly suited the character of our political institutions and pecuniary needs'. Benjamin Latrobe, one of the architects of the United States Capitol, in an address in 1811 added, 'Greece was free, p 132–(9) in Greece every citizen felt himself an important . . . part of his republic.'

The single act which established the Greek revival most firmly was the competition for the design of the second building for the Bank of the United States in Philadelphia in 1818. Although it was p 204 (William Strickland, winner of the first prize, who gave the building its form, it was the program itself, stating that '. . . the Directors are desirous of exhibiting a chaste imitation of Grecian Architecture, in its simplest and least expensive form', which determined its character. So, as happens recurrently in the history of building, it was the client, in this case probably under the influence of Nicholas Biddle, who played the decisive role, and it was Biddle who asked Strickland to add a Greek Doric portico to his estate in Andalusia in 1836, agreeing with Robert Mills that the Greek style by '. . . its simplicity recommends its introduction into . . . private dwellings'.

As the devotion to the Greek ideal spread through an ever-enlarging territory a kind of architectural glow was diffused over the countryside. One can travel in extensive areas of New York State and the Middle West today and see farmhouse after farmhouse with classical Doric porticos, country churches with pilasters, cornices and Doric doorways, town houses with wooden p 202 (entablatures punctured by iron-grilled windows, and public buildings which still give out the aroma of the period in which Jefferson's agrarian ideals were envisioned as emulating those of f 7 Athenian democracy.

Industry comes to town

Jefferson himself came to the realization that his anti-urban policy, allowing Europe to do the manufacturing for an agrarian America, would not work and, in 1816, said, 'We must now place the manufacturer by the side of the agriculturist'. The trend of Jefferson's admonition was carried out but not its form because the manufacturer soon began to leave the agriculturist behind, with decisive effect on architectural expression, taste and the form of cities.

The growth of manufacturing meant concentration of more people in cities, and produced a new moneyed class whose aspirations and self image were not satisfied by Greek motifs, and who looked to a range of cultures and styles for an adequate expression of their new status. *The Architect's Dream*, painted by Thomas Cole p 204–(12) in the 1840s, embodies the new spirit in its mixture of styles and cultures from ancient Egypt through something vaguely Roman to Gothic and finally to an arch so indefinite in style as to seem an invention of the artist himself.

The period which followed saw the rejection of the Greek ideal and its substitution by an eclectic approach, by which architects might choose any European historical style that seemed suited to the moment. While this led to excesses and produced the sometimes discredited 'Brown Decades', it actually marked the beginning of a liberation from the rigidities of the rectangular Georgian structure and its survival in the discipline of the Greek revival. It was at this period that the seeds were sown for a new functional expression of American living which later flowered in the purely American p 211 (29) contribution to architecture in the work of Frank Lloyd Wright.

It was Andrew Jackson Downing, landscape architect turned architect, philosopher and journalist, who saw most clearly the route that should be followed, and, through his 1850 work, *The Architecture of Country Houses*, helped to open the way. His 'Design XXI, Villa in the Norman Style' may seem doubtful of detail, but its f 5 form is a direct expression of the functional elements of the house with a clarity of articulation that would have been impossible earlier. While we may smile at his views on architectural expression —'As regards the *style* to be given to the exterior, if we are to choose among foreign architecture, our preference will be given to modification of the Rural Gothic . . . or the modern Italian, with bold overhanging cornices and irregular outlines'—we must respect his vision of the course of future years in the comment: 'Our own soil is the right platform upon which a genuine national architecture must grow, though it will be aided in its growth by all foreign thoughts that mingle harmoniously with its simple and free spirit.'

The centennial accounting

The degree of progress in this and many other areas during the first hundred years of American national life was thrown into the spotlight of public consciousness at the Centennial Exposition in Philadelphia in 1876. Here were exposed technical achievements, managerial advances and artistic accomplishments (as well as gropings and uncertainties), a kind of national stock-taking.

p 206   The buildings in which the exhibits were housed were, of them-
(13) selves, a technical achievement for a country so young. The two largest buildings, architecturally expressing their construction of wrought iron columns and roof trusses, with a clear central span of 120 feet, were 1400 and 1800 feet long. One of them was completed in five months. These remarkable and austerely functional glass-skinned structures, their iron girders receding into the distance, gave to the ten million visitors quite a new vision of the
p 207 potential of the American environment, and were the precursors of
(17) a number of larger structures of much greater span, notably train
p 105 sheds in urban railroad terminals. Of the exhibits themselves,
(1) probably the most spectacular was the Corliss engine, built almost miraculously in ten months after everyone had said it couldn't be done, which drove some six miles of shafts, belts and flywheels, animating all the operating exhibits in Machinery Hall. This great bold embodiment of power and functional directness was a confident expression of one aspect of American culture and was recognized as such in the contemporary comment, 'The general proportions are exceedingly harmonious and graceful, and the details simple and in excellent taste.' But how uneasy was much of the rest of the culture, how uncertain were the forms of the objects produced by the power machines is shown by the selection of the
f 6 Eastlake Organ, as the example of a product which the same commentator declared to be 'free from all the abortions in the shape of ornament with which many pretentious instruments are disfigured. The public taste in this respect is rapidly improving.' Yet it was at the same Exposition at the Froebel Kindergarten display that Frank Lloyd Wright's mother first saw the pure-geometry pure-color child's building blocks which she acquired for her son, and which Wright said had so great an influence on his architecture.

It was at the Centennial that Alexander Graham Bell first publicly demonstrated his new invention, the telephone, person to person communication by mechanical means, but requiring a connecting
p 207 wire. It was this connecting wire that so rapidly proliferated, in-
(18) vading the urban environment with telling effect, producing the
p 113 urban scene shown on page 113, within ten years of the Centennial.
(21) Here the architectural environment is almost obliterated by the elements of communication which include telephone and telegraph wires and those manifestations of American commercialism—painted advertising signs. The struggle to preserve a desirable environment in the face of technological invention continues to this day. The overhead wires were eventually driven underground, but in their place sprang up a wilderness of trolley poles and wires, then traffic signals, trash baskets, no parking signs, overhead signs
p 202 to expressways, mercury vapor street lights—a never-ending
(54) welter of elements which, if uncontrolled, destroy the quality of the urban environment. These are manifestations of the elements in society which place secondary value on the human aspects of city living, and regard the development of technology as dominant.

Contrasting with this view, and establishing a counter-thrust, was a group of men concerned about the effect of growing congestion in cities on the lives of people who lived there. Rejecting the nostalgic and defeatist anti-urban sentiment that was and still is so much a part of American thinking, epitomized at this time by Thoreau and his musings at Walden Pond, this group set about to bring the restorative qualities of open space and living vegetation to city dwellers. Andrew Jackson Downing, shortly before his death in 1852, published an article urging a large park in the center of New York, and Frederick Law Olmsted, picking up the challenge, continued the agitation and finally assumed responsibility for making Central Park a reality. Armed with a clear philosophy

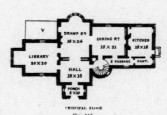

Design for a 'villa in the Norman Style' by an architect from Cincinnati, Ohio. Andrew Jackson Downing, in publishing it, commented: 'Of course, this is not a house to please a practical, commonsense man. It is not a rational house . . .' He believed, nevertheless, that Romanesque and Gothic could free architecture from the rigidities of the Greek Revival. (5)

The Centennial Exposition of 1876 showed a growing confidence in technological progress, but a curious uncertainty in taste. This organ designed by Charles Lock Eastlake was particularly recommended for the restraint of its decoration. (6)

225

p 208
(18, 19)

and purpose he produced there an urban amenity, whose influence continues to spread outward. These men, along with Calvert Vaux, Olmsted's partner, set into motion a force which established the American city as the battleground of a continuing struggle between the technologist and the humanist.

Culture comes to Chicago

p 158-9
(15-19)

As we have seen, while industry was producing huge agglomerations of workers and consequent congested slums, the vast agglomeration of capital was creating a new moneyed class, a new group of leaders referred to as Captains of Industry, Merchant Princes or Robber Barons, depending on the perspective from which they were observed.

p 158
(15)

It is appropriate that the most vigorous expression of this leadership should have moved from the east coast to heartland Chicago because here were produced more rapidly and more spectacularly than elsewhere great new family dynasties, the McCormicks, the Armours, the Potter Palmers, the Montgomery Wards. The environment in which these families developed and conducted their business was one of improvisation and rich experimentation, freed of the constraints of European institutionalization. It was Chicago, faced with the need for providing shelter for the flood of new arrivals, that in 1833 produced the balloon-frame structure, a light wooden building structurally strong because of the systematic interaction of all of its parts held together by factory-produced nails, a revolution in world building methods. It was Chicago which, in 1871, experienced what in contemporary

p 210
(23)

accounts was termed the worst civic catastrophe from fire in all history, a disaster which was the direct consequence of too many balloon frame buildings too close to each other. This bitter experience brought home in its own telling way that it isn't just the discrete object which is involved; it is the interrelation of objects with each other and with their environment. The holocaust brought in its wake a new appreciation of environment as an element in city building, formulated into new building regulations, laws and planning principles. The consequent necessity for speedy rebuilding on a vast scale was a challenge to the new leaders. The magnificent success with which they met it inspired the kind of self-confidence that made the next problem seem easy.

The role of these newly rich clients in the development of structure and architecture is often undervalued. True, it was the inventive brain of architect William LeBaron Jenney that produced in Chicago, in 1884, the iron-framed Home Insurance Building. This contained the elements that were to figure in the future

p 210
(24)

development of the American skyscraper, and the generally experimental and inventive atmosphere of Chicago leadership provided a rich milieu in which to carry on the experiment. True, the

p 210-11
(25, 28)

design profession produced men of sensitivity and genius, Louis Sullivan, Dankmar Adler, William Holabird, Daniel Burnham, John Root, whose work effloresced into the great buildings of the Chicago School after the fire of 1871 and before the 1893 World's Columbian Exposition. Here, again, the role of the client is mis-

p 210
(25)

understood. The Monadnoch Building, perhaps the most beautiful of all of the Chicago School group, was originally designed by John Root, Daniel Burnham's partner, encrusted with elaborate ornamentation. It was the client, Owen Aldis, who wanted all of the ornament eliminated, a desire he achieved working with a draftsman in Root's office while Root himself was away on vacation.

A decisive achievement of this group of Chicago titans was the wresting from East Coast New York the honor of holding the World's Columbian Exposition, the White City. This was to celebrate the four-hundredth anniversary of Columbus's landing and opened on 1 May 1893, in Jackson Park, on the shores of Lake Michigan. The layout was by Frederick Law Olmsted, brought into the picture by Chicago industrialist James W. Ellsworth, but the architecture of the most conspicuous buildings was the work of New York architects, Richard Morris Hunt, Charles Follen McKim, George B. Post, imported for the purpose by Daniel H. Burnham, uneasy about the competence of his fellow Chicago architects to present to the world the state of American culture in its best light. Added to the mixture was sculptor Augustus Saint Gaudens and fellow artists, and, in one of the most remarkable

decisions in American artistic history, all of these temperamental creators decided to subjugate their individual predilections to the good of the whole, and actually did produce, on the splendid land and water sites of Olmsted, a series of buildings related to each other and to the landscape. A second decision was made to clothe the iron-framed structures in all-white stucco forms of classical

p 209
(21)

derivation, a decision which caused consternation among many architects, and which inspired a string of fulminations against the Fair by Louis Sullivan, but which did accomplish what no other architect had been able to accomplish in 19th-century America, a harmonious environment on a large scale.

The effect was immediate and electric. The millions of people who poured through the gates, some twenty-one million over the course of the summer, saw, felt and moved through a kind of miniature world different from anything they had seen or dreamed of before. They then went back to their cities, towns and hamlets from one coast to the other, imbued with a new vision of the possibilities of the American city. These consequences have to be taken into account in reckoning everything which happened since.

The immediate consequence for Chicago was the acquisition of a fine new public park. Olmsted, armed with his experience in developing Central Park in New York, as well as his earlier studies for the ultimate development of the then wasteland of Jackson Park, had kept one eye cocked on the long-range usefulness and beauty of the land forms created for the Exposition, and indeed did succeed in leaving a topographic and horticultural legacy which became Jackson Park of today.

A longer range result of the Exposition was the mobilization of 'disinterested men of wide experience', the business leadership of Chicago, by the Commercial Club, in an avowed attempt to secure for all of Chicago the vision contained in the White City, the consequence of which was the 1908 publication *Plan of Chicago*. This, in turn, was restructured into the 'Wacker Manual', a summary account of the Plan and its objectives and woven into the curriculum of the high schools of Chicago, making an impression on a generation. The immediate physical consequence was the great lakefront park development connecting Jackson Park with Grant

p 209
(22)

Park at Center City and its extension northward. On a broader scale the influence of the Exposition was felt across the country as many cities expressed their concern for environmental quality,

p 213
(34)

with varying degrees of success. In Cleveland, Ohio; Denver, Colorado; San Francisco, California; Philadelphia, Pennsylvania; and many others, civic centers and monumental malls were built in emulation of the principles of the White City.

But there was a subtler alchemy at work in American thought. Burnham himself pointed out one effect in a speech in Paris in 1910, in his statement that, prior to the Columbian 'Exposition', there had never been a plan commission in the United States, but '. . . there are many hundreds of plan commissions at work at the present time.' It was beyond his powers to foresee that these same municipal plan commissions or their successors, only twenty years later, would reject the very concept which fathered them, with the epithet, 'City Beautiful Movement', with Burnham as the arch enemy. It may be Burnham, however, who will have the last word for, in this same speech, he went on to say with a strangely contemporary sound, 'only a few are able . . . to live in delightful surroundings; the rest have to take things as they come . . . but will not the people of a continuing democracy awaken some time to the fact that they can possess as a community what they cannot as individuals, and will they not then demand delightfulness as a part of life, and get it?'

The White City and Washington

The most spectacular legacy of the now-vanished White City was the development in 1902 of the so-called McMillan plan for the reconstitution of the capital city of Washington. Initiated by a resolution of the United States Senate, the work was carried on by a galaxy of geniuses transplanted from the Chicago Exposition, Daniel Burnham, Charles Follen McKim, Augustus Saint Gaudens and Frederick Law Olmsted, Jr, landscape architect and son of the site planner of the Chicago Fair. They formed themselves into what was known as the McMillan Commission, reviving and

Thomas Jefferson planned the University of
Virginia as three sides of a rectangle, open
to the west. In the engraving above we are
looking east, away from the vista and
towards the Rotunda. In 1901, however,
McKim, Mead and White completed the
rectangle and closed the vista by a new range
(shaded, at the bottom of the plan; the
lateral blocks were not in fact built). The
same insensitivity, springing from the same
desire for symmetry and completeness, is
seen in the modification to L'Enfant's plan
of Washington, illustrated on pages 212 and
213. (7, 8)

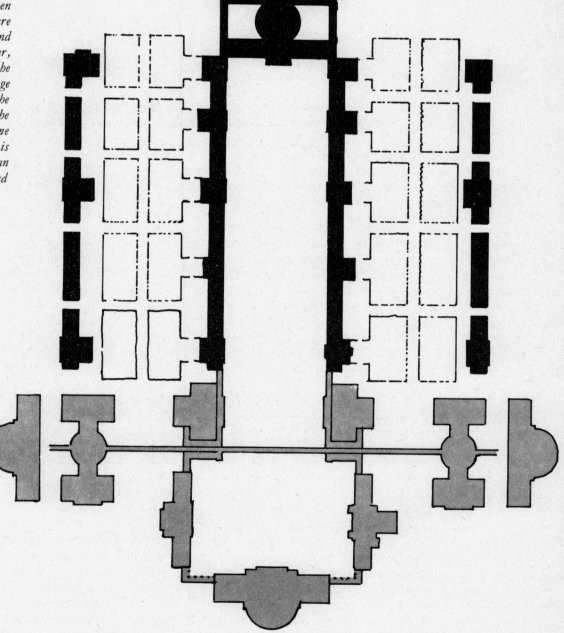

New provision for the pedestrian has become a preoccupation of modern America city planning. In Philadelphia a whole new network of walkways has been integrated into the road and rail systems. Mostly below road level, this bursts into the open in three ways—into a glass-walled prism of space in the Municipal Services Building on the left, into a sunken garden before the 1870 City Hall in the center, and into a three-storeyed glass-roofed galleria between two towers on the right. (9)

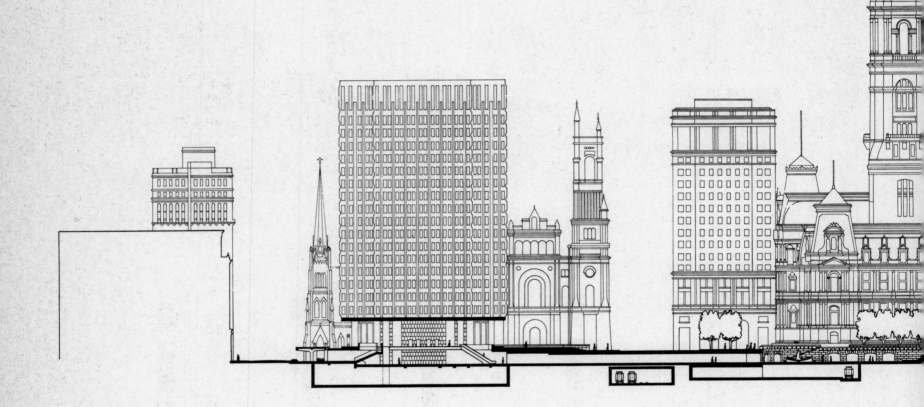

clarifying many of the basic ideas behind the 1791 Pierre Charles L'Enfant plan for Washington, and rescuing its essential features from the virtual obliteration which had resulted from Victorian counter-purpose accumulations. Burnham's conversation with his client, Pennsylvania Railroad President Alexander Cassatt, requesting the removal of the discordant tracks and station from the monumental portions of the Mall inspired Cassatt's suggestion that a single Union Station be established north of the Capitol with the tracks extending south underground where they crossed the monumental axis. The station was built with Burnham as architect and the report of the Commission proudly remarks that it was eight feet eight inches longer than the Capitol. The models and the beautiful Jules Guerin paintings of the new Washington gave lay people and politicians a new vision of possibilities and set into motion a series of plans and action programs for improving Washington which still continue.

The titans of business and their professional associates who constituted the leadership group at the turn of the century were a proud and self-confident lot, secure in their belief that they had achieved in America a stable society that would endure indefinitely, bulwarked against the onslaught of eroding social change. This inward-looking, finite, delimited view of the world was in sharp contrast with the vision of the founding fathers, who saw the new nation in time and space expanding beyond the limits of the immediately evident. In terms of architecture, the closed, finite designs of the late Victorians came into violent collision, sometimes with disastrous results, with the work of the early republic forebears. Thomas Jefferson, for instance, had designed the campus of the University of Virginia in such a way that one end of his beautiful quadrangle would always be open to the vista of the Virginia hills, generating an awareness of the nourishing hinterland, the larger

p 212–13
(30–32)

p 212
(33)

f 7

system of which the University is but a part. The plugging up of this vista by Charles Follen McKim in 1901 is one of the most wanton acts of architectural vandalism in American history, yet it seemed all right to the Victorians because they thought in terms of finite, inward-looking things.

A more significant but less odious product of this type of thought is what McKim, Burnham and their associates did to the two main axes of the original plan of Pierre L'Enfant for Washington. That the plan survived at all during the difficult days of the new republic is due to the breadth of political, geographical and architectural vision of one man, George Washington, and his dogged, unwavering and tenacious pursuit of that vision in the face of detractors, inadequate resources, and obstructionists at every turn. Even Thomas Jefferson saw the issue in much more limited terms. But the vision did persist and the plan was followed, and continues to be followed, yet our judgment of it is based more on the Burnham, McKim restructuring of it than on the original vision which Washington and L'Enfant shared. True, the original plan was influenced by Versailles, but Versailles comes to a completed resolution at both ends, with the King's bed at one end and the star crossing of planted *allées* at the other. The original L'Enfant plan, on the other hand, was based on a vision of unlimited extent; of two great vistas, one from the President's House and one from the Capitol, not of some man-made work of art, structure or planted trees, but across the Potomac to the Virginia hills, and, from the President's House, in L'Enfant's own words 'down the Potomac with a prospect of the whole harbor'. Moreover, the actual point of contact between the city and the river, unprecedented in classical design, was defined by a diagonal line.

It was this expression of outreach, this design connection with the river as an embodiment of regional forces, that made the original

f 8

p 212
(30)

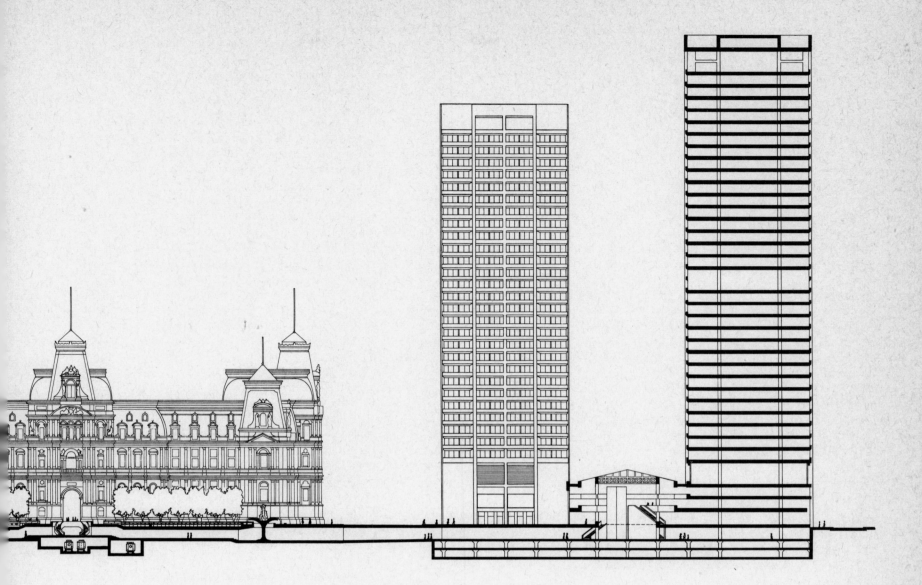

p 212
(33)
L'Enfant Washington plan so fresh and daring, and it was this very quality that was invisible to the short-viewed Victorians, and which they destroyed by imposing man-made structures in these views. Certainly the Lincoln Memorial and the Jefferson Memorial are handsome buildings and a pleasure to see, but one may, on occasion, wistfully wish the great natural vistas had been preserved.

Megalopolis

The kind of expansive vision of time and space which both George Washington and Thomas Jefferson possessed was never totally absent from American thought, and was given rich and powerful expression in the middle of the 19th century in the poetry of Walt Whitman. The feeling for the vastness of the country, for the great wind-swept plains and prairies which Whitman had, and which flowed through the narrow Victorian parlours like a breath of fresh air, was translated into architecture at the beginning of the century following by a man who was himself reared in the Middle p 211
(29) West, Frank Lloyd Wright. The free flow of space through his structures, the integration of indoor and outdoor spaces, the freedom from the rigid confines of static geometry, the outreach to the spaces immediate and beyond, all these are the legacies to world architecture of Wright, who neither loved nor understood cities.

Yet there were people who cared for cities too, and who strove to bring the very qualities which Wright's work embodied to the people who lived there. Earliest of the series of great humanitarian issues to surface was that of deprivation of contact with open spaces and growing things because of growing congestion over larger and larger areas. We have already traced the idea of the public park as an integral part of American cities. Easily the most far-reaching design in its effect on subsequent development was Olmsted's for

Central Park in New York in 1857. This plan went far beyond the bare requirements for public open space; it dealt with the growing issue of how to provide ways for people to get about without getting in each other's way. Olmsted's solution was a circulation p 208
(20) network which integrated four distinct kinds of movement into a single system. The transverse city traffic having no business in the park was separated from it in depressed roadways. The park drives, curved to prevent speeding, passed over the transverse roads on bridges. The bridle paths were at quite different locations separated from vehicular traffic by bridges also, and the network of footpaths had its own integrity, preserved by overpasses and underpasses as required. In addition to its naturalistic sections the plan had its formal architectural features as well, the Mall, Bethesda Fountain, stairways and plazas at the lake's edge which is the scene of civic festivals today. That this seemingly technological traffic plan had its roots in humanitarian considerations is affirmed in Olmsted's words, prophetic of new attitudes relating to the wider city, 'The value of these grade separations lies not so much in the greater safety to pedestrians, and still less in the speeding up or continuity of flow of traffic attainable, but chiefly in the freedom from distraction and in the greater comfort for the people who have come to the park for its enjoyment.' And that a half century before the appearance of the automobile!

Whether or not the New York Central Railroad engineer William J. Wilgus consciously regarded the planning of Central Park as the forerunner of his own work on the New Grand Central Terminal at Forty-Second Street, New York, he did carry forward, into the very core of the commercial city, the principles of traffic separation that Olmsted initiated. The actual work on Grand Central followed by only nine days the initiation, by its rival railroad, the Pennsylvania, of its track extension under the Hudson to a new terminal on Seventh Avenue between Thirty-First and Thirty-Third Streets, where it connected with the Long Island Railroad tracks, extended from the east. The brilliant and costly Pennsylvania Railroad plan was again the product of the brain of Alexander Cassatt, worked out this time with Charles Follen McKim. It included the monumental Pennsylvania Station, most p 207 notably the steel and glass structure over the tracks, now un-(17) fortunately destroyed.

The Vanderbilts of the New York Central resolved to do the Pennsylvania Railroad one better, and in this they succeeded. Under the guidance of Wilgus there was built not only a railroad p 206-7 terminal remarkable for its two-level system of tracks, twenty-(16) seven lower for suburban trains and forty-three upper for through p 214 trains, but also a new street, Park Avenue, over the sixty acres of (35-37) tracks adjacent to the station and to the north, and cross streets that had been closed for forty years, and between them in the air rights, commercial buildings, apartment buildings and hotels. The greatest contribution to urban development lay, however, in the complex and extensive development of interwoven means of circulation, an extension of Park Avenue street traffic on an elevated roadway around the station, interlocking pedestrian connections between train tracks and subway, and, in a series of passages under the street, direct pedestrian routes to buildings surrounding the station. All the principles contained in the Olmsted statement about Central Park were incorporated here, and what was created was not an isolated building but an extension of the city's functional network.

The next great effort on the more-than-one-building scale was the *f10* development by the Rockefeller family, starting in 1931, of Rockefeller Center between Fifth and Sixth Avenues from Forty-Eighth to Fifty-First Streets in Manhattan.

The architect Wallace Harrison, in his planning for Rockefeller Center, had the advantage of dealing with a large enough site, twelve acres, to contain a new urban principle, and this he produced.

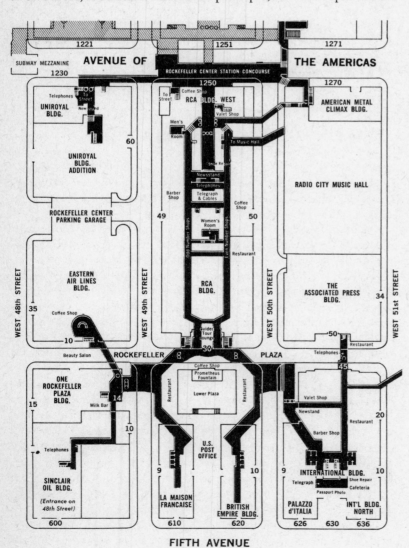

Rockefeller Center, New York. The areas in black are the underground connecting concourse, which transforms the whole complex into a tightly-knit city within a city, a setting for both work and leisure. (10)

The structures along Fifth Avenue were of modest size, six storeys in height, with open courts with sculpture and fountains. The great seventy-storey RCA tower rising sheer from the ground was set p 215 back behind a landscaped mall from Fifth Avenue leading to a (41) sunken court before a great cascade, open air restaurant in summer, skating rink in winter, which served as a forecourt to the tower. The fourteen original buildings and those that have been added since are placed in an asymmetrical relationship to each other, and are seen in an endless variety of changing views as one moves about the open spaces at their base.

Perhaps the greatest single contribution of Rockefeller Center to city building was the idea of providing pleasure to the general public. The role of pleasure in American life went through many changes from the Puritan communities in which, in some minds, it was to be excluded altogether, through the Victorian era in which, again in some minds, it was thought to be the exclusive property of the rich. Olmsted held that it was the right of everyone to have access to the pleasures of associating with nature, and furthered the municipal park movement. The more urban types of pleasure, traditionally part of European piazzas and boulevards, were excluded in the customary American land development which included nothing but the public street and the private structure. Rockefeller Center broke down the division between the two, p 216-17 opened the gates to public participation in the privately-built (42-45) magnificence of the open spaces, and enriched the image of urban possibilities. In his book, *Time, Space and Architecture*, Sigfried Giedion said that Rockefeller Center 'accomplished for town planning what the small Chicago house of Frank Lloyd Wright in the nineties had accomplished for the free and open planning of the single house'.

In a functional sense Rockefeller Center carried forward the concept established in Grand Central of extending the network of urban movement systems, and it added the basically new vision of urban development as a series of skyscrapers rising out of such a fabric as a base. The plan included a series of lower level shop-lined pedestrian connections passing under the streets, tying the subways and the buildings together; but, although these footways passed close to the sunken court and were at the same level, they never made direct contact with it.

It was in Philadelphia in Penn Center some twenty years later p 217 that this connection finally was made, the lower level pedestrian (46) system opening directly into sunken courtyards and gardens, bringing light, air and beauty to the pedestrian plane one level below the street.

This concept was first presented by the Philadelphia City Planning Commission in its proposal for Penn Center, a development on fourteen acres adjacent to City Hall to replace the then elevated railroad and Broad Street Station, made in 1952. The vision of a large garden open to the sky, penetrating four blocks one level below the street, a handsome entrance to Center City for the workers arriving by underground train or subway (77% in Manhattan), was too far removed from prevailing practice to be accepted by the leaders of the Pennsylvania Railroad at that time. But the basic principle of an unbroken lower level pedestrian system was built *f9* into Penn Center, and this lower level is being enriched by a proliferating number of smaller gardens puncturing the roof and bringing the sun at least to strategic spots. The dream of greeting Center City arrivals on subways with a view of sun-drenched fountains from the car windows has finally been achieved at Penn Center, bringing the pleasure principle into the subway where the people are.

In the continuing American process of moving from idea to experiment and back to idea again, the basic principles which were set forth in the Olmsted plan for Central Park, in Grand Central and Rockefeller Center and in the Philadelphia plan for Penn Center, have been expanded and enlarged to cover the entire central part of Manhattan as a theoretical exercise in a publication, *Urban Design Manhattan*, by the New York Regional Plan Association.

Here for the first time is a view of the whole urban center recast to meet simultaneously the technological demands of the movement of masses of people, and the humanistic demand on the part of the individual for light, air, room and a pleasurable experience. The planner sees the land area from which the city rises not as a

The plan of Canberra, Australia's new capital, was the work of an American planner, Walter Burley Griffin, and carries on the tradition of L'Enfant's Washington. Its eight urban centers, of which the most prominent is the Capitol (c), are connected by straight roads which focus on natural features—Mount Ainslie (b) and Black Mountain (a)—and are separated by ingeniously used, and partly artificial, expanses of water. Like Philadelphia, it also allows for indefinite future growth. (11)

static surface of ground, but as a pulsating network of movement systems with interlocking conduits, interweaving at different levels, at, above and below the ground; according to the report, 'a design philosophy . . . which considers the horizontal transportation by train, the vertical transportation by elevator, and their pedestrian link as parts of a single system'.

Within this vast functionally efficient technological system there must be pleasure and identity for the individual. Here the plan provides public squares below street level breaking through the street membrane. According to the report, 'the shaft of light descending below grade provides orientation and identity . . . the interest of the cityscape is enhanced for pedestrians at the street level since they can look down as well as up, seeing a world that is now judiciously concealed'. The report suggests that 'not just the public transportation system but the water and waste, the energy and communication systems, should be viewed and designed as one "mega-building", to which the interchangeable above-ground portions of the urban structure are continuously attached, removed and again attached'. When combined with fountains, trees and sculpture in sun-drenched plazas this system within the complex interaction of public and private facilities provides both efficiency for the masses and a true sense of place for the individual, out of which may grow a new urban aesthetic.

Occasionally in history, in addition to the day-to-day building from which new principles gradually arise, there are moments of dazzling vision, of startling insights into new scales and new systems of order. One such moment occurred in this century in the mind of Walter Burley Griffin, (a product of the Chicago School, nurtured in the experience of the Columbian Exposition, an

associate of Frank Lloyd Wright), in his design for the new capital of Australia, Canberra. It is a curiosity that, in 1791, the capital of the United States should be the projection of a design of one from old-world France, and that today the design of one of the very few capital cities built in this century should be the projection of one of the Chicago School halfway around the world. The full significance of the Canberra plan has not yet been grasped, either here or in Australia. Its meaning will grow as time goes on, for it embodies the great American striving for freedom within order, for some system of overall organization that still allows for individual creativity and initiative. Like L'Enfant's Washington, the Canberra plan provides a web of connecting thoroughfares, but here the business and residential streets which lead into them are carefully tailored to avoid acute angles. In a form markedly similar to the 1898 diagram by Ebenezer Howard for the English Garden City, these streets surround a focal center in hexagonal and octagonal patterns, discouraging their use by through traffic and always providing an evident relationship with a focus. It has eight clear and definite urban centers connected together by straight thoroughfares, and two foci in open space, one at the peak of Mount Ainslee, the other at Black Mountain. The whole system is integrated with the natural features, mountains, lakes, plains— indeed, like the L'Enfant plan, it derives directly from them.

Griffin saw that he was relating to the long pull: 'Any arrangement looking forward one hundred years has to be elastic, permitting street improvements and construction to proceed little by little, no faster than the city growth demands, but at the same time in a way that will be adequate ultimately without constant shifting of site uses in the various sections'.

f11

The plight of the people

Behind the gleaming façades of the Chicago towers facing the parks along the shores of Lake Michigan, and supporting and making possible Grand Central Park and the Rockefeller Center in New York, lay the vast massive city and the people who live in it, and here all was not well. The same industrial production that produced the vast agglomeration of wealth produced vast agglomerations of workers also, a method of working that tended to dull the identity of the individual, and a method of living that took a heavy toll on his vitality and the integrity of the family. To meet the labor needs of the growing industrial machine, wave after wave of immigrants arrived from Europe during the latter half of the 19th century, bringing the problems of congestion and overcrowding to cities, and the problems of unassimilated cultures, languages and ways of doing things as well. The spectacular slum conditions in the tenement houses in New York, brought to the public eye by the writings of Jacob Riis in the *New York Sun* in 1885, were representative of slum problems in every large city throughout the United States. Exploitation of labor during the later 19th and early 20th century had reached appalling proportions. Women and children worked incredible hours for a pittance and, in the abortive strike of 1886, the eight-hour day proved to be just a radical dream.

p 218
(47)

Unease manifested itself occasionally at the top. Frank Leslie in his Historical Register of the Centennial Exhibition in 1876 quotes a statement, 'the rich are getting richer and the poor are getting poorer', scarcely a gratifying fulfilment of the first hundred years of democratic effort. At the World's Columbian Exposition seventeen years later Mrs Potter Palmer, the remarkable president of the Board of Lady Managers and wife of a highly successful merchant, hotel keeper and real estate developer of Chicago, at the opening of the Women's Building said, 'The struggle for bread is as fierce as of old. We find everywhere the same picture presented— overcrowded industrial centers, factories surrounded by dense populations of operatives, keen competition, many individuals forced to use such strenuous effort that vitality is drained in the struggle to maintain life under conditions so uninviting and discouraging that it scarcely seems worth living. It is a grave reproach to modern enlightenment that we seem no nearer the solution of many of these problems than during the feudal days'.

p 158
(15)

p 218
(48)

Such sentiment was thought to be tolerable in women, but the male leadership remained secure in its belief in the permanency of its way of life.

As a philanthropic gesture, George Pullman, Mrs Palmer's neighbor, built for his sleeping-car workers a model town, Pullman. During the depression of 1893 he cut the workers' wages 25% but maintained the rents on their houses at the previous level, and seemed surprised when they objected. The destructive and bloody strike which followed was just one of a series. It had been preceded by an even more serious strike at Homestead, Pennsylvania; where Henry Clay Frick of the Carnegie Steel Company refused to negotiate with the Amalgamated Association of Iron, Steel and Tin Workers' Union. He imported strike-breakers and armed guards, giving the union a setback in the steel industry from which it recovered only many years later. Efforts on the part of the State Legislatures and even of Congress itself to legislate improved conditions of work, hours and wages and to eliminate child labor were frustrated by decisions of the Supreme Court which ruled such legislation unconstitutional. Attempts at direct action by the workers themselves were countered by state and Federal troops; during the American Railway union strike in 1894 two thousand Federal troops were sent to Chicago, in response to the railroad's request for intervention. This strike was really broken by the insistence of the Attorney General of the United States on the issuance of injunctions in the Federal courts based in part on the Sherman Anti-Trust Law.

The stock market crash of 1929 and Depression which followed undermined the confidence of the business leaders in their own system of values and ways of doing things, and left the country virtually directionless until the election of 1932. The man who was elected President at that time, Franklin Delano Roosevelt, was a nephew of Frederick Delano, a leader in the development of the 1908 Chicago Plan, who later on founded the New York Regional Plan Association, and was appointed by Roosevelt as a member of the short-lived National Resources Planning Board. This is not intended to indicate that Frederick Delano had an important direct influence on his nephew, but rather that Franklin Roosevelt, born of wealthy parents, had a wide background to draw upon in the formulation of the social policy of his administration during that remarkable period of frenetic activity, the first hundred days of his administration. Out of this grew policies and programs, unheard of or totally rejected before, but now an accepted part of the American scene—unemployment insurance, public welfare, labor relations boards, medical care, Federal control of securities, social security, and, of deep significance to cities, public housing. The next four decades were to see the deep impact of these policies on the form of cities, and, perhaps even more deeply, on their state of mind.

p 148
f 5

The cities which Franklin Roosevelt faced, and which he proposed to change in his zeal for a 'New Deal', were, in large measure deteriorated, crowded, congested and confused, an accumulation of long years of unbridled private speculation and exploitation, and public neglect. In New York low-income families were jammed into six-storey tenements, cheek by jowl in street after street, with no open space but the street and a paved back alley. Conditions in other cities never achieved the density of New York, which at the end of the 19th century was the highest anywhere in the world, but they contained most of the New York slum characteristics, overcrowding, deterioration, monotony and just plain misery. Despite the fact that the environment of cities had ceased to express in physical form the sense of place and sense of community that was the hallmark of early American towns, the spirit of these qualities proved to have remarkable staying power and to be capable of surviving in the minds and hearts of people, even in the most hostile environment. It has received continually changing expression in public policies and private action in cities, and has been a deep undercurrent in all that has been done.

p 218–1
(49)

American idea of community

In the 1690s, speaking of Philadelphia, a German pastor remarked that Penn 'will not give any man his portion separately, but all must dwell together in townships and towns, and this is not without weighty reasons . . . the children can be kept at school and much more conveniently brought up well. Neighbors also can better offer each other loving and helpful hands'. The wagon train communities that crossed the prairies to the West learned principles of co-operation and mutual help necessary for survival. The immigrants who came steerage to this country had some of the same problems as their Pilgrim predecessors two centuries before. As they transplanted their shipboard experience into the walkup tenements where many of them came to live, they translated their sense of community into the names they gave to places in the anonymous physical extent of tenements, the Bowery, Greenwich Village, Harlem and the rest. It was natural that the politicians, then close to the people, would understand this quality and would exploit it. Lincoln Steffens in his 1902 *Shame of Cities* speaking of ward politics says, 'The leader and his captains have their hold because they take care of their own. They speak pleasant words, smile friendly smiles, notice the baby, give picnics up the River or the Sound, or a slap on the back, find jobs. . . . Tammany kindness is real kindness, and will go far, remembering long, and take infinite trouble for a friend.' Politicians were only one element of a complicated web of mutual help and interdependence that had been built up in poverty areas on a community basis, the local priest, minister or rabbi, the private charity, the settlement house, the services administered on a face to face basis, and indeed care of each other's children, aged and sick. All of this existed, invisible within the rows of anonymous tenements along the streets, but the very fiber of life which gave deep and strong association with place.

p 16 (1

p 39–4
(1, 2)

p 41 (6)

It was understandable that, as the Great Depression of the 1930s took center stage, and the problems of poverty were newly exposed because they were shared by the formerly affluent, a kind of panic would erupt which would discredit the old ways of doing things and would set up a cry to discard the entire old structure, the good with the bad.

'I feel I should warn you. They've taken down most of Boston and they're putting up something else.' (Drawing by Saxon; © 1969 the New Yorker Magazine, Inc.) (12)

This is what actually occurred. The undermining of confidence in the old value systems affected not only the bankers but the intellectual and academicians as well, and left a great vacuum of thought. Into this vacuum rushed Europeans ideas of systems of order, aided by the youthful reform administration of the New Deal, and abstract values took over from human ones.

The first thing that happened was acceptance of the super-rationalistic approach to analysis of the problem. The 'City Beautiful' movement was discarded with anathema along with the old American pragmatism. Detailed social statistics were produced from surveys done by the unemployed, supposedly to replace 'intuitive' judgment as the basis for action. Elaborate techniques were designed by the American Public Health Association to evaluate, record statistically and map housing factors such as structural condition, sanitation and environment. In many parts of the United States maps blossomed forth showing in solid black those areas which fell below the standards of the Public Health Association for conservation, substituting statistics for human judgment, and paving the way for indiscriminate and total destruction in these areas in the name of progress. The interesting thing about this procedure is that it treated land as a blank piece of paper, devoid of associations and human sentiments; it treated the institutions connected with the land as placeless entities, and it treated the people who lived on the land as grouped statistical averages. It set up a process which automatically excluded as significant variables individual differences between properties on the land and between the families which occupied them. It laid the foundation for massive programs of total clearance which followed, and set in motion a way of thinking which was guaranteed to destroy the sense of community and sense of place.

Exacerbating the problem was the new image of what was to rise in the place of the old 'slums', as the land was made pure and clean by the total removal of all of the buildings and people who formerly occupied it. Here the crude vision of 'safe and sanitary housing' grafted onto the rationalistic formula of multi-storey, 'high rise' elevator apartment slabs spaced wide apart, developed at the Bauhaus in Germany, in a kind of adulation of abstract rather than human values, 'low land coverage', open space, light angle and the like. The consequence was massive subsidized public housing projects, open only to families of low income, the families

p 219
50, 51)

'piled one on top of another like objects in a filing case', to make way for open areas dotted with signs, 'keep off the grass'. One might almost say of some of the planning of this era that families were removed to make way for the grass.

Construction of such projects is widespread. In Saint Louis, the thirty-six million dollar Pruitt-Igoe project with its thirty-three identically designed eleven-storey buildings, the barren open space between being strewn with tin cans and broken glass, has now been partially demolished. The growing crime in such projects, notably in the elevators, and increasingly wide expression of resentment at the anonymity of the accommodations, gradually caused changes in the public attitude toward housing the poor. Indicative of the intensity of the change is the fact that the Housing Act of 1968 has prohibited the construction of any further low rent public housing projects with high rise elevator structures for families with children, unless the Secretary of Housing and Urban Development agrees that there is no practicable alternative. Thus what only a few years before was considered an act of civic virtue has been declared to be illegal by an act of Congress.

The really powerful opposition to wholesale clearance in cities and consequent social disruption came only after the program moved out of the area exclusively confined to low income housing into the broader, more varied field of urban redevelopment, first authorized in the Housing Act of 1949.

It is strange that redevelopment planning at its outset would show no respect for the old American tradition of a sense of place and a sense of community. Huge areas of cities throughout the United States were wiped clean in a way and on a scale that would have been impossible without national government help. Valuable sections of cities representing significant periods of development and sensitive and beautiful texturing of the city's surface were swept away, making a tear in the city's fabric, and a gap in the evidence of the flow of history. Historically valuable buildings, such as the very great Metropolitan Building in Minneapolis, were destroyed in the name of improvement, the continuity of Larimer Street in Denver, even the feeling of association with a place was obliterated, as expressed by a bellboy in Boston—'they have taken away Scollay Square'. And these are only a few of a very much larger catalogue.

It is strange that, at the outset, the financial support programs

p 219
(51)

p 213
(34)
f 12

providing subsidy for the landowner, the builder, the home-owner, and the renter should ignore the human factor, the differences between families, the individual dignity. People were shunted about ruthlessly to meet the convenience of the legal and financial programs. Thus those families which had managed to better themselves were thrown out of public housing projects as being 'over income', and left to seek housing in the slums again because of their new affluence. Housing officials and politicians sought sites for clearance for huge housing projects while thousands of scattered vacant lots and vandalized shells of houses went begging for users, and finally sank into such a state of degradation that they infected their neighborhood as cancerous sores, offering attractive facilities for arson, petty crime, rape and murder. Vast Federal supports were available for cheap mortgage money and low down-payments for speculative housing in the suburbs, drawing people from the older areas where it was virtually impossible to obtain a loan for necessary repairs. Gone was the great vision of Walt Whitman of huge masses of people in cities, but masses in which each individual stood out as a special person, each with his own special feelings, sets of sensory responses, appearance and even smell. The individual became blurred in the standardization implied in Henry Wallace's 'Common Man' and Franklin Roosevelt's 'One Third of a Nation'.

It is a curious thing that, in the initially euphoric reaction to urban redevelopment, no one seemed to notice that, since the purpose of the legislation was to clear the land of 'blighting factors' and to resell it at a lower cost to private developers for new development, and since private enterprise unaided never had succeeded in providing housing for the poor, the consequence of its application on a wide scale would be removal of the poor for projects of the rich. Since the great majority of the poor in large cities were also black, this also meant in many cases dislocation of black for white. Charles Abrams, in his great aphorism, 'urban renewal is Negro removal' sharpened the issue and exposed the fact.

As the cumulative effects of these policies became evident in the things that were actually done in their name across the nation, and which fell so far short of their objectives, a widespread popular reaction set in. As this reached the halls of Congress it was reflected in the many changes introduced into the Housing Legislation. The simple sequence of language used by Congress to express its housing intentions offers a fascinating indicator of evolving national attitudes.

In the National Housing Act of 1939, first in the nation, the objective placed top in sequence in the bill is 'to alleviate recent and recurring unemployment' and only secondarily to remedy the shortage of 'decent, safe and sanitary dwellings for families of low income', which, of itself, is a rather forbidding and limited objective. By the time of the Housing Act of 1949 Congress had gotten away from specifying 'families of low income' as a special class isolated from the rest of Americans, and also from considering dwellings separately from community, in the statement, 'the realization . . . of the goal of a decent home and a suitable living environment for every American family'. This legislation introduced the concept of urban redevelopment and provided funds for the clearance of blighted areas for private reuse for a variety of purposes. The 1954 Act contained for the first time the words 'urban renewal', which encompassed both construction and regulatory programs. In 1965 grants were made for community facilities, health centers, community meeting halls, cultural centers, strengthening the possibilities for expression of community in the city. The Model Cities legislation of 1966 envisioned a broad experimental program 'containing new and imaginative proposals', in which social services were given equal weight with physical changes, and, for the first time, specified 'widespread citizen participation' in planning the program. The Housing Act

of 1968 set up the revolutionary concept of replacing the project-by-project approach with a total 'Neighborhood Development Program' carried out on an annual incremental basis, the amount of funds provided to any city would be governed by the actual performance in the previous year. The Department of Housing and Urban Development provided for locally selected Project Area Committees consisting of residents in the neighborhoods, and provided them with technical staff for the planning of their neighborhood, either by direct loan of personnel or by providing funds to enable them to hire their own staff or consultants. Legislatively at least, the basis exists for a radically new and deep-rooted approach to rebuilding cities.

It is not just the theoretician, the planner and the social reformer who are reimposing the sense of place, the sense of community in the city; it is the people who live there, who are doing it in response to the impact of these programs from the outside. Out of the depressed communities, many in the black ghetto, are arising more and more community groups, generated by the people in the communities themselves, planning groups, church groups, non-profit development corporations, planning and rebuilding their community to their own image. Some of these started totally outside any governmental program, such as the Young Great Society in Mantua in Philadelphia, a group of young black people who started by rehabilitating abandoned houses with their own hands. Many have been formed in response to Federal programs giving financial assistance to non-profit corporations, and many struggling groups have moved into new dimensions of effectiveness as they are enabled to obtain their own technical help. p 220 (55)

Out of the resurgence of self-assertion of the black community, out of rejection of integration as the primary objective and the acceptance of blackness as such growing out of the Black Power Movement, has come a reactivation of community planning on what is practically a village basis in even the largest of the megalopolitan agglomerations. Although, of course, such activities are not confined to the black communities, it is really the black people, so long denied full recognition of citizenship or human dignity, who are now reconstituting and making alive the principles of community-interchange and community-action which animated and made viable the towns of the first settlers on these shores.

Fraught with difficulty, frustration and dangers, the basic process of community self-determination in the great city is, at last, provided for in Federal legislation and financial programs. The principle of development of plans for community improvement by the community itself has become accepted in government circles, Federal, state and local. Here and there significant plans have been made and significant work accomplished on the ground.

Throughout the world the fundamental problem is continually being expressed in its increasingly dangerous proportions, of how to maintain individual identity within the vast metropolitan complex. The solution to this problem may well prove to be the most important issue in world cities over the next century. Because, unlike most countries, the United States contains a wide variety of racial groups, and because, however traumatic it may have been, and continues to be, the United states has a long history of experience of interaction between nationality backgrounds and races, it may be the place where the function of the community in determining its own form will first become clearly established, simply because, under these circumstances, the community residents have most aggressively asserted these functions. It may well prove that the most valuable contribution of American cities to world city development is the re-establishment, within the metropolitan complex, of a sense of place of the individual, of a sense of community, of the expansibility of community 'nucleation' throughout the urban complex, and of the principle that each person should have a hand in shaping his own environment.

X

ENTERTAINMENT ARTS

Theater, music and film

RICHARD SCHICKEL

'Music rots when it gets too far from the dance.'

EZRA POUND

'There's No Business Like Show Business.'

IRVING BERLIN

'The Cathedrals of Broadway'

(opposite) are—or were—its theaters and cinemas. 'High art', until fairly late in the 20th century, usually meant something imported from, or closely modeled on, Europe. 'Entertainment', born of folk-song, technology and commerce, was something uniquely American, which America, in its turn, gave to the world. By 1929, the date of Florine Stettheimer's painting, jazz was enjoying its golden age, with pioneering Negro artists and big white bands flourishing side by side; the silent film had reached perfection and had been replaced by the less perfect, most promising 'talkie'; and the musical revue had been brought to that peak of sophistication that it was to maintain for the next decade. In all these fields American leadership was acknowledged and secure. (1)

The early cinemas, cramped and uncomfortable as they were, unfolded new worlds of realism and magic. (2)

The Western: John Ford's first essay in the type was *The Iron Horse* (below) of 1924. (4)

'Ben Hur' was made in 1925 at a cost of four million dollars. Here Fred Niblo shoots the chariot-race scene in a recreated Circus Maximus. (3)

Laurel and Hardy (left, in *Hog Wild*, 1930) were among the formative geniuses of silent comedy. (5)

With 'Intolerance' in 1916 Griffith proved that the long film with a complicated plot and serious theme could justify itself aesthetically, if not at the boxoffice. Above: Griffith directing. Right: the Babylonian scene, one of the most lavish ever filmed. (6, 7)

The Golden Triplets

The richest trio in the film industry: Douglas Fairbanks, Mary Pickford and Charlie Chaplin in 1917. (8)

Erich von Stroheim (below, directing *Greed*, 1925) gave the screen a flavour of Central European cynicism. (10)

Busby Berkeley transformed the screen musical by expanding tradition to a previously undreamed of scale. Above: *Dames*, 1934. (9)

The star system is almost as old as the industry itself. Left: a scene from *Morocco* (1930) with Marlene Dietrich and Adolphe Menjou. (11)

Orson Welles's first film, *Citizen Kane* (below) told its story in a particularly cinematic way, using sophisticated techniques of shooting and editing. (13)

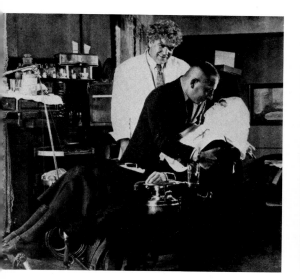

'Forbidden Paradise': Ernst Lubitsch directing the exotic Pola Negri in 1934. (12)

The American theater was very early rivaling the Old World in both acting and scenic effects. The Park Street Theatre, New York, in 1822, (left) embodied the most up-to-date features of theater design, though the projecting stage and proscenium doors are English features soon to disappear. (14)

American actors were soon challenging visiting Europeans, such as Kean, in the classic roles. Above: a caricature of Edwin Forrest as Spartacus. (15)

'Hold! I will reach you!' Melodrama was the staple fare of the theatre during the second half of the 19th century. This poster of 1896 advertises *The War of Wealth*. The vivid illusionistic effects upon which so much ingenuity was vainly spent in the theater were to be achieved in the medium of film. (16)

Buffalo Bill, William Cody, was all that he pretended to be – rider, buffalo hunter, scout, Indian slayer. After a colorful early career he formed his Wild West Show in 1883, taking it to Europe four years later. Along with popular fiction and melodrama, it helped to create the image of 'the West' that later became a film mainstay. (17)

The Leaders of Modern Minstrelsy and The Genuine Negro Minstrels

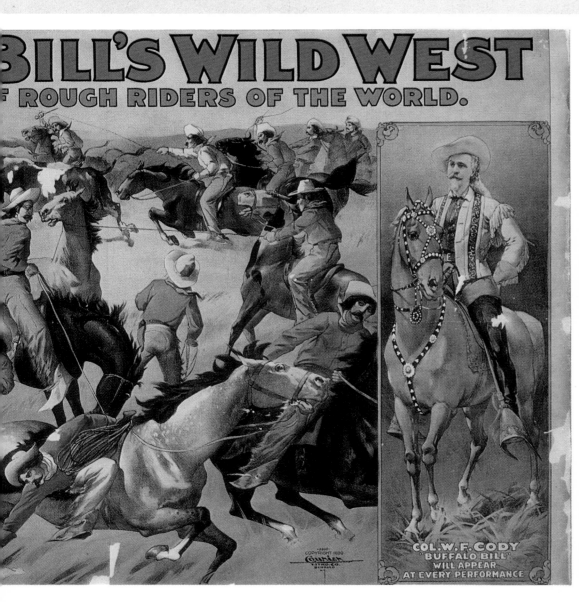

'Minstrels' exploited the vogue for Negro ballads, dressed up after 1880 with lavish decor and costumes. (18)

'Vawdvil' – straw hat, cane, synchronized dance – epitomized on a *Life* cover of 1928. (19)

Jenny Lind's tour in 1850 (left) illustrates not only the fact that America was now part of the European 'circuit' but also the growing importance of the impresario. She was brought over by the showman P. T. Barnum. (20)

Isadora Duncan (below), born at San Francisco in 1878, created a new form of dance that rejected the artificiality of classical ballet in favour of a more natural 'freedom'. The drawing is by Gordon Craig. (21)

Ruth St Denis (below, in 1906), following Isadora, turned to India and the East for inspiration. In a typically American way, her ambition was to express in dance 'the whole range of thought and philosophy'. (22)

Ragtime was a version of jazz, diluted to suit popular taste. Irving Berlin's famous song was among the earliest examples. (23)

Professional efficiency, 'the steady, incorruptible purr of the dynamo', made the musical revue eminently characteristic of 20th-century America. Above: *The Passing Show*, 1913. (26)

The authentic voice of jazz was first heard in the deep South, where it represented a true product of Negro culture. Far left: the Cake Walk, New Orleans, 1890. Left: King Oliver's Band before 1922, also in New Orleans. But white professionalism soon transformed it into something shallower and slicker. Bandleaders like Paul Whiteman (right) exploited the talents of musicians better than themselves. (24, 25, 27)

The picture palace – that is literally what it was – dominated entertainment of the twenties and thirties. All over the world, in surroundings as splendid as could be devised, millions paid their devotion to the gods and goddesses of Hollywood. Most palatial of all was the Roxy, New York (right), built in 1927 in a style that combines Gothic, Renaissance and Moorish. (28)

American history: the ballroom scene from *Gone with the Wind* (1939), one of the most expensive and successful films ever made. (29)

Full length cartoon (bottom center) owed its existence to Walt Disney. After the success of fairy tales like *Snow White* he attempted something more ambitious in *Fantasia* (1940), which supplied visual equivalents to famous pieces of music. This scene is from Ponchielli's 'Dance of the Hours'. (30)

Space-fiction led to a new kind of epic 'spectacular', which curiously enough retained many of the religious overtones of the old. Below: a preliminary drawing for *2001: A Space Odyssey*. (31)

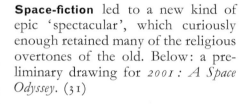

Biblical epic (right): Pharaoh's chariots are overwhelmed by the Red Sea in a scene from Cecil B. De Mille's second version of *The Ten Commandments*, 1956. (32)

The musical acquired a new seriousness in Gershwin's *Porgy and Bess* (right), which in 1935 united opera and jazz, with a revolutionary all-black cast. (33)

'Oklahoma!' (below), a slick blend of Broadway professionalism and folkish themes, revolutionized theatrical expectations. (34)

Alwin Nikolais seeks to eliminate human emotions from ballet and to produce abstract visual experiences that come closer to sculpture than to drama. Above: a scene from *Imago*. (35)

'West Side Story' (above) of 1957 tried to introduce realism – gang clashes and violence – into the conventions of the musical. (36)

In 'Hair' (right) all the preoccupations of young people in 1968 – civil rights, drugs, sex, the Vietnam War – were put on to the stage with unprecedented directness. (37)

Serious drama produced interesting experiments but only one playwright of genius, Eugene O'Neill. Above: scenes from *Desire under the Elms* (1924) and *The Iceman Cometh*. (38, 39)

The new dramatists reflected the stresses of modern society in various ways. Clifford Odets was overtly political (*Waiting for Lefty*, 1935, above left); Arthur Miller concentrated on society and the individual (above: design for the set of *Death of a Salesman*, 1949); Tennessee Williams went to psychology (*A Streetcar Named Desire*, 1947, far left) and Edward Albee (left: *Who's Afraid of Virginia Woolf?* 1962) to the personal crises of intellectuals. (40–43)

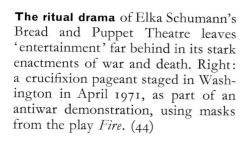

The ritual drama of Elka Schumann's Bread and Puppet Theatre leaves 'entertainment' far behind in its stark enactments of war and death. Right: a crucifixion pageant staged in Washington in April 1971, as part of an antiwar demonstration, using masks from the play *Fire*. (44)

Theater, music and film

RICHARD SCHICKEL

p 248
(45) ON 16 MAY 1969, the composer John Cage and his collaborator, a musician and computer expert named Lajaren Hiller, took over a huge assembly hall at the University of Illinois to put on the first (and only) performance of a new work they called HPSCHD (or *Harpsichord*, when it is unnecessary to reduce the word to computer language). It was, by any standard, a peculiar composition. In the center of the sports arena several huge (100 by 40 foot) semi-transparent sheets were hung. On them a collage of abstract and semi-abstract images was projected, with the images, in effect, encouraged to leak through from screen to screen. All the way around the hall, near the ceiling, a 340-foot screen was hung. On it more images, randomly mixed, were projected—computer instructions, musical scores, abstract blobs and blotches. Lights played across the ceiling, spinning mirrored balls fragmented and reflected light from other sources. Fifty-two loudspeakers, scattered about the hall, played computer-generated music and seven other loudspeakers picked up and amplified the playing of the seven harpsichordists present. Three of them were playing versions of Mozart's *Introduction to the Composition of Waltzes by Means of Dice*, each of them under instructions to play the sections of the work in any order they chose. Two others played differing, fixed montages of harpsichord music from Mozart to the present. Another played something called *Computer Print-out for 12-tone Gamut* and the seventh had carte-blanche to play any Mozart composition for his instrument any time the spirit moved him. Finally, each player was free, at any time, to play any of his colleagues' solos. The audience at this event did not sit down in neat rows. Instead, they were asked to wander about in the din, 'grooving' on whatever combination of sounds and images happened to arrest their attention at any given moment. A few chose to paint their faces with day-glo colors. Others occasionally broke into dances. They were, on the whole, very orderly, perhaps in compensation for the deliberately anarchical character of the work they were experiencing. (Another composer who was present commented to the man from the *New York Times*: 'It was insured that no order can be perceived.').

The tradition of universality

One has come to expect, in the art of our time (especially in America) a degree of formlessness, a rejection of artistic order as that term is traditionally defined. In the last decade or so, Happenings, the theater of mixed means, the discothèque, folk and rock festivals, the determined efforts of even the more traditionally-oriented theatrical directors to break down the wall that formerly separated performers from spectators, have all become familiar phenomena.

The Happening has evolved in recent years as an attempt to combine all the arts and to break down the barriers between them. In May 1969 the composer John Cage staged HPSCHD (left), in which abstract images were projected on sheets while loudspeakers relayed the sound of harpsichords and computer music played without order or co-ordination. The audience wandered around, 'grooving' on whatever took their fancy. The whole enterprise, surprisingly, fits into an American tradition which aims at encompassing a huge range of experience in a single work of art. (44)

Naturally, all this activity reflects a recent, general and still growing sense that our essential organizational systems, based on rationalism, materialism and the ideal of a liberal democracy, are failing, have perhaps already failed. It is, of course, impossible to say whether this sense of the way things are in America is a permanent or transitory mood, whether we are experiencing a peculiarly sharp social tremor that will merely give the nation a severe shaking-up or whether we are in the midst of a full-scale revolutionary earthquake that will destroy it as we have known it—and imply a total rebuilding.

Nevertheless, it is a mistake to believe that the so-called 'cultural revolution' of the 1960s and 1970s is totally without historical roots. I would, in fact, argue the opposite—that it is possibly a culmination, certainly an important way-station, in a very long-term trend, a trend one can trace back at least a century. There is precedent both in our high culture and in our popular culture for HPSCHD. For over a century, ever since it began to look as if technology might be able to help them achieve it, American artists have dreamed of creating works that would blend several—perhaps all—media in new forms that would enable them to encompass something like the entire range of the American experience in a single work of art or, at the very least, in a series of works.

To understand this, let us look, for a moment, at the career of an earlier American musician—a man who labored mostly unrecognized and unrewarded, to find a means of expressing the national spirit in huge, strangely sophisticated yet utterly charming works—Charles Ives. Son of a bandmaster in Danbury, Connecticut, student of Horatio Parker (composer of operas in an imitative and genteel tradition) at Yale, and successful insurance broker, Ives composed the bulk of his great work prior to 1920; most of it was not publicly performed until the 1950s and it is only in the past few years that it has been heard with any frequency. Even so, he is best known in musical circles for his purely technical pioneering—experiments in atonality that preceded Schoenberg, successful uses of multiple rhythms that preceded anyone else's, even the deployment of tone clusters and of piano techniques (the use of fists, palms, rulers) that we like to think of as the inventions of our own musical moment. Yet all this experiment was not, so far as one can tell, an end in itself for Ives. Rather, he was trying to synthesize (particularly in his symphonies) the sounds of the American experience. No less than Whitman, he heard our varied carols, and he made use of them in his music. He quoted Brahms and Bach, Wagner and Dvořák, suggesting our ties to the culture of the Old World. But this material exists in Ives side by side with contrasting material from the New World—hymns, folk songs, college tunes, Stephen Foster, the marches his father had conducted on the town green. Altogether, it formed a most delightful cacophony, suggestive, above all, of the rude bustle of a nation creating itself. Yet mingled with this simple stuff—often, it seemed, struggling to free itself from it—was another, more idealistic strain, a strain that one might reasonably risk terming transcendental, one that surely was intended to suggest the old American notion that the nation had a redemptive, possibly even Utopian, role to play in the world.

Of particular interest to anyone hoping to establish the historical connection between the work of Charles Ives and the modern avant-garde is his so-called *Universe Symphony*. He began thinking

249

MY OLD KENTUCKY HOME, GOOD NIGHT!

NEGRO SONGS

Stephen Foster's minstrel songs conveyed a nostalgic, idealized picture of the South, with happy 'darkies' singing in the cotton-fields. 'My Old Kentucky Home,' written in 1853, perhaps yields only to 'The Old Folks at Home' as the most popular of his sentimental ballads. It was adopted as Kentucky's official state song in 1928. (1)

'Mr Price: Please don't try to make things nice. All the wrong notes are right. Just copy as I have—I want it that way'—Charles Ives's instruction to the engraver. The score for his composition 'Fourth of July' is typical of his experimentation with highly complex and original techniques. (2)

about it in 1915 and he was still making sketches for it in 1937, by which time he had decided that it should remain unfinished because as Henry and Sidney Cowell, his biographers, express it, 'it is his culminating expression . . . so gigantic, so inclusive, and so exalted that he feels no one man could ever complete it; anyone else may add to it if he cares to do so.' Since Ives's scheme was to create 'the full expression of the universe in sound', there was a certain daft—and inspiring—logic to his dream. In any case, his plan was for a work in three parts—'Formation of the countries and mountains', 'Evolution in nature and humanity' and 'The rise of all to the spiritual'. Perhaps of more interest to modernists was Ives's idea of scoring the work for several orchestras and choruses which he saw (heard is perhaps a better term) placed about in the lowlands, on hillsides, on the tops of mountains, perhaps in the Keene Valley of New Hampshire where this great vision first overtook him.

New World, new culture

The point is obvious: There is a strain in American music—and, I believe, in all American art (including the non-performing ones, which are beyond my purview here)—that has long aspired to break the restraints and constraints of good form as it was traditionally defined. Classicism simply does not have a very strong hold on the American imagination. And the reason for this is simple; America is—so far—the only nation that has created its culture almost entirely within the context of an industrial society. The great European cultures all rested—still rest (as we can often see even in the works of their most avant-garde film-makers)—on a living, or at least lively, sense of what the intellectual community of a pre-industrial society was like. And though many Americans, both artists and members of the audience, have yearned for that state of grace (which may account for the extensive deployment of nostalgia as a theme in our art), the fact is that culturally we knew very little about that older world. Yes, of course, we had read histories, but our hearts were blank and uncomprehending. Perhaps our literary culture, when New England flowered and the Southern poets flourished, had some small sense of it. But in the performing arts, there was no such knowledge. We had to invent—and many of our better minds thought it was a high duty—a culture that stressed the uniqueness of the American experience of pioneering on a frontier and pioneering in the construction of vast industrial complexes.

It is fair to note that theorists of popular culture like Dwight MacDonald have always been appalled by our cavalier attitude toward traditional forms, the sheer jumble and mess of popular creativity. But if we are to understand what we have made here in the way of a culture, we must keep firmly in mind the quite direct relationship between the development of the American industrial system and the technologies on which it was based and the growth of new entertainment forms. Prior to the Civil War it is not too much to say that ours was essentially a parlor culture. There were, to be sure, flourishing lecture circuits, a fair number of stock companies in the nation's major cities and the beginnings of a system of touring companies (particularly after gold was discovered in California and the west coast began to look like an El Dorado for actors as well as miners). Nevertheless, in ante-bellum America, there were virtually no playwrights (and none of world class), no symphony orchestras operating on more than a catch-as-catch-can basis, no firmly established opera companies, no dance companies.

One gains a sense of the quality of American cultural life in the early 19th century if one notes, with the brilliant critic and historian, Wilfred Mellers, that the exemplary American composer of the time was Stephen Foster. His work, in Mellers's view, was the first consciously to exploit his audience's sense of nostalgia for times gone by, the sense of rootlessness and lack of tradition which were already endemic in this new found land. In any case, although Foster's songs were written for that most popular of theatrical forms, the minstrel show, their true environment was the parlor, their greatest devotees the middle-class family groups that gathered around the piano to harmonize on them.

It is perfectly true that Foster's contemporary, Louis-Moreau Gottschalk, who was America's first major, native-born concert artist, was able to make a career for himself in the middle of the 19th century, but only at a certain cost to his art. He had studied in Europe and his pianistic virtuosity had been praised by Liszt, Chopin and Berlioz, but on his American tours he assiduously wooed his audiences with a combination of Fosterian sentimentality and Lisztian pyrotechnics. He also composed—material based more directly than Foster's on the authentic Negro folk music he had heard as a child in New Orleans—but his work has lasted less well than Foster's, largely because he embellished it with unfelt, if technically showy, devices derived from the European piano virtuosi. The point of these two careers—really the first American

f 1

*p 241
(18)*

musical careers—is simple. There simply was no serious audience for serious music. So Foster and Gottschalk pandered to the unformed musical tastes of the time in one way or another—by keeping things simple or by turning oneself into a kind of a freak (it is perhaps significant that the promoter of Jenny Lind's first American tour was none other than P. T. Barnum, the circus impresario).

And what is true of music was true of the other performing arts as well. The American theater throughout the 19th century was a star's theater and, latterly, a producer's theater. John Howard Payne, the first important American playwright, was famous largely for his *Brutus, or the Fall of Tarquin*, and its success was based on the fact that it provided a meaty role for such stars as Edmund Kean, Junius Brutus Booth and his son Edwin, Edwin Forest and James William Wallack. Like many of the author's other works it was a pastiche (in this case of no less than seven European plays) and Payne himself, in an introduction to a later work, commented rather wistfully that because of 'the peculiarities of leading performers' and the 'restive spirit' of the public it was 'almost hopeless to look to the stage of the present day for a permanent literary distinction'. In that atmosphere, he said, 'good poets . . . often make bad dramatists'.

Nevertheless, there was abroad in the land a vague hope, a wild surmise. It was expressed by Edgar Allan Poe who was, incidentally, the son of a sometime actor: 'The next step may be the electrification of all mankind by the representation of a play that may be neither tragedy, comedy, farce, opera, pantomime, melodrama or spectacle, as we now comprehend these terms, but which may retain some portion of the idiosyncratic excellence of each, while it introduces a new class of excellence as yet unnamed because as yet undreamed-of in the world.' In short, there was a belief that a new country should, naturally, spawn new artistic forms. And implicit in that belief was another: that those forms should be as ambitious as the American Dream itself, should attempt somehow to encompass all of the national experience, if not all of human experience.

Drama and melodrama

The trend in the theater, from the end of the Civil War until the triumph of the movies, was toward romantic stories acted before settings that strived for greater and greater realism. These melodramas, though mostly laughable as literature, were all-encompas-

sing in their scenic ambitions. 'Photographic Realism' is the term most often applied to the stagecraft that was the ideal in the theater by the turn of the century, with Henry Irving acknowledged as the great master of this style. There was, however, more to this ideal than the realistic representation of a railroad train rushing toward the heroine bound, in classic fashion, to the tracks or of the chariot race in *Ben Hur*. Here, too, one observes a powerful desire to compress somehow within the confines of the stage, if not all of life, then at least huge chunks of experience. In the metropolitan centers elaborately equipped theaters vied to present the most elaborate productions of new works in the classic genres—the western, the mystery, the temperance drama, the rustic comedy. Of course, *Uncle Tom's Cabin*, especially in the version prepared by George L. Aiken, became an industry unto itself, the first American play to make any sizable impression on the rest of the world and, with its morally uplifting message, the play that broke down the lingering, puritanically-inspired resistance of 'nice' people to the theater. No matter what the subject of these pieces, no matter how naive their sentiments, no matter how feeble their wit and intellect, they offered the public an increasingly complex view of the world. Indeed, it is possible to say that there was no corner of the physical world, no corner of history, that the theater did not feel confident it could represent with some verisimilitude on stage —crowds, fights, frights, natural and man-made wonders, all the stuff of the cinema (which was, of course, waiting in the wings during the last decade of the century) was reproduced before the endlessly startled, if increasingly critical, eyes of the theatrical patron in this period. The two-dimensional conventions of melodrama, the simple stage trickery that had been tolerated in the middle of the century was greeted, as time wore on, by derision and, in the work of men like Irving, David Belasco and Steele MacKaye, the outworn conventions of melodramatic stagecraft were replaced by new ones, in which three-dimensional solidity of setting was emphasized, though not at the expense of the number of scenes a work might encompass or of the smooth flow of one scene into another. In effect, these men were attempting, with cumbersome mechanical methods and with lighting equipment that was not particularly flexible, qualities that, in a few years, movies would achieve with the greatest of ease.

The career of David Belasco—and there was no more successful career than his in the American theater of the time—is worth a few moments of study in this regard. His first great success was

p 242 (20)

p 240 (15)

p 240 (16)

f 3

Steele MacKaye, playwright, actor and inventor, as Paul Kauvar in his own play 'Anarchy', set in the time of the French Revolution. The carefully organized excitement of its mob scenes was an anticipation of the cinema. MacKaye was also a technical innovator—he patented over a hundred theatrical inventions. (3)

achieved in San Francisco where, in 1878, he adapted (perhaps 'inflated' would be a better word) an old play called *Not Guilty*, billing it as 'a Grand Production of the Magnificent, Musical, Military, Dramatic and Spectacular Christmas Piece', including in it 'with my customary leaning to warfare' a 'Battle Scene, with several hundred people in an embarkation, as well as horses and cannon'. Later, his adaptation in New York of H. Rider Haggard's adventure novel, *She*, contained so many flaming torches, fire-sprouting skeletons and other spectacular flame effects that a reviewer claimed 'the stage looks like a smelting works on a dark night, and the auditorium is perfumed with the exhalations of all the illuminating chemicals known to the stage mechanician.'

History, so dependent upon the written word for its view of culture, has not treated either the melodramatic or the spectacular theater kindly and it must be admitted that on the page they at best read quaintly, if not comically. Worse, it is economically unfeasible to revive the spectacle plays in anything like their intended grandness and impossible for audiences to reacquire the innocence necessary to respond appreciatively to the simpler melodramas. If they are seen at all today, they are seen in productions that intentionally call forth our condescending laughter. And yet, glancing at the prompt books and the working scripts of these works one senses that there was more here than we now realize—an attempt to create an expressive form that would blend the American's skill with, and delight in, technological invention, his delight in the expensive, expansive gesture, his joy in thronging spectacle, his distrust of the overly-intellectual, the overly-delicate.

The film takes over

In Russia, the great director Sergei Eisenstein commented very simply on why, in the 1920s, he transferred his allegiance from the stage to the screen: 'The cart fell to pieces and the driver fell into the cinema.' In the United States the cart fell apart sooner. Movies were first shown publicly in 1896 and they attracted, these short, undramatic successors to the kinetographs of the penny arcades, considerable interest. Still, they functioned largely as novelty attractions on vaudeville programs for almost a decade, despite the fact that the charming fantasy films of Georges Méliès, suggestive of the most exhilarating possibilities, were widely shown in America. It was not until the experiments of Edwin Porter, an employee of Thomas A. Edison, out of whose laboratories the first practicable American movie cameras and projectors came, that the possibilities of the film as a dramatic medium were convincingly demonstrated. His second story-film, *The Great Train Robbery*, though no more than ten minutes long, was an epochal film. No one knows how many nickelodeons used it as an opening day program, but the

growth of the movies in the years after its 1903 debut was, to borrow a word, stupendous. By 1906 there were at least a thousand little movie houses running in the US, by 1910 there must have been ten thousand of them.

p 238 (2)

To supply them there were, at one point, two hundred producing firms. They were at first, however, dominated by nine large manufacturers banded together as the Motion Picture Patents Co., a trust based on the fact that members used equipment protected by Edison's patents. They contended, with some basis in law, if not, perhaps, morality, that they and only they had the right to make films in this country and that only exhibitors they licensed to use their projection equipment had the right to show films. The problem with the patent companies was that they were managed by businessmen of a rather conventional sort. That is, they were not showmen and thus did not understand that there was something more to film production than grinding out so many feet of celluloid per week. Art was not yet an economic necessity, but a certain care in developing stories, in exploring the unique potentials of the medium for visual excitement and, later, a more enthusiastic response to the audience's desire for star personalities to identify with, would have stood them in good stead. For the most part, they failed in these and other respects, notably in their reluctance to attempt films longer than a couple of reels in length. The patent companies placed more reliance on defending an established position—mainly through legal maneuver—than in aggressively pursuing change and development in the art through paths that were admittedly strange to sober souls.

No such inhibitions afflicted their competitors, sometimes known as 'blanket outfits', because they kept a bed covering handy to throw over their equipment to disguise it from the trust's spies. They also went on location armed, because the trust's agents were in the habit of shooting at their cameras, hoping to put them out of commission and, of course, to frighten their operators. The small businessmen (some of whom were to become very large businessmen very quickly) who took on the trust were by no means scrupulous in their business methods. Immigrants and the sons of immigrants, they were a clawing, colorful, combative crew. No one ever accused them of being aesthetes, but in a way their lack of fine sensibilities served them well. They were willing to take a flier on anything, including art, which might expand their businesses.

An early historian of the movies, Benjamin Hampton, felt that the trust lost its fight with its smaller, less well-financed competitors simply because it failed to see what these men seemed to sense in their bones, that movies were to be the first truly democratic art, an art which, to survive and prosper, had to sense and then respond to public demand for new methods, ideas, themes, personalities in film products. He insisted that audiences were 'creating for themselves a form of entertainment that carried with it an immeasurable quantity of stimulation, enlightenment, and education'.

No doubt Hampton oversimplified, and certainly the idyllic free market conditions he described did not survive the great era of consolidation which took place in the 1920s, when studio theater combines came to dominate and, by ways ranging from publicity to booking methods, manipulate the market as surely as any other oligopoly in the more basic industries did. In their way, this handful of giants was as ruthless as the trust had been, and far more effective in driving out small competitors and preventing the emergence of new ones. Nevertheless, for a brief moment in time, conditions something like those Hampton described did, in fact, exist. Short films were inexpensive to make and since no one had any qualifications for working in this new medium, none were imposed on the talents that jumped, fell or were pushed into the infant industry. They were free to succeed or fail as they might, since there were no rules, aesthetic or otherwise, to hamper them. At first, it is fair to say, the movies were a people's theater. The craftsmen and artists of the movies in their first decade and a half of this century were of precisely the same economic level as their audiences. As a result, never in the history of art were art objects created for a large audience by people so closely identified with that audience's tastes, interests and aspirations. The prevailing wage for actors, directors, cameramen and all the others who toiled in the infant industry was $5 a day. The scenarios they shot—in a day or two or three, never more—were paid for at the same rate—though a clever man could turn out many more than one in a day's labor at his desk. Now, obviously, a little film, taking no more than ten minutes to flap through the projector, could not aspire to the kind of large vision the melodramatists could project for their audience. And yet, like the vaudeville described earlier, a program of these little films could, if well selected, touch 'us and our lives at many places'. For the historian there is no better way to gain a sense of the quality of American life in pre-World War I America than to spend an afternoon in a screening room at the Museum of Modern Art or George Eastman House in Rochester, NY, looking at a typical array of films from Biograph or Vitagraph or one of the other studios that attempted a degree of seriousness and realism in these little movies. Whatever the plots of these films—and they very often were no more than excuses to get a chase going—one still gets the authentic feel of the American street or farm, of the decor of homes at every level of society, the costumes of their inhabitants. The need to glamorize the ordinary was not yet felt by the industry or by its customers. More important, in the course of a single program, one might catch glimpses of every class, and of the boundless variety of human types to be found in all of them.

Let us take, for example, a representative sampling of D. W. Griffith's work for Biograph in the period 1908–13. There were adaptations from great or at least greatly popular literature—including poetry—that were models of intelligent and sympathetic adaptation (*Resurrection, The Call of the Wild, Pippa Passes, The Cricket on the Hearth, The Song of the Shirt*). There were films that took up social problems ranging from the white man's treatment of the red man (*The Indian Runner*) to gang warfare in the slums (*The Musketeers of Pig Alley*) to demon rum (*The Drunkard's Reformation*). There were stories aplenty that made use of such staples of movie historicism as the Civil War and the opening of the West. But Griffith was willing to work on less familiar ground, too. He was much interested in the War of Independence, court life in Renaissance Europe, even in prehistoric times (*Man's Genesis*). He ranged over America to give his audience stories of fishermen and hillbillies, anarchists and desert dwellers, musicians and suburban matrons, children at play and in peril. He did comedies and pastorales, social criticism and melodrama (lots of that), mysteries and action films. Taken together, the films of his Biograph period became a panorama of American life and thought in this era. And all the while he was creating this panorama, turning out close to two films a week, he was inventing a grammar of the film, developing that repertory of shots and editing techniques on which the art is still based.

But in thinking about Griffith one reaches the conclusion that his innovations were motivated—at least at first—not so much by a high regard for the new medium, as by cultural aspiration. He had been, with a truly remarkable lack of success, a stage actor and he had also failed in an attempt to become a playwright before economic necessity forced him into accepting the five dollars' daily wage of the movie player. When he was given a chance to direct he still saw his opportunity as no more than a blessed chance at steady work for a guaranteed year. When he was a success, and Biograph offered him bonuses that pushed his income up toward a thousand dollars a week in a couple of years, he realized that he could never hope to duplicate this kind of economic well-being on the stage. So, since he wanted respectability as the theater defined it, he had no option but to attempt to make the movies respectable. He did so, to put it briefly, by adapting the romantic-realistic mode most popular in the theater as he had known it, and by introducing the most popular devices of that theater to the movies.

The melodrama had long used the device of parallel action—two or more plot lines running side by side through the stage piece with cutting back and forth between them (through the use of quick scene shifts or area lighting), the climax arriving when these threads were drawn together in some concluding burst of action. Obviously the much more flexible cinema could use this device with greater ease and realism than the stage had ever managed. One had only to talk the essentially conservative businessmen of the movies into letting one try it, and by the end of his stay at Biograph Griffith had achieved complete acceptance of it both in front offices and with audiences. Then, too, it was obvious that, with all outdoors to make movies in, the opportunities for spectacle were boundless. No matter how sophisticated its technology became, no theater could stage, as Griffith could by 1913–14, the pageantry of *Judith of Bethlia* (which was an adaptation of Thomas Baily Aldrich's popular play), or the panoramic sequences of warfare that he gave movie-goers in *The Battle of Elderberry Gulch*. Indeed, the only real trouble he had was in convincing film executives that the humble nickelodeon crowd would sit still for movies of a length comparable to plays. He left Biograph over the dispute on this point (the studio released the four-reel *Judith* one reel at a time, as if it were a serial, at the same time criticizing him for its expense) and after a brief interval of making 'features' of similar length, turned to *The Birth of a Nation* and *Intolerance*—in the process firmly establishing the popularity of long pictures and ending the last purely technical advantage the stage had over film.

p 238 (6, 7)

Since the growth of movies coincided with the rise of Progressivism in America, many reformers hoped they would, as one put it, 'show justice and teach goodness and happiness'. Another suggested that 'No better field lies open to insert entirely without the person's knowledge a few grains of profitable and instructive matter.'

Vachel Lindsay, that most democratic of poets, and one of the few literary people to think seriously about the film's potential, went even farther. He thought that California, where by 1915 (when he wrote) most films were being made, was a kind of last frontier of innocence and emptiness and therefore a place where, free of the East's restrictive rules of good form, this new art could flourish in a truly democratic way. 'The piles beneath the castle of our near-democratic arts were rotting for lack of folk-imagination', he wrote. 'The man with the Hoe had no spark in his brain. But now a light is blazing. We can build the American soul broad-based from the foundations. We can begin with dreams the veriest stone-club warrior can understand, and as far as an appeal to the eye can do it, lead him in fancy through every phase of life to the apocalyptic splendors.'

He urged producers to grant democratic man a vision of his ideal future in all-encompassing detail. He wrote: 'let the Spirit conduct you till you see in definite line and form the throngs of the brotherhood of man, the colonnades where the arts are expounded, the gardens where the children dance.' And: 'Let us resolve that she [America] shall dream dreams deeper than the sea and higher than the clouds of heaven, that she shall come forth crowned and transfigured with her statesmen and wizards and saints and sages about her, with magic behind her and miracle before her.'

Rich stuff! And yet even as Lindsay wrote, Griffith was making a picture he called *The Clansman*. And when he showed it to Thomas

Dixon, the author of the book on which he had based his scenario, Dixon informed him that his working title did not begin to suggest the range of material he had managed to encompass in the two-and-a-half hours of the film's running time. Why not, he suggested, call it *The Birth of a Nation*? Griffith's point of view, glorifying Ku Klux Klansmen, showing black men as bestial children was, and is, reprehensible. And yet, in tracing the history of a family through the Civil War and Reconstruction, and in interpolating vignettes of actual historic incidents, Griffith did create a vision of unprecedented breadth. In this one film he surpassed anything the stage had ever accomplished. And though he failed the ideal of brotherhood and general spiritual uplift which Lindsay and others had enjoined upon the filmmaker, he was not yet finished.

His next movie was, of course, *Intolerance*, and he subtitled it, significantly, 'A Sun Play of the Ages'. In its four stories—of the Fall of Babylon, the Passion of Christ, the Massacre of the Huguenots in the France of Charles IX and a modern story of labor strife and a boy falsely accused of murder—he did not wish to show events 'set forth in their historical sequence, or according to accepted forms of dramatic construction, but as they might flash across a mind seeking to parallel the life of the different ages'. His theme was the havoc wrought by prejudice and intolerance (and just plain meddling, since Griffith was a radical individualist), but his plaything was *all* of human history. The film had its defects, but they seem modest indeed compared to the grandeur of its ambitions and its success in realizing them.

'The shadows of great forms'

The culture in which Griffith accomplished his greatest work was a culture that looked to many as if it were about to undertake huge, reformative change. In the very year *The Birth of a Nation* was released, Van Wyck Brooks published his little book with the hopeful title, *America's Coming-of-Age*. He included in it his now-famous description of America as 'A vast Sargasso Sea—a prodigious welter of unconscious life, swept by ground-swells of half-conscious emotion . . . a welter of life which has not yet been worked into an organism, into which fruitful values and standards of humane economy have not been introduced, innocent of those laws of social gravitation which, rightly understood and pursued with a keen faith, produce a fine temper in the human animal.' Nevertheless, he thought he detected stirrings, new beginnings, which would free the United States from the seemingly contradictory thrall of puritanism and materialism that had crippled its creativity.

In 1912, for example, Harriet Monroe had founded her *Poetry* magazine in Chicago and Lindsay and another of her discoveries, Carl Sandburg, cast aside the traditional forms and genteel subject-matter of the art as it had been practiced here since Whitman had been domesticated as 'the good, gray poet'. Moreover, they stormed up and down the land, reading their works in the colleges, attempting to revive the bardic tradition—poetry as a performing art. The next year, the famous Armory Show placed the works of the European post-Impressionists on display side by side with Americans of 'the black revolutionary gang', otherwise known as 'the Ashcan School', with an effect on intelligent sensibilities known to every reader of popular cultural history. A year after that, the Provincetown Playhouse, harboring in its midst the only playwright of world-class this nation ever developed, Eugene O'Neill, was founded. And by this time, America was evolving, in the work of Isadora Duncan and the Denishawn group, a new dance style, free-form and as respectful of the primitive and the archetypal as the new poetry was. Perhaps more significant, there were creeping into the intellectual journals a few articles that dwelled respectfully, if not with any profound understanding, on the virtues of a popular music that was more often referred to as 'ragtime' rather than jazz.

When Edward MacDowell, the first serious American composer to make any impression on the rest of the world, died in this period, Olin Downes, the critic, noted that 'the shadows of great forms' could be discerned beating in his work, but that MacDowell, himself trapped in the genteel culture of his day, could never quite free them—allowing them to remain the merest intimations of what Ives, his work unheeded, was already capturing on his

The music of Edward MacDowell, whose first Piano Concerto was praised by Liszt, was appreciated for its poetical and romantic style. His 'Indian Suite' (1896) became a popular concert piece. (4)

score paper. It is, therefore, fair to say that the only music of any vitality that was heard in public was ragtime. And it was despised in polite circles. Hiram K. Moderwell wrote in *The New Republic* in 1915: 'It has been nearly twenty years, and American ragtime is still officially beyond the pale. As the original and indigenous type of music of the American people, as the one type of American popular music that has persisted and undergone constant evolution, one would think it might receive the clammy hand of fellowship from composers and critics. There is very little evidence that these gentlemen have changed their feeling about it.' This blindness, the writer thought, was based on their distrust of 'the primitive love of the dance' which lay at the heart of this music. There may also have been a deal of racial and social prejudice involved.

But how stupid they were! 'I cannot understand how a trained musician can overlook its purely technical elements of interest. It has carried the complexities of the rhythmic subdivision of the measure to a point never before reached in the history of music. It has established subtle conflicting rhythms to a degree never before attempted in any popular or folk-music, and rarely enough in art-music. It has shown a definite and natural evolution—always a proof of vitality in a musical idea. It has gone far beyond most other popular music in the freedom of inner voices (yes, I mean polyphony) and of harmonic modulation. And it has proved its adaptability to the expression of many distinct moods.'

In short, in all the arts, but in the popular performing arts in particular, it appeared that the time was right for a breakthrough, for a full-scale cultural revolution.

The American revue

What happened was this: the movies and popular music were industrialized while the theater and serious music were isolated, cut off from the mainstream of national concern. One can, in part, blame World War I for this. It directed creative energies and mass attention away from art at a crucial moment and it blunted the thrust of Progressivism on which, to a larger degree than anyone realized, the new reformist spirit in the arts was based. Then, too, the climate of opinion in the postwar decade was radically altered. Many artists withdrew physically from the United States; more withdrew intellectually and spiritually from the mass of their fellow citizens. The great audience was regarded, if it was contemplated at all, cynically, satirically, as a hopeless case, and the popular arts unfit areas for intelligent sensibilities to engage in.

p 241
(19)
p 244
(28)
p 243
(26)

First let us look at what was going on in the theater. The melodrama was dead and vaudeville was entering upon its decline, both victims of the movies, which drew off the audience of the former and began occupying the theaters of the latter. This did not mean that all vitality was suddenly drained out of the theatrical enterprise. Gilbert Seldes, for one, was struck by the liveliness, in the 1920s, of the revue. In a singular passage, he compared it to the opera and found that 'the superiority of the lesser art is striking'. Here, again, we return to the main theme of this essay, which is that very often the difference between success and failure in popular art is determined by a work's ability successfully to incorporate a diversity of material unimaginable in the more formal arts. Seldes wrote that alone of all the forms available on the stage, the revue aspired to the virtue most prized by the typical American—efficiency. 'It shows a mania for perfection; it aspires to be precise and definite, it corresponds to those *deluxe* railway trains which are always exactly on time, to the millions of spare parts that always fit, to the ease of commerce when there is a fixed price; jazz or symphony may sound from the orchestra pit, but underneath is the real tone of the revue, the steady, incorruptible purr of the dynamo . . . the revue is the most notable place in which this great American dislike of bungling, the real pleasure in a thing perfectly done, apply even vaguely to the arts.'

p 242
(23)
f 5
p 246
(33)

The form is now moribund, but in the 1920s, when book shows were in intellectual disfavor (they smacked too much of the operettas that had littered stages before the war), this was the one theatrical form which could trace its line cleanly back to the prewar era; from Ziegfeld to the Music Box and the Little Shows and the Greenwich Village Follies the development was obvious and delightful. And perhaps more important, nearly all the outstanding composers of popular songs—Rodgers and Hart, Irving Berlin, Cole Porter, Arthur Schwartz, Gershwin—did more than develop their talents in this form; for it they created work that was among their finest, most polished.

A self-caricature by George Gershwin, whose compositions ranged from popular songs to tone poems and the celebrated 'Rhapsody in Blue'. (5)

Drama's new voices

There were, of course, playwrights of ambition and some distinction working in the postwar theater besides Eugene O'Neill. There was, for example, the witty and consistently underrated George Kelly (*The Show-Off, The Torchbearers*) with his expert ability to deflate middle-class pretense and pomposity. There was Maxwell Anderson, with his pathetic belief that 'if we are to have a great theater in this country, somebody has got to write verse, even if it is written badly'. (Anderson wrote more of the latter variety than any one man has a right to produce.) But O'Neill towered above them all and one cannot help but think that perhaps he acquired some of his ambition to cram all of life, all of history, on to a stage from his father, a great star of the melodramatic and spectacle stage, noted for his endless association with the title role in *The Count of Monte Cristo*.

In any case, O'Neill's range was immense, his courage in attempting new forms and revising old ones prodigious. There were short plays, full of a romantic realism comparable to that which animated Griffith's best work in the short films; there was the diversity of theme and style evident in his first four hits—*The Emperor Jones, Anna Christie, The Hairy Ape, Desire Under the Elms*; p 247 (38) then there was the ambitious use of masks in *The Great God Brown*, employed to suggest the difference between the outward image and the inner truth of characters; the soliloquies and asides employed in *Strange Interlude* which, in nine long acts, attempted to tell the complete psychological truth of a woman's life; the comic spectacle of *Marco Millions*, never properly appreciated as the delicious satire on go-getting American Babbitry that it was; *Mourning Becomes Electra*, another work of such length that it required a dinner-break as it re-set the *Oresteia* in bleak New England; the great late tragedy about the necessity for dreaming great dreams, *The Iceman Cometh* and, perhaps the finest of all his p 247 (39) works, the autobiographical *Long Day's Journey into Night*, a play 'of old sorrow, written in tears and blood'. Even his silences were interesting, as when, for over a decade, he retired from active production to wrestle with a cycle of eleven plays that were to present 'the continuity of family lives over a space of 150 years'. Throughout his career, critics plagued O'Neill with niceties—his language and his theatrical devices were crude, they said, and he was constantly overreaching himself. What was insufficiently stressed was that in a theater of under-achievers, he alone reached out and tried to capture the lonely tragedy that lay at the center of a people that, without deep roots, and without sustaining traditions, had constantly to reinvent themselves and, as O'Neill himself did, the forms that might contain and structure that experience. He remains, flawed and sometimes desperate, the only giant of a theater that produced no one remotely comparable to him. One has only to compare him to the 'major' writers who came after him —Odets, Williams, Miller, Albee—two of them sustained by p 276 (40–43) limited leftist ideology, two of them by the homosexual mystique—to understand the loneliness of his eminence.

The descent of jazz

One must note also that the other threatened art of the 1920s, serious music, discovered no O'Neill. Abroad, there was a renaissance of sorts. Stravinsky and Schoenberg were, as Leonard Bernstein was to describe them later, 'the heap big chiefs' of opposing schools, and between them were ranged such artists as *Les Six* in France, Delius in England, Prokofiev in Russia. The Americans were still studying, like Copland, or knocking on doors, like Roy Harris, or nurturing their ambitions, like Gershwin, who *f 5* described his *Rhapsody in Blue* as 'a sort of musical kaleidoscope of America'—the dreams of an all-encompassing work restated. Nor could it be said that the musical establishment was showing any particular interest in creating conditions where the new works from abroad could be consistently heard or in which native talent could gain a decent hearing.

Nor could one claim that the popular musical establishment was p 242–3 (24, 25) much more receptive to jazz. To be sure, there was an infusion into popular music of jazz motifs (as in the music of Paul Whiteman and p 243 (27) Vincent Lopez), a growing vogue for black singers and instrumentalists, but, as the historian H. F. Mooney comments, this was a trend 'limited by compromises with middle-class conventions'. He adds: 'Most Negroes were little short of outcasts, too poor and too segregated from the mainstream of life to maximally influence taste.' They were actively discriminated against in dance bands, radio and even recording sessions. From the twenties at least until the fifties, what most people conceived of as jazz was a watered-down, 'whitened' version. There was, undoubtedly, a substantial difference between the orchestras of Whiteman and Lopez and the swing bands that succeeded them in popular regard in the thirties—the Dorsey brothers, Benny Goodman, *et al*. But even the great Duke Ellington, it has been said, was for a time influenced by Guy Lombardo. The big bands, Mooney writes, 'presented a music which, despite solo variations, emphasized precise, lush, ensemble harmony. The highest compliment most of the public could pay to big-band jazz between 1928 and 1950 was "symphonic" or "advanced"'. He notes that late in this period the orchestrations of the coolest, most sophisticated groups reflected the influence of Ravel, Debussy and the post-Impressionists more than they did New Orleans, Chicago and Kansas City. Here was a very strange manifestation of the American drive to incorporate diverse elements in a popular art.

But what is more significant is that music became, in this period, a big business. The bands were booked on their tours by large organizations like the Music Corporation of America (MCA) and their success was dependent on the production of hit records, the content of which was dictated by the few large corporations that achieved national distribution for their labels. The Depression drove the smaller companies, which offered pure jazz to a limited audience, out of business and if it was recorded at all thereafter it was on 'race' labels aimed at the small, and desperately unprosperous, Negro market. Negro musicians spoke of 'coming up' and by that meant finding places in white bands or aping their styles in their own organizations.

f 7

A young and gifted critic of the modern pop scene, Nik Cohn, has very well evoked the spirit of the thirties, forties and fifties in popular music: 'songs about moonlight, stardust, roses, and bleeding hearts were duly churned out by the truckload. The big bands lined up strict and formal in penguin suits, the crooners slicked their hair back heavy with grease, the close harmony groups went oo-wah-oowah in the background, and everybody danced. It was warm and snug like a blanket.'

'All this time, the music industry was controlled by middle-aged businessmen, uninterested in change of any kind. They were making money as things were, so they made no effort to find anything very new. They'd switch a few details, dream up some small novelty gimmick, and leave it at that. And the only reason they got away with it was that nobody offered any alternatives. Mostly showbiz survived on habit.'

It is easy, now, to be sentimental about the merits of the popular music of the swing era, just as it is easy to be sentimental about MGM musicals and comedies of the same era. And, indeed, there were transcendent moments in both: there was Benny Goodman's famous 1937 concert at Carnegie Hall, in which a swing band, from which smaller groups might splinter off for effective, intimate improvisation, played with an excitement, an abandon that was extraordinary; there was Astaire with his casual yet elegant dances in the movie musicals and there were the Marx Brothers blending the earthy and the surreal on film.

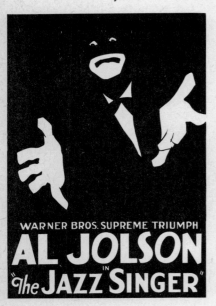

'The Jazz Singer' was intended as a silent film, with recorded songs but no speech. But Al Jolson ad-libbed several lines of dialogue, including the famous 'You ain't heard nothin' yet!' and caused a sensation. (6)

Processed film

Even so, and perhaps more completely than in popular music, the system for producing movies had been thoroughly industrialized. Prior to World War I, no fewer than two hundred small companies had been turning out films. A decade or so later, there were less than a dozen—very large—film producers operating successfully in the United States. Before World War I was over Charles Chaplin and Mary Pickford had attained million dollar contracts, setting the precedent for incredibly heavy payments to talent. Longer films,

p 239
(8)

'Jail Bird Love Song' was one of the many numbers recorded by the Mississippi Sheiks, a popular small black group, on the OKeh 'race' label in the 1930s. (7)

and more elaborate ones, sent costs up still further and it became clear that the era of the individualist in films was over almost before it had got started. Increasingly the film companies had to turn to banks for financing and that meant they had to prove that they were efficiently organized. Indeed, even if they had been able to finance themselves, something like a factory system would have had to be organized if they were to supply the needs of their theater chains, which demanded a weekly change of bill. The essence of this system was product mix—so many comedies, so many Westerns, so many musicals, so many romances, so many crime and detective films per year, with stars type-cast in familiar roles helping to guarantee the return on each discrete unit by their presence. The coming of sound, late in the twenties, further solidified this method of work, by doubling the cost of each film, doubling the length of time required for production. Irving Thalberg, the literate bookkeeper who brought this system to its highest flowering at MGM early in the decade, was famous for the impersonality of his operations. Staff directors were moved on and off projects at will, he set what is regarded as the Hollywood record by assigning no less than a dozen screenwriters to one project, and he was ruthless in the cutting room and in ordering re-takes not in the interest, so far as anyone could see, of art, but to realize the film's commercial potential as he (with admitted shrewdness) conceived it. He and some of the other producers salved their consciences periodically with 'special' productions, generally ponderous, if lavish, adaptations of 'great' literature like *The Good Earth*. Nevertheless, they were ruthless with talent. Unreliable directors, that is men who insisted on pursuing private visions, or merely men who could not bring their pictures in on time and on budget were weeded out. Rebellious stars, especially those whose private lives did not match their screen images, were forced into line or out of the business.

p 238
(4, 5)

f 6

Griffith could not survive in this world and, once he lost his bid for independence when his own company failed, he was a broken man. Erich von Stroheim, once an assistant to Griffith, latterly the director of the legendary *Greed*, in which to all intents and purposes he attempted line-by-line faithfulness to Frank Morris's novel, *McTeague*, was driven out at the same time Griffith was, and *Greed* was re-edited by Thalberg, the boy genius. Chaplin, clinging resolutely to silence and to his own vision, has kept his independence but has only managed to make eight films in the last forty years, the last four of which were done abroad. None of his peers in the realm of silent comedy did even as well as he did—the studios making no effort to adapt their enormous gifts to sound films, allowing them simply to fade into obscurity. About the only people who were allowed a measure of independence in the studio system were foreigners whose strange ways and accents were taken by the status-hungry executives as signs of genius. Happily for the movies, some of them, like Lubitsch and Von Sternberg and Hitchcock were geniuses. Happily, too, some Americans, like John Ford and Howard Hawks, learned to preserve that which was best in themselves while living under the Moguls' often oppressive rule.

p 239
(10)

p 239
(10, 11)
p 238
(4)

Did the movies, in the days of the great studios, divert us? Of course. Did good and intelligent and even serious work somehow get accomplished? Naturally—to say otherwise would be to betray all the emotions of childhood. But as Seldes suggested in his article on the revue form, the work that reaches out to encompass our diversity, to summarize democratic virtues and values must be, perhaps paradoxically, the product of a single hand, moving freely. Orson Welles, given that freedom, produced *Citizen Kane*, and somehow managed to give us a vision of our grandeur and folly that is without parallel in film history, a summary of a life (Kane's) that is also a summary of the first forty years of the American experience in this century. His next film, *The Magnificent Ambersons*, has intimations of the same quality, but we will never know what he planned, for the film was taken away from him, re-edited by others and now Welles's original climactic footage is lost. For the rest, we can with some great directors (Ford and Hitchcock come to mind), read each film as a chapter in a long, continuing serial, at the end of which we can begin to define the dimensions of their worlds. But very few men had the strength to create such extensive metaphors in the company town that Hollywood became.

p 239 (13)

Television: the ultimate weapon

Sometime in the 1950s it all started to fall apart. In 1948 the east coast was linked to the west coast (and they, in turn, were linked to all other regions of the nation) by television's coaxial cable. It was an event the importance of which we still do not fully understand, though we can at least make a few tentative observations about it. The first is simply that television was something more than radio with pictures. Radio had frightened the executives of competing media—it did, after all, offer free information and entertainment—but it had not finally posed a real threat to the more established competitors. Indeed the media learned to co-exist quite comfortably, cross-fertilizing in the realms of talent and publicity. Some things radio did superbly well—news, for example, certain forms of spooky drama (like Orson Welles's *The War of the Worlds*), cheerful situation comedies. Because its effects were limited to the auditory, its range was narrow (which may have meant that of all mass media it had the greatest potential for high, or at least highly stylized, art) and though a companionable, habit-forming medium, it never really jeopardized anyone or anything—politicians, the arts, the print media—and it was as easily domesticated as a stray dog. Television, however, was very like its contemporary, the H-Bomb, an ultimate weapon changing the lives of all who lived under its threat.

f 8

f 9

To take just a few examples: TV immensely speeded up the process by which information was disseminated and this posed a threat to the traditional methods of diplomacy and domestic politics. The emphasis now was not on the judicious response to events, but on a quick one. Moreover, it used up public figures very quickly. The strong highly individualistic performer, whether he was Milton Berle or Joseph R. McCarthy or Lyndon B. Johnson wore out his welcome very quickly in this medium. Cool, low

'*The loudspeaker (cheerily): HELLO, FOLKS!' A 'Life' cartoon of 1926 illustrates the democratizing influence of the radio, with its chatty informality. (8)*

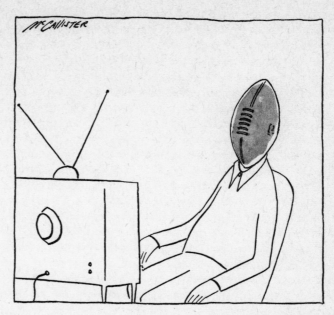

Sport was only one of the instant entertainments offered to television viewers, turning them into a nation of armchair spectators. (9)

profile types ranging from Captain Kangaroo to Richard M. Nixon, after he had retrained his natural instincts, fared rather better, but this placed an arbitrary limit on the personality types (and, for that matter, on the types of art and entertainment) that could be purveyed via TV. Worse, it became clear that it was less an informational medium than one that dealt in images, and images are far more easily blurred than facts.

Finally, one began to perceive that it was pointless to evaluate television in terms of discrete time-intervals. One show blended into another, one evening into another, and what one was dealing with was a collage full of weird congruities and incongruities. Somehow, as Michael Arlen showed in a brilliant essay in *The New Yorker*, the 1968 Tet offensive in Vietnam got jumbled up with the afternoon golf matches, the kiddie cartoon shows and Ted Mack's Amateur Hour and all that stuff, if one did not keep one's wits about one, got mixed into the domesticity of—in Arlen's case—a rainy, hung-over Sunday in a too-small New York apartment, the inhabitants of which were already suffering from a too-large informational input from the Sunday edition of *The New York Times*.

It was ghastly. And perhaps the most ghastly thing of all was the sense one had of drowning in disorder. Everything began to seem unstructured, connections between words and events were unclear, hierarchies of information were jumbled, all the old categories by which we organized thought were dismantled, as it were, before our very eyes. It was the incorporative mode in the popular arts unconsciously parodied, running riot.

Next moves

The immediate direct effect on competing media was profound. Radio, as it had been known for two decades, simply disappeared, to be replaced by disc-jockeys and capsuled news summaries on the hour and half-hour. The deejays didn't know it at first, but they were to be the leading factor in what came to be known, by the late sixties, as a counter-culture. For their audience was the youth, and the youth were uninterested in the old styles of popular music. When an enterprising Cleveland deejay named Alan Freed, having nothing better to do, rummaged through the rhythm and blues (nice name for 'race') discs that were piling up, unplayed, in his studio and started airing them along with the country music that had formerly had only a regional audience in the South and Middle West, he gave his audience something that could be theirs and theirs alone—since no one else wanted it. And when he gave this material a catchy new name—'Rock 'n' Roll'—he started what was to become a national and then an international phenomenon. It required only the emergence of a super-star named Elvis Presley to focus the phenomenon and bring it up from the youth underground into general, if usually dismayed, consciousness. After The Beatles and The Rolling Stones gave the movement a second enormous boost in the sixties, the old popular music simply

f 7

disappeared from the face of the earth (excepting, of course, from such adults-only pleasure domes as Las Vegas and Miami Beach). It is beyond the abilities of anyone not 'into the rock scene' (as the catch-phrase has it) to define all the sophisticated variations that have been piled on the primitive, four-beat, melodically predictable, lyrically banal early rock material. 'Nobody even attempts to define it any more,' a critic named Jonathan Eisen says. It just is.

There is only one thing that attaches it to the old popular cultural tradition in America and that is its ambitious desire to be all-encompassing. Eisen again: 'Born a hybrid of blues and country-western, it is now a full-throated school that incorporates everything from blues to Indian classical raga, from Bach to Stockhausen and Cage. Rock music is now much more than music for its devotees, it is a subculture in the strictest sense of the word.' He points out that in the pop world the old divisions between artist and audience have blurred, that taste-makers do not—at least quite so obviously—attempt to impose their views on listeners, that, especially under the influence of Bob Dylan, a new sense of poetry has come into the lyrics, and he might well have added that the incorporation of highly sophisticated electronic effects into the scoring of recordings has accomplished a blending of technology and sensibility many, in other fields, articulately envy. He might also have noted that the Rock revolution has closed the door at last on the institution known as Tin Pan Alley and pretty much killed the last evidence of vitality the American theater had to offer, the musical play. There is no young talent coming into it and the older talents have not been able to advance beyond Rodgers and Hammer-stein's *Oklahoma-South Pacific* level. Indeed, shows like *Hello Dolly* are far beneath it. Worse, the new Broadway tunes simply don't have a chance to reach out beyond New York. They aren't played by the disc-jockeys, are not needed by the youth culture if by rare chance they are heard by it at all, *Hair* and, perhaps, *Jesus Christ, Superstar*, being the exceptions that prove the rule.

This simple statement suggests a profound truth about the situation of the theater, which is that as an institution it no longer has any real social power. Such creative energy as exists in it is concentrated in the avant-garde, where companies like The Living Theater, such figures as Joe Chaikin seek, in improvisational works, to break down the traditional barrier between actor and audience by forcing the latter to become active participants in the theatrical event. Elsewhere, in the Happenings that are arranged by painters and sculptors, in the musical works of John Cage, who now incorporates film, dancers, actors, light shows and anything else that strikes his fancy in scores that are often dictated by chance, the barriers between the arts themselves are being broken. The one thing that tends to be missing from all this is the formally-structured verbal element—play*writing*, as it were. But it may be that this is only a reaction against the traditional over-emphasis on this element. It may be that if this new theater is to find any kind of audience this imbalance will have to be redressed. Still, it must be seen as a response to the imbecile articulateness of television, to the bombardment of words that afflicts the whole society. In any case, as I tried to suggest in the first section of this essay, there is a con-nection between a long-dreamed American ideal and present reality. It may be that we are approaching an historical moment in which the old division between high art and low is erased, where elements of both, and the audiences for both, are mingled. It may also be that we stand on the brink of anarchy, have already entered what John Simon calls 'the dark night of the arts'.

Perhaps the key element in determining where we go from here will be the movies. They were the most grievously afflicted of all the arts when television arrived. Almost immediately the film audience was cut by two-thirds—the sale of tickets dropping by some two billion annually in the fifties. This forced the abandonment of old-style studio production and the temporary embrace of numberless panaceas—spectacular films, wide screen, three-dimensional projection, a super-star system (in which those few personalities known to be able to pull the people in attained unprecedented economic power). Of late, there has been talk of 'small pictures', in which the risk of failure is minimized by tight budgeting, and of catering to the so-called youth market, since it is young people who have remained most faithful to film, again it would seem because it seems to be an alternative to the television which so dominates middle America. Again, as the proliferation of guitars has placed musical creativity within the reach of everyone interested in music, the creation of inexpensive, easily portable movie cameras has made the audience potentially a creative element in film, rescuing them (so they think) from the passivity of pure consumerism.

There are, however, other alternatives. Within the near future new technologies will become available and they might force a whole new direction on film and, perhaps, on the other arts. There is, for example, cable television, which may offer the subscribing viewer alternatives to network programing and provide an opportunity to movie-makers to experiment with an entirely new, non-theatrical method of distributing their products. Then, too, there are soon to be on the market devices which will play back, through the television set, video recordings and these seem to offer the possibility of marketing films in much the manner that phonograph records now are.

Finally, it must be said that the old dream remains and that movies also remain as the one medium technically capable of realizing it. One still thinks that it is not beyond the devising of the American mind somehow to combine all the arts, all the technologies that have come into being over the last century or so, in some grand, yet flexible symphony which will, as Poe and Ives and Cage have dreamed, orchestrate the democratic ideal, break down all the barriers between men and races, forms and genres, and give us a great vision of our best selves. All one has been trying to say is that the great custodians of that dream have been found in the popular performing arts as often as—and perhaps more often than—they have been in the fine and literary arts, and that for all the defects one can find in the history of those arts, for all the missed and failed opportunities one observes in them, the dream is still alive, still animating at least some of those who create in these often benighted forms.

p 246
(34)

p 246
(3)

p 247
(44)

f 10

p 245
(32)

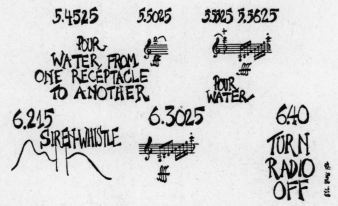

'Water Music.' John Cage's humorously revolutionary notation matches his music, whose form is often dictated by pure chance in a spirit of liberating anarchy. (10)

XI

WRITTEN WORDS

The making of American literature

R. W. B. LEWIS

*'The poet's, the writer's duty is to write
about these things. It is his privilege
to help man endure by lifting his heart,
by reminding him of courage and honour and hope
and pride and compassion and pity.'*

WILLIAM FAULKNER

To find the roots

of American literature in the 20th century, we have to look back to the 19th, and especially to the latter half. During that period the United States produced a body of writing that established a literary tradition comparable with any in Europe. This is not to say that it embodied a consistent program or even a consistent point of view. On the contrary, one of its distinguishing marks was its diversity, its emphasis upon the individual. Nevertheless, the best writers did share certain qualities that have come to be seen in this century as peculiarly American—respect for hard fact, social concern, an obstinate insistence on the personal self, and an urge to work out in literature values by which a civilization can live. They are qualities which we have met in other chapters of this book, and which seem to spring from the crucial experience of building a new nation in a new land. At the same time, the knowledge that culturally America was the child of Europe gave many writers a nagging obsession which had barely been overcome by the dawn of the new century.

Top row: Ralph Waldo Emerson was above all a moralist, concerned in general with the position of man in relation to God and to Nature, and in particular with that of the American in relation to England. Nathaniel Hawthorne, a natural story-teller, found his deepest theme in the violation of the human soul, 'the unpardonable sin' beside which all other sins paled. He lived part of his life in Europe and saw the meeting of European and American as already a clash of cultures. Washington Irving was the first American writer to win fame abroad, and in fact lived for seventeen years in Europe. He is the father of both American satire (based ultimately on the English 18th century) and of American biography.

Second row: Henry Wadsworth Longfellow struck a more sentimental note. In technique and feeling his poetry was hardly different from that of Europe, but his choice of American subjects gave him wide popular appeal. But with Walt Whitman American poetry came of age. Free in form, direct in expression, boundless in moral sympathy and appetite for experience, his verse seemed to speak for ordinary Americans as no literature had done before. Edgar Allan Poe, a writer of startlingly original talents, infused a new note of fantasy and horror into the literature of America and of the world. Morbid and grotesque as his stories often are, they broke through literary conventions, and created those eminently characteristic 20th-century forms, the thriller and the detective story.

Bottom row: Mark Twain stands at the beginning of several fertile developments—American humor, American reportage based on journalism, and the portrayal of life outside the cultured circles of New England. Herman Melville moved from factual accounts of his voyages in the Pacific to the complex, many-leveled allegory of *Moby Dick*. Henry James typified the dilemma of the 'provincial' American confronted by the sophisticated European. In James's case it ended with his decision to become a naturalized Englishman in 1915; but the nature of his interests—the nuances of moral choice in aristocratic society—perhaps made this inevitable. Out of the mainstream of both American and European literature, he is still the most intriguing link between the two. (1–9)

The **real world** seen through an intensely personal vision is the paradoxical subject-matter of the best 20th-century American fiction. In it journalism and introspection go hand in hand, and all the richness of regional American life is gathered and analyzed.

F. Scott Fitzgerald (left) set his novels in the fashionable resorts of Europe and America in the 'Jazz Age' and in the Hollywood film world of the wealthy, the talented and the neurotic. (10)

Thomas Wolfe aimed at condensing the whole of one man's experience – his own – into a series of novels which would comprehend the American spirit itself. In this photograph (right) he sits with his mother on the porch of the boarding house in North Carolina where he spent his childhood. (11)

The Negro world is a 'region' in the midst of white society which has found a voice in this century. The 'Harlem Renaissance' of the 1920s brought many new talents to the fore. This group shows Langston Hughes, Charles Johnson, E. Franklin Frazer, Rudolph Fisher and Hubert Delany. Hughes used blues and ballad meters to express personal and racial dilemmas. Johnson was a teacher, editor and author who wrote mainly on Negro history and culture. (12)

Small-town America entered literature in the pages of Sinclair Lewis, the first American novelist to receive the Nobel Prize. Above: the original jacket of *Main Street* (1920), based on a town in Minnesota. Right: Lewis and his wife Dorothy Thompson on their honeymoon in England. (13, 14)

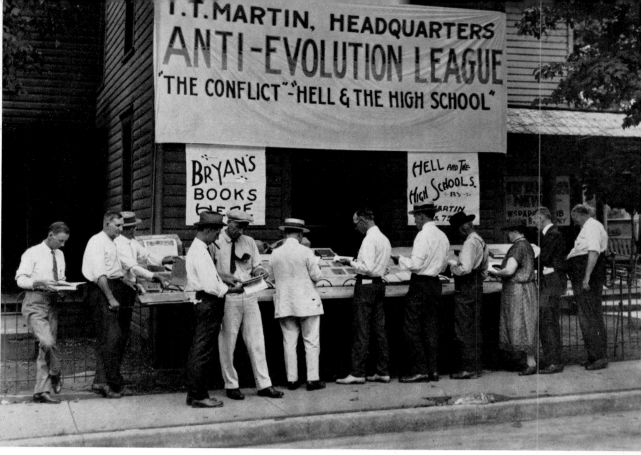

The journalist craftsman is exemplified in H. L. Mencken (above), whose career was punctuated by crusades against prejudice and ignorance. His coverage of the 'Monkey Trial' in 1925, at which a schoolteacher in Dayton, Tennessee, was convicted of blasphemy for teaching Darwinian evolution, was a masterly instance. (15, 16)

Commerce and success were explored by Theodore Dreiser. Well aware of – and fascinated by – the part that making money had played in American history, he showed the ultimate hollowness of a materialized society. With him in this photograph in 1944 is Willa Cather, poet and novelist of the traditional pioneering values. (17)

Formal experiment has characterized American poetry at least since Whitman. e.e. cummings (above) used typographical novelties to refurbish what were essentially quite simple sensations and thoughts. (18)

The hardness of nature and of man is the subject of many of John Steinbeck's novels, set among the migrant workers of the 1930s. Right: Dorothea Lange's photograph of an abandoned farmhouse in land taken over by mechanized agriculture during the years of *The Grapes of Wrath*. (19, 20)

Between literature and painting there have always been close connections of theme and attitude. In recent years, as we shall see in the next chapter, these connections have become closer and more self-conscious until in some areas the distinction between one art and another threatens to disappear altogether.

'I Saw the Figure Five in Gold' is the title of a painting (left) of 1928 by Charles Demuth illustrating 'The Great Figure' by William Carlos Williams (below).

'Among the rain
and lights
I saw the figure 5
in gold
on a red
firetruck
moving
tense
unheeded
to gong clangs
siren howls
and wheels rumbling
through the dark city.' (21, 22)

'The Bridge': two artists – the painter Joseph Stella in 1922 and the poet Hart Crane (right) eight years later – were inspired by the Brooklyn Bridge and the newly realized beauty of modern technology. Stella's work (opposite) is purely visual and geometrical. Crane's goes deeper, into the spiritual experience of which the bridge stands as a symbol. He was handling, he said, 'the Myth of America . . . I am really writing an epic of the modern consciousness'.

'Through the bound cable strands, the arching path
Upward, veering with light, the flight of strings –
Taut miles of shuttling moonlight syncopate
The whispered rush, telepathy of wires.' (23, 24)

264

Robert Frost (right, teaching a seminar at Dartmouth College in 1954 when he was over eighty) became the best loved poet of his time partly because he spoke for the traditional American virtues (independence, common sense, stoicism) and partly because he wrote in accepted literary forms without feeling the need to experiment. His subject was man and nature – the nature of New Hampshire viewed not sentimentally but with a harsh realism that enabled him to raise the most fundamental questions. (25)

Carl Sandburg (left, a composite study by Edward Steichen) also took his stand as a 'man of the people' but at a more populist level. Both Frost and Sandburg looked back to Whitman, but where Frost refined and deepened, Sandburg inclined to repetition and chauvinism. (26)

William Faulkner (right) took the South, where he lived, and made it a symbol of America, even of the world. Through long family sagas (often using difficult stylistic techniques) he showed a land rich in natural and human resources being raped by corruption and greed. (27)

In T. S. Eliot the need to find a stable tradition proved stronger than the lure of American vitality and freedom. He came to Europe in 1914 and became a British subject in 1927. After brilliantly expressing the sense of futility after World War I he found his own personal solution in Christianity and a kind of intellectual conservatism. In this photograph, he is seen with members of the cast of his first play, *Murder in the Cathedral*. (28)

Robert Penn Warren (left) was one of the originators of the 'new criticism', which held that the critic should pay attention only to the words on the page, not to the poet's biography. His later novels show him turning to the problem of defining American civilization itself. (29)

Ernest Hemingway came to literature from journalism, and his novels were usually based firmly on his own concrete experiences. He is seen here (right) as a war correspondent in England, 1944. In two ways he stands in the center of the American tradition as it was forged in the 19th century: in his almost obsessive emphasis on 'the real thing', on action and physical courage, and in his energetic quest for ways to preserve the essential self. (30)

Saul Bellow (right) sets the struggle for the self in the context of modern society. In several American writers – Bellow is one – their Jewishness has become suddenly important in the midst of a disintegrating world. (31)

Wallace Stevens (far right) explored ways of knowing reality in poetry that is intellectual and dense with symbolism. Resembling Eliot in many respects, he found a solution the opposite of Eliot's – the liberating realization of God's 'disappearance'. (32)

John Dos Passos (above) drew together almost every element in the American tradition to create the trilogy *USA* (1930–36), a massive indictment of capitalist society. (33)

For Norman Mailer (right) and **Joseph Heller** (far right) World War II was the formative experience of their art. Both are mordantly critical of contemporary America, and both have developed a highly individual brand of fantastic humor. (34, 35)

More books are written and published today than at any time in the past. Future directions are hard to predict, but the major motives at work during the 19th century still do not seem to be played out: the urge to document and record, to contribute to social evolution, and through writing to find the essence, the spirit, of America. (36)

The making of American Literature

R. W. B. LEWIS

THE AMERICAN WRITER has always been remarkably individualistic. He has been more concerned to assert a self and a unique impression of life than to participate in a movement or further a literary cause. By contrast, say, with the French, American *literati* have only rarely banded together, issued manifestos, conferred with and encouraged one another. W. H. Auden observed this a good many years ago, asking, as examples, who could be more unlike than Emerson and Hawthorne, or Melville and Whitman? To this we may add, turning to the present age, who could be more unlike than Dreiser and Fitzgerald, or T. S. Eliot and Wallace Stevens, or Faulkner and Hemingway?

p 261
(1, 2, 3)

The consequence, for anyone seeking to appraise the American literary achievement in this lengthening century, is that he is confronted by a rich welter of highly distinctive and uncommonly varied work. What follows, accordingly, is anything but a chronological charting of successive literary movements. So little is this my purpose that I have not paused to date either authors or texts except where the date seems especially pertinent. For what connects one novelist or poet with another is not that both belong to the same 'school', but rather some shared respect for concrete fact, or some comparable involvement with the personal self, or some similarity of posture towards the cultural environment, or some commitment to allegedly outworn values, or some compassion for the socially oppressed.

Those, anyhow, are among the phenomena that most strike the critic inquiring into this thick body of material, and it is to them that I shall pay the closest attention.

The expanding literary scene

A first sign of expanding variety is this—that over the past seven decades, almost every aspect of the American scene and American society has eventually earned literary representation. From the 17th century beginnings of literature in this country for more than two hundred and fifty years, American culture was largely a New England affair: it emanated from, and it was shaped by, the intellectual climate of a tiny northeastern section of the continent, from the early Puritans through the libertarians of the revolutionary period to the romantics of the age of Emerson. And when the culture began to extend beyond the boundaries of New England, it ventured at first only as far as New York City. A symbolic date in this regard is 1889, when William Dean Howells—who had gravitated from Ohio to Massachusetts as a matter of course in his early manhood, and had spent twenty years in Boston as editor of the *Atlantic Monthly*—abandoned Boston and settled once and for all in New York. (There are a few obvious, if partial, exceptions to this summary: Edgar Allan Poe, though born in Boston, worked in Philadelphia, Baltimore and New York. Walt Whitman was born on Long Island and for long made his home in Brooklyn, though he found his chief inspiration in Emerson. A generation later, Mark Twain looked back from his home in Hartford, Connecticut, to his childhood days in Missouri.)

261 (6)
261 (5)

261 (7)

But it was exactly in 1900, by a useful coincidence, that there appeared a novel of genius about a young girl from Wisconsin, who undergoes her first initiations in Chicago—*Sister Carrie*, by an Indiana-born writer named Theodore Dreiser. In the decades that followed, the vicissitudes of life in the small Midwestern town were

p262
(17)

explored by Sherwood Anderson, and those of the burgeoning industrial city by Sinclair Lewis. The slow artistic awakening (or better, perhaps, re-awakening) of the American South led at last to its presentation on an extraordinary, indeed a mythic, scale in William Faulkner's unfolding saga of Yoknapatawpha County, Mississippi.

The northwestern prairies of Nebraska had much earlier appeared on the literary landscape in Willa Cather's strong, nostalgic novel *O Pioneers!* (1913). By the end of the thirties, California had been added to the resources of American fiction in the stories of California-born John Steinbeck about the farmers, fruit pickers and *paisanos* of his native region; and soon after, the oddities of the Hollywood film world were also added, in Nathanael West's *The Day of the Locust* and F. Scott Fitzgerald's incomplete and posthumous, but artistically glowing, *The Last Tycoon*. The entire process may be said to culminate in John Dos Passos' trilogy (the last volume published in 1936), appropriately called *U.S.A.*

p 263
(19)

fs

But the sociological expansion in American literature during the same years has been still more arresting than the geographical spread. If American writing had for so very long been the province of New England and New York, it had also been pre-eminently the issue of a single segment of the society at large: bourgeois, native-born, white, more or less affluent, Protestant, Anglo-Saxon, and male. The very title of an excellent novel which came out in 1930—*Jews Without Money* by Michael Gold—signaled the entrance into literature at once of the Jew and the impoverished; and though the title does not say so, this account of a sensitive youth growing up in the New York slums is also one of the first reflections of immigrant experience. Henry Roth's still neglected masterpiece of 1934, *Call it Sleep*, is another story of the moral and psychological education, in the New York streets, of the child of poor Jewish immigrants; and Jewish writing today is exemplified by such expert craftsmen as Saul Bellow, Bernard Malamud and Philip Roth.

p 267
(31)

In fairness to those latter, it should be stated emphatically that as artists they share virtually nothing except the accident of a common racial ancestry. What we notice about writings by American Jews is what we are beginning to notice about writings by black Americans, and what we shall perhaps some day notice about writings by American women: namely, that if the first wave is characterized by a total absorption in the complex fate of being a member of a particular minority (women, of course, being in the economic and psychological but not the numerical minority), the second wave tends to be concerned rather with the fate of being a human individual in modern America.

As to black writing, it has in fact a long history in this country, stretching back to the antislavery editorials of Frederick Douglass in the previous century, and on through the urgent defenses of the Negro cause of W. E. B. Dubois and Booker T. Washington, to the so-called Harlem Renaissance in the 1920s, the poetry of Langston Hughes and the novels of Richard Wright. Wright's *Native Son* (1940) was a major breakthrough: a black version, as it were, of Dreiser's *An American Tragedy*. Since then, black writing has come into its own; names proliferate and fresh talents seem to appear daily. For entirely cogent reasons, the principal theme continues to be the sheer experience (usually, the agony) of the black man in a

p 262
(12)

p 263
(17)

The frontispiece for Mark Twain's 'A Tramp Abroad (1880) shows the author recording his European travels. Though Twain's most popular writings are set in his native Missouri, his travel books are full of lively, consciously philistine humor, expressing an irreverent Americanism in the face of Old World culture: 'On the whole, I think that short trips to Europe are better for us than long ones. The former preserve us from becoming Europeanized …' (1)

white society. But Ralph Ellison's *Invisible Man* (1952)—probably the best work of fiction composed by any American since the second war—points to the more all-embracing vision. If his title refers to the black man as invisible because the white man refuses to *see* him as a human reality, it also refers to modern man generally with his humanity concealed beneath layers of prejudice, convention, and the lust for power. 'Who knows', the black narrator concludes, addressing all his readers, white and black, 'but on the lower registers I speak for you?'

In the case of writing by women, the sequence has been somewhat different. The earlier decades were not lacking in accomplished 'women writers', as they were invidiously called: Edith Wharton, Willa Cather, Ellen Glasgow among them. Their work, however, was on the whole traditionally humanistic: feminine sensibilities engaging familiar human materials. It is only recently that writing not only by but also, often aggressively, *about* women has begun to emerge—so recently that one is wary of taking stock at this stage.

For an assortment of reasons, the American Indian experience has never received satisfactory literary expression, and it is unlikely

that it will. Nor has the Puerto Rican and the Chicano (Mexican-American) element in our society yet found its proper voice, though here one can be more confident. Otherwise, the record is impressively complete. And no doubt related to these different modes of expansion, of ever greater inclusiveness, has been a growing self-consciousness about American literature generally, a series of attempts to take hold of whole ranges of American writing, from Van Wyck Brooks's *America's Coming-of-Age* in 1915, to the studies of V. F. Parrington in the twenties and F. O. Matthiessen in the forties, through a plethora of other books down, on a decidedly lower register, to the present essay.

Respect for fact

As we move beyond the locales and the social origins of some of the work already alluded to, we become aware very rapidly—at least as we scrutinize the fiction—of the persistent respect for *fact* reflected in it: for hard, concrete, positivistic, reportorial fact. This is in part the legacy of literary realism, which also had its 19th-century beginnings; but realism in turn has been a shifting

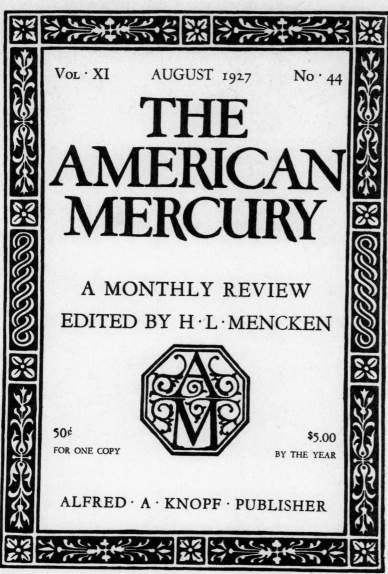

The American Mercury's sober appearance belied its brilliantly iconoclastic contents. Mencken's editorial team aimed 'to keep to common sense as fast as they can, to belabor sham as agreeably as possible, to give a civilized entertainment'. (2)

The same phenomenon helps explain the modern American writer's addiction to journalism. Several individuals who would go on to become novelists of the highest distinction began their careers as newspaper reporters—most notably, Dreiser and Hemingway. Their subsequent compulsion to get the facts straight in their fiction is not very surprising; but the process has also and more significantly been reversed. Hemingway was at the height of his creative powers when he accepted an invitation to report on the Spanish Civil War; and he may or may not have known that the *New York Times*, in 1915, sent Edith Wharton to the front lines in France on a similar mission. When the editors of *Sports Illustrated*, offering large sums of money, persuaded the Nobel Prize winner, William Faulkner, and later Norman Mailer to cover major sporting events for their pages, they may or may not have known that such—with writers of only slightly lesser reputations—had been common practice forty and fifty years before.

p 267 (30)

Alongside these reporters-turned-novelists and novelists-turned-reporters, there have been a host of writers who, more or less uninterruptedly, pursued journalism as a career rewarding in itself. One thinks of H. L. Mencken, who began as a reporter in Baltimore, went on to become a magazine editor, and in a series of volumes called *Prejudices* exuberantly denounced American culture as vulgar, antiquated, and hopelessly in thrall to the arid puritanism of what Mencken called 'the booboisie'. One thinks also of Edmund Wilson: for though Wilson may be thought of as the most vigorous, not to say the longest-lived, literary critic of his generation, he is content to describe himself, quite accurately, as a journalist—at one moment reporting at length upon the discovery of the Dead Sea Scrolls, at another probing into the sexual aberrations of Algernon Charles Swinburne, at still another investigating the plight of the Iroquois Indians.

p 263 (15) f 2

p 263 (16)

But there have been countless others: reform-minded muckrakers, tenacious crime reporters, adventurous foreign correspondents, skilled and eloquent commentators on the national and international scene. A catalogue of actual names would only be bewildering. But, while vastly enhancing the prestige of their profession, they have also provided a constant challenge to the writers of fiction—a challenge to be as scrupulous about detail as they have sought to be; to 'tell it the way it was', in Hemingway's

response to the increasing domination of the theoretical and applied sciences in American culture, then to such social studies as sought to display the rigorous methods of the sciences, and today to the overwhelming impact of technology. Those developments belong to the larger historical context described in other contributions to this volume. But it is within that context that the American writer's passion for the factual takes on much of its meaning.

Scott Fitzgerald was the disillusioned chronicler of the 'lost generation'. Right: an illustration to one of his Hollywood stories in the 'Saturday Evening Post'—a temperamental actress holds up work on a film set. (3)

phrase; to 'get it right', as Thomas Wolfe regularly admonished himself.

p 267 (34)

In the past few years, it has been Norman Mailer who has best illuminated the significant interplay of the three components mentioned: science or technology; fiction; and reportorial journalism. In *The Armies of the Night* (about the huge antiwar march on the Pentagon in 1967), *Miami and the Siege of Chicago* (the two political conventions in 1968), and *Of a Fire on the Moon* (the first moon landing in 1969), he brought to the meticulous reporting of historic events all his abilities as a novelist (the first-named has indeed as part of its sub-title the phrase 'History as the Novel'). Personalities are portrayed in the round, drama explodes, the dialogue is swift and telling. But the determining presence in all three books—and dictating, as it were, this thoroughly successful marriage of fiction and journalism—is contemporary technology, its menace and its challenge. For Mailer, who is the main exemplar today of the long American romantic tradition, technology—cold, mathematical, impersonal, implacable—exerts the gravest threat to man's sense of himself as a human person, to that aura of mystery in human life which Mailer regards as a prime necessity for human development, to man's religious consciousness. By the same token, technology is by all odds the first thing the imagination must take account of. It must be met on its own terms: Mailer, who majored in engineering at Harvard, packs his story of the moon landing with the most carefully prepared technological information. But more than that, technology must be *experienced*, as history must be experienced; and hence we have, in Mailer's recent work, not merely a series of dazzling and accurate reports, but the image of a driving, thrusting ego, very explicitly named Norman Mailer, going forth to confront, to affect and be affected by, the phenomena reported on.

Before leaving this subject, it can be remarked that there have been outlets other than journalism for novelists who wished to experiment in different but neighboring modes of writing, or who simply needed the money. Some—like Faulkner, Fitzgerald and West—earned a living for periods of time by writing scripts for Hollywood film companies. The undertaking provided Fitzgerald and West with the materials for their last novels, and all three to a certain extent made use of the techniques of cinematography to enrich their narrative method (for example, the camera roving across the contorted faces in a mob scene). For a while, it even seemed that script-writing would replace journalism as the American novelist's second profession, but of late the evidence suggests otherwise; journalism, and especially autobiographical journalism, is once again all in fashion. At the same time, taking quite another direction, a good many writers have sought permanent posts on college campuses across the country. One predictable result has been a spate of novels dealing (rather glumly) with college life: academic politics, the restiveness of students, the sexual choreography of professors and their wives. American literature has not been much advanced by these books. But for more imaginative practitioners like Saul Bellow, John Barth and Bernard Malamud, the academic setting has not so much been a source of subject-matter as a source of intellectual and literary cultivation. These are cultivated men who believe in the nourishment of the mind and the disciplining of the imagination; their talents are sharpened, not limited, by the library, the lecture or seminar, the interchanges with students and colleagues.

p 267 (31)

The personal voice

The image we have just observed in Mailer's journalism—that of a particular *self* confronting history in the age of science, reckoning it up and giving it shape—is not of course unique or original with Mailer. It is no less potent in two earlier writers Mailer has especially admired, Ernest Hemingway and Thomas Wolfe; and those writers in turn share an impulse that goes a long way back (at least as far as Lord Byron)—the impulse to take one's own personality as one's motivating subject, and then to watch what happens to that personality as it becomes entangled with the world that surrounds it, or threatens it, or simply pours in upon it. The impulse is ever more palpable—to the point where Richard Poirier, in the title essay of *The Performing Self* (1971) can pronounce it the defining characteristic of modern American and English

literature. Taking Robert Frost, Mailer and Henry James as his central examples—on the grounds that 'each of them is of an extreme if different kind of arrogance'—Poirier writes:

> Whether it be confronting a page of their own writing, an historical phenomenon like the assassination of Robert Kennedy, a meeting with Kruschev, or the massive power of New York City—all three treat any occasion as a 'scene' or a stage for dramatizing the self as a performer. I can't imagine a scene of whatever terror or pathos in which they would not at every step in their account of it be watching and measuring their moment by moment participation.

By participation, Poirier means fundamentally the writer's involvement *as artist*: as the one who gives shape and verbal articulation, and hence enduring reality, to the events reflected on and described. But in the cases of Hemingway and Wolfe, and after them of Mailer, the participation has been more literal. The contrast with Faulkner is suggestive. We are always aware, in Faulkner's stories, of a particular presence—a voice behind all the other voices of his narrators; Faulkner's voice, wondering, pitying, brooding. Yet Faulkner was the most private of men; no one insisted more often that an artist's personal life must never be looked for in his work:

> I think [he once remarked] that if what one has thought and hoped and endeavored and failed at is not enough, if it must be explained and excused by what he has experienced, done or suffered while he was not being an artist, then he and the one making the evaluation have both failed.

p 262 (11)

With Hemingway and Wolfe, however, the felt presence of the artist brings with it a swarm of autobiographical fact. Not only the self but the life of the self have gone into *A Farewell to Arms* and *Look Homeward, Angel*; and we see that the obsession with self and the passion for fact are closely related, for the only facts a writer can be really assured of (in his effort to 'tell it the way it was') are those he has witnessed or personally experienced.

A Farewell to Arms, published in 1929, illustrates a deeper motivation for the absorption in self, and it is worth inspecting a little. For in one perspective, the novel can be seen as an imaginative act whereby Hemingway, through the exercise of his art, managed to restore a certain wholeness, a coherence and continuity, to his own inner being. The Hemingway of 1928 was anxiety-ridden and temporarily directionless as a writer. He had suffered several alarming physical accidents (in his habitual way); he had divorced his first wife and married his second, and the latter had given birth to a child after an excruciatingly painful period of labor; Hemingway's father had committed suicide. The very self that was Hemingway's main subject was losing its outline. But in a manner familiar to psychologists, these assorted events seem to have brought surging back into memory a cluster of incidents and relationships of ten years before, when Hemingway was driving an ambulance on the Italian front in the first war.

There were the severe leg wounds caused by mortar shell and machine-gun fire; there was the American nurse with whom Hemingway had an unconsummated affair while recovering in a Milan hospital; there were the friendly Abruzzese priest, the sophisticated Italian medical officer who addressed Hemingway as 'baby'; the aging Count Greppi with whom Hemingway played billiards in a hotel on the edge of Lago Maggiore. The two sets of incidents, separated by a decade, went into *A Farewell to Arms*; and by fusing them into the same single narrative in the same moment of time, Hemingway, consciously or no, established an organic relationship between the wounded but heroic self in 1918 and the fragmenting self of 1928. And by doing this, he regained a vital harmony of self—one imbued, now, by an all-sustaining tragic vision.

The self thus recreated is stoical, terse of speech, disdainful of conventional values and of the language that has expressed them, a self that has learned to appear emotionless even while vibrating with suppressed emotion—the kind of self best equipped, in Hemingway's view, to survive in a world characterized by brutal violence and presided over by powers inexorably hostile to human aspiration.

An illustration by Douglas Gorsline for Thomas Wolfe's first novel 'Look Homeward, Angel' (1929), a partly auto-biographical chronicle of the Gant family of Altamont, who ran a boarding house just as Wolfe's mother had done. Wolfe, said William Faulkner, 'made the best failure'; he 'tried to get it all said'. (4)

f 4 The self that massively evolves in *Look Homeward, Angel* and Wolfe's other novels is the polar opposite, and it is another instance of the irreducible variety of American literature that Hemingway and Wolfe, who so much resemble one another on one level, can be so utterly different, finally, on the printed page.

'Tom Wolfe', Faulkner told a friend, 'was trying to say everything, the world plus "I", or filtered through "I" or the effort of "I" to embrace the world in which he was born and walked a little while and then lay down again.' The words partly contradict what Faulkner has just been quoted as saying about biography and criticism, but they are cogent. In Wolfe, nothing is suppressed, nothing held back; and as against the tight-lipped quality of Hemingway's prose and his main characters, Wolfe releases a steady torrent of loquacity. Through his protagonists Eugene Gant and George Webber, Wolfe records a bulging world as filtered through or embraced by his own hugely hospitable sensibility. He stays very close to autobiographical fact, making only such minor adjustments as befit the romantic personality he was striving to realize: in *Look Homeward, Angel*, for example, a youthful affair that remained innocent in the life is sexually fulfilled in the fiction, and the young Wolfe who rather enjoyed himself at the University of North Carolina becomes the Eugene Webber who feels romantically alienated and alone at the fictive Chapel Hill. Out of the unchecked flow of experience, there emerges a self often described as a hungry giant: a physically towering individual, avid for experience, flinging himself into the churning realities of 20th-century American history. For it is, one feels, some essence of the American spirit, some greatness of national soul, that Wolfe-Webber seeks to comprehend, to ally with, to be ennobled by. But the outcome of the quest is indicated in the rhythmically repeated phrase: 'Lost, oh lost!'

On still another level, however, Hemingway and Wolfe once again resemble one another, for both—through their heroes and in the imaginative thrust of their fiction—offer instances of what the critic Lionel Trilling has called 'the opposing self'. In his preface to a volume of that name, Trilling traces this phenomenon back to late 18th-century Europe. Prior to that, he argues, gifted literary artists tended to be the spokesmen of their times, the voices of their culture and the embodiment of its best ideals. But starting with the French Encyclopedist Diderot and his strange work *Rameau's Nephew*, there began to appear an artistic personality whose posture was rather one of profound *hostility* to the culture he inhabited, a rejection of its chief values, an adherence to views of human nature and achievement radically other than those the culture had espoused.

Whatever the historical origins of the opposing self, it is undeniable that the major American writers of this century have, virtually without exception, assumed a hostile—or at the least, a deprecating or a satiric—attitude towards the dominant mores and value systems of the country. To say that almost every aspect of American life has been given literary expression in the past seven decades is not at all to say that those aspects have been celebrated or rejoiced in. On the contrary, every new phase invoked has been a new occasion for a statement of opposition ranging from pain through bewilderment to outrage—the latter, to be sure, not infrequently salted with liveliest humor. One could pick a series of novels almost at random—say, one per decade—to illustrate the theme.

Dreiser's *Sister Carrie*, in 1900, discloses the hollowness, the vague feeling of dissatisfaction that accompanies material success, that first of all American public values; and in a parallel story it follows the downward course of a seemingly strong and self-confident man, driven to defeat and suicide by the mysterious economic powers of the age. In 1913, Edith Wharton's *The Custom of the Country* shows the attractive but enfeebled old social order giving way before the onslaught of the two new forces of sex and business. In *Babbitt*, eight years later, Sinclair Lewis brought his confusedly yearning hero to the point of questioning, opposing and temporarily abandoning the only world he had previously known: a world spiritually shrinking while materially expanding, shaped not even by the crude values of the business tycoon, but by the cruder ones of the salesman, where thought has yielded to fuzzy dreaming and even religion is a matter of short-term profits.

Other propensities, darker or more foolish, of the American character were examined by Nathanael West in a superb short novel of 1934, *A Cool Million*. West (1899–1940) has slowly become recognized as one of the century's most original and piercing satirists; and here he takes on both the American dream of success and the American potential for its own brand of paranoid bigotry. West's luckless hero, Lemuel Pitkin, is bent on rising from rags to riches in the nearly effortless manner so often described by Horatio Alger, the enormously popular author of success stories for the young; but every conventional move he makes is met with disaster—he is physically 'dismantled', limb by limb and organ by organ (even while his sweetheart is being periodically raped), until at last he is shot dead by a paid assassin. But he lives on as the martyred hero of an American fascist party, whose rise to power under the leadership of Shagpoke Whipple comprises the other half of West's story.

Faulkner's *The Hamlet* (1940) is a comic parable of a different sort. What Faulkner here envisages is the irreversible moral decay of the south (by extension, of America and even the Western world) under the invasion of a proliferating clan of human rodents known as the Snopeses. In Faulkner's imaginative history of his region, the Snopeses represent the third and perhaps the fatal last phase, following the reign of such families as the Sartorises, Compsons and McCaslins, each with its ancestral traditions and its code of honor, though each also showing signs of moral and psychological decline. Those families were embedded in southern society, but the Snopeses come from nowhere to feed on the spirit of the land. Themselves too remote from the moral sense to be called corrupt, they corrupt everything they touch. Flem Snopes, the leader of the clan, is an invention of genius: soulless and sexless, a tireless and unsmiling deceiver who draws the townsmen into self-degrading practices against their moral judgment and outwits them at every turn, Flem stands for the demoralizing energy which, in Faulkner's opinion, is bringing about the spiritual ruin of the country.

p 266
(27)

The Hamlet is a triumphant instance of a fictional genre which the circumstances of the age have made ever more appealing, to writer and reader alike. This is the genre of apocalyptic satire (an apter phrase, I think, than the once popular 'black humor'), a genre in which the opposing self arrives at an extreme of exacerbated hostility. Confronted at once by the horror of history and the grotesque ineptitude of the human response to it, the imagination, working within this genre, describes the approaching end of the world, the ultimate holocaust, as a cosmically funny event. This was the vision enacted in West's *The Day of the Locust* as well as in *The Hamlet*. The novel of the fifties which best caught the comical apocalyptic mood was Ralph Ellison's *Invisible Man*, in which the narrator's misadventures lead him finally into the midst of a ferocious race riot which threatens to destroy the whole city—metaphorically, the whole of America's racially divided society.

p 267 (35) In the wake of *Invisible Man* and through the sixties further contributions to the genre have accumulated, among the best of them Joseph Heller's *Catch-22* and Thomas Pynschon's *The Crying of Lot 69*, in each of which modern history is seen dissolving, however hilariously, into a nightmare from which the only escape may very likely be into oblivion. It is not easy to imagine how far beyond such images the hostile creative self can go. One suspects that it will be impelled to find new ways, new scenarios, to convey its perceptions of the drift of things human.

Old and new virtues

What values has the modern American writer proposed as a replacement for those he has so resolutely rejected? In a memorable passage in *A Farewell to Arms*, Hemingway, speaking through the character of Frederick Henry, describes the problem and suggests one kind of answer:

> I was always embarrassed by the words sacred, glorious, and sacrifice and the expression in vain. We had heard them, sometimes standing in the rain almost out of earshot, so that only the shouted words came through, and had read them, on proclamations that were slapped up by billposters over other proclamations, now for a long time, and I had seen nothing sacred, and the things that were glorious had no glory and the sacrifices were like the stockyards at Chicago if nothing was done with the meat except to bury it. There were many words that you could not stand to hear and finally only the names of places had dignity. Certain numbers were the same way and certain dates and these with the names of the places were all you could say and have them mean anything. Abstract words such as glory, honor, courage, or hallow were obscene beside the concrete names of villages, the numbers of roads, the names of rivers, the numbers of regiments and the dates.

Henry is talking specifically about the patriotic rhetoric of the Italian high command, with all its customary histrionics and exaggeration. But his reaction has, needless to say, a far broader significance. It defines the central dilemma of the modern individual who is at once a moral being and a literary artist. What values genuinely live for him? What *words* are sufficiently alive to communicate those values? The grand old vocables come through to the moral man and artist only as to someone standing in the rain almost out of earshot, disconnected, sundered from life and meaning. Where can he turn?

Hemingway, here as always, turns away from the abstract to the concrete, from the moral term to the hard fact—the date, the number, the village, the river. But against Hemingway's meditation we may put the following conjecture by Jason Compson, Quentin's father, in *Absalom, Absalom!*, speaking in part for Faulkner:

> Have you noticed how so often when we try to reconstruct the causes which lead up to the actions of men and women, how with a sort of astonishment we find ourselves now and then reduced to the belief, the only possible belief, that they stemmed from some of the old virtues?

And Compson goes on to mention such 'old virtues' as love, pity, true pride. He is engaged in reconstructing for his son the causes that led to the behavior of Judith Sutpen; and since, as we learn,

he has got many of his facts wrong, his theory of human causation may not seem to carry much weight. But there is evidence elsewhere that Faulkner himself partially subscribed to that theory. No other major novelist of his time has referred with more strength of feeling to love, courage, pity, humility, pride, the will to endure, and the like.

Few other contemporary novelists have appraised human motivation in language like that—and those that do will usually turn out, like Faulkner, to be Southerners: Robert Penn Warren, for example, or William Styron. To find adherents of older virtues, one must look rather to the poets of the century. For while poetry in our time has been characterized by every kind of technical innovation, it has also, not infrequently, shown at its core a hard ethical conservatism.

Two poets who have in very different ways declared for the old virtues are T. S. Eliot and Robert Frost. For Eliot, in the course of time, the old virtues revealed themselves as those of traditional Christianity. In his earlier verse, Eliot measured the futility, the nervelessness, the postwar chaos of his culture by values derived from a sort of hodge-podge of Greek tragedy, medieval literature, Elizabethan drama, and the *Upanishad*. Traces of most of these are evident in the closing lines of *The Waste Land* (1922): p 266 (28)

> I sat upon the shore
> Fishing, with the arid plain behind me
> Shall I at least set my lands in order?
> London bridge is falling down falling down falling down
> *Poi s'ascose nel foco che gli affina*
> *Quando fiam uti chelidon*—O swallow swallow
> *Le Prince d'Aquitaine à la tour abolie*
> These fragments I have shored against my ruins
> Why then Ile fit you. Hieronymo's mad againe.
> Datta. Dayadvham. Damyata.
>   Shantih   shantih   shantih

Among those cultural fragments, we make out seriatim allusions drawn from the medieval grail legend, a child's nursery rhyme, Dante's *Purgatorio*, a Provençal lyric, a poem by Nerval, a 16th-century play by Thomas Kyd, and three imperatives from the *Upanishad* which mean 'Give, sympathize, control'—followed by the Sanskrit word, thrice repeated, of which the nearest English equivalent, Eliot tells us, is 'The Peace which passeth understanding'.

It is a remarkable display of literary learning, but it is not a display for its own sake. Like his close associate Ezra Pound—who, in *Hugh Selwyn Mauberly* and the exfoliating *Cantos*, was similarly drawing upon vast reaches not only of Western but of Oriental culture—Eliot was trying to put together his own cultural defense against the devastating loss of meaning in his time. But this particular cluster of fragments made an unstable compound, even if it concluded a poem of the very first rank; and Eliot gradually moved towards a more orderly system of ideas. In *Ash Wednesday* (1930), he re-enacted the tortuous process of his conversion to Christian belief, and (in Eliot's understanding of it) its stern and uncompromising demands. This is the most moving poem about religious conversion in English, especially since the elements that constantly deflect the heart away from the Christian vision are so tellingly invoked:

> And the lost heart stiffens and rejoices
> In the lost lilac and the lost sea voices
> And the weak spirit quickens to rebel
> For the bent golden-rod and the lost sea smell
> Quickens to recover
> The cry of quail and the whirling plover. . . .

What is so poignant about Eliot's Christian poetry is that, even as he is enunciating the old Christian virtues, he cannot conceal that anyone who truly holds to them will feel himself an utter alien in his own profoundly secular age. This is the outcome of *The Journey of the Magi*, in which the Eastern kings, having made the long winter journey to Bethlehem to gaze upon the newborn Christ, travel back to their kingdoms with the heavy-hearted awareness that they have become strangers—more, they are dead—to their worlds:

There was a Birth, certainly.
We had evidence and no doubt. I had seen birth and death,
But had thought they were different; this Birth was
Hard and bitter agony for us, like Death, our death.
We returned to our places, these kingdoms,
But no longer at ease here, in the old dispensation,
With an alien people clutching their gods.
I should be glad of another death.

A different set of old virtues may be seen lurking in the poetry of p 266 (25) Robert Frost—virtues appropriate, not to the darkening city of *The Waste Land*, but to the harsh New England farming country which was Frost's actual and his symbolic setting. They comprise the moral and mental fortitude of an individual closely if often solitarily involved with nature: a self-reliance, a toughness of spirit, and among other things the wisdom not to believe that nature is cordial to the emotions of men. In *The Need of Being Versed in Country Things*, Frost depicts a ruined farm—the house burned down, the barn abandoned, the once bustling scene now desolate— and then observes the reactions of some visiting birds who *seem* to share the onlooker's regret but who in fact are quite indifferent, busy about their own comfort:

The birds that came to it through the air
At broken windows flew out and in,
Their murmur more like the sigh we sigh
From too much dwelling on what has been.

Yet for them the lilac renewed its leaf,
And the aged elm, though touched with fire;
And the dry pump flung up an awkward arm;
And the fence post carried a strand of wire.

For them there was really nothing sad.
But though they rejoiced at the nest they kept,
One had to be versed in country things
Not to believe the phoebes wept.

Any one as well versed in country things as Frost knows about the well-nigh intolerable solitude that is sometimes part of the farm country experience. Frost's bleakest portrait of the solitary is *An Old Man's Winter Night*, where the aged farmer goes to sleep night after night entirely alone, his comfortless dwelling surrounded by a nature which appears threatening rather than friendly ('All out-of-doors looked darkly in at him'), conscious as he falls asleep only of snow on the roof and icicles on the wall. This, Frost says, is life at its most minimal:

One aged man—one man—can't keep a house,
A farm, a countryside, or if he can,
It's thus he does it of a winter night.

Such solitude, for Frost, is a psychic condition; it is of the modern world generally, and not only of New England. Given it, a man needs a talent for neighborliness, the capacity to make the gesture of friendship toward the human being nearest at hand. But the gesture may be repulsed; modern man often seems to prefer solitude. In *Mending Wall*, Frost tells of the annual task of repairing the gaps in the wall between his farm and that of his neighbor 'beyond the hill'. The other farmer insists on restoring the barrier that divides them, and keeps repeating that 'Good fences make good neighbors'. Frost is moved to query this:

Spring is the mischief in me, and I wonder
If I could put a question in his head:
'*Why* do they make good neighbors? Isn't it
Where there are cows? But here there are no cows.
Before I'd build a wall I'd ask to know
What I was walling in or walling out,
And to whom I was like to give offense.
Something there is that doesn't love a wall,
That wants it down.'

But there are few neighbors in Frost's poetry, indeed few human beings at all; and the season of spring is seen less often than that of winter. For Frost is the poet of the onset: the onset of winter, or of the night; a poet gazing into the approaching darkness, bracing himself against the confusion and the coldness to come. The very act of writing a poem thus becomes an exercise in an old virtue— the courage to face up to moral and psychological darkness. 'Every poem is an epitome of the great predicament', he has written; 'a figure of the will braving alien entanglements'. Elsewhere he has defined a poem as 'a momentary stay against confusion'. Perhaps Frost's representative poem, and certainly one of his finest, is *The Onset*, an account of the yearly moment when the first snow falls: winter is upon one again, and one must reckon up one's moral record over the year:

Always the same, when on a fated night
At last the gathered snow lets down as white
As may be in dark woods, and with a song
It shall not make again all winter long
Of hissing on the yet uncovered ground,
I almost stumble looking up and round,
As one who overtaken by the end
Gives up his errand, and lets death descend
Upon him where he is, with nothing done
To evil, no important triumph won,
More than if life had never yet begun.

And yet, he tells himself, this sense of moral failure, even of death, will not last any more than winter will last. Spring will return, and the streams of April: at least, that is what has always happened before. And meanwhile, the very poem which speculates about these things is Frost's way of resisting the darkness he feels setting in.

Late Romantics

Both Eliot and Frost may be considered 'classical'—using that word rather loosely—both in their literary affinities and in their adherence to the virtues of restraint, control, staunchness of spirit amid 'alien entanglements'. But the poetry that seems of late to have been gaining the ascendancy, at least in the academies, belongs really to the romantic tradition. That phrase, too, is used loosely enough: here it may seem to mean little more than a common esteem for the figure and the poetry of Walt Whitman.

For some of the romantic poets in our time, Whitman has stood p 261 (5) for a set of old virtues derived not from the classical or Christian worlds, but from the mid-19th century, when democracy was finally forged in America. They include a belief in radical freedom; in the sovereignty of the individual combined with a devotion to the democratic community (or 'the people'); in the absolute equality of human beings. Earlier in the century, Carl Sandburg p 266 (26) composed a large repertoire of Whitmanian songs, wordy celebrations in endlessly uncoiling lines of American greatness—sometimes, at his worst, sounding like a parody of Whitman:

I am the people—the mob—the crowd—the mass.
Do you know that all the great work of the world is done
   through me?
I am the workingman, the inventor, the maker of the world's
   food and clothes . . .

Sandburg—another avatar of Whitman's common man, wandering, guitar in hand, among the hog markets and the skyscrapers of the modern city—was the poetizing grandfather of the 'hippie' poets who twang their chords and chant their formless songs in the bars of New York's Greenwich Village.

Vachel Lindsay, a better if a noisier poet, was the ancestor of a related contemporary group. Shouting poems like *The Congo* from platforms across the land, his heavily pulsating verse accompanied by the thump of drums and the crash of percussion instruments, Lindsay originated the use of what has today evolved into 'rock music' as the deafening context for an insistent, driving kind of poetry. But Lindsay best fulfilled his poetic potential in poems where his Whitmanian love of the people took the form, not of Sandburg's indiscriminate embrace of the mob, but an evocation of the historical political movement called 'Populism' (its program calling for 'popular' control of railroads and lands). Perhaps his most memorable single work is the one that salutes the Populist leader William Jennings Bryan, his presidential campaigns of 1896, his crusade for a silver as against a gold standard:

I brag and chant of Bryan, Bryan, Bryan,
Candidate for president who sketched a silver Zion,
The one American Poet who could sing outdoors,
He brought in tides of wonder, of unprecedented splendor,
Wild roses from the plains, that made hearts tender . . .

p 264
(23) The poetry of Hart Crane reveals another facet both of American romanticism and of Walt Whitman. For Crane, the greatest virtue was the oldest one of all: the virtue, quite simply, of human love. In *The Broken Tower*, the last poem he wrote (Crane's short life—1899–1932—ended in an apparent suicide by drowning), Crane hauntingly summarized his lifelong poetic ambition—which had been to create a poetic vision in which love and harmony would be restored to a world broken by discord and ugliness, even though he knew that such harmony endures only in the instant of its utterance:

And so it was I entered the broken world
To trace the visionary company of love, its voice
An instant in the wind (I know not whither hurled)
But not for long to hold each desperate choice.

The major source of fragmentation, Crane felt, was technology, or in his own word 'the machine'. He was convinced that the task of poetry in the modern epoch was 'to absorb the machine, i.e., to *acclimatize* it as naturally and casually as trees, castles, galleons and all other human associations of the past.' It was because of this that he found in Whitman his exemplary predecessor. For Whitman, Crane said in a note on 'modern poetry', 'better than any other was able to co-ordinate those forces in America which seem most intractable, fusing them into a universal vision which takes on additional significance as time goes on.' Crane's effort to rival the achievement he attributed to Whitman was *The Bridge* (1930), an epic of sorts in which, taking Brooklyn Bridge as representing the technological world, he sought by the sheer resources of poetry to convert that construct of steel and concrete into a spiritual experience. At a key moment, Crane addresses Whitman, dedicates *The Bridge* to him, and acknowledges Whitman as the source of its theme:

Walt, tell me, Walt Whitman, if infinity
Be still the same as when you walked the beach
Near Paumanok. . . . .
For you, the panoramas and this breed of towers,
Of you—the theme that's statured in the cliff.

It would not be easy to tell from lines like those that Hart Crane was one of the most supremely gifted poets in American literary history: a master of the musical line, his best poetry charged with dramatic intensity, a manipulator of language (as it were, of words exerting vital pressure on each other) unique in any time. But the most compelling passages both in *The Bridge* and in the independent lyrics are of a special kind of obscurity, and would require much glossing; so while urging that they be read, I shall not risk quoting from them.

If romantic poetry in America is gradually superseding poetry of a classical temper in the affections of professors and critics, it is partly due to the belated impact of Hart Crane, but even more so to p 267
(32) the work of Wallace Stevens (1877–1955), as that richly complex body of verse has—even more slowly than that of Crane—been assimilated, appraised and interpreted.

Stevens, too, pays his respects to Whitman, and like Crane he images Whitman as characteristically moving along the seashore:

In the far South the sun of autumn is passing
Like Walt Whitman walking along a ruddy shore.
He is singing and chanting things that are part of him,
The worlds that were and will be, death and day.

But Stevens is a romantic in his own exceptionally original way. Not a prophetic bard like Whitman, and much less visionary than Crane, Stevens is essentially a philosophic, a meditational poet. The virtues he cherishes are those of the intellect: or more precisely, of the intellect in the service of the imagination. For what Stevens most frequently meditates is the ever-shifting relation between the human imagination and the reality that it engages, or collides with. This, for Stevens, is the major challenge to the human spirit

under the modern circumstance, for the major circumstance of our culture is the disappearance of religious belief.

Stevens is the representative *par excellence* of atheistic humanism in this century. He regards 'the disappearance of God' as total and as enormously liberating. Seven years before Eliot, in *Ash Wednesday*, described his painful conversion to the Christian faith, Stevens was proclaiming something like the opposite. In the beautiful meditation or internal dialogue, *Sunday Morning*, he offered a fifteen-line history of religion in the Western world: how classical mythology had its day and then yielded to the Christian doctrine of the Incarnation, and how the latter in turn vanished from men's minds, leaving them free to assert their own radically human natures.

Jove in the clouds had his inhuman birth.
No mother suckled him, no sweet land gave
Large-mannered motions to his mythy mind.
He moved among us, as a muttering king,
Magnificent, would move among his hinds,
Until our blood, commingling, virginal,
With heaven, brought such requital to desire
The very hinds discerned it, in a star.
Shall our blood fail? Or shall it come to be
The blood of paradise? And shall the earth
Seem all of paradise that we shall know?
The sky will be much friendlier then than now,
A part of labour and a part of pain,
And next in glory to enduring love,
Not this dividing and indifferent blue.

In Stevens's view, a belief in God or the gods had from the outset been simply a product of human desire, abetted by the imagination, and what had happened was that the desire had suddenly ceased. It was an extraordinary event, Stevens reflected in an essay called 'Two or Three Ideas': 'to see the gods dispelled in mid-air and dissolve like clouds is one of the great human experiences. It is not as if they had gone over the horizon to disappear for a time; nor as if they had been overcome by other gods of greater power and profounder knowledge. It is simply that they came to nothing.' For a while, Stevens observed, man felt like a child who has lost his parents, or been abandoned by them; but soon he came to realize the grandeur of his new freedom, and to discover that the 'human self' was 'all there was'.

It was here that the crucial importance of poetry became apparent. 'In an age of disbelief,' Stevens said in the same essay, '. . . it is for the poet to supply the satisfactions of belief, in his measure and in his style.' It is a subtle argument, for by 'poetry' Stevens does not merely mean verbal constructs with a measured beat, though such are the supreme examples of what he *does* mean. But 'poetry' means any act of the imagination as it grapples with and finds order in external reality. A man observing that twenty separate farmhouses (the example is taken in fact from Emerson) make up a unified landscape is, insofar, behaving as a poet. It is, anyhow, in poetry so conceived, Stevens insisted again and again, that all the great business of life is or must be transacted.

Poetry, replacing music, must take the place
Of empty heaven and its hymns.

So says the title-figure in *The Man with the Blue Guitar*. And in 'Adagaia'—a collection of aphorisms published in *Opus Posthumous* (1957)—Stevens constantly returned to the theme. 'After one has abandoned a belief in god, poetry is the essence which takes its place in life's redemption. . . . Poetry is a means of redemption. . . . God is a symbol for something that can as well take other forms, as, for example, the form of high poetry', and so on.

Over a long career in which Stevens's poetry grew stronger and stronger, ever more intellectually difficult but moving to ever higher reaches of accomplishment, he played literally innumerable variations on the theme. Since poetry was of such all-embracing importance, poetry itself was Stevens's obsessive subject. But to say so is like saying that Dante's obsessive subject was the relation between Christian theology and human experience. Within his strictly humanistic framework, nothing human and nothing of the natural world is missing from Stevens's verse.

'Nineteen Nineteen' was the second novel, set in World War I, of John Dos Passos' trilogy 'USA'. Above: a scene of horseplay among GIs in Italy, illustrated by Reginald Marsh. (5)

The disinherited

One serious reservation should perhaps be made to the claim of inclusiveness in Stevens's poetry: namely, that there is little consciousness in it of *history*, either as tendency or event. There is almost no echo of the three great historical upheavals in the century thus far—the First and Second World Wars, and the economic Depression of 1929. The spiritual after-effects of the First War are palpable enough in the fragmented rhythms and the apocalyptic language of *The Waste Land*; Hart Crane's poetry seized more than once upon air war and air raids as symbols of man's brutalizing of his higher instincts; and Hemingway's *The Sun Also Rises* (1926) became the classic image of 'the lost generation'—a phrase that, though as originally coined it meant something narrower, came to define a postwar generation that felt itself cut loose by years of war from its cultural moorings, from any traditional set of values. As to the Second War, it seems not to have elicited the large-scale response represented by Eliot and Hemingway: partly perhaps because it was precisely a *second* war, bringing with it only more of the same devastations; partly because there has been no talent hospitable enough to take it on even with the indirections of art.

The Great Depression was something else again. For one thing, novelists and poets writing, in the thirties, out of their experience of the Depression—the massive unemployment, the bread lines, the hunger marches, the bewildered desperation of sharecroppers and fruit pickers, the confrontations of union organizers and police—gave first important literary voice to the tenets of Marxism, one of the two most significant intellectual influences to come to this country from abroad in this century. (The second, of course, was Freudianism, but its impact has been too diffuse for analysis here.) There had always been the poor and the hungry in America, but there had also been the legitimate hope of escape from both the urban and the rural ghetto into a better life. What now was felt is suggested by the title of Jack Conroy's far-ranging proletarian novel of 1933: *The Disinherited*. Very many Americans felt deprived of a living they had once enjoyed; they were, so to say, the *dis*-employed. In their anger and frustration, they were convinced that they had been deliberately sold out; that their plight was due to what Franklin D. Roosevelt called the 'entrenched greed' of the big industrialists and bankers; that, in short, the true villain was the capitalist system itself, in unholy alliance with imperialism. The writings of Karl Marx were at hand to explain history, and the Communist Party was there to invite their participation.

As it turned out, not many writers and intellectuals accepted the invitation, though few escaped entirely the radical response. One or two literary critics engaged in an intellectual flirtation with Marxism, but they were too independent-minded to accept the official party doctrine that all imaginative writing must be judged solely by its contribution to the revolutionary cause. The writing that did obey this dictum, indeed, is interesting today almost exclusively to social historians. What has survived is, as usual, novels and poems which pierced the immediate historical situation to find images of a more general human predicament.

The now half-forgotten poems of Kenneth Fearing—particularly his collection of 1935, with its warm sympathy for the victimized and its sharp satire of the upholders of law and order—may belong on that list; and probably one or two plays by Clifford Odets, especially *Waiting for Lefty*, Odets' still stirring one-act play about a labor union meeting and its decision to strike. But the names that seem most secure in this context are those of John Steinbeck and John Dos Passos. Steinbeck's *In Dubious Battle* (1936) is the most incisive American novel yet written about the labor movement; and *The Grapes of Wrath* (1939) elevates a group of migratory refugees from the Oklahoma dust bowl into memorable embodiments of common humanity in a moment of nearly unredeemable distress. If Steinbeck, for all his earlier merit, is somewhat bypassed here, it is because the career of John Dos Passos is so archetypal—so exemplary of the fate of the novelist *engagé* in our time—that it warrants a somewhat detailed account. p 267 (33)

Before looking at it, however, we should consider another development during the Depression years which can itself help to appraise Dos Passos' career. This is something best described as documentary non-fiction—'a vast body of writing', Alfred Kazin has remarked (*On Native Grounds*, 1942, 1955), 'that is perhaps the fullest expression of the American consciousness after 1930.' It was an urgent, often a passionate response to the physical, economic and psychological dislocations caused by the Depression, and as Kazin pointed out, it had profoundly tragic overtones.

> Here, in the revealing—especially revealing because it was so often mechanical—effort of so many American writers to seek out the reality of America in a time of crisis, is an authentic and curiously unconscious characterisation of a tragic period. Here, in the vast granary of facts on life in America put away by the WPA writers, the documentary reporters, the folklorists preparing an American mythology, the explorers who went hunting through darkest America with notebook and camera, the new army of biographers and historians—here, stocked away like a reserve against bad times, is the raw stuff of the contemporary mass record. p 263 (20)

There were—to spell out Kazin's catalogue a little—the myriad guides, commissioned by the Works Project Administration as a device for employment, of the states and highways of the country. There were the accumulating and scientifically documented, first-hand studies of social and economic distress: among the rubber workers in Akron, Ohio (Ruth McKenny's *Industrial Valley*); in comparative urban centers (George Leighton's *Five Cities*); amid the dispossessed sharecroppers of the South (the WPA case histories, *These Are Our Lives*). And there was the rapidly developing genre of the 'picture book'—collections of photographs of the dispossessed, in camps and mills and fields, accompanied by captions and sometimes by texts.

The begetters of these books claimed to be originating a new genre, and to some extent they were right. In one of the best of them, *An American Exodus*—an inquiry by Dorothea Lange and Paul S. Taylor into the plight of migratory workers from Oklahoma and Arkansas—the authors maintained that theirs was neither a commentary with illustrations nor a mere book of pictures. 'Upon a tripod of photographs, captions, and text,' they argued, 'we rest themes evolved out of long observations in the field.' It is true, as Kazin shrewdly noted, that there was a danger in letting the camera do the work of the mind, in simply recording things as they flatly were without relating them to the needs of body and spirit. But the picture books produced an immensely valuable shock in the sensibility of more fortunate Americans—*An American Exodus* came out the same year as *The Grapes of Wrath* and set off much deeper vibrations; and they led to at least one authentic masterpiece, *Let Us Now Praise Famous Men*, a hauntingly effective study of the Alabama sharecroppers, with a poetic text by James Agee fusing beautifully with the photographic works of art of Walker Evans.

The most striking development along this line in recent years has been the television commentary—on hunger and poverty in America, for instance, or on the swollen budget of the Defense

Department. It is perhaps too early to reckon its full potential, but it is, one feels, evolving a genuine new language, the first attribute of which is not so much that its images are in motion but that they are accessible on a scale undreamed of by the authors of the picture books—to scores of millions of Americans at the same moment in time.

In addition to the more purely documentary work in the thirties, meanwhile, there were explorations of the state of things American in general, of the American psyche, of the American past and its relation to the present. A plethora of books explicitly announced their concern with America as such: *Perplexed America* (Sherwood Anderson), *Tragic America* (Theodore Dreiser), *The American Jitters* (Edmund Wilson), *Say, Is This the USA* (Erskine Caldwell). It was partly in an effort to get at the root causes of the perplexed, tragic and jittery condition of the country, that other writers still sought out the defining traditions of the native culture, and the lives and achievements of its vanished great.

All the above provides an explanatory context for the successive phases in the life and the literary methods of John Dos Passos. Born in Chicago in 1896, Dos Passos went to an exclusive private school and then to Harvard College; but before graduating from Harvard, he was already expressing a sort of high-spirited rage. After watching what he called 'the Cossack tactics of the New York police force' during a demonstration, he declared himself repelled by his own social class and drawn to the 'foreigners' who were helping to organize labor. The subsequent experience of driving an ambulance in France and Italy during the first war only deepened his disgust with the American establishment, military and civilian authorities alike. In his first literary success, *Manhattan Transfer* (1925: a kaleidoscopic portrait of New York City), his hatred seemed so all-embracing that more than one critic wondered if it were only the capitalist system that Dos Passos detested—or whether he was not consumed by 'a distaste for all the beings who composed' American society. It was after the execution in 1927 of Sacco and Vanzetti, two pacific anarchists accused of murder in Massachusetts, that Dos Passos announced that he had 'privately seceded' from the United States.

That event was the seed of Dos Passos' trilogy, *U.S.A.*, though it is only arrived at towards the end of the third volume, *The Big Money* (1936). Two thirds of that immense work—*The 42nd Parallel* (1930) and *1919* (1932)—were written during Dos Passos' most active involvement with radical politics. Though he never formally joined the Communist Party, he supported it vigorously for several years, lent his name to its manifestos, and his talent to its undertakings. He spoke urgently of the need for a 'new myth that's got to be created to replace the imperialist prosperity myth', and insisted that a new theater must be drawn from 'the conscious sections of the industrial and white-collar working classes which are out to get control of the great flabby mass of capitalist society'.

Along with its driving anti-capitalist impulse, *U.S.A.*—sometimes identified as 'the sad epic of the great American sell-out'—adopts and exploits, through its variety of narrative techniques, most of the devices mentioned above of documentary non-fiction. There are masses of documented facts; there is the verbal equivalent of the picture-book camera in the lyrically flowing autobiographical sections called 'The Camera Eye'; there is virtually an anticipation of the uses of television in those portions called 'News-Reel' (snatches of song, excerpts from political speeches, newspaper headlines); and there are the brief biographies of great or of merely popular and representative Americans (Thorstein Veblen, Henry Ford, Isadora Duncan). There is finally, as has been said, the ambition reflected in the title to embrace the whole of the country during a long period of intensifying crisis.

The American Communist Party regularly offered Dos Passos as their proudest example of the correctly dedicated American writer. Yet as early as 1934, he was questioning the disruptive tactics of the Communists at a socialist rally in New York; and when he returned from the war in Spain, in 1937, he denounced the hounding of the anarchists there by the Stalinist forces. The Communists began to suspect that, as their saying went, he must be politically confused; and most of his writings since 1937 have only persuaded them that he was a hopeless case.

They were right. Dos Passos was consistently for the underdog, but not for revolutionary reasons. Answering a questionnaire in 1939, he wrote:

> My sympathies, for some reason, lie with the private in the front line against the brass hat; with the hodcarrier against the straw-boss, or the walking delegate for that matter; with the laboratory worker against the stuffed shirt in a mortarboard; with the criminal against the cop.

In *The Big Money*, Dos Passos is tender with the solitary and the dispossessed, but the radical leaders appear dehumanized, doctrinaire abstractions. The time came when Dos Passos, in his own phrase, 'rejoined the United States'. By this he did not mean that he now looked benignly upon American social conditions, but rather that he had allied himself with the central American democratic tradition, something that he along with others in his generation—digging into the country's past—found in the writings over a hundred years of Roger Williams, Benjamin Franklin, Tom Paine, Thomas Jefferson, Emerson and Whitman. Whitman, he once remarked, was 'a hell of a lot more revolutionary than any Russian poet I've ever heard of'.

The literary consequences of Dos Passos' total disenchantment with radicalism have not been happy ones: *Midcentury*, in 1963, is as ambitious as *U.S.A.*, but it is aesthetically soggy, and Dos Passos is unable to invest his historical conservative heroes (General MacArthur, Senator Robert Taft) with anything like the vitality he could bring to their forerunners. Dos Passos' integrity was absolute, and so was his consistency. Moving from radical politics to a deepening distrust of them to an enlistment in a specific American tradition, Dos Passos has in a sense never 'moved' at all. He has held fast to his sympathy for the individual, the lonely ones. But, as Daniel Aaron has said, 'he spent his talents too lavishly and too emotionally on causes he has since repudiated. He left the best of his literary self behind.'

As to the immediate present and future, I see no reason to predict major changes of imaginative direction. Most of the non-fiction writers who have come into view recently have already been named; and it is perhaps enough to say that of the two poets who have especially emerged since the War, one—Robert Lowell—came out of the poetic tradition represented by T. S. Eliot, though he has since created a voice and a stance very much his own, while the other—Stanley Kunitz—has even clearer affinities with American romanticism, with Hart Crane and even more with Whitman.

A more unusual case is that of Robert Penn Warren, who is the most distinguished American man of letters alive today. That phrase 'man of letters' should be reserved for a writer who performs on the highest level in most or all of the branches of literature, and so understood it can be applied to very few figures in American literary history: Henry James, Edith Wharton, in later years Allen Tate and Norman Mailer, as well as Warren. Warren has written a number of novels of the highest excellence (*All the King's Men* and others), several volumes of poetry (*Audubon*, in 1969), many of the most penetrating critical essays of our time, and at least one play (*Brother to Dragons*, a verse drama, based on an historical incident, which involves Thomas Jefferson in a debate about innocence and evil).

If I conclude with Warren, it is because he too exemplifies the almost inevitable development of the American writer in this century. Sooner or later in this century, the best and most energetic of our writers have discovered that what absorbs them most is America itself.

p 267 (29)

f 5

XII

AESTHETIC AMERICA

The problem of reality

HAROLD ROSENBERG

*'Any style is correct; art whether inborn
or acquired is based on knowledge
and knowledge on fact.'*

THOMAS ANSHUTZ

Absence of style,

concentration upon the object as a truer source of art than aesthetic principles or conventions, can be seen as the connecting thread running through American painting and sculpture. George Catlin's attitude is typical in this respect. For him 'the wilderness of North America', in which nature appeared 'unfettered by the disguises of art' was 'unquestionably the best study or school of art in the world'. This insistence on representing the world as it really is can be seen as part of the tradition of *reportage* that has been noted in the chapter on literature. Catlin's travels in the West in the 1830s produced some of the few authentic records of Indian life before it was destroyed. This example shows him painting the Mandan chief Mah-to-tah-pa.

This same quest for 'the real' is advanced in justification of the apparently wilful experimentation of avant-garde artists today. (1)

The intensity of the image gives a unity of feeling, not of style, to the diverse creations of American art, from the 17th century to today. On these two pages we place side by side examples from various modes – folk-art, Realism, academic painting, Expressionism – which have become 'icons of the American imagination'.

'The Peaceable Kingdom' (right) is, one of nearly fifty versions of the same subject by Edward Hicks, a self-taught Quaker sign-painter. The title is taken from Isaiah XI; in the background Hicks has placed Penn's treaty with the Indians. (2)

'The Gross Clinic' by Eakins (below), 1875, applies the realistic approach to the most harrowing of subjects. Dr Gross's bloodstained hand created a sensation, but Eakins's aim was truth, not sensationalism. (3)

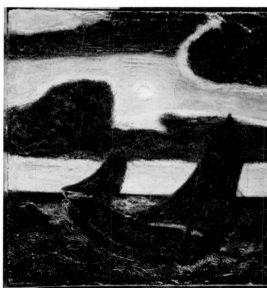

'Moonlight Marine', painted around 1900 by Albert Pinkham Ryder, conveys a visionary reality. Sea and sky are reduced to strong, simple shapes, whose heavy texture reflects the artist's emotional intensity. (4)

'**Mrs Freake and Baby Mary**' (right) by an anonymous painter of about 1674 is distinguished by strong characterization, despite the artist's inadequate technical training. (7)

'**Mrs John Montresor**' (far right) by J. S. Copley has a similar quality of forthrightness. The date is *c.* 1776–80. (8)

'**Bronco Buster**' (1895) by Frederick Remington. Remington, who had himself been a cowboy, succeeded in grasping the physical tensions of men and animals in action. (6)

'**Early Sunday Morning**' (below): the moods of the American city set down by Edward Hopper in 1930. (5)

'**The Artist's Mother**', carefully composed by Whistler of tones and spatial relations, remains a faithful mirror of its subject. (9)

In '**Woman, I**' (1950–52) by the Dutch émigré painter Willem de Kooning, immediacy of feeling brings into being the new language of Abstract Expressionism. (10)

283

The American landscape was romanticized to supply the setting for Thomas Cole's grandiose allegory of the history of mankind (1833–36). The first painting of the series (right), called *The Savage State*, shows the beginning of civilization, with a group of tents resembling Indian wigwams in the middle distance. Four other large canvases showed the scene transformed into an imperial city, like classical Rome, then sacked by barbarians and finally reduced to ruin. (12)

Careful study mixed with vivid imagination supply Audubon's watercolors of American birds with a unique directness comparable to that of folk-art. Above: the American egret (1832). (11)

The genre painters were more conscious of the tastes of their public. In Mount's *Cider Making* (1840–41) a farm scene is turned into a sentimental idyll. (13)

◄ **Truth to reality** reaches a climax in *trompe-l'oeil* paintings such as Harnett's *After the Hunt* (detail, left), exhibited in 1885. (14)

'In the Studio' (right), in its subject as in its style, reflects the ties of the artist, William Merritt Chase, with his beloved Europe. The room is filled with pictures and furniture collected on his frequent travels. It dates from about 1880 (15)

To bring the moving waters of *Niagara* to the very edge of the picture frame was a radical act in 1857. The 'rules' of composition demanded a solid foreground but to Frederick Church the subject was more important than the rules. In a similar frame of mind, Thomas Anshutz, a pupil of Eakins, described his style as 'painting what I see'; his *Steelworkers Noontime* (right) of c. 1882 takes a grim industrial subject but still cannot resist the urge to idealize the figures. (16, 19)

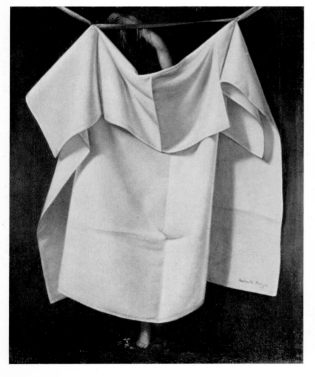

'After the Bath' plays with the socially troublesome subject of nudity by concealing an undressed figure behind a meticulously painted sheet. The artist was Raphaelle Peale, an early specialist in *trompe-l'oeil* (*After the Bath* was painted in 1823). (17)

The sea itself is the subject of Winslow Homer's *Gulf Stream*, of 1899. 'The boat and sharks', he told inquirers, 'are outside matters, of very little consequence.' Homer's beginnings were those of an illustrator of the Civil War (see p. 134). (18)

Eakins's refusal to idealize the nude led to his being expelled from the Pennsylvania Academy of Fine Arts. Above: *Masked Woman Seated.* (20)

'Backyards, Greenwich Village' by John Sloan reflects the artist's interest in the life of ordinary people. (21)

The turning point of American art came in 1913 with the Armory Show in New York. The work of avant-garde Europeans opened the way – paradoxically – for America's emancipation from Europe. As a nation without a firm aesthetic tradition, Americans were particularly qualified to 'discover the present'. This view of the show (left) includes sculpture by Brancusi and Lehmbruck; among the painters represented were Cézanne, Matisse, Picabia and Duchamp. (22)

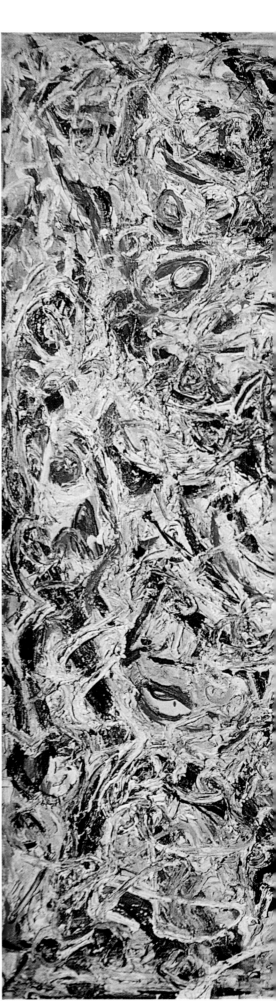

Charles Sheeler, according to his own account, took nine years 'to bail out and make a new beginning' after the Armory Show. His 'precisionist' painting *Upper Deck* (above) of 1929 approaches geometry but maintains its connection with real objects. (23)

It was Jackson Pollock who took the step which created the first distinctly American art movement – Action Painting. His *Eyes in the Heat, I* (below) of 1946 shows him on the brink of that achievement, but still retaining some links with stylistic models. During the next year, 1947, he inaugurated his technique of dripping paint on to the canvas under the guidance of 'contact' with the image that was in the process of forming itself, and without any reference to things. (24)

Mark Rothko's early works evoke a sense of mysterious, pre-civilized creation. Above: *Oil*, 1945. Later paintings go further towards abstraction, but the feeling of cosmic life remains. (25)

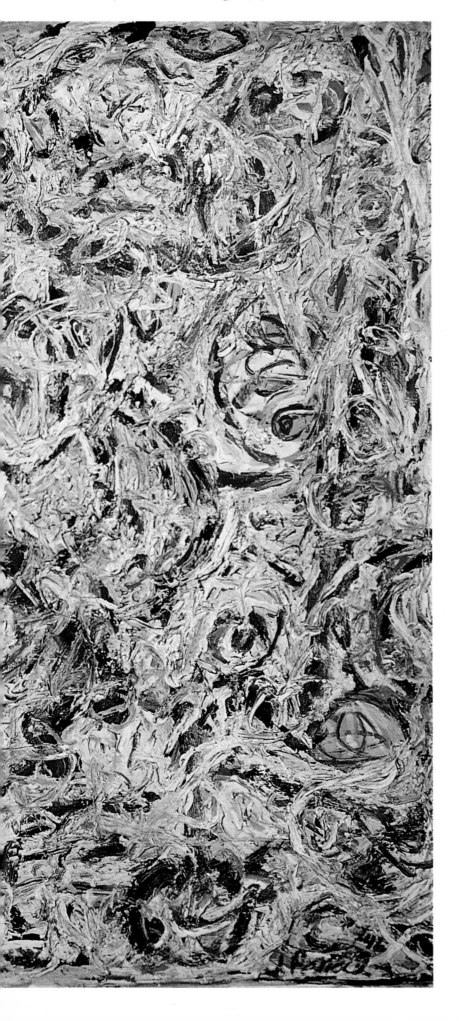

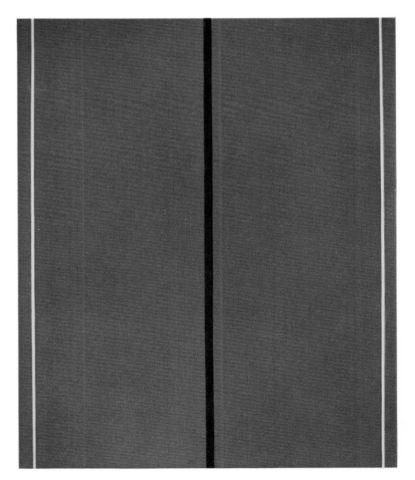

Barnett Newman took abstraction to the point of renouncing visual appeal altogether, another specifically American adventure. A painting like *Who's Afraid of Red, Yellow and Blue, II* (below), of 1967, aspires to the condition of 'pure idea'. (26)

289

Franz Kline's Action Paintings have been erroneously related to Chinese calligraphy. Below, about 1952, he uses a page from the telephone directory for his canvas. (28)

◀ **Arshile Gorky,** under the influence of European Surrealism, used semi-automatic drawing to free himself from the demands of art history. Left: *Virginia Landscape*, 1943. (27)

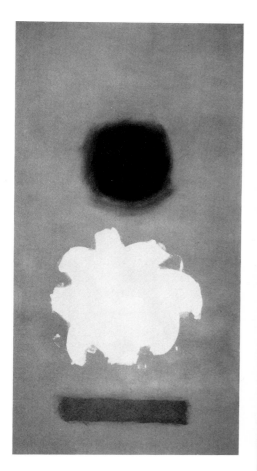

Adolph Gottlieb's effort to free himself from the European tradition led him first to primitive imagery then to a simplified symbolism of sun, earth, the sea: *Pale Splash*, 1971. (30)

David Smith's *Deserted Garden Landscape* of 1946 is composed of ambiguous forms which suggest at the same time organic growths and machinery. (29)

Barnett Newman's *Broken Obelisk* (1963–67) is a composition of triangles and rectangles that evokes, through its shape and its rust-colored surface, associations with the desert and with antiquity. (31)

291

Art and its double. Pop art turns abruptly away from abstraction not towards nature but to popular forms of art, to commerce and to technology. Earlier art is dealt with as a cliché of daily life. Below: Larry Rivers' mirror image of Manet, a three-dimensional, black and white *Olympia*. Right: Andy Warhol's multiple silk-screen image of the Pop heroine Marilyn Monroe (1962) – the crudely printed, commercial product is placed in the context of 'art' and given, if not a new meaning, a new impact. (32, 33)

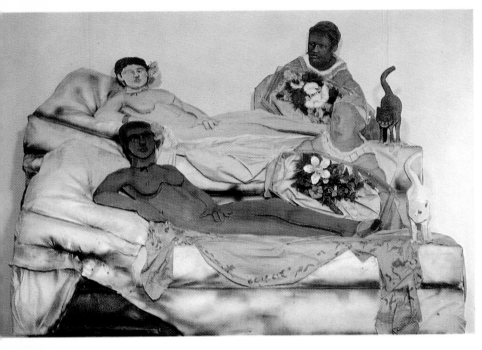

To paint the American flag as Jasper Johns has repeatedly done (in the example below, of 1958, three flags are superimposed) is another way of basing art on images familiar to everyone. Manet, Monroe, the flag, are identical in this respect. (34)

'**The Demuth Five**' by Robert Indiana (right), painted in 1963, uses a painting executed twenty-five years earlier – Charles Demuth's illustration of a poem by William Carlos Williams, reproduced on p. 264. Indiana's work appropriates stenciled commercial trade marks, but adds several sophisticated puzzles – the star and pentagon repeat 'five', but what is its relation to the five three-letter words? (35)

Technology offers artists a range of exciting new materials, which some have conceived as exclusively appropriate to the modern sensibility. Chryssa (below) in 1967 used colored neon tubes and plexiglass to make a construction of lights suggestive of an advertising sign. (36)

The levels of ambiguity in Roy Lichtenstein's *Red Painting*, 1965, are at least three: a brushstroke of oil paint is depicted as a coarse, enormously enlarged reproduction, but the picture is itself done in oil paint. It is a kind of badinage with the medium, art drawing fun out of itself. (37)

What is the museum's role in today's world? 'Harlem on my Mind' (right), an exhibition held in New York's Metropolitan Museum in 1969, involved the museum in local social problems. At the Museum of Modern Art, the Art Workers' Coalition, in 1970, staged a protest (far right) in front of Picasso's *Guernica*, pressing for art's commitment on political issues such as the war in Vietnam. (38, 39)

The dissolution of art was proclaimed at the opening exhibition of the Chicago Museum of Contemporary Art, 'Pictures to be Read, Poetry to be Seen' in 1967 (below right), at which Allan Kaprow staged a Happening. Subsequent exhibitions have included 'Art by Telephone' (below), featuring piles of dirt. (40, 41)

Junk provides the material for sculpture – as paper and bits of cloth and wood had provided materials for the collages of the Cubists. John Chamberlain uses smashed automobiles. Below: *Ruby, Ruby* of 1963. (42)

A 12-foot high banana commissioned in 1971 from Claes Oldenburg (below) by Walt Disney Productions was to unpeel mechanically and disappear as if being eaten. It went no further than the model stage. (43)

A less emotive assortment of *objets trouvés* come together in the work of Richard Stankiewicz (below, an example of 1961), offering another avenue of escape from 'high' style. (44)

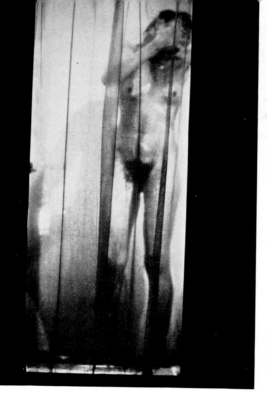

'Shower' by Robert Whitman consists of a real shower-curtain, the recorded noise of a shower, and the film image of a naked girl projected from behind the curtain. (45)

Clean smooth forms succeeded junk at the end of the sixties. Above right: a rationally calculated wooden structure by Ronald Bladen, made in 1971. (46)

Art in the street: this painted sidewalk (right) in New York was commissioned by gallery owners from Alexander Calder. (47)

The fairground imagery of Red Grooms's *City of Chicago*, 1968 (above) represents an attempt similar to that of Pop to draw 'low-style' visual experience into the net of art. (48)

Earthworks art returns to reality as such. Robert Smithson's *Spiral Jetty* (right) of 1970 projects into the Great Salt Lake in Utah. The causeway is about 15 feet broad and 1500 feet in length. (49)

Arguably the outstanding painting of 20th-century America, de Kooning's *Excavation* was completed in 1950 after strenuous months of making and un-making. Six feet eight inches by eight feet four inches, the canvas crowds invention upon invention, and in its austere solidity is like the conclusion of an almost unendurable drama. (50)

This Japanese-inspired garden by Isamu Noguchi was commissioned by IBM for their headquarters in New York – an example of patronage by a large business firm. The work reflects a complicated symbolic program expressing 'science and mankind's future'. (51)

The problem of reality

HAROLD ROSENBERG

ADVANCED modernist modes in art have been publicly accepted in the United States only since the middle of 1950. Yet with a speed typical of the transformation of attitudes among Americans, aesthetic avant-gardism now dominates production, exhibition, collecting and education in the fine arts. Earlier European experimental movements, from Neo-Impressionism to Constructivism and Surrealism, have been comfortably domesticated and, beginning with Abstract Expressionism and Action Painting, America, for the first time in its history, has proved capable of adding innovating modes of its own. The flood of aesthetic novelties has realized itself socially in the organization of new modern-art museums and the expansion of older ones, vastly enlarged museum and art-gallery attendance, multiplication of art dealers, art collectors and specialists in art-handling and explication, regular art features in the press and broadcasting, establishment of studio and history of modern art courses in universities, formation of state art councils and business committees to promote public support of the arts, and, finally, fine-arts appropriations by the Federal government. Most recent developments have included a phenomenal increase in the making and acquisition of lithographs, silkscreen prints and multiples, the organization of bank-backed international art-dealing syndicates and the publication of art investment-counseling bulletins.

In contrast to the socially alienated bohemianism out of which advanced art had sprung for the past one hundred years, art in America has increasingly taken on the features of a recognized profession. A major aspect of contemporary painting and sculpture in the United States is its mental and psychological orderliness, its rationale of conception, execution and social function. Although conservative middle-class aesthetic preferences have been superseded, much of America's new art appeals to middle-class tidiness and sense of intellectual security. In art modes prominent in the 1960s—Optical art, 'color field' painting, Constructivist and

p 247
(46)

Minimalist sculpture—individual emotion and sensibility are programmatically shunned in favor of aesthetic and technical systems. The ideal of art as embodying unique insights is denounced as outdated Romanticism, and works are conceived as artifacts made according to preconceived plans. It is consistent with the new objective professionalism that sculptures should no longer be made 'by hand' in the artist's studio but fabricated in machine or carpentry shops, and that paintings should be enlarged and re-processed in industrial materials.

The success of modernism in American art represents a revolutionary transformation of its relation to the European cultural past. Up to the war, American painting and sculpture were haunted by the masterpieces of Greece, Rome, and the Renaissance and, to some extent, the School of Paris, and bound by the versions of these taught in the academies: to political radicals in the 1930s anti-war painting meant copying Goya. Charles Willson Peale sounded the note of this dependence in a letter written before the American Revolution: 'A good painter of either portrait or History must be well acquainted with Grecian and Roman statues, to be able to draw them at pleasure from memory, and account for every beauty in all he sees.' There was a European, or a potential European inside every American artist, and aesthetic cultivation consisted in the subduing of the raw American by his alien *alter ego*.

A typical item in the biographies of American painters relates that, after the artist had trained himself by studying nature, copying engravings of European masters and following manuals on drawing and composition, some businessmen of the city, 'impressed by his talent', raised money to send him abroad to acquire polish. 'My God,' exclaimed William Merritt Chase in the 1870s when he was offered the opportunity to study in Europe, 'I'd rather go to Europe than to heaven.' As late as the 1920s the Jewish immigrant in New York City's East Side who wanted to become an artist was sent to Paris to learn how to paint like an American. Art in America was a European thing. Almost a hundred years after Chase's paean, Willem de Kooning testified to a similar view as to where art was domiciled. 'We never heard in Holland', he told an interviewer, 'that there were artists in America. There was still the feeling that this was where an individual could get places and become well off, if he worked hard—while art, naturally, was in Europe.'

p 287
(15)

Aware of its historical handicap, American art was preoccupied with the ideal: it sought to overleap time by seizing the essence of Beauty in the masterpieces of the past. Searching for the aesthetic philosopher's stone, American artists, from the birth of the Republic, landed in the academies of London, Rome, Munich and Paris. The European vanguard movements of the second half of the 19th century reached the Americans late and usually in a diluted form—such exceptions as Mary Cassatt and James Whistler were sufficiently expatriated to be considered Europeans.

p 285 (9)

'Make it new'

The conservatism of American art was dramatically disclosed at the Armory Show held in New York in 1913—perhaps the most decisive single event in the history of American painting and sculpture. The exhibition, whose official title was the International Exhibition of Modern Art, began a process which terminated in nothing less than changing the relation of American art to art history. Displaying, among others, Cézanne, Matisse, Brancusi, Picabia and, above all, Marcel Duchamp, the exhibition made clear that the issue of art in the revolutionary 20th century was no longer that of adding to the list of Great Works but, as Baudelaire had conceived it, of discovering the present. In effect, the Armory Show challenged the Americans to place themselves culturally on the same plane as their European contemporaries.

p 290
(22)

Once having taken this position the Americans, far from being crippled by their lack of tradition, had certain advantages, if largely negative ones. They might be incapable of creating a new aesthetic culture, but they were especially equipped to explore the conditions of living without one—a condition toward which the peoples of the globe seemed headed. American objects lacked the dimension of long human association, but the industrial world would cause this to be the norm everywhere. The poet Rilke was to point out that 'a house in the American understanding, an American apple, or a grapevine there, has nothing in common with the house, the fruit, the grape into which went the hopes and meditations of our forefathers.' But Rilke added, 'We are perhaps the last still to know such things.' The very object-ness of American objects made them symbols of the 20th century. 'To detach a fact from its origins', wrote the French philosopher Levinas, 'is precisely to live in the modern world.'

'*The Greek Slave*', *an idealized statue by Hiram Powers (1805–73), was shown at the London Crystal Palace Exhibition in 1851, along with other* '*American notions*', *and attracted a great deal of attention. (1)*

p 290
(23)

Between the two world wars, American painters endeavored to live up to Ezra Pound's slogan 'make it new', which already prevailed in American poetry. Charles Sheeler noted that after he first met the works of the Europeans shown at the Armory, it took him nine years 'to bail out and make a new beginning.' The 1920s was the decade of the American artist in Paris, the 1930s of the artist as a social radical active in programs to change the world politically. From both the aesthetic Left Bank and the political Left Front, the American painter acquired an awareness of history, and of the fact that art and society could be changed to meet the needs of the time. By the 1940s, a generation of younger artists had learned to trust their sensibilities as the measure of what was vital in painting, regardless of its date or place of origin. Thus Arshile Gorky found support for abstract art in Uccello; Adolph Gottlieb, Mark Rothko and Barnett Newman discovered suggestive signs in the pictographs of the American Indians and in pre-Christian art; Pollock began with magical emblems based on Mexican art and moved on to those of his own unconscious. The founders of the new American painting might have exclaimed with Whitman, 'As if it were necessary to trot back generation after generation to the eastern records!'

p 291–2
(25–27)

p 293
(30)

p 290–91
(24)

Not only did American art cease to look to Europe for models but, in a historical development of incalculable consequence, the United States itself became after the war the primary source of aesthetic innovation for the art capitals of the world. Not that New York replaced prewar Paris, as some observers maintain; rather that, having shaken off the uneasy conviction of cultural inferiority, American painters took the lead in dealing with the problems of creating art in the new global situation in which regional and national traditions were being demolished. After all, the inhabitants of 'the melting pot' were the most experienced people in the world in regard to just such a demolition of older cultures.

p 44–5
(13)

Along with the collapse of the European standard came a decline in the prestige of the American gentry who had represented that standard. Since Colonial times, American paintings and sculpture

had had to contend with the tastes and notions of propriety of the American middle class. Paintings that might be emotionally upsetting—such as Vanderlyn's of the tomahawking of Jane McCrea —were rarities in American fine art (though not in popular picture making). As the catalogue of a recent Metropolitan Museum survey of American painting and sculpture points out, violence is an aspect of American life that 'most artists governed by 19th-century ideas of suitability and decorum, chose not to emphasize'. The same was true of nakedness, a fact wittily commented on by Raphaelle Peale in his well-known *After the Bath*, which presents a presumably undressed lady completely concealed behind a *trompe l'œil* hanging.

p 288
(17)

America was reflected in its painting and sculpture only to the extent that its features were found acceptable in the drawing room. The wild vistas, country folk and daily objects and activities of uncultivated America entered art under a veil of idealism or in costumes of theatrical quaintness. There is an air of self-conscious posing not only about the people but even the countryside. For Thomas Cole, 'father of American landscape painting', scenic grandeur was given the added pomp of serving as a setting for allegories of the death of civilization and the Ages of Man. George Caleb Bingham's *The Concealed Enemy* is pure grand opera, and the figures, including the captive bear cub in his *Fur Traders Descending the Missouri*—probably the most frequently reproduced painting of mid-19th-century America—face the spectator, the old trader with a sour grimace, his son with an inviting smile, as if reacting to the interest in them of the art-loving public. The huge landscapes of the Hudson River School pardonably swagger, as their overpowering distances are accentuated by microscopic human beings spotlighted in a corner of the composition or near the bottom. In Asher Brown Durand's *Kindred Spirits* a painting like a colored engraving that is a favorite in histories of American art, Cole, standing on a rock platform with a pointer in his hand, lectures his companion, William Cullen Bryant, and the spectator of the painting, too, on the transcendent significance of the scene.

p 13 (
p 286-
(12)

In contrast to the romantic landscapists, the genre painters bring their figures closer to the picture plane, in order to identify them as country types. In the left foreground of William Sidney Mount's *Cider Making*, a young girl gazes tenderly at a youth, who, however, is more concerned with the impression he is making on the person standing in front of the painting than with his admirer, while a girl and a boy sitting on a rail in the background also keep their eyes fixed on the onlooker. The theatricality of American landscape and genre painting is magnified by the fondness of the painters for sharp highlighting and deep shadows calculated to bring out the contours and textures of every fold of sleeve, pebble, leaf and water ripple. This mode of painting, which the historians call luminism, with its smooth, glossy and thinly pigmented surface, comes close to printed illustrations and reproductions, and it anticipates color photography. Magnificent exceptions to the audience-conscious art of the time are Audubon's birds and an occasional landscape, such as Frederic Church's *Niagara*, whose uneven paint thicknesses are rhythmically modulated to match the swirlings and stillnesses of the waters. For Thomas Eakins, America's greatest realistic painter of the 19th century, freedom from coercion by the art public demanded open defiance of it, and his refusal to stylize (i.e. idealize) his nudes, in the manner, for example, of Hiram Powers's *The Greek Slave*, made him a scandal to his neighbors and led to his ouster from the Pennsylvania Academy of Fine Arts.

p 286
(13)

p 286
(11)

p 288
(16)

p 289
(20)

The Armory Show and the turn of American artists towards avant-gardism were the signal for a shift from reliance upon the monied and conservative sponsors of portraits and landscapes (to whom the show was an abomination) to a newly emerging public favorable to innovation. Less a public than a cult, this avant-garde audience has, despite profound changes in the past half-century, retained traces of its original dedication to a cause—the cause of the New. It is a curious amalgam of international financiers and businessmen, society and fashion leaders, upper and lower bohemians, art-world and mass-communication professionals, academic radicals, united by an alertness to novelty more or less essential in the practice of their vocations. Hospitable to unfamiliar images and ideas, even to shock, and to moral and intellectual permissiveness coupled with a new kind of conformism,

p 290
(22, 2

this cult keeps expanding, continually augmented by the crowds inducted by educational programs and the mass media, into the mysteries of modernism. The growth of the vanguard audience has submerged, apparently forever, the remnants of the old socially cohesive, upper-class tastemakers. For all its intellectual limitations and its susceptibility to fads and catchwords, the new aesthetic leadership undoubtedly represents the most sophisticated sensibility of contemporary America, and its recently acquired authority with respect to the physical forms of things—from beach costumes and house furnishings to public monuments—constitutes a cultural revolution of the first magnitude.

The recession from style

Such a revolution has to do, first of all, with style, and it is in regard to style that developments in American art go to the heart of the changing social character of the nation. Since the beginning of American painting the question of style has been a passionate issue, if a partly hidden one. In transforming visual experience to conform to dominant conventions, style has a political dimension; it reinforces the norms of existing social authority and renders invisible data, qualities and moods inimical to those norms. A

popular synonym for style is 'class', and if style in 19th-century America meant 'suitability and decorum', an opposite strain condemned style as fashion and falsification. The need to break through the barrier of manner in order to reach the new American fact kept cropping up among naives and self-taught craftsmen as well as among the most thoroughly European-educated professionals. From George Catlin, painter of Indians, through Thomas Eakins and the early 20th-century 'Ashcan School', the alternative to aesthetic artifice has been 'nature as is'.

p 281 (1)
p 284 (3)
p 289
(20, 21)

'Black and blue cloth and civilization', wrote Catlin, 'are destined not only to veil but to obliterate the grace and beauty of Nature', and he went on to argue that 'the wilderness of North America', in which man appeared 'unfettered by the disguises of art', was 'unquestionably the best study or school of art in the world'. Here, Chase's conception of Europe as the heavenly destination of the American artist is met by the counter-sentiment that to be in America is already to be in heaven. Catlin's statement is a way of testifying, as did Whitman, that everything in the American landscape, just as one finds it, is art, or something higher than art: Beauty. In today's aesthetics the found, non-art object or random fact is similarly considered to be art in that it transcends

'Anshutz on Anatomy', by John Sloan (1871–1951). Several members of a group of realist painters called 'The Eight' were taught by Thomas

Anshutz in night classes at the Pennsylvania Academy of Fine Arts. Sloan himself, Glackens and Henri, among others, are seen in this etching. (2)

299

style. Instead of Beauty the unstyled object possesses today the quality of being *New*—a mystery equivalent to Beauty in the modern historical consciousness.

Fashionable academicism in 19th-century America is complemented by a realism that defies style. In the eye-fooling still-lifes of Harnett, Peto, Haberle and others, the magical illusion of things the spectator can touch—a frayed banknote, a letter in a rack, a dead bird—reaches past style to the wonder shared by people of all social classes at seeing nature duplicated on a flat surface. The *trompe l'œil* artist could dispense with both an individual manner and formal conceptions of composition, drawing, color harmony in favor of a kind of side-show performance—Harnett's rabbit with red bullet holes in its white fur is like a rabbit pulled out of a hat by a magician. The verisimilitude of this kind of painting in rendering everyday things relates it to the waxworks museum, the stereoscope, the photograph and other forms of popular visual entertainment. In its informational aspect, it falls into the tradition of the illustrators who accompanied the first exploring expeditions in the New World of Audubon and Catlin, of the sketch artists of the Civil War, of the magazine illustrations of Winslow Homer, of the front-line draftsman of World War II and of current travel and court-trial visual reporting.

p 287
(14)

p 15 (8)

p 110
(11)
f 3

Academically trained Americans also exalted visual fact as possessing its own style or providing a substitute for style. 'What I mean by truth in a painting', wrote Thomas Anshutz, 'is as follows: Get up an outfit for outdoor work, go out to some woe-begotten, turkey chawed, bottle-nosed, henpecked country and set myself down, get out my materials and make as accurate a painting of what I see in front of me as I can. If I draw it well and color it as I see it and if I see it well (which is the hardest part) my pictures is true . . . so my style now is painting and drawing what I see.' It is surely interesting that Anshutz, who studied in academies both in the United States and abroad, and who replaced Eakins as a teacher at the Pennsylvania Academy, adopts a folk dialect to state his credo, and maintains a makeshift approach to style hardly different from that of the folk artist, the self-taught artist, and artists with purpose beyond art such as Audubon and Catlin—all of whom rank high in American painting because their visual testimony can be trusted. As Anshutz summarized his view twenty years after the statement quoted above, 'Any style is correct . . . art whether inborn or acquired is based on knowledge and knowledge on fact.'

p 289
(19)

f 2

Anshutz's 'any style is correct' is a radical affirmation that in America no inherited style exists, and that style is an individual quality that comes into being through the activity of each artist. Traditional styles in painting are extensions of styles outside of painting—for example, Elizabethan portraiture resembles the masklike Elizabethan physiognomy and the habitual concealment of character traits recorded in literature. Colonial Boston is a 'work of art' in the British mode, the Hudson Valley in the Dutch. Robert Feke's *General Samuel Waldo* is posed like a manikin, but there is reason to assume that Feke's mid-18th-century gentleman resembled a manikin, at least in public. Copley acquired his British-related style in New England less through knowledge of British painting than through careful study of his models during unusually numerous sittings—with the change in the style of New Englanders after the Revolution, Copley had no successors.

p 285 (8)

Both in life and in art, America has been receding from style since Colonial times. The firmest style in the history of American painting is Colonial portraiture, with its strongly contoured images of strongly contoured souls. Later, outlines soften in both paintings and sitters, as in Eastman Johnson's *The Funding Bill*, a painting of two late-19th-century worthies suffused in moral chiaroscuro. Once the original settlements had been left behind, the choice for the artist was either to adopt a manner temporarily fashionable abroad or to ignore style in favor of 'knowledge based on facts'. The common solution was to vacillate between the demands of art and the truths of nature. Even Bingham, pre-eminent among painters who converted the American scene into taste-satisfying pictures, and whose ambition for high style led him, when he was already a successful and mature painter, to study for several years at Düsseldorf, was convinced that art was inferior to reality, though on the rather simple-minded basis that in paintings things don't

p 13 (1)

move or make noise—a deficiency rectified in contemporary American art by kinetic images and tape recordings.

A frontier is not a landscape—Gainsborough could not have painted it. Nor, since the Civil War and industrialization, is the American city. For generations, the American countryside and town have been raw scene, and this becomes increasingly the case each decade, as the land fills up with ruins left by logging and strip mining, oil derricks, rivers of factory discharges, superhighways, business and university building complexes, military installations, advertising billboards. The American outdoors acquires style only when style is imposed upon it. The alternative is the snapshot ('facts'), whose a-formal features began to appear in American painting long before the invention of the camera. In the panoramas of the Hudson River School the edges of the canvas are simply limits, like those of the camera lens, by which the scene is cut off; they do not denote a space to be composed. The painter of the American scene applies his technique to whatever holds promise as a 'good subject', either to satisfy his idea of art or to attract the public. For him the relation of form to the spectacle depicted is as fortuitous as the relation of a tractor to the site marked for an excavation; 'any style is correct' so long as the spectator 'gets the picture'.

p 114
(24)
p 220
(53)

History, too, in this discontinuous setting is a quantity, an expanse of uncomposed happenings, as in the endless cycloramas done in the 19th century depicting Indian battles or events of the Civil War. Segments of the recently discovered scenic roll by Carl Christian Anton Christensen, a Mormon, which was designed to illustrate his lectures on the principal events of the first decades of his cult, owe their power to pictorial and formal improvisations separately conceived by the artist to convey each incident, and without the aid of any overall style.

p 64 (1

The best examples of American painting and sculpture consist of individual creations, the value of which lies not in their stylistic distinction but in the intensity of their images, like an obsessive dream or memory. *Mrs Freake and Baby Mary*, a limner's portrait of a dressed-up dummy clutching a dressed-up doll, John Singleton Copley's aristocratic *Mrs John Montresor*, Audubon's birds, Mount's *Eel Spearing at Setauket*, Edward Hicks's *The Peaceable Kingdom*, Winslow Homer's *The Gulf Stream*, Whistler's mother, Eakins's *The Gross Clinic*, Frederick Remington's *Bronco Buster*, Hopper's *Early Sunday Morning*, Willem de Kooning's *Woman I* mingle on equal terms as icons of the American imagination.

p 284–
(2–10)
p 286
(11)
p 288
(18)

With style an individual matter, or an import soon superseded by a newer import, American art has a fragmented history, not unlike folk art, which is inherently lacking in development. (Survey exhibitions of American art ought therefore to combine painting and sculpture with folk decorations and even with popular art and kitsch.) Audubon, for instance, one of America's most consummate artists, is much closer to folk art than to his academically oriented contemporaries; even more than Christensen, his formal inventions arise from singular responses to his subjects. American genre painters frequently began as engravers and sign painters, and works by them often differ from Currier & Ives prints only in being done in oil on canvas and in being less visually incisive. As noted above, the *trompe l'œil* still-lifes of Harnett and others also exist on the edge of popular art.

p 286
(11)
p 64 (1

p 287
(19)

In stressing that 'seeing well' is the 'hardest part' in painting realistically, Anshutz acknowledged the force of style in controlling the reflex of the eye, as well as the action of the hand. American visual reality has tended to vanish somewhere between the 'henpecked country' and the salon. On-the-spot sketches and drawings were more likely to escape the intervention of aesthetic recasting than full-dress oil paintings. Some of Cole's tiny studies for landscapes have firmer structure and better distribution of light and tonal values than his huge chromos. The longer the American painter worked on his canvases the more his aesthetic ideal bled through the retinal fact. In his way of finishing his picture he revealed his notion of Great Art and succumbed to it.

p 286–
(12)

In actuality American art, before the beginning of this century, rarely broke through style to the American visual reality—exceptions might include Eakins's *Max Schmitt in a Single Scull*, some of the more photographic oils and watercolors of Winslow Homer (of whom Henry James said that 'things came already

A drawing of a cavalryman by Winslow Homer (1836–1910), one of a series of sketches drawn for 'Harper's Weekly' during the Civil War, when he was with the troops at the front. He later turned to painting, and continued to depict men of action as well as landscapes and the sea. (3)

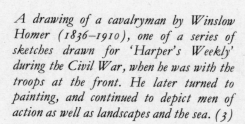

284 (4)

20–21
(21)

modeled to his eye' but that the result was 'horribly ugly'), and the inner visions of Albert Ryder. Instead of discovering America, American artists discovered art on the American continent—that is to say, scenic effects in any style the artist might admire, as tourists have found their choice in Alps, fjords and Saharas. Speaking of a group of early American painters who settled in East Hampton, Long Island, in the 1870s (they included William Merrit Chase, who had preferred Europe to heaven), Van Wyck Brooks noted that they had chosen this spot for its English lanes, Dutch windmills and meadows of Brittany, and concluded that 'they could see America only when they saw it as European.' From wilderness to tourist paradise America has retained the scenic versatility of a theatrical lumber room. Jacques Le Moyne, one of the first artists to leave a record of America, painted the Florida

Indians in the middle of the 16th century as if they were French courtiers inhabiting an Oriental harem. Mansions along the Hudson took on the shape of castles on the Rhine, and to this day a house in Aspen, Colorado, becomes, inevitably, a Swiss chalet. In the realistic 1930s, girls on Union Square were given the look of ballet dancers by Degas in costumes from Klein's bargain basement, and in West Coast figure paintings of the 1950s people on a porch looking out on the Pacific basked in the light of Bonnard. The American artist has browsed through his native land in search of his conception of art, not unlike the vacationist who snaps the shutter of his camera when he spots a scene that resembles a picture postcard. Aiming at a museum piece, the painter has copied segments of the American landscape that come closest to museum pieces. The actual countryside has served much the same function as the models which some realistic artists—e.g. Thomas Benton, Ivan Albright—have built to reproduce on their canvases. American pictorial reality has tended to be the aesthetic modification of an artifice.

To disentangle New World fact, physical and mental, from forms inherited from Europe, the most strenuous efforts have been required—efforts by no means concluded today. The wrestle with style is the dynamic of America's postwar aesthetic revolution. The powerfully influential teachings of Hans Hofmann in New York and Provincetown from the early 1930s through the 1950s were epitomized in his program of 'learning to see' and his rejection of the use of reproductions and slides of great paintings in the classroom. For Hofmann good painting would come directly from accurate seeing in accordance with correct principle, without help from the masters, new or old—an approach different in content but similar in attitude to Eakins's scientism. Some pioneers of the new American painting—Gottlieb, Rothko, Still—polemicized against surrender to European influences and, as noted above, sought an independent idiom in primitive art. The late David Smith summed up the still-prevailing suspiciousness toward European artificiality in a latter-day variation on Catlin and Anshutz. 'Provincialism or coarseness or unculture', wrote Smith in 1953, 'is greater for creating art than finesse or polish Creative art has a better chance of developing from coarseness and courage than from culture. One of the good things about American art is that it doesn't have the spit and polish that some foreign art has. It is coarse.'

To eradicate the last traces of European sensibility, which he found surviving even in the extreme abstraction of Mondrian and the Neo-Plasticists, the late Barnett Newman went so far as to propose an art without visual appeal and, claiming that Americans were 'at home in the world of the pure idea', he called for works that evoked 'an experienced moment of total reality'. Newman was to become the major influence in American art of the sixties. Arshile Gorky, for years helpless in the grip of his European models—Cézanne, Picasso, Miró—finally released himself into a vocabulary of his own through semi-automatic drawings executed in the fields of Virginia. Jackson Pollock eluded the pressure of stylistic models through by-passing the process of conscious shaping—he gave himself up to guidance by 'contact' with the canvas, and his celebrated observation, 'When I am *in* my painting, I am not aware of what I am doing' was followed by the conclusion, 'I am nature', which eludes the problem of stylization faced by those who study nature's appearances. De Kooning, denouncing style on historical grounds, took its social role into account and extended his condemnation to the European avant-garde movements. 'Style is a fraud', asserted this veteran of eight years' study at the Rotterdam Academy of Fine Arts and Techniques. 'It was a horrible idea of Van Doesburg and Mondrian to try to force a style. The reactionary strength of power is that it keeps style and things going. Actually, there *is* no style in painting now. The desire to make a style is an apology for one's anxiety.' At length, de Kooning arrived in his paintings at an explicit practice of 'no-style'.

The end of art history

Catlin's 'grace and beauty of Nature', Anshutz's 'any style', Pollock's 'contact', de Kooning's 'no-style', *Mrs Freake and Baby Mary*, Hicks's *The Peaceable Kingdom*, Eakins's *The Gross Clinic*, Jasper Johns's American flags, Warhol's silk screen serials of Marilyn Monroe snapshots, Newman's *Who's Afraid of Red, Yellow and Blue*, Kaprow's released balloons, Red Grooms's cut-outs of early movie stars—these ideas, images and doings coalesce in today's conviction that anything is art that is accredited by art history, which includes Dadaist anti-art and Surrealist non-art. The art object is suspended in a web of references to earlier art—a web woven partly of the works themselves, partly of the words that interpret these works. Why is a Happening primarily art, not theater? Because the Happening was born out of the history of painting, not out of the history of drama, specifically out of the idea of Action Painting.

A pivotal figure in contemporary American painting and sculpture is Marcel Duchamp, star-villain of the Armory Show, whose display of an object obtainable in plumbing supply houses redefined works of art as artifacts of modern civilization, a definition that conforms to the outlook of cultural anthropology. In this perspective, current art is seen as if from some point in the future, when all the ideas and associations that distinguish a painting from other images, objects and events produced in contemporary society will have faded away and only its physical traces remain. With Duchamp's 'ready-made', art as a separate category of objects has ceased to exist.

This is another way of saying that the history of art has come to an end. Past styles no longer point toward future ones. The act of the artist intervenes as an aesthetically arbitrary fact between one work and another. People continue to create, of course, but the formal qualities established by centuries of painting have disintegrated into the aesthetics of objects unrelated to art. Painting exists as one means among many by which individuals assert their relation to the general concept 'art'. Inherent in all the significant postwar art movements is the breakdown of barriers between art and life. An outstanding place in the past quarter of a century is reserved for works accelerating the breakdown—they range from Pollock's 'drips' to Les Levine's 'disposables'.

As the sole arbiter of what shall be displayed and discussed as art, art history has entered into a crisis of self-consciousness related to the break in continuity of art itself. The historian's tracing of the stylistic relations among works (including works lacking in style) becomes the power to magnify their effect upon the future or to nullify it. But this very power of art history to intervene in the shaping of art undermines its stability as a form of knowledge. Like the political historian, the art historian has been recast into a maker of history, not merely a narrator of past events. In his freedom to participate in determining the direction of art he has become an agitator. Since art movements in our time arise more out of ideas about art than out of admired works (for example, Cubism out of Cézanne's methods, rather than imitation of his paintings), the account of these movements cannot avoid being interpretative and partisan. Every major period-survey exhibition presented in the past two decades—the 'Toward a New Abstraction' exhibition at the Jewish Museum, the exhibition on 'The 1930's' at the Whitney in New York, the exhibition on 'The 1960's' at the New York Museum of Modern Art, the 'New York School' at the Los Angeles County Museum, the 'New York Painting and Sculpture: 1940–1970' exhibition at the Metropolitan Museum, to name but a few—has been a more or less aggressive use of art history in an attempt to direct future creation in the United States. In that its contemporary subject-matter lacks definition and is contingent on ideology, the history of art has drawn to a close.

The new American scene is either an after-image imprinted on the mind by the mass media (for example, magazine photos and movies of glamorous mountains, lakes and shorelines, or of rat-infested slums); or it is actually man-made (for example, highway systems, shopping centers, airports). In the imagination the landscape, the communications media version of it, and industrial construction and damage introduced into it become inseparable. The made American world, discovered in the early 20th century by the Henri group of big-city reportorial draftsmen, was recaptured as a motif in more trenchant form by American Pop painters and sculptors, and has been investigated along other lines by Op artists, Constructivists, lights artists and kineticists. Art as cultural anthropology recognizes itself inescapably as an extension of the physical and social scene. One of the current art movements, Earth Art, disdains to produce an 'art object'—'the artist', declares a spokesman, 'is not in competition with other artists but with everything in the environment.' Verbal and photographic descriptions of what an artist has experienced and conceived are taken as preferable to art products, which by their nature imply emphasis on aesthetic purposes. The utilitarian strain in American painting and sculpture, from 'views' of the first settlements and village shop signs to modern advertising art, reaches its culmination in the current self-affirmation of the artist as a reporter of facts and ideas. The filtration between the arts and the communications media becomes continuous, as exemplified in a recent exhibition at the Museum of Modern Art entitled 'Information'. The adulteration of forms and intermixing of the arts to create an 'environment' for the spectator, or to make him aware of his actual environment,

p 291
(25)
p 293
(30)
p 292
(29)
p 291
(26)
p 292
(27)
p 290–91
(24)
p 285
(10)
p 298
(50)
p 294
(33)
p 291
(26)
p 297
(48)
p 296
(41)
p 114
(24)
p 163
(33)
p 297
(49)
f 4

```
PROPOSAL FOR WALL DRAWING, INFORMATION SHOW



Within four adjacent souares,

each 4' by 4',

four draftsmen will be employed

at $4.00/hour

for four hours a day

and for four days to draw straight lines

4 inches long

using four different colored pencils;

9H black, red, yellow and blue.

Each draftsmen will use the same color throughout

the four day period,

working on a different square each day.
```

The description of the work takes the place of the work itself: an example of conceptual art by Sol Le Witt, entitled 'Proposal for Wall Drawing', from 'Information', an exhibition held in New York in 1970. (4)

constitutes the kind of advanced development that is beyond stylistic evaluation, hence outside the compass of art history.

The traditional notion of the high arts (museum art) as holding the commercial, popular and folk arts at bay has ceased to apply and is being abandoned. Mass production and distribution, the identifying characteristic of the media, exert an increasingly powerful pull on painting and sculpture. In addition to the surging interest in prints and multiples mentioned earlier, reproductions of paintings in magazines, books, exhibition catalogues and announcements play an ever-larger role in the studio, and in the appreciation of art and in art education than the paintings themselves. As for art history, its present intellectual character is entirely determined by its almost exclusive perusal of reproductions and slides.

The rapid popularization of American postwar avant-garde art is unquestionably indebted in large part to the dissemination of reproductions of the works, and of explanations of them, through large-circulation news and fashion magazines, TV programs and other organs of popular education. In the 1950s American painting and sculpture entered, for the first time, into the mass media *system*; since then they have been a regular ingredient of the world communications package.

'Burn the museums!'

The passage of art out of the separated realm of the history of styles into interaction with industrial and social phenomena and current events has introduced a perilous imbalance in museums of modern art. As the physical embodiment of art history, the museum has been the supreme authority by which contemporary works have been accredited as art. What is art goes into the museum, what goes into the museum is art. The soup-can label is the product of a professional designer and is calculated to stimulate the eye and the appetite through color and form. The label, however, exists outside the museum and is not art—until a Pop artist by slight alteration brings it into harmony with past events in art—for example, with Dada gesture and Art Nouveau design—at which point the label passes from the grocery shelf to the museum wall. Applying the aesthetic of displacement established by Duchamp, the museum proclaims a work to be art by means of its cultural location.

Besides its function of art-historical discrimination, however, the museum has become a mechanism of mass education and enter-

tainment; in keeping with this new role it can no longer be oriented toward the past, toward excavating works of earlier periods and arranging them in accordance with principles of sound historical interconnection. To arouse interest in the museum audience by appearing relevant to modern life, masterworks of all times must be put forward as *news*. Far from being a final resting place for creations that constitute the standards of art, the museum is compelled to activate all works as novelties capable of intriguing an ever-expanding self-engrossed public.

As its role as a mass medium disseminating cultural propaganda becomes unmistakable, the museum is increasingly pressed to change its identity by abandoning its scholarly and art-critical functions and rededicating itself as a mass-educational and community service center for visual novelties and neighborhood beautification projects. Ambitious for avant-garde status, museum staffs often take the lead in proposing to liquidate the preferred status of painting and sculpture. The Chicago Museum of Contemporary Art opened in 1967 with an exhibition by artists who had proclaimed the end of art and the inutility of museums, and with a statement by its director to the effect that painting and sculpture no longer represent vital forms in the latter decade of the 20th century. A participant in the exhibition, Allan Kaprow, founder of Happenings, had denounced museums as 'a fuddy-duddy remnant from another era that ought to be turned into swimming pools and night clubs . . . or . . . emptied and left as environmental sculpture'. The crime of the museum, according to Kaprow, was the old American complaint that it set paintings and sculpture apart from the rest of nature. p 296 (38) p 296 (41)

In the face of rising attacks on institutional culture, American museums today seem willing to go all the way with Kaprow, stopping just short of not existing. With the elimination of middle-class cultural patterns and values, the populist tradition is in strong ascendancy—perhaps it has already won a final victory. The present stress of the institutions is on informality and popular demand—jazz concerts in the sculpture courts, discothèque dancing, kinetic shows for the kids—and they exercise profound caution to avoid enveloping paintings and sculptures in an aura of high culture or setting art apart from anything. The prevailing sentiment is that in a democracy nothing ought to exist, at least in public, that is not for everyone. 'Elitism' is firmly repudiated (though this has not obliterated manifestations of the old genteel snobbery). The very idea of art is challenged in the name of cultural egalitarianism. Art is conceived as a kind of protean, or catch-all, mass medium that flows into the gaps between the more stabilized media, such as motion pictures and broadcasting.

A recent interview on TV with the then director of the Museum of Modern Art provided a synthesis, or dictionary, of the accepted ideas underlying the behavior of museums, from the Metropolitan's 'Harlem on My Mind' exhibition to artist/industry collaboration arranged by the Los Angeles County Museum. p 296 (38) p 296 (43)

In reply to a question as to 'what people should experience in museums', the spokesman for the Museum of Modern Art declared that 'first of all it ought to be fun', and he added that spectators might also obtain in the Museum 'some sort of visual experience that they may not get anywhere else' (presumably, an underwater expedition would qualify). Having conceded its evolution into a mass medium, including the profit-making aspect for what the Museum of Art director called 'the club' of trustees, collectors and an insider group of artists and dealers, the Museum refused, however, to relinquish its authority as 'a kind of detached, unsullied, unbought and unbuyable critic'. It can, the director went on, 'recognize what is, essentially, a very valid artistic expression, whether it's gardening or pulling the bird out of the oven on Christmas day.' (He did not explain how.)

But the museum's critical function is doomed, if by nothing else than by its exaltation of 'visual experience' as such and its accommodation to the insistence of militants that questions of the quality of paintings and sculptures not only be equalized with that of exquisitely browned turkeys but be subordinated to displays considered 'relevant' by blacks, women, peace fighters and 'young artists'. p 296 (39)

With its authority no longer sustained by the museum, the art of the past has finally relinquished its hold upon present-day creation.

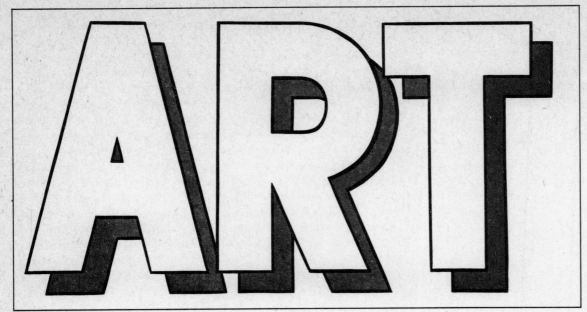

'Art', by Roy Lichtenstein, 1962, is a large oil painting over five feet long, yet its subject is a printed word, and that word is ART. Like many of Lichtenstein's works, it poses the question how far art can itself be the concern of art. (5)

'A large part of the pleasure of drawing is the awareness of shifting scale', said Claes Oldenburg. His 'Cake Wedge', 1962, is in fact a drawing not of a real slice of cake but of his own sculpture, 'Giant Cake Wedge'. Oldenburg has always been intrigued by scale—making, for instance, an electric plug six feet high, or seeing Manhatten as an ironing board. (6)

As a source of vitality, tradition in art expired in the self-consciousness generated by the pre-World War I vanguard movements, and was buried with Duchamp's mass-produced spade. The current defection of the museums in response to populist challenges consummates in this final portion of the 20th century the Futurist Marinetti's slogan, 'Burn the museums!' with which the century began. Whatever the Renaissance heritage still means to art, it means it only to individuals, not as a force determining the character of art generally. Formalist art movements of the sixties, that tried to consider art solely in relation to its own past, succeeded only in demonstrating with their shaped canvases, hard- and soft-edged paintings, reductionist and module sculptures, the fatal attenuation of inherited aesthetics. By the end of the sixties, formalism had been thrust aside by a new attention in American art to the social conditions of its existence.

Art as technology

For artists seeking an easy way to keep up with the times the obvious solution is affiliation with the laboratory and with engineering. The use of an electronic color-light keyboard or the computer as a substitute for the pencil and paint brush is the most effective means of dispelling uneasiness regarding art as an obsolescent trade. Technological avant-gardism identifies itself with advanced modes in the production and distribution of social artifacts and information. In American production, the object, whether a breakfast food or a beach house, is qualitatively identical with the means (pictures, rhetoric) used to sell it to the public. A new model is at once a new thing and an event. With the exception

of Abstract Expressionism, every postwar mode in American painting and sculpture has accommodated itself to techno-culture —the absorption of the arts by the mass media is an aspect of this accommodation. Art has been founded on mass-market commodities (Claes Oldenburg, Andy Warhol), on the billboard and package (Rosenquist, Tom Wesselman), on the comics (Roy Lichtenstein), on the electric sign (Chryssa), on commercial trademarks and insignia (Robert Indiana), on highways and traffic markers (Allan D'Arcangelo). Whatever the aesthetic distance between the individual artists, their works participate in the substance which the American imagination shares with the substance of American reality. In place of style, the American object has acquired the look of American fabrication.

Advertising and technology are also at the bottom of Op art that succeeded Pop in the early sixties. Like the *trompe l'œil* still-lifes of Harnett and Peto, Optical painting is related to eye-fooling attention-getters in shop windows or the figure in the poster who follows you with his stare. Op is related, too, to dazzling electric signs, retina-disturbing neons, strobe lights and laser beams, all of which have provided specialized directions in the art of the past decade. The increased sophistication of technological consciousness among American artists is indicated by the fact that today they are no longer content to paint pictures of factory workers in the manner of Anshutz's *Steelworkers' Noontime* or of factory buildings à la Sheeler. It is the technological *process* that intrigues them, as well as new industrial substances—even 'pure' painters, Expressionists and post-Cubist sculptors have succumbed to the lure of acrylics and sheets of tinted plastic. The inherent luminosity of

p 295 (35, 36 37)

p 289 (19)

synthetic pigments, from which some artists have gone on to Day-Glo, parallels the visual intensity of art lit by electricity. One feature of the sculpture of the sixties was the swing from the junk assemblages of artists such as Richard Stankiewicz, the smashed fenders of John Chamberlain, and the rags of early Oldenburg to the glass-and-chromium cubes of Larry Bell, the painted aluminum sections of Ronald Bladen, the tensed cables of Kenneth Snelson.

p 296 (42, 44)
p 297 (46)

The spread of new industrial tools and techniques into the studios and galleries has brought with it the intellectual habits and moral outlook of the manufacturing plant and front office, to say nothing of the sales and public relations department, and these attitudes have spread even among artists whose aesthetics are derived exclusively from the formal history of art. The immaculate surfaces and clean-cut forms of painters such as Kenneth Noland, Ellsworth Kelly, Frank Stella, Ludwig Sander, the late Ad Reinhardt not only envelop the spectator in a sheath of prophylaxis but reassure him of the operation in art of a rationale of conception, practice and utility comparable to that of an expertly managed corporation or bank—in sum, that art in America is an intellectually viable vocation within a viable socio-historical context. No wonder that in the past few years American business firms have shown a remarkable birth of interest in sponsoring museum exhibitions, acquiring paintings and sculptures for offices of executives and for display to customers, and collaborating with artists through their architectural, designing, public relations and engineering departments.

p 298 (51)

Consistent with the artist's new relations with industry, the traditional embarrassment regarding fame and financial success has given way to an open courting of both; it is not uncommon for contemporary painters to be represented by public relations firms. The aesthetics of technological rationalization, neatness and efficiency in meeting market demands reflects the integration of art and society; thus it has a political dimension, which has included the abjuration of politics in art. The notion of changing the world, or escaping from it, that motivated avant-garde art for a hundred years has been abandoned. Current political and cultural militancy express themselves against art (and the 'art establishment') rather than through it.

Machine-based art reaches back to 19th-century Europe, but until after the Second World War machine forms failed to take hold in the United States, where factory production needed no aesthetic reconciliation with traditional crafts. Since the war, European avant-gardism, with its nostalgia for the future, has often out-spaced United States art in light shows and color-sound intermixes, as well as in anonymous, teamwork art. Recently, however, America has been catching up with artist-engineer collaborations under Experiments in Art and Technology (EAT), the numerous industry-sponsored projects arranged by museums, an official representation of the United States at international exhibitions by collective works chosen by the Smithsonian Institution; recent selections emanated from such groups as Zomeworks Humano-factory of Corrales, New Mexico, Ant Farm of Houston, Envirolab of Los Angeles. American art has belatedly absorbed the tone of *RUR*, *1984* and German and Soviet technocracy of the 1920s. Spurred by, among others, the Massachusetts Institute of Technology and The Architectural League, collectivism has become a force in American art, with a corresponding drive toward the conversion of painting and sculpture into industrial design and new settings for 'dynamic individual-environment relations' (to quote a Smithsonian release).

p 296 (43)

As enriched visual and somatic experiences, whether of blinking lights or rocks displaced in the desert, art today can be summed up in the metaphor of a perpetual world fair or festival, whose attendance, in person or through the media, keeps spreading outward in ripples from the chief metropolitan art centers, with their exhibitions, special events, lecture programs, memberships and cut-rate catalogues and reproductions, to small-town art-tour programs and newspaper features on do-it-yourself converting of coffee-grinders into modernist lamp bases, on Op wallpaper and 'Homage To The Square' dress fabrics. America's backing away from style has reached fulfilment in the limitless dimensions of the new-look commodity market, fed by the inexhaustible streams of plagiarism,

p 262–3 (30)

improvisation, parody and revivalism. Today, all modes of visual excitation, from Benin idols to East Indian chintzes, are both contemporaneous and American. The quantity of formally competent creations presented in museums, art galleries and art publications is literally overwhelming. Since Dada, art has been steadily redefined by the mixing of aesthetic principles with audience-stimulating objectives and product design. Pop and Op art, kinetic constructions, chemical- and water-animated images, lights art, modular and machine-shop sculpture, microphotographic projections, silk screen and photomontage assemblages, painting and found-object combines, color-area wall-size compositions, computer-patterned figures, abstraction and cutouts, mixed-media theaters are aesthetically processed aspects of daily life.

p 297 (45)

Thus the artist and his public are offered a catalogue of art modes and art phenomena that are as boundless as the physical universe and human ingenuity. One rule of selection applies—the rule of novelty. Whatever its origins, the work must appear to represent fresh territory. But the object or form that is new today may be out of date tomorrow, hence drained of meaning and retarding in its effects. Everything that has been done in art in any place or period might open a door, but the door faces a blank wall. As soon as a move has been made, the exhaustion of its potentialities is under way. Duchamp spoke of the restricted life of a work of art—the same may be said of the ideas and models by which art continually redefines itself (or rather makes definition impossible). In effect, each invention plugs up another avenue of advance. Thus having canceled or deformed traditional styles, the new automatically cancels itself. All current modes of painting and sculpture are simultaneously legitimized as reflecting the present, and discredited as mere variations on the art of the past.

Hence in the midst of its enormous expansion and growing social acceptance, art is continually confronted by loss of its identity, either through dissipation into contiguous crafts or through lack of significant relation to the present. Insecurity is of the essence of modern art, an attribute of its historical consciousness. In becoming one with reality, art has delivered itself to time and change. The individual work exists as an 'anxious object', never assured of its present nature or its future status. Continuing crisis is the fundamental condition of art in this epoch—a condition periodically forced to the surface, despite efforts to normalize the practice of art or relegate its crises to the past. After a decade of complacency, art at the beginning of the seventies seems to be finding the issues of the existence of art and its function once more on the order of the day.

The crisis of art produces of itself characteristic aesthetic effects—for example, the attempt to separate painting from social history through concentrating exclusively on 'painting as painting', i.e., as color applied to a canvas of a given size and shape. Or the effort to meet the crisis of painting by substituting for it the 'intermedia' event or aesthetic hybrid, part object, part works or sound, part film or theater. In general, the crisis of art has caused speculation about art—its nature, function, value—to become the most pervasive content of the works of the past 25 years.

p 297 (45)

The difference between works of art and various categories of cultural artifacts has become a strictly subjective difference. Having ceased to inhabit a separate 'realm', art as such has been deprived of continuous being—it exists only when it is resurrected by individual artists. It is constituted by the will of Newman for the 'sublime', the curiosity of Albers concerning the interaction of hues. The qualities of fine art are materialized by acts different in kind from those responsible for TV shows and advertising layouts. The artist, no matter how conscious he is of art history, and of his opportunities for affecting it, is always in some respects a primitive (an embodiment of Smith's 'coarseness or unculture'), who sets into motion previously uncontrolled, or even undiscovered, powers of the mind. Art is a way of generating insights through the doing itself; it exists beyond what can be preplanned. A painting or sculpture is not only a transformation of matter but of its creator as well.

p 291 (26)

Beyond its technological explorations, and its efflorescences of design, modern American art has achieved greatness in enacting in painting the drama of individual identity. Its high point was attained in its Abstract Expressionist and Action Painting beginnings, in the work of Gorky, de Kooning, Pollock, Hofmann, Franz Kline, Gottlieb, Rothko, Newman, Still, Guston, Smith, Tomlin, Reinhardt, artists familiar with the art of the past but unwilling to follow its directions because each experienced inherited culture not as a standard to be emulated but as a personal problem. In his semi-automatic drawings, Gorky generated clues to his unknown 'I'; the thrown paint of Pollock was an incantation aimed at a magical dissolution of self into nature; in continuous experimentation de Kooning has found the means for seizing the immediacy of unformulated sensation and feeling. Investigating the unknown, American painting and sculpture have disengaged themselves again and again from the mass of qualitatively indifferent fabrications of machine production and the communications media and restored the autonomy of art as an idiom in which man can reflect upon himself.

p 290–91
p 292–93

p 292
(27)

p 285
(10)

p 298
(50)

The search for reality

In the union of art and technology, the idea of vanguard art as a vision that goes to the root of the times is replaced by the vigorous popularization of modernist phenomena and processes—an aim summed up in an American Motors statement regarding an art/technology show sponsored by it at a New York museum as 'a broader public understanding of the technical marvels of today and of innovative communication techniques'. The artist as designer and new-media experimenter cuts across the styles of earlier elites—Futurists, Constructivists, Neo-Plasticists—in an effort to educate the masses in aesthetic modernism through the objects they use or their curiosity about the mechanisms by which those objects are made or distributed. The filling station, teletype equipment, a display screen, a strip of film are aestheticized through art lectures and museum demonstrations. 'Software', writes an avant-gardist art professor about an exhibition of information-processing items organized by him, 'makes none of the usual distinctions between art and technology. Rather it defines technology as pervasive environment altering our consciousness vastly more than art. At a time when aesthetic insight must become a part of technological decision-making, such art/technology divisions seem nonsensical.' Vanguard art demands to be understood, and even that the spectator transform himself: the understanding and the transformation are the point of it. Art as technology, new design and 'communications' offers gifts of the new without the need for comprehension. It brings the aesthetically uneducated individual up to date, while leaving his beliefs, attitudes and prejudices intact. Like applied science, which bestows the advantages of the self-defrosting refrigerator and the electric toothbrush on the consumer regardless of his knowledge of electronics, applied modernism induces his participation in progress as effortlessly as enjoying an improvement in the weather. Art/technology is the ideal aesthetics for the consumer society.

While art has been driven deeper inward (the subjectivization predicted by Hegel), every aspect of American life, from funerals to food packaging to antiwar demonstrations, undergoes constant aesthetic refashioning and is reflected back to the public as an aesthetic phenomenon. The incessant modification of things and events to fit professionally-designed formats and the doubling of fact by fiction have transformed American public life into a semi-dream. At this far end of style America has become a nation of aesthetes—its prevailing quality is surreality (Surrealism never took on in the United States because American advertising displays made it seem too ordinary). The collapse of America's inherited forms—British, Dutch, minority group—is compensated for today by a popular theater of styles, each with its costume, manners and ethos. The revolution of the 20th century, which stimulates people of all races and social categories to demand a visible place on the stage of history, takes the form in the United States of a conflict of 'life styles'. Socially and politically, the American public has come to be the American audience, as when candidates for public office are reshaped by show-business professionals to arouse pre-planned responses, such as confidence.

In the postwar American world of fictions, the role of art has been ironically reversed: instead of being the creator and perpetuator of an imagined or stylized world, art in America today repeatedly rededicates itself to a 'search for the real'. Every movement, from pure abstraction to displays of 'software', claims the hallmark of New Reality. Characteristic American modes in art, such as Action Painting and junk sculpture, anti-form and random art, are efforts to purge visual creations of the element of artifice.

The contemporary American avant-gardist artist (as distinguished from the avant-gardist art manager) is a professed anti-aesthete—this is as true of the late Barnett Newman, a metaphysical painter, as of Robert Smithson, a young 'materialist' gatherer of gravel samples. Paint, stone, wood, bronze suffer the handicap of being too closely associated with art, and artists have preferred Plexiglas, epoxy, nylon filaments, fluorescent tubes, synthetics. In a still stronger resurgence of the American appetite for 'nature', even new laboratory materials are put aside or left unworked. Art is produced out of earth, boulders, animal matter or even out of living people and animals; forms are hacked or incised into the ground itself or into a rock face, to become, as one writer put it, 'a fragment of the real within the real'. Digging holes or trenches, making tracks in the snow or in a cornfield—the so-called Earthworks art—collaborates in the de-aestheticization of art with gallery exhibits of strips of felt, newspapers tacked on a wall, film produced by keeping the shutter of a camera open while speeding through the night—the so-called anti-form art. Another species of attack on the aesthetic is process art, in which materials are exposed to biological, chemical, physical or seasonal forces which either change their forms or destroy them, and in works incorporating growing grass and bacteria or inviting rust. In a 'final' gesture of leaving art behind (final gestures of this sort have been made for more than half a century), the new 'information' art consists of telegrams, newspaper clippings, computer-assembled data, typed proposals, diagrams, receipts and other evidence of a 'work' that remains invisible or never comes into being.

Nature itself cannot, of course, be rid of the aesthetic, and anti-art art has always proved subject to transformation into just another art movement—especially since its eager embrace by the museums. What is significant in the 'reality' movements, however, is their inherent intent, their character as protest against the myth-world of contemporary America. In this respect, the anti-art modes are a species of political art that stands in cultural opposition to the integrationist trend of technologically inspired design.

Reflection on the relation between art and reality is the verbal cement that binds the disparate modes of modern art with one another and with American 'realists' of the past—there is much to be said for the recently expressed notion that art has become 'speculative philosophy'. In any case, art's current defiance of the aesthetic is the latest incident in the perennial resort to primitivism by art movements since the middle of the 19th century, the exaltation invoked by Smith, of ruggedness, simplicity and adherence to direct experience, without regard to 'polish', or to the tastes of the art public and its institutional representatives. In this context, the fixation in 19th-century American art on 'the reality of beauty in nature as is' (which Robert Henri found in the paintings of Eakins) and the belief that 'any style is correct' represent a central American outlook on creation.

p 291
(26)

p 297
(49)

p 295
(36)

XIII
MISSIONARY AND WORLD POWER

America's destiny in the twentieth century

ERNEST MAY

'Let every nation know, whether it wishes us well
or ill, that we shall pay any price,
bear any burden, meet any hardship, support any friend,
oppose any foe to assure the survival
and success of liberty.'

JOHN F. KENNEDY

Isolation or involvement

has been the crucial choice facing America ever since the Revolution. A sense of mission, an urge to transmit the gift of freedom to other nations, pulled against the desire to be dissociated altogether from the corruptions of the Old World. During the 19th century the two forces maintained a balance. Many Americans held a compromise philosophy, of intervention in the Western Hemisphere but isolation from the rest of the world.

The turning-point came with World War I. In spite of earnest efforts by President Wilson to remain outside the European struggle, America was finally forced to commit herself. In a wave of patriotic enthusiasm she linked herself firmly to the cause of Britain and France. This painting by Childe Hassam, *Allies Day, May 1917* (opposite), shows a parade held in New York less than a month after

the American declaration of war. The flags of the allies wave in symbolic unison. Yet no sooner was the war won, leaving the USA unmistakably the greatest power in existence, than a reaction asserted itself. Wilson's dream of America leading the world under the League of Nations was abruptly shattered. Isolationism seemed to many to be the means of returning to prewar 'normalcy'. But again, in 1941, international conflict made such a position impossible to maintain. Scenes like the Allies Day parade were repeated with even more fervor. Again, victory left America stronger than ever. Afterward there was little talk of isolation, but the concept of America's mission changed. From being idealistic, liberal and confident, it became defensive, with the 'containment' of Communism taking precedence over both democracy and self-determination. (1)

Latin America was a sphere in which political evangelism was deemed justified, though liable to be interpreted by the enemies of the US as nationalist aggression. War waged in 1847 to protect the Texans (above: General Scott entering Mexico City) resulted in the acquisition of territory that later formed several new states. (2)

Cuba's fight for independence against Spain appealed to American sentiment. In 1898 the battleship *Maine* was blown up in Havana Harbor (above) leading to a war in which President Roosevelt's 'Roughriders' (above right) were prominent and which ended with a triumphant march (above far right) through New York. (4, 5, 7)

Across the Pacific, another Spanish colony, the Philippines, was in revolt (right: insurrectionists in a prison camp). Spain's defeat promised the Filipinos freedom, but for some decades the islands remained under American tutelage. (6)

'I wish they wouldn't come so many in a bunch; but if I've got to take them I guess I can do as well by them as I've done by the others.' *Puck* in 1896 foresaw Hawaii, the Philippines, Puerto Rico and Cuba, all applying for membership in the U.S. (3)

A US-controlled Panama Canal had been under consideration since 1850. To facilitate it the US in 1903 aided a Panamanian revolt against Columbia (which ruled Panama) and a fortnight later signed a treaty with the new republic acquiring in perpetuity complete control of the Canal Zone. President Theodore Roosevelt (on the site in 1906) lost no time in 'making the dirt fly'. (8)

The road to Peking: relations with China in the 20th century began with the international expedition (below) to crush the Boxer Rebellion in 1900. (9)

'Pershing's Crusaders' (right) was the title of a silent film produced after the United States entered the war in 1917. It expressed the prevalent feeling of the time – which was essentially true – that America was fighting an ideological war, to make the world (in President Wilson's phrase) 'safe for democracy'. General Pershing, the commander of the US Expeditionary Force in Europe, had fought in Cuba in 1898 and in Mexico in 1916. In 1917 he insisted on the Americans fighting as a single national army, rather than being 'amalgamated' with the English and French. This meant a long interval of training and organization, and it was not until 1918 that American troops were ready to take a major part in the war. In the painting below they are shown embarking at Southampton for France. (10, 11)

At the peace conference Wilson exercised a dominating influence, both because of America's share in the victory and because of his own moral stature. In this painting, by William Orpen, he is sitting third from the left (the others are Orlando and Lansing, and on Wilson's other side Clemenceau, Lloyd George, Bonar Law and Balfour). Wilson's 'Fourteen Points' were a summary of America's mission – the extension of self-government and (preferably republican) democracy to the whole world. Yet the postwar forces of isolationism (strengthened by Wilson's tactlessness and rigidity) gained new influence in the 1920s. (12)

Anti-Communist hysteria led to some harassment and deportations. Above: 'Reds' awaiting the boat for Deer Island, the emigration station in the port of Boston, in 1920. (13)

Charity to Europe: food shipments in 1921 relieved European distress without involving the US politically. Here Herbert Hoover supervises a consignment. (14)

Industry to South America: General Motors branch in Uruguay in the 1920s. (15)

Pearl Harbor (below: a photograph taken from one of the a ing Japanese planes) in 1941 ended American hesitation. A President Franklin D. Roosevelt signs the declaration of Henceforward, America was one of a family (above rig a family in many respects ill-assorted. Roosevelt was I enough to be sitting with Churchill, but American comrad with Stalin was destined to be for the duration only. (16–

America's wealth furnished aid for her allies on a massive scale, as well as providing armies in the Pacific and Europe. These tanks (right) await shipment for Europe in 1940. (19)

Democratic ideals were linked by Roosevelt with World War II as closely as Wilson had linked them with World War I. His famous formula of the 'Four Freedoms' (right: a poster by Norman Rockwell) was a program for the postwar world like Wilson's Fourteen Points. But American postwar pursuit of this program tended to be dominated by the 'containment' of Communism. (20)

Victory over Germany came after nearly a year's hard fighting. Below: American troops driving inland off the Normandy beaches, June 1944. The defeat of Japan, on the other hand, was dramatically sudden. Atomic bombs were dropped on 6 and 9 August 1945. Japan surrendered on 14 August, and an armistice was signed (bottom) on 2 September. (21, 23)

SAVE FREEDOM OF SPEECH

BUY WAR BONDS

Yankee, go home.

Massive aid for Europe was offered by the Marshall Plan in 1947. The countries of Western Europe accepted it (below: West Germany) but those of the East saw in it an attempt to undermine their Communist regimes and rejected it (above: East Germany). (22, 24)

Freie Bahn

DEM MARSHALLPLAN

UNITED
we are strong

UNITED we will win

The solidarity of war (above: a World War II poster) seemed to promise a solidarity of peace. All agreed that when the war ended the mistakes of 1919 had to be avoided. Wilsonian ideals were reborn in the United Nations, and this time Congress gave America's entry almost unanimous approval. (25)

'Hot' war: American support for democratic regimes gradually ▶ developed into support for regimes threatened by Communism. In 1950 North Korea invaded the South. Presidend Truman immediately sent troops and fighting (right) lasted for over two years. (28)

Cold war: American efforts to rebuild West German industry in 1948 were seen as a threat by the Russians. Land access to Berlin was closed. America and Britain responded by bringing in supplies by an unprecedented 'air-lift'. In this painting (left) one of the supply planes approaches Tempelhof airport. (26)

'Ich bin ein Berliner', declared President Kennedy when he visited the city in 1963. It was a measure of the importance in American eyes of retaining a citadel of democracy in East Germany. Two years earlier the flow of refugees from east to west had been so great that the Russians built a concrete wall to prevent all traffic. It still stands. (27)

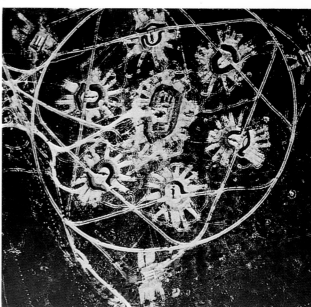

Crisis: Russia's provision of missile sites in Cuba in October 1962, established by aerial photographs (above), seemed a direct threat to American security. After Kennedy's demand Krushchev withdrew. (29)

The rival alliances — NATO (above: Macmillan and Eisenhower in 1957) and the Warsaw Pact – both claimed to be defensive but each appeared offensive to the other side. (30)

The crowning irony: America's championship of freedom branded as imperialism. Left: a vast crowd at Pyongyang, N. Korea, spells out slogans in October 1969. (31)

Communist conspiracy was the pretext for US intervention in the Dominican Republic. Left: anti-American demonstrations in Santo Domingo, September 1962. Three years later a revolution aiming to restore Juan Bosch (above with Lyndon Johnson in 1963) was forcibly suppressed by US troops. (32, 33)

The tragedy of Vietnam was not foreseen when President Kennedy sent in the first American troops in 1961, yet it was an outcome of the policy of containment. If South Vietnam were drawn into a Russian-dominated Communist sphere, it seemed inevitable that Laos, Cambodia and Thailand would follow. Limited action, however, was found to be inadequate. President Johnson took the decision to expand military involvements. Right: American troops near Khe Sanh. (35)

Russia comes to the US. In one of a series of summit meetings designed to relieve world tension, Nikita Krushchev came to Washington in September 1959. He is seen here with President Eisenhower. (34)

America goes to China. President Nixon's visit to Peking (left) in February 1972 marked the end of America's refusal to recognize Communist China. By dramatically reversing the policy of the previous twenty-five years, it offered the opportunity for new settlements in Asia. (36)

319

A war that could not be won: American public opinion, at first substantially in favor of the Vietnam War, gradually swung round to widespread disapproval. The demonstration shown here took place in Washington in November 1969. There was a new tendency toward isolationism, especially among the young. (37)

America's destiny in the twentieth century

ERNEST R. MAY

DURING AND AFTER the War of Independence, most reflective Americans regarded their new nation as unique. They conceived of it as destined to be an island of liberty in a corrupt world. As Thomas Paine put it in *Common Sense*: 'Freedom hath been hunted round the Globe. Asia and Africa have long expelled her. Europe regards her like a stranger, and England hath given her warning to depart. O! receive the fugitive, and prepare in time an asylum for mankind.'

The Revolution in France altered American perspectives. Many saw the French as having adopted American principles and set out to imitate the American example. The force of French arms then spread republicanism to Central and Southern Europe. Later, republics sprang up spontaneously in South America. Often, their very constitutions aped America's. People in the United States felt reason to believe that they had started a movement which would sweep the world.

In short order, of course, all the European republics disappeared. Spain temporarily regained her American colonies. By 1815, the United States was once again the world's lone republic. But Americans could not forget what had passed. Many had become convinced that republicanism would not only survive in the New World but ultimately triumph in the Old. The United States thus became not 'an asylum for mankind' but, as Jefferson had said in his first inaugural, 'the world's best hope'. There emerged a widely shared conviction that the United States had a mission to perform on behalf of other lands and peoples.

The national mission

This mission was seen as primarily that of extending republicanism or, later, democracy. It was also seen as upholding the principle of national self-determination. 'Every man and every body of men on earth,' Jefferson had written, 'possesses the right of self-government.' Not everyone shared his opinion that England and her allies infringed such a right when they intervened in the French Revolution. On the other hand, nearly everyone agreed in principle with those portions of President Monroe's famous message which applauded Greece's revolution for independence and defended the right of Spain's former American colonies to retain the independence they had won. And almost all Americans supported in sentiment later independence or national unification movements in the Balkans, the Italian peninsula, Poland, Germany, and Cuba.

For many, America's national mission had other components. Of great importance in the early decades of the country's history was simple territorial expansion. Movements in favor of annexing New Orleans, the Louisiana territory, the Floridas, Texas, and the Great Southwest were all, at one time or another, elevated to the level of noble national objectives. Similarly, opportunities for expanded trade and, later, for investment and natural resource exploitation were on occasion converted into components of the national purpose. To the confusion of both contemporaries and later historians, rhetoric sometimes mingled these self-serving goals with larger political aims. Thus, in the most notorious example, the 'Open Door', as urged for China and the Ottoman Empire, embraced both encouragement to national self-determination and the maintenance of trade and capital investment openings. It was possible to reason out linkages. Territorial expansion was said to

increase the 'area of freedom' and enhance America's potential influence elsewhere. Promotion of economic progress through trade and investment was defended as bringing less advanced lands nearer to the level of development necessary for democracy. Nevertheless, service to America as a nation or to individual Americans as producers or entrepreneurs was never central to the national mission as most Americans understood it. The essence of that mission was disinterested advancement of republicanism (or democracy) and national self-determination.

If there existed some consensus about the mission, there existed no agreement at all about the best means of carrying it forward. Most of the time, the majority of Americans probably believed that the nation's purposes should be achieved by eschewing involvement in the politics of other countries.

Such a view was consistent with tradition. The Puritan settlers of New England had sought to establish a 'City on a Hill'. The concept of America as 'an asylum for mankind' involved its standing alone, inviting lovers of liberty to its shelter. It was not contradictory to accept the wider concept of America as leader of a worldwide movement and yet to hold that Americans should exercise that leadership primarily by setting a pattern for others to imitate.

At times, however, some Americans felt dissatisfaction with this essentially passive role. During the Spanish-American wars for independence, Henry Clay and others urged that the United States officially support the rebels and perhaps even intervene militarily to secure their independence. The Monroe Doctrine involved some concessions to their viewpoint. Later in the century, Spain's one remaining American colony, Cuba, experienced two uprisings for independence. On both occasions, significant numbers of Americans championed intervention against Spain. The second time around, they won. The Spanish-American War of 1898 was the result.

p 310
(4, 5, 7)

Many who advocated activism in the Western Hemisphere supported strict non-entanglement elsewhere. In doing so, they kept alive a tradition that had its origins before Columbus. In the 15th century, the Pope had drawn an imaginary line dividing the unknown world between Spain and Portugal. Until the 18th century, European states treated that line as the boundary between two political systems. It was possible for powers to make peace in Europe but to remain at war 'beyond the line'. Americans building a new nation were heirs to this concept.

f 2

Even before there existed movements for independence in the Spanish colonies, Jefferson opined that the Western Hemisphere might require 'a different code of national law to govern relations with other nations'. Clay talked later of 'an American system' embracing the United States and Latin American republics. In the fourth quarter of the 19th century, James G. Blaine championed a Pan-Americanism somewhat counterpart to the Pan-Germanism and Pan-Slavism then in vogue in Central and Eastern Europe. Despite the distances in the Hemisphere, the fact that tourism and trade tended to develop on an east-west rather than north-south axis, and the fact that economic and political evolution made the United States and Latin American republics less and less alike, the mystique survived. It was thus comparatively easy for an American to hold that, in regard exclusively to Latin America, fulfilment of the national mission might sometimes require more than the mere establishment of an example.

On occasion, small groups of Americans advocated action elsewhere. In the 1820s, a few philhellenes urged aid to the Greeks. In 1848–49 some voices spoke for American support of beleaguered revolutionaries in Europe. During the 1850s a curious group called 'Young America' called for America's taking leadership in a worldwide nationalist revolution. In the 1890s a small number championed assistance to Armenians suffering persecution in the Ottoman Empire. None of these causes, however, developed much political strength. For practical purposes, there were in the 19th century only two alternative views of how the United States should carry out its national mission. One was isolationist: set an example but meddle nowhere. The other was isolationist in regard to all the world except the Western Hemisphere.

Meanwhile, however, the United States changed. Relative to other states, it grew increasingly powerful. Annexations gave it territorial vastness matched only by Russia, China, and Brazil. A high birth-rate and continuous immigration made America, by the end of the 19th century, more populous than any industrialized state except Russia. Economically, it also outstripped most European competition, becoming by the early 20th century the p 110 chief producer of petroleum, coal, iron, and steel. Although the (14) United States maintained only a small standing army, the Civil War proved its ability quickly to mobilize, train, and maneuver large forces. And, except for a brief period after the Civil War, it always maintained a respectable navy. As of 1900, indeed, its fleet ranked second only to that of Britain. On account of these facts, added to the rapid victory over Spain in 1898 and the attendant acquisition p 310–11 of territories and colonies in the Pacific, the United States won (3) general acknowledgment by the beginning of the 20th century as one of the great powers.

Given this status and the strength which it betokened, the nation had to face in the new century the issue of whether it should, or could, pursue its mission within the limits earlier observed.

Pan-Americanism gained force in 1889, when James G. Blaine presided at a conference of all the American nations. In this 1900 cartoon, Uncle Sam gallantly offers his protection to the whole continent of America. (2)

Uncle Sam 'opens' China to free trade with the key of American diplomacy, while his competitors, Russia and England, look on. American support of self-determination through the 'Open Door' policy was not entirely disinterested. (1)

'A world safe for democracy'

The Spanish War had represented a victory for those who advocated a more than passive American role within the Western Hemisphere. The early 20th century saw an enlarged vision of the active role that the United States might take. President Theodore Roosevelt encouraged Panama's separation from Colombia. His chief interest was, of course, an interoceanic canal which Colombia p 311 blocked. Nevertheless, his action involved a new form of support for national self-determination, for he employed both diplomacy and naval power to protect Panama. Earlier, he and the Congress had arranged for Cuban self-government under the limitations of the Platt amendment. This gave the United States title to intervene 'for the preservation of Cuban independence, the maintenance of a government adequate for the protection of life, property, and individual liberty, and for discharging its obligations with respect to Cuba.' In effect, the United States undertook to ensure that democracy flourished on the island, and Roosevelt in fact sent in troops when advised later that chaos threatened.

Roosevelt also established an arrangement with the Dominican Republic which involved America's assuring economic stability. Part of the rationale was that the Latin nation would thus progress more rapidly toward effective democracy. Subsequently, President Woodrow Wilson sent troops into both the Dominican Republic and Haiti. In both instances, the stated objective was to permit the development of stable democratic institutions. In the interval, money, advisers, warships, and marines had been used on occasion to promote the same ends in various Central American republics. In addition, Wilson had used non-recognition and various types of diplomatic and military pressure in an effort to bring down a Mexican regime that, in his judgment, had subverted democratic process and illegitimately taken power. All these moves involved a new kind of activism within the Western Hemisphere—overt use of American power for the purpose not only of protecting self-determination but also of hastening the inevitable success of American-style democracy.

The results of this activism, however, were not encouraging. Wilson's efforts to influence events in Mexico seemed an utter failure. Although the regime which he attacked did eventually fall, American pressure seemed least among the causes. Indeed, well-informed observers judged that its tenure had been lengthened because nationalists supported it against Yankee interventionism. By the late 1920s, the other Latin countries which the United States had sought to influence were not conspicuously more democratic than others. In fact, Cuba, the Dominican Republic, and Nicaragua were ruled by dictators.

Acknowledging the ill-success of his predecessors, President Herbert Hoover took steps to disentangle the United States from the internal affairs of Latin America. His successor, Franklin Roosevelt, continued the same course, advertising it as a 'Good Neighbor policy'. By the 1930s the United States had retreated in the Western Hemisphere to the traditional posture of merely setting an example which it hoped that other states would copy.

Between 1900 and 1940, Americans also gave intermittent consideration to becoming active champions of self-determination and democracy outside the Western Hemisphere. As mentioned earlier, *f 1* the declaration of 1899 in support of an Open Door in China had at least the color of a statement in favor of national self-determination. A declaration in 1900, urging preservation of China's territorial integrity, represented more clearly an extension of this principle to Asia.

P 311 (9) Theodore Roosevelt and his successors adopted various diplomatic measures designed to contribute to self-determination for the Chinese. Roosevelt so represented his efforts before and during the Russo-Japanese War to maintain some balance of power between those two strong neighbors of China. Wilson protested in 1915 when Japan presented China with twenty-one demands, some of which would have involved Chinese acceptance of Japanese political tutelage. The Harding administration successfully pressed Japan to hand back to China the German-leased territory which Japan had seized during World War I. The Hoover administration voiced strong disapproval of Japan's annexation of Manchuria in 1931-32. Franklin Roosevelt did likewise when Japanese armies commenced in 1937 a campaign for conquest of all of China. The United States thus evidenced continuous interest in self-determination for the Chinese. At no point, however, did any significant number of Americans advocate use of military power for this end.

In that respect, Asia remained distinguishable from Latin America. Also, almost no one proposed furthering democracy in China by means other than example and exhortation.

The most serious question which Americans faced during the first half of the 20th century concerned their roles in Europe and in those large areas of the globe where Englishmen and Europeans owned colonies or spheres of influence.

This question presented itself as a result of World War I. In the first place, that war so wasted the resources of the Old World as to make the United States no longer merely a great power but the greatest of all powers. In the second place, the intervention of the P 312 (11) United States, provoked by Germany's challenge to American maritime interests, had led to the dispatch of a huge American army to Europe, more than 250,000 American casualties, and, inevitably, P 313 (12) American participation in the framing of peace terms for all of Central and Southern Europe.

President Wilson himself believed devoutly in the American mission. When he concluded that the United States had no choice other than war with Germany, he immediately sought to make the impending sacrifices serve ends nobler than mere punishment of the enemy. His war message of 1917 spoke of a 'world safe for democracy'. His later statements about war aims emphasized ensuring a right of self-determination for Poles and nationality groups subject to Austro-Hungarian and Ottoman rule. When negotiating for an armistice in 1918, he made a virtual condition that Germany cease to be a monarchy and become a republic. In P 312 (10) some respects, Wilson converted the war into a crusade for self-determination and democracy.

In the peacemaking, Wilson continued to support self-determination. Also, he insisted on the creation of a League of Nations. *f 3* Through it, international issues could be aired, and public opinion in all democratic states could be aroused to concern. Through it,

President Wilson delivers his olive branch to the Dove of Peace ('Punch', 1919). Dove: 'Isn't this a bit thick?' In America the skeptics triumphed and Congress refused to ratify Wilson's plan. (3)

too, the democratic states could pool their resources so as to resist any autocrat who sought to conquer or subjugate some land or people. Underlying this conception of the League was, of course, the premise that democracies were by nature peaceable and disposed to permit self-determination—a premise which America's own history did not wholly support. But Wilson believed that the League would, in fact, defend self-governing democracies, and he expected the United States to exercise leadership within the League.

Various elements in America combined to oppose Wilson's project and to bring about votes in the Senate that prevented the United States from even becoming a member of the League. Thereafter, through the 1920s and 1930s, it was assumed that American public opinion had decisively rejected any active policy *vis-à-vis* Europe or colonial areas in the European orbit.

In the mid-1930s Fascist Italy conquered Ethiopia. Together, Italy and Nazi Germany lent support to Fascist or semi-Fascist forces in a civil war in Spain. Germany annexed Austria, then sectors of Czechoslovakia, then all the Czech nation. Finally, Germany marched into Poland, precipitating World War II. At *f 4* each stage, some Americans argued that the United States ought to act either to defend the principle of self-determination or to oppose European dictatorships which were clearly outspoken enemies of democracy.

At first, such clamor seemed to come only from a small minority. During the Ethiopian affair and the Spanish Civil War, Congress passed Neutrality Acts designed to demonstrate and ensure that the United States would not become involved. Gradually, however, the ranks of those advocating a non-passive policy expanded. After World War II commenced, Congress modified the Neutrality P 314 (19) legislation so as to permit the supplying of the British and French.

In 1940, after Germany suddenly defeated the French armies and converted a rump France into a Nazi satellite, millions of Americans became concerned lest democracy be extinguished on the other side of the Atlantic, and the United States be left alone to face a Nazi behemoth.

'*Laocoön 1938*'. *In the years leading to World War II, dissension between isolationists and those favouring a non-passive policy grew acute. Finally only a minority still supported non-intervention.* (4)

The years 1940–41 saw a swift turnabout in America's stance. Aid was extended to Britain. When British funds ran low, a Lend-Lease Act provided for continuing the supply virtually free of charge. American warships waged an undeclared naval war in order to ensure that weapons and goods reached Britain. In Asia, the United States threatened Japan with war in order to deter the Japanese from striking against British possessions in Asia.

Many Americans continued to contend that the United States should not depart from its earlier path. Former President Hoover, among others, held that the Western Hemisphere could be defended no matter what the fate of Europe or Asia, and he argued that in the long run self-determination and democracy would be best advanced if Americans conserved their isolation and employed their resources exclusively for improvement of their own still imperfect society. Such voices were, however, those of a dwindling minority.

Concluding that the American threats were not bluffs, the Japanese launched a war against the United States; Germany and Italy promptly joined in. From that moment, it became almost unanimously accepted that Americans had been mistaken in rejecting Wilson's interpretation of what the national mission entailed. They should, it was agreed, have joined in defending the right of self-determination against the challenges in Manchuria, Ethiopia, Spain, and Central Europe. Probably, too, Americans should have shown more concern about the subversion of democracy by military elements in Japan and by Fascists and Nazis in Europe.

Renewed commitment

From official declarations, speeches and editorials, almost any observer would have forecast America's emerging from World War II with renewed commitment to its traditional national mission and with a determination to pursue that mission more actively in all regions of the world. This did not occur. To be sure, the United States became involved as never before in the affairs of nations on many continents. Meanwhile, however, the national mission was redefined in new and much narrower terms. Within a quarter-century, even this definition had come under challenge, and Congress and the public were laboring with the question of whether any high purposes at all were served by America's extensive and elaborate foreign entanglements. The rest of this essay centers on this puzzling development—the transformation of the American sense of mission in the third quarter of the 20th century.

The United States emerged from World War II as incomparably the strongest nation on this planet. Only Hawaii and outlying Pacific islands carried burns from the war. The mainland was completely unscarred. By contrast, the other great states of the

world had been ravaged. Bombs had fallen on Britain daily for almost five years. France and Italy had been battlegrounds. The richest and most populous areas of the Soviet Union had been scorched and scorched again. Some 7,500,000 Russian soldiers had died in battle. This was almost twenty times the total of American combat deaths. Most of Germany consisted of battered ruins. Japan had felt the touch not only of TNT and fire bombs but of nuclear weapons as well, and both Germany and Japan had ended the war as conquered territories.

The American economy had not only escaped damage from the war but had thrived. In the early postwar years, America's factories produced much more than all the rest of the world together. The holdings of American citizens, companies, and banks, together with those of the United States government, constituted the lion's share of the world's wealth.

During the war, Americans had only dimly foreseen how immense would be their later power. The first half-year after Pearl Harbor had, after all, seen one serious defeat after another. No one had been certain that German or Japanese bombers or missiles would not hit the mainland. Millions of Americans took part in earnest air raid drills, even in cities deep in the Middle West. Moreover, all Americans remembered nervously how shaky had been the domestic economy as recently as 1937–38. No one felt confident that the end of the war would not bring a return of the Great Depression.

Given such a high level of uncertainty, and memories of how Wilson's plans had been frustrated after World War I, American political leaders were loath during the war to define with too sharp precision the means by which the nation might pursue its mission in the postwar years immediately ahead. They did agree on two guidelines. First, the enemies should be defeated as quickly and completely as possible. Second, the United States should repair the cardinal mistakes made after World War I. Specifically, it should see to it that an international organization, with America as a member, replaced the League of Nations and that the economic settlement promoted stability and co-operation rather than instability and conflict.

In retrospect, Wilson was thought to have erred by failing to win bipartisan support for the League, failing to involve senators in its planning, and failing to take adequate account of isolationism among the public. Franklin Roosevelt's administration devoted itself to avoiding those errors. The President did not make any firm commitment to American participation in an international organization until after Republican leaders, meeting at Mackinac Island in 1943, endorsed the principle. In preparing drafts of a Charter for a new United Nations organization, State Department officials scarcely altered commas without consulting Senators Tom Connally (Dem., Texas) and Arthur Vandenberg (Rep., Michigan) of the Foreign Relations Committee. So concerned was Roosevelt about possible postwar isolationism that he toyed for some time with the concept of obligating the United States to action only in the Western Hemisphere. Strong evidence of Republican and senatorial interest in other regions changed his mind. The whole effort culminated, shortly after his death, in a conference at San Francisco, approval of the Charter by the conference, and 89–2 ratification by the Senate.

There also existed a widespread consensus that Wilson and the other peacemakers of 1919 had paid too little attention to economic factors. In consequence, it was believed, the interwar years had seen quarrels over reparations and debts, the hoarding of financial reserves, harmful competition for exclusive trade advantages, and sluggishness in the international flow of foods and manufactures. Economic nationalism was held to have contributed to the Great Depression, and the Depression enabled militarism to triumph in Japan, the Nazis to gain power in Germany, and totalitarianism to win adherents elsewhere. Men in the American government were united in concern about the economic aftermath of the war.

This concern manifested itself in creation during the war of the United Nations Relief and Rehabilitation Administration, the United Nations Food and Agriculture Organization, the International Bank for Reconstruction and Development (the World Bank), and the International Monetary Fund. These agencies were supposed to provide supplies and food for the poor and hungry,

f 5

p 314
(18)

p 315
(27)

p 314–
(17)

p 137
(21)

f 6

capital for the nations needing to rebuild or to progress, and money for governments temporarily in financial straits. By the standards of the time, these bodies were generously funded. In addition, Congress quintupled the capital of the US Export-Import Bank so that it could facilitate trade between the United States and other nations. There were some notes of caution. When agreeing to continued Lend-Lease shipments in 1944–45, Congress exacted from the executive branch a promise that Lend-Lease would not be used as a cover for postwar aid to allies. Nevertheless, there seemed a general determination that the United States should do what it could to promote economic recovery and stability in the postwar world.

Besides this objective and the creation of a new world organization, there was little else to which the executive branch or Congress seemed prepared to commit themselves until the outlines of the future became more distinct.

To be sure, the administration had a general commitment to the propagation of democracy. The 'unconditional surrender' declaration at Casablanca made clear that the United States would not willingly see the survival of the regimes then existing in enemy countries. When Italy surrendered suddenly in 1943, Roosevelt reluctantly yielded to Churchill and his own military commanders in allowing Victor Emmanuel to remain as King. He insisted, however, that all real power be vested eventually in a parliament. Similarly, Truman agreed with the utmost hesitancy to offer Japan surrender terms not requiring dethronement of the Emperor. He did so only because persuaded that such a concession might save many American lives. And planning for the occupation of Germany and Japan led men to expect not only a purge of elite groups but also an educational effort aimed at indoctrinating youth with democratic principles.

It was an open question, however, whether the same objective was to be pursued elsewhere. In accordance with the Good Neighbor policy, the United States had looked on unprotestingly while dictators seized power in Argentina, Brazil, Venezuela, Colombia, and other Latin American states. With the approach of war, Washington had shown some concern about those possibly

p 315
(23)

The insignia of the Food and Agriculture Organization, one of several specialized agencies within the United Nations framework, created during World War II to assist economic recovery. (6)

susceptible to Nazi influence, especially Argentina. After Pearl Harbor, an effort was made to draw Latin American nations into the war. Argentina held out. There seemed no doubt that its military regime, headed by Juan Domingo Perón, had a Fascist flavor. If Americans were to pursue the goal of spreading democracy, Argentina was a likely place to start.

Even ardently anti-Fascist Americans felt some qualms, however, about a campaign to unseat Perón. They could recall the ill success of past attempts to influence political developments in Latin America. There was no apparent reason why a new interventionism might be more productive, and the result might be to sacrifice the good will built up through renunciation of intervention. Moreover, if the American government acted in Argentina, it might have to act elsewhere, for, while Perón was conspicuous for his pro-Axis sympathies, he was no more brutal a despot than some of his contemporaries. Americans acquainted with Latin America could see that a general policy of promoting democracy in the world might lead to their government's returning within the Western Hemisphere to a policy that had proved futile in the past, that was sure to be unpopular among Latin Americans, and that might lead to deep involvement in the intricate internal affairs of a number of Latin states.

Spain stood as yet another problem. Generalissimo Francisco Franco had won power there with aid from Italy and Germany. His final victory had come just before the outbreak of general war in Europe. Throughout the war, the Allies had feared that Spain would join the Axis, and allow German troops to cross the Straits of Gibraltar and strike the communication lines of American forces operating in Tunisia. Much effort and much money had gone into purchasing Spanish neutrality. The issue was whether, with the war over, the United States should make some effort to bring about the downfall of Franco's Falangist regime.

Other, somewhat comparable, situations existed in Eastern and Southeastern Europe. During the interwar years, only one state in those regions had been regarded by most Americans as a democracy. That was Czechoslovakia. All the others had been seen as authoritarian regimes. On the other hand, while Austria, Hungary, Rumania, and Bulgaria had also qualified as Axis countries, Poland, Yugoslavia, and Greece had, through governments in exile, been at least nominal members of the United Nations. Since they would be liberated rather than occupied states, the United States would have an obligation to accord them somewhat different treatment. But the same policy issues confronted Americans with regard to all nations in Eastern and Southeastern Europe. Should it be an objective of the United States to establish democracies in these regions? Should the American government permit or even assist restoration of the oligarchies that had ruled before the war? To the extent that the Soviet Union sought to impose its own non-democratic system of exclusive governance by members of the Communist Party, should the United States acquiesce or resist?

Perhaps most puzzling of all was the question of what position the United States should adopt with regard to mainland Asia. Wartime propaganda had pictured Chiang Kai-shek as the popular leader of a Chinese republic. Most Americans who knew Asia recognized that portrait as inaccurate. Chiang bore more resemblance to a warlord. He governed by means of intricate bargains with cliques of corrupt officials and military commanders. Moreover, significant areas of China lay under the control of Communists who did not acknowledge Chiang's sovereignty. Had large numbers of American ground forces been sent to China, the United States

'The Way of a Stork', an Illingworth cartoon referring to the Lend-Lease Act of 1941. The American eagle wings its way across the Atlantic bringing aid to Britain in the form of aircraft, tanks and guns. (5)

might have been inescapably involved in Chinese affairs. As it was, the American government had a broad range of choices: among them, to back Chiang, to attempt mediation between Chiang and the Communists, and to leave the Chinese to work matters out for themselves. Though more complex and mysterious than other areas, China posed for Americans the same basic problem that presented itself in Latin America, in Spain, and in Eastern and Southeastern Europe. Was the United States to use its postwar power to promote actively the spread of democracy?

Or would the United States confine itself to defending national self-determination? It would not have been illogical for Americans, remembering their experiences in Latin America, to take the position that, while they hoped for and expected the eventual extension of democracy, they would employ their resources only to ensure that the world's nationalities had sufficient self-government to make their own choices. This would have meant that, in Eastern and Southeastern Europe, the American government would concern itself more with territorial boundaries than with the make-up of cabinets. It would also have meant continuing along lines that Roosevelt broached when, to Churchill's vexation, he advocated independence for India and flatly opposed the reintroduction of French forces into Indo-China.

'Containment'

In the event, however, Americans pursued neither the goal of spreading democracy nor that of protecting national self-determination. Instead, they developed a new and curiously limited definition of America's international purpose. It was simply to prevent the spread of Communism. Rather than freedom or democracy or self-determination, or any of the shibboleths of the past, 'containment' became the watchword of American foreign policy.

This new goal emerged relatively slowly. The concluding phase of the war in Europe saw friction between the United States and the Communist USSR over Rumania, Yugoslavia, Bulgaria, Austria, and especially Poland. Roosevelt and Stalin had agreed at Yalta on a Polish government to be formed by a coalition of Communists and non-Communists. Controversy arose over the question of whether the non-Communists should have more than token representation. Since the principal American contention was that preparation should be made for a prompt free election, the US government seemed to stand for both democracy and self-determination. In the meantime, further dispute developed over efforts by the Soviet-backed Yugoslav Communist government of Marshal Tito to seize territory around Trieste, where the population was primarily Italian. President Truman authorized American and British forces to fight if Tito's partisans marched into the territory. This seemed a vigorous stand for self-determination.

For many months after the end of the European war, the United States seemed doggedly committed to defend these principles in Eastern Europe. The American government did not extend recognition to Poland until June 1945, when Stalin agreed to broaden the Polish cabinet and reaffirmed a pledge of eventual free elections. Protesting against the exclusion of non-Communists from any major governmental roles, the United States government continued to withhold recognizing the Rumanian and Bulgarian regimes installed and supported by the Soviets. It grudgingly agreed in December 1945 to accord such recognition in return for promises of at least token representation for non-Communists.

At Foreign Ministers' Conferences and other meetings, American representatives persistently complained that democracy was not being given an adequate chance in Eastern Europe. Non-Communists continued to be systematically excluded from power, they declared, and, except in Hungary, free elections were not taking place. All through 1946, tension persisted over Trieste. Also, the United States became engaged in open dispute with the Soviet Union about Iran, where Soviet troops remained despite a wartime pledge of prompt withdrawal and where Russian agents seemed to be encouraging a Communist separatist movement. Relations between the United States and the USSR grew less and less friendly. But the issues dividing them appeared at first to grow out of an American commitment to both democracy and self-determination, not out of hostility to either the Soviet Union as a state or to Communism as an ideology.

In the meantime, moreover, the American government manifested the same commitment in other contexts. When preparing for creation of the UN, Washington had bowed to Latin American pressure for Hemispheric solidarity. The United States accepted Argentina's last-minute declaration of war against the Axis as evidence of repentance, restored diplomatic relations, and joined in sponsoring Argentina for membership in the world organization. With the war over, the UN functioning, and a new Organization of American States beginning to be discussed, the United States returned to the tack it had followed earlier in the 1940s. US Ambassador Spruille Braden voiced open criticism of Perón. In anticipation of Argentina's presidential election, the State Department released a 'Blue Book', documenting Perón's collaboration with the Nazis. Its preface asked explicitly 'whether the military regime, or any Argentine government controlled by the same elements, can merit . . . confidence and trust.'

With regard to Spain, the American government had initially seemed more cautious. When Stalin proposed at Potsdam that the Allies overthrow the Franco government, Churchill voiced vehement opposition. Truman proposed successfully that the Big Three merely refuse Spain membership in the United Nations Organization. In December 1945, however, the United States removed its ambassador from Madrid, and in March 1946, in company with a British Labour government and a Socialist-led French cabinet (that of Félix Gouin), Washington issued a public appeal to 'patriotic and liberal-minded Spaniards' to 'find means to bring about a peaceful withdrawal of Franco, the abolition of the Falange, and the establishment of an interim or caretaker government under which the Spanish people may have an opportunity freely to determine the type of government they wish to have and to choose their leaders.'

During early meetings of the UN, the United States delegation supported Syria and Lebanon in asking for withdrawal of French and British forces and prompt independence for those former League of Nations mandates. There, and in other forums, the American government backed independence, or at least autonomy, for British, French, and Dutch colonies in Southeast Asia.

During 1945 and 1946, disputes with the Soviet Union drew more sustained public attention than did such gestures as the Argentine 'Blue Book', the declaration on Spain, appeals for liberation of colonial areas, or fulfilment of the prewar promise that the Philippine Islands would receive independence. Nevertheless, there existed these and other items of evidence, indicating that the goals of the United States were simply democracy and self-determination. Moreover, any appearance that the American government regarded the Russian government or its ideology as a hostile force was at least partially offset by two facts. First, American officials were in process of elaborating the so-called Baruch Plan, the effect of which would be to associate the USSR with the United States in an international agency controlling all information about, production of, and control over nuclear weapons. Second, General Marshall, as a personal representative of President Truman, engaged in an intensive effort to mediate between the Chinese Nationalists and Chinese Communists with a view to their establishing a coalition government.

Gradually, however, US policy shifted in a distinctly anti-Soviet and anti-Communist direction. In March 1946, President Truman looked on approvingly while former Prime Minister Churchill spoke of an 'iron curtain' in Eastern Europe. In the autumn, he fired his Secretary of Commerce, Henry Wallace, for stating in public his opinion that the State Department showed excessive mistrust of Russia. At almost the same moment the Secretary of State, James Byrnes, declared at Stuttgart that the Western powers should adopt a new policy with regard to occupied Germany. Independently of the Soviets, they might take measures to restore the German economy, hoping thus to contribute to recovery throughout Western Europe.

At the end of 1946, the prolonged negotiations within the Council of Foreign Ministers seemed at last to achieve some headway. The United States, the USSR, and the other wartime allies agreed on peace treaties for Italy, Bulgaria, Rumania, Hungary, and Finland. In the early spring of the following year, however, President Truman went before Congress to proclaim the 'Truman

Doctrine' and to ask funds for economic and military aid to enable Greece and Turkey to 'maintain their institutions and their national integrity against aggressive movements that seek to improve upon their totalitarian regimes'.

Until then, the United States had avoided open involvement in Greek or Turkish affairs. British forces had landed in Greece in 1944. They had helped a reactionary monarch and military oligarchy to install themselves in office. The British treasury then provided arms and funds to sustain this regime in a civil war against Communist-led partisans supplied and assisted from Bulgaria and Yugoslavia. At international gatherings, Soviet representatives had responded to Western complaints about Poland, Rumania, and Bulgaria by pointing to British activities in Greece. Americans stood by as mute spectators. Meanwhile, Moscow pressed Ankara for the retrocession of border areas annexed by Turkey during the Russian civil war of 1918–20 and for acceptance by the Turks of Soviet control over the Black Sea and the straits. The United States lent verbal assistance to Turkey, citing the principle of national self-determination, but it left the provision of material aid to the British. With the Truman Doctrine and the passage of the Greek–Turkish aid bill, the United States took over the British role. It began thus to provide large-scale assistance to two states that American officials could only blushingly describe as democracies.

p 315 (24) In mid-1947, Truman's new Secretary of State, George Marshall, proposed a massive economic aid program for Europe. The terms of the offer permitted participation by the USSR and Communist nations in Eastern Europe. In the upshot, they refused to ask for American money. p 315 (22) The Marshall Plan thus became a multi-billion-dollar investment exclusively in non-Communist states.

In the year 1948, the relationships between the United States and the Soviet Union earned Walter Lippmann's appellation 'cold war'. Acting on the principle suggested by Byrnes's Stuttgart speech, the Western powers consolidated their occupation zones and launched an effort to increase Germany's agricultural and industrial productivity. When the Soviets responded by shutting off land communication with Berlin, the United States and Britain risked p 317 (26) war by operating a continuous airlift of supplies. During an Italian general election, American officials openly exerted themselves to prevent a victory by the Communist Party. At the same time, they encouraged Western European governments receiving US aid to purge their cabinets of Communist ministers.

Earlier, the United States had established a defensive alliance with Latin America. The Rio Treaty of 1947 led to the creation of the Organization of American States. In 1948, a congressional resolution authorized exploration of a comparable alliance with nations in Western Europe. There followed in 1949 the North Atlantic Treaty and, not long afterward, formation of NATO.

In East Asia, meanwhile, Marshall's mediation failed. During 1948 and 1949, the Chinese Communists routed the Nationalists, winning control of the entire mainland. Maintaining relations with Chiang, who retained Formosa, the United States withheld recognition from the new regime. In the Korean peninsula, an American-p 317 (28) backed South Korean government confronted a Russian-backed Communist North Korea.

In June 1950, the North Koreans launched a military invasion. Truman immediately sent in American forces. After initial setbacks, the Americans and South Koreans repelled the northerners. They continued into North Korea, seeking to achieve unification by force. When they neared the Yalu River, Chinese Communists intervened and drove them back to the vicinity of the original partition line. After two years of stalemated warfare, the two sides agreed to an armistice and, in effect, to restoration of the *status quo ante*.

While fighting continued in Korea, the United States effected a large-scale military build-up, much of which had little to do with Korea itself. The economic aid program for Europe was largely transformed into a military aid program. American divisions and air and naval squadrons went to Europe as elements of a NATO force, all of which was to be under an American supreme commander. Plans were laid for rearming West Germany and incorporating it in NATO. Economic and military aid and, in some instances, small contingents of US forces also went to other

'*The Tumult and the Shouting Dies: The Captains and the Kings Depart*' (*from '*The Herblock Book*', Beacon Press, 1952*). *After the war Truman faced new responsibilities, including an economic aid program for Europe. (7)*

quarters of the world. And the central justification offered for these outlays and deployments was the need to prevent any expansion of Soviet power, either physically through conquest by the Red Army or ideologically through the capture of a government by a Soviet-controlled Communist Party.

In the process, the historic ideals of democracy and self-determination dropped by the wayside. Perón having survived the State Department's effort to unseat him, Argentina was invited to join the inter-American alliance. In 1951, the Perón government began to receive US military assistance. In the same year, the United States negotiated an agreement with Franco, exchanging aid for military base rights in Spain. An alliance treaty was signed with Chiang Kai-shek, whose regime was not only an out-and-out dictatorship but also one imposed by a Chinese minority on a population ethnically and linguistically Formosan. A military assistance agreement was concluded also with a military dictatorship in Thailand, headed by the very general who had allied the Thai with Imperial Japan in 1941. The course of US policy toward Yugoslavia after Tito's break with Stalin indicated that the United States could now become a supporter even of a Communist dictatorship so long as it was prepared to take sides against the Soviet Union.

When forming NATO, the American government allied itself with French and Dutch cabinets engaging in resisting independence movements in Southeast Asia. Although Washington consistently urged these cabinets to accord greater self-rule to their colonies, it knowingly provided funds that went into waging war for the maintenance of colonialism. Truman, Secretary of State Dean Acheson, and other officials expressed regret at this result but said almost explicitly that the ideal of national self-determination had to be set aside for the sake of containing Soviet Communism. This had become the overriding objective of the United States.

The growth of distrust

How is such a swift change to be explained? The fears felt during World War II had proved groundless. The US mainland had not been attacked. The economy had not gone into a new slump. Public opinion had not relapsed into isolationism. Americans could hardly fail to perceive how rich and powerful was their country in comparison with all others. If ever they had the strength and status to press forward toward fulfilment of their historic national mission, it was in the late 1940s and early 1950s. Why did they retreat instead to a limited and apparently defensive aim?

The turn must be explained by the convergence of a number of factors. First and foremost was the apparent behavior of the Soviet government. For a long time, most Americans regarded Soviet actions as the sole cause of the Cold War. The view prevailed that Soviet provocations left the United States no choice but reluctantly to draw lines and say, 'Thus far; no farther.' Recently, it has become fashionable to question the portrait of the Soviet Union previously accepted and to suggest that the United States may not have been so patient, so tolerant, and so free of blame as previously assumed. On the whole, this new skepticism has salutary results. It involves, however, the risk of one's forgetting or ignoring such truth as was embodied in the older version of events.

The fact is that Soviet acts from 1944 onward were such as to lead almost any Western observer to conclude that the Soviet government meant to install Communist regimes wherever possible, was indifferent to the wishes of the people concerned, and was wholly ruthless in its choice of methods. This conclusion was all the more plausible because it agreed with what was known of Leninist-Stalinist doctrine.

In September 1944, advancing Red Army units approached Warsaw. Soviet radio broadcasts encouraged an uprising in the city by the Polish underground. The uprising commenced. Meanwhile, Russian forces halted. They sent no aid to the embattled Poles. The Soviet government refused to co-operate in schemes proposed by the Americans and British for airlifting supplies to Warsaw. In consequence, the uprising led only to the Polish underground's being decimated by the Nazis. Since that underground contained much of the potential non-Communist leadership for postwar Poland, it seemed a logical surmise that Soviet authorities had deliberately sacrificed it.

In early 1945, Roosevelt, Churchill and Stalin met at Yalta. For practical purposes, the Western leaders accepted Soviet-created regimes as the nuclei for new governments in Eastern and South-eastern Europe, subject to two qualifications. First, the provisional cabinets should be broadened to include representatives of major non-Communist parties. Second, free elections should be held at the earliest feasible date.

Hardly had the conferees returned to their homes than the Soviets forced upon Rumania a predominantly Communist government. Deputy Foreign Minister Andrei Vyshinsky ordered King Michael to seat such a government. When the King attempted to protest, Vyshinsky cut off debate by walking away and slamming a door behind him. With the Red Army occupying Bucharest, the King had no choice but to comply.

In Bulgaria and Yugoslavia, non-Communist elements received equally short shrift. With regard to Poland, lengthy negotiations produced no tangible results. When confronted with American refusal to recognize a predominantly Communist government, Stalin agreed to the inclusion of certain prominent non-Communists in the cabinet. These individuals were not, however, given real power. Soon, some of them not only resigned but fled the country. The free election also promised by Stalin never took place. Balloting for parliamentary delegates in 1947 took place under such conditions as to give Communists all but a handful of seats.

The picture, it is true, was not in monochrome. The Soviet Union had not sent occupation forces into Finland, and it had accepted the installation of a non-Fascist but also non-Communist government as a result of relatively free elections. In Hungary, Soviet authorities seemed loath to intervene. They permitted the formation of a government in which Communists held only a few posts. In Czechoslovakia, Russian representatives approved a coalition government in which Communists were to be in a minority.

Hungary and Czechoslovakia became Soviet satellites well after the war. In both countries, the Soviets insisted that Communist ministers control the police. During 1946, those in Hungary bent their efforts to subverting the non-Communist parties. The Red Army lent them support. Beginning in 1947, the Communists assumed a larger and larger share of control. When new elections were held in 1947, they were rigged so as to produce a Communist

majority. In short order, Hungary enjoyed a relationship with the Soviet Union comparable to that of Poland, Rumania, or Bulgaria. In Czechoslovakia, the Communist ministers pursued a similar course. In February 1948, they effected a coup, ousting their non-Communist colleagues and seizing complete power.

Apologists for the USSR could, of course, point to Greece, to Syria, and to Southeast Asia. They could argue, moreover, that Communist takeovers in Hungary and Czechoslovakia occurred only after the United States had given clear indications of turning toward an anti-Soviet policy.

Finland, pre-1947 Hungary, and pre-1948 Czechoslovakia did not, however, draw much attention among Americans. After all, free elections and coalition regimes were what the Yalta declarations and other inter-Allied accords had led Westerners to expect. They were not news. And nothing that occurred in Greece or the Levant or Southeast Asia matched in forcefulness, crudity, or apparent disregard for sworn agreements the actions of Soviet and native Communists in Poland, Rumania, Bulgaria, and Yugoslavia.

In the Foreign Ministers' Conferences of 1945–47, the Soviet Union had the misfortune, moreover, to be represented by Vyacheslav Molotov. At least since his appointment as Foreign Minister in 1939, he had been regarded in the West as the pre-eminent hard-liner among Bolsheviks. His name was inseparably connected with the Nazi-Soviet pact. Cold, suspicious, harsh, and doctrinaire, Molotov appeared a polemicist and an obstructionist, not a diplomat bent on smoothing differences.

From 1945 onward, almost everything that occurred in Eastern Europe or in Foreign Ministers' meetings or at sessions of the new UN organization conspired to confirm an impression of Soviet intransigence and bellicosity.

In retrospect, one can understand why Stalin and his associates probably attached low priority to offsetting such impressions. With survival uncertain during the war, they had concentrated on gaining popular support in Russia. With the war over, they undoubtedly judged it imperative to restore the discipline of the prewar era. Critical to the maintenance of discipline had been popular belief in the capitalist peril: that is, belief in capitalism's undying hostility to Communism and belief that an active or latent conspiracy united capitalist states in a design to suppress Communism and subvert, conquer, or destroy the Communist motherland. Soviet leaders must have feared that the temporary wartime alliance with capitalist states might cause the people, and perhaps even members of the Party, to become insensitive to the long-term threat. In their eyes, therefore, it must have seemed positively advantageous that co-operation be replaced by conflict and that Western politicians and journalists be provoked into anti-Soviet or anti-Communist declarations.

A second preoccupation of Soviet statesmen must surely have been economic reconstruction. Some no doubt thought of seeking postwar aid from the United States. On the other hand, the resources of the occupied and liberated territories in Eastern Europe represented birds in the hand. The installation of docile Communist regimes in Warsaw and Bucharest meant that the USSR could have Silesian coal and Rumanian oil. Given the common interest of Soviet leaders in restoring public understanding of the capitalist peril, this means of securing resources for Russia's reconstruction must have seemed much preferable.

In all probability, the war had had the result of improving the standing of the military within the Soviet government. Red Army generals had some specific interests. One was security of access to occupied Germany and Austria. A second was priority for defense in postwar budgeting. The first interest was served by having obedient Communist governments in the countries through which ran the Red Army's lines of communication. The second was served by renewal of belief that the USSR was in constant danger of attack from the West.

It is possible thus to surmise that Soviet leaders were not driven by a desire for limitless expansion. Rather, they saw control over certain parts of Eastern Europe as convenient for economic and logistical reasons. What was most important to them was not territory but evidence of Western, and especially American, hostility.

It is important to remember, too, that it was the West, and not merely the United States, that interpreted Soviet behavior as aggressively imperialistic. Postwar regimes in France, Belgium, and the Netherlands necessarily involved Communists, for after June 1941, Communists had formed one of the best organized elements in the Resistance. In the early postwar period, Communist politicians played constructive roles, promoting public housing and improved public health. Their chief effort went, however, to building up their Party. They tried to blacken the reputation of all non-Communists, sometimes trumping up charges of collaboration against former colleagues in the Resistance. By force as well as persuasion, they attempted to gain control of labor unions. And, as in the past, they often seemed slavishly pro-Soviet. Before the war, politicians in Western Europe had seen Communist Parties perform astonishing intellectual somersaults following signals from Moscow. They had also seen Nazi groups in Austria, Czechoslovakia, and elsewhere effect political takeovers as a result of the application of pressure and terror by the German Nazi state. Little wonder then that nervous non-Communist politicians and bureaucrats in postwar Western Europe should regard the actions of the Soviet Union in Poland, Rumania, and Bulgaria as overtures to campaigns to place Communists in power elsewhere.

These politicians and bureaucrats were all the more apprehensive because they remembered America's behavior in the aftermath of World War I. Many had heard American friends predict fearfully that a retreat to isolationism would occur again. In conversations with and communications to American soldiers, diplomats, newspapermen, and others, non-Communist ministers in postwar Western European governments painted as darkly as possible the picture of what might occur should the United States fail vigorously to oppose the extension of Soviet influence.

The English occupied a special position. They had no significant Communist Party. But their statesmen, diplomats, and colonial administrators shared a general concern about possible dominance of the European Continent by any single power and a more specific

'*Don't mind me—just go right on talking*' (*from 'The Herblock Book', Beacon Press, 1952): the atom bomb addresses a group of diplomats in 1947, when the US still held the monopoly of nuclear weapons. (8)*

concern about possible Russian inroads in British spheres of influence in the Eastern Mediterranean, the Middle East, and Southern Asia. Aware that they had weathered the struggle with the Axis only because of massive US aid, they feared being left alone to face the USSR. Hence, Englishmen did all they could to persuade Americans of the reality of the fears voiced by Western Europeans. They also emphasized for Washington evidence of Soviet ambitions in other sectors of the world. Since their military and diplomatic establishments had become intertwined with those of the United States during the war, the English were well situated to convey these messages to American officialdom. The Labour victory of July 1945 enhanced British influence, for, while Churchill and Eden had been viewed with mistrust by many Americans, Clement Atlee and Ernest Bevin could hardly be mistaken for old-fashioned English imperialists.

Thus, at the end of World War II, Americans not only observed at first hand Soviet actions that could be construed as provocative, aggressive, and imperialistic, but they were told by most of their friends that these actions should be so construed. Regarding themselves as somewhat naive about international politics and feeling a deep sense of guilt about their failure to play a more active world role in the interwar years, Americans found it difficult not to view Stalin's moves as counterparts to the moves effected by Hitler in the 1930s.

Acceptance of this outlook was facilitated by convergent developments within the United States. Some took place within the American bureaucracy, where the years 1944–48 saw significant readjustments.

Hard liners

During the war, the State Department had been dominated by newcomers dedicated to creating the UN and solving postwar economic problems. At the war's end, career diplomats waged a successful battle to regain control. As a result, Roosevelt in his final months and Truman throughout his first term received information and diplomatic advice primarily from men who had practiced the diplomatic trade prior to the war—among them Joseph C. Grew, James Clement Dunn, George F. Kennan, and Loy Henderson. These men had seen Soviet agents play by their own rules in the 1920s and 1930s. They were anxious that the politicians and political appointees whom they served should not be taken in by Communist trickery. Professionally, they desired the opportunity to prove that, as negotiators, they could drive hard bargains. Above all, they wanted to prevent their government from adopting any stance that might even suggest a return to isolationism. On balance, therefore, they were inclined to credit the warnings that came from Continental capitals and London, to emphasize for their superiors the evidence of parallelism between Stalin's behavior and Hitler's, and to recommend firm stands on issues in negotiation with the USSR.

The military services also underwent internal change. Concern with combat operations gave way to preoccupation with preparedness for unforeseeable future wars. Civilians and officers in the services all remembered the dismantling of the army and navy in the aftermath of World War I. They were eager, if at all possible, to prevent the armed forces from being starved once again. Each service, moreover, felt that it had a special stake, for advances in technology had lengthened the lead time involved in getting ready for war. To service Secretaries, chiefs of staff, and planning officers, it seemed vitally important that the executive branch, Congress, and the public, should not be insouciant about the danger of a conflict that might develop in five or ten years' time. Since the most plausible enemy was the USSR, spokesmen for the services seized on any piece of evidence suggesting that at some date the United States might need stockpiles, trained ground forces, armor, warships, and bombers in order to counter Soviet aggression.

Representatives of the armed services occupied important places within the bureaucracy. Partly because of mistrust of the State Department, Roosevelt had relied heavily on the service Secretaries and especially the chiefs of staff. Through various co-ordinating committees and, after 1947, the statutory National Security Council, the services retained an important voice concerning foreign policy. In general, spokesmen for the military establishment underlined warnings from Continental states and Britain, supported the professional diplomats, and argued that the United States had an interest in blocking any extension of Soviet power.

None of the factors thus far described was decisive. The American government could have viewed Eastern Europe, the Black Sea region, and northern Iran as naturally and historically a Soviet sphere of influence. It could have taken the position that the USSR would prove itself dangerously imperialistic only if it began to make demands for some degree of control outside that sphere. Similarly, Washington could have discounted fears expressed in Continental capitals and London, and President Truman could have resisted pressures from his own bureaucracy. After World War I, neither appeals from erstwhile allies nor arguments by professional diplomats and proponents of preparedness had determined the major lines of US foreign policy. The controlling force had been trends in public opinion.

After World War II, however, the public gave powerful support to a policy of implacable opposition to Communism. The potential support for such a policy had been present throughout the war. Despite the heroism of the Red Army, the extolling of the Soviet Union by American and British leaders, and intensive official and private pro-Soviet propaganda campaigns, public opinion polls at the height of the war showed more than 40% of the American people regarding Communism as evil and the Soviet Union as a p 314 potential enemy. Hostility to Communism as an ideology and to (13) Russia as a nation were ingrained in the large majority of Roman Catholics and in many others of Central or East European descent. Communism as synonymous with atheism was also anathema to a great many devout Protestants. And a number of labor unions were led by men who carried scars from past battles with Communist organizers.

There existed relatively few groups offsetting those with strong anti-Communist or anti-Russian leanings. The American Communist Party never enrolled significant numbers. While Communists had garnered some allies in the 1930s, they had sacrificed nearly all popular support by applauding the Nazi-Soviet pact and, until June 1941, opposing American aid to the anti-Nazi Allies. A handful of union leaders, mostly Communists themselves, and a small number of intellectuals, chiefly writers and actors, constituted the only friends of Communism in America. And since the bulk of Americans of Russian descent were either anti-Bolsheviks or Jews whose families never identified with Russian nationalism, there was almost no ethnic group to counterbalance the millions of Poles, Bohemians, Hungarians, Rumanians, Bulgars, south Slavs, and Czechs who, on historic or racial or religious grounds, were either anti-Russian or anti-Communist or both.

Even during the war, it had been evident that anti-Communism would be popular and would rouse relatively little opposition. As the Republican presidential nominee in 1944, Thomas E. Dewey had tried to attack the Democratic administration as unduly influenced by Communist labor leaders and as unlikely to uphold the interests of nationalities bordering the USSR. Roosevelt had dealt with this line of attack not by countering it but by ignoring it. Two years later, in 1946, many Republican candidates for the House and Senate campaigned on charges that the Democrats were insensitive to the danger of Communism both at home and abroad. The Republicans made large gains, sweeping control of both chambers. Public opinion thus seemed overwhelmingly to back the kind of opposition to the Soviet Union counselled by Western Europeans and Englishmen and, on the whole, by the diplomatic and military bureaucracies in Washington.

Alternative or supplementary policies gained little momentum. Had either the move against Perón or that against Franco proved a success, American policy might have developed a different character. But the 'Blue Book' proved an embarrassment. Perón used it as a campaign document, claiming that the voter's choice lay between him and Yankee imperialism, and he won handily. Similarly, the pronouncement against Franco produced no result in Spain. Its chief consequence was to revivify right-wing Roman Catholic groups in America that had supported Franco during the Spanish Civil War. Marshall's mediation efforts failed to produce a democratic solution in China. And the outcome there—total victory by the Communists—tended to discredit any future effort

to further democracy in any area where the result might involve Communist participation in power. Without these failures, US policy might have been pro-democratic rather than simply anti-Soviet and anti-Communist.

Had circumstances differed, American policy might have at least retained a positive emphasis on self-determination. Outside of Eastern Europe, however, opportunities for upholding that principle had proved few and unattractive.

Since Communists and other dissidents observed a truce in Greece from early 1945 until late 1946, no occasion presented itself there for a display of even-handed American support for self-determination. Nor did such occasions offer in the Levant or Southern or Southeast Asia, for Western European governments, eager for the good opinion of Americans, either championed self-determination on their own or so masked their colonialism as to make difficult the drawing of clear-cut issues. Thus the Attlee cabinet offered India, Ceylon, Burma, and the former Middle Eastern mandates independence. The French and Dutch governments conducted negotiations with their Southeast Asian colonies ostensibly leading in the same direction. President Truman could and did encourage them to imitate the American example in the Philippines and grant self-government promptly, but there were limits on what he could say, and these limits became more and more narrow as the United States involved itself in efforts to restore economic and political stability in the French and Dutch homelands. Had the Tories retained power in Britain and reneged on the prewar pledge to free India, then there might have arisen an issue as interesting to the American public as the issues that emerged in Eastern Europe. Since this did not occur, concern for national self-determination became absorbed in concern about Soviet Communist expansion.

The one other alternative for Americans might have been a simple return to the concept of their nation as a self-perfecting model for the world. But if the generation of political leaders that came to power during and after World War II shared one set of tenets, it was that the United States should *not* avoid involvement in the politics of the rest of the world, should *not* fail to risk its own peace for peace on other continents, and should never shirk 'responsibility'. Given the convergence of developments—the internal pressures that caused the Soviets to act provocatively, the fears their behavior aroused among Europeans and Englishmen, the postwar changes within the US bureaucracy, the evidence of hostility to Communism and to the Soviet Union among the American electorate, the failure of pro-democratic efforts in Argentina, Spain, and China, and the progress of national self-rule independently of encouragement from the United States—it is very difficult to see in retrospect how the Truman administration might have taken a different tack. So the nation was left with opposition to 'Communist imperialism' as almost the only remnant of its global mission.

On occasion, statesmen tested variations. When campaigning against a Democratic administration in 1952, Republicans condemned containment as a static concept. They advocated 'liberation' as an alternative. Once in office, however, they became more cautious. When presented in 1956 with an opportunity to support a popular uprising in Communist Hungary, they took the safe course of standing by while Soviet forces subjugated the rebels. President Eisenhower initiated an effort to achieve a *détente* with the Soviet p 319 Union. Presidents Kennedy, Johnson, and Nixon continued it, (34) with minimal results. At most, however, these gestures indicated willingness to accept a *status quo*. At no point did any administration relent from the stand that Soviet or, after the Sino-Soviet split, Chinese Communism should not extend its sway over any new territory.

This objective dominated. The *cordon sanitaire* erected in Europe by NATO was extended to other parts of the globe. Counterparts to NATO were set up in Southeast Asia and the Middle East. The complex relationship between Israel and the Arab states was represented in most official American commentary as primarily a contest for influence between the West and the Soviet Union. And for a time in the early 1960s, the United States engaged in a strenuous effort to prevent Soviet-dominated factions from taking power in the Congo!

So dominant did anti-Communism become that American officials and the American public hardly noticed corollary policies quite out of keeping with the nation's traditional stances. Neither the extension of aid to anti-democratic governments in Latin America nor *de jure* or *de facto* alliances with Franco, Tito, Chiang, and the Thai military drew significant critical comment in Congress or the press. Only tiny minorities voiced protest when the American government used its power to block or oppose national self-determination in situations in which victory for foreign-dominated or foreign-influenced Communists seemed a likelihood—as, for instance, in Guatemala in 1954, in Indo-China on repeated occasions, and in the Dominican Republic in 1965.

p 318
(32)

Vietnam—escalation and withdrawal

Only in the late 1960s did widespread questioning begin to develop about the world mission which Americans had defined for themselves after World War II. The precipitant was Indo-China. There, the French had become engaged in a war against nationalist forces led by Communists. By 1954, they had suffered both military and psychological defeat. President Eisenhower considered sending in American forces to rescue their hold over the colony. On account of doubts as to whether the war could be waged successfully and whether American action would command support among a public just recovered from the war in Korea, he decided against armed intervention. He helped, however, to arrange a diplomatic settlement dividing Indo-China into four states: a Communist North Vietnam, an anti-Communist South Vietnam, a neutral Laos, and a neutral Cambodia. The American government then supplied large-scale material aid to South Vietnam.

Despite American aid, a major civil war developed in South Vietnam, with Communist insurgents receiving support from the north and, indeed, with North Vietnamese military units operating in the South Vietnamese back country. In these circumstances, President Kennedy decided to take the step which Eisenhower had declined to take seven years earlier. He sent ten thousand American soldiers to help the South Vietnamese wage this war.

p 319
(35)

Given the national mission which the United States had defined for itself, this action had a quality of inevitability. At the end of the 1950s Americans had perceived the Soviet Union as starting on a new and more ambitious program of expansion. On more than one occasion, Premier Nikita Khrushchev threatened seizure of Berlin. Soviet and East European aid missions appeared in Egypt and even in central Africa. In Cuba, Communist revolutionaries won power and immediately received backing from the USSR. Simultaneously, Southeast Asia became a theater in which the Soviet Union appeared eager to extend its influence, for civil warfare had broken out in Laos as well as in Vietnam, and the USSR had suddenly begun to airlift large quantities of weapons and supplies to a Laotian faction led by Communists. Kennedy and his associates thus saw Southeast Asia as one of a number of sectors in which the Soviets were testing the strength of America's commitment to the mission it had taken upon itself.

p 317
(29)

Information about Laos persuaded Kennedy that there existed little likelihood of America's being able to create or sustain a durable anti-Communist regime. He decided therefore to demonstrate that the United States would not permit a victory by the Communists but at the same time to negotiate with Moscow about re-establishment of a neutral coalition regime. Given the lessons commonly drawn from the failure of US mediation in China and the overthrow of the coalition government in Czechoslovakia, this was a relatively venturesome course. It seemed to succeed. That is, an agreement was eventually signed, providing for a truce and a coalition in Laos. But Kennedy and his associates regarded it as imperative that the Russians understand America's determination not to permit this or other such arrangements elsewhere in the globe to yield Communist successes. When fighting threatened to resume in Laos, Kennedy fielded five thousand US troops on the Thai side of the Thai-Laotian border.

The President and his advisers saw Vietnam in this context. Even if North Vietnam were somewhat independent of the USSR and China, its takeover of South Vietnam would nevertheless represent an enlargement of the area that looked to Moscow for guidance. Perhaps more important still, a Communist victory in South

Americans have tended to think that their own democratic system is equally suitable for all people at all times. Occasional bitter experiences in Southeast Asia have begun to suggest the contrary. (9)

Vietnam would make almost impossible maintenance of the American-Soviet bargain over Laos. That kingdom would also come under Communist control. Neutralization arrangements elsewhere on the globe would become out of the question. The Russians might be encouraged to attempt adventures elsewhere. The chances for any kind of *détente* would diminish. The danger of all-out war would become greater. Or so it seemed to the White House, the State Department, the Pentagon and, indeed, nearly all well-informed American observers. Hence the necessity for risking some American lives in an effort to prevent Communist success in South Vietnam.

The North Vietnamese, however, stepped up their activity in the South. The demand for American manpower grew. The tasks of American troops multiplied, but the prospect for maintaining a non-Communist regime in Saigon became dimmer rather than brighter.

By early 1965, the American government faced an apparent choice between abandoning South Vietnam or significantly expanding American military involvement. In the interval, Presidents Kennedy and Johnson, a number of presidential advisers, and a number of congressmen and other public figures had justified earlier commitments of force in terms which made difficult even contemplation of the alternative of acquiescence in a Communist takeover. Prevention of such an eventuality had been represented as important, indeed essential, to accomplishment of the American mission in the world. Hence President Johnson selected what seemed to him and to nearly all his advisers the only fitting course of action. He ordered the bombing of North Vietnam in the hope that Hanoi would thus be persuaded to desist from intervention in the South. He dispatched large numbers of US troops to South Vietnam in the hope that they could subjugate the insurgents and give the non-Communist political forces a new lease on power.

These measures did not succeed. The North Vietnamese and the South Vietnamese continued to fight. In an offensive staged during the Tet holidays early in 1968, the North Vietnamese demonstrated that the massive American military effort had not even given the non-Communists secure control over major cities in the South. Soon afterward, Johnson suspended bombing of the North. His successor, President Nixon, commenced a slow withdrawal of US forces from South Vietnam.

This turn of events was not due primarily to non-success in Vietnam. It came about chiefly because of a new change in American public opinion. While the abstract objective of combating Soviet

p 320
(37)

or Communist imperialism had commanded almost universal popular support, the extent of the public's willingness to make sacrifices for that objective had never been clear. Polls showed approval of President Truman's initial decision to act in Korea, but enthusiasm for the Korean War paled quickly. From the early 1950s through the 1960s, congressional willingness to appropriate foreign aid funds steadily diminished. For practical purposes, Congress came to vote large sums only when appealed to on national security grounds by representatives of the military establishment.

Even when there seemed the broadest consensus on an anti-Soviet or anti-Communist policy, some influential voices questioned whether the interests of the nation were actually bound up in the fate of non-Communist governments on other continents. In 1950–51, former President Hoover and Senator Robert Taft led a campaign to prevent the assignment of American troops to NATO. In 1954, certain Republican and Democratic senators (among them, Lyndon Johnson of Texas) advised Eisenhower not to intervene in Indo-China. Later in the 1950s, when crises arose over Chinese Communist attacks on Nationalist-held islands close to the mainland, other public figures questioned whether defense of these islands or of Formosa itself justified a risk of war with China. Still others offered the suggestion that the United States should contemplate some form of 'disengagement' from Europe. Among these was Ambassador George F. Kennan, who had been responsible in the mid-1940s for publicizing the concept of containment.

Public reaction to the war in Vietnam paralleled in part reaction to the Korean War. At first, polls showed approval. Then approval diminished. By 1968–69, large majorities reportedly regarded the war as a mistake and hoped for its prompt ending. The difference between the early 1950s and the late 1960s lay in the existence of a fervent antiwar minority made up mostly of young people whose memories did not extend even to the Eisenhower administration.

This minority condemned the war not only as a failure but as an enterprise that should never have been undertaken. Declaring that the United States supported a military regime in Saigon and denied Vietnamese people the right to settle their affairs for themselves, this minority in effect revived advocacy of the national mission as it had been defined before World War II.

The numbers and the earnestness of this minority, together with obstreperous tactics by some of its members, reawakened long dormant questions about American national objectives. To many, it brought shamefaced awareness that the United States had somehow given up its pretensions to uniqueness. During its first decades as a great power, it had at least kept up some appearance of being devoted to ends other than those which preoccupied other nation states. After World War II, it had gradually set aside traditional ideals and begun to behave like all other powers, identifying a rival and employing all its energies to prevent that rival from gaining any apparent relative advantage.

In the 1970s, increasing numbers of American are asking whether such behavior is appropriate for a nation dedicated so long to loftier ends. Echoes of old debates begin to be heard again, with distinguished public figures declaring, in effect, that the United States can best attain its traditional goals by concentrating on its own ability to set an example for other states. Most concede that isolation, even as practiced in the 1930s, no longer exists as a realistic choice. The United States is far too rich and strong, far too great a factor in the affairs of other lands, and, in view of modern military technology, far too vulnerable. But hard questions are being posed once again about both the purposes of the nation and the strategies best suited to achievement of those purposes. There is enough stir so that a reckless prophet could chance at least a long-odds bet that by the decade of the 1980s there will have developed a definition of America's mission more limited than that of the 19th century but less limited and less negative than that of the Cold War era.

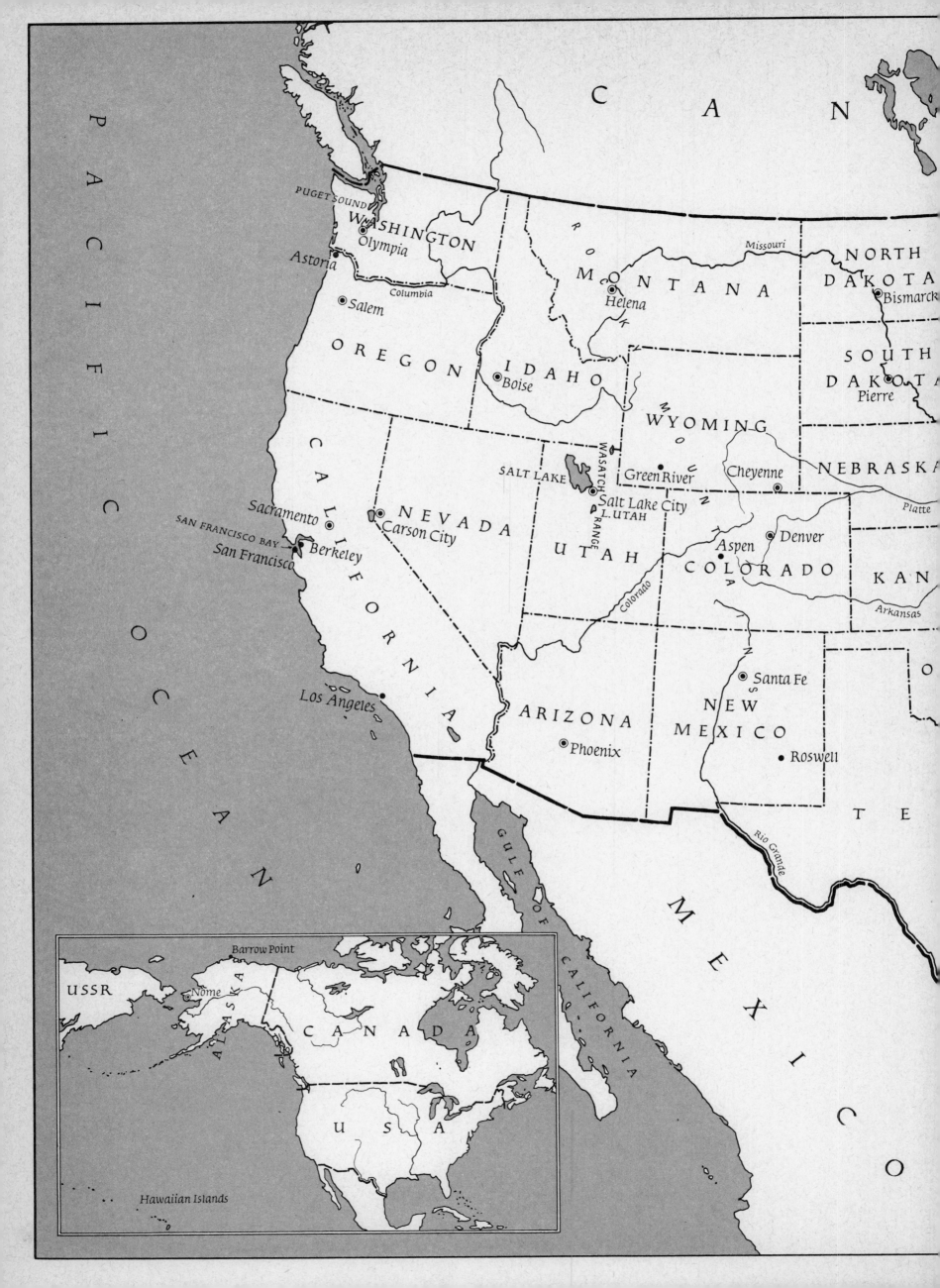

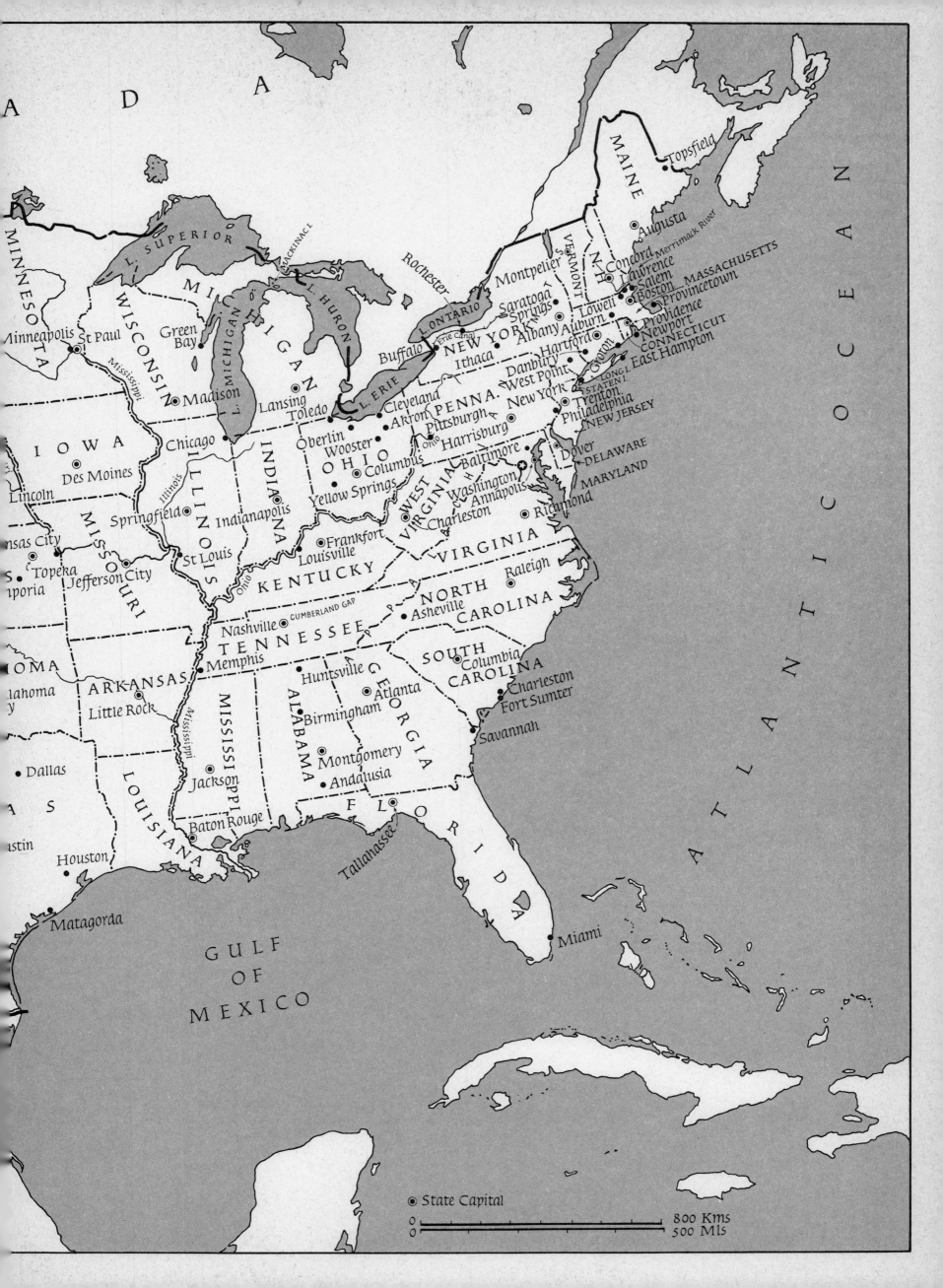

● State Capital

800 Kms
500 Mls

List and sources of illustrations

River expedition in 1857. *Collection W. H. Goetzmann*

9. Reptiles drawn by J. H. Richard, from the Pacific Railroad Survey *Reports* of 1853. *University of Texas Library*

32 10. Apache Indians attacking the US Boundary Survey Commission, 18 October 1852; after sketches by Henry Pratt and John Russell Bartlett. *Yale University Library*

11. Detail from T. H. Jefferson's *Map of the Emigrant Road from Independence, Mo. to San Francisco, California*, pt. III, 1840s. *Library of Congress, Washington, D.C.*

33 12. Cartoon of Othniel Charles Marsh; from *Punch*, 13 September 1890

13. Japanese woodcut showing the arrival of Commodore Perry's expedition of 1852–54. *Library of Congress, Washington, D.C.*

II A Nation of Nations

39 1. Ben Shahn: immigrants arriving in New York, detail of mural in the former Community Center of Jersey Homesteads, Roosevelt, N.J.; 1937/8. *Photo Scala, courtesy Ben Shahn Foundation*

40–41 2. Immigrants on an Atlantic liner; detail of photograph by Edwin Levick, 1906. *Library of Congress, Washington, D.C.*

3. Immigrants in 'pens' on Ellis Island, New York; detail of photograph by Underwood & Underwood, late 1905/ early 1906. *Library of Congress, Washington, D.C.*

4. Immigrants on Ellis Island, New York, waiting to be transferred; photograph by Underwood & Underwood, 1912. *Library of Congress, Washington, D.C.*

5. Italian immigrant woman carrying cloth for home work in New York; detail of photograph by Lewis W. Hine, 1909. *George Eastman House Collection*

6. Orchard Street, New York; photograph by Byron, c. 1900. *The Byron Collection, Museum of the City of New York*

7. Immigrant train on the Baltimore & Ohio line at the Station Terminus, Locust Point, Maryland; detail of photograph, c. 1910. *Smithsonian Institution, Washington, D.C.*

42–43 8. *St Patrick's Day Parade at Union Square, New York*; detail of lithograph, 1874. *The J. Clarence Davies Collection, Museum of the City of New York*

9. Samuel B. Waugh: *The Battery, New York*; detail of panoramic painting, c. 1855. The Chinese junk shown in the picture is the *Keying*, which visited New York in the 1840s; since Castle Garden (the Battery) did not open as a reception center for immigrants until 1855, its inclusion here is a fanciful reminiscence. *Museum of the City of New York*

10. 'They all do It'; cartoon from *Puck*, 3 April 1889. *Library of Congress, Washington, D.C.*

44–45 11, 12. Tom Torlino, a Navajo Indian, on his arrival at Carlisle Indian School (Carlisle, Pennsylvania) and three years later; photographs by Choate, 1880s. *Cumberland County Historical Society and Hamilton Library Association, Carlisle, Pennsylvania*

13. 'The Thing won't Melt!', cartoon by W. H. Walker from *Life*, 18 November 1915. *British Museum, London. Photo R. B. Fleming*

14. 'Uncle Sam's Thanksgiving Dinner', engraving by Thomas Nast from *Harper's Weekly*, 20 November 1869. *British Museum, London. Photo R. B. Fleming*

15. Americanization program in a school at Enfaula, Oklahoma; photograph by Russell Lee for the Farm Security Administration, February 1940. *Library of Congress, Washington, D.C.*

16. Evacuees of Japanese descent who arrived by train at Lone Pine, California, transferring to buses for Manzanar, California, a War Relocation Authority Center; photograph by the US War Relocation Authority, April 1942. *Library of Congress, Washington, D.C.*

46–47 17. '"Welcome to All!"'; lithograph by Joseph Keppler from *Puck*, 28 April

1880. *Victoria and Albert Museum, London. Photo A. C. Cooper*

18. Gambling saloon in Sonora, California, c. 1850–52; detail of illustration from Frederick S. Marryat, *Mountains and Molehills*, 1855. *The American Museum in Britain, Claverton Manor, Bath. Photo Eileen Tweedy*

19. 'Looking Backward'; detail of lithograph by Joseph Keppler from *Puck*, 11 January 1893. *Library of Congress, Washington, D.C.*

20. 'Remember your First Thrill of American Liberty'; illustration from a poster for US Government Bonds (2nd Liberty Loan of 1917) printed by Sackett and Wilhelms. *Library of Congress, Washington, D.C.*

48–49 21. Double-page spread of illustrations from *A Nation of Nations* by Louis Adamic, New York 1945. The family shown below right are in fact Polish Americans (information from Mr Alland). *Reproduced by kind permission of Harper and Row: photographs from the Library of Congress, Washington, D.C. (left) and Alexander Alland (right)*

22. Four generations of slaves all born on the plantation of J. J. Smith at Beaufort, South Carolina; photograph by Timothy O'Sullivan (who accompanied Northern troops as they moved into the South during the Civil War), 1862. *Library of Congress, Washington, D.C.*

23. Workers conditioning transparent plastic bomber noses for installation, Baltimore, Maryland, May 1942. *US Office of War Information photograph in the Library of Congress, Washington, D.C.*

24. Selection of newspapers published by ethnic groups in the US in 1959. *Photo BBC*

25. Chinese grocery in Chinatown, San Francisco; detail of stereo view, c. 1906. *George Eastman House Collection*

26. Celebration of Chinese New Year in New York. *Photo Edward Meyers*

50 27. Navajo children in Arizona collected from home by a school bus of the US Bureau of Indian Affairs, 1957. *Photo Carl W. Herbert (Camera Press)*

28. Detail of scene from the film *White Feather* showing, right to left, Robert Wagner, Jeff Hunter and Debra Paget; directed by Robert Webb and distributed by Twentieth Century Fox, 1955. *Photo courtesy John Kobal*

29. Detail of scene from the film *Little Big Man*, showing Dustin Hoffman with Indians (members of the Crow, Stony and Sarcee tribes, playing Cheyenne); directed by Arthur Penn and distributed by Twentieth Century Fox, 1971. *Photo courtesy John Kobal*

30. *Power to the People*; poster issued by the Committee to Defend the Panther 21, New York City; offset lithograph, 1969/70

52 1. '(Dis) "Honors are easy." Now both parties have something to hang on'; cartoon by Thomas Nast from *Harper's Weekly*, 20 May 1882. *Library of Congress, Washington, D.C.*

53 2. 'Just So'; cartoon by Bellew from *Harper's Weekly*, 15 March 1879. *Courtesy Arthur Bonner*

3. 'The only way to handle it'; cartoon by Hallahan from the Providence *Evening Bulletin*, reprinted in *The Literary Digest*, 7 May 1921. *Library of Congress, Washington, D.C.*

54 4. Illustration to show foreign-born population in the United States in 1920; from *The Literary Digest*, 7 May 1921. *Library of Congress, Washington, D.C.*

Detail of 'Our Common Schools as They Are and as They May Be'; cartoon by Thomas Nast from *Harper's Weekly*, 26 February 1870. *Library of Congress, Washington, D.C.*

55 6. Graph showing the composition of the foreign-born population in the United States by country of birth, 1850–1940; from *The Annals of The American Academy of Political and Social Science*, March 1949. *Reproduced by permission*

57 7. 'The Union as it was . . .'; cartoon by Thomas Nast from *Harper's Weekly*, 1874. *Library of Congress, Washington D.C.*

III Freedom and Faith

61 1. Sedona, Arizona: Chapel of the Holy Cross; by Anshen and Allen, 1956. *Photo United States Travel Service, London*

62 2. Adam van Breen: *The Departure of the Pilgrims from Delft Haven in the Speedwell to join the Mayflower*; first half of the 17th C. *Courtesy the H. Terry-Engell Gallery, London*

3. Pavel Petrovich Svinin: *A Philadelphia Anabaptist Immersion during a Storm*; watercolor, 1811–13. *The Metropolitan Museum of Art, Rogers Fund, 1942*

4. *French Expedition visiting San Carlos de Borromeo Mission in Carmel, California*; watercolor, 1786. *Museo Naval, Madrid. Photo Mas, Barcelona*

5. *Scene in a Quaker Meeting House*, c. 1790. *Museum of Fine Arts, Boston. Bequest of Maxim Karolik*

6. Tucson, Arizona: San Xavier del Bac; built by Franciscans, 1784–97. *Photo Camera Press*

63 7. *On the Great Plains*; Catholic, Lutheran and Baptist churches, near Winner, South Dakota; photograph by Dorothea Lange, 1938. *The Oakland Museum Collection, Oakland, California*

8. Newport, Rhode Island: pulpit of the Seventh Day Baptist Church; built 1729, now part of the Newport Historical Society. *Photo Camera Press*

9. Lewis Miller: *Interior of the Lutheran Church, York, Pennsylvania*; detail of drawing, 1800. *From the collection of The Historical Society of York County in York, Pennsylvania*

10. Newport, Rhode Island: interior of Touro Synagogue; by Peter Harrison, 1759–63. *Photo Library of Congress, Washington, D.C.*

64–65 11. Carl Christian Anton Christensen: *A Mormon campsite near the Mississippi where thousands of quail have descended*; from a panorama of 22 paintings illustrating the history of the Mormon Church, completed in 1890. *Courtesy Brigham Young University, Provo, Utah*

12. *Methodist Camp Meeting*; aquatint by M. Dubourg, 1819, after Jacques Gerard Milbert. *Library of Congress, Washington, D.C.*

13. *The Way of Good and Evil*; lithograph by John Hailer, 1862. *Library of Congress, Washington, D.C.*

14. Ben Shahn: *Women's Christian Temperance Union Parade*; gouache, 1933–34. Part of a mural project for Central Park Casino. *Museum of the City of New York*

66 15. John Wollaston (fl. 1742–70): *George Whitefield Preaching*. *National Portrait Gallery, London*

16. Sankey and Moody holding a meeting at the Agricultural Hall, Islington, London; wood engraving, 1875. *Mansell Collection*

17. Three day Biennial Meeting of college students in the First Church of Christ, Scientist, Boston. *Courtesy of Christian Science Center, Boston, Mass.*

18. Black Muslims attending a mass meeting. *Photo T. L. Blair (Camera Press)*

67 19. Aimee Semple McPherson preaching, 1933. *Photo United Press International*

20. Billy Sunday preaching in the late 1920s. *Photo United Press International*

21. A Billy Graham Crusade in Anaheim Stadium, California. *Photo Ray Hamilton (Camera Press)*

68 22. California girl giving the 'Jesus sign'. *Photo Julian Wasser*

23. 'Pass the Lord and Praise the Ammunition'; 1967 poster attacking Cardinal Spellman, then Archbishop of New York, for his support of the Vietnam War. *Photo BPC Library*

24. Pope Paul VI visiting St Patrick's Cathedral, New York, 1965. *Photo United States Information Service*

70 1. Richard Mather (1596–1669); woodcut by John Foster 1670. This is the first woodcut made in America. *Radio Times Hulton Picture Library*

71 2. Jonathan Edwards; engraving by Trotter, 1783. *Radio Times Hulton Picture Library*

72 3. Title-page of the Massachusetts Indian Bible, 1663; translated by John Eliot.

British Museum, London. Photo *John R. Freeman*

73 4. *Grand ascension of the Miller Tabernacle*; woodcut, 1844. *Courtesy of the American Antiquarian Society, Worcester, Mass.*

75 5. Map showing distribution of religious adherents in 1965; *drawn by Map Graphics, London*

77 6. *Church and State*; wood engraving by Thomas Nast from *Harper's Weekly*, 5 February 1871. *Library of Congress, Washington, D.C.*

IV Popular Politics

81 1. Inauguration of Lyndon B. Johnson, 20 January 1965, in Washington, D.C. *United States Information Service*

82–83 2. Town Meeting; engraving from John Trumbull's popular poem *M'Fingal*, 1795. This patriotic poem (begun 1775, completed 1782) was inspired by the Revolution. *Library of Congress, Washington, D.C.*

3. A French commentary on the Tea Controversy; engraving published in Paris, *c.* 1775. *The Metropolitan Museum of Art, New York, Gift of William H. Huntington, 1882*

4. *The Bostonians paying the Excise-man or Tarring and Feathering*; lithograph by Pendleton, 1830, after a print published in London in 1774. *Library of Congress, Washington, D.C.*

5. Pulling down the statue of George III by the 'Sons of Freedom' on Bowling Green, New York, July 1776; engraving by John McRae, after painting by Oertle, 1859. *Library of Congress, Washington, D.C.*

6. The Boston Tea Party, 18 December 1773; lithograph by Nathaniel Currier, 1848. Young men disguised as Mohawk Indians stole aboard a vessel in Boston Harbor and threw the cargo of tea overboard. Library of Congress, Washington, D.C. Photo *United States Information Service*

7. Inauguration of George Washington, 30 April 1789, at Federal Hall, New York City; engraving by Amos Doolittle, after a contemporary drawing by Peter Lacour. *The I.N. Phelps Stokes Collection, New York Public Library*

84–85 8. John Lewis Krimmel: *Election Day at the State House, Philadelphia, 1816. The Historical Society of Pennsylvania*

9. Fan with miniature portraits of the first eleven Presidents from Washington to Polk; between portraits are the coat of arms of the United States and the Goddess of Liberty. Fan was a gift from Polk to his wife and carried by her at his inauguration. *James K. Polk Home, Columbia, Tennessee*

10. Campaign ribbons of 1876. *National Museum of History and Technology, Smithsonian Institution, Washington, D.C.*

11. Campaign pins and buttons from 1888. *National Museum of History and Technology, Smithsonian Institution, Washington, D.C.*

86–87 12. *King Andrew the First*; cartoon by the political opposition of President Jackson as 'King Veto'; lithograph, 1832. *Library of Congress, Washington, D.C.*

13. General Harrison's Log Cabin March and Quick Step; music cover, lithograph by Ed Weber and Company, 1840. *Library of Congress, Washington, D.C.*

14. Parade in Presidential Campaign of 1840; watercolor by Francis Schell of later date. The procession is assembled at the Harrison headquarters in Philadelphia. *Courtesy Kenneth M. Newman, The Old Print Shop, New York*

15. *Phryne before the Chicago Tribunal* or *Tattoed Man*; cartoon by Bernhard Gillam parodying the then popular French painting by Gérome; from *Puck*, 1884

16. *Riot in Philadelphia*; lithograph by James Baillie, 1844. *Library of Congress, Washington, D.C.*

17. Inaugural procession in honor of President Buchanan on Pennsylvania Avenue, Washington, D.C.; wood engraving from *Frank Leslie's Illustrated Newspaper*, 21 March 1857. *Library of Congress, Washington, D.C.*

18. *Another Voice for Cleveland*; cartoon by Frank Beard from *Judge*, 27 September 1884

19. Armed Republicans occupying the Kansas House of Representatives after a disputed election in which both Populists and Republicans claimed a majority; photograph, 15 February 1893. *The Kansas State Historical Society, Topeka, Kansas*

88–89 20. Tammany Hall decorated for the National Convention, 4 July 1868; from *Shannon's Manual*, 1868. *Courtesy the New-York Historical Society, New York City*

21. *The Lost Bet*; lithograph after a painting by Joseph Klir, 1892. *Courtesy the Chicago Historical Society*

22. *The Sacrilegious Candidate*; cartoon by Grant Hamilton from *Judge*, 19 September 1896. The illustration depicts William Jennings Bryan in an allusion to his 'Cross of Gold' speech before the Democratic Convention in 1896. *Library of Congress, Washington, D.C.*

23. *Apostle of Prosperity*, election poster for Theodore Roosevelt; lithograph, 1903. *Courtesy The New-York Historical Society, New York City*

24. *'Ave Theodore!'*; cartoon by Joseph Keppler from *Puck*, 1 March 1905. Theodore Roosevelt is portrayed as a Roman emperor leading a procession of his political supporters and shackled opponents. *Library of Congress, Washington, D.C.*

90 25. President Franklin D. Roosevelt on a campaign tour in Springfield, Massachusetts, on 4 November 1944. Photo *Associated Press*

26. Franklin D. Roosevelt's plane in Chicago, 1932. Roosevelt flew from New York to Chicago to accept the nomination at the nominating convention. Photo *United Press International*

27. President Truman holding a copy of the Chicago Tribune erroneously announcing his defeat on 4 November 1948. Photo *Associated Press*

28. Franklin D. Roosevelt's first radio address to the nation after America's entry into World War II. *Paul Popper Ltd, London*

29. President Eisenhower and Vice-President Nixon celebrate their re-election in Washington, D.C., 7 November 1956. Photo *United Press International*

91 30. A supporter of Barry Goldwater holds a placard during election campaign in Longview, Texas. Photo *Burt Glinn (Camera Press)*

31. Hubert Humphrey, Vice-Presidential candidate in the 1964 campaign, speaks at a rally in Santa Fé, New Mexico. Photo *Ollie Atkins (Camera Press)*

32. Vice-President Nixon debates with Senator Kennedy on television during the 1960 presidential campaign. Photo *United Press International*

92 33. Adlai Stevenson addresses the Democratic Convention at Los Angeles in 1960. Photo *United States Information Service*

95 1. *The Election of 1764*; an engraving of the period showing voters in Philadelphia. *American Antiquarian Society, Worcester, Massachusetts*

99 2. Thomas Nast: the 'Republican Elephant' after a narrowly won victory in the presidential election of 1876; detail of a cartoon from *Harper's Weekly*, 24 March 1877

100 3. Thomas Nast: 'Let us Prey'; cartoon depicting 'Boss' Tweed of Tammany Hall, from *Harper's Weekly*, 23 September 1871

4. A Democratic cartoon of 1896 attacking big business profiting from the labors of Southern and Western farmers. *Library of Congress, Washington, D.C.*

101 5. A new role for the President, a commentary on televised press conferences; cartoon from *The Newark News. Courtesy of the Newark News, Newark, New Jersey*

6. Daniel Fitzpatrick: the 'Democratic Donkey' and the 'Republican Elephant' watch the results of the New Hampshire primary; cartoon from the *St Louis Post-Dispatch*

V Stages of Enterprise

105 1. The Corliss Engine; from *Treasures of Art, Industry and Manufacture Represented in the American Centennial Exhibition at Philadelphia*, Buffalo, New York, 1877. Victoria and Albert Museum, London. Photo *John Webb*

106 2. Interior of the New York Crystal Palace; colored lithograph by C. Parsons, printed by Endicott and Co., 1853. *The J. Clarence Davies Collection, Museum of the City of New York*

3. B. J. Harrison: *Fair of the American Institute at Niblo's Garden*; watercolor, *c.* 1845. *Museum of the City of New York*

4. William Giles Munson: *The Eli Whitney Gun Factory*, 1826–28. *Yale University Art Gallery, Mabel Brady Garvan Collection*

107 5. Christian Schussele: *Men of Progress*, *c.* 1860, an imaginary meeting of inventors. From left to right, standing: William T. E. Morton (introduced use of ether); James Bogardus (cast iron); Samuel Colt (revolving-breech pistol); Cyrus McCormick (reaper); Joseph Saxton (official system of weights and measures); Peter Cooper (constructed first American locomotive); Joseph Henry (physicist, discovered principles of dynamos, transformers, and wireless telegraphy); John Ericsson (designed ship *Monitor*); Erastus Bigelow (looms for carpet manufacture). Seated, left to right: Charles Goodyear (vulcanized rubber); Jordan Mott (anthracite stove); Eliphalet Nott (improvements in steam boilers and generators); Frederick Sickels (devices for steering ships by steam power); Samuel F. B. Morse (telegraph); Henry Burden (cultivators, plows); Robert Hoe (rotary printing press); Isaiah Jennings (dentistry tools); Thomas Blanchard (machine tools); Elias Howe (sewing machine). *National Portrait Gallery, Smithsonian Institution, Washington, D.C.*

6. *The testing of the first reaping machine near Steele's Tavern, Va.*; colored lithograph, 1831. Photo *The Science Museum, London*

108 7. Mary Keys: *Lockport on the Erie Canal*; watercolor, 1832. *Collection of Munson-Williams-Proctor Institute, Utica, New York*

8. *By industry we thrive*; lithograph by Kimmel and Voigt, 1873. *Courtesy The New-York Historical Society, New York City*

109 9. *The World's Railroad Scene*; advertisement poster for the Illinois Central Railroad; lithograph by Swaim and Lewis, 1882. *Library of Congress, Washington, D.C.*

10. *Ten Minutes for Refreshment*; chromolithograph published by the Great American Tea Company in New York, 1886. *Courtesy Chicago Historical Society*

110–11 11. Winslow Homer: *Bell Time*; wood engraving from *Harper's Weekly*, 25 July 1868. *Library of Congress, Washington, D.C.*

12. *Studebaker in a wagon-tire shop, Hangtown, California*; artist unknown, *c.* 1855. *Courtesy National Gallery of Art, Washington, D.C. Gift of Edgar William and Bernice Chrysler Garbisch, 1966*

13. John D. Rockefeller and his wife alighting from a train. Photo *Camera Press*

14. S. B. Shiley: *Bessemer converters in Bethlehem, Pennsylvania*, 1895. *Courtesy Bethlehem Steel Corporation, Bethlehem, Pennsylvania*

15. Dinner meeting of officials of the Carnegie Steel Company, celebrating the formation of US Steel, 9 January 1901. *Courtesy of the Carnegie Library of Pittsburgh*

16. A member of the Pioneer Automobile Party in his Toledo car at the rim of the Grand Canyon, Arizona; photograph by Aultman, *c.* 1902. *Library of Congress, Washington, D.C.*

17. *Park Row Stores*; engraving by Doty and Bergen, *c.* 1854. *Museum of the City of New York*

112–13 18. Orville and Wilbur Wright's glider being launched at Kitty Hawk,

North Carolina, 10 October 1902. Photo *The Science Museum, London*

19. Official program of the first American Aviation Meet, Los Angeles, 1910. *Aviation Museum, The Smithsonian Institution, Washington, D.C.*

20. 'Interior view of a modern first-class pork packing and canning establishment'; chromolithograph by Shober and Carqueville, 1880. *Courtesy Chicago Historical Society*

21. *Broadway*; lithograph by J. J. Fogerty, *c.* 1880. *Courtesy The New-York Historical Society, New York City*

22. Sears, Roebuck and Company catalog cover, Fall 1897. *Courtesy Sears, Roebuck and Company*

114–15 23. Norris Dam in east Tennessee, completed in 1936. This was the first dam built by the Tennessee Valley Authority created by the first New Deal Congress in 1933. Photo *TVA, Knoxville, Tennessee*

24. The Los Angeles Freeway. Photo *Infoplan*

25. Oil refinery in Tyler, Texas. Photo *Texas Eastern Transmission Corporation*

26. The Pushbutton Miner. This machine can move along a hillside on crawler treads and mines coal by remote control. Conveyor units are shown here stored on a spiral ramp when not in use. Photo *United States Information Service*

27. A Boeing 747 Jumbo Jet in airport hangar. Photo *Bob Kelley (Camera Press)*

116 28. At the Kennedy Space Center in Florida, men monitor a test performance of the countdown for the Apollo 14 moon shot, January 1971. Photo *NASA*

118 1. *The Lure of American Wages*; woodcut, *c.* 1855. *Museum of the City of New York*

119 2. Arrival of enormous quantities of grain at the New York Central and Hudson River Elevator; wood engraving from *Frank Leslie's Illustrated Newspaper*, 10 November 1877. *Library of Congress, Washington, D.C.*

120 3. Diagram of the Colt revolver; detail from an 1850s advertisement for Colt pistols. *Courtesy of Colt's Firearms Division, Hartford, Connecticut*

121 4. *The First Cotton Gin*; engraving after a drawing by William L. Sheppard, from *Harper's Weekly*, 1873. Library of Congress, Washington, D.C. Photo *United States Information Service*

122 5. *The First Oil Well*; detail from wood engraving, 1891; drilled by Col. Drake in 1859, near Titusville, Pennsylvania. *Library of Congress, Washington, D.C.*

123 6. *The Modern Ship of the Plains*; detail of wood engraving after drawing by R. T. Zogbaum from *Harper's Weekly*, 13 November 1886. *Library of Congress, Washington, D.C.*

125 7. Table showing product orientation of applied research and development by industry, 1960

VI A Changing Federalism

129 1. *Arms of the States and Territories of the American Union*; lithograph by A. J. Cornell, 1876. *Library of Congress, Washington, D.C.*

130–31 2. *Congress Voting Independence*, *c.* 1788; engraving by Edward Savage, after a painting by Robert Edge Pine, completed by Edward Savage. *Library of Congress, Washington, D.C.*

3. Mass meeting at Institute Hall, Charleston, South Carolina, to endorse a call for a State Convention to discuss secession from the Union; wood engraving from *Frank Leslie's Illustrated Newspaper*, 24 November 1860

4. Breaker boys; photograph by Lewis W. Hine, 1909. *George Eastman House Collection*

5. Textile workers' strike in Lawrence, Massachusetts, 1912. *Brown Brothers*

6. William Gropper: *The Building of a Dam*; part of a three-panel mural commissioned by the Department of the Interior; 1939. *Public Buildings Service photo no. 121-PS-3091 in the National Archives, Washington, D.C.*

7. US Bureau of the Census, Washington, D.C. Photo *United States Information Service*

132–33 8. Benjamin Latrobe: *Elevation of the south front of the President's House copied from the design as proposed to be altered in 1807*; watercolor, 1817. *Library of Congress, Washington, D.C.*

9. Charles Burton: *View of the Capitol, Washington, D.C., in 1824*; watercolor. *The Metropolitan Museum of Art, New York, Purchase, 1942, Joseph Pulitzer Bequest*

10. Samuel F. B. Morse: *The Old House of Representatives*, 1821–22. *The Corcoran Gallery of Art, Washington, D.C.*

11. George Catlin: *The Virginia Constitutional Convention*; watercolor, 1829–30. *Courtesy of The New-York Historical Society, New York City*

134–35 12. Chief Justice Roger Brooke Taney; photograph by Mathew Brady. *Library of Congress, Washington, D.C.*

13. *The Starting Point of the Great War Between the States*; detail of a lithograph by A. Hoen and Co., 1887, based on a photograph of the inauguration of Jefferson Davis as President of the Confederate States of America, at Montgomery, Alabama, 18 February 1861. *Library of Congress, Washington, D.C.*

14. Lincoln conferring with General George McClellan at Army Headquarters, Antietam, Maryland, October 1862. Photo *United States Information Service*

15. Lieutenant General Ulysses S. Grant, at City Point, Virginia; photograph by Mathew Brady or assistant, 1864. *Library of Congress, Washington, D.C.*

16. Winslow Homer: *Prisoners from the Front*, 1866. *The Metropolitan Museum of Art, New York, Gift of Mrs Frank B. Porter, 1922*

17. General Grant's Battery at City Point, Virginia; photograph by Mathew Brady, 1864. *National Archives, Washington, D.C.*

18. The ruins of Charleston, South Carolina. *Library of Congress, Washington, D.C.*

136–37 19. *The Fifteenth Amendment*; lithograph from an original design by James C. Beard, commemorating the celebration on 19 May 1870. *Library of Congress, Washington, D.C.*

20. *The Bosses of the Senate*; detail of a cartoon by Joseph Keppler from *Puck*, 23 January 1889. *Library of Congress, Washington, D.C.*

21. Ben Shahn: *Years of Dust*; poster issued by the Resettlement Administration to publicize government aid to farmers and victims of the Dust Bowl, *c.* 1935. *Library of Congress, Washington, D.C.*

138–39 22. Mrs Susan Fitzgerald, a suffragette, posting bills in Cincinnati, Ohio, 17 May 1912. *Bain Collection, Prints and Photographs Division, Library of Congress, Wahington, D.C.*

23. Negro woman registering to vote in a jailhouse in Haynesville, Alabama. Photo *Bruce Davidson (Camera Press)*

24. Ford workers voting at the first election of Union officials at the Ford plant, Detroit, 1942. Photo *United States Information Service*

25. George Meany and Walter Reuther jointly open the convention marking the merger of the AFL (American Federation of Labor) and CIO (Congress of Industrial Organizations), becoming the largest union group, 5 March 1955. Photo *United States Information Service*

26. Martin Luther King shaking hands with a fellow participant in the civil rights march in Washington, D.C., August 1963. Photo *United States Information Service*

27. Senator Joseph McCarthy testifying on Communist Party infiltration of the US Army, during the Army-McCarthy Hearings, 9 June 1954. Joseph N. Welch, counsel for the Army, listens to McCarthy's testimony. Photo *United Press International*

28. Air view of the 'Solidarity Day' march during the Poor People's Campaign, in front of the Lincoln Memorial, Washington, D.C., 19 June 1968. Photo *United States Information Service*

29. Eldridge Cleaver addressing a 'Free Huey Newton' rally, flanked by Black Panther guards, late 1968. Newton, the Panther 'Minister of Defense' was serving a prison term for the 1967 slaying of a California policeman. Photo *Yorum Kabana (Camera Press)*

140 30. Ben Shahn: *Integration, Supreme Court*; tempera on panel, 1963. The Supreme Court decision on school integration was handed down in May 1954. *Des Moines Art Center, James D. Edmundson Fund*

31. The US Senate in session, 24 September 1963. Photo *George Mobley/National Geographic (United States Information Service)*

142 1. *Join or Die*, from the masthead of the *Massachusetts Spy*. The serpent device was created by Benjamin Franklin and first appeared in his newspaper *The Pennsylvania Gazette* on 9 May 1754, bidding the colonists to unite against the French and Indians. It was later revived in other newspapers during the struggle with England, here represented by the griffin. *Library of Congress, Washington, D.C.*

2. *The Federal Edifice*, cartoon which appeared in the Massachusetts *Centinel* [sic] after eleven states had ratified the Constitution, 1788. *Library of Congress, Washington, D.C.*

145 3. L. G. Illingworth: *The Line of Least Resistance*; cartoon from *Punch*, 21 April 1937. Reproduced by permission of *Punch*

147 4. Thomas Nast: *The Rising of the Usurpers and the Sinking of the People*; cartoon, 1889. *Prints Division, New York Public Library*

148 5. Cartoon commenting on the recently passed Social Security Act of 1935. *Library of Congress, Washington, D.C.*

VII Society, Inequality and Manners

151 1. Henry Sargent: *The Dinner Party*; oil, 1822/3. *Courtesy, Museum of Fine Arts, Boston*

152–53 2. *The Sargent Family*; American School, 1800. *National Gallery of Art, Washington, D.C. Gift of Edgar William and Bernice Chrysler Garbisch*

3. The Haven family on the porch of Franklin Haven's house, Beverly Farms, Massachusetts; *c.* 1868. Seated far right with his host is Salmon P. Chase, Secretary of the Treasury under Lincoln; Mrs Haven appears at the center window. *The Society for the Preservation of New England Antiquities*

4. New York City: view down Broad Street showing Federal Hall in Wall Street; lithograph by H. H. Robinson after a drawing by John Joseph Holland of *c.* 1797, *c.* 1847. *Courtesy of The New-York Historical Society, New York City*

5. Rochester, Minnesota: Broadway, in 1920. *State Historical Society of Wisconsin*

6. Chimayó, New Mexico: the village seen from 'El Santuario'; from an old photograph. *Collections in the Museum of New Mexico, Santa Fé.*

7. 'American Family at Breakfast'; stereo view by the Keystone View Company from the series *Citizenship Lessons*, *c.* 1929. *Library of Congress, Washington, D.C.*

8. Los Angeles, California: air view of residential neighborhood, 1971. Photo *Associated Press*

154–55 9. Susan Merrett: *Picnic Scene—Fourth of July* at Weymouth, Massachusetts; watercolor and collage, *c.* 1845. *Courtesy of the Art Institute of Chicago*

10. Illustration from a home-made poster advertising a skating rink at the Town Hall, Brandon (subtitled *We use only Saml Winslows "Patent Vineyard" Roller Skates*); watercolor, late 19th C. *Bella C. Landauer Collection, courtesy of The New-York Historical Society, New York City*

11. Display of garden produce in the State Fair at Des Moines, Iowa. Photo *United States Information Service*

12. Ben Shahn: *Speakeasy Interior*; gouache, 1933/4. One of a series of designs for murals in Central Park

University, Washington, D.C. Photo *Paul Almasy (Camera Press, London)*

188–89 39. New Haven, Conn.: Kline Biology Tower at Yale University; by Philip Johnson and Richard Foster, 1965–66. Photo *Burkhard-Verlag Ernst Heyer, Essen*

40. San Diego, California: library building, University of California. Photo *courtesy Public Affairs Office, University of California, San Diego*

41. Chicago, Illinois: Crown Hall, Illinois Institute of Technology; by Ludwig Mies van der Rohe, 1952–56. Photo *Hedrich-Blessing, Chicago*

190 1. Page from *The New England Primer*, enlarged and improved version, Newburyport

191 2. Diagram of the monitor system; from Joseph Lancaster, *The Lancasterian System of Education, with Improvements*, Baltimore, 1821

192 3. The Ladies' Hall, Oberlin College, Ohio; from the catalog of 1854–55

193 4. 'The American River Ganges: the Priests and the Children'; cartoon by Thomas Nast from *Harper's Weekly*, 1871

195 5. Interior of the Cincinnati Public Library; pen and ink sketch by George W. Rapp, 1869. Photo *Cincinnati Public Library*

196 6. 'Course in advanced sandwich-making'; cartoon from *Life*, 1927

197 7. 'Training versus Muscle'; cartoon from *Life*, 16 October 1915

IX New World Cities

201 1. Philadelphia, Pennsylvania: view showing, from foreground to rear, the 18th-C. Shambles, 19th-C. Headhouse, and modern Society Hill Towers. Photo *Edmund N. Bacon*

202–03 2. *A View of Savannah as it stood the 29th of March, 1734*; engraving by P. Fourdrinier after Peter Gordon. *The I. N. Phelps Stokes Collection, New York Public Library*

3. Savannah, Georgia: bird's eye view; gouache/tempera by Firmin Cerveau, 1837. *Georgia Historical Society, Savannah*

4. Milan, Ohio: Mitchell-Turner house; by Zenas King, 1848. The doorway is based on a design in Minard Lafever's *The Beauties of Modern Architecture*, 1835. Photo *Emily Lane*

5. Philadelphia, Pennsylvania: plan; by John Reed, 1774. *Atwater Kent Museum, Philadelphia*

6. Philadelphia, Pennsylvania: High Street, from Ninth Street; engraving by W. Birch & Son, early 19th C. *Reproduced through courtesy of the New York State Historical Association, Cooperstown, New York*

7. Monticello, Virginia; designed by Thomas Jefferson, 1769 et seq. Photo *United States Information Service*

8. Joseph H. Hidley: *Poestenkill, New York*; 1862. *Reproduced through courtesy of the New York State Historical Association, Cooperstown, New York*

204–05 9. Philadelphia, Pennsylvania: Branch Bank of the United States, by William Strickland, 1818; lithograph by W. H. Bartlett. *Courtesy The Historical Society of Pennsylvania*

10. Bird's eye view of Trinity Church, New York, by Richard Upjohn, 1847; lithograph after the artist's drawing. *The J. Clarence Davies Collection, Museum of the City of New York*

11. New York: The Tombs, by John Haviland, 1838 (demolished 1897); lithograph by C. Autenrieth, published by Henry Hoff, 1850. *Courtesy of The New-York Historical Society, New York City*

12. Thomas Cole: *The Architect's Dream*; oil, 1840. *The Toledo Museum of Art, Toledo, Ohio. Gift of Florence Scott Libbey*

206–07 13. Centennial Exhibition, Philadelphia, Pennsylvania, 1876: detail of bird's eye view from the east, showing the great hall and railroad; lithograph by H. J. Toudy & Co. *Courtesy The Historical Society of Pennsylvania*

14. *Representation of the first Cast Iron House erected*, by James Bogardus of New York City; lithograph by Ackerman.

The building was Bogardus's own establishment at 63 Center Street, New York, built in 1848. *Museum of the City of New York*

15. Detail of John Randel's plan for an elevated railroad along Broadway in New York: cross-section; lithograph, 1848. *Courtesy of The New-York Historical Society, New York City*

16. New York: section through Grand Central Terminal, showing traffic flow, c. 1912. *Penn Central Archives*

17. New York: train concourse of Pennsylvania Station in the course of construction, 3 November 1909; station designed by McKim, Mead and White, built 1906–10. *Courtesy of the Avery Architectural Library, Columbia University, New York*

18. New York: view along New Street toward Wall Street after the blizzard of 1888. *Museum of the City of New York*

208 19. New York: air view, looking north across Central Park. Photo *United States Travel Service*

20. New York: bird's eye view of Central Park, looking south; drawn by John Bachman, c. 1870. *Courtesy of The New-York Historical Society, New York City*

209 21. Lewis Edward Hickmott: World's Columbian Exposition, Chicago, Illinois, *View from the south to the northwest from the west end of the Agriculture Building looking along the top of the 'T' of the lagoon. On the left is the Obelisk & Machinery Hall*; oil, 1893. *Courtesy Chicago Historical Society*

22. Plan of park development proposed for the lake shore of Chicago, Illinois (west is at the top). From D. H. Burnham and E. H. Bennett, *Plan of Chicago* (The Commercial Club, Chicago, 1909). *Courtesy Edmund N. Bacon*

210–23 23. *The Burning of Chicago*; lithograph by Currier & Ives, 1871. *Library of Congress, Washington, D.C.*

24. Chicago, Illinois: Monadnock Building, by Burnham and Root, 1889–91. Photo *Commercial Photographic Company, by courtesy of Professor Carl W. Condit*

25. Chicago, Illinois: erection of the steel frame for the Fair Store, by William LeBaron Jenney, 1890–91. From *Industrial Chicago*, 1891

26. Chicago, Illinois: Gage buildings, in their original state, by Holabird and Roche (left and center), 1898, and by Louis Sullivan (right: façade design only, built by Holabird and Roche), 1898–99. Photo *Chicago Architectural Photographing Co.*

211 27. Buffalo, New York: Guaranty (now Prudential) Building, by Adler and Sullivan, 1894–5, in its original state. Photo *Chicago Architectural Photographing Co.*

28. Chicago, Illinois: detail of ornament on the Carson, Pirie, Scott store, by Louis Sullivan, 1903–04. Photo *Richard Nickel*

29. Buffalo, New York: Martin House, by Frank Lloyd Wright, 1904. Photo *Jay W. Baxtresser*

212–13 30. Washington, D.C.: view looking west, with an imaginative rendering of the Capitol (showing portions not built at the time); lithograph by E. Sachse & Co., 1852. *Library of Congress, Washington, D.C.*

31. Washington, D.C.: detail of plan by R. King, Surveyor of the City, 1818, with superimposed drawing showing the alterations due to the McMillan Commission of 1901. *Library of Congress, Washington, D. C., and Edmund N. Bacon*

32. Washington, D.C.: bird's eye view from the Virginia shore; lithograph by Currier & Ives, 1892. *Library of Congress, Washington, D.C.*

33. Washington, D.C.: bird's eye view of 'The Ultimate Washington', according to the McMillan Commission of 1901; after F. V. L. Hoppin. *From The National Geographic Magazine, March 1915, by courtesy of the Commission of Fine Arts, Washington, D.C.*

34. Denver, Colorado: air view showing the Civic Center (left, the City and County Building; right, the Colorado Capitol). Photo *United States Travel Service*

214–15 35. New York: New York Central train lines, north of Grand Central Terminal in the area covered over to become Park Avenue; 1906. *Penn Central Archives*

36. New York: Park Avenue, over the lines of the New York Central, looking south toward Grand Central Terminal; c. 1925. The street at this point was lined with elegant apartment buildings. *Penn Central Archives*

37. New York: view down Park Avenue, showing office buildings, the tower of Grand Central Terminal, and the Pan Am building by Walter Gropius. Photo *Charles Eames*

38. New York: view south down Fifth Avenue before construction of the World Trade Center. Photo *Louis B. Schlivek—New York Regional Plan Association*

39. New York: view from the Hudson River, showing Castle Garden in the right foreground. *Fox Photos*

40. *Rivetting on the dome, a quarter mile up*, during construction of the Empire State Building; detail of photograph by Lewis W. Hine, 1931. *George Eastman House Collection*

41. New York: Lower Plaza (in the winter, an ice-skating rink) in Rockefeller Center, seen from the Prometheus Fountain (by Paul Manship). The original architects of the scheme, in 1929, were Reinhard & Hofmeister; Corbett, Harrison and MacMurray; and Hood and Foulhoux. The Center was built 1931–40. Photo *United States Travel Service*

216 42. Boston, Massachusetts: the Prado, laid out in 1933/4. Photo *Edmund N. Bacon*

43. San Antonio, Texas: riverside park, laid out c. 1935. Photo *Edmund N. Bacon*

217 44. Chicago, Illinois: Civic Center, by C. F. Murphy Associates; Skidmore, Owings and Merrill; and Loebl, Schlossman and Bennett; begun 1963. The sculpture, 65 ft 9 in. high, is by Picasso. Photo *Peter Mahony*

45. Portland, Oregon: cascade fountain by Lawrence Halprin, 1968. Photo *courtesy Edmund N. Bacon*

46. Philadelphia, Pennsylvania: ice skaters in part of the Penn Center development, 1964. Photo *Philadelphia City Planning Commission, courtesy United States Information Service*

218–19 47. *Five cents a Spot*, lodgers in a tenement in Bayard Street, New York; photograph by Jacob A. Riis, c. 1889. *The Jacob A. Riis Collection, Museum of the City of New York*

48. Pittsburgh, Pennsylvania: workers' homes and steel mills; photograph by Lewis W. Hine, 1909. *George Eastman House Collection*

49. Chicago, Illinois: children playing under the 'El' on the south side; detail of photograph by Russell Lee for the Farm Security Administration, April 1941. *Library of Congress, Washington, D.C.*

50. St Louis, Missouri: demolition of one of the blocks of the Pruitt-Igoe project, May 1972. Photo *Associated Press*

51. New York: air view of the Penn Station South housing project, looking north; March 1963. The project runs from West 23rd to West 29th Street, between Eighth and Ninth Avenues). Photo *courtesy New York City Housing and Development Administration*

220 52. Reston, Virginia: air view of Lake Anne Village center, 1971. Photo *courtesy Gulf Reston, Inc.*

53. Reston, Virginia: Washington Plaza, 1971. Photo *courtesy Gulf Reston, Inc.*

54. Leesburg Pike, Falls Church, Virginia. Photo *courtesy Gulf Reston, Inc.*

55. New York: painted wall in the Alfred W. Smith Recreation Center, June 1970. Photo *Cityarts Workshop Inc.*

222 1. Newport, Rhode Island. The following buildings are shown, left to right: by Richard Munday, the Jahleel Brenton House (1720) and the Colony House (1739); by Peter Harrison, the Redwood Library (1748) and the side elevation of the Brick Market (1761–72). Drawn by Suzanne Carlson, from J. F. Millar, *The Architects of the American Colonies*, 1968, © Barre Publishers

303 *4.* Sol Le Witt: *Proposal for a Wall Drawing, Information Show*; contribution to the catalogue of *Information*, 2 July-September 1970. The Museum of Modern Art, New York

304 *5.* Roy Lichtenstein: *Art*; oil, 1962. Locksley/Shea Gallery, Minneapolis, Minn.
6. Claes Oldenburg: *Cake Wedge*; crayon, 1962. Collection: Mr and Mrs Robert C. Skull

XIII Missionary and World Power

309 *1.* Childe Hassam: *Allies Day, May 1917*; oil, 1917. *National Gallery of Art, Washington, D.C. Gift of Ethelyn McKinney in memory of her brother, Glenn Ford McKinney*

310–11 *2.* General Scott's entrance into Mexico City; lithograph by Bayot after C. Nebel, from George W. Kendall, *The War between the United States and Mexico*, 1851. *Library of Congress, Washington, D.C.*
3. 'Gosh! I wish they wouldn't come quite so many in a bunch; but if I've got to take them I guess I can do as well by them as I've done by the others!'; cartoon from *Puck, c.* 1896
4. Destruction of the US Battleship *Maine* in Havana harbor, 15 February 1898. *Library of Congress, Washington, D.C.*
5. Theodore Roosevelt at the head of the Rough Riders; lithograph by W. G. Read. *Library of Congress, Washington, D.C.*
6. Captured Filipino insurrectionists during the Spanish-American War. *Library of Congress, Washington, D.C.*
7. Sousa's band leading the crew of the *Olympia* in the Dewey Land Parade, New York, *c.* 1900. *George Eastman House Collection*
8. Theodore Roosevelt on the site of the Panama Canal, 1906. Photo *Theodore Roosevelt Association, New York*
9. United States Cavalry unit between two stone elephants on the road to Peking during the Boxer Rebellion, *c.* 1900. *US Signal Corps photograph no. 111-SC-75112 in the National Archives, Washington, D.C.*

312–13 *10.* 'Pershing's Crusaders'; poster for the first official American war film,. *Huntington Hartford Collection, New York*
11. Thomas Derrick: *American Troops at Southampton Embarking for France*; oil, 1918–19. *By kind permission of the Trustees of the Imperial War Museum, London*
12. William Orpen: *A Peace Conference at the Quai d'Orsay*, 1919; oil. By kind permission of the Trustees of the Imperial

War Museum. Photo *Eileen Tweedy*

314–15 *13.* 'Reds' awaiting the boat for Deer Island, the emigration station in the port of Boston, 1920. Photo *United Press International*
14. Herbert Hoover supervising a food shipment to Germany, 1921. Photo *United Press International*
15. General Motors branch in Uruguay in the 1920s. *Bureau of Foreign and Domestic Commerce photograph no. 151-FC-100A-A2 in the National Archives, Washington, D.C.*
16. President Franklin D. Roosevelt signing the declaration of war against Japan, 1941. Photo *Imperial War Museum, London*
17. Miguel Covarrubias: *United Nations*; caricature from *Vogue*, 1 May 1942. *Copyright 1942, 1970 by The Condé Nast Publications Inc., New York*
18. Japanese photograph taken during the attack on Pearl Harbor, 7 December 1941. Photo *Office of Defense, Washington, D.C.*
19. Tanks for shipment to Europe in New York harbor, 1940. *Office of War photograph in the Library of Congress, Washington, D.C.*
20. Norman Rockwell: *Save Freedom of Speech*; poster, 1943. *Library of Congress, Washington, D.C.*
21. US troops advancing to the fighting front from a beachhead during the Normandy invasion. Photo *Imperial War Museum, London*
22. Anti-Marshall Aid demonstration in East Germany, 1950. Photo *Röhnert, Ullstein Bilderdienst, Berlin*
23. Japanese Foreign Minister Mamoru Shigemitsu signing the surrender terms on board the USS *Missouri*, 2 September 1945. *Navy Department photograph no. 80-G-700777 in the National Archives, Washington, D.C.*
24. 'Free Pass for the Marshall Plan'; poster, 1950. *Bundesarchiv, Koblenz*

316–17 *25.* 'United We are Strong, United We will Win'; World War II poster. *The West Point Museum Collections, United States Military Academy, West Point, New York*
26. Bob Lavin: *Approach to Tempelhof. US Air Force Art Collection, Washington, D.C.*
27. President John F. Kennedy in Berlin, 1963. Photo *London Express News and Features services*
28. Korean Army aircraft gunners guarding the road from the UN base camp to Panmunjom, where armistice negotiations were in progress, 1951–53. Photo *US Department of Defence, Washington, D.C.*

29. Air view of the SA-2 missile site in Cuba, 1962. Photo *US Department of Defense, Washington, D.C.*

318–19 *30.* NATO summit conference, Paris, 16 December 1957. Left to right: Turkish Prime Minister, Aduan Menderes; British Prime Minister, Harold Macmillan; US President, Dwight D. Eisenhower; Secretary of NATO, Paul Henri Spaak; Luxembourg Premier, Joseph Bech, and Belgian Premier, Achille van Acker. Photo *United Press International*
31. The international journalists' conference against US imperialism at Pyongyang, Korea in October, 1969. Photo *Camera Press*
32. Demonstration against US imperialism in front of the US Consulate in Santo Domingo, 8 September 1962. Photo *Camera Press*
33. Juan Bosch embraced by Vice-President Lyndon B. Johnson on his election as President of the Dominican Republic, 27 February 1963. Photo *United Press International*
34. Eisenhower and Khrushchev in Washington, September 1959. Photo *United Press International*
35. American troops near Khe Sanh, North Vietnam. Photo *David Douglas Duncan*
36. President Nixon and Chairman Mao meeting in Peking, February 1972. Photo *United Press International*

320 *37.* Demonstration against US involvement in the Vietnam war, Washington, D.C., November 1969. Photo *Associated Press*

322 *1.* Cartoon on the 'Open Door' policy, 1900
2. 'No other arm around this waist!'; cartoon by W. A. Rogers, 1900. *Library of Congress, Washington, D.C.*

323 *3.* 'Overweighted'; cartoon from *Punch*, 26 March 1919

324 *4.* 'Laocoön 1938'; cartoon by Clifford Berryman. *Library of Congress, Washington, D.C.*

325 *5.* 'The Way of a Stork'; cartoon by Illingworth, from *Punch*, 29 January 1941
6. Insignia of the Food and Agriculture Organization. Photo *courtesy United Nations*

327 *7.* 'The Tumult And The Shouting Dies: The Captains And The Kings Depart'; cartoon by Herblock from *The Herblock Book*, Beacon Press, 1952

329 *8.* 'Don't Mind Me—Just Go Right on Talking'; cartoon by Herblock, 1947. From *The Herblock Book*, Beacon Press, 1952

331 *9.* 'It Don't Fit'; cartoon by Dennis Harper from *Dallas Notes*

Page numbers in *italic* refer to illustrations